MW00748517

COLLEGE COSTS & FINANCIAL AID HANDBOOK

1996

SIXTEENTH EDITION

College Scholarship Service

College Entrance Examination Board
New York

The College Scholarship Service (CSS) is an activity of the College Board concerned with improving equal educational opportunity. The CSS, through the determination of financial need, assists in the equitable distribution of financial assistance to students. Its services are offered to students and their parents, to secondary schools, to noncollegiate sponsors of financial aid programs, and to all institutions of postsecondary education.

The College Board is a nonprofit membership organization committed to maintaining academic standards and broadening access to higher education. Its more than 2,800 members include colleges and universities, secondary schools, university and school systems, and education associations and agencies.

This publication contains material related to Federal Title IV student aid programs. While the College Board believes that the information contained herein is accurate and factual, this publication has not been reviewed or approved by the U.S. Department of Education.

Copies of this book may be ordered from your local bookseller or from College Board Publications, Box 886, New York, New York 10101-0886. The price is $16.

Editorial inquiries regarding this book should be addressed to the College Scholarship Service, The College Board, 45 Columbus Avenue, New York, New York 10023-6992.

Photo credits: page 4, left; University of New Mexico; page 4, right, and page 25, Bill Sublette and the University of Virginia Alumni Association; pages 67, 68 and 73, Monkmeyer Press; pages 69 and 74, Michael Paras, Columbia High School, New Jersey; page 20, Hugh Rogers; page 37, Emile Wamsteker, Syracuse University.

Library of Congress Catalog Number: 80-648095

International Standard Book Number: 0-87447-508-2

Printed in the United States of America

Contents

Mission Statement

The College Board champions educational excellence for all students through the ongoing collaboration of member schools, colleges, universities, educational systems, and organizations. It promotes—by means of responsive forums, research, programs, and policy development—universal access to high standards of learning, equity of opportunity, and sufficient financial support so that every student is prepared for success in college and work.

The College Board

Educational Excellence for *All* Students

Preface

This book starts out from a simple premise: without advance planning, almost no one can afford to pay for college. But with planning, *anybody* can. It's true for families whose children are already high school juniors and seniors—and even truer for families whose children are still quite young.

You may have doubted that education or training after high school is within your family's reach. *That's probably not true.*

You may have assumed that there's nothing you can do to help yourself or improve your chances of finding the outside help you need. *That's definitely not true.*

This book is designed to help students and their families meet college costs. If you're worried about your family's ability to pay future educational expenses, early planning *can* help. The *purpose* of planning is twofold:

- to get as much mileage as you can out of your own resources, and
- to secure the additional outside help—the "financial aid"—you may need.

Planning ahead to meet college costs involves several different kinds of activities. This book will:

- show you how to estimate the full costs of attending the colleges you're considering,
- help you to estimate what share of those costs you and your family will probably be expected to bear,
- prove that you can make time work *for* you in covering your share of the costs,
- describe different ways that families can make their costs more manageable,
- help you estimate your own probable need and eligibility for financial aid,
- explain the various types and sources of financial aid available and what you need to do to apply, and
- assist you in developing a personal financing plan and timetable for gathering the resources *you* need.

Next to buying a home, the money that you and your family pay toward college costs may well be the largest financial investment you ever make in your lifetime. You owe it to yourself to investigate all your options beforehand, and then to manage that investment as carefully as you would any other.

The author gratefully acknowledges the contributions of the many individuals who assisted in the development of the 1996 edition of *College Costs and Financial Aid Handbook*. Data in Parts II and III were collected by the editorial staff of Guidance Publishing under the direction of Renée Gernand, using information collected through the College Board's Annual Survey of Colleges. The book was edited by Hannah Selby.

Mary Gaffney, Joan Greenberg, Laura Greene-Knapp, Jack Joyce, Maureen McDonough, and Kathleen Payea provided valuable assistance in various aspects of research and statistical analysis.

At the time this book went to press, a few aspects of financial aid delivery for academic year 1996-97 had not yet been finalized. Changes in program, application, and eligibility rules are always possible. Thus, it is very important that students seeking aid for the fall of 1996 take steps, early on, to ensure that they fully understand and comply with all application requirements.

To improve your chances of getting the help you need, you must know *what* you have to do, *when* you have to do it, and *how* to do it right—the first time. Missed deadlines, incomplete or inaccurate answers, and messy or illegible forms can hurt you. *If you have any doubts at all about which forms to file or which questions to complete, contact the financial aid offices at the colleges to which you are applying.*

Kathleen Brouder
Director
CSS Information and Training
The College Scholarship Service

Part I. Paying for college

1. What does college cost?

Some of the best things in life may be free, but unfortunately, college isn't one of them.

In fact, it costs even more than you may think. High as the prices may seem to the family that's facing them, the truth is, they represent only part of the real costs. Only a very few colleges charge you the *full* costs of providing an education.

Public colleges and universities receive large operating subsidies from state and local taxes. Most independent or private colleges and universities meet at least some of their operating expenses through endowments, contributions from graduates, and government or foundation grants. Virtually all of them invest money and use the return to help pay for their activities. The influx of federal and state institutional aid for research, facilities, and special programs is an important part of most colleges' operating budgets, helping to hold down the amounts that must be charged to students and their families.

However, all of this may not be much consolation to students and parents like you who actually have to find a way to pay the bills. Average annual costs of attendance continue to climb for virtually every postsecondary educational option, from commuting to a low-cost community college to living on campus at a high-cost private institution.

The purpose of this book is to help you plan to meet college costs. Because every family's personal and financial circumstances are different, each family's plan for meeting college costs will be different, too. The worksheets in Chapter 10 follow three sample students from different family and financial backgrounds—Andrea, Beth, and Carlos—as they plan to meet college costs. Space is also provided for you to make some preliminary plans.

Your first step in planning is to learn what college costs. Part II of this book lists the average student expenses at 3,000 colleges and universities for

the 1995-96 academic year (AY). The average expenses at different kinds of colleges for 1994-95 (the most recent year for which averages are available) are listed in Chapter 10.

The components of college costs

Regardless of where you enroll, your expenses include both direct educational expenses *and* living expenses, and typically consist of five parts:

- tuition and fees
- books and supplies
- room and board
- personal expenses
- transportation

Many students have additional expenses not covered under any of these categories, such as costs arising from medical care or a disability. Be sure to include these extra expenses in estimating the costs of attending the particular colleges you're considering.

Don't let the costs scare you! As this book explains, you may not have to pay the whole amount yourself, *and* there are ways of making more manageable the part you do have to pay.

Tuition and fees

Tuition is the charge for instruction. Fees may be charged for services such as the library, student activities, or the health center. The amount of tuition and fees charged by a particular college depends on many factors, but the most significant factor is what kind of college it is.

Because they receive funds from taxes, tuition and fees at public institutions are generally the lowest, particularly for legal residents of the state or district in which they are located. Most two- and four-year public colleges charge higher tuition for nonresidents, however. This "out-of-state" tuition (or "out-of-district"

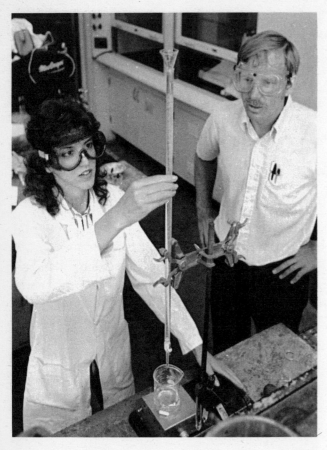

The budget for maintaining, staffing, and operating college facilities is met by federal and state aid, endowments, and investments in addition to charges to students.

tuition, in the case of two-year community colleges) often can make the cost of attending a public institution as high as the cost of attending many private institutions. (In rare instances, religiously affiliated colleges may add a surcharge for students who are not members of that religious group.) Tuition at private colleges is usually much higher than at public institutions because private colleges must charge a larger percentage of the real costs. Tuition at proprietary or profit-making institutions (such as many trade and technical schools) is usually set at a level to recover all of their operating costs plus a profit.

The tables in Part II of this book show the tuition and fees charged to most first-time, full-time students. Part-time charges, usually set by credit or semester hour, may work out to be higher per unit. Tuition and fees for upperclassmen and graduate or professional students may also vary.

Books and supplies

Every college student has to buy books, pencils, paper, and other supplies. The amount you spend for books

and supplies will vary only slightly by type of institution but is generally related to the curriculum or courses you select. In some academic fields, for instance, students may have to spend a good deal more than the averages cited in Part II of this book.

Art students, for example, may need more extensive supplies such as canvases, paints, brushes, and clay. Engineering students may need calculators or slide rules. Students in the sciences may have additional expenses for lab work. Computer science students may need to buy more computer time, or even purchase personal computers. In some programs, the textbooks are more expensive simply because the "information explosion" causes rapid changes in the field.

Room and board

Room and board means basic living expenses for food and housing. Regardless of the kind of institution you choose, you will have to consider these expenses.

You may choose to live in a dormitory on campus or in other college-operated housing located near campus (such as college-owned apartments). Although some private two-year colleges have college-operated housing available, most public community colleges do not.

Or you may want to live in privately owned housing, such as an apartment or rooming house near campus. At many large colleges and universities where on-campus housing is limited, students often live in dormitories for the first year or two and then shift to off-campus private housing.

Or you may choose to live at home with your parents and commute to campus.

The terms "resident student" and "commuter student" can be confusing. In this book, students who live in dormitories or in off-campus, college-owned housing away from their families are called "resident students" (not to be confused with the term "legal resident" used in the discussion of tuition and fees). "Commuter students" are those who live at home with their families. Many colleges have additional budget categories designed to cover students who live off campus in private housing; information about estimated expenses for such students is available in college catalogs and financial aid bulletins. Students who live off campus in private housing generally have expenses that are more like the resident budgets in this book than the commuter budgets.

Colleges with their own housing typically charge residents on a nine-month basis for room rental and most meals, excluding holiday and vacation periods. The room and board charge is built into the student expense budget. Colleges also expect that students living in privately owned, off-campus housing have a similar level of expense (although this is sometimes estimated as somewhat higher or lower than the college's own room and board costs, depending on the local housing market).

Commuter students, on the other hand, are generally assumed to have somewhat lower expenses than resident students because they do not have to pay for housing. However, families should remember that they will still need to buy food for the student and pay for other normal living expenses. For example, if classes start early in the morning and go on until late at night, commuter students will need to buy at least one meal a day, and possibly additional snacks, in the student union or coffee shop. Therefore, the estimated cost of food and other expenses at home is usually built into commuter student expense budgets for financial aid purposes. Take these costs into account in your planning.

Personal expenses

No matter what kind of institution you choose, you will have some personal expenses for such things as clothing, laundry, toiletries, recreation, medical insurance and care, and perhaps incidental furnishings for your dormitory room. This is an area in which you can economize, but colleges usually estimate that students spend at least $1,100 to $1,400 per academic year on such items.

Transportation

All students spend some money for travel. Resident students who live on or near campus must travel to get there at the start of the academic year and return home at the end; most also go home at least once during the year. If you plan to live at college but expect to travel home frequently, your transportation costs may be considerably higher than the averages shown in this book or reported by individual colleges. Include estimated travel costs in your planning. For financial aid purposes, colleges often budget students for two round-trips home per year by the lowest-cost means of travel possible.

Commuter students who travel to and from campus daily also have travel expenses, whether they use public transportation or a private car. The costs of gasoline and daily parking can add up quickly, so estimate carefully. These costs, too, are built into student expense budgets by colleges for financial aid purposes.

Total expense budget

The total expense budget for a particular college is determined by adding up these five categories of expenses. "Tables, sample cases, and worksheets" in Chapter 10 reflect sample total expenses for resident and commuter students. For your own estimates, remember to consider any additional costs that might result from medical bills or other extraordinary personal expenses.

The total budgets at public colleges are lower than those at private colleges largely because tuition and fees tend to be lower at the former. There is not, however, a lot of difference in the other costs. So don't rule out a private college because of its higher tuition. Private institutions often have more financial aid resources that can help you make up the difference between costs and financial aid. *The greater your overall expense, the greater is the possibility of your demonstrating need for financial aid.*

Questions and answers about college costs

Q All of these costs look greater than anything we can afford. How can we possibly manage to pay for college?

A First, you may be eligible for some financial aid to help you meet part of the costs. What *you* pay for college is not necessarily what the price tag says. Second, you may be able to cut your costs and stretch your resources, as described in later chapters, but be prepared to contribute *something*. In very rare cases, parents are judged too poor to contribute anything toward the costs. Third, remember that you and your family are already paying some of these expenses right now—your food, clothing, and personal expenses, for example.

That's not to say that your expenses as a member of the household aren't putting a strain on the household budget; they may well be. If you can manage it now, however, ask yourself seriously if your family can't manage it for another two or four years.

Q With college costs so high, as well as the rising cost of living in general, shouldn't I just look for the cheapest alternative?

A Not necessarily. Higher cost colleges often have more financial aid to help families bridge the gap between the costs and what they can afford to pay.

Q How do I know that the costs at a particular college won't keep going up during the years I'm enrolled?

A You don't. In fact, they probably *will* continue to rise. However, your family's income will probably rise, too. Whether your family's ability to pay will increase at the same rate as college costs depends on a lot of factors, including the overall state of the economy.

2. How much will you be expected to pay?

You should regard your family as the first—and probably primary—source of funds for education. Virtually all colleges, government agencies, and private student aid programs expect you to pay *something* toward college costs, according to your ability. Financial aid often makes up the difference between the costs of attendance and what a family can afford to pay. You may not have to pay as much as the prices listed in a college's catalog if you are eligible for financial aid. Thus, estimating how much your family can reasonably be expected to pay toward educational expenses is a major part of understanding financial aid—and a critical aspect of goal setting.

Whether your family's share of the total costs amounts to 5 percent or 100 percent, you have a better chance of achieving the goal if you know how much you are aiming for.

To help them evaluate a family's financial strength, most college financial aid administrators and aid sponsors use a set of federal formulas that take into consideration income, assets, expenses, family size, and other factors.

In addition, many colleges use an alternate set of formulas for awarding their own *institutional* student aid funds. This alternate guideline, informally known as the "Institutional Methodology," differs from the "Federal Methodology" in several respects. (For instance, the Institutional Methodology takes home equity into account and includes a minimum expected contribution from students in calculating a family's ability to pay, but also permits more generous treatment of medical/dental expenses, elementary and secondary school tuition payments, and child support paid.) In Chapter 10, you will see how the formulas actually work. But the two methodologies share some common general principles.

Evaluating a family's income

A family's total income for the previous calendar year is added up. Parents' wages and all other income (such as dividends, social security, or welfare benefits) are included, but not all of this income can be used to pay for college. For most families, the largest part of its annual income must be used to provide for basic living expenses—housing, food, medical care, clothing, and so forth.

In evaluating a family's financial strength, aid administrators also take into account other demands on the parents' income, such as taxes or unusually large medical or dental bills. Even the costs of working must be taken into consideration—clothing, transportation, meals away from home, and so forth. Elementary and secondary school tuition payments for other children may also be considered.

After all these family expenses are taken into account, the amount remaining to a family for other uses is quite a bit smaller than its original income. This remaining amount is called "available income." A family would be expected to use some of this remaining income to help pay college costs. The more available income a family has, the more would be expected of them.

Evaluating a family's assets

Many family's assets are considered, too, because a family with assets is in a stronger financial position than a family with similar income but no assets. All of the assets are added up—the value of a business or farm, cash, savings and checking accounts, stocks and bonds, and so forth. At lower income levels, home equity is not considered in the *federal* aid formulas.

In the same way that a family can't be expected to spend all its income on education, neither is it expected to use all its assets to pay for college. The system "protects" a portion of parents' assets for their use in retirement. The amount parents are allowed to protect gets larger as the age of the primary wage earner increases, because an older worker has fewer years to save for retirement than a younger one. The system also "protects" a substantial portion of family assets tied up in a business or farm, since a business or farm is also a source of income. If it were all used up to pay for college, there would be nothing left to generate income in the future.

Even when the various allowances are subtracted from total assets, a family is not expected to convert all its remaining assets into cash for college—only a portion called "income supplement from assets."

Available income (the discretionary part of a family's annual income) is added to the income supplement from assets to get a dollar amount called "adjusted available income." Not all the adjusted available income is tapped for educational expenses, only a percentage. A family with a higher adjusted available income is expected to pay a greater share of college costs than is a family with a lower adjusted available income.

If more than one family member is attending college at the same time, the amount parents are expected to pay is divided by the number attending, in order to find the expected contribution per student. This means that sometimes a family is not eligible for aid when the first child goes to college, but becomes eligible in subsequent years when a younger brother or sister starts college.

Evaluating a student's ability to pay

A student is usually expected to contribute toward college expenses, too, from savings and summer earnings. While *federal* student aid rules do not prescribe a minimum expected contribution from students, many colleges expect a freshman to contribute at least $900 a year from summer job earnings when it comes to awarding their own private funds. Upperclassmen are often expected to contribute even more from summer and part-time jobs—upwards of $1,100 a year at many colleges, and more than that at some.

Estimating your expected family contribution

Your family's "share" is the sum of what your parents can contribute from their income and assets *and* what

Table 2.1. Sources for educational expenses

Resources	Percentage of students having resource	Percentage of students receiving $1,500 or more from resource
Parents' assistance	76%	50%
Federal Pell Grant	24	6
Federal Supplemental Educational Opportunity Grant	6	1
State scholarship or grant	14	3
College scholarship or grant	24	12
Other scholarship or grant	9	3
Federal Stafford Loan	28	14
Federal Perkins Loan	8	2
College loan	6	3
Other loan	5	3
Federal Work-Study Program	12	1
Part-time job on campus	20	2
Part-time employment	22	2
Full-time employment	2	1
Savings from summer work	48	7
Other savings	28	6
Student's spouse	1	*
Other government aid	3	1
Other aid	4	2

Note: Asterisk indicates less than 1 percent.
Source: *The American Freshman: National Norms for Fall, 1993* (Los Angeles: American Council on Education and University of California at Los Angeles, 1993).

you can contribute from your earnings, savings, and so forth. In the financial aid process, this amount is also referred to as the "expected family contribution":

What parents can contribute from income
+ What parents can contribute from assets
+ What a student can contribute from income
+ What a student can contribute from assets
= Expected family contribution.

If you're simply curious about what magnitude of expense this represents, the Parents' Contribution table in Chapter 10 gives you a sense of what is expected of *parents* at different income and asset levels, assuming they meet the specifications as to age, family size, and other characteristics. Pick the combination of annual income and asset figures that most resembles your own, and you will have a *very* crude approximation of how your parent's share might work out.

You can make a much closer estimate of what might be expected of you and your family by fully completing the worksheets in Chapter 10. By subtracting your expected family contribution from the average costs of attendance at different kinds of colleges, you can get a sense of your remaining financial need. (In addition, computer software, such as the College Board's *College Cost Explorer FUND FINDER*, can be helpful when you're trying to determine how to pay for college. It provides a scholarship data base, detailed information about costs at 2,800 colleges, and also explains how expected family contribution is calculated and then translated into eligibility. Check to see if your guidance office or library has a copy of *FUND FINDER* for you to use.)

You are usually eligible for financial aid equal to the amount of your demonstrated financial need. (Whether you are able to obtain all of the financial aid you're eligible for depends on a variety of factors, such as the availability of funds in any given year.)

Setting a goal

Your estimate of your expected family contribution—be it 5 percent or 100 percent of college costs—should be your goal. Your plan should be organized to help you achieve, or even exceed, that goal. If the goal seems too *big* in relation to your household budget, don't panic! Chapters 3 and 4 give some ideas about ways to finance your share of the costs. If your goal seems too *small* in relation to actual college costs, don't worry! Chapters 5 and 6 demonstrate how financial aid can bridge the gap. Whatever your goal, write it down on a piece of paper and refer to it occasionally. *Writing goals down on paper helps to make them real.*

Special note on independent (self-supporting) students

So far the discussion has focused on students who are dependent on their parents for financial support. If you are truly financially independent of your parents, you are called an "independent," or "self-supporting," student. This does not mean that your resources are always sufficient to pay your direct educational costs as well as living expenses (for yourself and your family).

What it *does* mean is that, in considering your need for financial aid, colleges and other aid providers assume that your parents will not provide you with any support. (When it comes to awarding their own *institutional* funds, some colleges will expect parents to supply *information*, however, regardless of the student's dependency status.)

Your ability as a self-supporting student to contribute toward college costs is evaluated on the basis of your own income, assets, and expenses. Expenses are typically higher than a dependent student's because self-supporting students must provide for maintenance and living expenses year-round. You may also have extra expenses, such as child care, which may be considered in the student expense budget developed by a college for self-supporting financial aid applicants. Because they do not get help from their parents and because their expenses are usually higher than dependent students' expenses, self-supporting students often have a greater financial need. (They may also be expected to contribute more toward their own educational expenses.)

Who is considered self-supporting and who is not? There are certainly many students who really are self-supporting, such as younger students who no longer have financial support of their parents, or older students with families of their own. The problem is defining what really constitutes self-supporting status.

At the time this book went to press, it was assumed that for the 1996-97 academic year the federal definition of independence, as outlined in the Higher Education Amendments of 1992, will be used to determine eligibility for the Federal Pell Grant, Federal Stafford Loan, and campus-based programs. Most state, institutional, and private aid sponsors are expected to use a similar definition.

Under this definition, you are *automatically* considered to be self-supporting if:

- you are at least 24 years old by December 31 of the award year (e.g., by December 31, 1996, for the 1996-97 award year),
- you are a veteran of the United States Armed Forces, regardless of age,
- you are an orphan or a ward of the court,
- you have legal dependents of your own *other than* a spouse,
- you are married, or
- you are a graduate or a professional student.

Financial aid administrators can make exceptions for students who do not meet these criteria but are nonetheless self-supporting. Contact the financial aid offices at the colleges you're considering if you need more information about dependency status.

Even if you meet the federal criteria for self-supporting status, however, you may be required to submit parents' financial data as part of the aid application process at some colleges. Some colleges may also ask you to provide additional documentation of your income and expenses if you claim self-supporting status. Also, some private sponsors may use different definitions than the federal government for determining self-supporting status. Contact the financial aid offices at the colleges from which you are seeking help if you think you may qualify as a self-supporting student and wish further information.

Questions and answers about how much you will be expected to pay

Q We have special expenses that aren't talked about in this chapter that affect our ability to pay (for example, a handicapped child who requires special medical care or education). Does anybody take this into account?

A Colleges try to take into account the unique circumstances of each applicant. In Chapter 6, where applying for financial aid is discussed, you will learn about ways in which you can make sure that the colleges you're considering at least understand your situation fully. Whether they will be able to give you extra help depends on a variety of factors, one of the most important being how much money they have available to help students in any given year.

Q We live in a big city and the rents for apartments are very high. Does the need analysis system take this into account?

A The formulas do take housing costs into account, along with food, clothing, and other family living expenses. Financial aid administrators at some colleges also may consider the high cost of living in your particular residential area.

Q I've calculated our expected family contribution, and it's more money than we can possibly afford. How can we pay this out of our current earnings?

A You aren't necessarily expected to pay it out of your current earnings alone. The next chapter will explain that no matter how large that expectation may appear to you, it can be made smaller if you break it into monthly amounts. The earlier you start planning, the more choices you have about how to finance your share of the costs.

3. How to make time work for you

If you have estimated how much you may be expected to pay toward college costs, you may wonder how you can possibly squeeze that much out of current income.

In fact, you probably *can't* squeeze it all out of current income. Few people are wealthy enough to pay cash for houses, cars, or major appliances. Most of us save or borrow, sometimes both, to finance the purchase of "big-ticket" items. In fact, we may not even be able to figure out whether we can afford something until we see how it breaks down in terms of monthly payments.

The more time you give yourself, the more choices you will have about how to finance your share. If you still have several years left before enrollment, you have many more options than families who are facing enrollment within the next year or two. But even if you were to enroll next month, you would still have some choices.

What does "expected family contribution" actually mean?

Your expected family contribution is *not* a prediction of how much extra cash you actually have on hand, or even an assumption of how much you "ought to" be able to pull from current income. Rather, the expected family contribution is a measure of your family's overall capacity to absorb some portion of educational expenses, and you can cover your share in any number of ways.

If you start early enough, you may be able to *save* your entire share, and more. One of the advantages of starting early is that you *earn* interest toward your goal. If you start late, you may have to *borrow*. The downside is that you're *paying* interest, not earning it. You could use a combination of saving *and* borrowing—or even "leverage" your money by borrowing against your own savings. The toughest way to cover your share of educational expenses, though, is to force

them into your current household budget. Some families do it, but it's not easy.

Financing the parents' contribution

Students can get summer or part-time jobs to help finance their portion of the expected family contribution. Accommodating the parents' portion, or "parents'

Table 3.1. Relationship of family income to parental contribution (1995-96 Federal Methodology)

Annual family income	Net income (after tax)	Parents' contribution (annual)	Percentage of total	Percentage of net
$ 10,000	$ 8,435	$ 0	0.0%	0.0%
15,000	12,653	0	0.0	0.0
20,000	16,510	0	0.0	0.0
25,000	19,978	620	2.5	3.1
30,000	23,445	1,390	4.6	5.9
35,000	26,913	2,150	6.1	8.0
40,000	30,380	3,040	7.6	10.0
45,000	33,848	4,120	9.2	12.2
50,000	37,315	5,460	10.9	14.6
55,000	40,341	6,880	12.5	17.1
60,000	43,158	8,210	13.7	19.0
65,000	45,370	9,250	14.2	20.4
70,000	48,497	10,720	15.3	22.1
75,000	51,625	12,820	17.1	24.8
80,000	54,752	13,660	17.1	24.9
85,000	57,880	15,230	17.9	26.3
90,000	61,007	16,600	18.4	27.2
95,000	64,135	18,070	19.0	28.2
100,000	67,255	19,530	19.5	29.0

Note: Estimated parents' contributions in Tables 3.1-3.4 assume four family members; one family member in college as an undergraduate; older parent (age 45) is employed; the other parent is not employed; income only from employment; no unusual circumstances; standard deductions on U.S. income tax; asset neutrality (assets equal to Asset Protection Allowance). Values are approximate.

Table 3.2. Parents' contribution related to monthly net income (1995-96 Federal Methodology)

Annual family income	Annual net income (after tax)	Parent's contribution (annual)	Monthly net income (after tax)	Monthly net required to pay contribution
$ 10,000	$ 8,435	$ 0	$ 703	$ 0
15,000	12,653	0	1,054	0
20,000	16,510	0	1,376	0
25,000	19,978	620	1,665	52
30,000	23,445	1,390	1,954	116
35,000	26,913	2,150	2,243	179
40,000	30,380	3,040	2,532	253
45,000	33,848	4,120	2,821	343
50,000	37,315	5,460	3,110	455
55,000	40,341	6,880	3,362	573
60,000	43,158	8,210	3,597	684
65,000	45,370	9,250	3,781	771
70,000	48,497	10,720	4,041	893
75,000	51,625	12,820	4,302	1,068
80,000	54,752	13,660	4,563	1,138
85,000	57,880	15,230	4,823	1,269
90,000	61,007	16,600	5,084	1,383
95,000	64,135	18, 070	5,345	1,506
100,000	67,255	19,530	5,605	1,628

Table 3.3. Financing parents' contribution (PC) under four different scenarios: percentage impact on monthly budgets

Annual family income	Expected parents' contribution	Percentage of gross income required each month to finance PC			
		Pay from current income (0-4-0)	Borrow in full (0-4-10)	Borrow and save (4-4-4)	Save in full (8-4-0)
$ 10,000	$ 0	0.0%	0.0%	0.0%	0.0%
15,000	0	0.0	0.0	0.0	0.0
20,000	0	0.0	0.0	0.0	0.0
25,000	620	2.5	0.9	0.8	0.7
30,000	1,390	4.6	1.7	1.5	1.4
35,000	2,150	6.1	2.3	2.0	1.8
40,000	3,040	7.6	2.8	2.5	2.2
45,000	4,120	9.2	3.4	3.0	2.7
50,000	5,460	10.9	4.0	3.6	3.2
55,000	6,880	12.5	4.6	4.1	3.7
60,000	8,210	13.7	5.0	4.5	4.0
65,000	9,250	14.2	5.2	4.7	4.2
70,000	10,720	15.3	5.6	5.0	4.5
75,000	12,820	17.1	6.3	5.6	5.0
80,000	13,660	17.1	6.3	5.6	5.0
85,000	15,230	17.8	6.6	5.8	5.2
90,000	16,600	18.4	6.8	6.0	5.4
95,000	18,070	19.0	7.0	6.2	5.6
100,000	19,530	19.5	7.2	6.4	5.7

Values are approximate.

contribution," in the current household budget can be much harder, simply because the amount represents a large portion of annual income, as Table 3.1 illustrates.

At any point on the chart, you can see that the expected parents' share would require a pretty large percentage of income—*if* you were trying to take it all out of current income. At the $45,000 annual income level, for example, the expected parents' contribution would require *9 percent* of gross income, and a whopping *12 percent* of net (after-tax) income. As Table 3.2 demonstrates, that translates into a pretty big chunk of the monthly household budget.

You don't have to finance your share that way. You can if you want to and are able to, but spreading the expense out over time has a much smaller impact on your monthly budget. This is true whether you save, borrow, or both.

By way of illustration, consider these four very different scenarios for financing the *same* parents' contribution:

- Pay the entire contribution out of current income during the four years of enrollment.

- Borrow the full amount of the same contribution, starting at the point of enrollment and spreading repayment out over the four years of enrollment and the 10 years following graduation.
- Save some of the amount during the four years preceding enrollment, and then borrow the balance, with repayments spread out over the four years of enrollment and the four years following graduation.
- Save the full amount in the eight years preceding and the four years of enrollment.

The four approaches yield the same parents' contribution, but their respective effects on a household's monthly budget differ. Table 3.3 displays parents' contributions as constant percentages of total (pre-tax) income under each of the four scenarios.

To get a feel for how the percentages in Table 3.3 work out in dollar terms, see Table 3.4.

Look at the $45,000 annual income band again. Paying the parents' contribution entirely from current income would require modifying consumption by approximately $345 a month. Spreading the expense

Table 3.4. Financing parents' contribution (PC) under four different scenarios: dollar impact on monthly budgets

Annual family income	Expected parents' contribution	PC in monthly scenarios			
		Pay from current income	Borrow in full	Borrow and save	Save in full
$ 25,000	$ 620	$ 52	$ 19	$ 17	$ 15
30,000	1,390	115	43	38	35
35,000	2,150	178	67	58	53
40,000	3,040	253	93	83	73
45,000	4,120	345	128	113	101
50,000	5,460	454	167	150	133
55,000	6,880	573	211	188	170
60,000	8,210	685	250	225	200
65,000	9.250	769	282	255	228
70,000	10,720	893	327	292	263
75,000	12,820	1,069	394	350	313
80,000	13,660	1,140	420	373	333
85,000	15,230	1,261	468	411	368
90,000	16,600	1,380	510	450	405
95,000	18,070	1,504	554	491	443
100,000	19,530	1,625	600	533	475

over time by any of the other scenarios could reduce the effect on the monthly budget by more than half.

The other important point about Tables 3.3 and 3.4 is that it is *never too late* to plan. If you were to enroll tomorrow and hadn't yet saved any money, you could still make time work for you by borrowing. The differences in the monthly payouts between the borrowing, saving, and borrowing/saving options in Tables 3.3 and 3.4 are nowhere near as large as the difference between all three of them and the pay from current income options.

However, when you are actually at the point of determining what your family should do, analyze the total *costs* associated with each option. Depending on the length of time you will be making loan payments, the amount of interest you will be paying, the rate of inflation, and the general state of the economy, some borrowing options may be a lot more expensive than others.

NOTE: The values in Tables 3.3 and 3.4 are calculated by a computer model using standard annuity formulas to create a monthly "outlay" computed as a constant percentage of family income. The model also assumes a 7 percent yield on investments, an 11 percent interest rate on borrowed money, and 5 percent annual increases in income and parents' contributions over the period of years associated with each scenario. Note that

the model is designed to compare the relative effects of various financing scenarios on a monthly household budget. It cannot be used to compare the relative *costs* associated with those scenarios; borrowing, for instance, typically costs more than saving (except when inflation is high). Furthermore, the model deliberately fixes the monthly outlay as a constant percentage of income for comparison purposes, and thus Tables 3.3 and 3.4 cannot be used as amortization tables.

Questions and answers about making time work for you

Q My child will start college in less than a year. Isn't it too late to start saving?

A It is *never* too late to make plans. First of all, check your current finances to ensure you're getting as high a rate of return as possible. Second, take steps to make sure that you are creditworthy. If you are going to have to borrow, make sure that your credit history is accurate and that you have not exhausted your borrowing capacity. Third, look at the next chapters for some ideas about ways to finance your share—and reduce your costs. Fourth, investigate financial aid. Remember, even if your child *does* start college next year, he or she will be enrolled for four or more years. You don't just have one year to plan ahead; you have several.

Q Is it wise to borrow for education?

A Borrowing is an honorable way of paying for education; many students *and* parents take out loans to cover college costs. The important thing is not to get in over your head. Chapters 5 and 6 describe some current loan programs designed to help students and parents cover expenses, and Chapter 7 includes consumer advice about responsible borrowing.

Q How do I actually start saving for future educational expenses?

A The worksheets in Chapter 10 will help you estimate probable future college costs and what might be expected of your family toward paying those expenses. Once you have set an overall goal, break it down into annual, monthly, or even weekly goals.

The next chapter describes a variety of approaches to financing your share of the costs. If you have many resources already, you may wish to consult your financial adviser to make sure that your savings and investment programs are achieving your objectives.

4. Making the most of your own resources

Are you concerned that your family can't come up with enough cash to cover the contribution a college believes you should be able to make? What if a college can't give you any aid or can't give you enough to meet your need fully? What if you decide to attend college late in the year, and financial aid has already run out by the time you apply for admission?

Remember that colleges and most other student aid sponsors regard the student and his or her family as the primary source of funds for meeting the cost of education or training after high school. (There are rare instances where parents are considered unable to contribute anything whatsoever toward college costs, but even then, the student would be expected to contribute something from savings and summer earnings.)

This chapter will review some of the strategies that students and families have used to meet their share of college costs. Not all of these ideas will be applicable to your unique family situation, of course, but perhaps one or two will provoke some creative thinking. (Several commercial and not-for-profit organizations' programs are described in this chapter. Their inclusion is intended to illustrate the wide and growing array of options available to families in meeting college costs but does not imply any endorsement whatsoever.) The next chapter will describe how financial aid—grants and scholarships, loans, and jobs—can cover the gap between your best efforts and the costs of attendance.

If there is a "silver lining" to the rising costs, it is that colleges are working harder than ever not only to contain the costs but also to develop new mechanisms to assist students and families in meeting the costs. This chapter also describes some of the ways that colleges are trying to help families finance education after high school. Not all of these approaches will be available at the particular colleges you're considering, but they're worth asking about. Make sure that you review the lists in Part III of this book; you'll find the names of many colleges that offer special kinds of help to families in financing educational expenses.

Strategies for stretching your resources

Many students and families have used a variety of strategies for getting the most out of the resources they *do* have for meeting college costs. Some of these ideas may work for you, and some may make you angry! This section describes some possible strategies for getting more mileage out of family resources. Remember, the point is to do your share, *not* necessarily to cover the whole expense.

Rearranging your personal finances

Few families can cover their expected share from current earnings only, never mind bridge the gap that could be created by insufficient financial aid resources. To minimize the impact on your household budget when the time comes to start paying college bills, you should start planning as early as possible.

For instance, you might want to think about how your current assets can be resources for paying educational bills. Ask yourself, What are they worth now? What are they most likely to be worth when I want to use them? You may want to talk to your banker, a financial adviser, or an investment specialist about the best way of "saving" for college, given your financial situation. These professionals can offer you advice on financial planning for college based on your present situation, how much time you have left to save, and the risks involved in selecting certain financing alternatives.

The long-range approach

The earlier you start, the more time you have to arrange your personal finances to the greatest advantage. Families with young children, for instance, should think about creating a regular savings plan against the day when their children start college. Starting earlier rather than later really does make a difference. Deposited funds accrue interest, and the effect of compounding can be astonishing over a long period of time.

Many banks, savings and loan organizations, credit unions, investment firms, and other financial institutions market programs designed to help families accumulate resources for their children's future education. Under some programs, families make regular deposits to a savings account at interest rates that increase with the amount of the balance in savings; other programs provide for one-time or periodic payments into various kinds of investment funds or other financial products. Sometimes counseling and financial planning services are included as part of the program.

The Tax Reform Act of 1986 changed some of the rules governing ways in which families can accumulate money for college. Consumer guides to the tax law are widely available in bookstores, and you can also pose questions directly to the local office of the Internal Revenue Service (IRS). Or you may want to seek the help of a professional adviser, such as a Certified Financial Planner (CFP), a Certified Public Accountant (CPA), or a tax attorney. In any case, carefully investigate all the features of the programs offered by banks and investment firms. There is considerable variety in the safety, the yield, and the requirements of college savings programs and products now on the market. Shop around before you invest your hard-earned dollars.

More immediate options

Even if you have to start paying bills within the next year, it is worth your time to talk to your banker about your current savings and investment arrangements. Banks, savings and loan associations, credit unions, and investment firms never have been more eager for your money or have offered so many varieties of plans. The family with several thousand dollars in a passbook savings account is almost certainly not getting the most mileage out of its money.

No college expects you to sell the family homestead to pay for education, but when it comes to awarding their own institutioal funds, some colleges *are* quite explicit about their expectations of families with assets. The Higher Education Amendments of 1992 eliminated consideration of home equity in the case of families at lower income levels for purposes of determining eligibility for federal Title IV student aid. You may find that a college financial aid office wants to know your net return on investments, for instance. Others may suggest that you refinance the mortgage on your home. Others may inquire about the contribution that other members of the extended family (such as grandparents) might make to a student's educational expenses. Such observations from colleges may startle or even anger you, but they reflect a renewed emphasis on the family's central responsibility for financing education or training after high school.

There are some respects in which the family homestead has taken on potential new importance in paying educational expenses. Under the Tax Reform Act of 1986, the consumer interest deduction was phased out over a period of five years, effective December 31, 1986. One important exception is interest on indebtedness securing a taxpayer's principal residence or a second residence, up to the amount of the original purchase price plus improvements. (Taxpayers can't take out home equity loans on the appreciated value to make consumer purchases and deduct the interest, except in strictly limited cases where loans are to be used for education, medical expenses, or home improvements. Make sure you understand how the IRS rules are applied before you act.)

Many banks are marketing new loans and lines of credit based on home equity. Some of the new programs are geared specifically to educational expenses. As with most financial services, there is considerable variation in the terms of such programs, so you will want to shop both widely and cautiously. Make sure you understand all the implications of using your home this way, not just the tax-related ones.

Here are some other ideas.

Federal Parent Loan for Undergraduate Students

The Higher Education Amendments of 1992 expanded an important financial resource for families—the Federal Parent Loan for Undergraduate Students Program. (The Federal Stafford Loan Program will be described in the next chapter.)

As of July 1, 1994, parents may borrow up to the total cost of education *minus* any student aid awarded, per child. (There is no longer an annual limit or aggregate total.) The interest rate on a Federal PLUS Loan is variable, based on the 52-week T-Bill (treasury-bill) rate plus 3.1 percent, and is capped at 9 percent. Monthly repayment begins within 60 days of disbursement (although some lenders may permit borrowers to make interest-only payments while the child is still enrolled.) Federal PLUS loans are made without regard to financial need, but borrowers must demonstrate that they do not have an adverse credit history.

Because repayment generally must begin within 60 days, Federal PLUS loans are primarily assistance in meeting the cash-flow problems caused by college bills. Some parents borrow under the Federal PLUS program to meet all or part of the expected parental contribution, while others may borrow to make up the difference between costs and their contribution plus available financial aid.

Federal PLUS loans are widely available through programs like CollegeCredit™, sponsored by the College Board, as well as many banks, credit unions, and savings and loan associations.

Privately sponsored supplemental loans

Many organizations, banks, and credit unions sponsor special education loan programs that have more favorable interest rates and/or other special features that make the loans more attractive than other consumer borrowing options. Eligibility generally relates more to demonstrated creditworthiness than demonstrated financial need, and parents rather than students are generally the borrowers under such programs (although creditworthy students may be eligible as well).

For example, the College Board sponsors two privately insured supplemental loan programs as part of its CollegeCredit™ Program. The ExtraCredit™ Loan works like a line of credit for families who want to plan ahead for meeting up to four full years of college costs. Borrowers have up to 15 years to repay; competitive interest rates, high loan limits, fixed monthly payments, and a one-time application process afford families both convenience and control. The ExtraTime™ Loan provides funds for families who need help in paying for up to the total costs of attendance for a single year of college. Borrowers have up to 15 years to repay. An optional feature of ExtraTime Loans is that the borrower may choose to pay only the *interest* while the student is enrolled, so that monthly

payments are lower when the parents' expenses are the highest. (For more information about ExtraCredit and ExtraTime Loans, call 1-800-874-9390.)

A few private supplemental loan programs permit students and parents to borrow *jointly*. For instance, under the MassPlan℠ sponsored by the Massachusetts Educational Financing Authority, parents *and* students (from any state) may jointly borrow up to 100 percent of the costs of attendance (minus any financial aid) at 58 participating Massachusetts colleges and universities. Two options are available: a 15-year, fixed-interest-rate plan, and a 10-year, variable-interest-rate plan. Borrowers who secure their loans with a home mortgage option may be able to take advantage of the tax deductibility of interest payments. (For information about MassPlan, call 1-800-842-1531 or 1-617-261-9760.)

Chapter 7 contains extensive information about responsible borrowing, and includes some advice about evaluating the terms and features of private supplemental loan programs.

Combination savings/loan plans

This approach to financing a child's education is becoming more widely available. Under such plans, a participating bank will "leverage," or multiply, a customer's balance to give a family a line of credit for meeting college costs that is, in effect, a long-term loan, with the interest on savings offsetting to a substantial degree the interest on the loan.

Terms and conditions of these and similar programs can vary considerably from sponsor to sponsor, so prospective users will want to shop around. Inquire about the availability of programs at banks in your community.

College-sponsored financing programs

Many institutions of higher education participate in a tuition budgeting plan that permits families to spread out their payments over a longer period of time. Some colleges finance the programs themselves, while others participate in commercially available options. Because of the interest, insurance, and service fees involved in such programs, a family will typically end up spending more money than if the charges had been paid outright. However, for families with cash-flow problems or insufficient reserves, as well as for families who prefer to preserve their capital, such programs can be very helpful. Information about the options available at a particular college usually can be found in its catalog or financial aid bulletin; if you don't find it, ask.

Some insurance companies offer tuition budgeting programs to families. Insurance features on plans like these generally guarantee that the tuition will continue to be paid in the event of a parent's death or total disability. Some colleges offer variations on plans like this, financed through their own resources.

In evaluating these approaches to stretching your resources, get all the facts before you sign any contracts, promissory notes, or loan agreements. You should evaluate both what you pay and what you get back to ensure that you are getting the best possible deal.

Don't assume that you can always find financing plans or tuition installment plans at every college and university. Some public institutions, for instance, are prohibited by state law from extending credit to anyone. However, they may be able to direct you to commercial budgeting or installment plans offered by outside companies. Information about programs designed to help you manage educational expenses at a particular college can usually be found in the college's catalog or financial aid bulletin.

Strategies for cutting costs

In the absence of sufficient personal resources and financial aid, one obvious approach to financing a college education is to reduce the overall costs. There are many different ways to cut expenses, and your personal situation and ambitions will determine whether any of these approaches can work for you.

Reducing the time involved in earning a degree

By reducing the length of time involved in earning a degree, you can reduce the overall costs. (Reducing the amount of time you spend in education or training may also reduce your "forgone income," or the amount of money you could otherwise have earned if you were employed.) There are several approaches to cutting time and thus cutting costs.

For instance, many colleges award advanced placement and/or academic credit to students who can demonstrate proficiency in college-level studies through examinations such as those sponsored by the Advanced Placement (AP) Program and the College-Level Examination Program (CLEP) of the College Board. Credit-by-examination means the number of courses required to earn a degree is reduced, so the overall costs are cut. As you investigate colleges, you may want to ask about credit-by-examination policies.

Some colleges also grant advanced placement and/or academic credit to students who can demonstrate proficiency because of prior independent study and "life experience." A student might demonstrate particular competencies or skills, for example, by compiling a portfolio that documents prior learning experiences. College requirements for documenting prior learning tend to be quite rigorous, but if you can meet them, you can reduce both your time and your financial investment. (You may find that the approach is less commonly available than credit-by-examination options. You may also find that some colleges offering such opportunities restrict their use to older, "nontraditional" students who have spent several years working or raising a family.)

Some students also compress the time required to earn their degrees by taking more courses than the average student and/or attending summer school. (Obviously, attending summer classes will cut down on your ability to work during the summer to earn money for college.) Some students successfully complete a bachelor's degree in less than four years, thus reducing their overall costs, but this clearly requires a high degree of motivation. You may want to ask colleges you're considering whether it's possible to earn a degree in less than four years, since some colleges have policies limiting the number of credits a student can carry per semester.

Sometimes students can earn some college credit without actually attending classes, thus reducing transportation and possibly some living expenses. (This approach would also allow a student to work and save for full-time attendance later.) Check with the colleges you're considering if this appeals to you.

Reducing indirect costs

Living at home instead of on campus has helped many students reduce their overall costs. Some students live at home and commute to campus for the entire course of their studies, while others alternate between living in college housing (or off-campus private housing) and living at home with their families. Other students elect to attend a local, lower cost college (such as a community college) for the first two years and then transfer to a higher cost public or private college to complete their degrees.

Dormitory residents at some colleges have also discovered that savings can be achieved in the choice of college-sponsored meal plans. Investigate carefully the options open to you before you select a particular meal plan.

Some students work in return for room and board in private homes. Information about such opportunities is often available through a college's placement or student affairs office.

Students at many colleges have banded together to provide services for each other that can reduce both their direct educational expenses and their living expenses. The range of student-sponsored services is enormous and well worth investigating as part of your college-search process. Secondhand bookshops enable students to reduce textbook expenses. Food co-ops enable residents in private, off-campus housing to cut their food bills and still get adequate nutrition. Daycare programs provide help to students with dependents of their own. Revolving emergency loan funds can provide short-term financial assistance. Housing referral services or guides can help students to locate private housing, while tenant organizations protect and advocate their rights with landlords. Entertainment programs are specifically designed to provide free or low-cost recreation to students living on a budget.

College administrators, too, have instituted programs at many institutions, usually in conjunction with the student affairs or financial aid offices. The financial aid office may conduct workshops on money management, for instance, or the student activities office may issue guides to low-cost housing and shopping in the community. As the effects of rising costs and declining aid begin to be felt more widely, the number and range of such programs to help students live on a tight budget can be expected to grow.

Guaranteed or stabilized tuition plans

You can expect increases in tuition charges at least once, and probably annually, during your enrollment at a particular college. A few colleges guarantee their tuition for four years at the time of enrollment, at no obligation to the student. Under other plans, families can prepay tuition for four years in one lump sum and escape subsequent tuition increases.

Taking advantage of such programs could reduce your overall expenses, although you may want to consider whether you can get a return on your investments that's equivalent to or better than the rate of tuition increases, while still having the use of your money. For families who do not have enough disposable income to pay the entire sum at once, some colleges offer a borrowing option whereby payment is made in monthly installments over a period of years. However, with the gradual phaseout of consumer interest deductibility, you may want to make some

calculations to ensure that this option still makes financial sense for you.

Strategies for working your way through college

Working your way through college is certainly possible, but it's not easy, particularly if you want to attend college on a full-time basis. The problems include both money and time. Educational and living expenses are sufficiently high to make it difficult to earn enough money to cover them fully while maintaining a full course load, but here again, there are a variety of approaches to working your way through. One or more of them may work for you. An estimated half of all college students now hold jobs of some sort.

Part-time employment

Some students find that they can earn enough money through part-time employment to meet their costs. Many students work part time while enrolled full time, and find that a part-time job does not hamper their studies. The Federal Work-Study Program described in Chapter 5 provides employment opportunities for many students with demonstrated financial need. Other students work in jobs, on or off campus, that they find themselves.

Some colleges have made a special commitment to helping students pay some of their educational expenses through working. For example, Cornell University in New York sponsors a unique program that assists students in meeting their educational costs. The Cornell Tradition, a loan forgiveness fellowship program, recognizes students committed to the work ethic and service. Tradition Fellows receive awards that reduce the amount of their student loans up to $2,500 per year. Since the program's inception, over $10 million has been awarded in recognition of student work and service; about 600 students are recognized annually.

At Babson College in Massachusetts, students are encouraged to own and operate their own businesses, both to earn needed funds and develop hands-on business skills. A student Chamber of Commerce serves as a forum for exchanging ideas and sharing skills, while the Babson Entrepreneurial Exchange links students with alumni and nonalumni business people.

Some colleges have instituted special programs to help students find part-time employment. Check

To find out about employment opportunities, contact the job placement office or consult the job bulletin board.

the community for experienced waiters and waitresses, that might be useful to know when you're looking for summer and part-time jobs in high school.

Unless you have truly unusual and marketable skills, part-time work is not likely to earn you enough money to cover all your expenses, but, depending on your overall costs and your family's ability to contribute toward your education, plus financial aid, you may be able to cover the difference through part-time employment.

Cooperative education

Some students have found that alternating periods of full-time employment and full-time enrollment works best for them. Many colleges have even formalized such arrangements through cooperative education programs. In cooperative education programs, students alternate semesters of academic enrollment with semesters of full-time employment, usually in jobs directly related to their field of study. In addition to helping them finance their studies, cooperative education programs give students a chance to develop concrete job skills and experience that enhance their employability after graduation. About 1,000 colleges and universities across the country offer some form of cooperative education opportunities; inquire about the possibility at the colleges you're considering.

Deferred enrollment

Some students take a year or two off before going to college to get some money in their pockets. Some colleges have formalized this, too—it's called "deferred enrollment." You're accepted, but you don't actually start going to college until the following year. You might keep this in mind as a question to ask about the various colleges you investigate.

Employee fringe benefits

Some students decide to work full time and attend college part time at their employer's expense. Many employers offer educational opportunities as fringe benefits. Sometimes workers are reimbursed, in whole or in part, for successfully completed course work; other programs pay tuition expenses up front. (Check with the Internal Revenue Service for the most current tax treatment of employee educational expense benefits.)

Keep in mind, too, that some unreimbursed educational expenses may be considered tax deductible. However, under the Tax Reform Act of 1986, they

with the financial aid and student employment offices at the colleges you're considering.

You should begin lining up summer job prospects as soon as you are old enough to work. You might also think about acquiring and cultivating skills that will be useful in finding part time jobs to help finance your education. As you investigate colleges, you may want to inquire about the availability of part-time jobs on and off campus. Admissions recruiters, financial aid counselors, and job placement counselors may be able to give you some clues about the kinds of jobs most frequently available. If you're visiting a college, pick up copies of the student newspaper as well as local newspapers to check out the help-wanted ads.

You might be able to tailor some of your precollege courses or summer job experiences to improve your chances in the job market once enrolled. For example, if there's a typically heavy demand for typing term papers at the college you're aiming for, it may be worth your while to take a word processing course. If there are usually openings on campus and in can be deducted only if they meet specific criteria. Check with the IRS for more information.

Managing your time if you work

There have not been many studies of students who combine work and school. The information that does exist, however, tends to show that students who work part time do not usually seem to suffer academically for the time they put into their jobs. Some studies have indicated, in fact, that students who work part time achieve higher grade-point averages than their nonemployed fellow students. For most students who work, the discipline required to juggle their responsibilities and manage their time effectively pays off in academic work, too. (At the same time, some colleges try to minimize the necessity of part-time work for some groups of students, particularly freshmen, in order to ease their transition into college life.) Some students also like the opportunity to develop employment experience in anticipation of job hunting after graduation.

Questions and answers about making the most of your resources

Q My parents have scrimped and saved for my college education, but because we have savings, we won't have as much eligibility for financial aid. Aren't we being penalized for being thrifty?

A You and your parents *will* be expected to contribute something toward the cost of college from the money you and they have saved, but as subsequent chapters will illustrate, the system *also* takes into account your parents' ages and corresponding need to save for retirement. Remember, too, that a student whose parents have no savings must rely much more heavily on financial aid than you. That family may have a heavier work or loan burden than yours will have to carry. In a time when public appropriations for student aid programs are not keeping pace with increases in college costs, your reduced reliance on financial aid may give you a wider range of choices.

Q Didn't tax reform knock out all the incentives for college saving?

A The Tax Reform Act of 1986 affected many of the "income transfer" strategies that some parents have used in the past to accumulate college savings and shelter some assets from taxation by putting them in their children's names. "Clifford Trusts," for instance, were eliminated entirely, and new restric-

tions were imposed on "generation-skipping" bequests from grandparents.

The experts still have lots of ideas about how families can build up money for college, with or without tax advantages. The more time you give yourself to study the various ideas, the better off you'll be. The important thing is to take advantage of whatever time you and your family have before enrollment. The loss of a specific tax break that may have existed in previous years is no reason to stop saving for college.

Q Is the interest on educational loans tax-deductible?

A The Tax Reform Act of 1986 initiated a gradual phaseout of the deductibility of consumer interest on all nonmortgage loans, including loans assumed by students and parents to pay for education, such as Federal Stafford Loans (formerly Guaranteed Student Loans) and Federal PLUS loans. However, interest on home mortgages, including second mortgages up to the fair market value of the house, is still deductible, and interest on debt *in excess* of a house's value may still be deductible if used for educational or medical expenses. Always check with the IRS or your tax adviser before making any personal financial decisions on the basis of tax treatment. Laws change and so do regulations.

Since the passage of the Tax Reform Act of 1986, legislation that would *reinstate* the tax deductibility of student loans has often been contemplated, but is not yet enacted. This could change.

Q Is it better to take out a Federal PLUS Loan or a private supplemental loan?

A Like many financial questions, this one does not have a black-and-white answer.

The interest rate on Federal PLUS Loans will sometimes be lower than supplemental loans, and the rate is always capped by law, making it a better choice for some borrowers.

Other borrowers may prefer the comfort of fixed monthly payments and/or the security of a four-year credit line, available with some private loans such as ExtraCredit™. "Shop around" before you borrow. Terms and conditions vary widely from program to program. (See Chapter 7 for more advice on responsible borrowing.)

5. How financial aid can help

Financial aid is help for meeting college costs: both direct educational costs (such as tuition, fees, and books) and personal living expenses (such as food, housing, and transportation). People are sometimes surprised that students can get financial aid to help them pay for living expenses. Even colleges with comparatively low tuition, such as community colleges, can give qualified students some help in paying for food, rent, commuting, and other personal expenses.

Many students don't realize that financial aid is available to pay for noncollegiate education and training programs, too. If you are thinking about vocational or trade school after high school, financial aid could be a possibility for you.

Who gets financial aid?

While many scholarships are based on criteria other than demonstrated need, most financial aid today is awarded on the basis of need. (Sometimes factors such as academic performance, career plans, or special abilities are considered in addition to demonstrated need.) Chapter 2 explained that "need" is the difference between what it costs to attend a particular college and what you and your family can afford to pay toward those costs. Students are usually eligible for aid equal to the amount of their demonstrated financial need.

Since the amount a family can afford to pay stays the same whether the costs are high or low, you can see that you would be eligible for different amounts of aid at different colleges. In fact, if you get all the financial aid you're eligible for, you could end up paying the same amount at a high-cost college as you would at a low-cost one.

That's a pretty big "if." In academic year 1993-94, more than 5 million students received an estimated $42 billion in various forms of student assistance to help them meet the costs of education or training after high school. Large as that amount may seem, it still wasn't enough to fully meet the need of all the students who could have used some help.

You can improve your chances of getting the outside help you need. Financial aid doesn't just happen to you. You have to take an active part in the process—by identifying all possible sources of assistance for which you might be eligible (the topic of this chapter) and by applying in the right way at the right time (discussed in Chapter 6).

Types of financial aid

There are three types of financial aid generally offered to undergraduate students in college.

Grants and scholarships are sometimes called gift aid, because you don't have to repay them or work to earn them. Grants are usually awarded on the basis of need alone, while scholarship recipients may have to meet criteria other than or in addition to need (academic achievement, for example).

Educational loans are a form of self-help aid. These are usually subsidized by the state or federal government or by colleges themselves and carry lower interest rates than commercial loans. They have to be repaid, generally after you have graduated or left college.

Student employment or work aid is another form of self-help aid. The Federal Work-Study Program is perhaps the best known example of this kind of assistance. Students work, usually 10 to 15 hours a week, to "earn" their aid.

Financial aid comes from a variety of sources: the federal government, the state government, colleges themselves, and a wide range of private organizations.

Most students get a combination of gift aid and

self-help aid from a variety of sources. This is called a financial aid package. The financial aid administrator at the college you attend or apply to will help you put your package together.

Eligibility for financial aid

While each program has its own special criteria, certain basic eligibility requirements are common to almost all programs. For instance, to be eligible for many programs, you must be at least a half-time student (usually defined as six semester hours of courses per semester or the equivalent). In some cases, less-than-half-time students may be eligible for some federal funds, but other programs, such as those sponsored by colleges and private organizations, require recipients to attend on a full-time basis, usually at least 12 hours per semester.

You must be enrolled in an eligible program at an eligible institution, according to the aid program's definition. For some federal student aid programs, you can receive aid to attend more than 9,500 eligible institutions, including colleges, universities, and vocational and technical schools. State aid programs are sometimes limited only to accredited colleges and universities. Some programs have restrictions on providing aid to students in certain fields of study (for example, religious studies) or in vocational or technical courses (those that are shorter than six months in duration). Most programs require that you maintain satisfactory academic progress toward a degree or certification and that you be in good standing with the institution you attend.

Federal student aid programs require that a recipient be either a United States citizen, or a noncitizen who is a permanent resident; refugees or persons granted political asylum may be eligible, too. State student aid programs are usually restricted to legal residents of their particular state, although exceptions to this rule do exist, especially in loan programs. College-sponsored and private assistance programs usually require recipients to be citizens of the United States, too, except for a few programs designed for foreign students.

Financial aid from the federal government

The federal government is the largest single source of student assistance, providing over $31 billion— or about 75 percent of all available financial aid

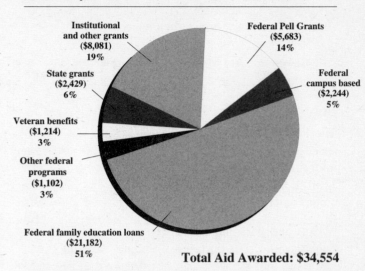

Figure 5.1. Estimated student aid by source for academic year 1993-94 (current dollars in millions)

Institutional and other grants ($8,081) 19%

Federal Pell Grants ($5,683) 14%

State grants ($2,429) 6%

Federal campus based ($2,244) 5%

Veteran benefits ($1,214) 3%

Other federal programs ($1,102) 3%

Federal family education loans ($21,182) 51%

Total Aid Awarded: $34,554

Note: "Other federal programs" include State Student Incentive Grants, Income Contingent Loans, military, other grants, and other loans.

dollars—in academic year 1993-94 (see Figure 5.1). About 67 percent of federal dollars were concentrated in the Federal Family Education Loans Program, and another 18 percent in the Pell Grant Program.

This massive commitment of taxpayer dollars to financial aid reflects the bipartisan national commitment to equalizing postsecondary educational opportunity that has prevailed in the United States since the 1950s— a commitment unparalleled anywhere in the world.

Despite real growth over the past decade, however, federal funding of student aid programs has not kept pace with educational costs. There are many reasons why: the rate at which college costs have been increasing annually, competing demands on the federal budget, the downward pressure of the federal deficit, and the effects of a recessionary economy on families' ability to contribute to educational expenses. But the net result is that federal funds—and indeed, *all* student aid funds—are being stretched further and further to meet growing needs.

In the summer of 1992, Congress "reauthorized" the Higher Education Act. The configuration of federal Title IV student aid programs remained fundamentally the same, but the authorized maximums for some programs were increased. (Whether the authorized maximums will actually be available in any given year depends on whether Congress subsequently appropriates more funds.)

The Higher Education Amendments of 1992 also modified the formulas for determining eligibility for federal Title IV funds. The result is expanded eligibility for many families.

For the most current and detailed information about federal programs, obtain a copy of the free pamphlet, *The Student Aid Guide,* published by the federal government and cited in "Further reading" at the end of this chapter.

Federal Pell Grant Program

The Federal Pell Grant Program is the largest need-based student aid program. An estimated 3.7 million undergraduates received Pell Grants ranging from $100 to $2,300 for the 1993-94 academic year. The amount a student receives depends on need, the costs of education at the particular college he or she attends, the length of the program in which he or she is enrolled, and whether enrollment is full or part time. Graduate students are not eligible, nor are students who have previously received a bachelor's degree.

Federal Supplemental Educational Opportunity Grant Program

The Federal Supplemental Educational Opportunity Grant Program (SEOG) is one of three federal campus-based programs. "Campus-based" means that while the money comes from the federal government, the colleges distribute the money to students who demonstrate need. Recipients must be United States citizens enrolled at least half time in an undergraduate program at an accredited college or university. Grants of up to $4,000 a year are awarded on the basis of need. About 991,000 students received Federal SEOGs in 1993-94.

Federal Perkins Loan Program

The Perkins Loan Program is another federal campus-based program administered by colleges and universities. Undergraduate and graduate students enrolled at least half time may borrow up to $3,000 a year for each year of undergraduate study, to a total of $15,000 for an undergraduate degree and $30,000 for graduate and professional study (including any amount borrowed as an undergraduate). Approximately 697,000 students borrowed Perkins Loans in 1993-94.

Federal Perkins Loans carry the lowest interest rate of any educational loans (5 percent) and repayment is deferred until a student graduates or leaves school. Nine months after a student leaves school, regular repayments are required over a maximum period of 10 years until the total amount (including interest) is repaid. A minimum monthly payment of $30 is usually required, unless the college agrees to a lower amount.

Repayment can sometimes be further deferred for up to three years for service in the military, the Peace Corps, or approved comparable organizations, or if study is resumed on at least a half-time basis. (In such instances, however, the student does not get another six-month grace period in which to defer payment.) A student who wants to have repayment of a Federal Perkins Loan deferred for any reason must complete a request form and submit it to the college from which the loan was originally borrowed. Perkins Loans are cancelled outright in the event of a student's death or total disability. (See Chapter 7 for more information about borrowing money from this and other programs, including legal requirements and advice.)

Federal Work-Study Program

The Federal Work-Study Program (FWSP) is also a federal campus-based program. Participating colleges provide employment opportunities for students with demonstrated need who are enrolled for at least half-time study at either the undergraduate or graduate level. Students are almost always employed on campus, although occasionally jobs are arranged off campus. In assigning work-study to aid recipients, financial aid administrators typically take into account their employable skills, class schedule, and academic progress.

Students are generally paid at least the prevailing federal minimum wage. Students may work as many as 40 hours a week under the program, although 10 to 15 hours is far more typical. The only limitation on Federal Work-Study is a student's demonstrated financial need.

Examples of on-campus jobs for students are faculty aide, dining hall worker, library assistant, grounds keeper, office secretary, and financial aid peer counselor. About 713,000 students received help under the Federal Work-Study Program in 1993-94.

Federal Stafford Loan Program

The Federal Stafford Loan Program (formerly called the Guaranteed Student Loan Program) permits students with demonstrated need to borrow money for educational expenses from private sources such as banks, credit unions, savings and loan associations, and educational organizations. For example, the CollegeCredit™ program sponsored by the College Board is a coordinated array of subsidized and unsubsidized educational loans available through participating colleges and universities. In some states, a public agency also acts as a lender; some colleges also participate in the program as lenders.

Because Federal Stafford Loans are subsidized by the government, the interest rate is lower than most commercially available loans (although higher than Perkins Loans). The government pays the interest while the student is enrolled—another big advantage. For new borrowers after July 1, 1994, the interest rate is variable, based on the 91-day Treasury-bill rate plus 3.1 percent, capped at 8.25 percent. Repayment on both interest and principal is deferred until six months after a student graduates or leaves school. In most states, a state government guaranty agency (or a private organization authorized by the state government) insures the loans; in those states where there is no guaranty agency, the federal government insures them, in which case they're called Federally Insured Student Loans. An estimated 5 million students borrowed under the Federal Stafford Loan Program in 1993-94.

Although some states permit half-time students to borrow under the Stafford Loan Program, most states require that borrowers be full-time students. Freshmen may borrow up to $2,625 a year, and upperclassmen may borrow larger amounts annually, to a maximum of $23,000 for dependent undergraduates ($46,000 for independent undergraduates). Graduate and professional students are currently eligible to borrow a maximum of $65,500 in *subsidized* federal Stafford Loans; they may also be able to borrow additional sums under the unsubsidized Stafford Loan program (see below).

If you borrow money under the Stafford Loan Program, you are charged an origination fee or service charge of 3 percent. Your guaranty agency may also charge you an insurance premium of up to 1 percent. This amount is subtracted from the amount of your loan money before you receive payment.

Stafford Loans are insured against the student's death or total disability, but there are no provisions for cancellation of any part of a loan for other reasons. Under certain circumstances (such as full-time study or service in the military or Peace Corps), repayment can be deferred temporarily. The schedule for repayment is worked out between the student and the lender; the borrower usually has between 5 and 10 years to repay, with the amount of monthly payments and the length of the repayment period depending on the total amount borrowed.

The Higher Education Amendments of 1992 created a new resource for students—the *unsubsidized*

ROTC offers college scholarships with a commitment of military service after graduation.

Federal Stafford Loan Program. Unsubsidized Stafford Loans are intended for use by students who *don't* qualify for a Federal Stafford Loan and/or who need additional funds. The amounts, interest rates, and terms are generally the same as for subsidized Federal Stafford Student Loans, with a couple of important differences. For example, repayment begins when the loan is disbursed instead of when the student borrower graduates or leaves school; the borrower may opt to postpone payments until leaving school, but interest begins to accrue immediately.

Students at some postsecondary institutions can borrow subsidized and unsubsidized Federal Stafford Loans from the federal government through the new Federal Direct Student Loan Program (FDSLP). If the college you attend is participating in the FDSLP, the financial aid office will tell you how to apply for these loans. (Parents of students enrolled at participating institutions will also be able to borrow Federal

PLUS Loans under FDSLP.) The interest rates, maximums, and other terms and conditions of Stafford and PLUS Loans available through the FDSLP are the same as described above.

Note: At the time this book went to press, the U.S. Congress was contemplating changes in the terms of the Federal Stafford Loan Program, chiefly the elimination of the in-school interest subsidy for some or all borrowers. If enacted into law, this change would not affect the availability of funds, but *would* increase the overall costs of borrowing under the Federal Stafford Loan Program.

For more information about Stafford Loans, contact the financial aid office at the colleges you're considering, your guidance counselor, or the guaranty agency for your state listed in Part II of this book. (See Chapter 6 for information about applying and Chapter 7 for advice on responsible borrowing.)

Military options

Military service options are a way of paying for education as you go. Service academies offer a college education at no cost to students, while the Reserve Officers' Training Corps (ROTC) programs help pay for your education at participating colleges and universities. (Still another approach is described elsewhere in this chapter under the heading "Assistance from Benefit Programs.")

Service academies

The United States service academies prepare both men and women for careers in the military, merchant marine, or coast guard. Students attending one of the academies have all expenses paid by the federal government and receive a monthly stipend for incidental expenses as well. Appointments to the academies (with the exception of the Coast Guard) are made through nominations from members of Congress. If you are interested, contact your senator or congressional representative early in the spring of your junior year in high school. Appointments to the Coast Guard Academy are based on national competition for admission. For more information write:

Director of Admissions
United States Air Force Academy
2304 Cadet Drive, Suite 210

United States Air Force Academy,
Colorado 80840-5025

Director of Admissions
United States Military Academy
606 Thayer Road
West Point, New York 10996

Dean of Admissions
United States Naval Academy
117 Decatur Road
Annapolis, Maryland 21402-5018

Director of Admissions
United States Merchant Marine Academy
Kings Point, New York 11024

Director of Admissions
United States Coast Guard Academy
15 Mohegan Avenue
New London, Connecticut 06320-4195

Reserve Officers' Training Corps

Reserve Officers' Training Corps (ROTC) programs are located at approximately 600 colleges and universities across the country; in addition to the institutions that serve as hosts or extensions, there are about 1,800 other institutions in which an ROTC student can cross-enroll. Graduating high school seniors may qualify for competitive four-year ROTC scholarships that typically cover the costs of tuition, fees, and books, and provide a monthly stipend. Students who receive ROTC scholarships must meet certain physical and academic requirements and agree to accept appointment as commissioned officers in the military after graduation. (A minimum of four years' active and two years' reserve duty is required.)

In addition, some ROTC in-college scholarships may be available for students who decide to join as sophomores or even juniors, as well as for students who originally joined ROTC units as nonscholarship students. The requirements and obligations are somewhat different than for four-year scholarship students.

There are different procedures, requirements, and benefits associated with the ROTC programs operated by the different military services. In addition to ROTC programs, there are also other special programs providing financial assistance for education to students who promise to fulfill a term of military service after graduation; the officer training occurs during summer vacations or after college. A good source for students interested in exploring the various military-related options for college assistance is *How the Military Will Help You Pay for College*, by Don M. Betterton (see "Further reading"), which describes each service's ROTC program, the service academies, and several other programs available to military personnel who want to continue with their education. The book also contains a comprehensive list of host and cross-enrollment institutions. Contact the ROTC units at the colleges you are considering, or write:

HQ AFROTC/RREC
551 East Maxwell Boulevard
Maxwell Air Force Base
Montgomery, Alabama 36116-6106

Army ROTC Scholarship Program
HQ—Cadet Command
Building 56/Scholarship Branch
Fort Monroe, Virginia 23651

Navy-Marine Corps NROTC Scholarship Program
Chief of Naval Education and Training
Code N-2/081
Naval Air Station
250 Dallas Street
Pensacola, Florida 32508-5220
Telephone: (800) NAV-ROTC

Assistance from the Bureau of Indian Affairs

Students who can demonstrate financial need and are registered as being at least one-fourth Native American or Alaskan native of a federally recognized tribe are eligible for assistance through the Bureau of Indian Affairs (BIA). Scholarship assistance may be used at any accredited postsecondary institution. For more information, contact your tribal education officer, BIA Area Office.

Assistance from benefit programs

Benefit programs are not quite the same as financial aid programs, but they provide many students with assistance in meeting college costs.

Assistance for military personnel and veterans

There are several programs designed to help servicemen and women pursue higher education, as well as

to assist veterans. Defense Activity for Non-Traditional Education Support (DANTES) permits military personnel to demonstrate job proficiency, qualify for college admission, or earn college-level credits by taking correspondence courses and/or examinations. Each of the services operates programs in which active duty personnel can take courses on an off-duty basis, and you also may be able to translate some of your on-the-job technical training into college credits later on. If you are thinking about enlisting, carefully explore the educational possibilities associated with the various services, including the requirements and obligations of each.

If you think you may want to go to college eventually but are also interested in the military, investigate the major initiative launched on July 1, 1985, called the New G.I. Bill, which replaced the former Veteran's Educational Assistance Plan (VEAP). Although an enlisted service person could use the plan to pay for college work while on active duty, it is more likely that people will use the New G.I. Bill to accumulate benefits for use after discharge. Under the terms of the New G.I. Bill, $100 per month would be automatically deducted from your paycheck during your first year of active duty for a total initial deposit of $1,200 in your "education account." (You can choose not to participate when you enlist, in which case the deduction would not be made.) Depending on how many years you serve on active duty, the government would add between $7,800 and $9,600 more to your account for later use in paying for education.

The New Army College Fund currently offers additional benefits beyond those cited above to men and women who enlist in the army. Men and women serving in the reserves can also participate in New G.I. Bill benefits in return for a service commitment. Because these programs are still new and subject to modification, they may be changed by the time you are ready to go to college; the most current information can be obtained from military recruiting offices.

If you are already a veteran and want to know whether you or your spouse or dependents qualify for educational assistance, contact your local Veterans Administration (VA) office.

Vocational rehabilitation benefits

Since 1977 the federal Rehabilitation Act has prohibited discrimination on the basis of a handicap and has provided for equal participation by handicapped people in programs and activities of postsecondary educational institutions that receive federal funds. The intent of the law is to assure qualified handicapped students of access to educational programs, including financial aid. Many colleges have tried to expand opportunities, particularly in the Federal Work-Study area.

State vocational rehabilitation agencies in most states can help students with handicaps meet the costs of education or job training after high school. In many states, these agencies are working with groups of financial aid administrators to develop cooperative agreements about financial aid and other assistance for handicapped students enrolled in postsecondary institutions. In developing an aid package for a handicapped student, the financial aid administrator at the college typically will consider both the amount of assistance and the type of services provided by the vocational rehabilitation agency. A handicapped student's expense budget may be larger than a nonhandicapped student's budget, in order to take into account their greater expenditures for such things as special equipment, noninsured and nonroutine medical expenses, assistants or attendants, and special transportation. To find out about special help for handicapped students, contact your state department of vocational rehabilitation.

Financial aid from state governments

Every state has a scholarship or grant program that provides some form of financial aid to eligible students who are legal residents of the state. Eligibility criteria vary from state to state. Most state programs award aid to students with demonstrated need, although a few states have some funds available to assist students who meet criteria other than or in addition to need (such as academic performance). Most programs require that students attend a postsecondary institution within the state. (A few states have reciprocal agreements with other states, meaning that students can use their state grants in other states, but this practice may decline as funds become more limited.) Over 1.8 million students received some form of state grant or scholarship in 1993-94.

Your high school guidance counselor can provide you with additional information about the programs and requirements in your state. Part II of this book contains summaries of the major scholarship and grant programs in each of the 50 states, with an address to which you may write for additional information.

Financial aid from colleges

Assistance programs sponsored and administered by colleges and universities themselves are another important resource. College-sponsored financial aid usually comes from one of two sources: tuition revenues and contributions from private donors.

Some scholarships and grants-in-aid are based on demonstrated need, while others are awarded to students who meet criteria other than or in addition to need (such as academic performance, proposed field of study, or special talents or abilities). See Part III of this book for lists of colleges offering various types of scholarships.

Student employment programs are also provided on many campuses to supplement employment provided through the Federal Work-Study Program. These college-funded job programs usually are not based on financial need but on the special skills of the student employees. Examples include laboratory assistant, business office aide, and dormitory resident adviser. At some colleges, need is also considered in addition to skills and experience.

Short-term and emergency loans usually are available to all students. The repayment period generally is confined to an academic year, and interest is either quite low or not charged at all.

The criteria and application procedures for college programs vary considerably, and your best source of information is the catalog or financial aid bulletin published by the college you're considering. Private colleges often have more college-sponsored aid available to assist students than do public institutions; proprietary or profit-making institutions generally have very little or none at all.

Financial aid from private sources

While aid from the federal government, state governments, and colleges and universities constitutes most of the financial assistance received by students, private student aid programs can offer important assistance. The total amount of funds available through such private programs is comparatively small. For an individual student, however, these programs can mean the difference between attending the college one likes best and the college one can afford. So it's well worth investigating the private programs for which you may be eligible.

There are literally thousands of private student aid programs in the United States that award grants, scholarships, and low-interest loans to students to help them further their education or training after high school. One of the best known programs is the National Merit Scholarship Program, which awards over $26 million each year to about 6,700 students. High school juniors compete for these awards by taking the Preliminary SAT/National Merit Scholarship Qualifying Test (PSAT/NMSQT) each October at more than 20,000 high schools around the country that offer the test.

Eligibility criteria, application procedures, number of awards given annually, and average award amounts vary tremendously from program to program. Some programs base their awards on financial need, others on need plus other criteria, and still others don't consider need at all. You might qualify because of your:

- academic achievement
- religious affiliation
- ethnic or racial heritage
- community activities
- artistic talents
- leadership potential
- athletic ability
- career plans
- proposed field of study
- hobbies and special interests
- parents' employers or union membership
- parents' membership in a civic or fraternal group.

Since virtually everyone can claim to meet one of these general criteria, some perspective on the subject seems important. Frequently, stories appear in the press about the "millions of scholarship dollars that go begging every year." Strictly speaking, that's true, but that doesn't mean that if *you* go begging for some of them, you'll necessarily get any!

Many of the scholarships are tied to particular colleges and universities, or programs of study within those institutions. For instance, there actually may be an obscure little scholarship fund for students with a particular last name, but it has to be used at the particular college that administers that bequest. That means you have to be admitted to that college before you can claim any of the funds. If that happens to be a college you have been accepted to and want to attend anyway, terrific! But trying to finance your

education in this way is a little like using coupons to get a discount on a product you don't really want and would never buy under normal circumstances.

Many of the scholarships have very detailed and restrictive eligibility requirements—you might, for instance, have to live in a certain state or region, attend a particular college, pursue a particular course of study, meet certain high academic standards, and demonstrate financial need. If you don't meet them all, you don't qualify.

Nevertheless, it makes good sense to investigate all possible sources of assistance for which you might be eligible. Check with your guidance counselor, and periodically look for notices on your school bulletin board. If you are not yet a senior, read your hometown newspapers (especially in April, May, and June) for the names of scholarships given to graduating seniors in your area. If you think you might qualify, check with the sponsor.

Contact your church or synagogue to see if either the local unit or national organization offers any student aid programs. Contact local civic and fraternal organizations, religious groups, and veterans' posts; many local, state, and national units sponsor some scholarship programs, especially for members' children.

Ask your parents to check with their employers. Many employers have some form of scholarship or grant aid available to help employees' children meet educational expenses; sometimes these programs are competitive, with awards based on academic achievement, while others are based on demonstrated need alone. Some employer programs are even offered as employee fringe benefits, particularly in educational institutions and nonprofit organizations.

If your parents are members of labor unions or trade and professional associations, they may discover that these organizations have some type of aid available to assist members' children. If one of your parents is a military veteran, you might also qualify for some help.

Investigate programs that may be underwritten by local businesses and industries. Community-based Education Opportunity and Upward Bound programs sometimes can assist you in identifying private sources of aid, too.

Scholarship search services

The microcomputer is a powerful tool that can help you in your search for financial aid. Should you use the services of a company that matches you to appropriate scholarships? The Student Advisory Committee of the College Scholarship Service looked at that question a few years ago. Here are the questions that the committee suggests you ask when evaluating a service:

- If the company suggests that large amounts of aid currently are not being used, how does it document the statement?
- How many financial aid sources exist in the company's computer file? Does the company maintain its own file of sources, or does it use the file of some other company or service?
- Is there a minimum number of sources provided by the company? Are the listings in the form of scholarships, work, loans, or contests? Do they include federal and state programs for which the student will be considered through the regular financial aid application process?
- How often does the company update its list of aid sources? Does the company check to confirm that the source still exists, and that data concerning application deadlines and eligibility criteria are current?
- Can the student apply directly to the aid sources provided by the company, or must he or she be recommended for consideration by some other person or group? Are there application fees for the sources provided?
- How long will the student have to wait for the information? Will the list of aid sources be received prior to application deadlines?
- What characteristics are used to match students with aid sources?
- How successful have previous participants been in obtaining funds from aid sources identified by the company?
- Will the company refund the program fee if aid sources are incorrectly matched with the student's qualifications, if aid sources no longer exist or fail to reply to the student, or if application deadlines for aid sources have already passed when the information is received?

The College Board, in the interest of enabling families to get scholarship information *without* paying a fee, developed a new software program that includes a scholarship search. *College Cost Explorer FUND FINDER*, annually updated software developed in collaboration with The Education Resources Institute and American Student Assistance Corporation, enables you to:

- Search a data base of private and public scholarships for ones you are eligble for
- Get detailed cost and scholarship information about 2,800 undergraduate institutions
- Calculate your family's Expected Family Contribution to college costs under the federal methodology.

Students cannot be charged for using *FUND FINDER*. Check with your library or guidance office to see if they have the program.

You could be pleasantly surprised to discover that there is a local, regional, or national scholarship program aimed specifically at someone with your particular experiences talents, part-time employment history, career plans, or proposed field of study. Realize that there is no guarantee that you will receive any funds, even if through reputable sources you find and apply for scholarships that you are eligible for.

There are also many helpful publications that describe sources of financial aid. (Some are listed at the end of this chapter.)

Questions and answers about financial aid

Q With fewer scholarship and loan dollars available and jobs so hard to find, is financial aid available only to people with very low incomes?

A No. You don't have to be poor to receive financial aid, but you have to prove you need it. You are eligible for financial aid equal to the difference between college costs (tuition, living expenses, and so forth) and what you and your family can afford to contribute toward those costs

Q I've done an estimate of my expected family contribution and financial need on the worksheets in Chapter 10. Can I count on getting this much money to help me?

A Not necessarily. You may be eligible for a certain amount, but you may not be able to get all you're eligible for simply because there's not enough to go around. If you've done the estimate, you've got a rough idea of your financial need, but you should be aware of some important limitations on this estimate.

The methods and formulas used in analyzing a family's financial need can and often do change from year to year.

Family situations change. Your family may have

unusual personal or financial circumstances that could not be taken adequately into account in these calculations, but would affect your family's ability to pay for education. (An example might be unusually high expenses associated with an illness or a disability.) When the time comes for you to actually apply for financial aid, you can provide more detailed information than you used in completing these worksheets. At that time, you can explain your financial situation in more detail, and note any special family circumstances.

You should be aware that financial aid administrators at colleges can—and often do—adjust the family share calculated by CSS if a change in circumstances or additional information about your situation warrants a revision. This is because a national need analysis system can never accommodate all the special circumstances that make each family's situation unique. For any of these reasons, your expected family contribution and financial need could be different from your current estimate when the time actually comes for you to apply for financial aid. Use the estimates as a tool for planning, but count on doing as much as you can to help yourself.

Q If I am awarded aid, when will I actually get my money?

A You should get your money when you enroll (although not necessarily "on the spot") or at the start of the term or semester for which you enroll. The financial aid officer can tell you exactly when you will receive your award. Note that awards are not necessarily cash grants but may also be in the form of loans and jobs; most students get a combination or "package."

Q I plan to attend school half time, but I'll still need help with expenses. Will going to college part time lessen my chances of receiving aid?

A In awarding aid, many institutions give priority to full-time students; however, you may be eligible for some aid on a half-time basis. Depending on the priorities and availability of funds at a particular college, half-time students could be eligible for virtually all forms of federal aid. Depending on your financial situation, you could be eligible for a Pell Grant. Ask the financial aid office at the colleges you're considering whether part-time students are given any assistance.

Q Are noncitizens eligible for financial aid?

A In most cases noncitizens are not eligible for tax-supported financial aid (such as federal or state assistance). Usually, however, noncitizens who are permanent residents are eligible, as are some refugees. Some colleges may have limited private funds to assist foreign students.

Q Will I receive special consideration if I have brothers and sisters who are continuing their education beyond high school?

A Generally speaking, yes. Your parents will not be expected to contribute as much to your college costs if you have brothers and sisters whom they are also assisting.

Q My older brother was turned down for financial aid last year. Is there any point in my trying for financial aid?

A Definitely! College costs, institutional policies, and your family's financial circumstances change from one year to the next. The only way to know for sure whether you're eligible for financial aid is to apply for it. (See the next chapter for details.)

Q My older sister and my next-door neighbor both applied for financial aid at the same school last year. Their house is bigger than ours, and they make more money than our parents, so why did my neighbor get more financial aid than my sister?

A The formulas used to assess family financial strength are designed to treat families in similar circumstances equally. There are many reasons why your neighbor may have received more money than your sister:

1. Although her family has a larger house and a greater total income, they may also owe substantially more money on their home mortgage. If so, they would be able to contribute less to college costs and would be eligible for more aid.

2. The family might have financial circumstances of which you are unaware (more family members, extraordinary medical expenses, and so forth).

3. Your neighbor may have met the criteria for some financial aid award that your sister did not meet. For instance, the college may have been able to award her some aid because of her proposed academic major or because of her past academic achievement.

4. The college didn't have enough money to fully meet the needs of all the students who needed some assistance. Unfortunately, when the overall student need at a college exceeds the funds available, the financial aid administrator has to make difficult choices in deciding how much to give each recipient.

But *you* are not your sister. The only way to find out if you're eligible and how much you can receive is to apply for financial aid.

Q Do I have to pay income tax on my student aid award? How about FICA tax on my earnings from work-study jobs?

A The Tax Reform Act of 1986 included some new provisions related to the taxation of scholarships and fellowships. Under the new law, grants, scholarships, and fellowships *in excess of* the amount needed for tuition and fees plus related expenses must be included in taxable income. The Internal Revenue Service has ruled that this means that amounts of awards used for tuition, fees, and required books, supplies, and equipment are nontaxable, but amounts used for other indirect expenses—such as room and board—are subject to taxation.* (However, remember that even these portions of your student aid package would be taxable only if you make enough money overall that you are required to pay income taxes.) Ask at your financial aid office or local IRS office if you have questions about the taxability of your aid award.

Under current law, students are *not* required to pay social security (FICA) tax on wages they earn in jobs provided by the colleges and universities they attend, such as jobs in the Federal Work-Study Program. (Jobs with *other* employers are subject to FICA tax withholding.)

Further reading
Many of these publications are available in public and/or school libraries.

General
Annual Register of Grant Support, 1995. 28th ed. New Providence, N.J.: R.R. Bowker. Lists over 3,000 programs providing grant support in the humanities, international affairs, race and minority concerns, education, environment and urban affairs, social sciences, physical sciences, life sciences, technology, and other areas. Revised annually. $185 plus $12.95 shipping and handling. R.R. Bowker, 121 Chanlon Rd., New Providence, NJ 07974. Order ISBN 0-8352-3522-X.

Chronicle Financial Aid Guide, 1994-95.

Moravia, N.Y.: Chronicle Guidance Publications, Inc., 1994. Information on more than 1,600 financial aid programs for students at high school and undergraduate levels of study, including those offered by noncollege organizations, labor unions, and federal and state governments. Revised annually. $22.47 plus $2.50 postage and handling. Contact Chronicle Guidance Publications, 66 Aurora St., P.O. Box 1190, Moravia, NY 13118-1190.

College Blue Book: Scholarships, Fellowships, Grants, and Loans. 25th ed. New York: Macmillan Publishing Co., 1993. Lists sources of financial aid assistance for high school seniors through students in advanced professional programs. One of a set of five volumes, $50 per volume. Macmillan Publishing Company, Inc., Attn: Order Dept., 866 Third Avenue, New York, NY 10022.

College Costs and Financial Aid Handbook, 1996. 16th ed. New York: College Board Publications, 1994. This how-to reference for students and parents outlines major aid programs, discusses how financial need is determined, and lists current costs and scholarship opportunities at 3,200 two- and four-year public, private, and proprietary institutions. Indexes to colleges that award scholarships for achievement in academics, visual and performing arts, and sports. Revised annually. $16 plus $3.95 handling. Order item #004922 from College Board Publications, Box 886, New York, NY 10101-0886.

Financial Aids for Higher Education, 1995. Keeslar, Oreon, ed. 15th ed. Dubuque, Ia.: Wm. C. Brown Company, 1995. Updated biennially. Lists more than 3,000 programs for students entering as college freshmen. Information includes title, sponsor, nature of program, monetary value, rules for eligibility, basis for selection, application procedures, deadline dates, and addresses. $61.62 plus $2.50 shipping and handling. Order from Brown & Benchmark, a division of Wm. C. Brown Communications, 2460 Kerper Blvd., Dubuque, IA 52001.

Foundation Grants to Individuals. Mills, Carlotta, R., ed. 9th ed. New York: The Foundation Center, 1994. Lists undergraduate and graduate scholarship sources by general and specific requirements. Also includes fellowships, residencies, internships, and grants by U.S. foundations to foreign nationals and citizens and company-sponsored aid. $65 plus $4.50 postage and handling. Order from The Foundation Center, 79 Fifth Ave., 8th Floor, New York, NY 10003.

Fulbrights and Other Grants for Study Abroad,

---

*Department of the Treasury, Internal Revenue Service, Public Affairs Division, News Release IR-87-55, April13, 1987, page 1.

1996-97. New York: Institute of International Education, 1994. Information on Mutual Educational Exchange, Fulbright, and other grants offered by foreign governments, universities, and private donors. Free. Write U.S. Student Programs Division, IIE, 809 United Nations Plaza, New York, NY 10017.

Need A Lift? Educational Opportunities, Careers, Loans, Scholarships, Employment. 44th ed. Indianapolis: The American Legion Education Program. Updated annually. Sources of career, scholarship, and loan information for all students, with emphasis on scholarships for veterans, their dependents, and children of deceased or disabled veterans. $3 prepaid. Order from Emblem Sales, Attn.: Need A Lift, P.O. Box 1050, Indianapolis, IN 46206.

The Official Handbook for the CLEP *Examinations.* New York: College Board Publications, 1994. Information about earning college credit for college-level learning acquired elsewhere. Includes questions from general and subject CLEP exams, a description of each examination, test preparation advice, and a list of 1,200 CLEP test centers by city and state. $15 plus $3.95 shipping and handling. Order item #005279 from College Board Publications, Box 886, New York, NY 10101-0886.

The Scholarship Book: The Complete Guide to Private Sector Scholarships, Grants, and Loans for Undergraduates. 4th ed. Cassidy, Daniel J., and Michael J. Alves. Englewood Cliffs, N.J.: Prentice Hall, Inc., 1993. Lists over 50,000 private-sector scholarships, grants, loans, fellowships, internships, and contest prizes covering major fields of study. Includes sample form letters requesting information on scholarship application requirements and tips on applying for scholarship money. $21.95 plus $1.32 postage and sales tax where applicable. Order from Prentice Hall, Englewood Cliffs, NJ 07632.

The Student Guide. 1995-96. Washington, D.C.: U.S. Department of Education, Office of Student Financial Assistance, 1995. Detailed information on federal student aid programs, eligibility rules, application procedures. Free. Order from Federal Student Aid Programs, P.O. Box 84, Washington, DC 20044, or call 1-800-433-3243.

Specific population groups

Bureau of Indian Affairs Higher Education Grants and Scholarships. Washington, D.C.: Bureau of Indian Affairs. Free. Lists sources of assistance for students who are native American or Alaskan natives of a tribal group recognized by the Bureau

of Indian Affairs for certain benefits. Order from Office of Indian Education Programs, Code 522-Room 3516, 18th and C Streets NW, Washington, DC 20240.

Directory of Financial Aids for Minorities, 1995-97. 5th ed. Schlacter, Gail Ann. San Carlos, Ca.: Reference Service Press, 1995. Biennial. Over 2,000 references and cross-references to scholarships, fellowships, grants, loans, awards, and internships set aside for ethnic minorities. $47.50, plus $4 for shipping. Order from Reference Service Press, 1100 Industrial Rd., Suite 9, San Carlos, CA 94070.

Directory of Financial Aids for Women, 1995-97. Schlacter, Gail Ann. San Carlos, Ca.: Reference Service Press, 1995. Over 1,500 scholarships, fellowships, grants, loans, awards, and internships set aside for women. $45 plus $4 postage and handling. Order from Reference Service Press, 1100 Industrial Rd., Suite 9, San Carlos, CA 94070.

Educational Assistance and Opportunities Information for Army Family Members. Alexandria, Va.: Department of the Army. A general guide available to the Department of the Army on educational financial assistance of particular interest to dependents of active duty, retired, or deceased Army personnel. Free. Order from Commander U.S. Army Pers. Comm., Attn: TATC-POE, 2461 Eisenhower Ave., Alexandria, VA 22331.

Federal Benefits for Veterans and Dependents. Washington, D.C.: Veterans Administration, 1993. Comprehensive summary of benefits, updated every January. $3.25, prepaid. Order Fact Sheet IS-1 from Superintendent of Documents, U.S. Government Printing Office, Washington, D.C. 20402.

Financial Aid for the Disabled and Their Families. 1994-96. Schlacter, Gail Ann, & R. David Weber. San Carlos, Ca.: Reference Service Press, 1994. Lists hundreds of scholarships, fellowships, loans, grants-in-aid, and awards established for the disabled and their children or parents. Nearly 800 entries. Also identifies state educational offices and agencies concerned with the disabled. $38.50 plus $4 for shipping. Order from Reference Service Press, 1100 Industrial Rd., Suite 9, San Carlos, CA 94070.

Financial Aid for Minorities in Business and Law. Garrett Park, Md.: Garrett Park Press, 1994. Lists financial aid sources for minority students specifically in business and legal fields. Other books in the *Financial Aid for Minorities* series cover allied health, education, engineering, science, mass communications and journalism, and sources available regardless of major. $4.95

each *or* $27 for the series. Order from Garrett Park Press, P.O. Box 190, Garrett Park, MD 20896.

Financial Aid for Veterans, Military Personnel and Their Dependents, 1994-96. Schlacter, Gail Ann, and R. David Weber. San Carlos, Ca.: Reference Service Press, 1994. Identifies scholarships, fellowships, loans, grants-in-aid, awards, and internships for military-related personnel. More than 850 references to programs open to applicants at all levels (from high school through postdoctoral) for education, research, travel, training, career development, or emergency situations. $38.50 plus $4 postage and handling. Order from Reference Service Press, 1100 Industrial Rd., Suite 9, San Carlos, CA 94070.

Higher Education Opportunities for Minorities and Women. Washington, D.C.: U.S. Government Printing Office, 1991. Select listing of opportunities for minorities and women in higher education, including some information on scholarships, fellowships, and loans. $8. Order document #065-000-00458-5 from Superintendent of Documents, U.S. Government Printing Office, Washington, DC 20402-9325.

How the Military Will Help You Pay for College. Betterton, Don M. 2nd ed. Princeton, N.J.: Peterson's Guides, 1990. Information about scholarship and financial aid for students going directly to college after high school, including the service academies, ROTC, and other special programs, as well as scholarship and tuition-payment programs for members of the armed forces. $9.95. Available in bookstores.

Fields of study

Allied Health Education Directory, 1995-96. 21st ed. Chicago: American Medical Association, 1994. Contains a section on financial aid and a listing of allied health education programs. $49.95 plus $6.95 postage and handling. Order from American Medical Association, P.O. Box 10946, Chicago, IL 60610-9050.

Directory of Grants in the Humanities, 1994-95. 8th ed. Phoenix, Az.: Oryx Press, 1994. $84.50 plus $7.00 postage and handling. Contains more than 3,500 current funding programs that support research and performance in literature, language, anthropology, philosophy, ethics, sculpture, crafts, mime, etc. Order from Oryx Press, 4041 N. Central, Suite 700, Phoenix, AZ 85012-3397 or call 1-800-279-6799.

Financial Assistance for Library Education, Academic Year 1994-95. Chicago: American Library Association, 1994. Produced by Office of Library Personnel Resources. Lists assistance administered by state library agencies and associations, local libraries, and academic institutions. $1 (postage and handling). Order from Office for Library Personnel Resources, American Library Association, 50 East Huron St., Chicago, IL 60611.

Grants and Awards Available to American Writers. 18th ed. New York: PEN American Center, 1992. Updated annually. Lists awards granted to American writers to use in the United States or abroad. $10.00. Order from PEN American Center, 568 Broadway, New York, NY 10012.

Grants, Fellowships and Prizes, 1994-95. Washington, D.C.: American Historical Association, 1994. Lists over 400 history-oriented sources of humanities grants, fellowships, prizes, internships, and awards from undergraduate to senior postdoctoral level. $8 to members; $10 to nonmembers. Updated annually. Order from American Historical Association, 400 A St. SE, Washington, DC 20003.

A Journalist's Road to Success: A Career and Scholarship Guide. Princeton, N.J.: Dow Jones Newspaper Fund, 1994. Updated annually. Information on journalism programs, scholarships, and minority grants. $3.00. Order from Dow Jones Newspaper Fund, P.O. Box 300, Princeton, NJ 08543-0300 or call 1-800-DOW-FUND.

Medical School Admissions Requirements, U.S. and Canada, 1996-97. 44th ed. Washington, D.C.: Association of American Medical Colleges, 1995. Updated annually. Describes U.S. and Canadian medical schools, detailing entrance requirements of each school, selection factors, and curriculum features. It includes up-to-date information on medical education, premedical planning, choosing a medical school, the Medical College Admission Test (MCAT), the American Medical College Application Service (AMCAS), financing a medical education and other aspects of the medical school application and admissions process. Information for minority students, high school students, and applicants not admitted to medical school. $10 plus $5 for shipping and handling. Order from Association of American Medical Colleges, 2450 N St. NW, Washington, DC 20037. Attn: Membership and Publication Orders.

The National Directory of Grants and Aid to Individuals in the Arts. Fandel, Nancy A. 8th ed. Des Moines, Ia.: Washington International Arts Letter, 1993. Lists grants, prizes, and awards for professional work in the United States and abroad. Includes information about universities and schools offering aid to students in the arts, as well as retreats and residencies.

$30. Order from Washington International Arts Letter, Box 12010, Des Moines, IA 50312.

Scholarships and Loans for Nursing Education, 1994-95. New York: National League for Nursing, 1993. Lists fellowships, scholarships, traineeships, and loans for nursing education, including public funding—federal and state scholarships and loans and work study programs. Outlines packages offered by selected schools and universities; scholarships from community groups and membership organizations for specific purposes and constituencies; fellowships, traineeships, and grants for research and postdoctoral studies; and aid for minority students. Includes tips on how to apply for aid. Bibliography. Appendix of state boards of nursing and brief explanation of the licensing process and types of nursing programs. $15.95 plus $3.75 postage. Order from National League for Nursing, Publications Order Unit, 350 Hudson St., New York, NY 10014. Order No. 41-2638.

Scholarships for Architecture Students. New York: American Institute of Architects, 1993. Poster. Lists major scholarship programs in architecture; accredited schools of architecture; programs for minorities, postgraduates, and professionals. Free. Order from the American Institute of Architects, 1735 New York Ave. NW, Washington, DC 20006.

Student Financial Aid: Speech-Language Pathology and Audiology. Rockville, Md.: American Speech and Hearing Association, 1986. Mimeographed list of general information about grants, scholarships, and loans at the graduate level and aid for graduate education in the field. $1.50 prepaid. Order from American Speech and Hearing Association, 10801 Rockville Pike, Rockville, MD 20852.

Graduate study

Graduate Guide to Grants. Verba, Cynthia. Cambridge, Mass: Harvard University, 1993. Annual publication prepared by the Harvard Graduate School of Arts and Sciences. Designed to help graduate students locate grants and fellowships applicable to a wide range of fields in the arts and sciences. Most grants listed are to support specific research projects—usually dissertation research—but some support earlier stages of graduate study during course work. $25, including postage. Order from Harvard University, Byerly Hall, 8 Garden St., Cambridge, MA 02138.

Graduate Study in Psychology and Associated Fields, 1994, with 1995 addendum. Washington, D.C.: American Psychological Association, 1992. Information about financial assistance and foundations and agencies accepting fellowship applications, as well as information about graduate programs in psychology. $15.95 to members, $19.95 to nonmembers, plus $3.50 for shipping and handling. For charge card orders call 202-336-5570. Order from American Psychological Association, 750 First St. NE, Washington, DC 20002-4242.

Grants Register, 1995-97. New York: St. Martin's Press, 1995. Updated biennially. Lists scholarships and fellowships at all levels of graduate study. Includes specific awards for refugees, war veterans, minorities, and students in unexpected financial difficulties. $95 plus $6 postage and handling from St. Martin's Press, Attn.: Cash Sales, 175 Fifth Ave., New York, NY 10010.

Selected List of Fellowship Opportunities and Aids to Advanced Education for U.S. Citizens and Foreign Nationals. Washington, D.C.: The National Science Foundation, 1993. Prepared by the National Research Council of the National Academy of Sciences. Lists organizations, federal and private, offering fellowships at advanced levels of education. International sources included. Free. Order NSF 88-119 from the Publications Office, National Science Foundation, 1800 G St. NW, Washington, DC 20550.

The Directory of Biomedical and Health Care Grants, 1994. 8th Ed. Taken from the files of *The Grants* Database. Contains more than 3,100 sources. From pure research and health care services to facility expansion and in-service training programs, the directory features more than 200 sources for *graduate* scholarships and assistantships, fellowships, etc. Order from Oryx Press, 4041 No. Central #700, Phoenix, AZ 85012-3397, 1-800-279-6799.

The Graduate Scholarship Directory. Daniel J. Cassidy. 3rd Ed. $24.95 plus $3.50 postage and handling. A guide to scholarships, fellowships, grants, and loans for graduate and professional study. Compiled from the data base of the National Scholarship Research Service (NSRS), this guide lists sources of financial aid in all areas of study: business, education, engineering, and humanities. Order from Career Press, P.O. Box 34, Hawthorne, New Jersey 07507. 4th Ed. available Fall 1995.

Study abroad

Financial Aid for Research and Creative Activities Abroad, 1992-1994. San Carlos, Ca.: Reference Service Press, 1992. Approximately 1,100 entries.

$40. Order from Reference Service Press, 1100 Industrial Rd., Suite 9, San Carlos, CA 94070.

Financial Aid for Study and Training Abroad, 1992-1994. San Carlos, Ca.: Reference Service Press, 1992. Approximately 1,100 entries. $40. Order from Reference Service Press, Suite 9, 1100 Industrial Rd., San Carlos, CA 94070.

Fulbrights and Other Grants for Graduate Study Abroad, 1994-95. New York: Institute of International Education, 1993. Mutual Educational Exchange, Fulbright and other grants offered by foreign governments, universities, and private donors. Free. Order from U.S. Student Programs Division, Institute of International Education, 809 United Nations Plaza, New York, NY 10017-3580.

The International Scholarship Directory. Cassidy, Daniel J. 4th ed. 1993. Santa Rosa, Ca.: National Scholarship Research Service. Guide to financial aid for worldwide study. Lists scholarships, fellowships, grants, internships, and loans available for graduates and undergraduates in every major field of study. Can be used in many countries by both Americans and international students seeking educational opportunities anywhere in the world. $24.95 (subject to change) plus postage and sales tax where applicable. Order from National Scholarship Research Service, 2280 Airport Blvd., Santa Rosa, CA 95403 or call 1-707-546-6781.

6. Applying for financial aid

If you have estimated your expenses at the colleges that interest you, evaluated your family's financial situation, and concluded that you will need some extra help in meeting educational expenses, then you should apply for financial aid. Even if you are not certain that you will qualify, you should apply—that's the only way to find out if you are eligible. Simply applying for admission to college is not enough. If you think you need financial aid, you *must apply* for aid.

The process of applying for financial aid can be confusing and time-consuming, especially to the first-time applicant. (Yes, you must reapply for aid every year, but it really does seem a lot simpler and less confusing the second time around.) In Chapter 5, you learned about the various types and sources of financial aid. Application requirements differ from college to college (and program to program), but the good news is that you don't really have to file separate applications for each and every one.

In order to improve your chances of getting the aid you need, you must know *what* you have to do, *when* you have to do it, and how to do it right—the first time.

What do you need to do?

Financial aid doesn't just *happen* to you. You have to provide information about yourself and your family as the first step in the application process.

The process begins with identifying which form or forms you need to complete in order to meet the requirements of the various sources from which you are seeking financial aid. Don't guess! Find out for sure.

All applicants for *federal* student aid, including Federal Stafford Loans, *must* complete the Free Application for Federal Student Aid (FAFSA). The

FAFSA is available from high school guidance offices and college financial aid offices, generally in the late fall. Depending on where you are applying for admission, this may be the *only* form you need to complete.

Your high school counselor can probably tell you what form you need to complete to apply for assistance from your *state* scholarship or grant program. In some states, your FAFSA information is enough to establish your eligibility; in other states, a separate form may be required. If your counselor doesn't know what's required in your state, contact the appropriate agency at the address listed in Part II of this book.

The FAFSA may also be sufficient to apply for aid at many colleges and universities. However, many other colleges and most private scholarship programs require the completion of *additional* forms. Check with each college and private scholarship program from which you are looking for assistance.

Details about the form requirements for both colleges and private scholarship programs are generally found in the descriptive material they send to applicants, such as college catalogs and special financial aid information packets or brochures. If you do not see the information in these materials or are not certain what it means, contact the college or program and ask.

For purposes of awarding their own private funds, many colleges and universities require the submission of a form in addition to the FAFSA, such as the CSS/Financial Aid PROFILE. If a college you're considering advises you to complete the PROFILE process, ask your guidance counselor or the financial aid office for information about how to register with the College Scholarship Service (CSS) by mail, fax, or telephone.

When you register for PROFILE, you'll answer a few questions about yourself and where you're

The starting point in applying for financial aid is getting information about the need analysis form or forms required by the colleges that interest you. And make sure you meet the financial aid application deadlines.

applying for aid. That information forms the basis for your personal record in the CSS processing system, and also permits CSS to customize a package of forms and instructions for you personally.

That package, which you'll receive in the mail two to three weeks after you've registered, includes important information about how to complete the PROFILE form and when to return it to CSS for processing in order to meet all your deadlines. The first part of the PROFILE form itself contains questions for all filers, but Section Q includes questions unique to the particular colleges and private scholarship programs to which you are applying. If a particular college or program wants you to complete additional CSS supplemental forms, copies will be included in your package.

Most of the institutions that require or accept the CSS/Financial Aid PROFILE will be listed on a special CSS code list available to registrants. Some colleges may use PROFILE only for certain subsets of their populations, such as Early Admission candidates. Read the college's material carefully to determine whether and when you need to complete a PROFILE form. Use the four-digit CSS codes when you register

for PROFILE (not the six-digit federal codes you list on the FAFSA).

Other colleges and universities do not accept or require PROFILE. Do not list a college, university, or private scholarship program on your PROFILE registration *unless* it appears on the CSS code list *or* the institution or agency has supplied a four-digit CSS code to you privately.

You pay a fee for the CSS/Financial Aid PROFILE service to cover the costs of processing your information and sending it to the colleges and programs from which you are seeking aid. The fee is payable at the time you register, but you may subsequently add more colleges or programs to your list for an additional charge.

Note that PROFILE is *not* the same as a federal form and may not be used to establish eligibility for federal student aid programs. All students who want to apply for federal student aid must complete a FAFSA.

Some colleges, universities, and private scholarship programs may ask you to complete their own financial aid application in order to be considered for private funds. Institutional applications do not usually carry a fee, although a few do. If a college wants you to complete its own institutional application, it will send you the form directly. Private programs sometimes have other requirements as well, such as personal essays or biographical statements.

If you are not sure what forms a particular college wants you to complete, don't guess. *Contact the financial aid office and ask.*

Later in the process, you may receive requests from colleges or other aid sponsors for clarification of information you provided on your original forms. For example, you may be asked to provide copies of your own or your parents' most recent tax return. Or you may receive a letter asking for additional information about some aspect of your application.

Respond to any such inquiries promptly and in as much detail as is requested. Don't assume that something is "wrong" with your application just because you're asked for additional detail. Colleges that administer federal funds are required to verify information from at least a portion of their applicants; some routinely request tax returns from all their aid applicants.

When do you need to do it?

Here again the key is to find out what colleges and programs want from you, and to follow their instructions as closely as possible. Some colleges have deadlines for the receipt of all application materials; others have preferred filing dates; still others will accept applications at any time.

For most types of aid, you start the application process in the fall or winter *preceding* the academic year for which help is needed. Try to submit your FAFSA at least four weeks before the earliest college deadline you need to meet. However, do not file your FAFSA before January 1.

If one or more of the colleges and programs from which you are seeking aid requires completion of a PROFILE form, determine what your earliest deadline is and plan accordingly. Count on two to three weeks between the time you register and the time you receive your customized package; add a minimum of a week to fill out the enclosed form and supplements (if any); then assume another two to three weeks for processing and reporting. In other words, you'll want to start the registration process about seven to eight weeks before the college on your list with the earliest deadline for completed applications.

Some colleges may establish different PROFILE completion deadlines for different sets of applicants.

For instance, a college may request Early Decision candidates to submit a PROFILE form to CSS by November 15, all other first-time applicants by January 15, and all renewal applicants by April 15. If you are in doubt about when a college wants you to submit forms, *ask the financial aid office.*

Many private scholarship programs use CSS/Financial Aid PROFILE, including the National Merit Scholarship Corporation. Some programs may decide *not* to be listed on the CSS code list, but will provide applicants with the four-digit CSS code privately.

Still other private scholarship programs use their own applications, and some have deadlines that are far earlier than college deadlines. Some entail substantial effort, such as writing an essay, entering a competition, or compiling a portfolio or dossier of materials. Private sponsors will provide the information to you directly, but don't hesitate to contact the sponsor if you have questions.

After you have started the application process, the important thing is to respond promptly to any follow-up requests for information that you receive from a college or a program.

Generally speaking, it's unwise to wait until you've found out whether you're *admitted* to a college before you apply for financial aid. There are two reasons for not waiting.

First, most colleges try to tell you what financial aid is available before you have to accept their offers of admission; if you *need* financial aid, the colleges understand that you need information about what's available before you can make informed decisions about where to enroll.

Second, if you wait until after you've heard from colleges about your admissions applications, their grant and scholarship funds may be exhausted. Colleges don't have enough money to meet fully the needs of all the students who could use some help, and grants and scholarships usually run out first.

How do you do it *right*?

The forms you complete as part of the application process collect information about your family and finances much like that reviewed in Chapter 2—information about income, assets, family size, unusual circumstances, and so forth. Detailed step-by-step instructions are provided.

Read the instructions. Then read them again. If you don't understand what an instruction means, ask your counselor or call the financial aid office. Enough said.

Get organized. Before you sit down to complete your forms, gather together your most recent income tax returns, W-2 forms, pay stubs, interest statements, home mortgage debt information, records of medical and dental expenses, business or farm records, notices of social security payments for veterans benefits, and other financial records. You will need the records for the calendar year preceding the academic year for which you are seeking assistance. For example, for the 1996-97 academic year, you will need to collect information for calendar year 1995.

Know which federal income tax forms you plan to file, and draft your responses. The tax form you are eligible to file—an IRS 1040, 1040A, or 1040EZ—is one of the factors that influences how your eligibility for federal aid programs will be determined. You don't actually have to *file* your income tax return before you complete financial aid applications, but it's a good idea to at least rough it out. Some questions on the FAFSA are cross-referenced to the most common IRS forms in order to make them easier to complete. Besides, figuring out your answers to your IRS forms in advance—even if you don't actually file your tax return until later—increases the likelihood that if your case is verified, the answers on the financial aid applications will match up with the answers on your tax forms.

Complete all forms accurately, completely, and legibly. Inaccurate or missing information, or unreadable answers, could cause costly delays in the processing of your documents.

Provide all the information requested in the form it's requested. For instance, if the answer calls for a zero, enter a zero. Don't just leave the question blank. (A blank and a zero and a "not applicable" may seem like the same thing to you, but the computers may not interpret them the same way.)

At the same time, don't provide more information than you're asked for. If there's something you want to communicate to a college, for example, and there doesn't appear to be any place to enter it on the form you're completing, don't try to *force* the information into another answer. Send the college a letter. (If you are completing a CSS/Financial Aid PROFILE form, a blank space is provided in which you can explain special circumstances.)

Keep photocopies of every form you complete. If you are asked for follow-up information, you may need to refer to your original answers. Don't trust your memory.

Identify yourself consistently on all forms you complete. Don't call yourself "John James Doe" on one form and "Jack Doe" on another. Take special care to check that you always write social security numbers correctly. Colleges and programs sometimes need to match up records from multiple sources in order to complete your file, and incorrect social security numbers and variations on your name can slow the process down.

Review carefully all the communications that you receive back from programs and colleges. For example, within a few weeks of completing a FAFSA, you will receive back a Student Aid Report (SAR). If there are errors in the information, make corrections directly on the special page provided, and mail it back to the processor; within another few weeks, you will get a revised SAR. If you complete a CSS/Financial Aid PROFILE form, within a few weeks you will receive from CSS an Acknowledgment. Check the Acknowledgment carefully and follow the instructions provided about correcting information or adding more listings to your original request. You may also receive letters from colleges or private programs requesting additional information.

Respond promptly. If additional information is needed, send it as soon as possible. If you find errors, fix them quickly. When it comes to applying for aid, time *is* money.

Chapter 8—*"Pulling It All Together"*—describes what happens to your forms in the final stages of the application process. Don't skip it! It includes some important information about what *you* need to do to nail down your financial aid award.

Questions and answers about applying for financial aid

Q Must I be accepted for admission before I apply for financial aid?

A You should apply for financial aid at the time you apply for admission. Remember, too, that simply applying for admission is not the same as applying for financial aid. To receive aid, you must *apply* for aid; this means that you must file the appropriate form(s). In some cases, you may also be required to submit a separate institutional or state application as well. You will not actually receive aid until you have enrolled.

Q Is it necessary for me to apply for financial aid every year?

A Yes. At most colleges you must apply each academic year, but applying is almost always easier the second time around because there is less paper-work and you are familiar with the process.

Q I want to apply for a scholarship only. Do I have to fill out the FAFSA or the CSS/Financial Aid PROFILE form or both?

A Check with the sponsor of the scholarship and/or the financial aid office at the institution to which you are applying. Find out what forms should be completed and when they are due.

Q How can I find out what the deadline is for applying for aid at the college I am interested in?

A Look for the deadline in Part II of this book or in the college's catalog. If you cannot find it there, ask the college's financial aid office. Be aware that many institutions have "priority filing dates," which you should meet if you possibly can. After that date, some aid may still be available; check with the financial aid office if you are applying later than the deadline or priority date given.

Q One college I'm applying to *requires* the FAFSA plus the CSS/Financial Aid PROFILE form and another *requires* only a FAFSA. What should I do?

A List the college that requires the FAFSA plus the PROFILE form on both forms. List the college that requires *only* the FAFSA on the FAFSA only.

Q My parents are divorced. Who should complete the form?

A The parent with whom you lived for the longest period in the last 12 months should fill out the form. If you didn't live with either parent, or lived with each parent for an equal number of days, the form should be filled out by the parent who provided things such as housing, food, clothes, car, medical and dental care, and college costs.

Q Can a college legally require each of my divorced or separated parents to fill out forms.?

A To be considered for financial aid, you need to provide FAFSA information only from the parent with whom you live. However, an aid administrator at a particular college can make his or her decision about whether to require both parents to file the PRO-FILE or other need analysis forms when you are being considered for institutional aid. The current marital status and other obligations of the parent who doesn't have custody would be considered in this situation.

Q My parents are divorced, but the parent who qualifies and who must complete the form doesn't want to provide the necessary data. However, the parent who doesn't qualify is willing. What should I do?

A According to criteria established by federal programs, the qualifying parent *must* provide information unless an exception is made by a financial aid administrator. However, for purposes of qualifying for aid administered by colleges, the aid administrator at the college may resolve the problem. The administrator may determine, for instance, that there are sufficiently adverse home circumstances that information from the responsible parent cannot be obtained and that information from the other parent is acceptable. This situation should be explained in a letter to your college's financial aid administrator.

Q My parents refuse to file any forms. What should I do?

A In order to be considered for financial aid, you must file a need analysis form. However, aid administrators will sometimes consider special circumstances if they are documented by your clergyman, counselor, or social worker. You must realize that resources will be limited because no state or federal funds can be distributed without documented financial need. (You also may be asked to provide a notarized statement of parent nonsupport.)

Q I plan to start college in the fall of 1996. So why do all the forms ask questions about my parents' income from *this* year when I need the money next year?

A 1995 is the last complete year for which your parents' income can be verified through tax returns. If your parents' income in 1996 will differ substantially from their 1995 income, explain this situation. The financial aid administrator may be able to take these special circumstances into consideration in making your award.

Q Will anyone else see the information we provide on a FAFSA or CSS/Financial Aid PROFILE form?

A Information is shared with the colleges and programs you list as recipients because you are seeking financial aid from them. (You should be aware, however, that the federal government *does* routinely perform some data base matches of federal student aid applicants' records with the Selective Service and Immigration and Naturalization Service, for instance.)

Q Should I attach receipts? Will anyone ever ask for receipts? Should I attach my IRS Form 1040 to my FAFSA or CSS/Financial Aid PROFILE form?

A No. Don't enclose receipts. However, financial aid offices at colleges to which you apply may ask for documentation of unusually high expenses that occur during the academic year. It is more likely that they will request a copy of your tax returns to verify expenses that occurred in the prior calendar year. More and more colleges are requesting tax returns to validate information reported on applicants' forms. Do *not* attach a copy of your tax returns to the PRO-FILE or other need analysis document. If a college or program wants to see your tax returns, send them directly to the address indicated.

Note: A copy of the 1996 CSS/Financial Aid PROFILE is reproduced at the back of this book.

7. Borrowing for education

As costs rise and financial aid resources get tighter, fewer and fewer students will be able to escape the necessity of borrowing some amount of money to complete their education.

Almost half of the student aid dollars available today are in the form of loan dollars, predominantly in the Federal Stafford Student Loan Program. Other federal loans available to students include Federal Perkins Loans and Federal Supplemental Loans for Students. (See Chapters 4 and 5.)

Parents, too, are increasingly turning to public and private loan programs to help finance some or all of their "expected contribution." Federal PLUS Loans and private supplemental loans are among the options available to parents of college students. (See Chapter 4.)

Keep borrowing in perspective

The idea of borrowing to pay for college makes some students and parents anxious. This is especially understandable among people who have never before borrowed money, or who have had a negative experience with borrowing.

But without borrowing, few people could afford houses or cars or major appliances—*or* college. Borrowing can be a useful and appropriate way to help meet college expenses.

If you are worried about your ability to repay a student loan, remember that education usually makes people more employable and thus increases their earning power. U.S. Census data make it clear that the average lifetime earnings of *college* graduates far exceed the average lifetime earnings for high school graduates. By earning a degree or certificate, you will be better prepared to find a job that allows you to repay your student loan.

At the same time, remember that a loan *is* a loan, and not a gift. You are legally responsible for *repay-* ing student loans when you graduate or leave school, and you will have to repay both the *principal*—or the total amount you borrow—and *interest,* which is a fee that you pay for using someone else's money. (There are provisions for certain loans that allow the fulfillment of some or all of the obligation through specific kinds of service.)

How serious are you?

When you borrow, you commit a portion of your *future* income to pay for a *current* expense. That makes it a serious business, so it's important to know how serious *you* are about your education.

If you have grave doubts about your ability to do college-level work, or if you're honestly not sure you're interested in education or training after high school, you might want to hold off on borrowing until you have a clearer sense of what you really want. Taking out a large student loan just to "see how you like college" may not be as sensible as taking courses part time at a low-cost institution or working for a while to save the first semester's tuition.

On the other hand, if you *are* sure about your desire for education, a student loan can be a wise investment in your own future. The education that you purchase with your student loan dollars is something that you'll have forever—not a product that will wear out or get used up.

Credit where credit is due

Thinking of your loan as "credit," rather than as "debt," may ease your mind a little. When people lend you money, they extend credit to you because they believe you will be willing and able to repay the money, with interest. That makes it a good deal on both sides of the transaction—and it's why the federal government has put so much money into subsidized student loans.

And, contrary to the headlines, the vast majority of citizens *do* repay their student loans. Furthermore, they go on to participate fully in the social and economic life of the country in a way that justifies the nation's investment in them.

Repayment of student loans *does* leave borrowers with less money in their pockets than they'd like, especially in the first few years out of college—but they manage. And as their salaries grow over time, repaying their student loans becomes less burdensome. If financial setbacks occur, they can and do take steps to arrange for temporary relief of student loan payments until their financial situations improve again.

Educate yourself about loans

Your student loan may be the first big legal obligation you've assumed. And it may well be the largest single financial obligation you ever take on, short of a home mortgage. Many students borrow during their undergraduate years, and then borrow more funds for graduate or professional school as well.

Protect yourself by becoming an informed consumer. Take the time to educate yourself about loans in advance of applying for them. Familiarize yourself with the key terms and concepts, and know what questions you should ask *before* you sign on the dotted line.

Learn the language

Know your terms. The amount of money you borrow is called the *principal*. When you pay back a loan, you pay both principal and the *interest*—which is the fee you pay for using someone else's money. Interest is expressed as a percentage.

When you investigate the interest rates on different loans, look for the annual percentage rate (APR). (This is also sometimes called the *simple interest rate*.) Your lender is required by law to tell you what this rate is. Don't be confused by a description that talks about *compound monthly interest*. A 1 1/2 percent monthly compounded interest rate may sound like a better deal than a 10 percent annual interest rate, but spread out over one year, that 1 1/2 percent compounded monthly amounts to nearly 18 percent (12 x 1 1/2 = 18).

How much you pay each month is called the *minimum monthly payment*. Your lender or your financial aid office can help you estimate your minimum monthly payment, which varies by the amount borrowed and the number of years for which you've borrowed it.

The *term* of a loan is how long you have to repay the obligation. This can vary substantially, up to 10 years or more. Some loan programs, such as the Federal Stafford and Federal PLUS Programs, permit you to *prepay* your loan, or pay it off early; that can save you considerable interest. (In other programs, you may pay a penalty if you pay off early.)

The *grace period* is how long you can wait before you have to *start* repaying; this, too, varies by program. With Federal Stafford Loans, for example, you have a grace period of six months after you graduate, leave school, or drop below half-time status. With some supplemental loans, including several privately sponsored loan programs, the borrower (usually the parent) has to begin making payments within 30 to 60 days of the date the loan is *disbursed* (made available).

An *origination fee* is a charge deducted from a loan to pay for the costs of making the loan; some programs have an origination fee and others do not. Some programs also charge an *insurance premium* or a *guaranty fee* to insure your loan, while others may charge an *application fee*, which may or may not be refundable, depending on whether you qualify for the loan. Read the lender's literature carefully to make sure you understand what costs you may be incurring.

Subsidized loans—such as Federal Stafford, Perkins, and PLUS Loans—are loans backed by a guarantor; they usually have a lower interest rate and/or other more favorable features than *commercial* loans. A *guarantor* (or *guarantee agency*) is an organization that agrees to pay the loan if the student doesn't; state agencies, the federal government, and authorized private organizations are the most typical guarantors for student loans. Some loans are *privately insured* rather than backed by a guarantor.

A *lender* may be a bank, a savings and loan association, a credit union, a finance company, a college or university, a public or quasi-public agency, or a private organization.

Check out several lenders before you make a decision about where to borrow. Even in the case of the government-backed loans, there are some important differences among lenders, such as what kind of *repayment options* they offer. Repayment options can include *graduated repayment*, where payments are smaller in the first few years after you leave school (when earning power is less), and increase later on; and *consolidation*, where you combine multiple loans into a single obligation for smaller monthly payments but a longer repayment term. (Knowing that these *options* are available is important. You should also be aware, however, that exercising such repayment options can add to the *overall* cost of borrowing.)

Regardless of where you borrow or from what loan program you borrow, you will have to provide some information about yourself on a *loan application*; this information may be checked before a loan is actually made to you. A *promissory note* is another name for a legal agreement or contract you sign when you borrow money.

A *cosigner* or *cosignatory* is a person who signs for your loan with you. You don't need a cosigner for Federal Stafford or Perkins Loans, but you may be asked for one if you borrow from other loan programs, particularly if you are a minor.

If you *default*, or fail to repay your loan when it comes due, a cosigner is legally responsible for your debt. There are other things that can happen, too, if you default on a loan. Your *credit record* (or *credit history*) will most likely be damaged, which will create problems for you if you want to borrow money for other purchases, like a car or a house (or more education). Your salary may be *attached* (or *garnished*), which means that your employer is legally required to turn over part of your earnings to your lender; your federal income tax refund may also be withheld.

People sometimes default because they don't know that other options are available to them—options that would protect their credit records and help them meet their obligations. Under certain circumstances, for example, you may qualify for *deferment*, or temporary postponement of payments (*forbearance*); interest may or may not continue to *accrue* (or add up) during this time.

Evaluate how much you need

Make a realistic but conservative estimate of how much you really *need* to borrow. Remember, you don't have to borrow the maximum amount available. Have you exhausted other alternatives for meeting your expenses? Could you cut your expenses a little, or perhaps work a bit more and borrow a bit less?

Borrowing *more* than you really need just because the yearly or aggregate maximums are higher than your immediate need can be risky. It could impede your eventual ability to repay your loans, or at least reduce your borrowing capacity at a point in the future when you genuinely need more money.

At the same time, borrowing *less* than you really need can also be risky, but in a different way. You

Table 7.1. Selected average starting salaries[1]

College major	Starting salary
Chemical engineering	$ 39,863
Mechanical engineering	36,025
Electrical engineering	35,943
Industrial engineering	35,244
Computer engineering	34,914
Allied health	33,810
Computer science	32,607
Nursing	31,798
Management information systems	30,654
Civil engineering	30,348
Accounting	27,873
Economics/finance	26,597
Business administration	25,142
Marketing	24,726
Political science/government	23,812
English	22,520
Sociology	22,298
Psychology	20,487

[1] Excerpted from the National Association of Colleges and Employers March 1995 *Salary Survey*. Data are compiled from offers extended to students graduating between September 1, 1994, and March 13, 1995, as reported by 365 college and university career service offices nationwide.

don't want to jeopardize your enrollment by trying to get by on a lot less money than is really required to meet your educational expenses. For one thing, if you drop out of school *before* achieving your degree, you'll be at a disadvantage in the job market, but you'll still have a loan to repay!

Estimate how much you can repay

Estimating how much debt you can manage becomes more critical every time you borrow (and many students borrow more than once, and from more than one program). Take into account the amounts you've already borrowed, how much more you'll need to complete your education (including graduate or professional school, if that's in your plans), your estimated monthly payments, and starting salaries for the kinds of jobs you're likely to get once you graduate.

According to the U.S. Census Bureau, the average monthly income for persons with a bachelor's degree is $2,109, while monthly incomes for persons with professional degrees average $4,323. Of course, those figures are for all workers with degrees. A somewhat better frame of reference for estimating your own future earnings are the data in Table 7.1, which displays average starting salary data for students with bachelors' degrees in various disciplines. (If you want to check out the job and salary prospects for the career field you're thinking about, a good place to start is the *Occupational Outlook Handbook* published by the U.S. Department of Labor Bureau of Labor Statistics and available in many public libraries.)

Repaying your student loans may seem far in the future when you're first starting college, but a loan *is* a loan. Student loan payments may become difficult to manage if they exceed 8 to 15 percent of your available income once repayment begins. That's why it's not smart to borrow any more than you really need—particularly if graduate or professional school is in your future.

It's also why you should find out *before* you borrow whether your lender makes available any special plans for graduated repayment (with lower payments in the first few years, when earnings tend to be lower) or other financial incentives for making on-time payments.

A special note to parents about borrowing

Many parents find that they must borrow to help their children meet college costs. While many families elect to use privately insured supplemental loans or lines of credit, many other families turn to the Federal PLUS Loan Program, which was dramatically expanded by the 1992 reauthorization of the Higher Education Act. But before you take out a Federal PLUS loan or any other private supplemental loan, it's important to understand your cash flow so that you know exactly how much you can afford to repay each month.

The worksheet on the next page was prepared by the College Board's CollegeCredit Education Loan program to help parents calculate their monthly expenses.

Financial planners generally recommend that a family's *total* outstanding debt should not exceed 38 to 40 percent of its *net* annual income. That's why you need a close approximation of your cash on hand after monthly expenses before you can assess your ability to manage monthly loan payments under the Federal PLUS Loan Program or any other program.

In Chapter 4, the Federal PLUS Loan Program was described as having a variable interest rate, capped at 9 percent. The following chart from the CollegeCredit Program illustrates repayment over 10 years for various loan amounts at various interest rates.

Amount of loan	Interest rate (%)		Repayment factor		Monthly payment
$ 10,000	7.00	x	.011611	=	$ 116.11
	7.25	x	.011740	=	$ 117.40
	7.50	x	.011870	=	$ 118.70
	7.75	x	.012001	=	$ 120.01
	8.00	x	.012133	=	$ 121.33
	8.25	x	.012265	=	$ 122.65
	8.50	x	.012399	=	$ 123.99
	8.75	x	.012533	=	$ 125.33
	9.00	x	.012668	=	$ 126.68
$ 20,000	7.00	x	.011611	=	$ 232.22
	7.25	x	.011740	=	$ 234.80
	7.50	x	.011870	=	$ 237.40
	7.75	x	.012001	=	$ 240.02
	8.00	x	.012133	=	$ 242.66
	8.25	x	.012265	=	$ 245.30
	8.50	x	.012399	=	$ 247.98
	8.75	x	.012533	=	$ 250.66
	9.00	x	.012668	=	$ 253.36
$ 30,000	7.00	x	.011611	=	$ 348.33
	7.25	x	.011740	=	$ 352.22
	7.50	x	.011870	=	$ 356.10
	7.75	x	.012001	=	$ 360.03
	8.00	x	.012133	=	$ 363.99
	8.25	x	.012265	=	$ 367.95
	8.50	x	.012399	=	$ 371.97
	8.75	x	.012533	=	$ 375.99
	9.00	x	.012668	=	$ 380.04

To calculate a monthly payment for a Federal PLUS Loan amount other than those on the chart, multiply the amount borrowed by the repayment factor for your interest rate. (For example, if you borrowed $12,500 at 7.5 percent, your monthly payment would be $148.38 ($12,500 x .011870.)

If you are considering a private supplemental loan program or line of credit, ask your lender for sample monthly repayment schedules.

Understand what you're doing

Make sure you know what you're doing before you sign on the dotted line. Sometimes students borrow without even realizing that they're doing it; they fail to read award letters carefully and aren't paying attention when they sign a promissory note. Some students also have borrowed from more than one program on the mistaken assumption that their loan will automatically be consolidated in a single obligation

Monthly family expenses

Housing and Maintenance

- ☐ Mortgage or rent payment $_____
- ☐ Electricity   _____
- ☐ Gas   _____
- ☐ Water and sewer   _____
- ☐ Telephone   _____
- ☐ Property taxes   _____
- ☐ Homeowner's insurance   _____
- ☐ Household help   _____
- ☐ Furniture and appliances   _____
- ☐ Other household items   _____
- ☐ Home maintenance   _____
- ☐ Other   _____

Family

- ☐ Groceries $_____
- ☐ School lunches   _____
- ☐ Clothing   _____
- ☐ Laundry and dry cleaning   _____
- ☐ Toiletries   _____
- ☐ Prescription drugs   _____
- ☐ Child care   _____
- ☐ Education expenses   _____
- ☐ Children's camp expenses   _____
- ☐ Children's allowances   _____
- ☐ Gifts   _____
- ☐ Medical expenses   _____
- ☐ Medical insurance   _____
- ☐ Dental expenses   _____
- ☐ Dental insurance   _____
- ☐ Life insurance   _____
- ☐ Other   _____

Transportation

- ☐ Automobile payments $_____
- ☐ Gasoline   _____
- ☐ Auto insurance   _____
- ☐ Auto maintenance   _____
- ☐ Other   _____

Subtotal Monthly Expenses $_____

Subtotal from previous column $_____

Leisure

- ☐ Movies and theater $_____
- ☐ Cable television   _____
- ☐ Books/magazines/newspaper   _____
- ☐ Vacations   _____
- ☐ Restaurants   _____
- ☐ Club memberships   _____
- ☐ Other   _____

Other

- ☐ Installment loans $_____
- ☐ Credit card debt not accounted for above   _____
- ☐ Investment expenses   _____
- ☐ Accountant's fees   _____
- ☐ Attorney's fees   _____
- ☐ Charitable and political contributions   _____
- ☐ Other   _____

TOTAL Monthly Expenses $_____

Monthly Income

- ☐ Net monthly income after taxes and payroll deductions $_____
- ☐ Rent paid to you   _____
- ☐ Alimony received   _____
- ☐ Interest and dividend income   _____

TOTAL Monthly Income $_____

TOTAL Monthly Income $_____

Minus

TOTAL Monthly Expenses $_____

Equals

Cash on Hand After Monthly Expenses $_____

later on; that's not the case, although sometimes it may be possible.

Whether you are considering a subsidized government loan or a commercial loan, you should know the answers to all of these questions before you commit yourself:

- What is the simple interest rate?
- When will you have to begin repayment?
- How large will the monthly payments be, and how long will you be paying back the loan?
- Are there any extra charges involved in borrowing the money? (For instance, you may have to pay an origination fee, service fee, or insurance charges up front.)
- Are there any restrictions?
- Can the lender terminate the loan, and under what conditions?
  Do you have to be notified before cancellation?
- Can you terminate the loan before the contract is up? How much notice must you give the lender? Are there any prepayment penalties, such as additional costs for paying the loan off early?
- Does the loan agreement contain a "balloon clause"—one payment, usually larger than the rest, that is tacked onto the end of the contract? (Sometimes borrowers can't afford to pay this larger sum when the time comes and must get their loans refinanced.)
- Does the contract include a clause allowing wage assignments or garnisheeing? Such a clause allows the lender to ask your employer to take out a specified sum from your monthly earnings and send it to the lender if you default on your loan for any reason, and without any legal procedure. Most banks have eliminated such clauses from their loan contracts, and you should avoid any contract with such a clause.
- What kind of repayment options does the lender offer? Can you count on graduated repayment and/or consolidation options later on?
- Have you taken out other loans from this lender already? If you plan to borrow under the Federal Stafford Student Loan Program for each of your years in school, it makes sense to borrow from a single lender. That will make it easier for you to manage your obligations when you go into repayment, as well as to request consolidation if you decide you want it.

Before you sign any contract or promissory note, make sure you understand what it is all about. If something is unclear, don't be embarrassed to ask for an explanation. You have the right to seek outside counsel and advice before entering into any binding legal agreement.

Questions and answers about borrowing for education

Q Our family didn't qualify for need-based aid. Is any help available?

A A Federal PLUS Loan is a possibility, because you don't have to demonstrate financial need. A Federal PLUS Loan is a government-sponsored loan for *parents* of dependent students. Parents at all income levels may apply; these are "signature loans" that require no collateral. You may borrow from any lender approved by the U.S. Department of Education.

If you are creditworthy, you may also be able to qualify for a privately insured supplemental loan. These programs take many forms, from lines of credit and tuition budgeting plans to more conventional installment loans for students and/or parents. (See Chapter 4 for some examples, or ask your financial aid office for suggestions.)

Q My child is taking out a Federal Stafford Loan. May I take out a Federal PLUS Loan, too?

A Yes. In many families, both students and parents help to pay for college. Your child is legally responsible for Federal Stafford Loan repayment, and you are legally responsible for Federal PLUS Loan repayment. (You may also borrow under a private supplemental loan program, if you are creditworthy.) In some loan programs, both the student and the parent(s) are actually co-signatories on the loan, and legally share the obligation for repayment.

Q How much should I borrow?

A Ask yourself two questions: How much do I really need, and how much can I eventually repay?

Estimating how much debt you can manage becomes more critical each time you borrow. Take into account amounts you've already borrowed, how much more you'll need to complete your education (including graduate or professional school, if that's in your plans), your estimated monthly payments, and starting salaries for the kinds of jobs you're likely to get. (If you're a *parent*, and you're thinking about a Federal PLUS Loan or a privately sponsored supplemental loan, you may want to consider how much you've already borrowed for education as well as for other purposes, how much more you're likely to need to educate other children, other family needs and goals, your current salary and your prospects over the next several years, and how much debt you can handle for a sustained period.)

Q Can I borrow more than once, or from more than one program?

A Yes, many students borrow under the Federal Stafford Loan Program for each year in school; many also borrow from other loan programs.

Keep in mind, though, that each time you borrow from a new loan program, you create a new repayment obligation. Unless you eventually consolidate your loans, you may have separate minimum monthly payments to make on *each* loan program.

Q What is consolidation?

A Once you've entered your grace period or actually started repayment, you may be able to combine your Federal Stafford Loans and most other government-sponsored student loans into one debt. The result is a single monthly payment for the consolidated debt, which is smaller than the total of the separate monthly payments, at least in the initial years. You generally get more time to pay off the consolidated debt, but you'll also pay more in interest.

Investigate consolidation options before you borrow. The option is not available with all lenders.

8. Pulling it all together

Most of this book has been about how you interact with other people and agencies and institutions in the process of planning to pay for college. (That's partly because most of this book has been about getting other people's help for meeting college costs!) You have read about *guidelines*—for estimating costs, for demonstrating need, for determining eligibility. You've learned about *questions* you'll be asked—questions about your income and your assets, your hopes, and your needs. You've heard about *decisions*—how colleges, the federal government, state student assistance agencies, and private scholarship programs make them.

In the end it comes down to the student and his or her family. There are a lot of people who will help you to pull together a personal financing strategy, get financial aid, or offer you advice. But advice is cheap—college isn't. At some point in the process (the earlier the better), you need to develop your own guidelines, ask yourself some questions, and make some personal decisions.

Understanding financial aid awards

Elsewhere in this chapter you'll see a sample financial aid award letter. In mid-spring of your senior year of high school, you will begin to receive notices from financial aid administrators at the colleges to which you applied. Most selective institutions tell you about their admissions and aid decisions at the same time, often around April 15. Other institutions may have a "rolling" admissions schedule—that is, they make admissions decisions as soon as applications are complete—and use either a rolling or a fixed schedule for telling admitted students about their financial aid awards.

Sometimes financial aid administrators will not know exactly how much money is available in the aggregate to help their applicants; uncertainty about state or federal student aid appropriations, for example, can make estimating difficult. Many colleges issue tentative or preliminary award notices in the spring, which are subsequently confirmed in the summer when more information becomes available. In such a circumstance, a college will try to meet its original commitment to a student, but if government funds are reduced, the college may have to adjust the original award offer. The colleges find this process just as frustrating as do families, but in a time of uncertainty, it may simply be unavoidable.

Comparing award offers

If you are considering more than one college, you may want to compare the financial aid awards offered by the colleges. Resist the temptation to look only at the amount of the awards! College A may offer you $1,500 and College B may offer you $3,000. You need to look at the total student expense budgets at College A and College B before you can determine which award comes closer to meeting your need. The smaller award from College A may be all the extra help you need to attend, while the award from College B may not be enough to bridge the gap.

Here are some points to consider in comparing financial aid awards:

- What is the budget that the college used in determining your award offer? Does it coincide with your estimated budget for that college?
- What is the amount determined by the college that you and your family can be expected to pay toward college costs?
- How much of your need is met at each college—costs minus family contribution?
- What portion of each financial aid package is made up of gift aid (scholarships and grants) and

what portion consists of self-help aid (loan and work)?

- Which college would you most like to attend from an educational standpoint? From a financial standpoint, is this college also your best choice? If not, is the aid offered sufficient to permit you to attend?

Worksheet 6 in Chapter 10 provides a simple framework in which to analyze and compare your financial aid awards from various colleges. Remember, the point is not so much how many dollars you are awarded as how much of your need is met.

Accepting a financial aid award

After you have received award letters from the colleges to which you applied and have compared the offers, accept the award at the college you choose by signing the award letter. Complete and return any additional forms that were sent with the award letter. Also notify the other colleges that you are declining their aid offers, so that the funds can be distributed to other students.

If you have any questions about your award, contact the financial aid office at the college. Sometimes revisions in the composition of your award package are possible. For example, you may be able to shift a loan to a work opportunity. You are usually not required to accept the entire financial aid package as offered. If you decide not to accept a part of your aid offer, it may not be possible for the financial aid office to restore that aid later, should you change your mind.

Particularly in a time of declining resources, you should understand that if you need financial aid to meet college costs, you will almost certainly have to accept some of that aid in the form of self-help aid— that is, loans and/or jobs—during the course of your education. Many colleges gradually increase the self-help portion of a student's financial aid package over the four years he or she is enrolled, so you cannot necessarily expect the same package every year, even if your need is the same. For instance, some colleges try to minimize the Federal Work-Study awards offered to freshmen so that they can devote more time to studying and adjusting to college life, but colleges that do this may replace some of the grant aid in the freshman packages with jobs in subsequent years.

Appealing your award package

If you believe that your financial aid package is insufficient to meet your needs, you may want to contact the financial aid office at the college. Inquire about how your expense budget was put together and how your family contribution and financial need were determined. If there are special circumstances that you think have been overlooked, bring these to the aid administrator's attention. It may be that the aid administrator can take your particular situation into account and adjust your award offer.

After visiting with the aid administrator, if you still feel that you have unmet needs or that you have been treated unfairly, you may want to consider appealing your award. Some colleges have a formal administrative procedure with a review board to hear your appeal. Others have a much less formal process: usually the award decision is reviewed by the aid administrator's superior to see that institutional policies have been followed. Contact the financial aid office to find out what the appeal procedures are, and follow them.

Understand, though, that a college's inability to meet your full need probably reflects nothing more than insufficient funds. There has never been enough aid to fully meet the needs of all the students who could use some extra help, and when this book was written, resources were shrinking, not expanding. You have a right to a full explanation of a college's policies and practices with regard to determining need, eligibility, and priorities for distribution of funds, and a college will probably be happy to provide you with this information. The answers to your questions will not necessarily provide the answers to your financial problems. (You may want to review Chapter 4 for some ideas on getting the most mileage out of your own resources.)

Loans and your aid award package

Your financial aid award letter may include the recommendation that you borrow from the Federal Stafford Student Loan Program as part of your aid package.

You will need to complete a separate application for the Federal Stafford Student Loan Program. Your award letter will tell you how to proceed. Some colleges send applications directly to their students; in other situations, you may receive a loan application from your state guaranty agency or be directed to pick one up from your local bank.

The processing of Federal Stafford Student Loan applications varies somewhat from state to state, but the basics are the same. As the borrower, you com-

BROOKDALE COLLEGE

Ms. Juanita L. Student   Date   06/28/95
21 Cornwall Lane
Centerville, CA 95007   ID#   123-45-6789

Dear Juanita:

We have completed our review of your application for financial assistance from Brookdale College. Listed below is the financial aid that we can offer to you at this time, showing how it will be paid to you during the year.

SOURCE:	FALL	WINTER	SPRING	TOTAL
Jacobson Family Grant	667	667	666	2,000
Federal Work-Study Employment	779	778	778	2,335
Federal Pell Grant (ESTIMATED)	284	283	283	850
State Award: Cal Grant	367	367	366	1,100
	2,097	2,095	2,093	6,285

Our decision was based on an analysis of your estimated costs and projected family and other resources. In addition to the awards listed above we recommend that you apply for a Federal Stafford Loan in the amount of $2,625. For information or an application for the loan, contact the Financial Aid Office.

The Jacobson Family Grant was provided by Mr. E.C. Jacobson. If you wish to write him a thank you letter, it should be addressed to him care of my office. We will forward it to him with our annual accounting for the fund.

Please read the enclosed financial aid brochure carefully. If you wish to accept these awards, please complete and return the form enclosed within 30 days. If you have any questions or would like further information, please telephone my office.

Kathleen M. Brouder
Dean of Admissions and Financial Aid

A Fictional, Non-Degree-Granting Institution

plete one section of the application. Your financial aid administrator completes another, certifying that you are enrolled or have been admitted and providing other information about the cost of education and the financial aid awarded. The application is sent to your lender, and once the loan has been made, the application is sent on (either by mail or electronically) to your guarantor for approval.

At some colleges and universities, students may now apply directly to the government for subsidized and unsubsidized Federal Stafford and Federal PLUS Loans. If the college or university you choose to attend is a participant in the Federal Direct Student Loan Program (FDSLP), the financial aid office will explain to you exactly how and when to apply for loans through the institution. (Note that the terms and conditions of the Federal Stafford and Federal PLUS Loans are the same, regardless of whether you borrow from a private lender or through your college.)

Read carefully any information about how to borrow from the Federal Stafford Student Loan Program that accompanies your award letter. Follow the instructions completely and promptly. If you are uncertain how to proceed, call or write the aid office for additional details.

Your aid package may also contain an award of a Federal Perkins Loan. If you are awarded a Federal Perkins Loan, you will not have to complete a separate loan application. However, you will be required to sign a promissory note for each loan advance. A copy of the promissory note and other loan information is provided to recipients in accordance with federal loan disclosure laws. Recipients may also have to provide additional information at some point in the process, such as a list of personal references.

When you review your award letter, make sure you understand exactly what kind of aid you are being offered and what you must do to receive it. Take particular notice of any loans you are awarded, and whether you need to file separate applications in order to get the funds. (And remember the advice in Chapter 7 about borrowing only as much as you *really* need.)

Work and your aid award package

Many students receive a work-study job as part of their aid packages, generally through the Federal Work-Study Program (although some colleges also sponsor work-study programs of their own). Your aid award will tell you how much of your package you are expected to earn through your work-study job, but will not typically tell you what kind of job you'll get. The aid award notice will explain to you how to find out about and apply for eligible jobs, usually on campus.

A student who receives funding under the Federal Work-Study Program will be required to file a federal income tax witholding form (Form W-4) or witholding exemption form (Form W-4E) with the college before he or she can earn any funds. The financial aid office will provide you with full information and copies of the necessary forms.

Private scholarships and your aid award package

Thousands of organizations other than colleges and universities and state and federal governments provide scholarships to thousands of students every year. The way that these outside awards "fit" into a financial aid package can sometimes cause confusion—or even bad feelings—among recipients *and* donors. Often students receive outside scholarships *after* they have already received notification about colleges' financial aid awards. If a student's package was designed to fully meet demonstrated financial need, as discussed earlier in this book, then the college *must* make adjustments in the original award to comply with federal regulations that prohibit recipients of federal aid from getting *more* money than they need. Even if their original awards from colleges did not fully meet their demonstrated need, outside scholarship winners sometimes find that their packages are nonetheless reduced; this might occur because the colleges have a policy of reducing packages to maximize limited resources.

A few years ago, the New England Regional Office of the College Board asked an advisory committee of college financial aid administrators, high school guidance counselors, and foundation personnel to look at some of the problems that were occurring in that particular region of the country. The advisory committee discovered wide differences in colleges' policies regarding financial aid packaging, the percentage of demonstrated financial need met, and how outside awards were treated—a diversity repeated across the country. The committee helped create a pamphlet addressed to high school students who were applying for or had received outside scholarship assistance. Here is some of the good advice included in that pamphlet:

Organizations other than colleges, universities, and state and federal governments routinely award scholarships to worthy students to help them pay college expenses. These "outside" scholarships come from various sources including business and industry, church and civic organizations, unions, local scholarship boards, or school-related groups. Such scholarships vary in value anywhere from one hundred to several thousand dollars and are often renewable. Students fortunate enough to be awarded both an outside scholarship and financial aid from a university, college, or government source may encounter reductions of or revisions to their institutional aid because of the outside scholarships. And, if federal funds are involved, federal regulations forbid over-awards, thereby requiring institutional adjustments in cases where a student's full need has been met by an institution before knowledge of an outside scholarship. A review of the institution's policy in advance can prevent disappointment or surprise about the nature of the reduction.

Q. *If I receive financial aid from the college I'm planning to attend, and then I am awarded a scholarship from a civic group or business organization, how do I know if the college will change its financial aid award?*

A. The only way to be sure if your financial aid award will be adjusted is to check the policy of the institution you plan to attend. The financial aid officer at the college or university is your best source of information. A quick review of the institution's financial aid materials might also provide the answers. Remember, policies differ greatly from one institution to another. What may be true for your classmate's college may not be true for yours.

Q. *Is it true that my institutional financial aid can be reduced by as much as the full amount of any outside scholarship I receive? That seems really unfair.*

A. The answer depends primarily on whether or not your institution has already met your financial need (as measured by the institution). The answer: probably yes if your need has been met; probably no if your need has not been met.

Q. *What if I decide to avoid all this and don't report an outside scholarship to my college?*

A. That's a bad idea. Institutional policies and state and federal regulations require that, if you are a candidate for financial aid, you must report your outside scholarships to the financial aid office of the institution you're planning to attend. Remember, the information you and your parents provide about your financial situation and your outside scholarships must be complete and accurate. If it is not, you risk losing your entire financial aid package.

So what happens if a student's need has already been fully met and he or she receives an outside scholarship? The advisory committee noted that different colleges have different ways of handling the situation. Some reduce the gift aid (grants or scholarships) in the institutional offer by the same amount as the outside award. Others reduce the self-help (work and/or loan) portion of the package, while still others adjust both the gift and the self-help portions. If a student's need has *not* been fully met, however, the committee noted that many colleges would apply the amount of the outside award against the student's remaining unmet need, and not reduce the aid package until the student's need was fully met.

The advisory committee noted that students were still better off receiving outside scholarships even if their institutional awards were reduced, simply because "only a small number of New England institutions will reduce your institutional gift aid by the full value of your outside scholarship," a situation that holds true in most areas of the country. Investigating institutional policies in advance is certainly advisable, as the committee recommended, and high school counselors and college financial aid administrators continue to be good sources of information and advice on this subject.

Your rights and responsibilities

Education or training after high school requires an investment of time, money, and energy. Some people think of students as consumers, and feel that students, like other consumers, have both rights and responsibilities. The federal government has outlined a series of rights and responsibilities that you may want to keep in mind as you develop a personal financial plan and pursue financial aid opportunities.

Student rights

You have a right to receive the following information from a college:

- what financial aid is available, including information about federal, state, and institutional programs
- what the deadlines are for applying for each kind of aid
- what the cost of attendance is, and what the refund policies are if you withdraw
- what criteria the college uses to select aid recipients
- how the college determines your financial need, including how student expenses are figured in your budget
- what resources, such as parents' contribution, other financial aid and benefits, assets, etc., are considered in determining your need
- how much of your financial need has been met
- what aid resources make up your financial package
- what part of the aid received must be repaid and what part is grant aid
- if you receive a student loan, what the interest rate is, what the total amount is that must be repaid, what the procedures are for paying back the loan, how long you have to repay, and when repayment is to begin
- what the procedures are for appealing a financial aid decision if you feel you have been treated unfairly
- how the college determines whether or not you are making satisfactory academic progress, and what happens if you are not.

Student responsibilities

You have a responsibility to:
- review and consider all information about a college's program before you enroll
- pay special attention to your application for student financial aid, including completing it accurately and submitting it on time to the right place. (Errors can delay your getting aid, and intentional misreporting of information is a violation of law subject to penalties under the United States Criminal Code.)
- return all additional documentation, verification, corrections, and/or new information requested either by the financial aid administrator or the agency to which you submitted your application, read and understand all forms that you are asked to sign and keep copies of them, accept responsibility for all agreements signed by you
- if you receive a loan, notify the lender of any change in your name, address, or school status
- if you are assigned student employment, perform in a satisfactory manner the work that is agreed upon in accepting the aid

- know and comply with the deadlines for applying and for reapplying for aid
- know and comply with your college's refund policies and procedures.

Questions and answers about pulling it all together

Q If I accept a college's financial aid offer, how can I be sure of getting the same amount of money next year? How do I renew my award?

A The terms and conditions of your award will be spelled out in your award letter and/or accompanying literature from the aid office. Review this information carefully to make sure you understand exactly what you have to do to maintain your eligibility.

For several reasons, you may not receive exactly the same financial aid package next year. Your parents' income could go up (or down), or the college's tuition and room and board charges could increase. The college may have more or fewer aid dollars to distribute, or government funding could increase or decrease. Factors like these could influence the amount for which you qualify.

It's also possible that the *contents* of your financial aid package may change somewhat, even if its overall value stays approximately the same. Some colleges don't like to give first-year students too much work-study, for example, lest jobs distract them from academics in the critical first year. Others try to minimize loans until students have demonstrated their persistence by successfully completing a year or two.

The important thing to remember is that the financial aid office is there to *help* you. The staff are as anxious to see you make it—academically and financially—as you are. If you're worried about getting help for future years, or have any questions at all about what your package means or what you need to do to maintain your eligibility, call the aid office and *ask*.

Q I decided really late in the school year that I want to go to college in the fall. Is there any chance that I can still get some financial aid?

A It's possible, but you'll have to act quickly!

If you've already initiated the *admissions* application process, call the aid office to find out what you need to do to apply for assistance. If you haven't taken any action whatsoever yet, call the admissions office and explain that you need information about applying for admissions and financial aid.

If you are eligible for a Federal Pell Grant and/or a Federal Stafford Student Loan, you can still apply. However, you are likely to find that you've missed the deadline for state aid, college scholarships, and other programs administered by the college, like work-study. (You *may* be able to get consideration for some of these during the second semester.)

Q My parents say they just can't (or won't) come up with the amount of the expected contribution, and the aid offer from the college I like best just doesn't go far enough. What should I do?

A You can call or write the aid office to explain your situation and see if the staff have any suggestions. Some colleges have installment payment programs or tuition budgeting plans that might make it easier for your parents to finance their contribution. You could also investigate Federal PLUS Loans (for parents) or one of the privately sponsored supplemental loan programs.

If you truly have extenuating circumstances that affect your family's ability to contribute to your educational expenses, the aid office *may* be willing to reconsider your application. Just keep in mind that an aid administrator is likely to be more interested in factors that influence your family's *ability* to pay, not its *willingness* to do so.

It's not always easy—for the aid administrator or the family—to tell the difference between ability and willingness. Another child with exceptional needs or continuing medical expenses, or a parent who's lost a job, affect ability. Not wanting to "spend down" a child's educational trust fund, or wanting more grants in order to avoid borrowing, may reflect more on willingness than on ability. Be prepared to answer some questions.

Q I didn't get nearly as much aid as I needed to attend the college I like best. What now?

A You still have options. Find out if your preferred college will defer your enrollment for a year, giving you time to earn some money. Or consider enrolling in a less expensive college for a year or two, and transferring to your preferred college later on.

You could also go to college part time while you work. Look for an employer that offers tuition payment or reimbursement as a fringe benefit. (As a matter of fact, colleges and universities often give their staffs free or reduced tuition as a benefit of employment. The advantage is, you're already on campus.)

Financial aid checklist

❑ **Develop a list of colleges that interest you** and that seem to match your educational and career goals. You may want to use a comprehensive guide, such as *The College Handbook* or *Index of Majors and Graduate Degrees*, to help you do this. Software packages like *College Cost Explorer FUND FINDER* can also help; see if it's available in your counselor's office, or obtain a copy to use at home.

❑ **Write to the admissions office** at each college on your list for an admissions application form. Remember also to inquire about financial aid opportunities and application procedures. It is best to do this early in the fall of your senior year of high school.

❑ **Make certain you know what forms to file.** You can usually get forms from your high school guidance office or a college financial aid office.

❑ **Register for CSS/Financial Aid PROFILE if one or more of the colleges to which you are applying requests it.** You may register by completing a short form (available at high school guidance offices starting in September) or by telephone. Within two or three weeks of registering, you'll receive a personalized package of forms and instructions. If possible, complete and return your PROFILE form to CSS for processing four weeks in advance of your earliest deadline.

❑ **Mail your completed FAFSA as soon after January 1 as possible.** The form should be sent for processing at least four weeks before the earliest financial aid deadline set by the colleges or state scholarship or grant programs to which you are applying (but no earlier than January 1). Carefully follow the instructions for filling out the form. Make sure your answers are complete and correct.

❑ **Apply for all forms of student financial aid.** Determine early on whether you must fill out additional application forms. Find this out well in advance and make certain you file the appropriate forms by the deadlines.

❑ **Supply additional information promptly.** If you

or your parents receive requests for additional information about your need analysis form, respond promptly so that there will be no further delay in processing your request for aid.

❏ **Review the acknowledgment you get back.** After submitting your need analysis form, you will receive some type of acknowledgment from the processor. Make certain that all entries on the acknowledgment are correct.

❏ **Review your award letters carefully.** The director of financial aid at each college and scholarship program is responsible for determining a student's need, knowing which funds a student is eligible for, and making a decision about who will receive financial aid and how much. Once that decision is made, you will receive an award letter describing the contents of your financial aid package and outlining any conditions attached to the award.

❏ **Check to see if other financial aid application forms are required** by the colleges to which you are applying and find out the deadline dates for each. Complete these forms as early as possible.

❏ **Check with your guidance counselor, high school library, and public library** for books and pamphlets about other aid sources. Follow the directions for applying. You may qualify for a private scholarship, grant, or loan program because of your:

    academic achievement
    religious affiliation
    ethnic or racial heritage
    community activities
    hobbies or special interests
    organizational memberships
    artistic talents, athletic abilities, or
        other special skills
    career plans or proposed field of study

❏ **Find out if your parents' employers, professional associations, or labor unions** sponsor any aid programs.

❏ **Investigate community organizations and civic, cultural, and fraternal groups** to see if they sponsor scholarship programs at the local, state, or national level. Also check with local religious organizations, veterans' posts, businesses, and industries.

❏ **If you or either of your parents is a military veteran,** you may be eligible for special assistance. Contact the nearest office of the Veterans Administr-ation for information.

❏ **Ask about benefits from vocational rehabilitation or other social service agencies** if you think you qualify for assistance.

❏ **Pay close attention to award notices from state and federal student financial aid programs.** Review your federal Student Aid Report (SAR) carefully.

❏ **Learn how the payments from each aid source will be made.** Generally, payment of financial aid awards is made at the time you actually enroll. Also find out if there are additional procedures you should be aware of or forms you must fill out in order to receive aid.

❏ **Explore alternatives.** Some colleges offer tuition and/or fee waivers to certain categories of students, such as adults, children of alumni, or family members enrolled simultaneously. If you qualify, you may want to take advantage of this type of discount. (See Part III of this book for lists of colleges that offer tuition and/or fee waivers.) Colleges that offer special tuition payment plans—installment, deferred, or credit card—or tuition discounts for prepayment also are listed in Part III of this book.

❏ **Educate yourself about loans.** Investigate all the options before you borrow, and make sure that you understand the interest rates, repayment requirements, and other terms and conditions for each loan program you're considering. Give yourself plenty of time—at least six weeks—before the start of the semester to have your loan application processed.

❏ **Make a decision about which college to attend on the basis of your education and career goals.** Remember to notify the college whose offer you are accepting and to communicate your decision to other colleges so that the financial aid they reserved for you can be freed for other applicants.'

9. Long-range planning: A special message to parents

If your child will not be enrolling in college for several years, or if you have one enrolling now but others coming up. you have more time to plan. This chapter is written especially for you.

If you have not already done so, turn now to the tables in the next chapter showing average costs, or look up the average expenses for a few colleges with which you are familiar. And then think about this question:

When it is time to enroll in college, will you have enough ready cash to cover these expenses, in a single lump-sum payment, at the start of the semester?

Most people don't. Even what is generally regarded as the *least* expensive of the various educational options—living at home and commuting to a nearby community college—requires over $5,600 a year on average. The budget for students living on campus now averages about $9,000 per year at an in-state public college or university and more than $18,700 at a private one. And no one is sure how much higher the costs are going to go.

If your family saves little or no money before enrollment, it will be almost impossible to change your household budget fast enough or radically enough to pay for all your college expenses out of current income alone. People with low or fixed incomes don't have the extra money to spend. Even people with high incomes can't afford to divert large chunks of current income to make big payments once or twice a year. However, if you do the best you can for yourself, you may be able to get enough outside help to cover the difference between what you can afford and what college costs.

The purpose of planning

Remember that the purpose of financial planning to meet educational costs is twofold:
- to get as much mileage as you can out of your own resources, and
- to secure the additional outside help—the "financial aid"—you may need in order to make up the difference between what you can afford and what it costs to attend the college of your choice.

The two objectives are inseparable. The entire financing system for American postsecondary education is based on the assumption that you and your family have the *primary* responsibility for meeting college costs, to the extent of your ability.

You may wonder, Why should we use *our* resources at all if financial aid is available? Why not "plan" to have financial aid pay for it all?

The answer is that the bulk of financial aid awarded in the United States is, and always has been, based on "demonstrated need"; that is, it comes into play only after a family has done as much as it can reasonably be expected to do for itself, according to formulas that are applied to all aid applicants. Also, every dollar that you save in advance is probably one less that your child will have to borrow.

Some students come from families that have few or no resources to contribute toward college expenses. Others come from families that can easily foot the bill for even the most expensive educational options. But most students come from families that fall somewhere between the two extremes.

The Smiths and the Joneses

Imagine two families whose overall income pictures have been very similar over time and whose current

The Smiths

Two parents, both working outside the home, older parent age 45. Two children, one in junior high school, the other starting college in the fall. No unusual expenses; standard U.S. income tax deductions and exemptions

The Smiths saved $75,000.

Income before taxes	$50,000
Total assets	75,000
Expected from parents	
from income:	$4,377
from savings:	1,842
First-year costs	$15,000
− Expected from parents	6,219
= Demonstrated need	$8,781

The Joneses

Two parents, both working outside the home, older parent age 45. Two children, one in junior high school, the other starting college in the fall. No unusual expenses; standard U.S. income tax deductions and exemptions

The Joneses saved $15,000.

Income before taxes	$50,000
Total assets	15,000
Expected from parents	
from income:	$4,377
from savings:	0
First-year costs	$15,000
− Expected from parents	4,377
= Demonstrated need	$10,623

*Parental expectations are based on the Federal Methodology formulas for the 1995-96 academic year. Values are approximate.

incomes are identical. Both the Smiths and the Joneses have two children, one of whom will be in college, and the parents are of the same age.

The one big difference between the families is that the Smiths have done a much better job of saving over the years. They started saving a portion of both incomes each month when their children were very young, in anticipation of needing some of those assets to pay for college. They have accumulated $75,000 in savings while the Joneses have spent more of their current income each year and have saved only $15,000.

It is obvious that when the time comes for their respective children to enroll in college, the Smiths will have more money available to put toward college costs than the Joneses. But, won't the Joneses simply qualify for more financial aid?

The answer is, to a degree, yes—but the Smiths will be much better off than the Joneses. Here's why.

Assets, such as savings, *are* considered in the formulas for estimating a family's ability to pay for educational expenses. A family with assets is considered to be in a much stronger financial position than a family without assets. Despite this, the contribution from *income*

has a much greater influence on the expected contribution, as demonstrated with the Smiths and Joneses.

As shown above, the Federal Methodology will assume that the Smiths will be able to contribute $1,842 from their assets for the first year of their child's college expenses. That's only $1,842 out of the $75,000 saved! The Joneses, however, are not expected to make a contribution from assets since their assets are so low. Both families will be expected to contribute $4,377 toward educational expenses from their current incomes.

While some might argue that the Smiths are being "penalized" for saving, let's take a closer look. The Smiths have options the Joneses don't have.

Many families find it difficult to contribute the amount assumed available from current income. Families often accumulate financial obligations related to choices they have made in selecting a home or car, or in acquiring more consumer debt than they would like. These obligations can make it difficult to divert enough current income to educational expenses.

Because they have saved, the Smiths have the option of substituting some of their savings for part of the contribution expected from income, thus freeing up current income and lessening their need to borrow to meet educational expenses. This is a choice the Joneses can make for a year or two for their first child's college expenses, but doing so would leave them without that option for their second child and would leave the parents with very little savings toward their retirement.

In addition, both the Smiths' and Joneses' college-bound children will be asked to take out student loans to meet part of their expenses. The Smiths are in a much better position to use more of their savings to reduce the need for their child to go into debt.

If the families do find it difficult to contribute the amounts expected from their incomes, the availability of assets can make the difference between selecting a college on the basis of *educational value* rather than on the basis of *cost*.

Saving for college makes good sense. It puts a family in a strong position when decisions about college are to be made. It provides a family with options that might not otherwise be available. And as far as being "penalized" for saving is concerned, it's important to note that under the current Federal Methodology, the maximum amount that parents can be expected to contribute from their assets in a given year is *less than six percent of their total assets*. And, home equity is excluded. That leaves a great deal of a family's wealth unassessed by the formula, giving the family a real chance for receiving financial aid while leaving them with the ability to make sound educational decisions.

How to plan

The *basics* are the same for long-range planning as for short-range planning, and have been described earlier in this book: educating yourself about college costs, estimating what you will be expected to pay toward those costs, developing a timetable, choosing strategies to get the most mileage out of your family resources, and finding out about financial aid programs.

The details of your plan to meet college costs will necessarily be very different from a family whose child will enroll within the next few months. If your children are still quite young, time is on your side—a big advantage. On the other hand, you also have the disadvantage of uncertainty about what circumstances will influence both college costs and your ability to pay between now and enrollment. However, you still can—and should—plan.

Setting realistic goals

Setting realistic goals is the first step. A goal is not a wish but a statement of purpose, a description of an objective to be achieved. It should be as concrete and specific as possible.

Reviewing Chapters 1 and 2 will help you:

- learn what college costs today, and
- estimate what share of those costs *you* would be expected to pay if your child were enrolling in the near future.

Once you have done so, you will have to make some *additional* assumptions about what college costs and family expectations will look like when it's time for your children to enroll.

No one is really sure what college will cost in 5 or 10 or 15 years, and the further into the future you look, the murkier becomes the crystal ball. In the short run, at least, the prices charged by institutions for tuition, room, and board are *not* likely to go down, because operating costs continue to rise. Although colleges and universities are working harder than ever to achieve economies in their operating budgets, higher education continues to be very labor intensive. That means that one of their largest continuing expenses is salaries and benefits for employees —faculty members, administrators, librarians, cafeteria and maintenance workers, health service and security personnel, etc.

Does that mean that the costs charged to students and parents will continue to rise at the same rate as they have in recent years? For the last several years, overall increases have averaged 6 to 8 percent, a somewhat slower rate of increase than the double-digit annual increases that characterized the early 1980s.

A family whose children will start college in the fall of 1996 will probably not be too far off in their estimates of total expense if they add 7 or 8 percent *per year* to the 1994-95 averages in Chapter 10. Beyond that, you will have to keep track of annual increases and revise your own projections.

Nor is anyone certain that the formulas for assessing a family's ability to contribute will remain stable over time. However, the basic *principles* embodied in the current methodology have been in place for over 30 years. The same kinds of factors will probably continue to be considered in evaluating a family's financial strength as are discussed in this chapter, although they may be treated or weighted differently.

If you are trying to make some ballpark estimate of what will be expected of you when the time comes, you might want to complete the worksheets in Chapter 10, estimating what you think your income, assets, etc., will be at the time of enrollment. Subtract that estimate from your estimate of future college costs. Alternately, use current figures for estimating both total costs and family share, and inflate the resulting goal statement by your assumption of annual inflation between now and the point of enrollment.

Update your assumptions and goals annually. Revise your estimates of probable future expenses by incorporating new data about actual college costs and periodic changes in the formulas for assessing family ability to contribute. Keep your eye on changes in other leading economic indicators, too.

Developing a timetable

Developing a realistic timetable is closely related to goal-setting. The amount of time—in months or years—that's left before your children *start* college is an important factor. It represents the period in which you can *save* money and *look* for extra outside help. However, your plans could also include assumptions about the periods of time *during and after* college in which you may *spend* money to repay loans. Developing a timetable also lets you translate big goals into more manageable terms. To save $1,200 in one year you have to put aside $100 a month or $25 a week or $3.50 a day—actually a little less, assuming your money earns some interest.

Review Chapter 3 to prove to yourself that time really *is* on your side. It demonstrates that the longer the time period over which you finance any purchase, the smaller its impact will be on your monthly budget. For most families, the hardest possible way to finance their fair share of college costs—whether that share is 5 percent or 100 percent—is by cramming it into their household budget during the four-year period of enrollment. Don't assume, however, that you can, or should, defer saving with the intention of relying on loans when your children are ready to enroll.

Under some economic conditions, borrowing is certainly a feasible and even sensible way of making major purchases, but planning to borrow may not be your wisest strategy. The farther into the future you look, the harder it is to be sure about credit availability, your borrowing capacity, the state of the economy, etc.

If you are fortunate enough to have many years before your children enter college and considerable discretionary income, consult your financial adviser for recommendations about various savings and investment strategies to achieve your goals for meeting college costs. A lot is going to be expected of you. Even if you don't have much to spare, plan to save as much as you can in advance. Regular, systematic savings—even of small amounts—add up, and compounding of interest multiples your money powerfully.

Strategies for paying your fair share

Deciding how to pay your fair share is the next step, once you've established goals and timetables. Review Chapter 4 for descriptions of many of the options that are available today. Some are used far in advance of enrollment to save money, while others are designed to make the burden more manageable at the time of enrollment. To keep education affordable, many colleges and universities have instituted new financing programs in the last several years.

Not every choice is appropriate for—or even available to—every student and family. But the earlier you start, the more choices you'll have, and the more time to investigate the potential benefits and risks.

The dilemma, of course, is that other concerns and expenses may push college savings to the back burner. In particular, you may not feel as though there's much to be saved at the end of the month, once the basic bills have been paid.

Financial planning to meet college costs *isn't* just for wealthy people. It's true that particular financial accounts or products may be appropriate for (or even available only to) families at higher income levels. But financial planning itself isn't a product. It's a *process*, a way of thinking about how to organize whatever resources you do have—including your own time and energy—to meet college costs. In fact, the fewer financial resources you have, the more you need to plan the most effective way of using those you do.

- If you can afford to invest several hundred dollars a month to cover future college costs, *do it*. You'll need every penny of the principal *and* interest when the time comes.
- If you can carve $50 or $75 a month out of your household budget to save toward future college costs, *do it*. You may not be able to finance the whole amount that way, but you'll be able to man-

age a good piece of it. If you cover your fair share, then financial aid may be available to cover the rest.

■ If your best effort is only $2 or $5 a week, *do it*. Even a few dollars a week in the jar beside the kitchen sink is important, not just in a financial sense, but as a statement of faith in the future. The important thing is to make it *regularly*.

Evaluating savings and prepayment plans

Should you use one of the many new public and private plans that have recently been developed to help families engage in long-term saving for college costs? The answer will be different for each family, depending on its resources and its goals.

To help families assess the strengths and weaknesses of the different options, the College Board issued a set of guidelines, some of which are cited below.*

1. Is there a minimum contribution required to enter the program? Are incremental additions possible?
2. Is there a maximum annual amount that can be contributed? Will any such maximum restrict the accumulation below a realistic projection of future college costs?
3. Can anyone in the family, or an agent of the family, contribute to the plan? Are there exclusions?
4. Can the proceeds from the plan be transferred to another family member if educational plans change?
5. Are there eligibility restrictions to a particular class of institutions, either within a state or within an institutional sector, such as independent colleges? Are there penalties associated with these restrictions?
6. Is the yield from the plan guaranteed? How is it guaranteed? How is the family protected from investment deficits below college cost levels?
7. Is the plan insured? Can the investment be recovered if the plan sponsor ceases to exist?
8. Does the plan cover all college costs, or just tuition?
9. Are there any residency requirements for eligibility? What happens if the family moves during the plan years?
10. Are there age restrictions or time limits on use? Do proceeds from the plan have to be used within a certain number of years after high school?

11. How many years of study are covered by the proceeds? Undergraduate only? Is graduate study possible? Full time only? Is part-time attendance possible?
12. Are there restrictions as to who might match funds contributed to the plan? Could an employer or state contribute?
13. What are the refund conditions in the event of a student's nonadmission to college, disability, or death?
14. Does the family benefit from any investment surplus over the necessary cost levels, or is that a profit to the sponsor?
15. Will the plan benefits be taxable, either for federal or state taxes? Will any tax accrue to the contributor, plan sponsor, or student?

Finding extra outside help

Will financial aid continue to be available to help families cover the gap between their best efforts and the costs of attendance? Probably, although its form may change over time. Federal funding of student assistance programs has not kept pace with rising costs in recent years, but Congress has consistently resisted proposals to reduce the level of federal support. Many colleges, states, and private organizations actually have increased their support of student aid programs.

There is not very much you can do in advance of your child's senior year in high school about finding financial aid, beyond educating yourself about it (and expressing your continuing support of it to your legislators). The vast majority of federal, state, and institutional programs do not permit you to apply before January 1 of the year in which your child will actually enroll in college.

Private scholarship programs constitute one exception to this general rule. Review the section on private aid sources in Chapter 5. Competition for some of these private awards begins in the junior year of high school, or even earlier. One of the things you *can* do in advance of your child's senior year is check out the terms, conditions, and application procedures of any private aid source for which you think he or she might be eligible.

A closing note

A college education *is* within the reach of every qualified student in the United States. Paying for it is hard—but planning for it makes the paying easier.

---

*The *College Board Review*, Spring 1988, No. 147, p. 11.

If you do as much as you can for yourself, chances are you will find the extra outside help—the financial aid—you need to take care of the rest.

The other kind of planning you should do is academic. Watch what courses your children are taking in school, and make sure that they're taking the right courses for college. This can save time and money in the future—the curricular choices that children make, as early as the seventh grade, can either open doors or close them.

The College Scholarship Service wishes you well in your planning, and looks forward to serving you when the time comes to apply for financial aid.

Questions and answers about planning

Q Isn't educational financial planning complicated?

A A little. Certainly some savings and investment programs can be pretty complicated! The more money you have, the more sophisticated are the options that may be open to you, and the more you may want to get professional advice.

The basic principles are simple. Dr. Karl E. Case, a professor of economics at Wellesley College who has done a lot of thinking about how families can prepare themselves to meet future educational expenses, cites three important ideas:

1. if you pay over more years, your payment is lower
2. if you decide to pay early, you will earn some interest on this investment
3. compound interest can yield surprisingly large gains (8% compounded annually doubles your money in nine years).*

Besides, educational financial planning isn't as complicated as figuring out how to pay for college when you *haven't* done any planning at all.

Q I've done some calculations, and I don't think we're going to be able to save our full share between now and the time of enrollment. Can we count on loans being available?

A Review Chapter 4 for some insight into the kinds of financing options available today. You'll note that most of the loan programs aimed at parents (as distinct from many of the student loan programs) require a credit check. So it's important that you not arrive at the point of enrollment with your borrowing capacity already exhausted.

Also, don't assume that installment payment plans are necessarily going to be available at all colleges; state laws may even prohibit them at some public institutions. (Remember that installment plans and budgeting plans typically carry some additional costs, too.)

---

*Case, Karl E. "The Office of Family Finance and Planning" (formerly "The Financial Aid Office") in *Educational Financial Planning: A New Concept for the Financial Aid Office*. Columbus, Ga.: Southern Association of Student Financial Aid Administrators, 1986, page 34.

10. Tables, sample cases, and worksheets

The first table in this chapter provides average college costs for the 1994-95 academic year. These costs are based on information from all colleges that provided data for two consecutive years. Average tuition and fees are weighted by total undergraduate enrollment; room and board charges for resident students are weighted by the percentage of undergraduates living in college housing. Additional out-of-state tuition and fees are the mean charges reported by public institutions; they are not weighted by enrollment. (Private colleges rarely have additional nonresident tuition and fees.)

All other figures are average student expenses in each category. Average costs for books and supplies are weighted by total undergraduate enrollment; transportation and other expenses for resident students are weighted by the percentage of undergraduates living in college housing; and board, transportation, and other expenses for commuters are weighted by the percentage of undergraduates who commute.

This table is followed by sample expense budgets based on these average 1994-95 costs for resident students and commuters at different types of colleges.

By the time that *you* are ready to enroll in college, these costs will almost certainly be higher, but the patterns will probably be similar.

The table on estimated parents' contribution shows estimates used to determine how much parents would be expected to pay based on income and family size according to the 1995-96 Federal Methodology. (Average costs and estimated parental contributions are likely to be different for students enrolling in subsequent years. The 1996-97 Federal Methodology is virtually the same as the 1995-96 FM, but is adjusted for inflation.) See Chapter 3 for a discussion of how you can use this in your early financial planning.

Sample cases and worksheets

Meet our three sample students—Carlos, Beth, and Andrea—whose family backgrounds, financial situations, and educational goals have been made up from many of the characteristics of students who are facing the choices of a college education and how to pay for it. Following them through the process of determining financial need and applying for aid may help you develop your own financial plan.

All three begin their planning by estimating on Worksheet 1 their probable expenses at the colleges that interest them. Carlos, Beth, and Andrea come from families with very different financial situations. Before they can tell how much they will be expected to pay toward these educational expenses, they need to evaluate their own circumstances in relation to the costs of attending the particular colleges they're interested in. You will see that Worksheets 2-5 have been completed to help in this process. Worksheet 6 is a record of financial aid they are offered.

You can use Worksheets 1-6 for your personal plan.

Average student expenses, 1994-95

	Tuition and fees	Add'l out-of-state tuition	Books and supplies	Resident			Commuter		
				Room and board	Trans-portation	Other costs	Board only	Trans-portation	Other costs
National									
2-year public	1,298	2,644	566	—	—	—	1,746	934	1,095
2-year private	6,511		552	4,040	569	973	1,850	908	1,192
4-year public	2,686	4,169	578	3,826	592	1,308	1,684	892	1,314
4-year private	11,709		585	4,976	523	991	1,809	844	1,123
New England									
2-year public	2,236	3,424	489	—	—	—	1,812	1,024	1,164
2-year private	9,503		528	5,858	528	838	1,649	865	1,779
4-year public	4,168	4,901	543	4,492	437	1,176	1,686	1,013	1,146
4-year private	15,593		578	6,023	493	950	1,746	916	1,117
Middle States									
2-year public	1,978	2,619	545	—	—	—	1,484	855	1,065
2-year private	8,827		575	4,985	498	1,143	2,184	884	1,425
4-year public	3,490	3,581	589	4,456	490	1,263	1,607*	856	1,397
4-year private	12,396		573	5,678	374	916	1,651	756	1,074
South									
2-year public	1,002	2,378	547	—	—	—	1,802	1,104	1,054
2-year private	6,586		613	3,778	575	910	1,535	1,022	936
4-year public	2,265	3,869	584	3,449	598	1,189	1,653	997	1,229
4-year private	10,096		578	4,264	670	1,014	1,647	828	1,023
Midwest									
2-year public	1,554	2,711	566	—	—	—	1,740	1,000	1,075
2-year private	6,301		583	3,186	519	961	1,457	1,189	948
4-year public	2,930	3,912	526	3,477	527	1,335	1,534	855	1,294
4-year private	11,203		575	4,158	518	960	1,839	917	1,136
Southwest									
2-year public	756*	1,364	610*	2,543*	647*	996*	1,783*	946*	1,104*
2-year private	3,989	—	—	—	—	—	—	—	—
4-year public	1,707	3,448	449*	3,382	1,065	1,382	1,598	1,121	1,266
4-year private	8,691		568	3,918	663	1,182	1,685	1,034	1,179
West									
2-year public	812*	3,313	601*	—	—	—	1,905	724*	1,174*
2-year private	3,407*		—	—	—	—	—	679	1,078
4-year public	2,467	5,894	642	4,569	639	1,528	1,934	755	1,421
4-year private	11,616		687	5,241	614	1,224	2,310	799	1,292

Sample expense budgets

	Resident	Commuter
2-year public		$ 5,639
2-year private	$12,647	11,013
4-year public	8,990	7,154
4-year private	18,784	16,070

Note on the table: Calculations are enrollment-weighted and utilize only those institutions for which two consecutive years' worth of price and enrollment data are available. Institutions do not necessarily provide cost data in all fields. A dash (—) indicates that the number of institutions reporting data on this item was too small to support an analysis. A blank indicates that the data are not generally applicable for the type of institution. An asterisk (*) following an average indicates that while the number of institutions reporting data on this item was large enough to support an analysis, the sample size was marginal.

1995-96 Estimated parents' contribution

Net assets	$25,000				$50,000			
Family size	3	4	5	6	3	4	5	6

1994 income before taxes

	$25,000				$50,000			
$20,000	$ 496	$ 0	$ 0	$ 0	$ 789	$ 152	$ 0	$ 0
30,000	2,021	1,385	786	112	2,330	1,678	1,079	405
40,000	3,926	3,037	2,327	1,638	4,379	3,423	2,660	1,931
50,000	6,767	5,460	4,375	3,370	7,393	6,086	4,899	3,787
60,000	9,416	8,206	7,076	5,786	10,042	8,832	7,702	6,412
70,000	11,925	10,715	9,585	8,296	12,551	11,341	10,211	8,922
80,000	14,865	13,655	12,525	11,235	15,491	14,281	13,151	11,861
90,000	17,805	16,595	15,465	14,175	18,431	17,221	16,091	14,801
100,000	20,706	19,531	18,405	17,115	21,332	20,157	19,031	17,741

Net assets	$100,000				$150,000			
Family size	3	4	5	6	3	4	5	6

1994 income before taxes

	$100,000				$150,000			
$20,000	$ 2,109	$ 1,472	$ 872	$ 117	$ 3,743	$ 2,881	$ 2,192	$ 1,437
30,000	4,061	3,152	2,426	1,725	6,566	5,240	4,192	3,214
40,000	7,006	5,646	4,525	3,485	9,826	8,466	7,187	5,747
50,000	10,213	8,906	7,626	6,187	13,033	11,726	10,446	9,007
60,000	12,862	11,652	10,522	9,232	15,682	14,472	13,342	12,052
70,000	15,371	14,161	13,031	11,742	18,191	16,981	15,851	14,562
80,000	18,311	17,101	15,971	14,681	21,131	19,921	18,791	17,501
90,000	21,251	20,041	18,911	17,621	24,071	22,861	21,731	20,441
100,000	24,152	22,977	21,851	20,561	26,972	25,797	24,671	23,381

Note: The figures shown are parents' contribution under Federal Methodology (FM), assuming the older parent, age 45, is employed; the other parent is not employed; income is only from employment; no unusual circumstances; standard deduction on U.S. income tax; 1040 tax return filed; and one undergraduate child enrolled in college. Net assets exclude primary place of residence and family farms.

Carlos, Beth, and Andrea plan for college costs

Worksheet 1: Estimating student expenses

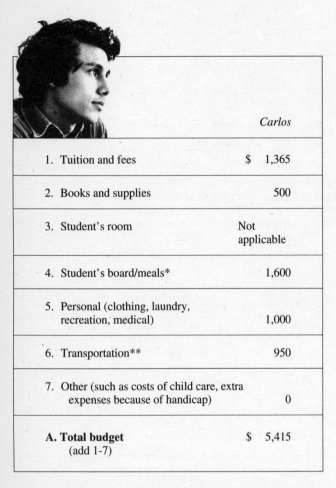

	Carlos
1. Tuition and fees	$ 1,365
2. Books and supplies	500
3. Student's room	Not applicable
4. Student's board/meals*	1,600
5. Personal (clothing, laundry, recreation, medical)	1,000
6. Transportation**	950
7. Other (such as costs of child care, extra expenses because of handicap)	0
A. Total budget (add 1-7)	$ 5,415

* You will want to consider these expenses to your family if you live at home.

** If you are planning to live on campus, estimate the costs of the round-trips you will have to make to your home. Colleges usually estimate a student makes two or three round-trips during the year. Students living at home should figure the costs of daily tranportation to college.

Carlos Fernandez age 18, graduated from high school in June 1995. He wanted to live with his family and attend a nearby community college to pursue an Associate of Arts degree in chemistry. He hopes to transfer to a four-year college of engineering when he completes his AA degree and eventually to become a chemical engineer.

Carlos' father, age 42, earns $21,300 per year as a maintenance worker; his mother, age 41, earns $9,100 as a part-time beautician at a local salon. His younger brother, age 16, is a junior in high school and also hopes to attend college after he finishes high school. The family owns a cooperative apartment and files IRS form 1040. They earn about $50 a year in interest from their savings of $5,320. Carlos earned $2,750 in 1994 working as a grocery clerk after school and full time during the summer. He expects to continue working part time at the grocery store while enrolled in college. He has saved $1,500 toward his college education.

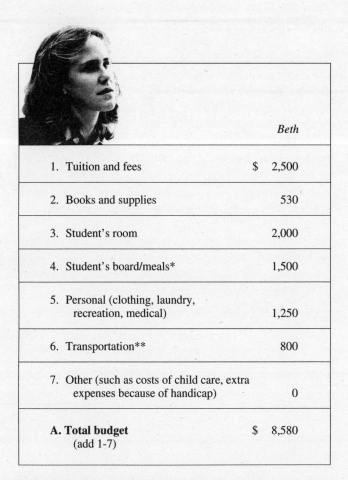

	Beth
1. Tuition and fees	$ 2,500
2. Books and supplies	530
3. Student's room	2,000
4. Student's board/meals*	1,500
5. Personal (clothing, laundry, recreation, medical)	1,250
6. Transportation**	800
7. Other (such as costs of child care, extra expenses because of handicap)	0
A. Total budget (add 1-7)	$ 8,580

* You will want to consider these expenses to your family if you live at home.

** If you are planning to live on campus, estimate the costs of the round-trips you will have to make to your home. Colleges usually estimate a student makes two or three round-trips during the year. Students living at home should figure the costs of daily tranportation to college.

Beth Edwards is 17 and graduated from high school in June 1995. She hoped to attend the state university to study journalism and plans to live on campus.

Beth's mother, age 45, does not work outside the home, but is kept busy looking after Beth's 5-year-old twin sisters. Beth's father passed away unexpectedly in December, 1993. The family is now supported by social security benefits of $17,350 (which will be reduced when Beth starts college). Her mother also receives about $950 in interest income from her savings of $30,000, the proceeds of Beth's father's life insurance policy. The family rents an apartment and Beth's mother files IRS form 1040A.

Beth earned $1,500 during the summer of 1994 as a summer camp counselor and spent the school year doing volunteer work. She has been unable to save since she has contributed most of her earnings to her mother for household expenses.

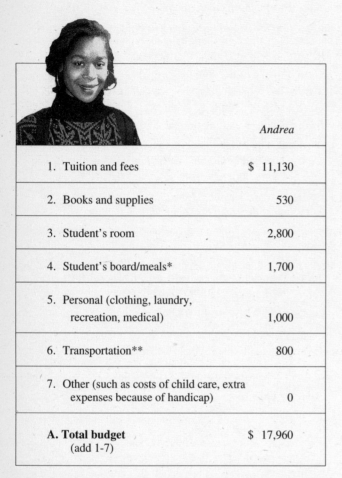

	Andrea
1. Tuition and fees	$ 11,130
2. Books and supplies	530
3. Student's room	2,800
4. Student's board/meals*	1,700
5. Personal (clothing, laundry, recreation, medical)	1,000
6. Transportation**	800
7. Other (such as costs of child care, extra expenses because of handicap)	0
A. Total budget (add 1-7)	$ 17,960

* You will want to consider these expenses to your family if you live at home.

** If you are planning to live on campus, estimate the costs of the round-trips you will have to make to your home. Colleges usually estimate a student makes two or three round-trips during the year. Students living at home should figure the costs of daily tranportation to college.

Andrea Daley, age 18, graduated from high school in June 1995. She planned to attend a private college to pursue premedical studies. She will live on campus.

Andrea's father, age 49, is the pastor of the community's Baptist Church and earns $19,500 per year. Her mother, age 50, is an assistant principal at the local high school, earning an annual salary of $49,750. Andrea's parents have additional income of $750 in interest from savings and also receive $1,000 per year from a part-ownership in a family dry-cleaning business. The Daley's assets include $25,000 in savings and $55,000 in home equity. Their part of the family business is worth $62,500. They file IRS form 1040.

Andrea has a sister, age 20, who is a junior in college. Her younger brother, age 14, is a freshman in high school. Andrea earned $1,050 in 1994 as the organist at her father's church and has saved $500. She has also been selected to receive two local scholarships totalling $1,000.

Worksheet 2: Parents' expected contribution (Federal Methodology[1])

	Carlos	Beth[2]	Andrea
A. 1994 income:			
1. Father's yearly wages, salaries, tips, and other compensation	$21,300	$ 0	$ 19,500
2. Mother's yearly wages, salaries, tips, and other compensation	9,100	0	49,750
3. All other income of mother and father (dividends, interest, social security, pensions, welfare, child support, etc.) *Include IRA/Keogh payments and 401(K) and 403(B) contributions.*	50	18,300	1,750
4. IRS allowable adjustments to income (business expenses, interest penalties, alimony *paid,* etc.) *Do not include IRA/Keogh payments.*	0	0	0
B. Total income (Add 1, 2, 3 and subtract 4.)	30,450	18,300	71,000
Expenses:			
5. U.S. income tax parents paid on their 1994 income (not amount withheld from paycheck)	$ 2,101	$ 0	$ 9,550
6. Social Security (FICA) tax (See Table for 6.)	2,325	0	5,298
7. State and other taxes (Enter 8% of B.)[3]	2,436	1,464	5,680
8. Employment allowance. If 2-parent family and both parents work, allow 35% of lower salary to a maximum of $2,500; if 1-parent family, allow 35% of salary to a maximum of $2,500. No allowance for a 2-parent family in which only one parent works.	2,500	0	2,500
9. Income Protection Allowance (See Table for 9)	17,150	17,150	18,330
C. Total allowance against income (Add 5, 6, 7, 8, 9.)	26,512	18,614	41,358
D. Available income (Subtract C from B.)	3,938	(314)	29,642
Assets:			
10. Other real estate equity (value minus unpaid balance on mortgage)	0	0	0
11. Business or farm (Figure total value minus indebtedness and then take percentage shown in Table for 11.) If your family is only part owner of the farm or business, list only your share of the net value.	0	0	25,000
12. Cash, savings, and checking accounts	5,320	30,000	25,000
13. Other investments (current net value)	0	0	0
E. Total assets	5,320	30,000	50,000
Deductions:			
F. Asset protection allowance (See Table for F.)	36,100	28,300	46,700
G. Remaining assets (Subtract F from E.)	(30,780)	1,700	3,300
H. Income supplement from assets (Multiply G by 12%, if negative, enter 0.)	0	204	396
I. Adjusted available income (Add D and H.)	3,938	(110)	30,038
J. Parents' expected contribution (Multiply I by taxation rate amount given in Table for J.)	866	0	10,100
K. Parents' expected contribution if more than one family member is in college (Divide J by number of family members in college at least half-time.)	866	0	5,050

1. Note that this and subsequent worksheets are based on the 1995-96 Federal Methodology (FM), and reflect the procedures that would have been used to estimate contributions in the 1995-96 academic year. Average student expenses displayed on page 64 reflect 1994-95 college costs. Average costs *and* average contributions are likely to be different for students enrolling in subsequent years.
2. Federal need analysis provisions provide a "simple needs test" treatment for families with total Adjusted Gross Income or earned income of $50,000 or less, who file the 1040A or 1040EZ federal income tax return or do not file taxes. Therefore, if neither Beth *nor* her parent filed a Form 1040 federal tax return, family assets would not be considered in the "simple needs test."
3. Note that state taxes vary substantially from state to state. This is an average. The FM itself uses a state-specific average.

Tables used for completion of Worksheets 2 and 3

Table for Social Security (FICA) Tax Allowance (Items 6 and 19)

When individual's yearly wage total equals	Allowance per wage earner for Social Security (FICA) tax is:
$ 1 to $ 60,600	7.65% of income earned by each wage earner (maximum $4,635.90 per person)
$ 60,601 or more	$4,635.90 + 1.45% of income earned above $60,600 by each wage earner

Table for income protection allowance (Item 9)

Family size* (including student)	Number in college**				
	1	2	3	4	5
2	$11,150	$ 9,240			
3	13,890	11,990	$10,080		
4	17,150	15,240	13,350	$11,440	
5	20,240	18,330	16,430	14,520	$12,620
6	23,670	21,760	19,860	17,960	16,060

* For each additional family member, add $2,670.
** For each additional college student, subtract $1,900

Table for business or farm adjustments (Item 11)

Net worth (NW)	Adjusted net worth
Less than $ 1	$ 0
$ 1 to 80,000	$ 0 + 40% of NW
$ 80,001 to 240,000	$ 32,000 + 50% of NW over $ 80,000
$240,001 to 400,000	$112,000 + 60% of NW over $240,000
$400,001 or more	$208,000 + 100% of NW over $400,000

Table for asset protection allowance (Item F)

Age	Two-parent family	One-parent family
39 or less	$ 32,000	$ 22,700
40–44	36,100	25,300
45–49	40,900	28,300
50–54	46,700	31,700
55–59	54,100	36,000
60–64	63,400	41,300
65 or more	70,200	45,100

Table for parents' expected contribution (Item J)

Adjusted available income (AAI) (Item I)	Total parents' contribution
Less than $–3,409	$ -750
$ –3,409 to 10,000	22% of AAI
$ 10,001 to 12,500	$ 2,200 + 25% of AAI over $10,000
$ 12,501 to 15,100	$ 2,825 + 29% of AAI over $12,500
$ 15,101 to 17,600	$ 3,579 + 34% of AAI over $15,100
$ 17,601 to 20,100	$ 4,429 + 40% of AAI over $17,600
$ 20,101 or more	$ 5,429 + 47% of AAI over $20,100

Worksheet 3: Student's expected contribution

	Carlos	Beth	Andrea
L. Student's 1994 income:			
14. Student's yearly wages, salaries, tips, and other compensation	$ 2,750	$ 1,500	$ 1,050
15. Spouse's yearly wages, salaries, tips, and other compensation	0	0	0
16. All other income of student (dividends, interest, untaxed income, and benefits)	30	0	21
M. Total income (Add 14, 15, and 16.)	2,780	1,500	1,071
Allowances:			
17. U.S. income tax student (and spouse) paid on 1994 income (not amount withheld from paychecks)	0	0	0
18. State and other taxes (enter 4% of M.)	111	60	43
19. Social security (FICA) tax (See Table for 19.)	210	115	80
20. Dependent student offset	1,750	1,750	1,750
N. Total allowances against student's income (Add 17, 18, 19, and 20.)	2,071	1,925	1,873
O. Available income (Subtract N from M.)	709	0	0
Resources:			
21. Contribution from income (Line O x 50%) cannot be less then $0	355	0	0
22. Contribution from assets (Multiply the total savings and other assets—such as stocks and bonds excluding home equity by 35%.)	525	0	175
23. Other gifts and scholarships already received	0	0	0
Q. Total student resources (Add 21, 22 and 23.)	$ 880	$ 0	$ 175

Worksheet 4: Total family contribution

	Carlos	Beth	Andrea
J. Parents' expected contribution (Use figure for K instead of J if there is more than one family member in college.)	$ 866	$ 0	$ 5,050
Q. Student's expected contribution from resources	880	0	175
R. Total family contribution (Add J and Q.)	$ 1,746	$ 0	$ 5,225

Worksheet 5: Student need

	Carlos	Beth	Andrea
S. Total college expense budget	$ 5,415	$ 8,580	$ 17,960
R. Total family contribution	1,746	0	5,225
T. Student need (Subtract R from S.)	$ 3,669	$ 8,580	$ 12,735

Worksheet 6: Financial aid awards

	Carlos
A. Total student budget	$ 5,415
R. Total family contribution	1,746
T. Demonstrated financial need	3,669
1. Federal Pell Grant	750
2. State scholarship	500
3. Institutional grant	0
4. Federal Work-Study	0
5. Federal Perkins Loan	0
6. Federal Supplemental Educational Opportunity Grant	500
7. Federal Stafford Loan	1,919
8. Private scholarships	0
Total resources for college	$ 5,415

	Beth
A. Total student budget	$ 8,580
R. Total family contribution	0
T. Demonstrated financial need	8,580
1. Federal Pell Grant	2,250
2. State scholarship	1,500
3. Institutional grant	0
4. Federal College Work-Study	1,205
5. Federal Perkins Loan	0
6. Federal Supplemental Educational Opportunity Grant	1,000
7. Federal Stafford Loan	2,625
8. Private scholarships	0
Total resources for college	$ 8,580

Carlos received a financial aid award from the community college that fully met his need. He received a Federal Pell Grant and a Federal Supplemental Educational Opportunity Grant along with a state scholarship The combined total of his grants was enough to cover his tuition and books. Since Carlos has an off-campus job at a grocery store, the college did not offer him a campus job, instead recommending that he take out a Federal Stafford Loan to meet his remaining need. Before applying for the loan, Carlos planned to carefully evaluate how much he might need to borrow. He might decide to increase his hours at the grocery store in an effort to mimimize his borrowing.

The financial aid award offer Beth received met her demonstrated need and included a wide variety of sources. Beth received a Federal Pell Grant from the federal government, a scholarship from her state student assistance agency, and—because her family income is quite low—a Federal Supplemental Educational Opportunity Grant. In addition, like almost all financial aid recipients, Beth will be expected to assume some "self-help" aid. In her case, she took out a Federal Stafford Loan, which she will repay after she graduates or leaves college, and she accepted the offer of a campus job through the Federal Work-Study Program.

		Andrea
	Federal Methodology	Institutional Methodology
A. Total student budget	$ 17,960	$ 17,960
R. Total family contribution	5,225	7,569
T. Demonstrated financial need	12,735	10,391
1. Federal Pell Grant	0	0
2. State scholarship	0	0
3. Institutional grant	4,515	4,515
4. Federal Work-Study	1,200	1,200
5. Federal Perkins Loan	1,050	1,050
6. Federal SEOG	0	0
7. Federal Stafford Loan	2,625	2,625
8. Private scholarships	1,000	1,000
Total resources for college	$ 15,615	$ 17,959

*included in R (above).

*Even though **Andrea's** family has the greatest resources of the three students, she also has the greatest need because the college she wanted to attend has the highest costs. The financial aid award Andrea received included awards from three federal programs, a scholarship from the college's own scholarship fund, as well as two local scholarships from her hometown. The federal funds Andrea received included a campus job through the Federal Work-Study program, and two loans including a Federal Perkins Loan and a Federal Stafford Loan. Because Andrea's parents' income was higher than average, she was not eligible for the Federal Pell Grant or a state scholarship, and the college was unable to offer her a Federal Supplemental Educational Opportunity Grant.*

All colleges awarding federal financial aid funds must determine need by using a mandatory Federal Methodology. Although this methodology establishes eligibility for federal funds, most colleges, particularly higher cost schools, do not have enough federal funds to meet their students' full federally determined need. Many colleges that award substantial amounts of their own funds use a need analysis methodology that differs from the Federal Methodology. Colleges using an institutional methodology to award institutional funds do so because they feel that it is a better means of assessing a family's true ability to pay for college costs. In Andrea's case, her eligibility for a scholarship from the college was based on an institutional methodology, which unlike the Federal Methodology, took into account her parents' home equity and depreciation-based business losses. Under the institutional methodology, her parents' contribution to costs is higher and the college also assumes that Andrea will make a minimum contribution of $900 from her summer savings.

Based on the college's own assessment of Andrea's need, Andrea received a scholarship from the college, which in addition to her awards from the federal programs and her local scholarships, met her institutionally determined need in full. Because Andrea's college uses an institutional methodology in awarding its own scholarship funds, two breakdowns of need are shown above.

Your personal plan

Now that you've followed Carlos, Beth, and Andrea through the financial aid application process, complete your own need analysis estimate. You can begin to make your own plans by filling in Worksheet 1 for the colleges you are considering. You can use the college cost information in Part II of this book, but *remember* that these costs are for the 1994-95 academic year; you should make a somewhat higher estimate. (Some colleges will have a greater increase, others a smaller one.) When you are actually applying for aid, the college catalog or financial aid bulletins for the colleges to which you are applying are the most authoritative sources of information about costs that will apply to you.

You can begin to get a sense of your need at these colleges by completing your own Worksheets 2-5. These will take you through the steps of estimating parents' expected contribution (Worksheet 2 and table of parents' contribution), estimating your own contribution (Worksheet 3), combining the total family contribution (Worksheet 4), and finding the difference between the contribution and the costs at each of the colleges you are considering (Worksheet 5)—that is, your financial need.

Worksheet 1: Estimating student expenses	College A	College B	College C
1. Tuition and fees	$	$	$
2. Books and supplies			
3. Student's room			
4. Student's board/meals*			
5. Personal (clothing, laundry, recreation, medical)			
6. Transportation**			
7. Other (such as costs of child care, extra expenses because of handicap)			
A. Total budget (Add 1–7.)	$	$	$

*You will want to consider these expenses to your family if you live at home.

**If you are planning to live on campus, estimate the costs of the round-trips you will have to make to your home. Colleges ususally estimate a student makes two or three round-trips during the year. Students living at home should figure the costs of daily transportation to college.

See Worksheet 2 for Carlos, Beth, and Andrea, and use the tables following their worksheet to help you estimate parents' expected contribution.

Worksheet 2: Parents' expected contribution (Federal Methodology)

A. 1994 income:

  1. Father's yearly wages, salaries, tips, and other compensation $

  2. Mother's yearly wages, salaries, tips, and other compensation

  3. All other income of mother and father (dividends, interest, social security, pensions, welfare, child support, etc.) *Include IRA/Keogh payments and 401(K) and 403(B) contributions.*

  4. IRS allowable adjustments to income (business expenses, interest penalties, alimony *paid,* etc.) *Do not include IRA/Keogh payments.*

B. Total income (Add 1, 2, 3 and subtract 4.)

Expenses:

  5. U.S. income tax parents paid on their 1994 income (not amount withheld from paycheck) $

  6. Social Security (FICA) tax (See Table for 6.)

  7. State and other taxes (Enter 8% of B.)

  8. Employment allowance. If 2-parent family and both parents work, allow 35% of lower salary to a maximum of $2,500; if 1-parent family, allow 35% of salary to a maximum of $2,500. No allowance for a 2-parent family in which only one parent works.

  9. Income Protection Allowance (See Table for 9.)

C. Total allowance against income (Add 5, 6, 7, 8, 9.)

D. Available income (Subtract C from B.)

Assets:

  10. Other real estate equity (value minus unpaid balance on mortgage)

  11. Business or farm (Figure total value minus indebtedness and then take percentage shown in Table for 11.) If your family is only part owner of the farm or business, list only your share of the net value.

  12. Cash, savings, and checking accounts

  13. Other investments (current net value)

E. Total assets

Deductions:

F. Asset protection allowance (See Table for F.)

G. Remaining assets (Subtract F from E.)

H. Income supplement from assets (Multiply G by 12%, if negative, enter 0.)

I. Adjusted available income (Add D and H.)

J. Parents' expected contribution (Multiply I by taxation rate amount given in Table for J.)

K. Parents' expected contribution if more than one family member is in college
  (Divide J by number of family members in college at least half-time.)

Student's expected contribution

Students, too, are expected to contribute toward college costs when they are employed and/or have accumulated assets. Worksheet 3 will allow you to estimate what your contribution will be for your first year in college based on the Federal Methodology. It is important to note, however, that many colleges will expect a minimum contribution, such as $900 for a freshman and $1,100 for an upperclassman, when consideration is given for nonfederal funds.

Worksheet 3: Student's expected contribution	
L. Student's 1994 income:	
14. Student's yearly wages, salaries, tips, and other compensation	$
15. Spouse's yearly wages, salaries, tips, and other compensation	
16. All other income of student (dividends, interest, untaxed income, and benefits)	
M. Total income (Add 14, 15, and 16.)	
Allowances:	
17. U.S. income tax student (and spouse) paid on 1994 income (not amount withheld from paychecks)	
18. State and other taxes (enter 4% of M.)	
19. Social security (FICA) tax (See Table for 19.)	
20. Dependent student offset	
N. Total allowances against student's income (Add 17, 18, 19 and 20.)	
O. Available income (Subtract N from M.)	
Resources:	
21. Contribution from income (Line O x 50%. Cannot be less than 0.	
22. Contribution from assets (Multiply the total savings and other assets, such as stocks and bonds, excluding home equity, by 35%.)	
23. Other gifts and scholarships already received	
Q. Total student resources (Add lines 21, 22, and 23.)	$

Total family contribution

Use *Worksheet 4: Total Family Contribution* to transfer figures from Worksheet 2 (line J, or line K if there will be more than one family member in college) and from Worksheet 3 (line Q). By adding together these two figures, you can determine your total estimated family contribution.

Worksheet 4: Total family contribution	
J. Parents' expected contribution (Use figure for K instead of J if there is more than one family member in college.)	$
Q. Student's expected contribution from resources	
R. Total family contribution (Add J and Q.)	$

Estimated financial need

Are you potentially eligible for financial aid? Use *Worksheet 5: Student Need* to compare your family contribution with the cost of going to college. Record the student expense budgets at the colleges that interest you. Enter your total family contribution (from line R in Worksheet 4) and subtract it from each of the student expense budgets. If your family contribution is less than the student expense budget, you have demonstrated financial need and may be eligible for financial aid equal to this estimate of your need.

It is important to remember that the figure you arrive at in line T is only an estimate, and you should consider this figure to be only a rough approximation of your eligibility for financial aid. It is also important

to remember that this estimate of need is based on 1995-96 need analysis methodology for *federal* financial aid programs. Colleges that award significant amounts of nonfederal funds may use a different methodology, as demonstrated in Andrea's case.

Your eligibility for financial aid, and the amount and type of aid you receive, will be determined by the financial aid administrator at each college. Many colleges lack sufficient funds to meet the need of all needy students, regardless of the methodology used. So it is most important that you apply for financial aid as early as possible and meet all deadlines. The only way you can find out how much you might receive is to apply for financial aid!

Worksheet 5: Student need	College A	College B	College C
S. Total college expense budget	$	$	$
R. Total family contribution			
T. Student need (Subtract R from S.)	$	$	$

Worksheet 6: Financial aid awards	College A	College B	College C
A. Total student budget	$	$	$
R. Total family contribution			
T. Demonstrated financial need			
1. Federal Pell Grant			
2. State scholarship			
3. Institutional grant			
4. Federal Work-Study			
5. Federal Perkins Loan			
6. Federal Supplemental Educational Opportunity Grant			
7. Federal Stafford Loan			
8. Private scholarships			
Total resources for college	$	$	$

Glossary

The definitions given here of terms commonly used by colleges to describe their programs, admissions procedures, and financial aid policies are necessarily general. Students should consult the catalogs of specific colleges and financial aid programs to get more detailed and up-to-date descriptions of their programs and procedures.

Accelerated program. A college program of study completed in less time than is usually required, most often by attending in summer or by taking extra courses during the regular academic terms. Completion of a bachelor's degree program in three years is an example of acceleration.

ACT. *See* American College Testing Program Assessment.

Advanced placement. Admission or assignment of a freshman to an advanced course in a certain subject on the basis of evidence that the student has already completed the equivalent of the college's freshman course in that subject. In some cases, the college also grants academic credit for the college-level work that has been completed.

Advanced Placement (AP) Program. A service of the College Board that provides high schools with course descriptions in college subjects and Advanced Placement Examinations in those subjects. High schools implement the courses and administer the examinations to interested students, who are then eligible at many colleges for advanced placement, college credit, or both, on the basis of satisfactory grades.

American College Testing Program Assessment (ACT). Test battery of the American College Testing Program, given at test centers in the United States and other countries on specified dates throughout the year. It includes tests in English, mathematics, reading, and science reasoning.

Bachelor's degree. The degree awarded after completion of an undergraduate college program that normally takes four years. Also called the baccalaureate degree.

Campus-based programs. The three federally funded student financial aid programs that are directly administered by colleges: Federal Supplemental Educational Opportunity Grant Program, Federal Perkins Loan Program, and Federal Work-Study Program.

Candidates Reply Date Agreement (CRDA). A college subscribing to this agreement will not require any applicants offered admission as freshmen to notify the college of their decision to attend (or to accept an offer of financial aid) before May 1. The purpose of the agreement is to give applicants time to hear from all the colleges to which they have applied before having to make a commitment to any one of them.

Certificate. An award for completing a particular program or course of study, sometimes given by two-year colleges or vocational or technical schools.

College-Level Examination Program (CLEP). A service of the College Board that provides examinations in undergraduate college courses so that students and other adults may demonstrate achievement at the first- and second-year college levels. The examinations are used by colleges to award credit by examination to adult applicants who have not attended college (or have not done so recently), students transferring from other colleges, and entering freshmen. They are also used by business, industries, government agencies, and professional groups to satisfy education requirements for advancement, licensing, admission to further training, and other purposes.

College Scholarship Service (CSS). A division of the College Board that assists postsecondary institutions, state scholarship programs, and private scholarship organizations in the equitable and efficient distribution of student financial aid funds.

College Work-Study Program. *See* Federal Work-Study Program.

Consumer Price Index (CPI). A measure of inflation or deflation at the consumer level, updated monthly by the U.S. Bureau of Labor Statistics. The index is determined by comparing the current price of a "market basket" of goods to the price at which the same "basket" could have been purchased during a given base year. The goods include food, shelter, clothing, transportation, and other items.

Cooperative education. A college program in which a student alternates between periods of full-time study and full-time employment in related work. Students are paid for their work at the prevailing rate. Typically, five years are required to complete a bachelor's degree program, but graduates have the advantage of having completed about a year's practical experience in addition to their studies. Some colleges refer to this sort of program as work-study, but it should not be confused with the federally sponsored Federal Work-Study Program.

CRDA. *See* Candidates Reply Date Agreement.

Credit by examination. Academic credit granted by a college for a student's having demonstrated proficiency in a subject as measured by an examination.

CSS. *See* College Scholarship Service.

Dependent student. A student dependent on his or her parents for financial support. A student's dependency status is determined by guidelines established by the federal government.

Early decision. Early decision admission plans are offered to applicants who are sure of the college they want to attend and are likely to be accepted by that college. An early decision admission application is initiated by the student, who is then notified of the college's decision earlier than usual—generally by December 15 of the senior year.

Early Decision Plan (EDP-F, EDP-S). Colleges that subscribe to this plan agree to follow a common schedule for early decision applicants. Colleges may offer either of two plans. A student applying under the first-choice plan (EDP-F) must withdraw applications from all other colleges as soon as he or she is notified of acceptance by the first-choice college. A student

applying under the single-choice plan (EDP-S) may not apply to any colleges other than his or her first choice unless rejected by that institution. If a college follows either type of plan, applications (including financial aid applications) must be received by a specified date no later than November 15, and the college agrees to notify the applicant by a specified date no later than December 15.

FAFSA. *See* Free Application for Federal Student Aid.

Family contribution. The total amount a student and his or her family are expected to pay toward college costs from their income and assets. The amount is derived from a need analysis of the family's overall financial circumstances. A Federal Methodology is used in determining a student's eligibility for federal student aid. Colleges, state agencies, and private aid programs may use a different methodology in determining eligibility for nonfederal sources of financial aid.

Federal Parent Loan for Undergraduate Students. The federal PLUS loan program permits parents of undergraduate students to borrow up to the full cost of education less any other financial aid the student may have received. The interest rate is variable, set at 3.1 percent above the one-year Treasury-bill, capped at 9 percent. The rate is adjusted annually each July 1.

Federal Pell Grant Program. A federally sponsored and administered program that provides grants based on need to undergraduate students. Congress annually sets the dollar range. Currently a Pell Grant cannot exceed $2,340 per year.

Federal Perkins Loan Program. A federally funded program based on need, administered by colleges, that provides low-interest (5%) loans of up to $3,000 per year during undergraduate study and up to $15,000 for the total undergraduate program. The combined cumulative total of loan funds available to an individual for undergraduate and graduate education is $30,000. Repayment need not begin until completion of the student's education or after limited periods of service in the military, Peace Corps, or approved comparable organizations.

Federal Stafford Loan Program. A federal program that allows students to borrow to meet educational expenses. Funds are borrowed directly from banks or other lending institutions, or, for colleges participating in the Federal Direct Loan Program, from the U.S. Government.

The federal government pays the full interest on subsidized Stafford Loans while students are enrolled in college if the loan is made on the basis of demonstrated need. For students who have not demonstrated need, unsubsidized Federal Stafford Loans are available. For unsubsidized loans, students will usually be asked to make interest payments while enrolled in school. Following a grace period, all students borrowing in the Federal Stafford Loan Program must begin repaying principal and interest after graduating or leaving school.

Federal Stafford Loans have a variable interest rate set at 3.1 percent above the federal 91-day Treasury-bill rate with a cap of 8.25 percent. The rate is adjusted annually on July 1.

The amounts that may be borrowed depend on the student's year in school. The undergraduate loan limits are as follows: first year, $2,625; second year, $3,500; third and fourth years, $5,500; to a total amount as an undergraduate of $23,000. Graduate and professional students may borrow $8,500 per year in subsidized funds and up to $10,000 in unsubsidized, to an aggregate limit, including undergraduate borrowing, of $65,000 in subsidized Federal Stafford Loans plus $13,000 in unsubsidized Stafford Loans.

Federal Supplemental Educational Opportunity Grant Program (SEOG). A federal program administered by colleges to provide need-based aid to undergraduate students. Grants of up to $4,000 a year may be awarded.

Federal Work-Study Program. A federally sponsored campus-based program. Participating colleges provide employment opportunities for students with demonstrated need who are enrolled for study at either the undergraduate or graduate level. Students are usually employed on campus, although occasionally jobs are arranged off campus. In assigning work-study to aid recipients, financial aid administrators typically take into account the recipient's employable skills, class schedule, and academic progress.

Financial aid award letter. A notice from a college or other financial aid sponsor that tells a student how much aid is being offered. The award letter also usually explains how a student's financial need was determined, describes the contents of the financial aid package, and outlines any conditions attached to the award.

Financial aid package. The total financial aid award received by a student. It may be made up of a combination or "package" of aid that includes both gift aid

and self-help. Many colleges try to meet a student's full financial need, but availability of funds, institutional aid policies, and the number of students needing assistance all influence the composition of a financial aid package.

Financial need. The amount by which a student's family contribution falls short of covering the student expense budget. Assessments of need may differ depending on the need-analysis methodology used. (*See* Family contribution.)

Free Application for Federal Student Aid (FAFSA). A form completed by all applicants for federal student aid. In many states, completion of the FAFSA is also sufficient to establish eligibility for state-sponsored aid programs. There is no charge to students for completing the FAFSA. Forms are widely available in high schools and colleges, and may be filed any time *after* January 1 of the year for which one is seeking aid (e.g., after January 1, 1996, for academic year 1996-97 assistance).

Gift aid. Student financial aid, such as scholarships and grants, that does not have to be repaid and that does not require a student's being employed.

Independent student. *See* Self-supporting student.

Need analysis form. The starting point in applying for financial aid. All students must file the federally sponsored Free Application for Federal Student Aid (FAFSA) to apply for the federal financial aid programs. For many colleges, this may be the only need analysis form you will need to file. For other schools, particularly private colleges, other forms may also be required. To apply for state financial aid programs, the FAFSA may be all that you will need to file, but you should check with your state agency to learn if any other application forms need to be submitted.

Open admissions. The college admissions policy of admitting high school graduates and other adults generally without regard to conventional academic qualifications, such as high school subjects, high school grades, and admissions test scores. Virtually all applicants with high school diplomas or their equivalent are accepted.

Parents' contribution. The amount a student's parents are expected to pay toward college costs from their income and assets. The amount is derived from need analysis of the parents' overall financial situation. The parents' contribution and the student's contribution together constitute the total family contribution, which, when subtracted from the student expense budget, equals financial need. Generally, students are eligible for financial aid equal to their financial need.

Pell Grant Program. *See* Federal Pell Grant Program.

Perkins Loan Program. *See* Federal Perkins Loan Program.

Parent Loan for Undergraduate Students (PLUS). *See* Federal Parent Loan for Undergraduate Students.

Preliminary SAT/National Merit Scholarship Qualifying Test (PSAT/NMSQT). A shorter version of the College Board's SAT I administered by high schools each year in October. The PSAT/NMSQT aids high schools in the early guidance of students planning for college and serves as the qualifying test for scholarships awarded by the National Merit Scholarship Corporation.

Reserve Officers' Training Corps (ROTC). Programs conducted by certain colleges in cooperation with the U.S. Air Force, Army, and Navy. Local recruiting offices of the services themselves can supply detailed information about these programs. Information is also available from participating colleges.

SAR. *See* Student Aid Report.

SAT I: Reasoning Test. The College Board's test of developed verbal and mathematical reasoning abilities, given on specified dates throughout the year at test centers in the United States and other countries. The SAT I is required by many colleges and sponsors of financial aid programs.

SAT II: Subject Tests. College Board tests in specific secondary school subjects, given at test centers in the United States and other countries on specified dates throughout the year. Used by colleges not only to help with decisions about admissions but also in course placement and exemption of enrolled freshmen. Formerly called Achievement Tests.

Self-help. Student financial aid, such as loans and jobs, that require repayment or a student's being employed.

Self-supporting student. For financial aid purposes, a student who is independent of support from his or her parents.

Stafford Loan Program. *See* Federal Stafford Loan Program.

Student Aid Report (SAR). A report produced by the U.S. Department of Education and sent to students who have applied for federal student financial aid. The SAR must be submitted to the college that the student attends to certify his or her eligibility for Federal Pell Grants and other federal financial programs such as the Federal Work-Study Program, Federal Perkins Loan Program, Federal Supplemental Educational Opportunity Grants, and the Federal Family Education Loan Programs.

Student expense budget. A calculation of the annual cost of attending college that is used in determining a student's financial need. Student expense budgets usually include tuition and fees, books and supplies, room and board, personal expenses, and transportation. Sometimes additional expenses are included for students with special education needs, students who have a disability, or students who are married or have children.

Student's contribution. The amount students are expected to pay toward college costs from their income, assets, and benefits. The amount is derived from need analysis of the student's resources. The student's contribution and parents' contribution constitute the total family contribution, which, when subtracted from the student budget, equals financial need. Generally, students are eligible for financial aid equal to their financial need.

Supplemental Educational Opportunity Grant Program. *See* Federal Supplemental Educational Opportunity Grant Program (FSEOG).

Tuition and fee waivers. Some colleges waive the tuition or tuition and fees for some categories of students, such as adults, senior citizens, or children of alumni. Colleges with such plans are listed in a separate section in this book.

Part II. College costs and financial aid

Table of college information

Introduction

This section provides detailed lists of expenses and financial aid at 3,000 colleges, universities, and proprietary schools. The data were compiled from information supplied by the institutions themselves on the College Board's Annual Survey of Colleges, 1995-96. The lists are alphabetical by state, and include the information provided by all participating institutions through the end of May 1995. Every effort is made to ensure that the data are as complete and accurate as possible. However, students are urged to contact institutions directly to confirm the information.

Institutions were asked to give expense figures for the academic year beginning fall 1995. If the 1995-96 tuition and fees were not yet set but a reliable forecast was available, the estimated tuition and fees are given with a single dagger next to them. If these figures were not yet available, the 1994-95 tuition and fees are listed with a double dagger next to them.

Details on each category of expenses and financial aid and what these figures can mean to applicants are explained here.

In an effort to collect comparable cost information, the College Board asked institutions to provide data for specifically budgeted items. The figures supplied under each column heading represent the following.

Educational costs

Tuition and fees

This figure indicates the annual tuition and general fees an institution charges most first-year, full-time students. Colleges were asked to report these costs based on a nine-month academic year of 30 semester hours or 45 quarter hours.

Additional out-of-state/district tuition

This item represents only the *additional* charges made to students who do not meet state or district residency requirements. The figure to the left of the diagonal mark shows additional charges for out-of-state students; the figure to the right shows additional out-of-district charges. These charges added to the tuition and fees in the first column will give you the total tuition and fees for out-of-state and out-of-district students, respectively.

Books and supplies

This figure is the average cost of books and supplies for the normal course load for full-time students. Supplies may be more expensive for students in certain areas of study (art, architecture, or engineering, for example) and institutions did not include these special costs unless the majority of their students are in these fields.

Living costs: Campus residents

Room and board for campus residents

For resident students, room and board includes the charge for living and eating for nine months in facilities operated by or for the college. These are average charges based on double-room occupancy and 21 meals a week in college facilities.

Transportation for campus residents

These figures include typical costs for two round-trips between home and campus during the nine-month academic year. If you anticipate more frequent trips between home and campus during the academic year, you should adjust this figure accordingly.

Other costs for campus residents

This column shows typical costs for miscellaneous

personal expenses, such as clothing, laundry, entertainment, snacks, medical insurance, and furnishings.

Living costs: Students living at home

Board for students at home

This column shows average costs for dependent students living at home, including three meals a day, seven days a week.

Transportation for students at home

The figures in this column represent the typical costs for daily travel to and from college for students who commute.

Other costs for students at home

This column shows miscellaneous personal expenses for students living at home. These include clothing, laundry, entertainment, and medical insurance.

Financial aid information

Total freshmen enrolled

This is the total freshman enrollment for fall 1994 on which the percentage of freshman students receiving aid is based.

Percentage receiving aid

This figure represents the percentage of enrolled freshmen (preceding column) who received some form of financial aid in fall 1994. The aid could be based on financial need or on other criteria such as talent or athletic ability. The financial aid could be in the form of grants, scholarships, loans, or jobs.

Freshmen judged to have financial need

This column shows the number of freshmen in fall 1994 who were judged to have financial need.

Percent offered aid

This figure is the percentage of freshmen with financial need (preceding column) who were offered aid. The financial aid could be grants, loans, or jobs.

Grants and scholarships

Need-based scholarships

An X in these columns indicates that the college awards scholarships on the basis of financial need combined with exceptional academic ability or talent in music or drama, art, or athletics.

Non-need scholarships

An X in these columns indicates that the college awards scholarships, without regard for financial need, on the basis of exceptional academic ability or talent in music or drama, art, or athletics.

Financial aid deadlines

Priority deadline for financial aid

The priority deadline is the date by which the college prefers that you submit your financial aid application. Missing this deadline may mean that most or all financial aid may have already been awarded, but it does not necessarily mean that *all* aid has been given out. It is best to meet the college's priority deadline in order to have the best chance of receiving aid if you qualify.

Closing deadline for financial aid

This is the final date by which the college will accept your application for financial aid.

Institutional aid form

An X in this column indicates that the college has its own financial aid form that you will have to complete if you are applying for aid. This requirement is in addition to the FAFSA. Be sure to verify with the college what it requires. (See "Need analysis form" in the Glossary for more information.)

Notes

Use this column to make notes about the colleges that interest you.

Part II.
College
costs and
financial aid

Institution		Tuition and fees	Add'l out-of-state/district tuition	Books and supplies	Costs for campus residents			Costs for students at home		
					Room and board	Transportation	Other costs	Board only	Transportation	Other costs
Alabama										
Alabama Agricultural and Mechanical University	†	1,794	1,700/—	550	2,550	1,000	850	1,500	1,000	850
Alabama Aviation and Technical College	‡	1,026	668/—	1,625		1,000	1,300	2,700	1,000	1,000
Alabama Southern Community College	‡	1,116	668/—	750		600				
Alabama State University		1,752	1,500/—	600	2,850	900	1,200	2,070	1,200	1,500
Athens State College		1,530	1,485/—	450	3,765	564	900	1,783	989	1,021
Auburn University										
Auburn	‡	2,100	4,200/—	600	3,873	633	1,275	1,500	633	1,275
Montgomery	‡	1,905	3,810/—	635		1,040	1,300	2,780	1,700	1,300
Bessemer State Technical College	‡	981	668/—	630				1,500	900	600
Bevill State Community College	‡	1,116	668/—	600				1,500	1,125	750
Birmingham-Southern College		12,510		400	4,730	500	900	1,500	1,500	900
Bishop State Community College	‡	1,026	668/—	400				1,500	610	738
Central Alabama Community College	‡	1,116		300				1,800	600	500
Chattahoochee Valley Community College	‡	1,116	668/—	500				1,900	600	500
Community College of the Air Force		0								
Concordia College		4,100		550	2,700					
Douglas MacArthur State Technical College	‡	945	608/—	595				1,800	1,560	668
Draughons Junior College		5,110		600						
Enterprise State Junior College	‡	1,215	743/—	450				1,900	650	550
Faulkner University	‡	5,550		630	3,150	680	1,030	830	735	870
Gadsden State Community College	‡	1,215	743/—	525	2,250	150	525	1,500	790	525
George C. Wallace State Community College										
Dothan	‡	1,215	743/—	600				2,000	720	300
Selma	‡	1,035	608/—	690				1,500	577	976
Harry M. Ayers State Technical College	‡	945	608/—	400				2,400	1,200	
Huntingdon College		8,765		500	4,165	500	730		300	530
International Bible College		4,210		450		700	1,500	2,100	1,000	1,500
J. F. Drake State Technical College	‡	900	608/—	500				550		
Jacksonville State University	‡	1,740	870/—	600	2,725	900	1,200	1,400	1,500	1,200
James H. Faulkner State Community College	‡	1,215	743/—	450	2,175	550	800	1,500	950	700
Jefferson Davis Community College	‡	900	608/—	525				1,500	300	600
Jefferson State Community College	‡	1,215	743/—					2,250	1,260	540
John C. Calhoun State Community College	‡	1,170	709/—	500				1,900	700	774
John M. Patterson State Technical College	‡	1,125	743/—	400					300	200
Judson College		5,780		650	3,600	376	1,600		624	1,600
Lawson State Community College	‡	1,116	668/—	400				1,550	725	700
Lurleen B. Wallace State Junior College	‡	1,125	743/—	375				1,800	600	600
Marion Military Institute		7,076		644	2,400	625	1,962		400	1,575
Miles College	†	4,350		400	2,700	500	1,000		500	800
Northeast Alabama Community College	‡	954	547/—	600				1,200	750	1,500
Northwest-Shoals Community College	‡	1,116	743/—	600	1,500	800	900	1,170	800	900
Oakwood College		7,064		600	4,160	2,112	1,500	2,688	462	768
Phillips Junior College: Birmingham		3,940		325				1,962	421	
Reid State Technical College	‡	990	675/—	400						
Samford University		8,648		524	4,129	700	1,650	1,575	990	1,650
Selma University		4,200		200	3,700		600			600
Shelton State Community College	‡	1,620	1,013/—	450				1,000	500	200

†Figures are projected for 1995-96. ‡Figures are for 1994-95.

| All aid | | Need–based aid | | Grants and scholarships | | | | | | | | Financial aid deadlines | | Inst aid form | Notes |
| Total freshmen | Percent receiving aid | Freshmen judged to have need | Percent offered aid | Need–based | | | | Non–need–based | | | | | | | |
				Acad	Music/drama	Art	Athl	Acad	Music/drama	Art	Athl	Priority	Closing		
784	69			X				X	X		X	4/1	6/1	X	
								X					none	X	
1,218	48	583	95	X	X	X	X	X	X	X	X	7/15	none		
1,071	90	1,051	100					X	X	X	X	3/1	none	X	
							X	X	X	X	X		none		
3,159	42	796	100	X	X			X	X	X	X	4/15	none		
826	40							X	X		X	4/15	none		
218	65	120	92	X				X				9/1	none		
3,353	65							X	X		X	7/1	none		
283	99	130	100	X	X	X	X	X	X	X	X	3/31	none		
1,399	40			X	X	X	X	X	X		X		none		
								X	X	X	X	7/15	none		
677	60							X	X	X	X	6/1	none		
													none		
													none		
427	80							X				6/1	none		
													none		
				X				X	X	X	X	4/1	none		
320	90							X			X	5/1	none		
1,301	33							X	X		X	4/15	none		
													none		
													none		
								X					none		
175	95	129	100	X	X	X	X	X	X	X	X	5/1	none		
35	71	9	89	X								7/1	none		
258	75			X				X					none		
876	47	429	100					X	X	X	X	3/15	none		
1,296	63							X	X	X	X	7/1	8/1		
													none		
808	37			X				X	X		X	5/1	none	X	
4,296	21							X	X	X	X	5/1	none		
376	50												none		
													none		
447	85			X	X	X	X			X	X	6/1	none		
336	70			X	X	X	X	X	X	X	X	6/1	none		
140	95			X				X	X		X	6/15	none		
368	84			X			X	X				4/15	none		
407	48							X	X	X			none		
		350	100					X	X	X	X	6/1	none	X	
342	64							X				4/15	9/11		
													none		
406	77			X									none		
596	78	285	100	X				X	X	X	X	3/1	none		
													none		
880	30	875	99	X	X	X	X	X	X	X	X	6/30	none		

Institution	Tuition and fees	Add'l out-of-state/ district tuition	Books and supplies	Costs for campus residents			Costs for students at home		
				Room and board	Trans-portation	Other costs	Board only	Trans-portation	Other costs
Snead State Community College	‡ 1,035	675/—	600	1,643	540	700	1,500	925	700
Southeastern Bible College	4,620		300	2,800	500		2,000	900	
Southern Christian University	5,310		600				5,240	1,233	1,610
Southern Union State Community College	‡ 1,116	668/—	400		600	1,100	1,800	600	600
Sparks State Technical College	‡ 1,035	709/—	820						
Spring Hill College	12,489		600	4,788	900	990	1,500	900	990
Stillman College	5,200		500	3,100	300	1,000	1,500	300	1,000
Talladega College	5,666		600	2,964	800	500	878	800	500
Trenholm State Technical College	‡ 1,125	675/—	575				2,350	850	350
Troy State University									
Dothan	‡ 1,890	1,501/—	600				2,160	1,785	1,425
Montgomery	‡ 1,845	923/—	625						
Troy	‡ 1,922	1,408/—	500	2,895	500	600	1,400		
Tuskegee University	† 7,070		665	3,620	700	1,207	2,100	300	210
UAB: Walker College	1,890	1,710/—	377	1,990	2,397	4,161	2,601	4,204	2,805
University of Alabama									
Birmingham	2,604	2,310/—	720		750	1,200	2,700	1,500	1,200
Huntsville	‡ 2,480	2,480/—	720	3,500	900	1,200	1,800	1,350	900
Tuscaloosa	‡ 2,172	3,252/—	610	3,530	590	1,654	1,910	950	1,654
University of Mobile	6,580		500	3,880	250	1,000	1,500	450	400
University of Montevallo	‡ 2,280	2,220/—	500	3,030	800	1,500	800	900	1,000
University of North Alabama	1,885	1,266/—	550	3,010	800	1,556	1,975	800	1,556
University of South Alabama	2,541	1,050/—	450	2,940					
University of West Alabama	1,965		570	2,541	900	1,200	1,500	1,500	1,200
Virginia College	6,400		300				1,700	100	100
Wallace State College at Hanceville	‡ 900	608/—	450		675	2,650	1,500	1,155	900

Alaska

Institution	Tuition and fees	Add'l out-of-state/ district tuition	Books and supplies	Room and board	Trans-portation	Other costs	Board only	Trans-portation	Other costs
Alaska Bible College	3,300		400	3,400	1,000	1,000		750	700
Alaska Pacific University	7,690		800	4,120	750	1,500	1,500	1,500	1,500
Prince William Sound Community College	2,120	4,090/—	500		936	1,125	2,520	936	1,125
Sheldon Jackson College	9,410		550	4,800	2,000	1,000	2,800	500	1,000
University of Alaska									
Anchorage	2,274	4,320/—	550		1,080	1,260	2,520	1,080	1,260
Fairbanks	2,950	4,320/—	550	3,690	324	1,980	4,010	1,710	1,980
Southeast	2,194	2,160/—	600		230	1,000	2,250	800	1,000

Arizona

Institution	Tuition and fees	Add'l out-of-state/ district tuition	Books and supplies	Room and board	Trans-portation	Other costs	Board only	Trans-portation	Other costs
Academy of Business College	‡ 5,050								
Al Collins Graphic Design School	14,950		1,400						
American Indian College of the Assemblies of God	3,020		450	3,000	1,100	1,400		1,100	1,400
Arizona College of the Bible	5,460		700			2,400	2,500		2,400
Arizona State University	‡ 1,894	5,606/—	700	4,200		2,210	2,390		2,210
Arizona Western College	‡ 780	4,320/—	350	2,800	350	952	1,100	924	950
Central Arizona College	‡ 700	3,590/—	400	2,870	700	1,500	1,500	700	1,500
Cochise College	‡ 750	3,810/—	600	3,006	680	1,125	1,800	800	675
DeVry Institute of Technology: Phoenix	6,335		550				2,217	1,831	2,045
Eastern Arizona College	‡ 628	3,252/—	400	2,772	950	900	1,700	950	900
Embry-Riddle Aeronautical University: Prescott Campus	8,380		570	3,462	1,800	1,220	1,300	1,860	1,220
Gateway Community College	‡ 960	3,750/—	700				2,500	1,150	1,150
Glendale Community College	‡ 960	3,750/—	700				2,504	1,150	1,150
Grand Canyon University	7,240		600	3,100	612	1,125	1,530	612	1,125

†Figures are projected for 1995-96. ‡Figures are for 1994-95.

All aid		Need-based aid		Grants and scholarships								Financial aid deadlines		Inst aid form	Notes
				Need-based				Non-need-based							
Total fresh-men	Percent receiving aid	Freshmen judged to have need	Percent offered aid	Acad	Music/drama	Art	Athl	Acad	Music/drama	Art	Athl	Priority	Closing		
								X	X	X	X	4/15	none		
44	85			X				X	X			5/1	9/8		
				X				X							
													none		
383	95			X				X				8/1	none		
224	81	132	100	X				X			X	3/1	none	X	
				X	X			X	X			6/15	none		
315	82			X			X	X			X	4/1	6/10		
													none		
19	15			X				X				5/1	8/1		
													none		
1,009	30			X	X	X	X	X	X	X	X	5/1	none		
669	90	110	100	X				X	X		X	3/15	3/31	X	
264	61	165	93	X		X	X	X		X	X	7/1	none		
1,117	55	700	87	X			X	X	X	X	X	5/1	none	X	
506	33	190	76	X			X	X	X	X	X	4/1	none		
2,570	34	787	97	X				X	X	X	X	3/15	none		
250	96	220	100	X				X	X	X	X	3/31	none		
573	61	291	100				X	X	X		X	4/15	none		
711	44	270	100	X				X	X	X	X	4/1	none		
1,303	47	555	100	X				X	X		X		none	X	
526	74	198	100					X	X	X	X	4/20	5/15		
1,938	50							X	X	X	X		none		
4	75							X	X				8/1		
29	100	16	100	X				X				3/15	none		
23	55			X				X				4/1	none		
36	90			X			X	X	X		X	4/1	none		
751	34			X				X	X	X	X	5/15	none		
				X	X	X			X	X	X	5/15	none		
85	75			X	X	X		X	X	X		6/1	none		
													none		
22	99	21	100	X				X				4/1	8/23		
16	75	15	100	X	X		X	X	X			4/15	9/15		
4,102	59			X	X			X	X	X	X	3/1	none		
								X	X	X		4/15	none		
													none		
1,166	45			X			X	X			X	4/15	none		
								X					none		
								X	X	X	X	4/15	none		
249	72	107	94	X				X				4/15	none		
				X				X				4/15	none		
4,932	25			X				X	X	X	X	5/15	none	X	
													none		

Institution		Tuition and fees	Add'l out-of-state/district tuition	Books and supplies	Costs for campus residents			Costs for students at home		
					Room and board	Trans-portation	Other costs	Board only	Trans-portation	Other costs
Lamson Junior College at Mesa		10,120		1,288						
Mesa Community College	‡	960	3,750/—	400					350	
Mohave Community College	‡	580	2,900/—	650				1,800	900	920
Navajo Community College	‡	620		450	2,740					
Northern Arizona University	‡	1,894	4,852/—	620	3,550	880	1,350	1,120	650	1,130
Northland Pioneer College	‡	600	1,650/—	520		670	1,150	1,730	920	1,150
Paradise Valley Community College	‡	960	3,750/—	400						
Phoenix College	‡	960	3,750/—	700		1,150	6,324		1,150	3,654
Pima Community College	‡	724	3,616/—	476					412	2,650
Prescott College		10,555		400				660	729	807
Rio Salado Community College	‡	960	3,750/—	400					1,038	800
Scottsdale Community College	‡	960	3,750/—	700		1,185	1,185	2,579	1,185	1,185
South Mountain Community College	‡	960	3,750/—	800				1,500	800	
Southwestern College		6,245		400	2,900	700	700			700
University of Arizona	‡	1,844	5,606/—	620	3,820	900	1,750	1,500	1,200	1,750
University of Phoenix	‡	5,940		500					500	200
Western International University		5,400		720						500
Yavapai College	‡	666	4,014/—	500	2,830	600	1,050	700	600	900

Arkansas

Institution		Tuition and fees	Add'l out-of-state/district tuition	Books and supplies	Room and board	Trans-portation	Other costs	Board only	Trans-portation	Other costs
Arkansas Baptist College		2,025		600	2,926	860	850	1,100	860	860
Arkansas State University										
Beebe Branch	‡	1,410	930/—	500	1,799	560	500		800	500
Jonesboro	‡	2,050	1,920/—	500	2,580	780	630	1,500	1,200	400
Arkansas Tech University		1,900	1,820/—	550	2,660	480	1,000	2,700	1,000	750
Central Baptist College		3,932		600	2,880	600	800	1,720	800	800
East Arkansas Community College		792	408/204	400					700	4,200
Garland County Community College		812	1,128/216	550				1,500	930	2,980
Harding University		6,420		630	3,635	945	2,750	1,953	945	1,765
Henderson State University	‡	1,888	1,728/—	600	2,840	1,400	2,000	1,250	2,000	1,600
Hendrix College		9,683		500	3,500	500	625	1,935	562	563
John Brown University		7,650		500	3,930	1,000	1,500	1,500	700	1,400
Lyon College		9,110		500	4,076					
Mississippi County Community College	‡	984	1,440/300	400				5,393	958	2,948
North Arkansas Community/Technical College		816	1,152/240	300				925	933	1,415
Ouachita Baptist University		7,070		500	2,900	650	920	1,600	650	920
Philander Smith College		3,048		400	2,540	700	750		700	750
Phillips County Community College		840	1,128/216	450				1,350	841	1,925
Rich Mountain Community College	‡	696	1,224/144	300					600	470
Shorter College	‡	2,225		300	2,400	200	200		200	300
South Arkansas Community College		840	1,200/216	500				1,500		450
Southern Arkansas University										
Magnolia	†	901	456/—	500	2,410	1,110	1,585	2,685	1,110	1,585
Tech		994	456/—	500		500	1,250		900	1,250
University of Arkansas										
Fayetteville	‡	2,148	3,096/—	650	3,375	1,250	950			950
Little Rock	‡	2,317	3,216/—	800		800	800	2,100	800	800
Medical Sciences	‡	1,908	2,852/—	470		831	1,600	3,874	1,152	2,413
Monticello	‡	1,706	2,016/—	450	2,310	475	850	1,150	950	850
Pine Bluff	‡	1,681	2,016/—	600	2,408	700	800		800	700
University of Central Arkansas		2,010	1,824/—	600	2,625	745	1,064	1,800		1,064
University of the Ozarks		6,520		600	3,300	1,800	2,700	1,400	1,300	1,215

†Figures are projected for 1995-96. ‡Figures are for 1994-95.

| All aid | | Need-based aid | | Grants and scholarships | | | | | | | | Financial aid deadlines | | Inst aid form | Notes |
Total freshmen	Percent receiving aid	Freshmen judged to have need	Percent offered aid	Need-based Acad	Music/drama	Art	Athl	Non-need-based Acad	Music/drama	Art	Athl	Priority	Closing		
													none		
				X	X	X	X	X	X	X	X	5/15	none		
1,827	30			X	X	X		X	X	X		4/15	none		
				X				X			X	4/15	none		
2,033	65			X	X	X	X	X	X	X	X	4/15	none		
		1,000	100					X	X	X	X	6/1	none		
				X				X					none		
				X	X	X	X	X	X	X	X	6/30	none		
4,924	20							X			X	4/1	none		
				X				X				4/15	none		
8,649	2			X								4/15	none		
3,801	20	1,155	46	X	X	X	X	X	X	X	X	4/15	none		
				X	X	X	X	X	X	X	X	5/1	none		
47	95											4/15	none		
4,481	40			X	X	X	X	X	X	X	X	3/1	none		
47	56												none		
													none		
													none		
555	60	365	96					X	X		X	5/1	none		
1,546	60			X				X	X	X	X	5/1	none		
956	51			X	X		X	X	X		X	6/1	none		
123	70	60	100	X	X		X	X	X		X	7/1	none		
360	50			X								4/15	none		
456	68			X	X	X		X	X	X	X	4/1	none		
867	85	408	100					X	X	X	X	4/1	none		
661	53	382	100	X				X	X	X	X	4/15	none		
299	88	159	100	X				X	X	X		2/15	none		
296	77	176	100	X	X		X	X	X	X	X	3/1	5/1		
190	98	138	100	X				X	X	X	X	3/1	none		
		154	95	X				X	X	X	X	4/15	none	X	
								X	X	X	X	5/1	none		
420	95	206	100					X	X		X	5/1	none		
419	90	185	90	X				X				5/1	none		
								X	X		X	4/1	5/1		
350	46			X				X				7/1	none		
186	70	25	100	X							X	5/1	none		
231	54			X				X	X		X	7/1	none		
488	63	263						X	X		X	6/1	none		
								X	X	X		7/15	none		
2,245	66	1,145	81	X	X			X	X	X	X	4/1	none		
847	60			X				X	X	X	X	5/1	7/1		
													none		
				X				X	X		X		none		
792	88			X	X	X	X					4/15	none		
1,574	70							X	X	X	X	2/15	none		
162	54			X				X	X		X	5/1	none		

Institution	Tuition and fees	Add'l out-of-state/district tuition	Books and supplies	Costs for campus residents			Costs for students at home		
				Room and board	Trans-portation	Other costs	Board only	Trans-portation	Other costs
Westark Community College	860	1,176/264	425				1,500	600	450
Williams Baptist College	4,550		600	2,522	700	600	1,500	700	800
California									
Academy of Art College	11,455		648		738	1,566		594	1,620
Allan Hancock College	‡ 414	3,210/—	648				2,196	594	1,620
American Academy of Dramatic Arts: West	8,975		460				1,652	448	1,232
American College for the Applied Arts:									
Los Angeles	‡ 9,525		750		800		800	800	2,000
American River College	‡ 390	3,600/—	630				2,124	400	880
Antelope Valley College	‡ 390	3,180/—	630				2,124	576	1,548
Antioch Southern California									
Los Angeles	9,450		1,050						
Santa Barbara	8,550		450						
Armstrong University	7,545		450						
Art Center College of Design	14,718		3,462					856	1,696
Art Institute of Southern California	10,224		1,216		1,327	2,312	4,587	1,327	2,312
Azusa Pacific University	12,468		600	4,020	700	1,250		1,000	
Bakersfield College	‡ 415	3,210/—	630	3,484	450	900	2,124	750	900
Barstow College	390	3,210/—	630				2,124	576	1,500
Bethany College	7,300		1,079	3,630	2,247	2,136	1,690	2,247	2,136
Biola University	12,652		648	4,932	540	1,278	1,062	576	1,548
Brooks College	7,140		800	4,480	1,300	1,100	1,100	900	1,100
Brooks Institute of Photography	† 13,025		4,000						
Butte College	‡ 500	3,750/—	630				907	684	1,430
Cabrillo College	484	3,270/—	630				1,512	600	1,595
California Baptist College	8,680		630	4,494	576	1,278	1,566	720	1,530
California College of Arts and Crafts	14,400		648		540	1,278	2,196	594	1,620
California Culinary Academy	12,470		1,315				7,000		
California Institute of the Arts	15,510		1,000	5,520	592	1,976		704	1,656
California Institute of Technology	17,586		765	6,620	600	1,443	1,800		1,443
California Lutheran University	13,680		630	5,450	540	1,584	2,400	720	1,530
California Maritime Academy	‡ 2,835	6,090/—	700	4,770	640	1,500			
California Polytechnic State University: San Luis Obispo	‡ 2,043	7,380/—	630	4,698	540	1,598	2,124	576	1,724
California State Polytechnic University: Pomona	‡ 1,752	7,380/—	630	4,724	540	1,638	2,124	576	1,764
California State University									
Bakersfield	‡ 1,858	7,380/—	630	3,857	530	1,164	2,124	530	925
Chico	‡ 2,006	7,380/—	630	4,632	540	1,368	2,124	576	1,600
Dominguez Hills	‡ 1,791	7,380/—	630		540	1,600	2,124	576	1,600
Fresno	‡ 1,802	7,380/—	630	4,398	540	1,176	2,124	576	1,164
Fullerton	‡ 1,800	7,380/—	630		540	1,638	2,124	576	1,764
Hayward	‡ 1,774	7,380/—	630		540		2,124	576	1,764
Long Beach	‡ 1,751	7,380/—	630	4,962	540	1,638	1,512	576	1,764
Los Angeles	‡ 1,713	7,380/—	630	4,709	720	1,584	2,124	576	1,584
Northridge	‡ 1,916	7,380/—	630	4,790	640	1,588	2,124	576	1,398
Sacramento	‡ 1,860	7,380/—	650	4,939	560	1,500	2,100	6,000	1,500
San Bernardino	‡ 1,878	7,380/—	630	5,256	576	1,584	2,124	720	1,530
San Marcos	‡ 1,700	7,380/—	630				2,124	576	1,406
Stanislaus	‡ 1,874	7,380/—	630	4,938	720	1,458	2,124	576	1,458
Canada College	450	3,390/—	630					650	1,450
Cerritos Community College	‡ 425	3,420/—	630				2,124	576	1,764

†Figures are projected for 1995-96. ‡Figures are for 1994-95.

All aid		Need–based aid		Grants and scholarships								Financial aid deadlines		Inst aid form	Notes
				Need–based				Non–need–based							
Total fresh-men	Percent receiving aid	Freshmen judged to have need	Percent offered aid	Acad	Music/ drama	Art	Athl	Acad	Music/ drama	Art	Athl	Priority	Closing		
107	92			X	X	X	X	X	X	X	X	5/1	none		
672	40	174	100	X		X		X		X		5/1	none	X	
				X	X	X	X	X	X	X	X	5/1	none		
149	57				X			X	X			7/1	none		
103	20											3/2	none		
3,500	12			X				X				3/2	none		
				X	X	X		X	X	X		3/2	none		
				X								8/4	none		
													none		
199	59	112	99									3/1	none		
24	45			X		X		X		X		3/2	none		
557	80			X	X		X	X	X		X	3/1	none		
3,300	20			X				X				3/2	none		
110	88			X				X	X	X	X	3/2	none	X	
577	80							X	X	X	X	3/2	none	X	
													none		
86	38	27	100	X		X		X		X		4/15	none	X	
				X		X	X	X	X	X	X	5/1	none		
3,000	58			X	X	X	X					3/2	none		
212	89			X				X	X		X	4/1	none		
72	64	45	100	X		X		X		X		3/2	none		
652	70												none	X	
					X	X			X	X		3/2	none		
231	75	147	100	X				X				2/1	none		
241	85			X	X			X	X	X		3/2	none		
107	56	65	100	X				X				3/2	none		
2,106	49	1,033	100	X		X	X	X		X	X		3/1		
1,754	40	848	87	X	X	X	X	X			X	3/2	none		
377	63			X	X	X	X	X	X	X	X	3/2	none		
1,329	24			X	X	X	X	X				3/1	none		
526	70							X	X	X	X	4/15	none		
1,427	33			X	X	X	X	X	X	X	X	3/2	none		
1,496	17			X				X	X	X	X	3/2	none		
				X				X				3/2	none		
2,301	48	1,459	99		X		X	X	X	X	X	3/2	none		
1,425	60	1,194	97	X				X	X	X	X	3/1	none		
				X	X	X	X	X	X	X	X	3/2	none		
1,399	28			X	X	X						3/2	none		
1,464	30			X	X	X		X				3/2	none		
				X				X				3/2	none		
498	25			X				X	X	X		3/2	none		
													none		
3,590	10							X				5/10	none		

Institution		Tuition and fees	Add'l out-of-state/ district tuition	Books and supplies	Costs for campus residents			Costs for students at home		
					Room and board	Trans-portation	Other costs	Board only	Trans-portation	Other costs
Cerro Coso Community College	‡	390	3,120/—	630				2,124	720	900
Chabot College	‡	396	3,300/—	750				2,124	750	500
Chaffey Community College	‡	410	3,210/—	630				2,124	900	1,584
Chapman University		17,902		600	6,220	650	1,100	2,000	650	1,100
Charles R. Drew University: College of Allied Health		3,100		2,268		1,683	2,832	1,440	720	1,460
Christian Heritage College		8,980		600	4,120	500	1,700	1,200	600	1,700
Citrus College	‡	415	3,690/—	630				2,124	640	1,000
City College of San Francisco	‡	410	3,510/—	600					550	3,880
Claremont McKenna College		17,840		600	6,260		900	3,434		900
Coastline Community College	‡	398	3,210/—	630				2,124	576	1,584
Cogswell Polytechnical College		7,010		600					620	1,232
Coleman College		5,050		425					1,000	1,000
College of Alameda	‡	394	3,510/—	630				2,124	720	1,584
College of the Canyons		410	3,120/—	630				2,124	684	1,584
College of the Desert	‡	410	3,000/—	630				2,124	684	1,584
College of Marin: Kentfield	‡	412	3,480/—	630				1,700	680	1,710
College of Notre Dame		13,500		648	6,100	636	1,314	2,196	636	1,314
College of Oceaneering		13,550						750	300	750
College of the Redwoods	‡	405	3,630/—	630	4,393	540	1,638	2,124	576	1,550
College of San Mateo	‡	410	3,390/—	648				2,124	684	1,000
College of the Sequoias	‡	412	3,510/—	648				1,890	594	900
College of the Siskiyous	‡	410	3,210/—	630	3,770	720	1,584	2,124	720	1,584
Columbia College	‡	418	3,360/—	650		400	1,200	2,124	500	900
Columbia College: Hollywood	‡	5,500		550					700	1,800
Compton Community College	‡	390	3,090/—	630						
Concordia University		12,500		580	4,740	560	980	2,180	840	980
Contra Costa College	‡	390	3,420/—	630				2,124	684	1,548
Cosumnes River College	‡	390	3,600/—	630				1,750	715	1,183
Crafton Hills College	‡	422	3,210/—	630				2,124	750	550
Cuesta College	‡	450	3,210/—	630				1,566	720	1,530
Cuyamaca College	‡	420	3,120/—	450				1,500	600	700
Cypress College	‡	415	3,420/—	630				2,124	750	750
De Anza College	‡	471	3,330/—	648				834	576	1,584
Deep Springs College		0				1,250	350			
DeVry Institute of Technology: Pomona		6,335		550				2,212	1,955	2,045
Diablo Valley College	‡	402	3,420/—	630				2,124	684	1,548
Dominican College of San Rafael		13,890		636	6,410	600	1,404		711	1,610
Dominican School of Philosophy and Theology		8,000		535				2,000	1,275	1,930
Don Bosco Technical Institute		4,930		400					450	400
D-Q University		3,800		500	4,352	517	1,622	1,680	550	1,402
East Los Angeles College		405	3,420/—	630				2,124	576	1,300
El Camino College	‡	410	3,510/—	612				1,998	684	1,728
Evergreen Valley College	‡	410	3,360/—	612				1,998	684	1,548
Fashion Institute of Design and Merchandising										
Los Angeles		11,950	150/—	1,350						
San Francisco		11,950	150/—	1,875				1,410	612	1,512
Feather River College	‡	410	3,750/—	550				1,998	700	1,638
Foothill College	‡	471	3,330/—	750				600	750	1,000
Fresno City College	‡	410	3,510/—	630				2,124	684	1,449

†Figures are projected for 1995-96. ‡Figures are for 1994-95.

| All aid | | Need-based aid | | Grants and scholarships | | | | | | | | Financial aid deadlines | | Inst aid form | Notes |
| | | | | Need-based | | | | Non-need-based | | | | | | | |
Total freshmen	Percent receiving aid	Freshmen judged to have need	Percent offered aid	Acad	Music/ drama	Art	Athl	Acad	Music/ drama	Art	Athl	Priority	Closing		
1,000	6			X	X	X		X	X	X		5/15	none		
3,218	25			X				X				8/1	none		
1,500	9			X				X				3/1	none		
388	74	289	100	X	X	X		X	X	X		3/2	none		
110	99			X				X					2/28		
94	85			X	X		X	X	X		X	4/1	none	X	
				X	X	X	X	X	X	X	X	3/2	none		
				X	X	X	X	X				3/2	none		
232	64	130	100					X					2/1		
5,797	10											3/2	none		
120	40			X				X				5/1	6/1		
130	87							X				3/2	none		
1,500	15											3/2	none		
													none		
				X	X	X		X	X	X		3/1	none		
780	15			X	X			X				3/1	none		
129	85	96	100	X				X	X	X	X	3/2	none		
													none		
1,384	50			X				X		X		4/15	none		
1,974	38	525	100									3/2	none	X	
2,036	38			X	X		X	X				3/2	none	X	
508	25							X				5/2	none		
598	13			X	X	X		X	X	X		3/2	none		
80	35			X								4/15	none		
1,450	75			X				X	X	X	X		5/15		
185	85	111	100	X	X		X	X	X		X	3/15	6/30	X	
1,994	37											3/2	none		
				X		X		X				5/1	none		
				X				X				5/1	none		
				X				X				3/2	none		
1,749	8			X								7/28	none		
2,299	15			X	X				X			5/31	none		
6,642	15			X	X	X		X	X	X		3/2	none		
								X					none		
4,364	10			X				X				3/2	none		
74	85	63	100	X	X	X	X	X	X	X	X	2/1	none		
														X	
													none		
													none		
													none		
4,329	8							X	X	X	X	6/1	none		
				X				X	X	X	X	5/31	none		
870	74											3/2	none		
												3/2	none		
482	40			X				X				3/2	none		
4,000	11			X	X	X	X	X	X	X	X	4/30	none		
3,800	11			X				X	X	X		4/15	none		

Institution		Tuition and fees	Add'l out-of-state/district tuition	Books and supplies	Costs for campus residents			Costs for students at home		
					Room and board	Trans-portation	Other costs	Board only	Trans-portation	Other costs
Fresno Pacific College		10,668		648	3,820	576	1,314	1,620	738	1,566
Fullerton College	‡	413	3,420/—	630				2,124	576	1,748
Gavilan Community College	‡	417	3,600/—	630				2,124	576	1,748
Glendale Community College	‡	446	3,390/—	630				2,124	576	1,748
Golden Gate University		7,990		400				2,050	2,176	3,330
Golden West College		410	3,210/—	630				2,124	720	1,584
Grossmont Community College	‡	410	3,120/—	630				2,124	700	800
Hartnell College		390	3,300/—	630				2,124	576	1,380
Harvey Mudd College		18,566		700	6,920		900			
Heald Business College										
Concord		6,000		600						
Fresno		5,400		800						
San Jose		5,850		500						
Heald College										
Sacramento		5,850		525						
Santa Rosa		5,550		450						
Heald Institute of Technology		7,800		1,000						
Hebrew Union College: Jewish Institute of Religion		7,000		750						
Holy Names College		12,700		648	5,330	576	1,314	4,050	738	1,566
Humboldt State University	‡	1,826	7,380/—	648	4,378	576	1,463	2,124	576	1,463
Humphreys College		5,460		630		540	1,530	1,566	720	1,530
Imperial Valley College	‡	390	3,210/—	630				2,124	576	1,638
Irvine Valley College		410	3,210/—	630				2,124	1,040	1,784
John F. Kennedy University	‡	7,944		504					675	
Kelsey-Jenney College		8,388						2,124	576	1,584
Kings River Community College	‡	410	3,510/—	630	2,980	684	1,200	2,124	684	1,748
La Sierra University		12,975		450	3,885	522	1,314	1,512	612	1,458
Lake Tahoe Community College	‡	411	3,735/—	630				2,124	576	1,386
Laney College	‡	394	3,510/—	630				2,124	720	1,584
Las Positas College	‡	396	3,300/—	630				2,124	720	1,530
Lassen College	‡	405	3,750/—	630	4,044	540	1,278	2,124	576	1,584
LIFE Bible College		4,640		400	2,600		475		225	475
Lincoln University	‡	6,475		400					360	
Loma Linda University		7,866								
Long Beach City College	‡	410	3,420/—	630				2,124	612	1,535
Los Angeles City College	‡	405	3,570/—	840					768	2,040
Los Angeles Harbor College	‡	390	3,570/—	630				2,124	576	1,530
Los Angeles Mission College	‡	405	3,570/—	630				2,124	576	1,548
Los Angeles Pierce College	‡	405	3,570/—	630				2,124	576	1,748
Los Angeles Southwest College	‡	405	3,570/—	630				2,124	576	1,530
Los Angeles Trade and Technical College	‡	405	3,570/—	630				2,124	576	1,584
Los Angeles Valley College	‡	405	3,570/—	630				2,124	576	1,584
Los Medanos College	‡	392	3,420/—	648				2,196	594	1,620
Louise Salinger Academy of Fashion	‡	12,180		1,000						
Loyola Marymount University		14,823		572	6,190	50	1,314	1,566	594	1,314
Marymount College		12,875		630	6,156	540	1,278	2,300	576	1,584
Master's College		9,992		612	4,314	576	1,000		684	1,548
Mendocino College	‡	410	3,288/—	630				2,124	684	1,584
Menlo College		15,460		600	6,200	700	1,625	1,500	250	1,625
Merced College	‡	410	3,210/—	630				2,124	576	1,728
Merritt College	‡	394	3,510/—	650				2,500	750	1,584

†Figures are projected for 1995-96. ‡Figures are for 1994-95.

| All aid | | Need-based aid | | Grants and scholarships | | | | | | | | Financial aid deadlines | | Inst aid form | Notes |
| Total freshmen | Percent receiving aid | Freshmen judged to have need | Percent offered aid | Need-based | | | | Non-need-based | | | | Priority | Closing | | |
				Acad	Music/drama	Art	Athl	Acad	Music/drama	Art	Athl				
163	90	102	100	X	X	X	X	X	X	X	X	1/31	none		
2,783	3			X				X	X	X	X	5/1	none		
				X				X	X	X	X	4/15	none		
1,320	20											7/1	none		
32	16	5	100	X				X				3/2	none		
													none		
4,672	10			X	X	X	X	X	X	X	X	4/1	none		
													none		
169	82	97	100	X				X				2/1	none		
													none		
													none		
													none		
													none		
													none		
				X									none		
65	54	62	100	X	X	X	X	X	X	X	X	3/2	none	X	
825	37			X	X	X		X	X	X		3/1	none		
53	60												4/4		
1,800	60							X	X	X	X	3/2	none		
				X				X	X	X	X	3/2	5/2		
				X				X				4/1	none		
													none		
2,260	30	1,510	99	X	X		X	X	X		X	6/1	none		
321	65			X	X	X	X	X	X	X	X	5/1	none	X	
				X	X			X	X	X		5/1	none		
												4/15	none		
1,320	2	55	100									5/1	none		
1,339	85			X								7/1	none		
59	35			X	X	X	X	X	X	X	X	6/1	none		
													none		
													none		
2,487	27			X	X	X		X	X	X		5/1	none		
7,597	20			X	X	X	X					3/2	none		
2,300	14			X				X				3/2	none		
								X				8/1	none		
				X				X				7/7	none		
				X				X				7/1	none		
												7/7	none		
3,200	5											6/12	none		
1,212	13			X				X	X			3/2	8/1		
													none		
766	77	482	97	X	X	X	X	X	X		X	2/15	none		
361	50	165	100	X	X			X				3/2	none		
								X	X		X	4/2	8/1		
												5/31	none		
192	74	87	100	X				X				3/2	none		
1,500	35			X				X				6/1	none		
1,323	28			X								4/1	none		

Institution	Tuition and fees	Add'l out-of-state/district tuition	Books and supplies	Costs for campus residents			Costs for students at home		
				Room and board	Trans-portation	Other costs	Board only	Trans-portation	Other costs
Mills College	14,982		550	6,180		1,370	1,500	600	1,500
MiraCosta College	‡ 430	3,300/—	600				2,223	585	1,287
Mission College	‡ 416	3,300/—	630				2,124	576	1,584
Modesto Junior College	‡ 418	3,360/—	630				2,124	576	1,584
Monterey Institute of International Studies	15,245		450				5,200	700	1,400
Monterey Peninsula College	‡ 430	3,300/—	630				2,124	720	1,548
Moorpark College	410	3,300/—	630				2,124	684	1,000
Mount St. Mary's College	14,185		648	6,020	576	13,141	2,196	594	1,620
Mount San Antonio College	428	3,420/—	630				2,124	684	1,728
Mount San Jacinto College	‡ 395	3,390/—	630				2,124	576	1,584
Napa Valley College	‡ 392	3,570/—	648				2,196	594	1,566
National University	‡ 6,255		500					650	
New College of California	‡ 7,500		600					800	2,268
New School of Art and Architecture	9,000		600						
Occidental College	18,000		648	5,660		1,152			1,152
Ohlone College	‡ 392	3,210/—	630				2,124	576	1,584
Orange Coast College	‡ 433	3,210/—	630				2,124	684	1,584
Otis College of Art and Design	14,236		1,650		550	1,375		550	1,375
Oxnard College	420	3,300/—	600				1,800	700	1,300
Pacific Christian College	7,820		630	4,250	540	1,278	2,124	576	1,584
Pacific Oaks College	13,110		500				3,000	2,400	3,600
Pacific Union College	12,360		612	3,945	576	1,350	1,500	576	1,350
Palo Verde College	‡ 390	3,210/—	648				2,124	594	1,600
Palomar College	‡ 410	3,210/—	630				2,124	576	1,584
Pasadena City College	‡ 410	3,510/—	630				2,124	576	900
Patten College	5,728		550		440	1,100	1,650	330	1,595
Pepperdine University	19,260		900	6,880	660	660	2,450	1,450	726
Phillips Junior College									
Fresno Campus	6,170		992					720	1,530
San Fernando Valley Campus	† 5,925								
Pitzer College	20,270		650	6,208		900			900
Point Loma Nazarene College	10,425		750	4,480	600	1,450	2,050	700	1,600
Pomona College	18,780		800	7,520	750	1,000	2,000	750	1,000
Porterville College	‡ 400	3,210/—	630				3,800	500	630
Queen of the Holy Rosary College	2,500		150						
Rancho Santiago Community College	415	3,210/—	630				2,124	576	1,764
Rio Hondo College	‡ 412	3,120/—	630				2,124	576	
Riverside Community College	‡ 410	3,060/—	630				2,124	648	1,008
Sacramento City College	‡ 390	3,600/—	630				1,971	648	1,383
Saddleback College	‡ 410	3,210/—	630				2,124	1,040	1,784
St. John's Seminary College	6,065		630	2,000	540	1,278			
St. Mary's College of California	14,250		648	6,608	576	1,314	2,196	594	1,620
Samuel Merritt College	13,395		900		1,053	3,600	2,500	1,053	3,600
San Bernardino Valley College	430	3,150/—	630				2,124	576	1,584
San Diego City College	‡ 410	3,180/—	630				2,124	684	1,548
San Diego Mesa College	‡ 410	3,180/—	630				2,124	684	1,548
San Diego Miramar College	‡ 395	3,180/—	648		2,196		2,124	738	1,620
San Diego State University	‡ 1,902	7,380/—	630	4,884	576	1,764	1,998	684	1,764
San Francisco Art Institute	15,486		1,100				2,000	684	1,512
San Francisco College of Mortuary Science	8,525		750				3,600	1,800	1,200

†Figures are projected for 1995-96. ‡Figures are for 1994-95.

| All aid | | Need-based aid | | Grants and scholarships | | | | | | | | Financial aid deadlines | | Inst aid form | Notes |
| Total freshmen | Percent receiving aid | Freshmen judged to have need | Percent offered aid | Need-based | | | | Non-need-based | | | | | | | |
				Acad	Music/drama	Art	Athl	Acad	Music/drama	Art	Athl	Priority	Closing		
142	72			X	X	X		X	X	X		2/15	none		
2,537	10	525	100					X	X	X		3/2	none		
				X				X				5/1	none		
3,000	30							X	X	X		3/2	none		
								X				3/15	none		
1,800	40	594	96	X	X	X	X	X	X	X	X	3/2	none		
													none		
				X	X	X	X	X				3/1	none		
													none		
1,500	40			X				X	X	X	X	3/2	none		
				X		X	X	X	X	X	X	4/1	none		
350	80			X								3/2	none		
85	85											3/1	none		
16	70	11	100	X		X		X		X		3/2	none		
357	83			X				X	X			2/1			
1,813	7	334	100	X	X	X		X	X	X		7/1	none		
6,300	3			X	X	X	X	X	X		X	6/1	none		
82	85			X		X						3/1	none		
													none		
102	98	70	100	X	X			X	X			3/2	none	X	
				X				X				3/1	none		
406	87							X	X			3/2	none		
													none		
4,799	20	550	82	X				X				4/1	none		
3,543	15			X	X	X	X	X	X	X	X	5/13	none		
130	89	78	97	X	X		X	X	X		X	3/2	7/15		
631	70			X	X	X	X	X	X	X	X	2/15	4/1	X	
													none		
													none		
175	40	83	100										2/1		
430	72			X	X	X	X	X			X	4/10	none		
379	55	191	100										2/1		
430	50			X				X				6/1	none		
												3/1	7/1		
													none		
2,570	11			X	X	X	X	X	X	X	X	7/15	none		
6,111	38			X	X	X		X	X	X		3/2	none		
2,591	35			X	X	X						3/2	none		
4,010	9			X				X	X	X		3/2	5/2		
11	50											4/30	none		
501	68							X			X		3/2		
12	93	10	100	X				X				3/2	none		
													none		
									X	X	X	X	5/1	none		
				X				X				5/1	none		
874	7											5/1	none		
2,791	67	1,461	91	X	X	X	X	X	X	X	X	3/2	none		
48	65									X		4/1	none		
													none		
22	85												9/5		

Institution	Tuition and fees	Add'l out-of-state/district tuition	Books and supplies	Costs for campus residents			Costs for students at home		
				Room and board	Trans-portation	Other costs	Board only	Trans-portation	Other costs
San Francisco Conservatory of Music	14,750		600				2,000	700	1,800
San Francisco State University	‡ 1,982	7,380/—	648	5,245	540	1,638	2,124	576	1,764
San Joaquin Delta College	‡ 390	3,390/—	700				2,200	650	1,300
San Jose Christian College	6,300		648	3,246	576	1,314	2,196	576	1,620
San Jose City College	‡ 410	3,360/—	630					576	
San Jose State University	‡ 1,970	7,380/—	630	5,112	540	1,548	2,124	684	1,548
Santa Barbara City College	‡ 410	3,210/—	630				2,124	639	1,440
Santa Clara University	14,772		648	6,522	576	1,314	2,196	594	1,620
Santa Monica College	‡ 410	3,570/—	630				2,124	585	
Santa Rosa Junior College	‡ 406	3,630/—	630		720	1,584	2,124	720	1,584
Scripps College	18,180		700	7,500		900			1,566
Shasta College	416	3,180/—	630		540	1,350	2,124	684	1,350
Sierra College	405	3,600/—	630	3,934	300	1,500	1,500	800	1,500
Simpson College	7,704		630	3,690	540	1,278	1,998	720	1,530
Skyline College	‡ 410	3,390/—	630				2,124	576	1,332
Solano Community College	‡ 401	3,540/—	630				2,124	576	1,386
Sonoma State University	‡ 2,070	7,380/—	630	5,500	292	1,370	2,124	536	1,121
Southern California College	10,288		648	4,690	576	1,314		594	1,314
Southern California Institute of Architecture	‡ 11,620		1,470				2,720	900	
Southwestern College	‡ 415	3,240/—	630				2,124	576	1,764
Stanford University	19,695		815	7,054		1,315			1,315
Taft College	‡ 450	3,210/—	250	2,300	576	1,566	2,196	576	1,566
Thomas Aquinas College	13,700		350	5,500	650	850		800	850
United States International University	10,566		630	4,350	774	1,836	2,124	900	1,836
University of California									
Berkeley	‡ 4,232	7,699/—	675	6,246	300	1,679	1,850	300	1,679
Davis	‡ 4,374	7,699/—	841	5,640	756	1,618	1,500	792	1,381
Irvine	‡ 4,050	7,699/—	790	5,323	540	1,278	2,124	576	1,584
Los Angeles	‡ 3,894	7,699/—	700	5,602	155	150	1,280	2,580	150
Riverside	‡ 4,093	7,699/—	882	5,430	576	1,260	1,500	684	1,260
San Diego	‡ 4,128	7,699/—	612	6,375	957	1,598	1,613	936	1,531
San Francisco	‡ 4,459	7,699/—	3,341		800	2,200	2,000	800	2,200
Santa Barbara	‡ 4,098	7,699/—	576	5,901	340	1,284	1,512	684	1,284
Santa Cruz	‡ 4,384	7,699/—	633	5,154	425	1,665	1,620	425	1,665
University of Judaism	12,468		800	6,300	725	1,600	2,125	725	1,600
University of La Verne	14,220		648	5,190	720	1,644	2,196	720	1,644
University of the Pacific	17,550		646	5,326	720	1,171	2,500	720	1,171
University of Redlands	17,110		600	6,515					
University of San Diego	14,325		650	6,800	576	1,314	1,170	594	1,620
University of San Francisco	14,108		750	6,670	600	1,900	2,000	600	1,900
University of Southern California	18,598		600	6,482	580	1,630	1,610	940	1,630
University of West Los Angeles	† 5,145		300					1,000	1,500
Ventura College	‡ 410	3,300/—	630				2,124	700	1,300
Victor Valley College	‡ 410	3,210/—	630				2,124	720	1,500
Vista Community College	394	3,510/—	630				2,124	720	1,584
West Coast University	‡ 10,355		630				2,124	576	1,584
West Hills Community College	‡ 390	3,480/—	630				1,566	576	1,530
West Los Angeles College	390	3,750/—	630				2,124	684	1,748
West Valley College	444	3,300/—	630				2,124	648	1,548
Westmont College	16,330		510	5,380	630	830		630	830
Whittier College	17,187		500	5,813	548	1,450	1,636	662	1,607

†Figures are projected for 1995-96. ‡Figures are for 1994-95.

| All aid | | Need–based aid | | Grants and scholarships | | | | | | | | Financial aid deadlines | | Inst aid form | Notes |
| Total freshmen | Percent receiving aid | Freshmen judged to have need | Percent offered aid | Need–based | | | | Non–need–based | | | | | | | |
				Acad	Music/drama	Art	Athl	Acad	Music/drama	Art	Athl	Priority	Closing		
11	72	8	100		X				X			3/1	none	X	
1,680	70			X				X	X			3/1	none		
4,571	22			X	X	X		X	X	X		4/15	none		
18	80			X	X		X	X	X		X	3/2	8/1	X	
2,897	6											5/31	none		
1,427	30	655	100	X							X	3/1	none		
2,097	26			X				X				5/1	none		
910	66	590	100	X	X	X		X	X		X	2/1	none		
3,493	23			X	X	X	X	X	X	X	X	5/15	none		
3,629	57			X				X	X	X	X	3/2	none		
167	53	84	100	X				X				2/1	3/2		
													none		
													none		
112	86			X	X		X	X	X		X	3/2	none	X	
1,563	8			X								5/13	none		
1,595	4											6/1	none		
668	58	270	100	X				X	X			3/2	none		
223	80	192	100	X	X		X	X				3/2	none		
16	49			X		X		X		X		3/2	none		
4,000	57	1,268	100									3/2	none		
1,588	67			X	X	X	X				X		2/1		
				X				X				8/1	none		
68	92	63	100					X				3/1	9/1		
								X				3/2	none	X	
3,516	55			X				X			X		3/2		
				X				X				3/2	none		
2,781	61							X	X	X	X	3/2	5/1		
4,130	70			X				X	X	X	X	3/2	none	X	
1,465	55			X				X	X	X	X	3/2	none		
3,839	40			X				X				3/2	5/1		
				X				X				7/1	none	X	
2,881	35			X	X	X	X	X	X	X	X	3/2	none		
1,788	42	801	100	X	X	X		X	X	X		3/2	none		
16	90	16	100					X				3/2	none		
473	80	182	100	X	X							3/2	none	X	
588	56	429	100	X	X	X	X	X	X	X	X	3/2	none		
308	79			X	X	X		X	X	X		3/1	6/30		
862	65	439	100	X	X		X	X			X	2/20	none	X	
527	66	290	99	X			X	X			X	2/15	none		
2,407	60			X	X			X	X	X	X	2/15	3/2		
				X				X				6/1	none		
				X	X	X			X	X		3/2	5/1		
				X				X				3/2	none		
													none		
				X									6/1		
780	68			X	X	X						3/2	none		
													none		
													none		
307	85	274	100					X	X	X	X	3/1	none	X	
347	83	261	100	X	X	X		X	X	X		2/15	none		

Institution	Tuition and fees	Add'l out-of-state/ district tuition	Books and supplies	Costs for campus residents			Costs for students at home		
				Room and board	Trans-portation	Other costs	Board only	Trans-portation	Other costs
Woodbury University	13,020		648	5,655	576	1,314	2,196	594	1,620
Yeshiva Ohr Elchonon Chabad/West Coast									
Talmudical Seminary	6,900		125	3,100					
Yuba College	‡ 412	3,420/—	630	3,400	566	1,568	2,124	576	1,570
Colorado									
Adams State College	‡ 1,785	3,430/—	520	3,670	800	1,336	750	800	1,336
Aims Community College	‡ 1,058	4,658/833	500					580	1,050
Arapahoe Community College	‡ 1,982	5,190/—	450				2,385	900	274
Bel-Rea Institute of Animal Technology	5,375		800				1,584	195	1,053
Beth-El College of Nursing	5,275		450					450	200
Blair Junior College	5,355								
Colorado Christian University	‡ 7,220		1,150	3,665	2,250	1,475			3,600
Colorado College	18,084		450	4,562	300	900	1,500	300	900
Colorado Institute of Art	‡ 8,450		1,200					675	1,250
Colorado Mountain College									
Alpine Campus	‡ 1,060	4,620/870	700	3,700	400	1,000	1,500	200	900
Spring Valley Campus	‡ 1,060	4,620/870	400	3,700	400	1,000	1,600	200	900
Timberline Campus	‡ 1,060	4,620/870	400	3,700	400	1,000	1,600	200	900
Colorado Northwestern Community College	‡ 390	3,500/950	500	3,530	400	2,250	1,953	207	3,105
Colorado School of Mines	† 4,760	8,738/—	800	4,400		1,400	2,000	1,100	1,400
Colorado State University	‡ 2,708	6,288/—	500	4,180	300	1,500			1,900
Colorado Technical College	‡ 6,045		700				800	800	200
Community College of Aurora	‡ 1,618	5,190/—	400						
Community College of Denver	‡ 1,803	5,190/—	415				1,115	720	916
Fort Lewis College	‡ 1,877	5,296/—	550	3,518	860	1,627	900	860	1,627
Front Range Community College	‡ 1,637	5,190/—	395				1,000	570	675
Lamar Community College	‡ 1,778	3,503/—	400	3,620	200	400	1,700	450	375
Mesa State College	‡ 1,814	3,582/—	425	3,610	350	800	650	360	750
Metropolitan State College of Denver	‡ 1,855	4,781/—	540				3,906	940	1,230
Morgan Community College	‡ 1,620	4,152/—	475				1,200	855	750
Naropa Institute	10,358		540						
National College	7,755		828					1,092	
Nazarene Bible College	4,220		500				1,600	750	600
Northeastern Junior College	† 1,920	3,930/1,500	460	3,600	720	800	1,944	587	800
Otero Junior College	‡ 1,698	3,503/—	400	3,690	600			800	1,200
Pikes Peak Community College	‡ 1,639	5,190/—	500					900	1,350
Pueblo Community College	‡ 1,727	5,190/—	540				1,680	944	950
Red Rocks Community College	‡ 2,019	5,190/—	450				2,000	805	875
Regis University	13,520		540	5,800	495	1,170	1,440	675	1,170
Rocky Mountain College of Art & Design	‡ 6,180		1,000				2,920	800	1,067
Technical Trades Institute	10,500								
Trinidad State Junior College	‡ 1,721	3,503/—	470	3,142	600	1,125	1,800	450	900
United States Air Force Academy	0								
University of Colorado									
Boulder	‡ 2,701	11,104/—	560	3,964	990	2,383	2,515	990	2,383
Colorado Springs	‡ 2,282	5,708/—	540				2,240	944	432
Denver	‡ 2,045	7,416/—	520				2,835	765	810
Health Sciences Center	‡ 4,102	8,868/—	865				1,575	100	2,340
University of Denver	16,284		555	5,004					1,887
University of Northern Colorado	‡ 2,227	5,902/—	500	4,128	350	1,730	1,700		520
University of Southern Colorado	‡ 1,968	5,456/—	500	4,004	950	1,500	800	800	1,500
Western State College of Colorado	‡ 1,915	4,520/—	500	4,279	750	1,250	1,500	500	1,000
Yeshiva Toras Chaim Talmudical Seminary	4,250			4,600					

†Figures are projected for 1995-96. ‡Figures are for 1994-95.

| All aid | | Need–based aid | | Grants and scholarships | | | | | | | | Financial aid deadlines | | Inst aid form | Notes |
| Total freshmen | Percent receiving aid | Freshmen judged to have need | Percent offered aid | Need–based | | | | Non–need–based | | | | | | | |
				Acad	Music/drama	Art	Athl	Acad	Music/drama	Art	Athl	Priority	Closing		
98	74	75	100	X				X				3/2	none	X	
2,080	12			X				X				3/2	none		
579	84	445	100	X				X	X	X	X	4/15	none		
				X				X				6/1	none		
5,706	9	607	100	X				X				3/15	none		
88	55							X				8/31	none		
													none		
155	85			X	X		X	X	X		X	3/15	none		
536	57	266	100	X				X			X	2/15	none		
526	80	491	100	X	X	X		X	X	X			none		
230	46							X			X	3/31	none		
238	46							X			X	3/31	none		
116	46							X			X	3/31	none		
172	95	145	100	X			X	X			X	5/1	none	X	
480	85	400	100	X	X		X	X	X		X	3/1	none	X	
2,295	55	1,284	100					X	X	X	X	3/1	none		
				X				X					none		
				X				X				6/1	none		
2,532	28							X	X	X		3/15	5/15		
1,604	66	534	100	X	X	X	X	X	X	X	X	4/15	none		
				X				X				5/15	none		
340	80			X			X	X		X	X	5/1	none	X	
1,016	70	762	100	X	X	X	X	X	X	X	X	3/15	none		
1,544	72			X				X	X		X	3/1	none		
270	90			X				X				3/1	none		
				X				X				3/31	none		
													none		
													none		
990	40			X	X	X	X	X	X	X	X	4/1	none	X	
381	70	304	94	X			X				X	5/1	none		
								X				7/1	none		
1,083	51			X				X				3/15	5/1		
													none		
317	76			X				X			X	3/15	none	X	
73	90			X		X		X		X		7/31	none		
79	100	79	100												
654	68							X	X	X	X	5/1	none		
3,603	54	1,463	100	X	X	X	X	X	X	X	X	4/1	none		
357	42	170	86	X			X	X			X	4/1	none		
294	25			X	X	X		X	X	X		3/31	none		
								X							
565	58			X				X	X	X	X	2/21	none		
1,625	71	845	95	X				X	X	X	X	3/1	none		
654	55	511	80	X				X	X	X	X	3/1	none		
608	70	384	100	X	X	X	X	X	X	X	X	4/1	none		

Institution	Tuition and fees	Add'l out-of-state/ district tuition	Books and supplies	Costs for campus residents			Costs for students at home		
				Room and board	Trans-portation	Other costs	Board only	Trans-portation	Other costs
Connecticut									
Albertus Magnus College	12,617		550	5,664		870	1,700	650	900
Asnuntuck Community-Technical College	1,646	2,976/—	600				2,000	1,500	950
Briarwood College	9,612		750		945	1,400	2,296	945	1,400
Capital Community-Technical College	1,646	2,976/—	500				2,000	820	1,700
Central Connecticut State University	‡ 3,140	4,120/—	500	4,666	191	1,075	1,500	685	1,075
Connecticut College			600			500	1,800		500
Eastern Connecticut State University	3,202	5,092/—		4,486					
Fairfield University	16,340		450	6,600	300	900	1,500	700	600
Gateway Community-Technical College	1,646	2,976/—	600				1,800	950	1,460
Holy Apostles College and Seminary	4,730		600	6,250	400	700		850	550
Housatonic Community-Technical College	1,646	2,976/—	500				1,800	925	960
Manchester Community-Technical College	1,646	2,976/—	600						
Middlesex Community-Technical College	1,646	2,976/—	500				2,000	1,500	700
Mitchell College	11,500		500	5,600	500	500	1,100	1,000	500
Naugatuck Valley Community-Technical College	1,646	2,976/—	700					1,100	
Northwestern Connecticut Community-Technical College	1,646	2,976/—	600				700	930	900
Norwalk Community-Technical College	1,646	2,976/—	400				900	1,800	1,600
Paier College of Art	10,120		600						
Quinebaug Valley Community-Technical College	1,646	2,976/—	600				2,000	1,200	1,000
Quinnipiac College	13,430		500	6,450	300	800	1,500	500	800
Sacred Heart University	12,100		600	6,080	700	700	1,500	700	700
St. Joseph College	13,020		550	4,810	200	900	1,500	600	900
Southern Connecticut State University	3,140	5,092/—	700	5,011	300	976	1,854		1,690
Teikyo-Post University	11,700		650	5,600			2,862		
Three Rivers Community-Technical College	1,646	2,976/—	450						
Trinity College	20,230		600	6,130		600			600
Tunxis Community-Technical College	1,646	2,976/—	420				1,800	1,400	1,210
United States Coast Guard Academy	0								
University of Bridgeport	12,825		550	6,020	400	500	778	500	500
University of Connecticut	4,810	7,900/—	725	5,124	725	1,700	2,604	1,000	1,700
University of Hartford	15,610		600	6,265	450	1,090	1,800	900	1,090
University of New Haven	11,400		500	5,310	200	1,000	1,600	720	1,000
Wesleyan University	20,820		600	5,810					
Western Connecticut State University	3,168	4,284/—	800	4,088	400	1,300	1,832	800	1,300
Yale University	21,000		630	6,630	547	1,510			1,510
Delaware									
Delaware State University	‡ 2,132	3,232/—	1,000	4,110	1,000	1,000		1,000	1,000
Delaware Technical and Community College									
Southern Campus	‡ 1,275	1,800/—	450				1,500	500	300
Stanton/Wilmington Campus	‡ 1,275	1,800/—	450				1,500	500	300
Terry Campus	‡ 1,275	1,800/—	450				1,500	500	300
Goldey-Beacom College	6,450		531		794	1,036	1,762	794	1,036
University of Delaware	‡ 4,100	6,530/—	550	4,230		1,350			1,350
Wesley College	10,295		500	4,674	450	900	2,224	2,000	1,000
Wilmington College	‡ 5,390		700				1,900	2,000	1,500

†Figures are projected for 1995-96. ‡Figures are for 1994-95.

| All aid | | Need-based aid | | Grants and scholarships | | | | | | | | Financial aid deadlines | | Inst aid form | Notes |
| Total fresh-men | Percent receiving aid | Freshmen judged to have need | Percent offered aid | Need-based | | | | Non-need-based | | | | | | | |
				Acad	Music/drama	Art	Athl	Acad	Music/drama	Art	Athl	Priority	Closing		
116	91	87	100	X				X				2/15	none		
		250	100									6/1	none	X	
149	70	115	100					X				4/30	none		
797	33			X				X				7/15	none		
1,070	47	371	100				X	X			X		3/15		
455	55	243	100									2/15		X	
573	60			X				X				3/15			
806	69	437	100	X				X	X		X	2/15			
1,589	19							X				none			
												none			
820	30	535	100									7/1	none		
												none			
				X								6/1	none		
247	70											3/1	7/15		
				X				X				4/7	none		
444	40			X				X				6/15	none		
1,526	25			X								4/15	none		
60	40											5/1	none		
357	27	135	100					X		X			10/1		
1,000	65			X				X			X	3/1	none	X	
587	83	472	100	X			X	X		X	X	3/1	none		
121	94			X				X				2/15	none	X	
985	33							X				3/16	none		
175	95	96	100	X			X	X			X	3/15	none	X	
1,206	40											7/15	none		
473	42	209	100										2/1		
351	20			X				X				7/1	none		
224	90	194	100	X			X	X	X		X	4/1	none		
1,897	76	1,387	100	X	X	X	X	X	X	X	X	3/1	none		
1,366	85	980	100	X				X	X	X	X	2/1	none	X	
384	70	235	100	X				X			X	3/15	none		
730	49												2/1		
537	65			X	X	X		X					3/15		
1,308	67	573	100										2/1	X	
734	83	204	75	X	X		X	X	X		X	4/1	none		
543	33			X			X	X			X	6/15	none		
1,149	25			X			X	X			X	7/1	none		
329	40			X				X					none		
372	89	206	100	X				X			X	4/1	none		
2,992	74	1,193	97	X				X	X		X	3/15	5/1		
401	70	240	100					X				4/15	none		
97	50	31	100					X			X	4/15	5/1		

Institution	Tuition and fees	Add'l out-of-state/ district tuition	Books and supplies	Costs for campus residents			Costs for students at home		
				Room and board	Trans- portation	Other costs	Board only	Trans- portation	Other costs
District of Columbia									
American University	17,115		450	6,710	700	600	1,600	700	600
Catholic University of America	15,062		480	6,614	500	1,524	700	500	1,224
Corcoran School of Art	11,550		1,800		1,050	1,800	1,700	1,050	1,800
Gallaudet University	5,380		700	5,700	947	2,232	741	947	1,945
George Washington University	19,032		700	6,800		950		600	950
Georgetown University	19,402		700	7,466	410	1,342	2,130	500	1,148
Howard University	8,205		700	4,440	250	2,250	2,000	967	2,250
Mount Vernon College	14,850		500	7,200	1,000	1,100	2,500	500	1,100
Oblate College	5,060		500					200	
Southeastern University	8,700		600				1,000	600	850
Strayer College	† 6,075		500				2,358	9,520	1,500
Trinity College	‡ 11,562		500	6,430	600	800		500	
University of the District of Columbia	‡ 1,046	2,808/—	600					800	1,400
Florida									
Art Institute of Fort Lauderdale	‡ 9,632		990		1,017	1,386	1,000	1,017	1,386
Barry University	12,190		500	5,520	650	800	700	800	800
Bethune-Cookman College	6,458		530	3,522	500	1,610	1,500	815	865
Brevard Community College	‡ 1,050	2,790/—	550				1,800	640	600
Broward Community College	‡ 995	2,778/—	640				1,620	1,552	1,080
Caribbean Center for Advanced Studies: Miami Institute of Psychology	‡ 5,660		600						
Central Florida Community College	‡ 1,093	2,917/—	540				1,620	1,125	666
Chipola Junior College	‡ 1,007	2,787/—	400	2,375	700	500	1,400	1,020	500
Clearwater Christian College	‡ 5,700		500	3,400	800	800	2,000	1,800	2,000
Daytona Beach Community College	‡ 1,289	3,543/—	485				1,700	1,000	1,000
Eckerd College	16,145		640	4,325	745	715	1,600	500	400
Edison Community College	‡ 1,073	2,857/—	450				1,500	876	732
Edward Waters College	‡ 4,300		500	3,850	500	750		600	550
Embry-Riddle Aeronautical University	8,380		570	3,462	1,800	1,220	750	1,240	1,220
Flagler College	5,350		600	3,318	750	1,520	1,680	800	1,520
Florida Agricultural and Mechanical University	‡ 1,835	4,902/—	600	4,292	718	2,000	1,120	740	2,000
Florida Atlantic University	‡ 1,791	4,902/—	600	4,060	1,150	1,120	1,700	1,770	1,120
Florida Baptist Theological College	† 2,634		500		1,000	750	2,000	1,000	
Florida Bible College	4,740		350	2,400	600	2,973	1,500	650	975
Florida Christian College	‡ 3,975		625		850	1,490	2,315	1,065	1,490
Florida College	‡ 4,800		800	3,220	1,250	950	1,800	500	
Florida Community College at Jacksonville	‡ 1,074	2,991/—	450				804	727	1,149
Florida Institute of Technology	14,346		660	4,264	1,500	1,500	2,472	1,500	1,500
Florida International University	† 1,791	4,918/—	800		1,380	1,775	1,650	1,950	1,390
Florida Keys Community College	‡ 1,035	2,775/—	500				2,000	800	1,000
Florida Memorial College	5,280		550	3,190	1,000	2,140	1,170	1,000	2,140
Florida Southern College	9,400		500	5,100	600	600		600	600
Florida State University	‡ 1,798	4,902/—	600	4,316	600	850		600	850
Fort Lauderdale College	‡ 5,244		150			360	1,600	1,075	360
Gulf Coast Community College	‡ 991	2,793/—	600				1,200	750	2,100
Hillsborough Community College	‡ 1,020	2,835/—					1,800	1,640	2,000
Hobe Sound Bible College	‡ 4,300		400	2,600	800	2,000	1,400	400	2,000
Indian River Community College	‡ 1,050	2,880/—	450					350	400
International Fine Arts College	9,975		1,000		1,000	1,900		1,200	2,015

†Figures are projected for 1995-96. ‡Figures are for 1994-95.

Total freshmen	Percent receiving aid	Freshmen judged to have need	Percent offered aid	Acad	Music/drama	Art	Athl	Acad	Music/drama	Art	Athl	Priority	Closing	Inst aid form	Notes
All aid		**Need-based aid**		**Grants and scholarships**								**Financial aid deadlines**		**Inst aid form**	**Notes**
				Need-based				Non-need-based							
1,003	60			X			X	X			X	3/1	none	X	
505	79	387	100	X	X			X	X			1/15	none		
80	64			X		X		X		X		5/1	none		
435	68	311	99	X				X			X		10/1	X	
1,568	78	817	98	X				X	X	X	X	2/15	3/15		
1,466	39	639	100	X			X				X	2/1	none		
				X				X	X	X	X		2/1		
92	90	84	100	X				X				3/1	none		
													none		
57	45							X				6/1	none		
824	37	304	100	X				X				7/1	none		
102	81			X				X				3/1	none		
1,304	5							X	X		X	3/15	none	X	
													none		
1,105	75			X			X	X	X		X	4/1	none		
711	91	647	100	X	X		X	X	X		X		none		
2,445	27	1,450	100	X	X	X	X	X	X	X	X	6/8	none		
								X	X	X	X	4/15	none		
				X				X	X	X	X	5/1	none		
774	60							X	X	X	X	6/15	none		
													none		
								X	X	X	X		none		
363	82	224	100	X	X	X	X	X	X	X	X	4/1	none		
1,500	35							X	X	X	X	6/1	none		
													none		
594	78	508	97	X				X			X	4/15	none		
321	75	159	100	X	X	X	X	X	X	X	X	3/15	none		
								X	X		X	4/1	none		
943	57	387	89	X				X	X	X	X	4/1	none		
43	85			X	X							5/1	none		
		10	100					X	X			5/31	none		
37	83							X	X			5/15	7/15		
212	80	101	100	X	X			X	X		X	6/1	4/1		
								X	X	X	X	3/1	none		
390	79	212	100	X				X			X	2/1	none		
1,395	40			X	X	X		X	X	X	X	3/15	5/1		
117	30	79	100					X		X		5/1	none		
467	95			X			X	X	X			4/1	none		
371	82	248	100	X	X	X	X	X	X	X	X	5/15	none	X	
3,323	52	1,786	100	X				X	X	X		3/1			
								X					none		
4,960	60	560	100	X				X	X	X	X	4/1	none		
								X	X	X	X	4/15	none		
32	75	31	100									6/1	none		
4,800	22	507	100					X	X	X	X		none		
395	45							X		X		7/1	none		

Institution	Tuition and fees	Add'l out-of-state/district tuition	Books and supplies	Costs for campus residents			Costs for students at home		
				Room and board	Transportation	Other costs	Board only	Transportation	Other costs
Jacksonville University	10,580		700	4,598	600	800	1,000	600	800
Jones College	4,350		750					950	1,700
Lake City Community College	‡ 945	2,557/—	500	3,057	500	750	2,901	500	750
Lake-Sumter Community College	‡ 1,088	2,895/—	500				1,600	980	500
Lynn University	15,250		800	5,950	1,200	1,200		600	600
Manatee Community College	‡ 1,020	2,610/—	548				6,458	1,128	1,045
Miami-Dade Community College	‡ 1,073	2,857/—	920				2,146	2,566	2,726
National Education Center: Bauder Campus	6,750								
New College of the University of South Florida	† 2,150	7,300/—	700	3,900	490	2,290		1,760	2,290
New England Institute of Technology	† 7,950		300				1,500	850	1,190
North Florida Junior College	‡ 810	2,318/—	450				1,700	300	475
Nova Southeastern University	8,770		700	4,750	1,900	1,950		1,900	1,950
Okaloosa-Walton Community College	‡ 860	2,410/—	665				2,606	960	1,750
Palm Beach Atlantic College	8,700		700	3,680			1,200		
Palm Beach Community College	‡ 1,074	2,862/—	650					1,061	800
Pasco-Hernando Community College	‡ 1,092	2,916/—	600				1,500	792	1,451
Pensacola Junior College	‡ 1,073	2,722/—	500				1,920	640	1,100
Phillips Junior College: Melbourne	4,995							113	
Polk Community College	‡ 1,084	2,890/—	400					1,000	600
Ringling School of Art and Design	11,500		1,500	5,950	500	500	2,000	500	500
Rollins College	17,995		400	5,555	750	550	1,500	350	51
St. John Vianney College Seminary	6,600		550	4,000	900	990			
St. Johns River Community College	‡ 1,050	3,060/—	550				1,500	600	781
St. Leo College	10,190		525	4,772	840	780	2,340	950	315
St. Petersburg Junior College	‡ 1,074	2,817/—	600				2,106	1,015	915
St. Thomas University	10,580		600	4,600	990	900	2,200	990	900
Santa Fe Community College	‡ 1,050	2,865/—	690					800	800
Schiller International University	11,440		350	5,950	990	3,000			
Seminole Community College	‡ 1,065	2,700/—	600				1,705	720	960
South College: Palm Beach Campus	6,780		750						
South Florida Community College	‡ 1,080	2,786/—	700	1,425				1,300	1,830
Southeastern College of the Assemblies of God	4,786		750	3,135	600	800		500	800
Southern College	5,172		565				2,151	608	210
Stetson University	13,615		600	4,589	550	850	1,100		1,050
Tallahassee Community College	‡ 1,043	2,722/—	500					775	1,000
Talmudic College of Florida	† 4,900		900	3,500					
Tampa College	‡ 5,472							600	700
Trinity International University	7,190		700				2,250	540	1,800
University of Central Florida	† 1,887	5,100/—	700	4,220	400	1,710	1,710	1,720	1,710
University of Florida	† 1,830	5,270/—	690	4,310	450	1,070	1,500	700	1,070
University of Miami	17,700		824	6,768	1,040	1,018	1,800	1,108	970
University of North Florida	1,731	4,902/—	600	3,926	1,836	660		1,836	660
University of South Florida	‡ 1,877	4,902/—	500	4,320	400	2,180	1,800	1,640	2,180
University of Tampa	13,612		775	4,570		1,100		1,200	1,100
University of West Florida	‡ 1,711	4,902/—	523	3,200	519	1,352	1,666	968	1,397
Valencia Community College	‡ 1,103	2,782/—	600					2,200	700
Warner Southern College	7,420		600	3,640	600	1,500	2,500	800	2,600
Webber College	6,540		500	3,000	800	100	1,200	300	100

†Figures are projected for 1995-96. ‡Figures are for 1994-95.

Total freshmen	Percent receiving aid	Freshmen judged to have need	Percent offered aid	Acad	Music/drama	Art	Athl	Acad	Music/drama	Art	Athl	Priority	Closing	Inst aid form	Notes
403	63			X	X	X	X	X	X	X	X	3/15	none		
255	85	81	100					X					none		
850	12			X	X		X	X			X	6/1	none		
600	23							X	X	X		6/1	none		
454	28	109	100	X			X	X			X	2/15	none		
1,130	32			X	X	X	X	X	X	X	X	6/5	7/5		
8,167	60			X	X	X	X	X	X	X	X	4/15	none		
													none		
131	66	115	100	X				X				2/1	6/1		
													none	X	
393	28	334	100	X				X	X	X	X	7/1	none		
424	82	219	100	X				X			X	4/1	none		
1,900	40							X	X	X	X	4/1	none		
348	90			X		X		X	X		X	5/1	none		
				X				X	X		X	7/1	none		
975	43			X			X	X			X	5/1	none		
1,681	30			X				X	X	X	X	4/1	none		
													none		
				X	X	X	X	X		X	X		5/15		
251	70				X						X	3/15	none		
417	50	149	100	X	X	X	X	X	X	X	X	3/1	none		
10	3	3	100										none		
								X	X	X	X	5/15	none		
174	74	128	100	X	X	X	X	X	X	X	X	4/1	none		
2,503	40			X				X	X	X	X	4/15	none		
530	97	160	100	X			X	X			X	4/1	none	X	
1,650	30			X	X	X	X	X	X	X	X	3/1	4/1		
				X				X				4/1	none		
				X	X	X	X	X	X	X	X	5/15	none		
													none		
1,083	30			X	X		X	X	X		X	4/1	none		
								X	X			5/1	none		
86	87												none		
466	90	294	99	X	X		X	X	X		X	3/15	none		
1,731	29			X			X	X	X		X	6/1	none		
				X				X					none		
				X				X					none		
106	80			X	X		X	X				4/1	none		
2,215	57	831	100					X	X	X	X	3/1	none	X	
3,258	28	1,246	99	X			X	X	X		X	4/15	none		
1,553	79	970	97	X	X			X	X		X	2/15	none	X	
883	30							X	X		X	4/1	none		
3,064	32	740	91	X				X	X	X	X	4/9	none		
225	95	175	100					X	X	X	X		none		
471	44			X				X	X	X	X	4/1	none		
				X	X	X	X	X	X	X	X		none		
55	98			X			X	X			X	4/1	8/1		
68	80	54	100	X			X	X			X	3/31	7/15		

Institution	Tuition and fees	Add'l out-of-state/district tuition	Books and supplies	Costs for campus residents			Costs for students at home		
				Room and board	Trans-portation	Other costs	Board only	Trans-portation	Other costs
Georgia									
Abraham Baldwin Agricultural College	1,356	2,043/—	675	2,490	648	1,146	1,011	648	1,146
Agnes Scott College	13,935		450	5,800	850	500	1,500	850	500
Albany State College	‡ 1,818	2,844/—	675	2,904	535	800	1,855	405	800
American College for the Applied Arts	9,210		600		560	960		560	960
Andrew College	5,343		600	4,020	700	1,200	950	200	1,100
Armstrong State College	‡ 1,623	2,844/—	450	3,546	500	750	1,575	800	1,425
Art Institute of Atlanta	9,514		1,500		500	500	1,100	200	500
Athens Area Technical Institute	649	612/—	450				2,895	750	750
Atlanta Christian College	5,312		400	3,030		500			4,490
Atlanta College of Art	‡ 10,145		850		375	1,245	1,575	375	1,245
Atlanta Metropolitan College	‡ 1,194	2,043/—	500						
Augusta College	‡ 1,632	2,844/—	480				975	975	1,950
Augusta Technical Institute	1,096	2,104/—	450						
Bainbridge College	‡ 1,119	2,043/—	600				1,800	1,734	450
Bauder College	7,550		750		1,000	1,100	1,100	1,000	1,100
Berry College	‡ 8,614		500	4,839	390	1,657	750	900	1,486
Brenau University	9,855		600	6,185	575	800	1,500	77	800
Brewton-Parker College	‡ 4,521		750	2,370		1,200	1,200	600	1,200
Brunswick College	‡ 1,209	2,043/—	600				1,600	1,000	500
Chattahoochee Technical Institute	† 672	612/—	950						
Clark Atlanta University	8,500		630	4,420	840	945	1,970	378	945
Clayton State College	‡ 1,548	2,844/—	600				1,700	945	1,080
Columbus College	‡ 1,653	2,844/—	650	3,375			1,500	600	600
Columbus Technical Institute	871	816/—	500				9,126	1,200	1,034
Covenant College	10,920		470	3,870	560	200	2,003	560	200
Dalton College	‡ 1,104	2,043/—	800				2,500	1,000	200
Darton College	‡ 1,149	2,043/—	450				1,100	450	600
DeKalb College	‡ 1,193	1,744/—	900					1,500	
DeKalb Technical Institute	984	768/—	400				2,000	660	600
DeVry Institute of Technology: Atlanta	6,335		550				1,818	1,759	2,045
East Georgia College	‡ 1,065	3,468/—	600				1,800	700	350
Emmanuel College	‡ 4,560		550	3,250	490	850	2,000	690	700
Emory University	19,000		600	6,220	390	490	2,400		480
Floyd College	‡ 1,119	2,043/—	400				1,150	200	250
Fort Valley State College	‡ 1,833	2,844/—	750	2,655	1,200	1,425	1,600	1,904	945
Gainesville College	‡ 1,137	2,043/—	600					1,850	1,000
Georgia Baptist College of Nursing	† 4,737		1,200	4,500	990	1,500	2,500	2,475	1,500
Georgia College	‡ 1,743	2,844/—	600	3,060	721	1,352	600	720	1,228
Georgia Institute of Technology	‡ 2,343	4,590/—	795	4,386		1,164	2,265	1,062	1,050
Georgia Military College	4,130		475	3,915		1,025		550	1,025
Georgia Southern University	‡ 1,878	2,844/—	540	3,312	525	735	1,761	705	735
Georgia Southwestern College	‡ 1,779	2,844/—	750	2,745					
Georgia State University	‡ 2,154	4,590/—	980				2,150	324	800
Gordon College	‡ 1,194	2,043/—	487	2,130	530	1,027	1,500	1,062	1,027
Gwinnett Technical Institute	‡ 756	360/—	500						
Kennesaw State College	‡ 1,605	2,844/—	600				2,500	900	935
LaGrange College	8,502		600	3,825	900	900		600	600
Macon College	‡ 1,161	2,043/—	525				2,416	902	998
Meadows College of Business	2,825								
Medical College of Georgia	‡ 2,148	3,798/—	700		315	1,170	1,173	495	1,170

†Figures are projected for 1995-96. ‡Figures are for 1994-95.

| All aid | | Need–based aid | | Grants and scholarships | | | | | | | | Financial aid deadlines | | Inst aid form | Notes |
| | | | | Need–based | | | | Non–need–based | | | | | | | |
Total freshmen	Percent receiving aid	Freshmen judged to have need	Percent offered aid	Acad	Music/drama	Art	Athl	Acad	Music/drama	Art	Athl	Priority	Closing		
1,338	76	600	100	X	X	X	X	X	X	X	X	5/1	6/1		
		113	100	X	X			X	X			3/15	none		
1,256	88			X	X		X	X				6/1	none		
273	75	240	100	X				X				6/1	none		
													none		
473	25			X	X	X	X	X	X	X	X	5/31	none		
													none		
				X									none		
54	90			X				X				6/1	8/1		
124	68	49	100	X		X		X		X		3/15	none	X	
397	25			X	X		X						7/21		
736	59	411	62	X	X	X		X	X	X	X	4/15	none		
770	25	453	100	X				X					none		
324	21							X				7/1	none		
													none		
483	97	260	100	X				X	X	X	X	4/1	none	X	
375	59	70	100	X				X	X	X	X	5/1	none	X	
458	96							X	X	X	X	4/1	none		
298	50			X				X			X	5/1	5/30		
1,164	31	420	100	X				X				4/1	none		
841	78			X	X		X	X	X		X	4/1	4/15		
1,409	25	192	100	X				X	X	X	X	4/1	none		
757	37							X	X	X	X	6/1	none		
265	90												none		
188	89	123	100					X	X		X	3/31	none		
				X				X				8/1	none		
				X				X	X	X		8/1	none		
				X			X						7/1		
				X				X				7/15	none		
				X				X					none		
175	18			X				X					none		
323	97	270	100	X	X		X	X	X		X	3/15			
1,129	56	467	100	X				X	X			2/15	4/1		
				X				X				4/30	6/30		
552	93			X	X		X	X	X		X	4/15	5/1		
1,538	27							X	X	X		4/15	none		
				X				X				5/1	none	X	
706	62	580	95	X	X	X	X	X	X		X	4/15	none		
1,719	42	1,430	100	X				X			X	3/1	none		
2,723	50											4/1	none		
2,895	75			X				X	X		X	3/1	none		
374	83							X	X	X	X	4/1	6/1		
1,311	25	323	84	X				X	X	X	X	5/1	none		
756	55							X	X	X	X	6/1	none		
				X				X				7/1	none		
1,218	30	488	97	X	X		X	X	X	X	X	3/31	none		
191	81	112	100	X				X	X	X		5/1	none		
833	34			X			X	X	X	X	X	4/1	none		
112	90												none		
				X				X				2/15	none		

Institution	Tuition and fees	Add'l out-of-state/ district tuition	Books and supplies	Costs for campus residents			Costs for students at home		
				Room and board	Trans-portation	Other costs	Board only	Trans-portation	Other costs
Mercer University									
Atlanta	7,110		450				1,607	675	800
Macon	‡ 11,988		450	4,122	400	600	1,500	300	672
Middle Georgia College	‡ 1,314	2,043/—	550	2,655	288	600	2,700	309	600
Morehouse College	† 8,930		700	5,770		2,772	1,766		2,272
Morris Brown College	8,280		600	4,750	500	650	1,982	500	650
North Georgia College	‡ 1,755	2,844/—	540	2,655	750	1,200	1,545	1,530	660
Oglethorpe University	12,960		600	4,340	1,720	2,390	1,500	1,720	2,390
Oxford College of Emory University	13,500		450	4,631	350	750		750	750
Paine College	6,324		500	2,960	2,564	1,850	1,756	2,553	1,850
Piedmont College	6,360		600	3,850	650	900	1,750	900	900
Reinhardt College	4,785		500	4,050	70	1,000	1,200	600	400
Savannah College of Art and Design	10,800		1,200	5,350	1,000	6,200	2,780	400	800
Savannah State College	‡ 1,818	2,844/—	750	2,520	700	700	1,300	700	700
Savannah Technical Institute	1,104								
School of Visual Arts: Savannah	9,620		1,435	3,000	735	1,815	2,525	735	1,815
Shorter College	‡ 7,210		520	3,600	630	1,470	1,750	1,350	1,400
South College	5,110		600				2,317	1,109	1,305
South Georgia College	‡ 1,182	2,043/—	600	2,880	600	750	2,100	600	750
Southern College of Technology	‡ 1,689	2,844/—	528	3,705	498	1,206	1,548	843	1,206
Spelman College	† 8,875		600	5,890	800	1,300		2,625	1,300
Thomas College	4,125		600				2,738	813	1,800
Toccoa Falls College	6,666		500	3,708	1,163	1,422	2,602	1,032	1,422
Truett-McConnell College	5,100		525	2,775	500	800	1,500	650	700
University of Georgia	‡ 2,352	3,798/—	525	3,600		1,338	1,830		1,797
Valdosta State University	‡ 1,785	2,844/—	600	3,063	1,142	964	895	1,142	1,087
Waycross College	‡ 1,127	2,043/—	500				1,500	600	900
Wesleyan College	12,500		515	4,800	412	957	1,500	412	957
West Georgia College	‡ 1,806	2,844/—	495	3,033	750	1,100	1,800	1,125	1,100
Young Harris College	‡ 5,900		500	3,405	450	900	1,500	750	600
Hawaii									
Brigham Young University-Hawaii	‡ 2,375		450	4,375		1,000			1,000
Chaminade University of Honolulu	10,600		721	5,000		1,076	1,950	158	759
Hawaii Pacific University	6,700		700	6,200	800	670	2,500	250	900
Heald Business College: Honolulu	6,300		1,000				180	180	1,200
University of Hawaii									
Hawaii Community College	554	2,592/—	500	4,270	225	1,000	2,414	225	1,000
Hilo	554	2,592/—	687	4,066	207	1,074	2,414	207	914
Honolulu Community College	524	2,592/—	582		180	1,097	1,524	180	953
Kapiolani Community College	519	2,592/—	554				2,011	207	777
Kauai Community College	514	2,592/—	582				2,515	180	953
Leeward Community College	514	2,592/—	560				2,414	180	914
Manoa	1,631	3,194/—	743	4,129	207	1,097	2,414	207	1,097
Maui Community College	524	2,592/—	554		207	1,074	2,414	207	914
West Oahu	914	2,182/—	687				1,463	207	1,865
Windward Community College	524	2,592/—	554				2,414	207	914
Idaho									
Albertson College	14,317		500	3,075	400	675	2,000	400	675
Boise Bible College	‡ 3,793		450	2,926	650	900	1,500	800	500
Boise State University	‡ 1,580	4,186/—	400	3,370	550	928	1,300	600	603
College of Southern Idaho	‡ 1,000	1,400/1,000	800	3,130	1,300	1,530	2,000	1,300	1,100
Eastern Idaho Technical College	‡ 960	2,362/—	1,000					1,300	630

†Figures are projected for 1995-96. ‡Figures are for 1994-95.

Total freshmen	Percent receiving aid	Freshmen judged to have need	Percent offered aid	Acad	Music/drama	Art	Athl	Acad	Music/drama	Art	Athl	Priority	Closing	Inst aid form	Notes
				X				X				5/1	none		
721	98	352	100	X	X		X	X	X	X	X	4/1	none		
751	32			X				X	X		X	7/1	none		
704	70			X				X	X		X		4/1		
720	81	581	98	X			X	X	X	X	X	4/1	6/15		
667	87			X			X	X	X	X	X	5/1	none	X	
222	84	147	100	X				X	X			3/1	none		
337	90	141	100	X				X				4/1	none		
377	82			X	X		X	X	X		X	5/15	none		
				X				X	X	X	X	5/1	none		
388	90			X	X	X	X	X	X	X	X	5/1	none		
620	60	298	86	X		X		X		X		4/1	none		
726	63			X	X		X	X	X		X	5/1	8/1		
													none		
30	85	29	100	X		X		X		X		3/1	none		
277	99	123	100	X	X	X	X	X	X	X	X	4/1	none		
89	85							X				9/1	none		
440	68	334	100			X		X			X	7/10	none	X	
318	38	231	100	X		X		X			X	3/15	5/31		
				X	X			X	X			4/1	4/15	X	
313	85			X	X		X	X				9/1	none		
290	75							X	X			4/1	none		
799	99							X	X		X		none		
3,555	40			X	X		X	X	X			3/1	none		
1,681	45	1,092	95	X	X	X	X	X	X	X	X	5/1	none	X	
				X				X				6/1	none		
126	96	113	100	X				X	X	X		3/1	none		
1,497	60	945	100	X				X	X	X	X	3/15	none	X	
272	70	175	100	X				X	X	X	X	6/1	none		
398	80			X				X	X	X	X		7/31		
218	50			X			X	X			X	3/1	none		
702	25	269	100					X	X		X	3/1	none		
													none		
400	33			X				X				3/1	none		
445	49			X	X	X	X	X	X	X	X	3/1	none		
2,204	7							X				5/1	none		
													none		
				X	X			X	X			5/1	none		
2,694	10							X				5/1	none		
1,706	26			X				X	X		X	3/1	none		
													none		
													none		
118	91	106	100	X	X	X	X	X	X	X	X	2/15	none	X	
51	85	31	100					X					none	X	
				X	X	X		X	X	X	X	4/1	none		
1,897	65	1,500	90	X	X	X	X	X	X	X	X	3/1	none		
124	81			X				X				6/1	none		

Institution		Tuition and fees	Add'l out-of-state/ district tuition	Books and supplies	Costs for campus residents			Costs for students at home		
					Room and board	Trans-portation	Other costs	Board only	Trans-portation	Other costs
Idaho State University	‡	1,500	4,500/—	500	3,140	360	1,575	1,800	360	1,575
Lewis Clark State College	‡	1,412	3,708/—	560	3,190	852	1,116	1,864	756	796
North Idaho College	‡	980	2,080/1,000	500	3,310	500	830	1,700	500	830
Northwest Nazarene College		11,145		1,000	3,105	700	800	1,749	600	800
Ricks College		1,790		550	3,365	900	1,000	1,880	700	1,000
University of Idaho	‡	1,620	5,380/—	832	3,600	894	1,786	1,800	894	1,786
Illinois										
American Academy of Art		11,280		800						
American Conservatory of Music		11,200		500					800	1,200
Augustana College		14,064		450	4,257	400	650	600	1,750	1,000
Aurora University		10,800		600	4,050	1,187	1,473	2,450	1,355	905
Barat College		11,190		800	4,680	1,100	1,700		1,600	1,700
Belleville Area College		1,200	3,240/1,350	500				1,500	1,200	1,320
Black Hawk College										
East Campus		1,560	4,440/1,830	500				1,334	677	1,418
Moline		1,590	4,200/1,680	500				1,334	677	1,418
Blackburn College		6,500		500	2,700	250	800	1,500	50	800
Blessing-Reiman College of Nursing		8,600		400	3,075	250	500	1,725	500	500
Bradley University	†	11,490		480	4,610	200	1,442	500	600	2,102
Carl Sandburg College		1,560	3,750/1,650	450				1,600	1,400	500
Chicago College of Commerce		5,700		450				4,536	540	1,305
Chicago State University		2,348	3,936/—	825				2,000	1,200	2,000
City Colleges of Chicago										
Harold Washington College	‡	1,225	3,224/2,381	600				1,500	540	1,761
Harry S. Truman College		1,225	3,224/2,381	600				1,500	702	1,761
Kennedy-King College		1,300	3,224/2,381	600				1,500	580	1,800
Malcolm X College		1,225	3,224/2,381	600				1,500	540	1,761
Olive-Harvey College	‡	1,225	3,224/2,381	600				1,500	540	1,761
Richard J. Daley College		1,225	3,224/2,381	600				1,500	540	1,761
Wright College		1,225	3,224/2,381	600				1,500	702	1,761
College of DuPage		1,170	4,095/2,970	929				1,500	1,550	1,150
College of Lake County		1,440	5,837/4,410	500						
College of St. Francis		10,770		410	4,340	340	900	1,500	710	900
Columbia College	‡	7,390		700		700	2,784	1,560	700	1,652
Concordia University		9,971		450	4,443	400	600	2,901	400	600
Danville Area Community College	‡	1,080	3,300/1,865	500				1,500	1,248	1,350
De Paul University		11,886		600	5,233	660	1,300	1,500	400	1,100
DeVry Institute of Technology										
Addison		6,335		550				2,298	1,788	2,045
Chicago		6,335		550				1,818	1,788	2,045
Eastern Illinois University		2,778	3,938/—	120	3,244	430	1,300	1,800	810	1,160
East-West University		6,270		600				1,200	500	1,800
Elgin Community College	‡	1,170	3,750/2,891	550				1,500	2,781	1,236
Elmhurst College		10,264		550	4,390		2,200	1,600	1,150	1,600
Eureka College		12,505		330	3,875	160	510	1,840	675	295
Finch University of Health Sciences/The Chicago Medical School	†	15,970		2,470				1,760	1,060	2,666
Gem City College	‡	3,150		600					400	1,350
Governors State University		2,098	3,936/—	500				1,600	800	800
Greenville College		10,960		500	4,750	300	600		300	600
Harrington Institute of Interior Design	‡	9,015		925					1,000	2,000
Highland Community College		1,200	3,270/2,340	565				1,800	1,800	1,000

†Figures are projected for 1995-96. ‡Figures are for 1994-95.

All aid		Need-based aid		Grants and scholarships								Financial aid deadlines		Inst aid form	Notes
				Need-based				Non-need-based							
Total freshmen	Percent receiving aid	Freshmen judged to have need	Percent offered aid	Acad	Music/drama	Art	Athl	Acad	Music/drama	Art	Athl	Priority	Closing		
1,713	80			X	X	X	X	X	X	X	X	3/15	none		
495	46	256	91	X			X	X	X		X	3/1	none		
1,588	39			X	X	X		X	X	X	X	4/15	none		
290	85			X	X	X		X	X	X	X	3/1	none		
2,349	78			X				X	X	X	X	5/1	none		
1,233	65			X	X	X	X	X	X	X	X	2/15	none		
155	68	144	100							X		7/1	none		
15	69								X			6/1	none		
551	95	433	100					X	X	X		4/15	none	X	
208	87	100	100	X				X				5/1	9/1		
117	70			X	X	X	X	X	X	X	X	3/15	none		
8,473	31			X				X	X	X	X	5/31	none		
													none		
				X	X	X	X	X	X	X	X	5/15	none		
232	98			X				X				4/1	none		
				X				X							
1,173	82	960	100	X				X	X	X	X	3/1	none		
1,336	70			X	X	X	X	X	X	X	X	5/1	none		
44	65	37	100										none		
530	80	649	100	X				X	X	X	X	3/15	none	X	
2,500	40			X								5/1	none		
													none		
				X				X			X	5/1	none		
													none		
555	70							X			X	8/10	none		
													none		
													none		
5,170	10			X	X	X		X	X	X		6/15	none		
									X	X	X		none		
159	84	106	100	X			X	X			X	5/1	none	X	
				X				X				5/1	none	X	
177	95	151	100	X	X			X	X			6/1	none		
900	80							X			X	6/1	none		
1,209	68			X	X	X	X	X	X	X	X	5/1			
								X					none		
								X					none		
				X				X	X	X	X	4/15	none		
													none		
5,640	28	556	100					X	X	X	X	3/1	none		
222	60	133	100	X	X			X	X			4/15	none	X	
100	90	80	100	X	X	X		X	X	X		5/1	none		
												8/20	1/31		
		90	100										none		
				X				X	X	X		5/1	10/1		
225	96	159	100	X				X				5/1	none		
97	39											6/1	none		
919	40			X	X	X	X	X	X	X	X	6/1	none		

Institution	Tuition and fees	Add'l out-of-state/district tuition	Books and supplies	Costs for campus residents			Costs for students at home		
				Room and board	Trans-portation	Other costs	Board only	Trans-portation	Other costs
Illinois Benedictine College	11,180		650	4,348		1,500	2,580		1,500
Illinois Central College	1,350	3,330/2,170	500				2,225	1,344	2,335
Illinois College	8,600		500	4,000	300	1,000		700	600
Illinois Eastern Community Colleges									
Frontier Community College	895	3,812/2,631	600				1,500	1,200	800
Lincoln Trail College	895	3,812/2,631	600				1,500	1,200	800
Olney Central College	895	3,812/2,631	600				1,500	1,200	800
Wabash Valley College	895	3,812/2,631	600				1,500	1,200	800
Illinois Institute of Technology	15,280		500	4,620		1,700	1,600		2,200
Illinois State University	3,544	5,382/—	500	3,627	430	1,867	1,800	900	1,937
Illinois Valley Community College	‡ 1,094	2,760/—	450				1,500	1,152	1,044
Illinois Wesleyan University	15,510		400	4,290	100	550	1,500	310	600
International Academy of Merchandising and Design	8,600		850				600	750	800
ITT Technical Institute: Hoffman Estates	6,165		1,100						
John A. Logan College	‡ 840	3,180/1,758	800				1,500	1,728	1,000
John Wood Community College	‡ 1,470	3,885/1,716	450				1,600	830	600
Joliet Junior College	1,270	3,090/2,120	450				1,727	1,097	1,300
Judson College	10,200		500	4,600	300	1,200	2,500	500	1,200
Kankakee Community College	1,216	4,320/720	480				1,008	768	855
Kaskaskia College	1,007	3,810/1,500	500				900	672	648
Kendall College	8,931		850	4,998	260	630	2,850	625	630
Kishwaukee College	1,153	3,419/2,466	400				1,500	1,152	943
Knox College	16,692		400	4,257	200	600	2,364	200	600
Lake Forest College	18,116		500	4,204	300	120		500	1,240
Lake Land College	1,275	2,836/1,080	205				1,800	1,530	858
Lakeview College of Nursing	6,475		475						
Lewis and Clark Community College	1,200	4,890/2,280	400				4,000	900	1,100
Lewis University	10,320		500	5,007	570	1,200	1,800	1,350	1,200
Lexington Institute of Hospitality Careers	‡ 5,250		600	3,300	1,200	400		800	400
Lincoln Christian College and Seminary	4,520		500	3,100	500	1,700	1,000	500	1,700
Lincoln College	8,860		450	3,800	200	1,000	2,300	500	1,000
Lincoln Land Community College	† 1,095	2,970/1,440	450					650	500
Loyola University of Chicago	13,400		700	5,910	420	1,500	1,750	900	1,500
MacCormac Junior College	7,155		600				1,650	444	1,200
MacMurray College	10,190		550	3,900	500	600		500	600
McHenry County College	1,117	3,960/3,090	440				1,600	1,160	1,400
McKendree College	‡ 7,335		500	3,570	250	800	250	600	800
Mennonite College of Nursing	7,938		600	2,330	250	650	1,500	250	650
Midstate College	5,006		940		400	690	2,500	1,500	
Millikin University	12,687		600	4,596	200	765	2,000	1,578	765
Monmouth College	13,660		500	4,200	100	150	2,000	200	
Montay College	5,630		500				1,620	810	990
Moody Bible Institute	1,209		600	4,100	250	500		500	500
Moraine Valley Community College	‡ 1,232	3,300/2,700	400				1,500	1,044	1,307
Morrison Institute of Technology	6,810		800	2,000	400	1,200	1,000	800	1,200
Morton College	1,395	4,325/3,372	400				2,000	500	900
NAES College	4,220		250						
National College of Chiropractic	8,352		830		950	1,945		1,160	2,130
National-Louis University	10,440		700	4,821	400	1,171	2,230	1,316	1,116

†Figures are projected for 1995-96. ‡Figures are for 1994-95.

| All aid | | Need–based aid | | Grants and scholarships | | | | | | | | Financial aid deadlines | | Inst aid form | Notes |
| Total fresh-men | Percent receiving aid | Freshmen judged to have need | Percent offered aid | Need–based | | | | Non–need–based | | | | | | | |
				Acad	Music/ drama	Art	Athl	Acad	Music/ drama	Art	Athl	Priority	Closing		
267	94	201	100					X	X	X		4/15	none		
													none		
306	94	259	100	X				X	X			5/1	none		
				X	X	X		X					none		
				X	X	X	X	X					none		
				X	X	X	X	X					none		
				X	X	X	X	X					none		
621	100	419	100	X			X	X				5/1	none	X	
								X	X	X	X	3/1	none		
								X	X	X		5/1	none		
510	85	345	100	X	X	X		X	X	X		3/1	none	X	
													none		
													none		
1,372	65			X				X	X	X	X	5/1	none		
500	50			X	X	X	X	X	X	X	X		none		
2,535	25	1,300	77					X	X	X		7/1	none		
144	93			X				X	X	X	X	5/1	none		
													none		
		313	96					X	X		X	7/1	none		
201	60			X				X				6/1	none		
													none		
275	92	237	100					X	X	X		3/1	none	X	
229	72	162	96									3/1	none	X	
1,605	46			X			X	X	X	X	X	5/1	none		
														X	
1,836	40			X	X	X	X	X	X		X	6/1	none		
497	80	231	100					X	X	X	X	5/1	none		
21	85	16	100	X				X				6/1	none		
120	90			X				X				8/10	none		
													none		
6,941	47							X	X	X	X	4/15	4/21		
1,287	65			X				X	X	X	X	3/1	none		
350	80							X					none		
168	87	152	100	X	X	X		X	X	X		5/1	8/1		
3,415	15	300	83					X	X	X	X	6/1	none	X	
136	90			X	X	X	X	X	X	X	X	6/1	none	X	
													none		
443	91	387	100	X	X	X		X	X	X		4/1	8/24	X	
309	98	304	100	X	X	X		X	X	X		4/30	none		
													none		
305	2			X	X								none		
								X				6/1	none		
92	60							X					none		
		85	100	X				X	X	X	X	6/1	none	X	
													none		
													none		
313	85			X	X			X				6/15	none		

Institution	Tuition and fees	Add'l out-of-state/district tuition	Books and supplies	Costs for campus residents			Costs for students at home		
				Room and board	Trans-portation	Other costs	Board only	Trans-portation	Other costs
North Central College	12,633		450	4,692	320	1,180	1,500	1,050	1,180
North Park College	13,280		813	4,560	550	900	1,674	850	900
Northeastern Illinois University	2,523	3,936/—	552				2,007	810	2,178
Northern Illinois University	3,746	5,382/—	450	3,416	350	1,376	2,116	350	1,376
Northwestern University	17,184		813	5,781		1,143	2,325	984	1,143
Oakton Community College	† 1,048	3,000/2,550	400				1,790	1,100	1,000
Olivet Nazarene University	9,440		600	4,360	400	800		400	800
Parkland College	† 1,290	3,750/2,242	500				1,800	920	860
Prairie State College	1,500	2,910/1,830	700				2,300	1,000	1,500
Principia College	13,578		450	5,640		750			
Quincy University	10,910		450	4,260	460	620	1,500	480	620
Ray College of Design	8,880		1,000				2,241	540	1,260
Rend Lake College	960	2,863/1,842	380				878	1,189	1,053
Richland Community College	1,185	3,155/1,169	400					1,000	
Robert Morris College: Chicago	9,300		600				1,313	540	1,145
Rock Valley College	1,268	5,490/2,972	500					1,100	2,400
Rockford Business College	5,430		720		916	2,855	2,500	916	2,855
Rockford College	13,500		800	4,400	500	1,440	1,500	792	1,440
Roosevelt University	9,770		600	5,866	600	1,456	1,580	600	1,456
Rosary College	11,600		550	4,600	50	900	1,500	500	900
Rush University	10,460		500		235	1,200		510	1,200
St. Augustine College	4,640		835				1,570	650	750
St. Francis Medical Center College of Nursing	6,643		800	4,200	350	1,557	1,500	350	1,937
St. Joseph College of Nursing	7,844		750				1,800	1,200	1,500
St. Xavier University	11,600		600	4,800	340	794	2,030	830	794
Sangamon State University	2,833	4,914/—	625		740	1,475	1,500	1,220	854
Sauk Valley Community College	1,200	2,498/299	500					1,000	900
School of the Art Institute of Chicago	† 15,480		1,956		580	1,280	2,800	580	1,280
Shawnee Community College	844	4,380/1,530	300				1,500	1,632	540
Shimer College	12,600		700			1,300			
South Suburban College of Cook County	1,357	4,349/2,664	500				1,500	300	1,000
Southeastern Illinois College	810	3,360/3,150	450				2,500	1,200	1,400
Southern Illinois University									
Carbondale	† 3,338	4,800/—	600	3,369	700	1,908	1,500	700	1,208
Edwardsville	‡ 2,265	3,557/—	221	3,498	1,203	1,046	1,500	1,203	1,046
Spoon River College	1,320	4,159/218	500						
Springfield College in Illinois	5,540		400		276	3,225	390	1,700	878
State Community College	1,044	3,600/—	200				1,550	425	1,300
Telshe Yeshiva-Chicago	7,300			2,400					
Trinity Christian College	10,200		515	3,900	715	1,110	1,956	1,185	1,110
Trinity College	11,140		600	4,420	400	900	2,030	400	900
Triton College	† 1,404	4,590/2,670	450				1,100	1,020	
University of Chicago	20,193		675	7,258		579	2,500		579
University of Illinois									
Chicago	‡ 3,628	4,710/—	630	5,088	702	3,100	1,800	702	2,526
Urbana-Champaign	3,956	5,174/—	540	4,736	400	1,646			
VanderCook College of Music	9,350		300	4,600	450	400	3,300	500	250
Waubonsee Community College	1,138	4,600/3,756	500				1,712	1,584	1,000
West Suburban College of Nursing	8,720		400	4,191	400	600	2,736	400	600
Western Illinois University	2,702	3,936/—	650	3,413	649	1,391	925	1,125	1,325
Wheaton College	12,300		660	4,370		1,300	1,760		1,155
William Rainey Harper College	1,248	4,719/3,880	502				1,924	920	1,492

†Figures are projected for 1995-96. ‡Figures are for 1994-95.

All aid		Need-based aid		Grants and scholarships								Financial aid deadlines		Inst aid form	Notes
				Need-based				Non-need-based							
Total freshmen	Percent receiving aid	Freshmen judged to have need	Percent offered aid	Acad	Music/drama	Art	Athl	Acad	Music/drama	Art	Athl	Priority	Closing		
336	92	253	100	X				X	X	X		4/1	none	X	
203	85	154	100	X	X	X		X	X	X		4/1	8/1		
738	22							X	X	X	X	4/1	none		
2,705	76			X				X	X	X	X	3/1	5/1	X	
1,867	49	859	100						X		X		2/15		
				X				X	X	X	X	6/1	none		
374	77			X	X	X	X	X	X	X	X	3/1	none		
2,523	65							X	X	X	X	3/1	none		
													none		
128	82	97	100	X	X			X				2/15	none	X	
302	97	243	100	X				X	X	X	X	2/15	none		
330	90			X				X		X		1/1	none		
2,250	66							X			X		none		
				X				X					none		
1,827	90							X				6/1	none		
								X	X			6/1	none		
													none		
156	98			X				X				4/15	none		
239	60			X	X	X		X	X	X		5/1	none		
131	80	101	100	X				X			X	5/1	none		
				X								5/15	none		
													none		
648	85	212	100	X	X		X	X	X		X	3/1	none		
				X				X			X	4/1	none		
													none		
215	75	163	100	X		X				X		4/1	none		
													none		
36	80			X	X	X		X	X	X		6/1	7/31		
													none		
1,679	70			X	X	X	X	X	X	X	X	5/1	none	X	
2,315	90							X	X	X	X	4/1	none		
1,048	70	660	90	X	X	X	X	X	X	X	X	3/1	none		
1,263	80			X	X	X	X	X	X	X			none		
													none		
												7/1	none		
216	96	126	94					X	X	X	X	2/15	8/15		
218	87							X	X		X	4/1	none		
				X				X				4/15	none		
924	68	571	100					X	X	X			2/1		
2,572	66	2,250	100	X			X	X	X		X	3/1	none		
5,744	75	4,478	97	X				X	X	X	X	3/15	none		
13	90								X			3/1	none		
													none		
1,467	57	989	93					X	X	X	X	3/1	none		
553	66	328	99					X	X			3/15	none	X	
3,580	74			X				X	X	X		5/1	none	X	

Institution	Tuition and fees	Add'l out-of-state/district tuition	Books and supplies	Costs for campus residents			Costs for students at home		
				Room and board	Trans-portation	Other costs	Board only	Trans-portation	Other costs
Indiana									
Ancilla College	3,060		400				1,000	900	735
Anderson University	11,240		550	3,750	400	700	2,500	400	700
Ball State University	3,048	4,776/—	500	3,768	352	1,100	1,500	1,078	1,100
Bethel College	† 9,750		600	3,100	600	700	1,900	1,000	700
Butler University	13,990		500	4,730	340	1,260	2,480	340	1,260
Calumet College of St. Joseph	5,300		600				1,545	775	1,130
DePauw University	15,475		550	5,245	250	700	1,500	600	350
Earlham College	17,160		550	4,305	600	650	2,220	400	600
Franklin College	10,810		590	4,210	455	895		750	895
Goshen College	9,900		600	3,760	360	960	1,503	360	960
Grace College	9,230		300	4,070	600	800	1,500	750	800
Hanover College	9,135		600	3,710	500	800	2,100	500	800
Holy Cross College	5,890		500				1,900	2,060	1,460
Huntington College	10,800		550	4,120	550	850	2,100	850	750
Indiana Business College	‡ 5,085		900				2,500	504	1,143
Indiana Institute of Technology	9,530		700	3,970		600		1,050	600
Indiana State University	‡ 2,802	4,090/—	600	3,706	600	1,100	1,700	968	600
Indiana University									
Bloomington	‡ 3,373	6,783/—	600	3,863	410	1,528	1,500	962	1,436
East	‡ 2,485	3,771/—	606				1,953	1,115	1,086
Kokomo	‡ 2,459	3,771/—	658				1,584	990	1,108
Northwest	‡ 2,474	3,771/—	500				2,050	1,705	1,436
South Bend	† 2,652	4,349/—	574				1,810	1,356	1,356
Southeast	‡ 2,415	3,771/—	576				1,890	910	1,225
Indiana University—Purdue University									
Fort Wayne	‡ 2,495	3,558/—	500				1,800	810	900
Indianapolis	‡ 2,978	5,724/—	528	3,260	378	1,359	1,827	1,233	1,359
Indiana Vocational Technical College									
Central Indiana	‡ 1,724	1,413/—	561				1,997	640	1,392
Columbus	‡ 1,724	1,413/—	561				1,997	640	1,392
Eastcentral	‡ 1,724	1,413/—	561				1,997	640	1,372
Kokomo	‡ 1,723	1,413/—	561				1,997	640	1,392
Lafayette	‡ 1,724	1,413/—	561				1,997	640	1,392
Northcentral	‡ 1,724	1,413/—	561					640	1,392
Northeast	‡ 1,724	1,413/—	561				1,997	640	1,392
Northwest	‡ 1,724	1,413/—	561				1,997	640	1,392
Southcentral	‡ 1,724	1,413/—	561				1,997	640	1,392
Southeast	‡ 1,724	1,413/—	561				1,997	640	1,392
Southwest	‡ 1,724	1,413/—	561			1,600	1,997	640	1,392
Wabash Valley	‡ 1,724	1,413/—	561				1,997	640	1,392
Whitewater	‡ 1,724	1,413/—					1,997	640	1,372
Indiana Wesleyan University	9,726		700	3,932	680	2,000		680	
International Business College	‡ 8,490		725						
Lutheran College of Health Professions	5,882		486		1,331	1,800	1,920	1,700	1,800
Manchester College	11,470		525	4,080	550	900	2,080	550	900
Marian College	† 10,834		550	4,060	700	1,000	1,500	640	1,000
Martin University	6,080		600			2,400	2,700	300	2,400
Oakland City College	7,666		800	2,996	1,200	1,600	2,500	1,200	1,800
Purdue University									
Calumet	‡ 2,448	3,607/—	505				1,916	1,086	1,204
North Central Campus	‡ 2,430	3,607/—	580				2,060	1,300	1,200

†Figures are projected for 1995-96. ‡Figures are for 1994-95.

| All aid | | Need–based aid | | Grants and scholarships | | | | | | | | Financial aid deadlines | | Inst aid form | Notes |
| Total fresh–men | Percent receiving aid | Freshmen judged to have need | Percent offered aid | Need–based | | | | Non–need–based | | | | | | | |
				Acad	Music/ drama	Art	Athl	Acad	Music/ drama	Art	Athl	Priority	Closing		
561	60	160	100	X		X	X	X			X	5/1	none		
517	88	461	99	X	X	X		X	X	X		3/1	none		
3,597	60	2,165	98	X		X		X	X		X	3/1	none	X	
204	90							X	X		X	3/1	none		
710	80	484	82				X	X	X		X	3/1	none		
110	52			X				X				3/1	9/1		
659	85	391	100	X				X	X	X		2/15	none		
272	81	177	100	X	X	X		X				3/1	none		
275	94	225	100	X				X	X	X		3/1	none	X	
227	87	150	100	X	X	X	X	X	X		X	3/1	none	X	
161	95	145	100					X	X	X	X	4/1	none		
367	80	219	100	X				X				3/1	none		
282	47											3/1	none		
132	90	101	100	X				X	X	X	X	3/1	none	X	
165	92			X			X	X			X	3/1	none		
2,839	76							X	X	X	X		3/1	X	
6,052	70	2,343	98	X	X	X	X	X	X	X	X	3/1	none		
609	75	282	98	X				X				3/1	none	X	
713	45			X				X				4/30	none		
888	40			X				X				3/1	none	X	
911	40							X	X	X	X	3/1	none		
1,140	60	263	95	X	X	X	X	X	X	X	X	3/1	none		
1,590	55			X				X	X	X	X	3/1	none		
2,049	49	922	91					X		X	X	3/1	none		
								X				3/1	none		
								X				3/1	none		
								X				3/1	none		
								X				3/1	none		
								X				3/1	none		
								X				3/1	none		
								X				3/1	none		
								X				3/1	none		
								X				3/1	none		
								X				3/1	none		
				X				X				8/31	none		
								X				3/1	none		
								X				3/1	none		
462	90			X				X	X	X	X	4/1	none		
74	51	44	100	X				X				3/1	5/1		
271	94							X	X	X		3/1	none		
285	97	230	100	X	X	X	X	X	X	X	X	8/15	none		
215	80							X					3/1		
225	97	218	100	X	X	X	X	X	X	X	X		3/1		
1,500	41			X				X			X		3/1		
872	25	675	100					X				3/1	none		

Institution	Tuition and fees	Add'l out-of-state/ district tuition	Books and supplies	Costs for campus residents			Costs for students at home		
				Room and board	Trans- portation	Other costs	Board only	Trans- portation	Other costs
West Lafayette	‡ 2,884	6,672/—	600	4,080	270	1,110	1,950	1,280	1,110
Rose-Hulman Institute of Technology	14,300		1,200	4,400	300	600	1,500	800	600
St. Francis College	9,550		450	3,954	250	1,000	2,200	1,000	500
St. Joseph's College	‡ 11,530		600	4,250	350	600		1,840	3,360
St. Mary-of-the-Woods College	‡ 11,170		775	4,260	750	900	2,620	1,000	700
St. Mary's College	† 14,477		500	4,785	275	1,250	1,800	425	1,250
St. Meinrad College	6,725		500	4,226	1,100	900			
Taylor University	11,914		450	4,150		1,250	1,800		1,250
Tri-State University	10,407		468	4,350	441	882	1,701	831	1,032
University of Evansville	12,630		700	4,520	400	690	1,650	1,570	690
University of Indianapolis	11,730		525	4,200	415	990	1,615	835	940
University of Notre Dame	18,030		600	4,500	500	850	2,500	500	850
University of Southern Indiana	‡ 2,188	3,450/—	500		500	925	1,660	900	925
Valparaiso University	12,860		500	3,450	200	600	750	500	600
Vincennes University	‡ 2,310	3,237/917	500	3,882	700	550	1,360	700	550
Wabash College	13,950		500	4,405		635	2,797		635
Iowa									
American Institute of Business	5,725		780	2,955	480	990	930	855	1,620
American Institute of Commerce	6,075		900					1,008	1,206
Briar Cliff College	11,100		600	3,942	500	1,000	2,000	500	1,000
Buena Vista College	‡ 13,306		450	3,797	450	950	1,800	450	950
Central College	11,836		650	3,660	550	76	2,022	550	76
Clarke College	11,520		400	3,860	300	600	2,500	300	300
Clinton Community College	‡ 1,575	720/—	900				1,500	900	900
Coe College	14,875		500	4,455	500	1,200	890	500	1,200
Cornell College	16,440		550	4,453	500	950		500	950
Des Moines Area Community College	1,560	1,380/—	500				1,360	1,200	640
Divine Word College	6,500		400	1,200	800	800			
Dordt College	10,360		600	2,770	1,100	1,700	2,250	1,500	1,700
Drake University	14,100		560	4,950	175	1,500	1,500	500	1,500
Ellsworth Community College	1,800	1,650/—	400	2,860		1,800		1,000	1,800
Emmaus Bible College	2,200		400	4,150	800	800	2,000	500	800
Faith Baptist Bible College and Theological Seminary	5,800		500	3,160	1,000	1,330	2,300	1,000	1,330
Graceland College	9,760		600	3,380	370	1,000	1,870	370	880
Grand View College	10,470		570	3,500	400	2,000	1,333	800	2,000
Grinnell College	16,628		400	4,782	500	400			400
Hamilton Technical College	5,250								
Hawkeye Community College	‡ 2,085	1,830/—	1,000				1,237	1,710	2,916
Indian Hills Community College	1,455	480/—	675	2,115	1,361	750	2,016	1,361	750
Iowa Central Community College	1,898	825/—	600	2,860	630	1,240	750	630	945
Iowa Lakes Community College	‡ 1,662	1,020/—	405	2,330	820	455	1,645	820	455
Iowa State University	‡ 2,455	5,260/—	640	3,224	388	1,980	1,694		1,870
Iowa Wesleyan College	10,920		500	3,840	600	1,200	2,600	900	1,200
Iowa Western Community College	1,950	885/—	600	2,600	470	1,100	640	2,800	1,000
Kirkwood Community College	† 1,590	1,590/—	450					1,000	900
Loras College	11,826		600	4,370	500	450	3,000	300	450
Luther College	14,100		600	3,600	400	400	1,900		400
Maharishi International University	13,976		500	3,728	600	1,100	2,288		1,100
Marshalltown Community College	‡ 1,800	1,650/—	425					630	630
Morningside College	11,226		500	3,870	500	1,000	1,812	500	1,000
Mount Mercy College	11,020		560	3,090	700	800	1,800	700	

†Figures are projected for 1995-96. ‡Figures are for 1994-95.

| All aid | | Need-based aid | | Grants and scholarships | | | | | | | | Financial aid deadlines | | Inst aid form | Notes |
Total freshmen	Percent receiving aid	Freshmen judged to have need	Percent offered aid	Need-based Acad	Music/drama	Art	Athl	Non-need-based Acad	Music/drama	Art	Athl	Priority	Closing		
5,486	96	3,820	85	X				X			X	3/1	none	X	
351	90							X				12/1	4/1		
115	76	87	100	X				X		X		3/1	none		
223	93	217	100	X				X	X		X	5/1	8/1	X	
85	90							X	X	X	X	3/1	none	X	
393	71	249	100	X	X	X		X				3/1	none		
27	100							X				3/1	none		
431	79	251	100	X				X	X	X	X		3/1	X	
253	85	220	100					X			X	3/1	none		
752	97	542	100					X	X	X	X	3/1	none	X	
406	76	307	99	X				X	X	X	X	3/1	none	X	
1,878	69	954	100	X							X		2/15		
1,292	53	646	86	X				X	X	X	X	3/1	none		
549	75	400	100					X	X		X	3/1	none		
3,700	60			X	X	X	X	X	X	X	X	3/1	none		
240	83	155	100	X	X	X		X	X	X		2/15	none	X	
276	77	271	100					X				4/1	none		
171	80												none		
173	99			X	X	X	X	X	X	X	X	3/1	none		
320	99	297	100	X	X	X		X	X	X		4/20	none		
337	98	278	100	X	X	X		X	X	X		3/1	none		
175	96	124	100	X				X	X	X		3/15	none		
													none	X	
298	88	246	100	X	X	X		X	X	X		3/1	none		
355	95	340	100	X	X	X		X	X	X			3/1	X	
2,929	60			X				X			X	3/1	none		
													none		
353	98	261	100					X	X	X	X	4/1	none	X	
750	80	529	100	X				X	X	X	X	3/1	none		
													none		
89	88	67	100	X	X			X				4/1	none		
272	93	221	99	X				X	X	X	X	3/1	none		
252	99			X	X	X	X	X	X	X	X	3/1	none	X	
337	86	287	100	X				X					2/1	X	
61	90												none		
1,146	74			X				X				4/20	6/30		
1,224	85			X				X	X	X	X	4/1	none		
1,489	75			X	X	X	X	X	X		X		none		
850	80			X	X	X	X	X	X	X	X		none		
3,356	75			X	X	X	X	X	X	X	X	2/15	none		
100	94			X	X	X	X	X	X	X	X	4/20	none		
1,540	76	703	91	X				X			X	5/1	none		
3,334	65			X	X		X	X				3/15	none		
459	80			X				X	X	X	X		4/15		
621	85	433	100	X	X	X		X	X	X		3/1	6/1		
68	79	58	74	X				X				4/15	7/15		
798	55			X		X	X	X			X	3/15	none	X	
230	96							X	X	X	X	3/1	none		
125	85							X	X	X		3/1	6/1		

Institution	Tuition and fees	Add'l out-of-state/district tuition	Books and supplies	Costs for campus residents			Costs for students at home		
				Room and board	Trans-portation	Other costs	Board only	Trans-portation	Other costs
Mount St. Clare College	10,300		600	3,750	350	700	2,000	400	500
Muscatine Community College	‡ 1,575	720/—	900				1,500	900	900
North Iowa Area Community College	1,920	857/—	600	2,832	308	1,153	2,050	945	1,153
Northeast Iowa Community College	‡ 2,048	1,800/—	1,000				1,500	1,155	945
Northwest Iowa Community College	1,883	810/—	550		500	690	1,000	1,900	690
Northwestern College	† 10,200		500	3,150	500	1,200	1,800	500	1,200
St. Ambrose University	11,180		500	4,200	500	1,000	3,200	1,000	500
Scott Community College	‡ 1,575	720/—	900				1,500	900	900
Simpson College	‡ 11,355		550	3,980	300	1,100			2,500
Southeastern Community College									
North Campus	‡ 1,463	668/—	300	2,392				500	
South Campus	1,463	668/—	600				1,350		
Southwestern Community College	‡ 1,872	720/—	600	2,400	648	1,500	1,240	2,400	1,500
Teikyo Marycrest University	10,690		525	3,790	630	700	1,800	630	700
Teikyo Westmar University	‡ 10,260		560	3,640	800	880	1,740	800	880
University of Dubuque	† 11,610		600	4,340	250	1,500	2,110	900	1,500
University of Iowa	‡ 2,455	5,858/—	668	3,468	400	2,112	668	590	2,112
University of Northern Iowa	‡ 2,455	3,806/—	595	2,915	545	1,835	1,400	545	1,835
University of Osteopathic Medicine and Health Sciences	9,020		450				832	445	843
Upper Iowa University	8,840		700	3,360	180	800	1,800	672	1,000
Vennard College	6,458		500	3,220	690	1,280	2,500	800	1,280
Waldorf College	9,600		505	3,525	535	960	1,275	515	960
Wartburg College	12,370		300	3,730	430	520	1,500	250	700
Western Iowa Tech Community College	1,600	1,470/—	425		150	800		825	660
William Penn College	10,290		500	3,240	500	750	1,130	1,000	800

Kansas

Institution	Tuition and fees	Add'l out-of-state/district tuition	Books and supplies	Room and board	Trans-portation	Other costs	Board only	Trans-portation	Other costs
Allen County Community College	‡ 990	1,245/—	300	2,600	500	1,620	1,200	500	1,670
Baker University	9,600		650	4,300	920	1,440	2,200	1,370	1,440
Barclay College	4,275		430	2,700	750	1,800	1,900	375	1,800
Barton County Community College	‡ 1,020	1,305/—	500	2,200	800	1,000	1,500	800	1,000
Benedictine College	10,020		550	4,200	570	1,250	2,000	570	1,250
Bethany College	9,375		550	3,475	600	1,092	550	2,500	1,474
Bethel College	9,270		475	3,800	550	925	1,600	760	925
Brown Mackie College	7,175		750				1,500	952	1,008
Butler County Community College	‡ 1,050	1,275/—	600	2,800	600	1,200	1,700	600	900
Central College	7,650		400	3,200	500	500	1,600	400	500
Cloud County Community College	‡ 1,110	1,215/—	475	2,650	475	875	1,600	475	875
Coffeyville Community College	‡ 900	1,440/—	350	2,500	300	1,200		200	900
Colby Community College	‡ 1,088	1,536/—	500	2,700	400	500	1,000	500	500
Cowley County Community College	‡ 990	1,305/—	500	2,440	450	1,000	1,800	1,000	1,000
Dodge City Community College	‡ 1,140	1,290/—	400	2,800	400	900	1,080	400	900
Donnelly College	2,700		500						
Emporia State University	‡ 1,730	3,672/—	464	3,120	515	1,458		515	
Fort Hays State University	‡ 1,787	3,672/—	500	3,090	1,200	1,250	1,500	400	1,000
Fort Scott Community College	‡ 1,080	1,410/—	500	2,214	700	2,100	1,450	700	1,800
Friends University	9,092		650	3,700		2,300			2,300
Garden City Community College	‡ 990	1,320/—	550	2,650	900	1,350	1,500	900	1,350
Haskell Indian Junior College	130		175	25	870	1,400		668	
Hesston College	9,150		700	3,750	500	1,000		300	1,100
Highland Community College	‡ 1,080	1,320/—	350	2,438	400	750	900	750	750
Hutchinson Community College	‡ 990	1,275/—	500	2,480	600	900	1,800	1,388	900

†Figures are projected for 1995-96. ‡Figures are for 1994-95.

| All aid | | Need–based aid | | Grants and scholarships | | | | | | | | Financial aid deadlines | | Inst aid form | Notes |
| Total freshmen | Percent receiving aid | Freshmen judged to have need | Percent offered aid | Need–based | | | | Non–need–based | | | | | | | |
				Acad	Music/drama	Art	Athl	Acad	Music/drama	Art	Athl	Priority	Closing		
													none		
1,859	60	900	100	X	X		X	X	X	X	X	3/1	none		
680	76			X				X				4/1	none		
429	70	305	100	X				X				4/20	none		
395	95	296	100	X	X	X	X	X	X	X	X	4/1	none		
273	92	190	100	X	X	X	X	X	X	X	X	3/15	none		
													none		
251	99	217	100	X	X	X		X	X	X		4/20	none		
				X				X					none		
													none		
755	75			X	X		X	X	X		X	4/15	none		
57	90			X	X	X	X	X	X	X	X	3/1	none		
91	85	87	100					X	X		X	4/1	none		
134	85	115	100	X				X	X			4/1	none		
3,367	65			X				X	X	X	X	1/1	none		
1,902	82	1,121	95	X				X	X	X	X	2/15	none		
													none		
134	93			X	X	X		X	X	X		5/1	none		
													none		
304	95	211	100		X	X	X	X	X	X	X	4/20	8/1		
327	88	278	100	X	X	X		X	X	X		3/1	none		
													none		
491	48							X	X		X		none		
226	92			X				X	X	X	X	3/1	none		
22	100	23	100	X	X			X	X			4/1	none		
				X	X	X	X	X	X	X	X	3/1	none		
196	96	162	100	X	X		X	X	X		X	4/15	none		
229	96	129	100	X				X	X	X	X	3/15	none		
124	96	98	100					X	X	X	X	2/1	none		
													none		
1,832	20							X	X	X	X	5/1	none		
114	90			X	X		X	X	X		X	6/1	none		
													none		
1,545	66							X	X	X	X		none		
1,291	78							X	X	X	X	6/1	none		
				X	X	X	X	X	X	X	X	4/1	none		
949	85			X	X	X	X	X	X		X	4/1	none		
65	85			X				X				6/1	8/1		
752	85			X	X	X	X	X	X	X	X	3/15	none		
790	70			X	X	X	X	X	X	X	X	3/15	none		
1,694	40	500	100	X	X	X	X					5/1	none		
376	93							X	X	X	X	4/1	none	X	
								X	X	X	X	6/1	none		
560	65			X								5/15	none		
177	95	150	100					X				5/1	none		
													none		
2,012	30	562	91	X	X	X	X	X	X	X	X	3/1	none		

Institution	Tuition and fees	Add'l out-of-state/district tuition	Books and supplies	Costs for campus residents			Costs for students at home		
				Room and board	Transportation	Other costs	Board only	Transportation	Other costs
Independence Community College	‡ 1,050	1,455/—	300	2,350					
Johnson County Community College	‡ 1,020	1,980/—	600				1,503	1,458	2,700
Kansas City Kansas Community College	‡ 990	1,440/—	750				1,850	1,800	
Kansas Newman College	8,100		597	3,556	1,221	1,487		1,668	1,487
Kansas State University	‡ 2,085	5,344/—	600	3,220	425	2,000	2,000	550	2,000
Kansas Wesleyan University	‡ 8,020		500	3,200	400	500	1,500	400	500
Labette Community College	‡ 990	1,650/—	400	2,200	400	450	1,300	750	425
Manhattan Christian College	4,730		700	2,946	600	700		400	
McPherson College	8,868		600	3,750	700	2,182	2,200	700	4,652
MidAmerica Nazarene College	7,928		1,100	3,928	231	1,050	1,776	756	1,050
Neosho County Community College	‡ 900	1,305/—	400	2,600	350	350		350	350
Ottawa University	8,100		700	3,570	150	650			
Pittsburg State University	‡ 1,754	3,672/—	450	3,034	500	1,000	1,600	700	1,000
Pratt Community College	‡ 1,050	1,320/—	450	2,640	600	1,430		800	1,430
St. Mary College	9,006		600	4,120	600	910	1,500	600	910
Seward County Community College	‡ 960	1,290/—	600	2,700	900	700		900	700
Southwestern College	‡ 7,200		550	3,532	600	900	1,500	600	900
Sterling College	8,926		550	3,514		650	1,972	1,250	
Tabor College	9,270		550	3,620	750	2,500	1,200	750	2,500
University of Kansas									
Lawrence	‡ 2,038	5,344/—	700	3,336	1,031	1,650	2,062	1,131	1,650
Medical Center	‡ 1,782	5,344/—	600				1,500	1,125	2,070
Washburn University of Topeka	‡ 2,732	2,430/—	450	3,110	963	1,000		773	950
Wichita State University	‡ 2,116	5,344/—	600	3,299	800	900	1,425	800	900
Kentucky									
Alice Lloyd College	360	—/3,800	500	2,560	350	885	1,350	640	885
Asbury College	9,819		550	2,876	810	810	1,590	1,026	
Ashland Community College	‡ 960	1,920/—	450					460	848
Bellarmine College	‡ 8,840		750	2,950	473	750	1,200	608	700
Berea College	‡ 188		450	2,835	250	800	1,400	975	800
Brescia College	‡ 7,550		700	3,200	600	1,000	2,200	755	1,000
Campbellsville College	† 6,420		650	3,210	300	1,000	2,400	900	1,000
Centre College	13,100		630	4,550	250	650	1,550	150	300
Clear Creek Baptist Bible College	‡ 2,110		200	2,260		100			
Cumberland College	7,130		500	3,526	400	600		400	600
Eastern Kentucky University	‡ 1,780	3,160/—	275	3,196	475	625	1,725	625	625
Elizabethtown Community College	‡ 960	1,920/—	490				2,926	495	
Georgetown College	8,890	100/—	550	3,950	650	550	1,800	900	550
Hazard Community College	† 980	1,960/—	450				1,500	460	848
Henderson Community College	‡ 960	1,920/—	500						
Hopkinsville Community College	‡ 960	1,920/—	450						2,808
Institute of Electronic Technology	5,910		50				1,500	727	2,000
Jefferson Community College	‡ 960	1,920/—	450				1,500	460	848
Kentucky Christian College	5,088		700	3,670	1,044	1,530	1,650	1,044	1,030
Kentucky College of Business	5,496		495						
Kentucky State University	‡ 1,680	3,160/—	510	2,816	300	800		350	800
Kentucky Wesleyan College	9,175		700	4,300	350	1,000	1,300	850	1,000
Lees College	4,870		450	2,700	400	1,280	800	1,600	520
Lexington Community College	‡ 1,938	3,240/—	450	3,534				223	
Lindsey Wilson College	7,128		350	3,820	200	900	1,575	900	900
Louisville Technical Institute	8,545		600			1,830		810	
Madisonville Community College	‡ 960	1,920/—	475				1,725	550	300

†Figures are projected for 1995-96. ‡Figures are for 1994-95.

| All aid | | Need-based aid | | Grants and scholarships | | | | | | | | Financial aid deadlines | | Inst aid form | Notes |
| Total fresh-men | Percent receiving aid | Freshmen judged to have need | Percent offered aid | Need-based | | | | Non-need-based | | | | Priority | Closing | | |
				Acad	Music/ drama	Art	Athl	Acad	Music/ drama	Art	Athl				
218	70			X	X	X	X	X	X	X	X		none		
1,804	25			X	X	X	X	X	X	X	X	4/15	none		
3,844	22	426	70	X			X	X	X		X	4/15	none		
114	58	103	100	X	X		X					3/15	none	X	
3,263	38			X	X	X	X	X	X	X	X	3/1	none		
161	99			X	X		X	X	X	X	X	3/1	3/15		
													none		
94	70			X	X			X				3/1	none		
32	95	84	98	X	X	X	X	X	X	X	X		none		
255	94	205	100	X	X		X	X			X	3/1	none	X	
244	65			X	X	X	X	X	X	X	X		none		
154	95			X	X	X	X	X	X	X	X	4/1	none		
1,330	47	329	100	X	X	X	X	X	X	X	X	3/15	none		
727	65							X	X	X	X	5/1	none		
103	67	72	100	X			X	X	X	X	X	3/16	none		
844	91	316	100	X	X	X	X	X	X	X	X	5/1	none		
147	83							X	X	X	X	3/1	none		
182	93			X	X	X	X	X	X	X	X	5/1	none		
138	99	112	100	X	X		X	X	X		X	5/15	none	X	
3,278	43	1,183	100	X				X	X	X	X	3/1	none		
				X				X				4/15	none		
779	80			X	X	X	X	X	X	X	X	3/15	none		
1,150	25	933	59	X				X	X	X	X	3/15	none		
206	100							X			X	2/15	8/31		
285	76	214	100	X	X	X		X	X	X		3/15	none		
618	40			X				X				4/1	5/1		
351	90	229	100					X		X	X	3/15	none		
406	100	406	100					X				2/28	none		
83	77	106	100	X	X	X	X	X	X	X	X	4/1	none		
338	88			X	X	X	X	X	X	X	X	4/1	none	X	
253	84	146	100	X				X					3/1	X	
17	95	40	100	X				X	X			7/15	none		
387	88	340	100					X	X	X	X	3/15	none		
4,952	71							X	X	X	X	4/15	none		
960	60			X				X				4/1	none		
354	95	244	100	X	X	X	X	X	X	X	X	3/1	none		
								X				4/1	none		
517	55							X			X		none		
								X				4/1	none		
78	80												none		
1,793	35							X				4/1	none		
157	92	119	100	X				X	X			4/1	none		
													none		
407	82							X	X		X	3/15	4/15		
156	95	138	100	X				X	X	X	X	3/1	none	X	
													none		
950	5							X				4/1	none		
359	96			X	X	X	X	X	X	X	X	4/15	none		
													none		
1,120	72	836	100	X				X				4/1	none		

Institution	Tuition and fees	Add'l out-of-state/ district tuition	Books and supplies	Costs for campus residents			Costs for students at home		
				Room and board	Trans-portation	Other costs	Board only	Trans-portation	Other costs
Maysville Community College	‡ 960	1,920/—	450				1,500	460	848
Mid-Continent Baptist Bible College	1,740		250	2,832	250	600		900	600
Midway College	‡ 7,360		600	4,050	320	500	1,100	640	500
Morehead State University	‡ 1,880	3,160/—	600	2,900	200	850	1,500	1,050	850
Murray State University	‡ 1,860	3,160/—	700	3,022	350	600	1,770	340	600
Northern Kentucky University	‡ 1,800	3,160/—	500	3,340	700	800	1,500	700	800
Owensboro Community College	‡ 960	1,920/—	500						
Owensboro Junior College of Business	‡ 3,913		600				—	493	
Paducah Community College	‡ 960	1,920/—	400				1,325	975	425
Pikeville College	6,000		500	3,000	400	800	1,800	800	800
Prestonsburg Community College	‡ 960	1,920/—	450					400	2,808
RETS Electronic Institute	5,005						2,608	750	896
St. Catharine College	4,850		400	3,100	520	900	1,800	800	900
Somerset Community College	‡ 960	1,920/—	450						
Southeast Community College	‡ 960	1,920/—	450				1,500	425	425
Spalding University	9,120		600	2,890	500	1,000	1,500	500	800
Sue Bennett College	† 6,100		550	3,788	1,050	740	2,100	2,100	1,050
Thomas More College	10,094		530	4,086	600	1,020	1,000	1,000	1,020
Transylvania University	12,020		500	4,630	200	800	1,000	600	800
Union College	‡ 7,800		500	2,950	900	600	1,500	900	600
University of Kentucky	‡ 2,510	4,360/—	450	3,476	460	850	850	460	850
University of Louisville	‡ 2,390	4,360/—	530	3,468	500	1,680	1,500	850	1,850
Western Kentucky University	‡ 1,860	3,160/—	500	3,100	400	1,100	1,812	1,400	1,100
Louisiana									
Bossier Parish Community College	‡ 645	720/120	600				1,680	945	1,050
Centenary College of Louisiana	10,122		650	3,690	700	1,250	2,000	1,150	1,250
Delgado Community College	1,136	1,560/—	500				1,500	860	930
Dillard University	7,000		600	3,750	442	1,200	1,882	1,076	1,166
Grambling State University	‡ 2,088	1,950/—	576	2,612	428	1,259	1,480	1,034	1,259
Grantham College of Engineering	3,600								
Louisiana College	† 5,236		535	3,024	410	1,040		970	1,040
Louisiana State University									
Agricultural and Mechanical College	‡ 2,628	3,300/—	617	3,310					2,153
Alexandria	‡ 1,060	1,104/—	617				1,937	1,107	1,200
Eunice	‡ 1,056	1,200/—	823		1,476	1,600		1,476	1,600
Medical Center	‡ 2,702	2,500/—	1,658		385		880	979	2,492
Shreveport	‡ 1,620	2,840/—	634				1,989	1,137	1,232
Louisiana Tech University	‡ 2,262	1,695/—	618	2,325	456	1,200	1,938	1,107	1,200
Loyola University	12,031		600		800	750	1,100	350	750
McNeese State University	‡ 1,968	2,540/—	660	2,310	442	1,166	1,882	1,076	1,166
New Orleans Baptist Theological Seminary: School of Christian Education	1,350		500						
Nicholls State University	‡ 1,987	2,592/—	600	2,550	400	1,000		859	930
Northeast Louisiana University	‡ 1,926	2,400/—	617	2,060	455	1,200	1,937	1,107	1,200
Northwestern State University	‡ 2,067	2,220/—	550	2,216	981	1,051	1,696	981	
Nunez Community College	† 900	1,870/—	617				3,900	1,107	1,200
Our Lady of Holy Cross College	4,694		600				1,882	1,076	1,166
Phillips Junior College: New Orleans	3,630					25			
St. Joseph Seminary College	5,740		800	4,350	650				
Southeastern Louisiana University	‡ 1,910	2,088/—	520	2,470	898	972		898	972

†Figures are projected for 1995-96. ‡Figures are for 1994-95.

All aid		Need-based aid		Grants and scholarships								Financial aid deadlines		Inst aid form	Notes
				Need-based				Non-need-based							
Total freshmen	Percent receiving aid	Freshmen judged to have need	Percent offered aid	Acad	Music/drama	Art	Athl	Acad	Music/drama	Art	Athl	Priority	Closing		
265	51	145	100	X				X				4/1	none		
13	47	4	100					X				5/1	none	X	
336	87							X	X	X	X		8/1		
1,139	70	907	95	X				X	X	X	X	4/1	none		
1,141	57	600	92					X	X	X	X	4/1	none	X	
1,703	22	339	100					X	X	X	X	4/1	none	X	
													none		
				X				X			X	4/1	none		
144	80	122	100	X			X	X			X	3/15	none		
1,823	60			X				X				4/1	none		
80	85												none		
													none		
1,358	80			X	X			X	X			4/1	none		
1,751	73			X				X				4/15	none		
95	91			X	X	X	X	X	X	X	X	3/1	none		
128	93			X				X					none		
238	70	180	94	X	X	X		X	X	X		3/1	none		
258	82	233	100	X				X	X	X	X	3/15	8/1		
153	84	129	100					X	X		X	4/1	none		
2,625	48			X				X	X	X	X	4/1	none		
1,882	50	1,200	92					X	X	X	X	4/15	none		
2,295	60	1,451	88					X	X	X	X	4/1	none		
2,491	40			X	X		X	X	X		X	6/1	6/30		
211	83	116	100	X				X	X	X	X	3/15	none		
		388	100	X			X	X			X	4/15	6/1		
2,628	95							X	X		X	4/15	none		
209	80							X	X		X		5/15		
3,155	69	1,262	93	X				X	X	X	X	4/1	none		
541	44			X				X		X		6/15	none		
2,556	60			X				X				7/1			
				X				X					none		
				X				X					none	X	
1,596	77	780	100	X				X	X	X	X	4/1	none		
715	86	427	100					X	X	X		5/1	8/1		
1,429	60			X				X	X	X	X	5/1	none		
													none		
2,504	56			X				X	X		X	3/1	none		
1,849	65			X				X	X	X	X	4/1	none		
1,716	68			X	X		X	X	X	X	X	4/1	none		
237	58	190	100	X				X				4/1	6/1		
103	65			X				X				4/15	none		
													none		
7	100			X				X				5/1	none		
				X	X			X	X		X	5/1	none		

Institution	Tuition and fees	Add'l out-of-state/district tuition	Books and supplies	Costs for campus residents			Costs for students at home		
				Room and board	Transportation	Other costs	Board only	Transportation	Other costs
Southern University									
New Orleans	‡ 1,656	1,806/—	400						
Shreveport	‡ 1,110	1,130/—	500				1,700	1,076	1,420
Southern University and Agricultural and Mechanical College	‡ 2,028	2,322/—	500	3,042	425	500	750	200	275
Tulane University	20,218		350	6,130		800			
University of New Orleans	‡ 2,362	2,792/—	800	3,386	650	1,140	2,721	1,132	1,140
University of Southwestern Louisiana	‡ 1,898	3,000/—	500	2,082	353	930	1,500	859	930
Xavier University of Louisiana	7,500		617	4,300	458	1,200	1,937	1,107	1,200
Maine									
Andover College	† 5,050		700				4,570	1,050	1,000
Bates College			650		250	900			
Beal College	‡ 3,825		725		350	1,400	1,200	1,500	700
Bowdoin College	20,555		620	5,945		875			875
Casco Bay College	5,575		650	3,800	100		800	400	1,300
Central Maine Medical Center School of Nursing	5,476		833			700	1,500	766	700
Central Maine Technical College	‡ 1,860	2,070/—	500	3,200	1,000	1,000	2,500	1,050	1,000
Colby College	20,990		500	5,650	200	800	600	300	
College of the Atlantic	15,621		450	4,500		400	1,800		400
Eastern Maine Technical College	‡ 2,030	2,070/—	600	3,200	500	1,200	1,700	1,000	1,200
Husson College	8,140		375	4,300	650	1,100		1,200	1,400
Kennebec Valley Technical College	‡ 1,845	2,070/—	400						
Maine College of Art	‡ 11,245		1,490	5,020	500			1,935	
Maine Maritime Academy	‡ 4,710	3,050/970	750	4,550	700	650		800	650
Northern Maine Technical College	‡ 1,879	2,070/—	750	3,200	500	3,285	1,600	1,050	900
St. Joseph's College	‡ 10,280		500	5,180	300	1,200		1,000	1,200
Southern Maine Technical College	‡ 1,930	2,070/—	600	3,200	423	832	1,800	714	950
Thomas College	9,975		600	4,825	800	1,000	800	1,500	1,000
Unity College	‡ 9,175	800/—	450	4,750	400	600	1,950	225	600
University of Maine									
Augusta	‡ 2,685	3,660/—	520				800	1,100	600
Farmington	‡ 3,060	4,050/—	450	3,970	500	1,400	1,846	1,100	100
Fort Kent	‡ 2,850	3,900/—	500	3,600	800	1,000	900	1,000	1,000
Machias	‡ 2,875	3,900/—	600	3,680	900	1,600	1,800	900	1,600
Orono	‡ 3,661	5,760/—	500	4,678	400	1,150	1,455	1,100	650
Presque Isle	‡ 2,940	3,900/—	400	3,630	700	975	850	1,050	850
University of New England	‡ 11,950		900	5,045	450	650	500	1,000	1,500
University of Southern Maine	‡ 3,278	5,550/—	500	4,494	725	1,250	1,850	725	1,250
Westbrook College	‡ 11,650		550	4,900	450	800		800	800
Maryland									
Allegany Community College	‡ 2,075	1,290/540	500				1,530	1,056	966
Anne Arundel Community College	1,876	4,320/1,440	500				1,700	950	1,200
Baltimore City Community College	1,648	3,690/—	500					400	2,000
Baltimore Hebrew University	4,120		400					400	1,300
Baltimore International Culinary College	12,915		1,200	4,842	270	3,627	3,312	270	
Bowie State University	‡ 2,814	2,728/—	700	4,000	700	1,400	2,900	950	1,050
Capitol College	‡ 8,445		600		800	1,346	1,578	1,575	1,440
Carroll Community College	1,665	3,450/—							
Catonsville Community College	‡ 1,700	3,090/1,290	500					1,500	900
Cecil Community College	† 1,810	2,820/1,740	500				1,900	1,000	1,000

†Figures are projected for 1995-96. ‡Figures are for 1994-95.

| All aid | | Need–based aid | | Grants and scholarships | | | | | | | | Financial aid deadlines | | Inst aid form | Notes |
| Total fresh–men | Percent receiving aid | Freshmen judged to have need | Percent offered aid | Need–based | | | | Non–need–based | | | | | | | |
				Acad	Music/drama	Art	Athl	Acad	Music/drama	Art	Athl	Priority	Closing		
272	95			X	X	X		X					none		
													none		
1,311	55	715	99	X				X			X	2/1	none		
1,597	56	640	80	X	X		X	X	X		X	5/1	none	X	
2,726	75							X	X	X	X	3/1	none	X	
675	89	545	87	X	X	X	X	X	X	X	X	4/1	none		
								X					none		
448	54	204	100										2/9		
				X				X				5/1	none		
431	42	171	100										3/1		
		120	100										none		
48	71	31	100									3/15	7/1		
				X								5/1	none		
434	75	175	100									1/15	2/1	X	
68	75	50	100									2/15	5/1	X	
359	66			X				X				4/1	none		
323	90	307	100	X			X	X				3/15	none		
79	80	74	100			X		X		X		3/1	none		
202	82							X				4/15	none		
425	72			X				X				4/1	none		
197	90	156	100	X				X				3/15	none		
793	55	450	100	X								4/1	none		
128	92			X				X			X	2/15	none		
182	74	144	100					X			X	4/15	none		
513	80							X	X	X		4/1	none		
480	88			X				X				3/1	none		
89	75	74	100	X				X				3/15	none		
167	85	125	97	X	X	X	X					3/1	none		
1,460	60			X				X	X	X	X	3/1	none		
239	72	147	93	X		X		X	X	X	X	4/1	none		
210	85	200	100	X				X				5/1	none	X	
768	60							X	X			3/1	none		
117	86			X								5/1	none		
1,704	62			X			X	X			X	3/15	none		
				X		X	X	X			X	4/15	none		
1,731	75			X			X	X			X		none		
													7/1	X	
266	90	252	100					X				7/1	none		
399	70	279	92	X	X	X	X	X	X		X	1/1	4/1	X	
50	39	44	100	X				X				3/1	none		
				X				X					none	X	
2,353	10							X			X	3/1	none		
335	23	77	100	X	X	X	X	X	X	X	X	8/1	none		

Institution	Tuition and fees	Add'l out-of-state/ district tuition	Books and supplies	Costs for campus residents			Costs for students at home		
				Room and board	Trans- portation	Other costs	Board only	Trans- portation	Other costs
Charles County Community College	1,900	3,480/1,740	650				2,000	600	400
Chesapeake College	1,755	5,250/2,100	475				600	950	720
College of Notre Dame of Maryland	11,840		600	5,845	250	700	1,600	300	700
Columbia Union College	10,775		750	3,850	1,000	1,000	1,200	750	1,000
Coppin State College	‡ 2,605	2,572/—	500	4,640			1,500	2,050	1,031
Dundalk Community College	‡ 1,688	3,090/1,290	600				1,500	1,500	1,000
Essex Community College	1,796	3,090/1,290	500					1,500	
Frederick Community College	2,123	3,870/1,920	700				1,650	1,100	775
Frostburg State University	‡ 2,849	2,997/—	700	4,390	500	900	1,800	900	750
Garrett Community College	1,770	2,040/540	600	4,125	1,233	750	1,700	1,233	750
Goucher College	16,630		500	6,360	350	1,100	1,500	700	400
Hagerstown Business College	4,028		650		450	1,260	1,632	1,920	960
Hagerstown Junior College	2,068	1,590/780	480				1,800	380	200
Harford Community College	1,814	2,310/1,020	500				1,500	800	500
Hood College	14,930		400	6,400		744	2,284	885	2,400
Howard Community College	‡ 2,343	2,070/1,260	450				1,500	675	700
Johns Hopkins University	19,750		500	6,955		1,045	1,500		1,045
Johns Hopkins University: Peabody Conservatory of Music	18,230		450	6,560	1,500	800	1,700	1,500	800
Loyola College in Maryland	14,290		600	6,560	200	700	1,700	650	700
Maryland College of Art and Design	8,430		1,000				1,800	1,460	1,200
Maryland Institute College of Art	15,100		1,400	5,050	500	600	600	1,000	600
Montgomery College									
Germantown Campus	2,102	3,120/1,680	560				1,100	1,700	1,000
Rockville Campus	2,102	3,120/1,680	560				1,100	1,700	1,000
Takoma Park Campus	2,102	3,120/1,680	560				1,100	1,700	1,000
Morgan State University	‡ 2,634	3,202/—	1,000	4,840	300	1,600	750	450	2,350
Mount St. Mary's College	14,120		600	6,250	300	700	2,100	650	800
Prince George's Community College	‡ 2,506	4,320/1,890	515					825	825
St. John's College	18,830		275	5,890	350	700	2,000	200	700
St. Mary's College of Maryland	5,435	3,300/—	700	4,970	230	1,050	1,650	800	1,050
Salisbury State University	‡ 3,094	2,802/—	600	4,690	800	800	1,095	850	850
Sojourner-Douglass College	3,510		400				3,200	416	2,800
Towson State University	‡ 3,287	3,000/—	700	4,480	420	1,110	2,500	420	710
United States Naval Academy	0								
University of Baltimore	‡ 3,024	2,800/—	600				1,800	1,200	1,800
University of Maryland									
Baltimore	‡ 3,168	5,552/—	1,200		1,150	1,250		1,150	1,250
Baltimore County	‡ 3,570	5,064/—	500	4,674	60	1,100	1,650	2,200	1,100
College Park	‡ 3,480	5,804/—	566	5,003	546	1,644	1,442	546	1,644
Eastern Shore	‡ 2,741	4,660/—	525	4,284	525	1,025	1,825	1,025	1,025
University College	5,270	630/—	1,060				1,817	1,500	8,934
Villa Julie College	8,190		600						
Washington Bible College	5,938		400	3,590	500	1,000		500	1,000
Washington College	16,040		500	5,558		300	750		300
Western Maryland College	‡ 14,510		400	5,240	400	500	1,500	600	500
Wor-Wic Community College	1,705	2,670/2,040	500				1,700	1,000	450
Massachusetts									
American International College	10,174		550	4,910	575	900	1,475	675	600
Amherst College	21,065		660	5,560		1,358			
Anna Maria College	11,780		526	5,028	493	1,019	1,830	1,096	1,074
Aquinas College at Milton	7,950		450				1,500	1,200	9,000

†Figures are projected for 1995-96. ‡Figures are for 1994-95.

All aid		Need-based aid		Grants and scholarships								Financial aid deadlines		Inst aid form	Notes
				Need-based				Non-need-based							
Total fresh-men	Percent receiving aid	Freshmen judged to have need	Percent offered aid	Acad	Music/drama	Art	Athl	Acad	Music/drama	Art	Athl	Priority	Closing		
1,189	25			X				X	X	X	X	4/1	none		
697	35	105	84	X				X			X	6/1	none	X	
				X				X	X	X		2/15	none	X	
115	85							X	X		X	3/31	5/31		
419	48	348	100	X				X			X	4/1	none		
				X			X	X			X	4/15	none		
				X	X	X		X	X		X	7/1	none		
1,321	15			X				X	X	X	X	6/15	none		
849	58	683	100	X				X	X	X		4/1	none		
342	85			X		X	X	X		X		4/1	none		
256	70			X				X	X	X		2/15	none	X	
220	87							X					none		
2,410	50			X			X	X			X	6/1	none		
				X	X		X	X	X		X	6/1	none		
183	80	157	100	X				X				3/31	none		
835	30			X	X							3/1	none	X	
955	50	401	100	X				X	X		X	1/15	2/1		
43	97				X				X			2/17	3/2		
798	67	388	99					X			X	2/15	3/1		
32	50	9	100	X		X		X		X		4/1	none		
188	78	124	100	X		X		X		X		2/15	none		
												2/15	none		
												2/15	none		
												2/15	none		
1,202	80	940	96	X				X			X	4/1	none		
398	81	251	96	X				X			X		3/15		
1,956	46	900	100	X			X	X	X		X	5/31	none		
113	60	75	100									3/1	none		
304	72	149	95	X				X	X				3/1		
687	25	280	82	X				X				3/1	none		
													none		
1,486	42	982	100	X	X	X	X	X	X	X	X	3/15	none		
								X						X	
817	65			X	X	X	X	X	X	X	X	3/1	none		
3,814	42	1,480	96	X	X	X	X	X	X	X	X	2/15	none		
813	80							X	X	X	X	3/1	none		
				X		X		X					5/1		
242	67	208	93	X				X				3/1	none	X	
34	30	34	100		X		X	X	X		X	3/1	5/19		
236	81	108	98	X				X	X	X		2/15	2/15		
332	80	189	100	X	X	X		X				3/1	none	X	
241	70			X			X	X			X	4/15	none		
426	60	189	100										2/1		
131	66	80	100	X	X			X	X			3/1	none	X	
													none		

Institution	Tuition and fees	Add'l out-of-state/district tuition	Books and supplies	Costs for campus residents			Costs for students at home		
				Room and board	Trans-portation	Other costs	Board only	Trans-portation	Other costs
Aquinas College at Newton	‡ 7,250		500				1,900	1,000	1,600
Assumption College	‡ 12,125		500	5,900	400	715	2,000	400	715
Atlantic Union College	11,100		600	3,600	600	800		600	800
Babson College	18,115		520	7,275		1,225	1,500	1,000	1,225
Bay Path College	10,700		600	6,350	300	900	600	1,000	900
Bay State College	9,200		500	6,400	675	2,405	2,500	810	2,180
Becker College									
Leicester Campus	8,945		500	4,460	300	600	1,500	700	600
Worcester Campus	8,990		500	4,580	300	600	1,500	700	600
Bentley College	14,835		630	6,340	420	1,450	1,590	1,320	1,450
Berklee College of Music	12,825		530	7,190	975	1,100	3,050	1,235	1,100
Berkshire Community College	‡ 2,400	4,500/—	480				1,800	900	900
Boston Architectural Center	4,570		1,210				1,800	1,430	935
Boston College	18,356		500	7,270	500	1,000	1,500	1,000	500
Boston Conservatory	14,125		500	6,280	500	1,000	1,500	800	1,000
Boston University	19,700		475	7,100	275	750	1,800	1,975	750
Bradford College	15,080		425	6,490	450	950	1,650	550	950
Brandeis University	20,934		410	6,780		1,000	1,800	2,400	1,000
Bridgewater State College	‡ 3,470	4,134/—	500	4,196	500	1,250	2,490	1,250	1,250
Bristol Community College	‡ 2,460	4,440/—	500				2,525	1,000	1,175
Bunker Hill Community College	‡ 2,250	4,440/—	540				3,700	1,117	2,959
Cape Cod Community College	‡ 2,400	4,440/—	400				2,000	500	1,000
Clark University	19,140		500	4,250	100	700	1,780	250	700
College of the Holy Cross	19,265		400	6,500	100	900	1,500	300	1,815
Curry College	14,550		600	5,500					
Dean College	11,810		600	6,000	300	600	2,500	800	600
Eastern Nazarene College	† 10,160		500	3,600	350	700		350	700
Elms College	12,470		475	5,000	500	960	1,500	800	2,200
Emerson College	‡ 15,545		500	7,782		937	1,500		1,577
Emmanuel College	13,450		500	6,275	200	900		200	900
Endicott College	12,220		400	6,400	600	1,000		1,000	1,000
Essex Agricultural and Technical Institute	‡ 2,079	—/3,700	500				3,000	1,700	3,000
Fisher College	11,300		600	6,300	800	900	1,500	1,000	
Fitchburg State College	‡ 3,234	4,134/—	500	4,030	350	1,538	590	1,000	1,538
Forsyth School for Dental Hygienists	13,578		400	7,800	175	450		675	450
Framingham State College	‡ 3,314	4,134/—	475	3,426	500	1,200		1,000	1,200
Franklin Institute of Boston	8,740		700	6,500	600		660	600	1,390
Gordon College	13,950		400	4,440	400	400	1,590		400
Greenfield Community College	‡ 2,478	4,500/—	550				2,153	1,030	1,351
Hampshire College	21,645		375	5,740		1,120	1,665		1,120
Harvard and Radcliffe Colleges	20,444			6,710					
Hebrew College	8,340		300				1,000	300	
Hellenic College	‡ 7,325		800	5,200	800	1,500	2,000	800	1,500
Holyoke Community College	‡ 2,482	4,440/—	520				2,500	1,170	1,600
Katharine Gibbs School	17,250		500						
Laboure College	‡ 9,438		800				1,200	960	900
Lasell College	12,700		600	6,300	450	1,700	1,600	450	1,700
Lesley College	12,900		550	6,075	350	850	1,900	735	850
Marian Court College	‡ 7,250		465				808	1,198	1,638
Massachusetts Bay Community College	‡ 2,310	4,440/—	400				2,015	800	860
Massachusetts College of Art	‡ 4,078	4,959/—	1,800	5,839	600			600	2,200

†Figures are projected for 1995-96. ‡Figures are for 1994-95.

All aid		Need-based aid		Grants and scholarships								Financial aid deadlines		Inst aid form	Notes
				Need-based				Non-need-based							
Total freshmen	Percent receiving aid	Freshmen judged to have need	Percent offered aid	Acad	Music/drama	Art	Athl	Acad	Music/drama	Art	Athl	Priority	Closing		
70	64			X				X					none		
490	65			X							X		3/1		
132	90							X	X		X	4/15	none	X	
404	53	206	100	X				X					2/1		
218	85			X				X	X				none		
289	85							X				3/1	none		
197	71	158	100	X				X			X	2/15	none	X	
348	80	204	100	X				X			X	4/1	none	X	
754	59			X		X		X			X	12/1	2/1		
741	59	307	89	X	X			X	X			3/31	none		
600	29											5/1	none		
15	47							X		X		6/15	none		
2,250	69			X				X			X	2/1	none	X	
67	78	41	95		X				X				3/1	X	
3,728	67	2,275	95	X	X	X		X	X	X	X	2/15	none		
223	75			X		X		X		X		2/15	none	X	
761	73	501	100	X				X				2/15	4/15		
1,105	54	880	100					X				3/1	none		
				X	X	X		X		X		4/15	none	X	
												5/1	none	X	
1,243	48											4/1	none		
475	69	331	100	X	X	X		X					2/1		
672	63	431	100					X				2/1	none		
294	60	162	100										3/15		
1,060	65			X	X	X	X					1/31	none		
209	80			X	X			X	X			3/1	none		
120	90	105	100	X				X				2/15	none	X	
447	80			X	X			X	X			3/1	none		
110	93	106	100	X		X		X				3/1	9/15		
335	84	267	100	X								3/15	none		
215	25	141	64									5/1	8/26		
372	80							X				3/1	none		
777	82	354	98	X				X	X	X		3/30	none	X	
48	70			X				X				3/1	none		
479	50	239	100	X				X				4/1	none	X	
189	90	126	100	X								4/1	none		
269	94			X	X			X	X			3/15	6/15	X	
				X								4/15	none		
301	60	201	100					X				2/15	none	X	
1,619	78	950	100									2/1	none		
												6/15	none	X	
36	80	20	100	X				X					4/1	X	
				X				X	X	X	X	5/15	none	X	
179	65			X									none	X	
														X	
225	90	204	100					X				5/1	none	X	
103	70	103	100	X				X				2/15	none	X	
74	84	65	100	X								4/1	none		
1,803	52			X				X					5/1		
168	59	103	100									5/1	none		

Institution	Tuition and fees	Add'l out-of-state/district tuition	Books and supplies	Costs for campus residents			Costs for students at home		
				Room and board	Trans-portation	Other costs	Board only	Trans-portation	Other costs
Massachusetts College of Pharmacy and Allied Health Sciences	‡ 11,875		500	6,720	320	1,600	1,700	750	1,600
Massachusetts Institute of Technology	21,000		800	6,150	500	1,650		1,175	1,650
Massachusetts Maritime Academy	‡ 3,464	4,959/—	450	4,083	350	1,250		1,300	1,200
Massasoit Community College	‡ 2,490	4,440/—	508				1,700	900	900
Merrimack College	13,300		600	6,600	1,000	450	1,600	1,000	450
Middlesex Community College	‡ 2,820	4,440/300	500				1,850	900	400
Montserrat College of Art	9,730		470		800	900	1,600	800	900
Mount Holyoke College	20,290		750	5,950		750	2,310		750
Mount Ida College	‡ 10,546		715	7,220	580	525		990	525
Mount Wachusett Community College	‡ 2,850	4,440/600	500				1,500	1,305	1,165
New England Banking Institute	‡ 2,034		300						
New England Conservatory of Music	‡ 15,400		400	7,300	550	1,350	1,700	800	1,800
Newbury College	‡ 10,430		520	5,990	585	900	350	585	900
Nichols College	10,332		500	5,904	250	650		500	650
North Adams State College	‡ 3,903	4,134/—	500	4,180	407	1,246	1,900	1,172	1,246
North Shore Community College	‡ 2,490	4,440/—	600				1,200	1,004	1,200
Northeastern University	14,241		600	7,710	750	900	2,250	750	900
Northern Essex Community College	‡ 2,280	4,440/—	500				1,700	1,175	1,400
Pine Manor College	16,050		500	6,660	500	450	1,500	315	450
Quincy College	‡ 2,120		400				500	200	400
Quinsigamond Community College	‡ 2,210	4,440/—	500				2,475	720	1,448
Regis College	13,700		450	6,250		750	1,500	900	750
Roxbury Community College	‡ 2,295	4,440/—	600				1,600	1,075	1,470
St. Hyacinth College and Seminary	4,000		425	5,000	400	725	1,300	800	700
St. John's Seminary College	5,000		400	2,600	400	600			
Salem State College	‡ 3,198	4,134/—	450	3,622	450	900	1,422	1,233	900
School of the Museum of Fine Arts	‡ 13,875		1,000		1,000	1,500	1,800	1,000	1,500
Simmons College	16,960		496	7,228		1,149	1,500	948	1,149
Simon's Rock College of Bard	20,270		400	5,860	400	450	2,880	250	400
Smith College	19,814		550	6,970		550			550
Springfield College	11,596		700	5,325	400	1,000	1,800	1,500	1,200
Springfield Technical Community College	‡ 2,640	4,440/—	400				1,450	800	1,500
Stonehill College	13,344		510	6,350	180	581	1,500	1,015	581
Suffolk University	11,360		500		700	2,400	1,500	700	2,400
Tufts University	21,086		600	6,250		964			3,414
University of Massachusetts									
Amherst	‡ 5,467	6,346/—	500	4,162	400	1,000	1,800	600	1,000
Boston	‡ 4,303	6,348/—	568				2,000	1,026	1,231
Dartmouth	‡ 3,835	5,083/—	600	4,850	450	1,000	2,026	1,275	1,000
Lowell	‡ 4,605	5,144/—	400	4,377	200	1,160	1,695	900	1,010
Wellesley College	19,610		500	6,200	435	700	1,000		700
Wentworth Institute of Technology	10,500		850	6,050		500	1,500	850	
Western New England College	10,310		500	5,740	300	840	1,625	925	1,140
Westfield State College	‡ 3,279	4,134/—	450	3,998	400	1,280	750	1,350	1,280
Wheaton College	19,140		710	6,050		850	1,550		850
Wheelock College	‡ 13,472		400	5,528		850	2,500		850
Williams College	20,790		500	5,990	350	800			
Worcester Polytechnic Institute	17,160		550	5,640		730	1,500		730
Worcester State College	‡ 2,653	4,134/—	500	3,880	500	1,150	1,250	1,000	1,150

†Figures are projected for 1995-96. ‡Figures are for 1994-95.

| All aid | | Need-based aid | | Grants and scholarships | | | | | | | | Financial aid deadlines | | Inst aid form | Notes |
| Total freshmen | Percent receiving aid | Freshmen judged to have need | Percent offered aid | Need-based | | | | Non-need-based | | | | Priority | Closing | | |
				Acad	Music/drama	Art	Athl	Acad	Music/drama	Art	Athl				
106	75							X				4/1	none		
1,095	75	697	100									1/13	none		
160	79			X				X				5/1	none		
810	65			X			X	X			X	4/15	none		
527	80	445	100	X			X				X	2/1	3/1		
2,460	40	900	89										none		
98	54	49	100	X	X					X		3/15	none		
454	70												1/15	X	
831	70			X		X	X					5/1	none		
898	63												none	X	
75	70				X				X			1/15	none		
1,400	72	490	100					X				5/1	none	X	
269	80			X				X				4/1	none		
241	66	166	100					X				4/1	none	X	
829	63	519	100									3/15	none		
2,558	71	1,820	100	X				X			X	3/1	none		
1,650	50											4/1	none		
119	94			X				X				3/15	none		
1,251	60							X				4/1	5/15		
842	44							X	X	X	X	7/1	none		
183	94	144	98	X				X				2/15	none	X	
670	85											5/1	none		
3	60			X				X				6/1	none		
8	60												none		
974	63	607	100	X	X	X		X	X	X		4/15	none		
214	53	98	100		X							3/15	none	X	
294	81	219	100	X				X				2/1		X	
137	90	123	100									6/30			
648	47	315	100									2/1		X	
492	77	407	100	X								4/1	none	X	
								X	X	X	X	4/1	none		
520	91	364	99	X				X	X		X	1/1	none		
445	76	317	100	X				X				3/1		X	
1,170	41	415	100	X				X				2/1			
3,910	50	2,400	100	X	X	X	X	X	X	X	X	3/1	none		
662	60			X				X				6/1	none		
												3/1	none		
										X		3/1	none		
572	54												1/15		
407	62	252	98	X				X				3/1	none	X	
409	80			X								4/1	none		
858	86							X				4/1	none	X	
392	70	276	100	X								2/1			
175	81	142	100	X								3/1		X	
498	43	189	100									2/1		X	
697	80	559	100									3/1			
561	42							X				3/15	none		

Institution	Tuition and fees	Add'l out-of-state/district tuition	Books and supplies	Costs for campus residents			Costs for students at home		
				Room and board	Transportation	Other costs	Board only	Transportation	Other costs
Michigan									
Adrian College	11,740		400	4,120	300	700	1,870	300	700
Albion College	15,334		525	4,850	425	425	2,325		
Alma College	13,332		700	4,762	400	600	1,300	700	700
Alpena Community College	‡ 1,500	1,260/630	500						
Andrews University	10,623		960	3,210	645	735		645	735
Aquinas College	11,852		380	4,124	470	700	2,500	940	700
Baker College									
Auburn Hills	6,070		750					1,600	
Cadillac	6,070		750				1,675	2,000	
Flint	6,070		650		1,000	2,500	1,575	900	2,494
Jackson	6,070		650				1,575	1,825	2,000
Mount Clemens	6,070							900	2,494
Muskegon	6,070		750		1,675	2,000	1,600	2,000	2,000
Owosso	6,000		750		1,600	2,000	1,650	1,600	2,000
Port Huron	6,070		650				1,575	1,825	2,000
Bay de Noc Community College	‡ 1,625	1,876/—	400		409	586	1,500	818	586
Calvin College	10,995		400	3,895	530	680	1,850	1,100	660
Center for Creative Studies: College of Art and Design	‡ 11,890		2,340	4,100	1,235	824	2,503	1,235	494
Central Michigan University	3,142	4,586/—	650	4,036	500	983	1,800	750	1,208
Cleary College	6,690		800				2,000	1,500	1,000
Concordia College	† 11,473		550	5,016	154	1,100	2,460	154	1,055
Cornerstone College and Grand Rapids Baptist Seminary	7,516		500	4,032	792	1,150	3,300	1,230	1,150
Davenport College of Business	‡ 7,400		675		982	843		982	843
Delta College	‡ 1,625	1,470/570	500					900	600
Detroit College of Business	‡ 7,020		600				2,500	955	825
Eastern Michigan University	‡ 3,050	4,140/—	500	4,148	600	600	1,500	1,200	600
Ferris State University	‡ 3,457	3,499/—	590	4,171	412	670	1,800	660	670
Glen Oaks Community College	1,503	630/180	480		800		800	1,320	775
GMI Engineering & Management Institute	‡ 11,730		600	3,462	3,130	2,320	1,325	3,130	2,320
Gogebic Community College	† 1,020	—/390	450		750	750	800	750	750
Grace Bible College	† 5,200		300	3,400	1,115	650		915	650
Grand Rapids Community College	‡ 1,384	1,120/672	1,050				2,575	915	500
Grand Valley State University	‡ 2,992	3,586/—	600	4,060	550	450		950	550
Great Lakes Christian College	‡ 4,368		500	2,800	500	1,500		500	1,500
Great Lakes Junior College of Business	4,830		300					2,400	490
Henry Ford Community College	1,720	1,110/810	500				2,650	940	525
Highland Park Community College	1,700	300/—	250				1,650	675	1,300
Hillsdale College	11,970		600	4,940	1,000	900	2,600	1,000	900
Hope College	13,318		480	4,516	255	875	1,500	470	485
Jackson Community College	‡ 1,366	600/360	386				2,430	890	634
Kalamazoo College	16,713		510	5,262	180	600	598	180	600
Kalamazoo Valley Community College	1,116	1,922/961	480				3,617	964	964
Kellogg Community College	‡ 1,290	1,960/810	510		915	600	3,310	915	600
Kendall College of Art and Design	† 10,550		1,610				3,790	935	990
Kirtland Community College	1,564	1,170/510	450						
Lake Michigan College	‡ 1,350	600/300	500				1,800	750	950
Lake Superior State University	3,396	3,282/—	600	4,290	375	600	1,850	375	600
Lansing Community College	1,320	1,740/870	540				2,250	945	945
Lawrence Technological University	‡ 7,400		1,300		1,000	800	2,200	1,200	800

†Figures are projected for 1995-96. ‡Figures are for 1994-95.

All aid		Need–based aid		Grants and scholarships								Financial aid deadlines		Inst aid form	Notes
				Need–based				Non–need–based							
Total fresh–men	Percent receiving aid	Freshmen judged to have need	Percent offered aid	Acad	Music/drama	Art	Athl	Acad	Music/drama	Art	Athl	Priority	Closing		
247	93			X	X	X		X	X	X		3/15	none		
433	88	299	100					X	X	X		2/15	none		
368	95	286	100					X	X	X		2/15	5/1		
676	57	390	100	X				X			X	5/15	none		
356	94	262	100	X				X	X			3/31	none	X	
225	95	183	100	X	X	X	X	X	X	X	X	2/15	none		
				X				X				2/15	none		
				X				X				3/15	none		
				X				X				3/15	9/1		
				X				X				9/1			
				X				X					9/1		
				X				X				9/1	none		
				X				X					none		
				X				X				9/1	none		
651	75			X				X				4/15	none		
938	89	701	100	X				X	X	X		2/15	none	X	
96	65			X		X				X		2/15	none	X	
2,748	65			X				X	X	X	X	2/21	none		
116	90	92	100	X			X	X	X	X	X	3/15	5/31		
193	90	147	100					X	X		X	3/1	9/1		
919	75							X				3/15	none		
								X					none		
1,476	82	901	99	X				X			X	2/15	none		
2,242	58			X	X	X	X	X	X	X	X	3/15	none		
1,819	70	1,420	100	X				X	X		X	4/1	none		
282	22			X				X	X	X	X	5/15	none		
559	66			X				X				3/15	none		
350	75			X			X	X			X	5/1	none		
46	94	43	100					X	X			7/15	none		
8,768	14	2,200	100	X	X	X	X	X	X	X	X	4/1	none		
1,738	68	1,059	100	X	X	X	X	X	X	X	X	2/15	none		
40	91							X	X			8/1	none		
													none		
5,100	40	2,399	100	X	X	X	X	X	X	X	X	4/1	none		
1,194	85											3/15	5/1		
355	70	240	100	X	X	X	X	X	X	X	X	3/15	none		
679	87	431	100	X				X	X	X		2/15	none		
				X				X	X			4/1	none		
337	90	223	100					X	X	X		2/15	none		
				X				X			X		none		
884	60			X	X	X	X	X	X	X	X	5/1	none		
92	85	79	100					X		X		2/15	none		
296	75			X				X				5/15	none		
													none		
584	75	370	100	X				X			X	4/1	none		
2,157	35			X	X	X	X	X	X	X	X	8/1	none		
651	60			X				X				6/1	9/1		

Institution	Tuition and fees	Add'l out-of-state/district tuition	Books and supplies	Costs for campus residents			Costs for students at home		
				Room and board	Transportation	Other costs	Board only	Transportation	Other costs
Lewis College of Business	4,900		500						
Macomb Community College	1,440	1,200/750	440				2,200	840	700
Madonna University	5,480		425	4,090		655		940	655
Marygrove College	7,504		500	3,840	560	1,325		1,178	1,325
Michigan Christian College	‡ 5,420		300	3,332	455	640	1,500	1,000	640
Michigan State University	‡ 4,660	6,556/—	552	3,764	269	877	1,500	2,304	1,076
Michigan Technological University	‡ 3,636	4,617/—	600	3,978	450	750	1,500	450	750
Mid Michigan Community College	‡ 1,390	1,470/825	500				1,600	1,200	1,000
Monroe County Community College	1,150	1,200/960	700				2,200	750	945
Montcalm Community College	1,421	1,323/738	600				1,325	940	480
Mott Community College	‡ 1,600	1,440/690	550					600	600
Muskegon Community College	† 1,290	1,005/570	400				1,600	1,000	800
North Central Michigan College	1,320	780/390	550	3,450	515	400	1,990	915	660
Northern Michigan University	† 2,595	2,256/—	450	3,965	400	800	1,800	400	1,800
Northwestern Michigan College	‡ 1,700	1,352/1,032	525	3,900	500	750		850	825
Northwood University	10,163		750	4,605			1,600		
Oakland Community College	‡ 1,485	1,890/960	400				2,300	1,900	360
Oakland University	‡ 3,110	5,610/—	400	4,030	500	650	1,800	900	650
Olivet College	11,580		550	3,860	500	530	1,760	530	530
Reformed Bible College	6,490		400	3,350	530	680		530	680
Sacred Heart Major Seminary	‡ 4,185		500	4,100	600	1,500	5,400	1,000	1,350
Saginaw Valley State University	‡ 3,003	3,030/—	550	3,820	420	830	1,520	815	835
St. Clair County Community College	† 1,630	1,600/738	500				2,500	1,000	500
St. Mary's College	‡ 5,520		500	3,300					
Schoolcraft College	‡ 1,445	1,620/690	500				2,000	800	800
Siena Heights College	9,630		500	4,100	530	580		530	580
Southwestern Michigan College	† 1,395	744/372	500				1,500	1,500	600
Spring Arbor College	10,106		400	3,850	530	680	2,090	530	680
Suomi College	9,500		500	3,700	700	800	1,800	1,125	600
University of Detroit Mercy	11,838		616	4,612	578	382	1,930	1,052	382
University of Michigan									
Ann Arbor	‡ 5,215	10,692/—	460	4,659	212	1,207		212	1,207
Dearborn	‡ 3,870	6,564/—	440				1,500	850	1,040
Flint	‡ 3,092	6,442/—	500					1,050	916
Walsh College of Accountancy and Business Administration	‡ 5,090							800	900
Washtenaw Community College	1,544	1,200/630	500				2,000	600	600
Wayne County Community College	1,730	1,050/480	400				2,575	915	495
Wayne State University	‡ 3,220	3,600/—	510		1,283	831	2,055	1,283	831
West Shore Community College	1,372	1,170/750	400				1,900	1,015	650
Western Michigan University	‡ 3,060	4,080/—	530	4,100	410	1,270	2,378	410	1,270
William Tyndale College	5,800		500		425	550		810	550
Yeshiva Beth Yehuda-Yeshiva Gedolah of Greater Detroit	† 3,500		500	3,000		500			200
Minnesota									
Alexandria Technical College	‡ 2,050	1,990/—	450				1,800	1,350	900
Anoka-Ramsey Community College	‡ 1,882	1,733/—	600		900	600	1,500	500	600
Augsburg College	12,704		540	4,591	100	850	1,500	100	850
Austin Community College	‡ 1,882	1,733/—	625		900	450	1,620	900	450
Bemidji State University	‡ 2,492	2,462/—	660	2,660	525	1,291	1,600	689	1,000
Bethany Lutheran College	8,163		450	3,432	150	900	2,142		900
Bethel College	12,260		500	4,460	800	1,500		3,250	1,500

†Figures are projected for 1995-96. ‡Figures are for 1994-95.

All aid		Need–based aid		Grants and scholarships								Financial aid deadlines		Inst aid form	Notes
				Need–based				Non–need–based							
Total freshmen	Percent receiving aid	Freshmen judged to have need	Percent offered aid	Acad	Music/ drama	Art	Athl	Acad	Music/ drama	Art	Athl	Priority	Closing		
													none		
195	62	40	100	X	X	X	X	X	X	X	X		2/21		
													none		
								X	X		X	8/1	none		
6,574	50	3,000	90	X	X	X	X	X	X	X	X	2/1	5/1		
1,028	65	440	90	X				X			X		3/1		
545	55	343	100	X				X				5/1	none		
914	43			X	X	X		X	X	X		6/1	none		
381	70			X				X	X			8/1	none		
								X	X	X	X		none		
4,648	60			X				X	X	X	X	5/1	none		
													none		
1,133	72	694	100	X	X	X	X	X				2/1	none		
1,090	34	380	92	X	X	X		X	X	X		4/1	none		
439	79	312	100	X			X	X			X	3/15	none		
				X				X			X	5/19	none		
1,295	35	420	98	X				X	X		X	4/1	none		
214	93	199	100	X	X			X	X			4/1	8/15		
33	88			X				X				4/1	6/1		
												2/15	none		
726	70	442	100					X	X	X	X	4/1	none		
1,979	45	241	100	X	X	X		X	X	X	X	6/1	none		
46	60	20	90	X				X					3/15		
1,344	25			X	X	X	X	X	X	X	X		none		
302	97	177	100					X	X	X		2/15	none		
1,527	55	1,200	100	X	X	X	X	X	X	X	X	6/1	none		
191	90							X	X	X	X	2/15	none		
228	94			X	X	X		X	X	X		5/1	none		
532	95			X				X			X	4/1	5/1		
4,892	40	2,300	96	X				X	X	X	X	2/1	9/29		
715	46			X				X			X	4/15	none		
512	31	250	100	X	X			X	X			4/15	none	X	
				X				X				8/1	none		
2,844	52							X		X		6/1	none		
													none		
1,720	45	743	88	X	X	X	X	X	X	X	X		5/1		
820	50	195	100	X				X	X			5/1	none		
2,793	68	1,877	100					X	X	X	X	3/1	none		
96	60			X	X			X	X			2/15	5/1		
													8/1		
1,006	85							X				5/1	none		
1,695	50			X				X	X			6/1	none	X	
287	91	222	100	X	X			X	X			4/15	none	X	
435	67							X	X			5/15	none		
582	82	346	100	X				X	X	X	X	8/15	none		
231	97	203	100					X	X	X	X	5/1	none		
481	90			X	X	X		X	X	X		4/15	none		

Institution	Tuition and fees	Add'l out-of-state/district tuition	Books and supplies	Costs for campus residents			Costs for students at home		
				Room and board	Trans-portation	Other costs	Board only	Trans-portation	Other costs
Carleton College	20,300		550	4,125	500	550			
Central Lakes College	‡ 1,882	1,733/—	510				1,500	720	1,230
College of Associated Arts	‡ 8,100		1,600				2,200	300	1,200
College of St. Benedict	13,089		500	4,370	100	600	1,000	600	500
College of St. Catherine: St. Catherine Campus	12,380		450	4,282	200	800	345	400	630
College of St. Catherine-Minneapolis	† 9,490		600		500	900	500	750	900
College of St. Scholastica	12,534		450	3,807	456	721	720	456	721
Concordia College: Moorhead	10,720		450	3,280	200	600	1,830	200	600
Concordia College: St. Paul	10,815		450	3,930	100	750	1,800	100	750
Crown College	‡ 8,075		500	3,700	700	700	2,000	600	700
Dunwoody Industrial Institute	‡ 4,151		90					1,170	2,340
Fergus Falls Community College	‡ 1,882	1,733/—	550				1,773	500	622
Gustavus Adolphus College	14,855		450	3,760	500	750	1,985		750
Hamline University	13,650		450	4,318		700			700
Hibbing Community College	‡ 1,882	1,733/—	600		900	900	900	900	900
Inver Hills Community College	‡ 1,882	1,733/—	500				2,000	550	590
Itasca Community College: Arrowhead Region	‡ 1,882	1,733/—	600		425	810	1,500	535	1,125
Lakewood Community College	‡ 1,882	1,733/—	600		1,500	1,805	1,500	970	650
Macalester College	16,686		550	4,975		700	2,390		700
Mankato State University	‡ 2,525	2,462/—	570	2,660	650	1,500	760	650	1,500
Martin Luther College	4,035		635	2,010	630	735	2,010	420	735
Mesabi Community College: Arrowhead Region	‡ 1,882	1,733/—	510				1,700	470	1,000
Metropolitan State University	‡ 2,180	2,462/—	600					960	2,100
Minneapolis College of Art and Design	† 13,852		1,200		300	500	1,500	300	500
Minneapolis Community College	‡ 1,882	1,733/—	525				900	1,800	1,350
Minnesota Bible College	4,839		375		300	1,150	1,200	300	1,150
Moorhead State University	‡ 2,381	2,462/—	600	2,660	600	1,734	850	600	1,734
National College	‡ 6,575		675				1,080		
National Education Center: Brown Institute Campus	10,943			4,473	648	1,330			
NEI College of Technology	‡ 4,785		700				2,500	1,430	2,000
Normandale Community College	‡ 1,882	1,733/—	600				1,700	1,000	500
North Central Bible College	6,370		638	3,450	500	1,190	1,095	500	1,190
North Hennepin Community College	† 2,007	1,618/—	600				1,618	1,000	400
Northland Community College	† 1,901	1,800/—	550				1,950	500	975
Northwest Technical Institute	8,425		300						
Northwestern College	11,985		430	3,600	660	1,225	1,500	883	500
Oak Hills Bible College	5,850		530	2,400		4,000	2,300		4,000
Pillsbury Baptist Bible College	† 4,300		935	3,060	808	1,722	2,835	808	1,155
Rainy River Community College	‡ 1,834	1,733/—	510	2,550	650	1,200	1,500	400	900
Rasmussen College-Minnetonka	6,625		750		900	1,575	1,275	1,200	1,575
Rochester Community College	‡ 1,834	1,733/—	500				2,000	750	950
St. Cloud State University	‡ 2,471	2,462/—	600	2,660	645	1,284	1,350	900	1,160
St. Cloud Technical College	‡ 1,908	1,836/—	850				1,800	500	500
St. John's University	13,089		500	4,224	100	600	2,230	100	600
St. Mary's College of Minnesota	11,280		400	3,770	110	710	1,675	110	710
St. Olaf College	15,000		550	3,850		550		300	550
St. Paul Technical College	‡ 1,778	1,733/—	700				4,300	450	900
Southwest State University	‡ 2,661	2,462/—	750	2,660	500	1,500	1,600	600	1,500

†Figures are projected for 1995-96. ‡Figures are for 1994-95.

Total freshmen	Percent receiving aid	Freshmen judged to have need	Percent offered aid	Acad	Music/drama	Art	Athl	Acad	Music/drama	Art	Athl	Priority	Closing	Inst aid form	Notes
All aid		*Need–based aid*		*Need–based*				*Non–need–based*				*Financial aid deadlines*			
527	82	312	100	X				X				2/15	3/15		
909	79	527	100	X	X	X	X	X	X	X	X	6/1	none		
33	80	19	100					X		X		5/1	none		
487	91	368	100	X				X	X	X		8/15		X	
221	92	183	100	X	X			X	X			4/1	none	X	
463	77			X				X				6/1	none		
264	94	350	100	X	X			X	X			3/15	none	X	
811	86	650	100					X	X			5/1	none	X	
150	96			X	X	X		X	X			4/15	none		
176	95							X	X			4/1	none		
				X				X				6/3	none		
703	85							X	X	X		6/1	none	X	
604	81	508	100	X	X			X	X			3/1	5/1	X	
354	78	283	100	X	X	X		X				3/15	none	X	
350	64			X	X		X	X				7/1	none		
4,341	40							X	X	X	X	5/1	none		
782	70	350	100	X				X				5/1	none		
1,691	40	850	100	X				X				6/15	none		
452	81	330	100	X				X				1/15	3/1		
1,545	65			X				X	X	X	X	3/15	none		
135	94	107	100	X	X			X	X			5/15	none		
229	82							X				4/22	none		
				X								5/1	8/1		
81	72	98	95			X		X		X		4/1	none	X	
				X				X				6/1	none		
28	83	25	100	X				X	X			6/1	none	X	
1,121	88	867	100	X				X	X	X	X	3/1	none	X	
								X				8/21	none		
													none		
96	68	45	100					X					none		
2,392	33			X				X				6/1	none		
								X	X	X		4/1	5/1		
1,957	26	625	100	X	X	X			X	X		8/15	none		
206	75			X	X	X	X	X	X	X	X	5/1	none		
													none		
331	87	299	100	X	X	X	X	X	X	X	X	3/1	8/1	X	
33	95			X				X				4/1	none	X	
55	68			X				X	X			3/1	none		
231	82			X	X	X	X	X	X	X	X	8/1	none		
		47	100					X				2/1	none	X	
1,312	50			X				X					none		
1,899	46	875	100	X	X	X	X	X	X	X	X		none	X	
1,234	70												none		
430	75	321	100	X	X	X		X	X	X		3/1	none		
384	87	308	100	X	X	X		X	X	X		3/15	none		
759	95	708	100	X				X	X			3/1	none		
													none		
597	82			X	X	X	X	X	X		X	4/15	none		

Institution	Tuition and fees	Add'l out-of-state/district tuition	Books and supplies	Costs for campus residents			Costs for students at home		
				Room and board	Trans-portation	Other costs	Board only	Trans-portation	Other costs
University of Minnesota									
Crookston	‡ 2,953	5,332/—	500	3,210	400	800	1,500	400	800
Duluth	‡ 3,301	5,835/—	693	3,474	663	1,401		663	1,401
Morris	‡ 3,806	6,818/—	465	3,291	500	1,200	1,200	350	1,200
Twin Cities	‡ 3,391	5,796/—	714	3,774	660	2,250	1,980	660	2,250
University of St. Thomas	13,106		500	4,374	510	950	1,750	510	950
Vermilion Community College	‡ 1,834	1,733/—	510	3,270	365	1,160	1,400	200	1,865
Willmar Community College	‡ 1,834	1,733/—	650				2,400	525	375
Willmar Technical College	† 1,986	1,911/—	470		900	900	1,800	1,800	900
Winona State University	‡ 2,367	2,462/—	400	2,660	300	600		300	600
Worthington Community College	‡ 1,834	1,733/—	500						
Mississippi									
Alcorn State University	‡ 2,389	2,142/—	650	2,159	950	1,035	955	1,800	1,035
Belhaven College	8,040		1,400	3,100	900	4,110		900	4,110
Blue Mountain College	4,090		500	2,170	300	1,500	1,390		
Coahoma Community College	‡ 910	1,900/—	500	2,037	200	200		200	200
Copiah-Lincoln Community College	‡ 1,000	1,200/—	500	1,680					
Delta State University	‡ 2,294	2,234/—	500	1,880	500	3,090	1,500	500	1,000
East Central Community College	1,000	1,200/—	500	1,830	640	800	1,000	960	800
East Mississippi Community College	† 1,000	1,000/—	500	1,960	800	400			
Hinds Community College	† 1,070	2,206/—	400	1,770	431	1,309	1,531	1,497	1,052
Holmes Community College	‡ 1,010	1,000/—	500	1,500	1,600			600	1,600
Itawamba Community College	900	850/—	600	1,740	400	800		600	800
Jackson State University	‡ 2,380	2,234/—	500	2,413	750	750	1,500	750	750
Jones County Junior College	792	1,260/—	310	1,782	200	325		180	300
Magnolia Bible College	† 2,860		400	1,390	500	4,990	1,000	750	2,200
Mary Holmes College	4,100		400	3,890	500	700	1,000	1,500	500
Meridian Community College	† 960	1,040/—	600	2,200				620	
Millsaps College	12,700		600	5,868	500	950	1,900	600	950
Mississippi College	‡ 5,888		700	2,830	700	1,500	1,500	1,500	1,500
Mississippi Delta Community College	‡ 790	1,100/90	400	2,000		400	1,410	320	240
Mississippi Gulf Coast Community College									
Jackson County Campus	‡ 860	900/—	150				1,600	1,100	
Jefferson Davis Campus	‡ 860	900/—	150				1,600	1,300	260
Perkinston	‡ 860	900/—	150	1,298			365		
Mississippi State University	† 2,561	2,460/—	480	3,084		1,579	2,018		1,579
Mississippi University for Women	‡ 2,244	2,142/—	600	2,467	500	1,200	1,500	500	1,200
Mississippi Valley State University	‡ 2,189	2,142/—	450	2,425	450	800	1,800	875	700
Northeast Mississippi Community College	950	1,100/—	600	1,800			1,100	600	600
Northwest Mississippi Community College	1,000	1,000/—	300	1,000		375			375
Pearl River Community College	‡ 910	1,000/—	200	1,648	300	1,085		550	1,085
Phillips Junior College of Jackson	‡ 4,475						660	1,040	1,612
Rust College	4,625		225	2,175	225	150	1,100	375	300
Southeastern Baptist College	‡ 2,220		300	1,800	200	350	500	300	350
Southwest Mississippi Community College	‡ 850	1,050/—	400	1,650		1,300	1,100	1,300	
Tougaloo College	† 5,680		500	2,400	300	800	1,500	300	500
University of Mississippi									
Medical Center	‡ 2,106	1,959/—	660		450	4,950		900	2,250
University	‡ 2,546	2,460/—	500	3,810	550	1,304	1,900	950	1,119
University of Southern Mississippi	‡ 2,429	2,460/—	750	2,385	250	1,380	800	970	1,380
Wesley College	2,200		400	2,200	300	650		500	1,150

†Figures are projected for 1995-96. ‡Figures are for 1994-95.

Total freshmen	Percent receiving aid	Freshmen judged to have need	Percent offered aid	Need-based Acad	Need-based Music/drama	Need-based Art	Need-based Athl	Non-need Acad	Non-need Music/drama	Non-need Art	Non-need Athl	Priority	Closing	Inst aid form	Notes
385	85							X			X	4/30	none		
1,603	80	1,278	100	X	X	X	X	X	X	X	X	3/31	none		
532	83	353	100	X	X			X	X			4/1	none		
3,645	55	2,025	95	X	X	X	X	X	X	X	X	2/15	none		
769	95	540	100	X				X	X			4/1	none		
434	93			X				X				4/30	none	X	
343	84			X				X	X	X		4/23	5/1		
875	80			X								5/1	none	X	
1,200	72	720	100	X	X	X	X	X	X	X	X	4/1	none		
642	65	285	100	X	X	X		X	X	X		6/1	none		
615	92	578	100	X	X		X	X	X		X	4/1	none	X	
143	91	89	100	X	X	X	X	X	X	X	X	4/1	none		
48	70			X	X		X	X	X		X	5/1	none		
													none	X	
520	80			X				X	X	X	X	4/1	none		
507	67						X	X	X	X	X	6/1	none	X	
660	80	396	100					X	X	X	X	5/1	none		
2,954	40							X	X	X	X	4/1	none		
1,387	85			X	X	X	X	X	X	X	X		none		
				X	X	X	X	X	X	X	X		none		
													5/1		
													none	X	
5	88	1	100	X				X				8/1	none		
157	95			X	X		X					6/1	none		
1,682	45							X	X	X	X		none		
336	68			X	X	X		X	X	X		3/1	none		
282	75	177	100	X	X	X	X	X	X	X	X	4/1	none	X	
								X	X	X	X		none		
2,446	50			X	X			X	X			6/1	none		
1,981	70	992	100	X				X	X		X	6/1	9/1		
								X	X	X	X	6/1	none	X	
1,507	84			X	X		X	X	X		X	4/1	none		
362	88							X	X	X	X	6/1	none		
519	95	355	100	X	X		X	X	X		X	4/1	none		
														X	
3,000	75			X	X		X						3/1		
1,666	70	944	100	X				X	X		X	5/1	none		
													none		
241	94	232	97	X	X	X	X	X	X			5/1	none	X	
7	33	3	100	X	X							7/1	none		
742	45											8/5	none		
235	92			X	X		X	X	X		X	4/15	none		
				X				X				4/1	none		
1,595	56			X				X	X	X	X	4/1	none		
1,123	69	757	95	X				X	X	X	X	3/15	none	X	
10	26			X	X			X	X				5/15		

Institution	Tuition and fees	Add'l out-of-state/district tuition	Books and supplies	Costs for campus residents			Costs for students at home		
				Room and board	Trans-portation	Other costs	Board only	Trans-portation	Other costs
William Carey College	5,340		900	2,500	1,500	1,440	1,463	1,500	1,440
Wood College	3,050		400	2,560	100	1,000		1,100	1,000
Missouri									
Avila College	9,600		650	3,950	600	1,600		1,200	1,450
Baptist Bible College	2,602		300	2,812	450	1,300	1,000	500	1,300
Berean College	2,095		500						
Calvary Bible College	3,924		400	2,950		350	1,550	374	800
Central Bible College	4,200		550	2,930	850	1,000	1,300	850	2,000
Central Christian College of the Bible	3,750		350	2,386	400	1,300	1,330	150	2,600
Central Methodist College	9,430		650	3,600	400	1,800	1,570	400	1,300
Central Missouri State University	‡ 2,310	2,310/—	300	3,348	500	1,750	650	750	1,000
College of the Ozarks	100		500	1,900		1,200	2,400	800	1,200
Columbia College	8,546		800	3,830	500	900		500	900
Conception Seminary College	6,704		400	3,174	550	800	1,750	550	800
Cottey College	6,500		500	3,400	1,000	800			1,500
Crowder College	‡ 1,140	1,110/420	500	2,500	900	1,000	960	900	1,000
Culver-Stockton College	‡ 8,000		400	3,700	500	1,200	1,500	500	1,200
Deaconess College of Nursing	6,934		866	3,500	300	300	1,600	400	300
DeVry Institute of Technology: Kansas City	6,335		525						
Drury College	9,250		450	3,600	300	250	2,000	300	250
East Central College	‡ 1,310	1,230/476	600				1,865	1,312	500
Evangel College	7,300		500	3,240	800	1,500	1,700	800	500
Fontbonne College	‡ 8,540		615	4,180	380	1,100	1,795	1,350	1,100
Hannibal-LaGrange College	6,688		500	2,610		1,300		300	1,300
Harris Stowe State College	† 2,070	2,010/—	750				2,600	1,000	1,600
Jefferson College	‡ 1,110	720/360	460				1,800	800	1,070
Kansas City Art Institute	14,785		1,600	4,340	980	800	3,740	980	800
Kemper Military School and College	9,500		1,800	3,200	900	1,080			
Lincoln University	† 3,812	3,792/—	480	2,728	926	1,496	2,057	1,466	1,496
Lindenwood College	9,700		1,050	4,800	1,250	2,975	1,500	2,050	3,575
Longview Community College	1,350	1,860/900	550				1,627	1,639	1,306
Maple Woods Community College	1,410	1,860/900	550				1,627	1,627	1,972
Maryville University of St. Louis	‡ 9,250		500	4,550	685	850	2,125	1,890	850
Mineral Area College	‡ 1,050	510/450	550					1,460	1,900
Missouri Baptist College	7,670		600	3,600	275	1,500	1,800	1,500	1,500
Missouri Southern State College	‡ 2,160	1,920/—	400	2,856	460	900	1,500	600	600
Missouri Valley College	9,500		1,000	5,000	1,500	3,030	9,480		
Missouri Western State College	‡ 2,206	2,374/—	350	2,444	600	1,500	1,600	500	1,500
Moberly Area Community College	1,030	2,250/750	600	1,200	980	1,500		2,200	1,500
National College	7,730		600					500	
North Central Missouri College	‡ 1,141	541/—	460	2,170	890	976	1,500	1,000	976
Northeast Missouri State University	‡ 2,704	2,152/—	450	3,416	730	1,700		730	2,500
Northwest Missouri State University	2,280	1,695/—	250	3,330	700	1,200	1,290	700	1,200
Ozark Christian College	3,620		450	2,980	250			100	
Park College	† 3,990		800	4,100	400	2,300	1,800	350	1,200
Penn Valley Community College	1,410	1,860/900	550				1,627	1,627	1,972
Phillips Junior College	3,686		305				1,700	2,025	1,260
Ranken Technical College	5,175		1,700						
Research College of Nursing	‡ 10,050		700	4,532	800	890	2,600	1,210	890
Rockhurst College	10,520		525	4,200	600	1,373	1,800	1,000	1,500

†Figures are projected for 1995-96. ‡Figures are for 1994-95.

Total freshmen	Percent receiving aid	Freshmen judged to have need	Percent offered aid	Acad	Music/drama	Art	Athl	Acad	Music/drama	Art	Athl	Priority	Closing	Inst aid form	Notes
174	70			X				X	X		X		4/1		
													none		
116	97	84	100					X	X	X	X	7/1	none	X	
								X					5/1		
													none		
				X				X					7/15		
216	68	132	100	X				X	X			5/1	none		
57	82			X	X			X	X				4/1		
210	95			X	X		X	X	X		X	4/1	none		
1,489	55	899	90				X	X	X	X	X	3/1	none		
310	100	310	100	X	X	X	X	X	X	X	X	4/1	none		
120	59							X	X	X	X	3/15	8/22	X	
								X	X	X		5/1	none		
246	60							X	X	X	X	8/1	none		
278	96	224	100	X				X	X	X	X	3/15	none		
								X					none		
307	83	280	99	X	X	X	X	X	X	X	X	4/1	6/15	X	
441	50			X	X	X	X	X	X	X	X	7/1	none		
394	79	310	98					X	X	X	X	4/1	none		
113	92	105	99	X	X	X		X	X	X		4/1			
													none		
155	51	80	100	X	X		X	X	X		X	4/3	none	X	
2,044	37							X	X	X	X		none		
136	78										X	2/15	8/25		
													none		
								X	X	X	X	3/1	none		
407	90	305	100	X	X	X	X	X	X	X	X	4/30	none		
1,672	17							X	X	X	X	5/31	none		
													none		
180	89	95	100	X		X		X				2/1	none		
968	50			X	X	X	X	X	X	X	X	4/15	none		
148	82							X	X		X	4/1	none	X	
2,018	72	589	100					X	X	X	X	2/15	none		
406	75	305	100	X	X	X	X	X	X	X	X	4/15	9/1		
				X	X	X	X	X	X		X	4/1	none		
				X				X	X		X		6/30		
													none		
							X	X			X	8/1	none		
1,545	90	756	100	X	X	X	X	X	X	X	X	4/1	none		
1,312	79	953	100	X				X	X	X	X	4/1	none		
152	68			X	X			X	X			5/1	none		
154	60	74	100					X	X	X	X	4/1	8/1	X	
													none		
													none		
				X				X					none		
				X				X				3/15	none		
373	87			X				X			X	4/1	none		

Institution	Tuition and fees	Add'l out-of-state/district tuition	Books and supplies	Costs for campus residents			Costs for students at home		
				Room and board	Trans-portation	Other costs	Board only	Trans-portation	Other costs
St. Charles County Community College	1,247	1,620/600	600					900	500
St. Louis Christian College	‡ 4,086		350	3,730	400	600	1,500	405	1,200
St. Louis College of Pharmacy	‡ 9,845		350	4,350	400	1,400		1,100	2,100
St. Louis Community College									
Florissant Valley	‡ 1,200	630/300	600				1,200	700	1,500
Forest Park	‡ 1,260	660/330	500				1,200	770	1,440
Meramec	‡ 1,200	600/300	500				1,300	750	1,600
St. Louis University	12,800		800	4,900	2,500	4,550	4,160	2,500	4,550
Southeast Missouri State University	‡ 2,670	2,130/—	350	3,320	700	1,650		1,700	1,650
Southwest Baptist University	7,526		500	2,500		600			
Southwest Missouri State University	2,756	2,550/—	500	2,770	790	2,000	1,710	790	2,000
State Fair Community College	‡ 1,050	2,160/600	900				2,250	1,800	750
Stephens College	14,400		450	5,370	700	1,450	2,400	700	1,450
Three Rivers Community College	‡ 1,085	1,230/390	300				1,300	1,200	900
University of Missouri									
Columbia	‡ 3,444	6,030/—	650	3,327		1,900	2,120		1,900
Kansas City	‡ 3,475	6,030/—	610	3,690	760	1,780	1,500	2,160	1,780
Rolla	‡ 3,580	6,027/—	750	3,600		1,491			1,491
St. Louis	‡ 3,408	6,030/—	500	3,676	515	855	1,000	930	859
Washington University	19,291		766	5,961	500	1,552		1,264	3,254
Webster University	‡ 9,160		800	4,340	1,500	1,500	2,500	500	1,500
Wentworth Military Academy	11,250		700	3,125	1,350	1,800	600	1,350	900
Westminster College	† 12,080		630	4,225	350	1,300		350	1,300
William Jewell College	10,580		500	2,970	800	1,800	1,650	900	1,800
William Woods University	‡ 10,675		600	4,365	1,000	2,700		700	3,120
Montana									
Blackfeet Community College	1,523		600	4,950			900	1,200	1,200
Carroll College	9,789		390	3,915	350	700	1,500	350	700
College of Great Falls	6,560		600	4,500	750	900	850	750	900
Dawson Community College	1,344	2,653/602	550		1,049	1,048	1,500	1,049	1,048
Dull Knife Memorial College	1,134		600	4,150	455	656	3,950	455	656
Flathead Valley Community College	1,260	2,328/552	500		900	900	1,170	900	600
Fort Belknap College	† 1,890		450				4,680	1,539	1,431
Fort Peck Community College	1,230		440	3,000					700
Helena College of Technology of the University of Montana	‡ 1,700	1,857/—	400					1,260	
Little Big Horn College	1,650		420					1,092	468
Miles Community College	1,288	2,604/658	600	2,500	600	650	1,000	600	650
Montana State University									
Billings College of Technology	† 1,792	1,792/—	500		600		1,800	600	
College of Technology-Great Falls	1,402	1,692/—	1,200						
Billings	‡ 2,142	3,724/—	600	3,146	480	1,200	1,246	480	1,200
Bozeman	‡ 2,224	4,060/—	600	3,710	525	1,825	1,700	525	1,825
Northern	‡ 2,105	3,724/—	473	3,570	532	465	662	532	465
Montana Tech of The University of Montana	‡ 2,013	4,060/—	550	3,360	800	1,400	1,000	500	
Montana Tech of the University of Montana: Division of Technology	‡ 1,516	1,624/—	550				1,500	1,500	1,000
Rocky Mountain College	9,715		600	3,758		630	1,966	300	630
Salish Kootenai College	1,883	4,284/504	600				1,350	550	
Stone Child College	1,640	450/—	400						
University of Montana-Missoula	‡ 2,251	4,060/—	550	3,957		2,500	1,850		2,200

†Figures are projected for 1995-96. ‡Figures are for 1994-95.

All aid		Need–based aid		Grants and scholarships								Financial aid deadlines		Inst aid form	Notes
Total freshmen	Percent receiving aid	Freshmen judged to have need	Percent offered aid	Need–based				Non–need–based				Priority	Closing		
				Acad	Music/drama	Art	Athl	Acad	Music/drama	Art	Athl				
919	20							X	X			4/15	none		
41	85			X	X			X	X			7/1	none		
143	76			X				X				5/31	none		
1,468	18							X	X	X	X	8/1	none		
		1,758	20					X	X	X	X		5/1		
2,556	25			X	X	X	X	X	X	X	X	5/1	none		
1,088	89	857	100	X	X	X	X	X	X	X	X	1/1	none		
1,217	45			X	X	X	X	X	X	X	X	3/1	none		
1,122	90							X	X		X	4/30	none		
2,875	50			X	X	X	X	X	X	X	X	3/31	none		
470	63			X				X	X	X	X	7/1	none		
185	65	117	100	X	X	X		X	X			1/15	none		
1,468	75			X	X	X	X	X	X	X	X	6/1	none		
3,635	71							X	X	X	X	3/1	none		
528	40			X	X	X		X	X	X	X	3/15	none		
822	62							X	X		X	3/1	none		
669	31	270	100	X				X			X	4/1	10/3		
1,257	58	575	99	X		X		X		X			2/15		
203	83	161	100	X	X	X		X	X	X		4/1	none		
		56	100	X				X				4/30	6/30		
167	87	102	100					X	X	X		3/31	none		
319	96	210	100					X	X	X	X	3/15	none	X	
195	83			X		X	X					4/30	6/1		
														X	
292	88	296	100	X				X	X		X	3/1	none		
35	95			X				X				4/1	none		
194	72	131	100					X	X	X	X	3/1	none		
													none		
													none	X	
													none		
													none	X	
215	75			X				X				4/1	none		
													none		
138	92			X	X		X	X	X		X	3/1	none		
													none		
													none		
637	63							X	X	X	X	3/1	none		
1,791	83	920	100	X				X	X	X	X	3/1	none		
				X	X		X	X	X		X		none		
643	60	235	100					X			X	4/1	none		
121	65	100	100	X				X				4/1	none		
		120	100					X	X	X	X	4/1	none		
													none		
				X				X				3/27	none		
1,677	60	982	100	X	X	X	X	X	X	X	X	3/1	none	X	

Institution	Tuition and fees	Add'l out-of-state/district tuition	Books and supplies	Costs for campus residents			Costs for students at home		
				Room and board	Trans-portation	Other costs	Board only	Trans-portation	Other costs
University of Montana College of Technology	‡ 2,200	1,200/—	500						
Western Montana College of the University of Montana	‡ 1,938	3,724/—	550	3,618	1,100	1,100			1,800
Nebraska									
Bellevue University	‡ 3,280		500				5,400	900	1,800
Central Community College	1,140	570/—	450	2,080	600	700	1,350	750	750
Chadron State College	1,759	1,200/—	600	2,814	500	450	750	250	352
Clarkson College	7,504		435		1,104	1,349	3,314	1,568	113
College of St. Mary	10,820		400	3,800	923	2,235	1,062	1,845	2,464
Concordia College	9,480		500	3,470	900	1,200	1,900	900	1,200
Creighton University	11,562		650	4,548	525	1,530	1,500	950	1,530
Dana College	‡ 9,580		450	3,322	300	1,000		300	1,000
Doane College	‡ 9,820		450	3,000	400	1,000	975	300	500
Grace University	5,350		400	2,850	600	1,700		1,100	1,700
Hastings College	10,164		650	3,472	400	1,364		400	1,364
Lincoln School of Commerce	5,500		450		450	800	1,450	450	800
McCook Community College	‡ 960	135/—	500	2,680	610	550	560	610	550
Metropolitan Community College	† 1,080	1,080/—	450				1,500	353	270
Mid Plains Community College	‡ 1,170	162/—	450		500	500	1,500	500	
Midland Lutheran College	10,990		400	3,060	400	900	1,000	400	900
Nebraska Christian College	† 3,620		310	2,570	390	1,665	1,390	380	1,665
Nebraska College of Technical Agriculture	1,678	1,548/—	500	2,800	500	1,100	680	1,000	1,100
Nebraska Indian Community College	‡ 2,020		400				1,860	710	800
Nebraska Methodist College of Nursing and Allied Health	7,320		550		531	949	1,594	1,063	949
Nebraska Wesleyan University	10,316		500	3,420		1,800		300	1,800
Northeast Community College	‡ 1,092	150/—	500		450	700	1,260	250	600
Peru State College	‡ 1,696	1,200/—	600	2,734	630	1,000	1,500	630	1,000
Southeast Community College									
Beatrice Campus	† 1,118	225/—	450		500	500		750	500
Lincoln Campus	‡ 1,094	225/—	900		700	1,200	1,500	700	1,200
Milford Campus	‡ 1,094	225/—	600	1,866	450	900	1,125	1,125	900
Union College	9,198		550	2,900				900	900
University of Nebraska									
Medical Center	† 2,600	3,600/—	550				1,650	500	1,500
Kearney	‡ 1,914	1,455/—	500	2,630	436	1,400	1,800	436	1,400
Lincoln	‡ 2,415	3,540/—	535	3,185		2,165	1,830		1,975
Omaha	‡ 2,057	3,195/—	600				1,090	600	650
Wayne State College	‡ 1,764	1,200/—	600	2,660	250	2,500	480	2,000	1,000
Western Nebraska Community College:									
Scottsbluff Campus	1,140	90/—	480	2,440	400	660	1,700	400	500
York College	5,350		600	2,785	800	1,600	1,575	350	
Nevada									
Community College of Southern Nevada	1,020	3,100/—	600				4,672	1,500	2,480
Morrison College: Reno	† 5,795		690						1,804
Northern Nevada Community College	† 1,020	3,100/—	500				1,350	960	1,195
Sierra Nevada College	† 8,850		500		500	2,820	2,000	500	820
Truckee Meadows Community College	1,020	3,100/—	440				1,575	525	470

†Figures are projected for 1995-96. ‡Figures are for 1994-95.

Total freshmen	Percent receiving aid	Freshmen judged to have need	Percent offered aid	Acad	Music/drama	Art	Athl	Acad	Music/drama	Art	Athl	Priority	Closing	Inst aid form	Notes
													none		
455	70			X		X	X	X	X	X	X	3/1	5/1		
110	61			X			X	X			X	4/15	none		
515	58			X	X	X	X	X	X	X	X	7/1	none		
42	75							X				4/1	none		
125	99	73	100	X	X	X	X	X	X	X	X	5/1	none		
110	99							X	X	X	X	5/1	8/15	X	
824	82	430	100	X				X			X	4/1	none		
177	93	142	100		X	X	X	X				4/1	none		
239	99	204	100	X				X	X	X	X	3/15	none	X	
128	71			X	X			X	X			3/15	none		
258	96	202	100					X	X	X	X	5/1	8/15		
255	95			X				X					none		
745	69	197	100	X	X	X	X	X	X	X	X	4/1	none		
2,231	31			X				X				3/30	none	X	
480	67			X				X	X	X	X	4/15	none		
295	93			X	X	X	X	X	X	X	X	5/1	none	X	
57	97			X				X				6/1	none		
				X				X				4/1	none		
45	90			X				X				7/15	none		
35	82	27	100					X				5/1	none	X	
337	92	228	100					X	X	X		11/1	none		
639	74			X	X	X	X	X	X	X	X		4/15	X	
272	81			X	X	X	X	X	X	X	X	3/1	none		
295	58	182	97	X	X	X	X	X	X	X	X	4/1	none		
1,125	50			X				X					none	X	
153	60			X				X				4/1	none		
128	71			X	X			X	X				5/1		
				X				X				5/1	none		
1,262	76							X	X	X	X	3/1	none		
3,357	54	2,189	100	X	X		X	X	X		X	3/1	5/6		
1,153	55			X	X	X	X	X	X	X	X	3/1	none		
748	80	477	95	X				X	X	X	X	5/1	none		
692	75	587	86	X	X		X	X	X	X	X	4/1	none		
168	92							X	X	X	X	8/1	none		
2,081	13			X								4/15	5/1		
30	81	52	100	X				X				5/1		
531	5			X		X		X				6/1		
				X				X	X	X	X		none		
5,455	18			X								4/10	none		

Institution	Tuition and fees	Add'l out-of-state/ district tuition	Books and supplies	Costs for campus residents			Costs for students at home		
				Room and board	Trans-portation	Other costs	Board only	Trans-portation	Other costs
University of Nevada									
Las Vegas	1,830	4,900/—	700	5,206	400	1,000	1,000	700	1,000
Reno	1,830	4,900/—	600	5,154	1,072	2,124		1,072	592
Western Nevada Community College	1,020	3,100/—	450				900	680	1,230
New Hampshire									
Castle College	‡ 4,850		500				1,935	1,160	1,540
Colby-Sawyer College	14,720		600	5,640	100	1,000	1,500	900	500
College for Lifelong Learning	‡ 3,690	300/—	650						
Daniel Webster College	13,152		500	5,262	450	500	1,500	450	500
Dartmouth College	20,910		1,590	6,129					
Franklin Pierce College	14,430		500	4,900	600	1,000		600	1,000
Hesser College	† 7,400		500	3,800	500	1,000	900	500	800
Keene State College	‡ 3,454	5,280/—	500	4,157	350	800	1,500	600	525
McIntosh College	† 3,755		440	3,750					
New England College	14,226		400	5,620	450	1,050		400	1,000
New Hampshire College	11,622		500	4,884	300	900	1,980	700	900
New Hampshire Technical College									
Berlin	‡ 2,344	3,112/—	450				1,575	1,000	1,800
Claremont	‡ 2,356	3,112/—	550				1,800	1,600	1,100
Laconia	‡ 2,344	3,112/—	500				1,000	1,400	800
Manchester	‡ 2,344	3,112/—	500				1,700	1,000	1,770
Nashua	‡ 2,368	3,112/—	500				1,100	1,000	500
Stratham	2,368	3,112/—	600				2,680	1,500	1,000
New Hampshire Technical Institute	‡ 2,392	3,112/—	400	3,699	750	1,600	1,500	1,500	1,600
Notre Dame College	‡ 9,990		650	4,900	375	925	1,500	950	925
Plymouth State College of the University System of New Hampshire	‡ 3,381	5,280/—	600	4,024	254	894	1,500	1,000	700
Rivier College	11,010		600	5,250	200	900	3,465	900	900
St. Anselm College	14,120		550	5,550	200	1,000	1,500	1,400	1,000
Thomas More College of Liberal Arts	7,635		400	5,635	1,500		500		
University of New Hampshire									
Durham	‡ 4,559	8,320/—	500	4,038	300	1,100	1,200	600	1,100
Manchester	‡ 3,240	6,470/—	500				1,700	1,000	1,000
White Pines College	7,950		600	4,000					
New Jersey									
Assumption College for Sisters	1,200		400	1,100					
Atlantic Community College	1,501	3,149/1,267	550				1,550	1,425	370
Bergen Community College	‡ 1,588	4,148/1,490	850						
Berkeley College of Business	10,425		744		1,335	1,044	1,530	1,335	1,044
Beth Medrash Govoha	‡ 2,900		450	4,075					
Bloomfield College	8,850		500	4,500	300	1,440	2,772	1,095	1,275
Brookdale Community College	† 2,277	3,960/1,980	550				1,500	1,248	941
Burlington County College	‡ 1,415	2,200/340	750				1,500	900	1,400
Caldwell College	† 9,560		425	4,900	500	1,000	2,400	1,200	1,000
Camden County College	‡ 1,542	—/196	500				1,050	525	825
Centenary College	12,094		500	5,500	300	600	2,500	1,500	600
College of St. Elizabeth	‡ 11,450		380	5,250	350	650	1,700	850	650
County College of Morris	‡ 2,110	3,205/1,835	500				2,000	1,000	900
Cumberland County College	‡ 1,694	4,422/1,474	450				1,500	727	1,429
DeVry Technical Institute	6,280		550				2,348	1,564	2,045
Drew University	19,638		520	5,833	230	370	1,500	600	500
Essex County College	2,131	3,705/1,862	600				1,500	900	1,061

†Figures are projected for 1995-96. ‡Figures are for 1994-95.

All aid		Need–based aid		Grants and scholarships								Financial aid deadlines		Inst aid form	Notes
Total fresh-men	Percent receiving aid	Freshmen judged to have need	Percent offered aid	Need–based				Non–need–based				Priority	Closing		
				Acad	Music/drama	Art	Athl	Acad	Music/drama	Art	Athl				
1,520	48	1,180	67	X	X	X	X	X	X	X	X	2/15	none		
1,212	65	366	89					X	X		X	4/15	none	X	
				X				X				6/1	none		
147	84	187	100					X				3/31	none	X	
218	62	123	100					X	X	X		3/1		X	
													none		
153	87			X				X				3/15	none		
1,086	47	508	100									2/1			
385	79			X			X	X			X	3/15	none		
430	70			X			X	X			X	3/1	none	X	
								X	X	X	X	3/1	none		
				X				X				7/1	none		
212	65			X	X	X		X				3/1	none	X	
287	73			X			X	X			X	3/15	none		
													none		
88	76			X				X				5/1	none		
548	83			X				X				5/1	none		
1,283	75	233	100	X								5/1	none		
				X								5/1	none		
													none		
				X				X				5/1	none		
135	90	105	100	X				X			X	3/15	none		
884	76	665	100					X	X			3/1	none		
153	80	191	100	X				X				4/1	none	X	
476	73			X			X	X			X	3/1	4/15		
2,478	72	1,567	95	X			X	X	X	X	X	3/1	none		
111	25	27	93	X				X				5/1	none		
35	50			X				X				3/15	5/1		
													none		
												5/1	none		
				X				X			X	5/15	none		
748	85			X				X					none		
352	90	228	100	X			X	X			X	6/1	none		
3,761	43	580	51	X				X			X	6/1	none		
1,235	50			X			X	X			X		none		
207	55	136	100	X		X	X	X		X	X	4/15	7/15		
3,305	20			X				X				7/1	12/2	X	
70	80	64	100	X				X				5/1	none	X	
114	90	72	100	X				X		X		4/1	none		
2,223	25	1,000	80	X	X	X		X			X	3/15	none		
												6/1	none		
								X					none		
318	82	198	99	X				X				3/1	none		
													none		

155

Institution	Tuition and fees	Add'l out-of-state/ district tuition	Books and supplies	Costs for campus residents			Costs for students at home		
				Room and board	Trans-portation	Other costs	Board only	Trans-portation	Other costs
Fairleigh Dickinson University									
Edward Williams College	11,480		623	5,550	588	1,396		1,944	4,326
Teaneck	12,254		623	5,550	588	1,396		1,944	4,326
Felician College	8,900		500					500	
Georgian Court College	10,075		500	4,150	800	800	1,900	1,600	800
Gloucester County College	‡ 1,680	4,500/30	600					1,000	800
Hudson County Community College	2,053	3,510/1,770	681					857	941
Jersey City State College	† 3,162	1,290/—	427	5,000	400	1,400	1,600	1,045	1,040
Katharine Gibbs School	7,545		500						
Kean College of New Jersey	† 3,089	1,200/—	500	4,250	650	800	1,000	875	800
Mercer County Community College	1,890	3,165/1,215	880				1,500	1,120	970
Middlesex County College	1,800	—/1,800	405					657	2,954
Monmouth College	13,140		540	5,770	390	1,410	2,470	690	1,410
Montclair State University	2,969	1,230/—	700	5,010	498	950	1,500	1,372	950
New Jersey Institute of Technology	‡ 4,980	4,344/—	700	5,376	450	1,000	2,000	850	1,000
Ocean County College	1,762	1,532/315	500				1,400	1,450	900
Passaic County Community College	‡ 2,055	1,785/—	735				2,250	850	945
Princeton University	20,960		700	6,116	395	1,624			
Rabbinical College of America	7,000			6,500					
Ramapo College of New Jersey	‡ 3,353	1,290/—	600	5,184	800	855	1,700	1,800	602
Raritan Valley Community College	1,721	4,488/1,496	750				1,500	1,080	1,000
Richard Stockton College of New Jersey	3,152	816/—	725	4,456	800	1,125	1,500	1,050	1,025
Rider University	14,135		700	5,630		1,200			1,200
Rowan College of New Jersey	† 3,095	2,014/—	600	5,109	230	1,000	1,500	800	1,000
Rutgers, The State University of New Jersey									
Camden College of Arts and Sciences	† 4,861	3,921/—	650	4,936					
College of Engineering	† 5,244	4,348/—	650	4,936					
College of Nursing	† 4,627	3,921/—	650	4,936					
College of Pharmacy	† 5,244	4,348/—	650	4,936					
Cook College	† 5,231	4,348/—	650	4,936					
Douglass College	† 4,798	3,921/—	650	4,936					
Livingston College	† 4,862	3,921/—	650	4,936					
Mason Gross School of the Arts	† 4,828	3,921/—	650	4,936					
Newark College of Arts and Sciences	† 4,644	3,921/—	650	4,936					
Rutgers College	† 4,836	3,921/—	650	4,936					
St. Peter's College	11,035		600	5,605	500	600	1,500	650	600
Salem Community College	2,176	—/213	700					1,100	700
Seton Hall University	12,250		650	6,710	630	1,200	2,270	1,020	1,330
Stevens Institute of Technology	18,088		500	6,156	180	570		1,500	570
Sussex County Community College	2,199	3,930/1,965	650				1,500		966
Talmudical Academy of New Jersey									
Trenton State College	† 4,168	2,420/—	700	5,600	100	1,000	1,600	900	600
Union County College	2,180	5,670/1,890	585				1,980	962	2,573
University of Medicine and Dentistry of New Jersey: School of Nursing	‡ 2,500	650/—							
Warren County Community College	2,094	5,670/3,780	500				1,080	864	900
Westminster Choir College of Rider University	‡ 13,580		500	5,420	150	700	2,280	1,000	700
William Paterson College of New Jersey	‡ 3,000	952/—	500	4,650	1,000	1,500	2,000	1,000	1,500

†Figures are projected for 1995-96. ‡Figures are for 1994-95.

Total freshmen	Percent receiving aid	Freshmen judged to have need	Percent offered aid	Need-based Acad	Music/drama	Art	Athl	Non-need-based Acad	Music/drama	Art	Athl	Priority	Closing	Inst aid form	Notes
316	73	198	100	X	X	X	X	X				3/1	none		
477	78			X	X	X	X	X			X	3/1	none		
107	60	55	100	X				X				6/1	none		
186	76			X	X	X	X	X	X	X	X	3/1	10/1	X	
				X				X				5/1	none		
1,151	50							X				4/1	none		
772	48	389	93	X				X	X			4/15	none		
													none		
1,001	55	982	62	X				X				3/15	none		
1,289	23			X	X	X	X	X	X		X	5/1	none		
													none		
765	88	476	100	X				X			X	3/1	none		
876	65	622	100					X				3/1	none		
550	78	327	100	X				X				3/15	none		
													none		
963	67	815	93	X				X				8/1	none		
1,158	70	507	100										2/1	X	
													none		
365	56	177	94	X				X				3/15	5/1		
													none		
778	67	385	100	X				X	X	X		3/1	none		
630	70	652	100	X			X	X	X		X	3/1	none		
824	70			X	X	X		X	X	X		5/1			
252	56	229	98	X	X			X				3/15	none	X	
510	59	335	99	X	X		X	X			X	3/15	none	X	
55	78	44	98	X	X		X	X				3/15	none	X	
198	62	110	98	X	X		X	X			X	3/15	none	X	
581	62	328	98	X	X		X	X			X	3/15	none	X	
582	67	364	99	X	X		X	X	X		X	3/15	none	X	
501	50	431	97	X	X		X	X	X		X	3/15	none	X	
97	65	56	100	X	X		X	X	X	X	X	3/15	none	X	
459	43	543	91	X	X		X	X			X	3/15	none	X	
1,871	67	1,095	97	X	X		X	X	X		X	3/15	none		
510	70							X			X	4/1	none		
				X				X			X		9/1		
938	74	780	97	X				X			X	4/1	none		
367	70	283	100	X				X				2/1	none		
851	40							X				3/1	8/1		
													none		
1,061	65	593	100	X				X	X			5/1			
1,338	17	669	91	X		X		X		X	X	3/15	none		
												3/1	none		
479	8	55	75	X				X				11/1	none		
70	87			X	X			X	X			3/1	none		
939	49			X	X			X	X			4/1	none		

Institution	Tuition and fees	Add'l out-of-state/district tuition	Books and supplies	Costs for campus residents			Costs for students at home		
				Room and board	Transportation	Other costs	Board only	Transportation	Other costs
New Mexico									
Albuquerque Technical-Vocational Institute	1,014	1,701/—	497				2,023	1,208	1,691
Clovis Community College	870	1,260/30	600					700	1,200
College of Santa Fe	11,796		500	4,300	200	1,200	1,800	200	1,200
College of the Southwest	4,100		500	2,480	1,000	600	1,760	1,380	600
Dona Ana Branch Community College of New Mexico State University	864	1,104/150	300				1,560		
Eastern New Mexico University									
Portales	‡ 1,518	4,068/—	500	2,600	1,000	1,200		1,000	1,200
Roswell Campus	654	1,212/24	580	2,700	1,300	600		1,300	950
Institute of American Indian Arts	† 7,410		1,700	3,166	500	1,144	1,800	1,400	1,144
National College	† 7,025		600					2,184	
New Mexico Highlands University	† 1,568	4,375/—	600	4,351	1,133	824	2,000	2,060	824
New Mexico Institute of Mining and Technology	‡ 1,858	4,074/—	600	3,440	500	1,100	2,600	250	1,100
New Mexico Junior College	† 506	384/264	700	3,200	720	1,575	1,500	1,060	1,575
New Mexico Military Institute	1,532	1,751/—	700	2,550	500	1,000			
New Mexico State University									
Alamogordo	900	1,530/150	325						
Carlsbad	‡ 744	1,224/120	600					1,054	1,168
Grants	624	1,224/120	400				1,214	754	
Las Cruces	2,088	4,710/—	550	3,210					
Northern New Mexico Community College	638	900/—	475	2,768	1,200	1,300	2,128	935	1,025
Parks College	† 5,750		625						
St. John's College	‡ 17,630		275	5,720	600	900	1,700	100	
San Juan College	360	240/—	440				2,000	900	650
Santa Fe Community College	434	672/72	500				2,500	650	440
Southwestern Indian Polytechnic Institute	60			3,450	600	1,000	2,000	1,000	1,000
University of New Mexico	1,997	5,545/—	546	3,968	926	1,816	1,890	850	1,168
Western New Mexico University	1,486	3,965/—	625	2,392	805	1,155	1,000	915	1,000
New York									
Adelphi University	‡ 13,000		750	6,450	1,900	900		3,025	3,225
Adirondack Community College	‡ 2,043	1,900/—	560				945	750	7,757
Albany College of Pharmacy	9,765		700	4,600	300	700	1,500	700	700
Alfred University	17,948		550	5,676	350	575	1,500	1,350	525
American Academy of Dramatic Arts	8,875		400				3,500	1,120	875
American Academy McAllister Institute of Funeral Service	5,625		400				2,600	800	1,500
Audrey Cohen College	8,260		300				1,000	690	640
Bard College	20,677		550	6,382	400	450	3,232	600	600
Barnard College	‡ 18,646		520	7,602		850	660	630	830
Berkeley College	10,425		700	7,200					
Berkeley College of New York City	10,400		700						
Beth Hamedrash Shaarei Yosher Institute	† 4,000			1,200		1,800			
Boricua College	5,925		450				6,515	560	844
Bramson ORT Technical Institute	6,180							475	1,300
Briarcliffe: The College for Business and Technology	7,550		700				1,100	1,200	1,500
Broome Community College	‡ 2,020	1,890/—	500				750	600	750

†Figures are projected for 1995-96. ‡Figures are for 1994-95.

All aid		Need-based aid		Grants and scholarships								Financial aid deadlines		Inst aid form	Notes
Total freshmen	Percent receiving aid	Freshmen judged to have need	Percent offered aid	Need-based				Non-need-based							
				Acad	Music/drama	Art	Athl	Acad	Music/drama	Art	Athl	Priority	Closing		
				X								3/1	none		
				X				X				9/1	none		
				X	X	X		X	X	X		3/1	none		
59	91	55	100					X	X		X	4/1	6/1		
998	21			X								3/1	none		
500	80			X	X	X	X	X	X	X	X	3/1	none		
1,420	70			X				X				5/1	none		
69	85	28	100										4/15	X	
33	75			X				X					none		
443	85	297	93	X	X	X		X	X	X	X	3/1	5/1		
211	90	112	100	X				X				3/1	none	X	
1,283	46			X	X	X	X	X	X		X	6/1	none		
277	88	80	100	X				X	X		X	5/1	none		
				X				X				3/1	none		
													none		
1,538	60			X				X	X		X	3/1	none		
													none		
103	73	69	100	X								2/15	none	X	
1,600	22	375	100	X	X			X	X			5/1	none		
													none	X	
													none		
1,741	60	679	100	X				X	X		X	3/1	none	X	
				X				X	X	X	X	2/15	none		
959	49			X	X	X		X				4/15	none		
132	79	98	100									2/15	4/15		
472	90	395	100	X	X	X		X		X			none	X	
136	65	115	100	X	X							7/1	none		
													none		
134	85			X								8/15	none		
310	68	215	99	X	X	X		X	X	X		2/15	3/15	X	
558	60	256	100										2/1		
													none		
298	86			X				X					none		
306	87			X				X							
500	95	240	100	X				X					none		
379	93			X				X					none		
1,294	60			X				X				4/1	none	X	

Institution	Tuition and fees	Add'l out-of-state/ district tuition	Books and supplies	Costs for campus residents			Costs for students at home		
				Room and board	Trans-portation	Other costs	Board only	Trans-portation	Other costs
Bryant & Stratton Business Institute									
Albany	6,252		750	3,800			1,600	450	1,100
Buffalo	2,064		750				2,241	450	1,305
Rochester	6,192		750						
Syracuse	6,252		750	3,800				540	360
Canisius College	11,976		400	5,500	430	700	1,500	430	630
Catholic Medical Center of Brooklyn and Queens School of Nursing	4,200		900				2,500		1,450
Cayuga County Community College	‡ 2,203	2,050/—	750				900	720	500
Cazenovia College	10,485		500	5,100	250	250	750	250	750
Central City Business Institute	5,400		600	3,200	1,173	700	1,500	642	800
City University of New York									
Baruch College	‡ 2,560	2,600/—	500		675		1,750	675	2,100
Borough of Manhattan Community College	‡ 2,184	576/—	500				1,802	675	2,100
Bronx Community College	‡ 2,204	576/—	500				1,802	675	2,100
Brooklyn College	‡ 2,631	2,600/—	500				1,802	675	2,100
City College	‡ 2,548	2,600/—	500				1,802	675	2,171
College of Staten Island	‡ 2,560	2,600/—	500				1,802	675	2,100
Hostos Community College	‡ 2,146	576/—	500				1,802	675	2,100
Hunter College	‡ 2,557	2,600/—	500		675	2,455	1,937	675	2,360
John Jay College of Criminal Justice	‡ 2,559	2,600/—	500				1,802	675	2,100
Kingsborough Community College	‡ 2,194	576/—	500				1,802	675	2,100
La Guardia Community College	‡ 2,204	576/—	500				1,802	675	2,100
Lehman College	‡ 2,564	2,600/—	500				1,802	675	2,100
Medgar Evers College	‡ 2,176	576/—	500				3,400	675	2,262
New York City Technical College	‡ 2,500	2,600/—	500				1,802	675	2,100
Queens College	‡ 2,637	2,600/—	500				1,802	675	2,100
Queensborough Community College	‡ 2,202	576/—	500				1,802	675	2,100
York College	‡ 2,536	2,600/—	600				1,835	676	2,262
Clarkson University	17,113		700	5,830	426	665	2,956		691
Clinton Community College	‡ 1,985	1,875/—	500		250		1,200	900	739
Cochran School of Nursing-St. John's Riverside Hospital	‡ 5,052		500				3,058	946	2,037
Colgate University	20,650		575	5,765	80	850	1,580	80	750
College of Aeronautics	5,366		1,050		1,350	1,950	700	1,350	1,950
College of Insurance	‡ 11,480		500	7,392	160	1,020	3,000	450	1,020
College of Mount St. Vincent	12,440		500	5,944	150	850	1,500	600	850
College of New Rochelle									
New Rochelle	12,300		500	5,550	250	100	1,500	250	100
School of New Resources	† 4,162		500					250	100
College of St. Rose	10,730		800	5,856	500	1,600	2,000	500	1,000
Columbia University									
Columbia College	‡ 19,110		800	6,664		1,060	1,680	400	750
School of Engineering and Applied Science	‡ 19,110		800	6,664		1,060	1,680	400	700
School of General Studies	17,784		900				2,529	414	400
School of Nursing	‡ 19,710		1,400	8,010	800	1,200	2,600	1,000	1,200
Columbia-Greene Community College	‡ 1,926	1,800/—	450				1,320	900	950
Concordia College	10,696		450	5,220	350	850	680	350	850
Cooper Union	400		1,255	8,915	150	1,260	1,350	500	1,260
Cornell University	† 20,066		510	6,762		1,060			
Cornell University: Statutory Divisions	‡ 8,556	7,970/—	510	6,762		1,060			
Corning Community College	‡ 2,266	2,100/—	550				1,880	850	400

†Figures are projected for 1995-96. ‡Figures are for 1994-95.

| All aid | | Need–based aid | | Grants and scholarships | | | | | | | | Financial aid deadlines | | Inst aid form | Notes |
| Total freshmen | Percent receiving aid | Freshmen judged to have need | Percent offered aid | Need–based | | | | Non–need–based | | | | Priority | Closing | | |
				Acad	Music/ drama	Art	Athl	Acad	Music/ drama	Art	Athl				
124	75	226	100	X									9/20		
													none		
													none		
155	95	146	100	X				X					none		
737	90	602	100	X			X	X			X	2/1	none		
2	34												none		
465	75			X				X				5/1	none		
429	87	358	100	X				X		X	X	3/1	none		
104	90			X				X				6/1	none		
1,537	70			X				X					5/1		
3,095	85												none		X
4,100	90												none		
3,316	65			X	X	X	X	X	X	X		5/1	none		
1,243	86			X				X				5/1	none		
1,687	33											5/25	9/30		
1,160	95			X				X				6/1	none		X
1,664	72	1,142	82	X				X				5/1	none		
1,435	75							X				6/1	none		
2,477	90											8/1	none		
2,216	83											7/1	none		
745	60	622	100					X				6/1	none		
633	90											6/1	8/31		
2,336	85											5/1	6/30		
1,775	60							X				5/31	8/1		
2,356	92	1,400	100					X				5/1	7/14		
692	80											4/1	8/1		
507	93	408	100	X	X	X	X	X	X	X	X		none		
673	82			X				X				6/1	none		
86	95	80	100	X				X					none		
862	61	362	100	X	X	X	X						2/1		
195	82	218	100	X				X				5/1	2/15		
10	88	10	100	X				X					none		
211	89	160	100	X				X				3/15	none		
243	95	115	100					X	X	X			none		X
490	96												none		X
287	85	464	100	X	X	X		X	X	X	X	3/1			
872	77												2/1		
268	65												2/1		
				X									5/30	X	
				X				X				3/1	none		
459	75							X				5/1	none		
88	100							X	X		X	4/15	3/31		
201	43	85	100	X				X				2/15	5/1		
3,103	65	1,570	100	X									2/15		
													2/15		
922	85							X				5/1	none		

Institution	Tuition and fees	Add'l out-of-state/district tuition	Books and supplies	Costs for campus residents			Costs for students at home		
				Room and board	Trans-portation	Other costs	Board only	Trans-portation	Other costs
Culinary Institute of America	‡ 12,715				600	1,300		600	1,300
Daemen College	9,780		700	4,900	700	800		700	800
Darkei Noam Rabbinical College	‡ 4,150		300	3,000			1,800		3,000
Dominican College of Blauvelt	9,230		600	5,740	900	900	1,800	1,000	900
Dowling College	‡ 10,290		450		800	1,413	2,105	1,106	1,413
Dutchess Community College	‡ 1,945	1,850/—	560				1,785	850	750
D'Youville College	9,420		680	4,470	640	680	1,500	640	680
Eastman School of Music of the University of Rochester	17,373		600	6,730	650	850	2,450	650	850
Elmira College	16,700		450	5,380		550	1,500		550
Erie Community College City Campus	‡ 2,186	2,100/—	500				1,008	750	750
North Campus	‡ 2,186	2,100/—	500				1,380	750	750
South Campus	‡ 2,186	2,100/—	500				1,008	750	750
Eugene Lang College/New School for Social Research	16,119		750	8,132				600	975
Fashion Institute of Technology	‡ 2,350	2,950/—	1,200	4,825	600	1,050	1,600	800	900
Finger Lakes Community College	‡ 2,130	2,000/—	500				1,800	600	480
Five Towns College	† 8,400		650	4,700		2,000	2,500	2,100	2,100
Fordham University	15,225		600	7,100	600	1,135	1,850	775	825
Fulton-Montgomery Community College	‡ 2,167	2,050/—	500				1,800	600	500
Genesee Community College	‡ 2,100	350/—	550					680	550
Hamilton College	20,700		450	5,250	200	600			
Hartwick College	19,300		600	5,310	350	250	1,400	1,100	250
Helene Fuld School of Nursing	‡ 7,169		1,000				2,700	400	1,575
Herkimer County Community College	‡ 2,000	2,850/—	500				500	600	660
Hilbert College	8,400		500	4,450	400	660	1,500	500	660
Hobart and William Smith Colleges	20,393		600	6,075	200	600	1,500	300	
Hofstra University	‡ 11,710		665	5,920	700	1,100	1,950	1,705	1,100
Holy Trinity Orthodox Seminary	1,400		100	1,400					
Houghton College	10,890		750	3,720	500	750	800	500	750
Hudson Valley Community College	‡ 1,831	1,710/—	550				1,700	900	800
Institute of Design and Construction	† 4,255		600					200	400
Interboro Institute	5,425		450				450	400	1,000
Iona College	11,615		635	7,050	612	1,287	907	1,055	1,287
Ithaca College	15,250		634	6,594		1,000	2,780	1,415	1,000
Jamestown Business College	5,850		550				500	1,792	1,386
Jamestown Community College	‡ 2,180	1,980/—	500				2,000	500	400
Jefferson Community College	‡ 2,035	1,776/—	600				1,500	310	500
Jewish Theological Seminary of America	7,100		500	3,750	400	5,000		450	2,500
Juilliard School	13,600		2,400	6,300	500	6,500	2,300	1,300	
Katharine Gibbs School Melville	8,546		550				1,100	1,315	1,053
New York	8,400		500					1,300	
Keuka College	10,230		600	4,780	750	750	1,500	750	750
Laboratory Institute of Merchandising	10,450		440				1,500	1,500	1,500
Le Moyne College	12,060		300	5,040		1,000	700	250	300
Long Island College Hospital School of Nursing	7,067		1,063				2,500	760	
Long Island University Brooklyn Campus	‡ 11,435		700	6,820	450	800	2,000	450	800
C. W. Post Campus	† 12,855		500	5,860	500	1,150	1,800	900	800

†Figures are projected for 1995-96. ‡Figures are for 1994-95.

| All aid | | Need–based aid | | Grants and scholarships | | | | | | | | Financial aid deadlines | | Inst aid form | Notes |
Total freshmen	Percent receiving aid	Freshmen judged to have need	Percent offered aid	Need–based Acad	Music/ drama	Art	Athl	Non–need–based Acad	Music/ drama	Art	Athl	Priority	Closing		
409	96	346	100	X				X					none		
				X		X	X	X			X	2/15	none		
81	79	65	100	X			X	X			X	3/1	none	X	
480	80	425	70	X	X	X	X	X			X	5/1	none		
1,203	50			X				X				5/1	none		
267	88			X				X			X	4/15	none		
116	88	82	100		X			X	X			1/15	none		
288	80	187	100					X	X	X		3/1	none		
744	82											4/30	none		
				X								4/30	none		
968	53			X								4/30	none		
77	70			X				X				4/1	none		
1,732	51							X					3/15		
2,757	75							X	X	X	X	4/1	none		
301	85	233	100	X	X			X	X			4/30	8/21	X	
1,051	85			X	X		X	X	X		X		2/1		
720	75			X				X				4/1	none		
1,578	75			X	X	X	X	X	X	X		3/1	5/1		
481	57	271	100									2/1		X	
416	88	303	100	X	X	X	X	X	X		X	2/15		X	
		33	76	X				X					none		
986	84	750	100	X			X	X			X		4/1		
129	64			X				X				2/28	none		
523	65	345	99	X	X	X						2/15		X	
1,278	73	834	98	X				X	X	X	X	3/1	none		
356	95	290	100	X	X	X	X	X	X	X	X	3/15	none		
2,670	60			X								5/30	none		
89	60												none		
934	80												none		
727	83	473	100	X				X		X	X	4/15	none		
1,328	66			X	X				X				3/1		
180	94			X				X					none		
1,212	80	1,074	100	X	X		X	X	X		X	3/1	none		
890	86			X				X				4/1	none	X	
27	68	21	100					X					3/1		
90	87			X	X			X	X				2/15		
94	90			X									none		
													none		
187	95	180	100	X				X				3/1	none	X	
44	80	32	100	X									none		
396	95	310	100	X	X	X	X	X			X	2/15	4/15		
													none		
1,022	90	800	100	X	X	X	X	X	X	X	X		none		
655	77	414	86	X	X	X	X	X	X	X	X	2/1	5/15		

Institution	Tuition and fees	Add'l out-of-state/district tuition	Books and supplies	Costs for campus residents			Costs for students at home		
				Room and board	Trans-portation	Other costs	Board only	Trans-portation	Other costs
Southampton College	† 12,925		400	6,447	200	840	1,580	360	840
Machzikei Hadath Rabbinical College	4,800			1,800					
Manhattan College	14,120		500	7,000	500	1,000	1,800	800	1,000
Manhattan School of Music	‡ 13,030		650	9,000	1,000	1,000	2,500	1,000	1,000
Manhattanville College	16,000		550	7,370	400	700	3,070	1,000	700
Mannes College of Music	13,850		1,200		600	1,000	2,850	600	1,000
Maria College	† 5,050		550					500	500
Marist College	11,716		500	6,339	300	550	2,000	600	550
Marymount College	12,500		550	6,750	425	650	1,600	1,000	650
Marymount Manhattan College	11,450		350	6,557	600	1,000	1,600	600	1,000
Mater Dei College	6,225		700	4,005	150	800	1,500	300	800
Medaille College	9,560		500	4,400	500	600		500	600
Mercy College	† 6,600		500	5,900			1,500	700	800
Mesivta Torah Vodaath Seminary	‡ 4,665		200	4,500			2,175		
Mohawk Valley Community College	‡ 2,215	2,100/—	750	3,890	510	1,262	1,698	660	750
Molloy College	9,700		700				1,500	1,700	1,200
Monroe College	‡ 5,280		555				1,500	520	680
Monroe Community College	‡ 2,236	2,100/—	450				1,000	700	1,475
Mount St. Mary College	9,010		300	5,150	500	700	1,500	1,000	750
Nassau Community College	‡ 2,050	1,950/—	576				2,248	1,024	1,030
Nazareth College of Rochester	11,605		550	5,234	150	900	1,500	650	900
New York Institute of Technology	10,990		500	5,980	410	1,200	1,500	1,270	1,200
New York School of Interior Design	‡ 10,400		1,000				5,000	800	
New York University	19,748		450	7,552		1,000	1,500		
Niagara County Community College	‡ 2,074	1,970/—	375				750	650	600
Niagara University	11,560		450	5,084	300	650	1,500	500	650
North Country Community College	‡ 2,235	2,100/—	500				700	800	700
Nyack College	9,450		500	4,130	300	600		600	900
Ohr Somayach Tanenbaum Education Center	3,600		300	3,600	150	725	1,800	1,000	725
Olean Business Institute	5,055		500				1,600		
Onondaga Community College	‡ 2,126	4,060/2,030	540				1,647	750	450
Orange County Community College	‡ 1,885	1,800/—	525				2,340	535	465
Pace University	† 11,850		550	5,240	150	925	1,750	500	875
Parsons School of Design	16,220		1,200			1,080	1,800	800	1,080
Paul Smith's College	10,980		750	4,500	400	1,000	1,500	600	1,000
Phillips Beth Israel School of Nursing	† 8,180		977				3,900	890	1,220
Plaza Business Institute	5,225		600					300	900
Polytechnic University									
Brooklyn	17,755		479	4,700	1,200	1,307	2,430	705	1,245
Long Island Campus	† 17,420		457		1,200	1,286	1,315	705	1,245
Pratt Institute	15,214		2,000	7,266	500	650	1,966	500	650
Rabbinical College Bobover Yeshiva B'nei Zion	3,600		400	2,800		500			500
Rabbinical College Ch'san Sofer of New York	4,000								
Rabbinical College of Long Island	6,300								
Rabbinical Seminary Adas Yereim	4,200								
Rensselaer Polytechnic Institute	18,565		825	6,155		440	1,500	1,175	440
Roberts Wesleyan College	11,077		520	3,744	450	950	1,156	1,000	950
Rochester Business Institute	5,700		600				1,000	900	1,200
Rochester Institute of Technology	14,937		600	5,898	300	600	1,500	300	600
Rockland Community College	‡ 2,135	2,050/—	600				1,800	800	600

†Figures are projected for 1995-96. ‡Figures are for 1994-95.

All aid		Need-based aid		Grants and scholarships								Financial aid deadlines		Inst aid form	Notes
				Need-based				Non-need-based							
Total freshmen	Percent receiving aid	Freshmen judged to have need	Percent offered aid	Acad	Music/drama	Art	Athl	Acad	Music/drama	Art	Athl	Priority	Closing		
246	85			X				X		X	X		none		
													none		
528	91			X				X			X	2/15	none		
73	78	42	88	X	X			X	X			3/15	none	X	
172	65	137	95					X	X	X		3/1	3/31	X	
22	81				X				X			5/15	none		
219	46											8/1	none		
876	77	614	100	X	X	X	X	X	X		X	3/15	none		
90	86	85	100	X		X		X	X	X		3/1	none		
328	93	289	99	X	X	X		X	X	X		2/25	4/1		
166	85	145	100	X			X	X			X	4/1	none		
97	70			X				X				5/1	none	X	
1,602	80							X			X	3/1	none		
1,540	85			X				X				4/15	none		
		130	100	X				X	X	X	X	4/15	none		
911	98	859	100										3/31		
4,236	70			X			X	X			X	5/1	none		
259	72	258	100	X				X				3/15	none		
				X	X	X		X	X	X		5/30	none	X	
297	89	249	100	X	X	X		X	X	X		3/1	none		
700	92							X			X	6/1	none		
16	30	14	86	X		X		X		X		7/1	none		
2,870	92	2,107	97	X	X			X	X			12/1	2/15		
1,726	70	1,029	100	X				X				4/1	none		
557	87	427	99	X	X		X	X	X		X	2/15	none		
												5/30	none		
199	87			X	X		X	X				3/1	none		
													none		
92	87	78	100	X				X				5/1	none		
2,063	80							X				3/1	none		
				X				X	X	X	X	5/1	none		
1,650	76	803	98	X	X		X	X	X		X	3/15	7/1		
366	73	231	94	X		X						4/1	none	X	
456	85	300	100	X			X	X			X	2/28	none		
8	98	8	100	X				X					6/1		
114	95			X				X					none		
189	99	258	100	X				X				3/1	none	X	
82	98	102	100	X				X				3/1	none		
348	80	238	100	X				X		X			2/1	X	
987	86							X			X	2/15	none		
193	91	184	100	X	X	X		X	X	X	X	5/15	none	X	
110	86												none		
1,462	80	1,129	100	X		X		X		X		3/15	none	X	
1,800	58			X				X				6/15	none		

Institution	Tuition and fees	Add'l out-of-state/district tuition	Books and supplies	Costs for campus residents			Costs for students at home		
				Room and board	Trans-portation	Other costs	Board only	Trans-portation	Other costs
Russell Sage College	13,270		500	5,560	200	650	1,500	300	700
Sage Junior College of Albany	‡ 7,370		500	5,240	300	650	3,300	300	700
St. Bonaventure University	11,604		500	5,000	400	650	1,500	600	650
St. Francis College	‡ 7,065		450				2,250	450	1,125
St. John Fisher College	† 11,230		400	5,600	200	600	1,500	600	600
St. John's University	10,550		600				2,700	750	1,800
St. Joseph's College									
Brooklyn	7,817		600				1,600	1,000	600
Suffolk Campus	8,047		500				1,500	1,000	600
St. Joseph's Hospital Health Center									
School of Nursing	4,672	2,788/—	650		120	780	1,500	320	780
St. Lawrence University	19,760		650	5,885		1,000		300	1,000
St. Thomas Aquinas College	9,450		500	6,050	750	1,000	3,100	1,000	1,000
Sarah Lawrence College	20,708		600	6,838	350	725	2,300	200	
Schenectady County Community College	‡ 1,943	1,840/—	550				1,750	900	900
School of Visual Arts	12,600		1,435		735	1,815	2,525	735	1,815
Siena College	11,650		575	5,270	350	565	850	575	575
Skidmore College	19,950		550	5,890	250	700	1,450	250	700
State University of New York									
Albany	‡ 2,936	3,900/—	500	4,543	260	900	1,600	525	900
Binghamton	‡ 2,961	3,900/—	750	5,120	400	709	1,468	740	1,054
Buffalo	‡ 3,078	3,900/—	800	4,808	690	784	2,200	690	784
Oswego	‡ 2,947	3,900/—	500	4,810	600	900		600	900
Purchase	‡ 2,943	3,900/—	775	4,760	315	1,204	1,800	609	900
Stony Brook	‡ 2,995	3,900/—	750	4,942	600	1,120	1,500	1,928	1,120
College of Agriculture and Technology at Cobleskill	‡ 2,994	3,900/—	500	4,740	200	600	1,500	550	600
College of Agriculture and Technology at Morrisville	‡ 2,940	3,900/—	600	4,800	350	600	1,600	2,700	1,000
College at Brockport	‡ 2,965	3,900/—	600	4,520	440	875	1,702	735	875
College at Buffalo	‡ 2,890	3,900/—	708	4,440	892	957	2,112	892	957
College at Cortland	‡ 2,942	3,900/—	650	4,400	400	845	1,575	700	520
College of Environmental Science and Forestry	‡ 2,994	3,900/—	600		200	450	1,800	600	300
College at Fredonia	‡ 3,009	3,900/—	620	4,420	671	800	1,920	981	800
College at Geneseo	‡ 3,083	3,900/—	600	4,170	650	650	1,700	650	650
College at New Paltz	‡ 2,985	3,900/—	600	4,760	600	900	1,500	900	900
College at Old Westbury	‡ 2,928	3,900/—	675	4,872	750	1,210	404	1,675	990
College at Oneonta	‡ 2,920	3,900/—	450	5,200	350	1,000	575	1,000	950
College at Plattsburgh	‡ 3,015	3,900/—	600	4,262	462	1,103	750	1,512	1,099
College at Potsdam	‡ 2,940	3,900/—	500	4,660	300	700	985	600	700
College of Technology at Alfred	‡ 2,927	3,900/—	600	4,490	448	700	700	858	700
College of Technology at Canton	‡ 2,941	3,900/—	500	4,737	400	700	1,660	1,500	700
College of Technology at Delhi	‡ 2,980	3,900/—	500	4,930	500	1,000	1,000	860	1,000
College of Technology at Farmingdale	‡ 3,065	3,900/—	600	5,190	500	800	2,100	1,100	800
Empire State College	‡ 2,922	3,900/—	600				2,730	405	1,500
Health Science Center at Brooklyn	‡ 2,865	3,900/—	685		330	820	1,155	520	820
Health Science Center at Syracuse	‡ 2,865	3,900/—	515		615	700	1,540	835	700
Health Sciences Center at Stony Brook	‡ 2,995	3,900/—	1,000	4,942	1,770	1,730	1,500	1,770	1,730
Institute of Technology at Utica/Rome	‡ 2,905	3,900/—	620	5,120	400	1,000	750	1,100	1,390
Maritime College	‡ 3,041	3,900/—	500	4,830	400	1,200			
Stenotype Academy	7,400		800					600	4,000

†Figures are projected for 1995-96. ‡Figures are for 1994-95.

| All aid | | Need–based aid | | Grants and scholarships | | | | | | | | Financial aid deadlines | | Inst aid form | Notes |
| Total freshmen | Percent receiving aid | Freshmen judged to have need | Percent offered aid | Need–based | | | | Non–need–based | | | | | | | |
				Acad	Music/ drama	Art	Athl	Acad	Music/ drama	Art	Athl	Priority	Closing		
196	85	148	100	X				X				3/1	none		
375	77			X				X		X	X	3/15	4/15		
465	79	279	100	X				X	X		X	3/1	none		
418	75	293	100	X			X	X			X	2/15	none		
322	92	314	100	X				X				3/1	none		
2,577	74			X				X	X	X	X	4/1	none		
77	90	54	100	X				X				2/25	none		
162	58	101	100	X				X				2/25	none		
96	85	73	100					X				5/1	none		
574	73	420	100	X				X					2/15		
292	65			X		X		X		X	X	3/1	none		
262	52	179	99	X	X								2/1	X	
1,209	70			X			X	X				5/1	none		
441	85	401	100	X		X		X		X		3/1			
640	84	432	100	X			X	X			X		2/1		
613	33	238	92						X				2/1		
2,089	63			X				X				3/5	none		
1,807	92			X	X	X		X	X	X		3/1	none		
2,263	75	1,581	100	X	X	X		X	X	X	X	3/1	none		
1,391	80	957	100	X	X			X	X			3/1	none		
374	80	204	100	X	X	X		X	X	X		2/15	none		
1,798	68							X				3/1	none		
1,047	65			X				X				4/1	none		
1,384	85	938	100					X				3/1	none		
923	87	577	100					X	X	X		3/15	none		
1,269	85			X	X	X	X	X	X	X	X	3/16	none		
1,100	79			X				X	X	X		4/1	none	X	
85	85	70	100	X				X					3/1	X	
873	74	634	100	X	X								none		
1,198	70			X				X	X			3/1	4/1		
971	85	439	100									3/15	4/15		
				X				X				4/19	5/1	X	
1,009	72	560	100	X				X				5/1	none		
901	66	562	93	X	X	X		X	X	X		4/15	none		
628	62	418	100	X				X	X				none		
1,629	75							X	X		X	5/1	none		
762	85			X				X				3/15	none	X	
942	60											3/1	none		
1,802	68			X				X				4/1	none		
				X									4/1		
												4/10	4/30		
				X								4/1	none		
				X				X				3/1	none		
				X				X				5/1	none		
223	90	227	100	X				X				4/15	none	X	
													none		

Institution	Tuition and fees	Add'l out-of-state/ district tuition	Books and supplies	Costs for campus residents			Costs for students at home		
				Room and board	Trans-portation	Other costs	Board only	Trans-portation	Other costs
Suffolk County Community College									
Eastern Campus	‡ 2,002	1,850/—	550				975	1,248	1,048
Selden	‡ 2,002	1,850/—	550				975	1,248	1,048
Western Campus	‡ 2,002	1,850/—	550				975	1,248	1,048
Sullivan County Community College	‡ 2,156	2,056/—	600				700	650	700
Syracuse University	16,305		770	7,140	300	660	3,380	504	660
Talmudical Institute of Upstate New York	‡ 4,250			3,300					
Talmudical Seminary Oholei Torah	4,500			2,100					
Taylor Business Institute	6,250						1,053	385	
Technical Career Institutes	‡ 6,150		450				2,000	487	1,430
Tompkins-Cortland Community College	‡ 2,270	2,100/—	500				1,500	1,000	900
Touro College	‡ 7,480		600		450	1,400	2,300	450	1,400
Trocaire College	‡ 5,800		700				1,500	700	600
Ulster County Community College	‡ 2,084	1,970/—	500				1,491	700	600
Union College	19,972		450	6,234	250	774	1,635	250	593
United States Merchant Marine Academy	4,570								
United States Military Academy	0								
University of Rochester	19,175		500	6,730	200	900	1,650	650	900
University of the State of New York:									
Regents College	‡ 535								
Utica College of Syracuse University	13,406		550	5,122	500	675	1,245	600	675
Utica School of Commerce	‡ 4,925		750						
Vassar College	20,250		600	6,150	300	600	2,600	150	600
Villa Maria College of Buffalo	‡ 6,180		425				1,750	475	675
Wadhams Hall Seminary-College	4,160		500	3,990	500	500	2,700	1,500	1,000
Wagner College	14,450		585	5,800	625	1,080	1,800	525	1,080
Webb Institute	0		750	5,500	2,000	600			
Wells College	16,880		600	5,800		500	1,300		500
Westchester Business Institute	9,999		600					2,055	1,281
Westchester Community College	‡ 2,217	3,000/—	600				2,000	900	500
Wood Tobe-Coburn School	8,640		1,000				2,490	1,200	2,800
Yeshiva Derech Chaim	4,000		400	1,500					
Yeshiva Gedolah Zichron Moshe	‡ 4,400		275	2,300	100	400		100	
Yeshiva Shaar Hatorah									
Yeshiva University	† 13,410		520	6,600	720	720	1,800	720	720
North Carolina									
Alamance Community College	† 578	3,959/—	600				1,900	750	800
Anson Community College	‡ 578	3,959/—	650				1,500	1,300	900
Appalachian State University	† 1,684	7,610/—	250	2,630	1,000	1,000	1,500	1,000	1,000
Asheville Buncombe Technical Community College	‡ 582	3,959/—	600				788	891	302
Barber-Scotia College	5,294		600	3,070	1,000	1,000	1,500	800	1,000
Barton College	8,396		850	3,600	1,150	1,100	1,032	1,350	1,100
Beaufort County Community College	‡ 575	3,959/—	800				1,400	1,500	400
Belmont Abbey College	10,276		500	5,044	1,200	1,280	2,500	1,400	960
Bennett College	6,875		750	3,190	1,500	1,000	2,300	400	1,500
Bladen Community College	† 588	3,959/—	300				500	800	1,550
Blue Ridge Community College	587	3,959/—	600				2,000	1,535	787
Brevard College	8,675		550	3,750	600	600	1,500	600	600
Brunswick Community College	‡ 581	3,959/—	390				1,500	1,184	660

†Figures are projected for 1995-96. ‡Figures are for 1994-95.

Total freshmen	Percent receiving aid	Freshmen judged to have need	Percent offered aid	Acad	Music/drama	Art	Athl	Acad	Music/drama	Art	Athl	Priority	Closing	Inst aid form	Notes
All aid		**Need–based aid**		**Grants and scholarships**								**Financial aid deadlines**		**Inst aid form**	**Notes**
				Need–based				**Non–need–based**							
				X	X			X				4/15	6/1		
				X	X			X				4/15	6/1		
2,053	50							X					4/15		
752	70			X				X		X		5/15	none		
2,518	75	1,450	100	X	X	X		X	X	X	X		2/15		
11	20												none		
													none		
													none		
													none		
607	80			X				X					none		
1,148	85			X				X				5/15	none		
134	86			X				X				3/31	none		
1,780	80			X				X				6/1	none		
543	57	302	100									2/1	none	X	
275	30	64	100									1/15	3/15		
1,246	78	794	100	X	X	X		X	X	X		2/1	none		
				X				X				7/1	none	X	
351	84	207	98	X				X				2/15	none		
215	85							X					none		
612	52	290	100										1/15		
94	65							X	X	X		5/1	none		
5	100							X				8/1	none		
406	87	229	100	X	X		X	X	X		X	4/1	5/1	X	
24	44	7	100					X					7/1		
94	93	77	100	X				X				2/15	5/1		
319	91							X					none		
2,837	30			X				X	X	X	X		none	X	
221	86							X					none		
													none		
704	75	322	100					X				4/15	5/1		
1,127	21	482	76	X				X				5/15	none		
134	30	95	100	X									none		
1,971	44	800	100	X				X	X	X	X	2/1	none		
													none		
86	94							X			X	5/1	none		
253	81	199	100	X	X	X	X	X	X	X	X	5/1	none	X	
141	26			X				X				7/1	none		
204	70	136	100	X		X		X			X	3/1	none		
180	84			X				X	X				4/15		
190	30	162	100									8/15	none		
712	15	280	100	X				X				6/30	none		
328	69	220	100					X	X	X	X	4/15	none		
340	30			X				X				8/1	none		

Institution		Tuition and fees	Add'l out-of-state/ district tuition	Books and supplies	Costs for campus residents			Costs for students at home		
					Room and board	Trans-portation	Other costs	Board only	Trans-portation	Other costs
Caldwell Community College and Technical Institute	†	578	3,959/—	475				2,300	1,000	1,305
Campbell University		8,982		600	3,370	570	1,927	1,600	1,575	1,154
Cape Fear Community College	‡	575	3,959/—	460				1,000	1,200	770
Carteret Community College	†	573	3,959/—	500				1,100	900	200
Catawba College		9,972		600	4,200	660	1,200	2,000	990	1,200
Catawba Valley Community College	‡	575	3,959/—	800					900	800
Cecils College	‡	4,450		400				1,503	911	1,080
Central Carolina Community College	†	578	3,959/—	666				3,237	1,342	1,204
Central Piedmont Community College	‡	572	3,959/—	800				2,400	2,400	1,500
Chowan College		9,200		550	3,660	470	1,000	2,100	1,250	1,000
Cleveland Community College	‡	587	3,959/—	490				2,000	750	1,175
Coastal Carolina Community College	‡	578	3,959/—	450				1,800	450	800
College of the Albemarle	‡	585	3,959/—	500				3,150	783	1,000
Craven Community College	†	584	3,949/—	750					612	918
Davidson College		17,464		550	5,070		903	2,304		903
Davidson County Community College		579	3,959/—	800				1,500	1,237	463
Duke University		19,996		656	6,320	571	1,108	2,950	600	1,108
Durham Technical Community College	‡	575	3,959/—	450				1,125	900	562
East Carolina University	‡	1,557	6,484/—	500	3,240	600	1,007	1,700	600	1,007
East Coast Bible College	‡	4,080		600	2,550					
Edgecombe Community College	†	578	3,959/—	700				2,550	925	1,800
Elizabeth City State University	‡	1,326	5,732/—	300	3,132	490	810	2,000	600	810
Elon College		9,910		500	4,088	640	1,180	2,130	640	1,180
Fayetteville State University	‡	1,334	6,484/—	350	2,550	190	750	1,500	185	750
Fayetteville Technical Community College	‡	569	3,959/—	600				1,600	495	525
Forsyth Technical Community College	‡	577	3,959/—	650				2,500	750	750
Gardner-Webb University		8,500		500	4,440	570	900		650	450
Gaston College	‡	575	3,959/—	1,000					1,000	1,000
Greensboro College	†	9,266		600	4,034	815	1,000	1,500	650	820
Guilford College		14,390		550	5,270	450	700	2,550	450	700
Guilford Technical Community College	‡	586	3,959/—	650				2,000	800	700
Halifax Community College	‡	576	3,959/—	377				1,500	1,031	896
Haywood Community College	‡	577	3,959/—	450				1,500	1,293	1,305
High Point University		9,050		600	4,470	550	950	750	1,070	950
Isothermal Community College		585	3,959/—	450				1,500	402	783
James Sprunt Community College	‡	581	3,959/—	600				1,800	1,350	800
John Wesley College	‡	4,534		300		100	1,500	1,500	765	1,500
Johnson C. Smith University	‡	6,643		638	2,438	938	1,608	1,500	618	773
Johnston Community College	‡	578	3,959/—	450				1,500	900	900
Lees-McRae College		8,998		425	3,276	530	790	1,300	1,000	790
Lenoir Community College		584	3,959/—	500				1,500	680	540
Lenoir-Rhyne College		10,960		400	4,000	600	400	2,500	600	400
Livingstone College	‡	5,500		600	3,400	850	1,000	1,904	800	800
Louisburg College		7,530		450	4,025	500	1,000	1,615	700	1,000
Mars Hill College		8,500		600	3,550	800	800	2,000	800	800
Martin Community College	‡	575	3,959/—	400				3,024	990	400
Mayland Community College	‡	581	3,959/—	750				980	893	1,087
McDowell Technical Community College	‡	575	3,959/—	600				2,358	693	1,386
Meredith College		7,100		500	3,400	320	1,200	1,500	325	1,200
Methodist College		10,000		800	3,975	500	1,625	2,200	600	2,550

†Figures are projected for 1995-96. ‡Figures are for 1994-95.

| All aid | | Need–based aid | | Grants and scholarships | | | | | | | | Financial aid deadlines | | Inst aid form | Notes |
| Total freshmen | Percent receiving aid | Freshmen judged to have need | Percent offered aid | Need–based | | | | Non–need–based | | | | Priority | Closing | | |
				Acad	Music/ drama	Art	Athl	Acad	Music/ drama	Art	Athl				
623	25	340	100	X				X				5/1	none		
673	85							X	X		X	3/15	none		
1,255	25			X				X				3/15	none		
283	60			X								8/1	none		
289	89	217	100					X	X		X	3/1	none	X	
													none		
													none		
513	40	350	100	X								3/31	none		
4,725	15			X								4/15	5/1		
338	85			X				X				3/1	none		
676	10			X				X					none		
													none		
516	35			X	X			X	X	X		6/1	none	X	
472	20	182	90	X			X	X				4/1	none		
452	63	135	100	X				X	X	X	X		2/15		
315	25	225	100	X				X				5/30	none	X	
1,719	48	679	100	X				X	X	X	X	2/1	none		
1,342	50	700	100	X				X					none		
				X	X	X	X	X	X	X	X	4/15	none		
33	77	21	100	X	X	X						5/1	5/15	X	
759	40	95	95	X			X	X			X		7/15		
391	91							X	X		X	5/1	none		
932	57	391	100	X	X		X	X	X		X	4/1	none	X	
607	74			X	X		X	X	X		X	4/1	5/1		
3,317	51	1,303	100	X				X				6/1	8/1		
				X				X				5/1	none		
282	65	188	100	X	X		X	X	X		X	4/1	none		
900	42			X				X				3/15	none		
238	65	200	99	X	X	X		X	X	X		3/1	none		
335	78	247	100	X	X	X		X	X	X			3/1		
													none		
750	43			X				X				7/1	none		
443	23			X				X				4/1	none		
341	56	280	89	X				X			X	3/1	none		
													none		
343	45			X				X				7/1	none	X	
11	67			X	X			X	X			5/1	none		
404	91	325	100	X				X	X		X	4/15	none		
1,286	55			X				X				6/30	none	X	
150	60			X	X		X	X	X		X	3/15	6/15		
												6/1	7/15		
68	60			X	X		X	X	X		X	3/1	8/15		
270	90			X	X		X	X	X		X	5/1	5/15		
282	80	213	100	X	X		X	X	X		X	3/15	none	X	
420	80	270	100	X	X		X	X	X		X	5/1	none		
													none		
256	68	187	99	X				X				3/15	none	X	
425	34	179	100	X				X				3/15	none		
395	47	164	100	X	X	X		X	X	X		2/15	none		
342	85	260	100	X				X	X			5/1	7/1		

Institution		Tuition and fees	Add'l out-of-state/district tuition	Books and supplies	Costs for campus residents			Costs for students at home		
					Room and board	Trans-portation	Other costs	Board only	Trans-portation	Other costs
Mitchell Community College	‡	582	3,959/—	525				1,771	772	1,501
Montgomery Community College	‡	575	3,959/—	600				1,500	1,936	1,885
Montreat-Anderson College		8,690		500	3,540	500	2,358	2,850	900	2,014
Mount Olive College		7,825		600	2,950	600	900	1,500	600	900
Nash Community College	‡	578	3,959/—	750				1,200	1,200	800
North Carolina Agricultural and Technical State University	‡	1,431	6,484/—	600	3,110	487	1,246	1,500	487	1,246
North Carolina Central University	‡	1,372	6,484/—	530	3,012	465	1,400	1,622	761	1,400
North Carolina School of the Arts	‡	1,974	7,407/—	595	3,606		1,565	1,680		755
North Carolina State University	‡	1,548	7,526/—	600	3,590	250	1,050	2,220	550	1,050
North Carolina Wesleyan College		9,150		500	4,500	432	863	2,500	757	938
Pamlico Community College	‡	572	3,959/—	380				3,180	1,370	1,630
Peace College		5,930		600	5,296	900	1,350	1,500	900	1,350
Pembroke State University	‡	1,146	5,732/—	598	2,760	606	900	1,800	898	700
Pfeiffer College		8,990		650	3,950	1,000	650	1,250	1,200	650
Piedmont Bible College		4,600		500	2,950	550	600	754	850	600
Piedmont Community College	‡	584	3,959/—	500				2,000	1,200	750
Pitt Community College	‡	575	3,959/—	600				3,600	2,294	400
Queens College		11,520		610	5,170	1,000	900	1,950	500	900
Randolph Community College	‡	579	3,959/—	500				2,385	832	1,305
Richmond Community College	‡	584	3,959/—	600				1,800	900	750
Roanoke Bible College		3,740		400	2,750	500	350	2,100	1,050	350
Roanoke-Chowan Community College	‡	581	3,959/—	360				1,500	1,620	150
Robeson Community College	‡	575	3,959/—	600				1,800	1,041	75
Rockingham Community College	‡	584	3,959/—	450				2,500	1,040	1,000
Rowan-Cabarrus Community College	‡	584	3,959/—	430				1,500	645	525
St. Andrews Presbyterian College		10,895		500	4,810	200	850			1,970
St. Augustine's College		5,872		450	3,708	1,166	1,300	2,088	980	1,300
St. Mary's College		7,600		200	6,300		1,000	1,300	575	1,000
Salem College	‡	10,700		500	6,300	800	2,000	1,700	800	2,000
Sampson Community College	‡	587	3,959/—	600				1,800	800	900
Sandhills Community College	‡	578	3,959/—	514				1,800	1,260	578
Shaw University		5,516		600	3,476	500	500		600	500
Southeastern Baptist Theological Seminary		4,000		500						
Southeastern Community College	†	588	3,959/—	425				1,500	1,300	900
Southwestern Community College	‡	575	3,959/—	500				1,500	1,650	630
Stanly Community College	‡	578	3,959/—	525				2,000	800	1,200
Surry Community College	‡	575	3,959/—	500				1,500	1,238	495
Tri-County Community College	‡	572	3,959/—	300				600	200	450
University of North Carolina Asheville	‡	1,538	5,732/—	600	3,290	1,203	750	1,500	1,124	680
Chapel Hill	‡	1,524	7,526/—	550	4,092	100	1,100	1,500	100	1,100
Charlotte	‡	1,457	6,484/—	600	3,260	900	1,000	1,500	1,600	1,000
Greensboro	‡	1,765	7,526/—	450	3,505	300	840	800	750	840
Wilmington	‡	1,528	6,484/—	500	3,800	800	1,090	2,240	560	1,090
Vance-Granville Community College	‡	584	3,959/—	475				1,500	900	400
Wake Forest University		14,750		500	4,585	500	1,000	1,500	500	500
Wake Technical Community College	‡	566	3,959/—	600		1,100	1,050	2,500	1,100	1,050
Warren Wilson College		11,165		500	3,152	560	738	1,500	900	738
Wayne Community College	†	584	3,959/—	600				1,500	1,100	400
Western Carolina University	‡	1,437	6,484/—	200	2,774	525	756	1,666	940	840

†Figures are projected for 1995-96. ‡Figures are for 1994-95.

Total freshmen	Percent receiving aid	Freshmen judged to have need	Percent offered aid	Need-based Acad	Need-based Music/drama	Need-based Art	Need-based Athl	Non-need Acad	Non-need Music/drama	Non-need Art	Non-need Athl	Priority	Closing	Inst aid form	Notes
		53	81	X	X	X		X	X	X		4/1	none	X	
188	52											7/15	none		
92	96	78	100	X			X	X			X	3/1	none		
122	100	72	100					X	X	X	X	3/1	none		
169	9			X				X					none		
				X	X	X		X	X	X	X	5/15	none		
767	69							X					3/31		
122	66				X	X		X	X	X		3/15	none		
3,530	43	1,135	90	X				X			X	3/1	none		
160	70			X				X				3/1	none		
110	80			X									none		
199	76	96	100	X	X	X	X	X	X	X	X	4/1	none		
433	45	297	89	X	X	X	X	X	X	X	X	4/15	none		
160	96							X	X		X	5/1	none		
													none		
													none		
		1,150	100	X		X		X				3/15	8/24		
182	90	124	99	X	X	X	X	X	X	X	X	3/1	none		
215	20			X				X				5/1	none		
103	65	560	100	X				X				7/15	none		
38	100	22	100					X	X			4/1	5/1		
99	68	101	100	X				X					none		
													none		
													none		
													none		
173	99	170	100					X	X	X	X	4/1	7/1		
555	80							X	X		X	4/30	7/1		
88	35	30	100	X				X	X	X		4/1	none		
152	93	97	99	X	X			X	X			3/1	8/1		
342	40	250	100	X				X				7/1	none		
565	40			X	X	X		X	X	X		6/1	none	X	
568	95	540	100	X	X	X	X					4/30	7/31	X	
				X				X			X	4/1	none		
474	36			X								6/1	none		
				X				X				5/1	none		
295	50			X				X				6/1	none	X	
243	44			X								5/31	none		
398	61	167	100	X			X	X	X	X	X	3/1	none		
3,497	36	1,049	99	X				X	X		X	3/1	none		
1,587	46	975	100	X				X			X	4/1	none		
1,427	42	695	93	X	X	X	X	X	X		X	3/1	none	X	
1,343	49			X	X	X	X	X	X	X	X	3/15	none		
823	50			X				X				7/15	none		
944	66	265	100	X				X	X	X	X	3/1	none		
515	18			X				X				8/1	none	X	
170	59	106	100	X				X				4/15	none	X	
				X								4/15	none		
1,248	64	575	89	X	X	X	X	X	X	X	X	3/31	none	X	

Institution		Tuition and fees	Add'l out-of-state/ district tuition	Books and supplies	Costs for campus residents			Costs for students at home		
					Room and board	Trans-portation	Other costs	Board only	Trans-portation	Other costs
Western Piedmont Community College	‡	579	3,959/—	500				1,500	800	1,200
Wilkes Community College	†	583	3,959/—	660				1,500	908	660
Wilson Technical Community College	†	578	3,959/—	800				2,200	800	2,500
Wingate College		8,800		550	3,600	700	850	700	700	850
Winston-Salem State University	‡	1,192	5,730/—	600	3,048	551	2,100	1,100	476	2,100
North Dakota										
Bismarck State College	‡	1,720	2,592/—	600	2,280	400	1,600	1,380	635	1,365
Dickinson State University	‡	1,856	2,806/—	618	2,146	1,000	1,000	1,740	1,000	1,000
Fort Bethold Community College	†	1,940		400				3,800	600	800
Jamestown College		7,970		400	3,080	250	400	775	450	450
Little Hoop Community College		1,160		175					650	875
Mayville State University	‡	1,920	2,806/420	600	2,516	600	2,000		600	2,000
Medcenter One College of Nursing		2,690		990		585	1,000	1,934	585	1,000
Minot State University	‡	1,960	2,974/446	600	1,987	500	1,401	1,776	500	1,401
North Dakota State College of Science	‡	1,701	2,592/—	400	2,010	500	1,255	1,500	500	500
North Dakota State University										
Bottineau	‡	1,742	2,592/—	600	2,252	600	1,200	1,000	600	1,200
Fargo	‡	2,310	3,524/—	600	2,744	270	2,000		500	2,000
Standing Rock College		1,870		500				1,350	1,000	1,125
Trinity Bible College	†	5,102		500	3,084	1,130	1,754	1,500	400	1,400
Turtle Mountain Community College		1,176		360				1,200	900	1,320
United Tribes Technical College		2,740		600	2,400	450	1,880	700	600	1,880
University of Mary		7,000		500	2,750	800	815		800	815
University of North Dakota										
Grand Forks	‡	2,428	3,524/—	500	2,753	500	1,300	1,500	500	1,300
Lake Region	‡	1,770	2,592/—	550	2,310	500	1,500	1,200	500	1,500
Williston	‡	1,758	2,592/—	600	1,080	550	500	1,500	550	500
Valley City State University	‡	1,889	2,806/420	600	2,340	641	1,359	500	641	1,359
Ohio										
Antioch College		17,376		400	3,436	400	700		400	700
Antonelli Institute of Art and										
Photography		7,390		1,500	4,242	1,408			1,408	1,000
Art Academy of Cincinnati	‡	9,420		1,200				2,000	1,140	590
Ashland University		12,474		600	4,832	399	1,333	1,500	1,387	1,333
Baldwin-Wallace College		12,270		500	4,635	250	250	1,700	250	250
Belmont Technical College	†	2,070	630/—	450				1,668	1,230	4,507
Bluffton College		10,620		500	4,377		700		700	800
Bowling Green State University										
Bowling Green	‡	3,730	4,382/—	618	3,352	460	1,320	2,232	1,200	1,320
Firelands College	‡	2,870	4,382/—	400					720	1,511
Bradford School		7,100		900						
Bryant & Stratton Business Institute:										
Cleveland West	†	6,300		750						
Capital University		13,700		520	4,000	120	670	630	540	1,510
Case Western Reserve University		16,430		535	4,940		1,205			1,205
Cedarville College		8,004		555	4,572		1,015	2,040		450
Central Ohio Technical College	‡	2,142	900/—	700				550	1,200	2,300
Central State University		2,895	3,537/—	604	4,575	1,452	1,929		1,739	
Chatfield College		4,605		488				760	580	1,460
Cincinnati Bible College and Seminary		4,950		500	3,450	500	1,600	1,536	1,200	1,600
Cincinnati College of Mortuary Science		7,955		750					750	375

†Figures are projected for 1995-96. ‡Figures are for 1994-95.

All aid		Need–based aid		Grants and scholarships								Financial aid deadlines		Inst aid form	Notes
				Need–based				Non–need–based							
Total freshmen	Percent receiving aid	Freshmen judged to have need	Percent offered aid	Acad	Music/drama	Art	Athl	Acad	Music/drama	Art	Athl	Priority	Closing		
146	40							X				4/15	none		
330	22	260	95	X	X	X		X	X	X		8/1	none		
217	30	200	75	X									none		
336	80	230	96	X				X	X		X	3/1	none	X	
342	77			X	X		X	X	X	X	X	5/15	none		
892	75							X	X		X	4/15	none		
337	82							X	X	X	X	4/15	none	X	
315	100	241	100	X	X		X	X	X		X	6/1	none		
160	75	100	82	X							X	4/15	none		
													none	X	
541	66			X	X	X	X	X	X		X	4/15	none		
842	67	512	100	X	X		X	X	X		X	4/14	none		
183	75			X	X		X	X			X	4/15	none		
1,622	66			X	X		X	X				3/15	4/15	X	
													none		
117	95			X				X	X			3/1	none		
													none		
319	100	286	100	X	X		X	X	X		X	3/15	none		
1,635	47	871	100					X	X	X	X	4/15	4/15		
482	78	180	100	X		X		X			X	4/15	none		
				X		X		X			X	4/15	none		
170	81	161	100	X	X	X	X	X	X	X	X	4/15	none		
164	77	130	100					X				3/1	none		
30	80												none		
34	95							X		X		4/1	none		
673	95	374	100					X	X	X	X	3/15	none		
641	95	436	100	X				X	X	X		3/1	none		
								X					none		
224	100	182	100	X	X	X		X	X	X		5/1	none		
2,956	55	1,692	100	X				X	X	X	X	2/15	4/1		
								X	X			4/1	none		
													none		
95	75	139	100					X					none		
411	90	362	100	X	X			X	X			3/1	7/15		
735	92	515	100	X	X	X		X	X	X		2/1	none	X	
591	84	392	100	X				X	X		X	3/1	none		
296	50			X				X				4/15	none		
33	65	28	100	X								7/15	none	X	
													none	X	
4	50	9	100									7/1	none		

Institution	Tuition and fees	Add'l out-of-state/ district tuition	Books and supplies	Costs for campus residents			Costs for students at home		
				Room and board	Trans-portation	Other costs	Board only	Trans-portation	Other costs
Cincinnati State Technical and Community College	‡ 1,881	1,749/—	650				1,700	450	900
Circleville Bible College	‡ 4,780		400	3,372	450	910	1,800	450	910
Clark State Community College	‡ 2,142	1,890/—	600				1,500	630	750
Cleveland College of Jewish Studies	3,915		150						
Cleveland Institute of Art	‡ 11,700		1,100	4,770	520	800	2,000	1,575	800
Cleveland Institute of Music	15,406		700	4,855	750	750		750	750
Cleveland State University	‡ 3,231	3,231/—	600	4,369	410	1,110	1,500	525	865
College of Mount St. Joseph	‡ 9,800		600	4,430	400	600	1,830	650	600
College of Wooster	‡		500		150	500			
Columbus College of Art and Design	‡ 9,940		1,600	5,400	300	750	3,200	350	800
Columbus State Community College	2,015	2,305/—	650				1,950	800	750
Cuyahoga Community College									
Eastern Campus	1,552	2,565/506	675				1,503	600	1,053
Metropolitan Campus	1,552	2,565/506	675				1,503	525	1,053
Western Campus	1,552	2,565/506	675				1,503	600	1,053
Davis College	6,000		700				1,995	900	1,800
Defiance College	10,850		500	3,670	446	928	1,730	928	1,000
Denison University	18,630		500	4,940		600	1,500		600
DeVry Institute of Technology: Columbus	‡ 5,962		525				1,839	2,027	1,978
Dyke College	‡ 6,600		600					814	1,035
Edison State Community College	2,010	1,740/—	744				3,500	809	500
ETI Technical College	5,280		1,500						500
Franciscan University of Steubenville	10,490		600	4,500	1,400	1,000	2,000	1,400	1,000
Franklin University	† 4,973		450				4,300	630	510
God's Bible School and College	‡ 3,910		400	3,050	800	800	800	1,100	1,275
Heidelberg College	14,606		530	4,674	500	500		500	500
Hiram College	15,435		400	4,722		900	1,860	500	900
Hocking Technical College	‡ 1,935	1,920/—	750		312	1,189	970	1,760	489
ITT Technical Institute: Youngstown	6,426		1,050				2,358	2,181	1,386
Jefferson Technical College	‡ 1,665	675/135	500				1,700	360	400
John Carroll University	12,390		600	5,550	800	450	2,500	1,600	450
Kent State University									
Ashtabula Regional Campus	‡ 2,885	3,596/—	560				1,745	940	1,370
East Liverpool Regional Campus	‡ 2,885	3,596/—	525				1,645	885	1,315
Kent	‡ 3,927	3,927/—	560	3,666	700	1,370		980	1,370
Salem Regional Campus	‡ 2,885	3,596/—	600				1,800	900	1,500
Stark Campus	‡ 2,885	3,596/—	560				1,745	940	1,370
Trumbull Campus	‡ 2,885	3,596/—	560				1,730	940	1,484
Tuscarawas Campus	‡ 2,885	3,596/—	580					980	1,385
Kenyon College	20,890		800	3,770	140	360			
Kettering College of Medical Arts	‡ 5,118		612	2,592	430		560	988	
Lake Erie College	‡ 10,220		500	4,630	1,390	1,900	1,500	1,390	1,900
Lakeland Community College	‡ 1,835	2,918/405	600				1,600	1,030	1,055
Lima Technical College	2,040	1,980/—	900				2,000	810	450
Lorain County Community College	† 2,174	3,195/450	580				1,500	500	950
Lourdes College	7,193		520				1,990	886	709
Malone College	10,345		450	4,020	400	800	800	640	640
Marietta College	14,850		500	4,030	430	350	430	350	
Marion Technical College	2,108	1,728/—	650				1,800	1,200	850
McGregor School of Antioch University	8,325		400					400	

†Figures are projected for 1995-96. ‡Figures are for 1994-95.

Total freshmen	Percent receiving aid	Freshmen judged to have need	Percent offered aid	Need Acad	Need Music/drama	Need Art	Need Athl	Non-need Acad	Non-need Music/drama	Non-need Art	Non-need Athl	Priority	Closing	Inst aid form	Notes
78	95			X				X			X	3/15	none		
				X	X								none		
				X			X	X					none		
													none		
103	74	72	100	X		X		X		X		3/15	none		
54	90	42	100	X	X			X	X			3/1	none		
1,131	52	570	88	X				X	X	X	X	4/15	none		
207	94	153	100					X	X	X		4/15	none		
449	70	255	100	X				X	X			2/15	none		
346	88									X		5/3	none	X	
5,100	35			X				X					3/31		
842	26			X	X	X	X	X					none		
				X	X	X	X	X	X	X			none		
2,111	45			X	X	X	X	X	X	X			none		
121	75							X					none		
													none		
508	73	243	100	X	X	X		X	X	X		4/1	none		
								X					none		
562	80			X				X				4/30	none		
								X			X	6/15	none		
													none		
246	92	191	100	X				X				3/15	5/1		
				X				X				5/30	none		
58	79			X	X			X	X			6/1	none		
262	91	207	100					X	X			3/1	none		
212	89			X	X			X	X			3/1	8/1		
				X				X				3/31	none		
165	76											9/29	none		
439	42			X				X				6/1	none		
791	85	605	100	X				X				3/1	none		
379	70			X				X				2/15	8/30		
142	63			X				X				4/1	none		
2,436	70	1,875	97	X				X	X	X	X	2/15	4/1		
								X				2/15	none		
800	45			X				X				2/15	none		
				X	X	X		X	X	X		3/15	none		
256	66	180	100	X				X				2/15	4/1		
434	55	182	95					X					2/15		
				X				X				4/1	none	X	
53	85			X	X	X		X	X	X		3/1	4/1		
				X	X	X	X	X	X	X	X	3/1	none		
4,616	34	850	100		X			X					none		
44	38			X								3/1	none		
418	94	401	100	X	X		X	X	X		X	3/31	7/31	X	
329	87	251	100					X	X	X		3/1	none		
1,237	65	380	84	X				X				7/1	none	X	
													none		

Institution	Tuition and fees	Add'l out-of-state/district tuition	Books and supplies	Costs for campus residents			Costs for students at home		
				Room and board	Trans-portation	Other costs	Board only	Trans-portation	Other costs
Miami University									
Hamilton Campus	‡ 3,000	5,116/—	550				2,260	896	1,420
Middletown Campus	‡ 3,000	5,116/—	500				1,800	890	1,198
Oxford Campus	‡ 4,538	5,116/—	550	3,960	330	1,118	2,260	896	1,118
Miami-Jacobs College	6,150		700				2,000	1,000	2,500
Mount Union College	‡ 12,950		450	3,530	1,000	550	2,130	1,000	550
Mount Vernon Nazarene College	‡ 8,590		600	3,576	610	970	2,610	400	900
MTI Business College	5,095								
Muskingum Area Technical College	‡ 2,130	1,350/—	675						
Muskingum College	14,240		600	4,090	400	800		400	800
North Central Technical College	‡ 2,221	2,221/—	705						
Northwest State Community College	‡ 2,528	2,198/—	660				750	1,230	450
Northwestern College	‡ 4,560		600	2,370	720	1,053		1,440	1,053
Notre Dame College of Ohio	‡ 8,064		650	3,690	550	700	1,890	850	700
Oberlin College	20,746		575	5,970		525	2,900		525
Ohio Dominican College	‡ 8,100		600	4,270	350	800	1,900	780	800
Ohio Institute of Photography and Technology	9,225		1,400						
Ohio Northern University	16,950		540	4,290	360	525	1,600	360	525
Ohio State University									
Agricultural Technical Institute	‡ 2,976	6,228/—	507		700	3,000	1,863	1,162	1,034
Columbus Campus	‡ 3,087	6,228/—	507	4,484	781	647	580	924	693
Lima Campus	‡ 2,976	6,228/—	650				1,991	810	400
Mansfield Campus	‡ 2,976	6,228/—	450				550	1,100	2,335
Marion Campus	‡ 2,976	6,228/—	502				1,040	1,135	2,600
Newark Campus	2,976	6,228/—	600				495	1,188	2,276
Ohio University									
Athens	‡ 3,552	4,077/—	425	4,095	425	1,200		1,800	
Chillicothe Campus	‡ 2,796	4,035/—	615					1,848	
Eastern Campus	2,796	4,035/—	390					1,995	
Lancaster Campus	2,796	4,035/—	500					400	
Southern Campus at Ironton	2,580	111/—	600				1,896	1,800	
Zanesville Campus	2,796	4,035/—	500					2,049	489
Ohio Valley Business College	2,995		500					450	
Ohio Wesleyan University	17,569		550	5,876		500			500
Otterbein College	13,611		400	4,569	210	720		1,250	550
Owens Technical College									
Findlay Campus	‡ 1,808	1,548/—	465				1,800	1,000	800
Toledo	‡ 1,808	1,548/—	930				1,800	1,000	800
Pontifical College Josephinum	5,587		350	3,780		2,500	550		2,150
Rabbinical College of Telshe	4,750			2,300	400	1,000			
RETS Tech Center	4,959		700				1,100	900	945
Shawnee State University	2,763	1,866/—	525		945	2,919	2,914	945	2,919
Sinclair Community College	‡ 1,395	2,025/720	774				1,854	465	2,000
Southeastern Business College	4,660		185						
Southern Ohio College	6,190		500				1,250	600	
Southern State Community College	† 2,574	2,164/—	600				1,500	750	
Stark Technical College	† 2,457	1,080/—	740				1,500	770	798
Terra Community College	‡ 2,019	2,856/—	675					928	400
Tiffin University	† 8,000		600	3,900	700	1,250	1,950	750	1,200
Union Institute	‡ 6,300		600						

†Figures are projected for 1995-96. ‡Figures are for 1994-95.

Total freshmen	Percent receiving aid	Freshmen judged to have need	Percent offered aid	Need-based Acad	Need-based Music/drama	Need-based Art	Need-based Athl	Non-need Acad	Non-need Music/drama	Non-need Art	Non-need Athl	Priority	Closing	Inst aid form	Notes
351	54	244	95	X				X				2/15	none		
496	23	237	87	X		X		X				2/15	none		
3,039	61	961	97	X				X	X	X	X	2/15	none		
162	85			X									none		
535	90	346	100	X				X	X	X		4/1	none		
348	98	284	100	X	X		X	X	X		X	4/15	none		
													none		
491	75	405	100	X				X				5/1	7/15		
153	96	257	100	X				X	X	X		3/1	8/1		
776	53	464	75	X				X				4/1	none		
400	51							X					none		
888	63	368	99					X				4/1	none		
36	100	27	100	X				X				4/15	none	X	
687	75							X	X			2/1		X	
239	82							X			X	3/1	none		
													none		
599	92	450	100	X	X			X	X	X		5/1	7/31	X	
		130	100	X				X				5/1	none		
				X	X	X		X	X	X	X	2/15	none		
355	45			X	X	X		X	X	X		4/1	none		
332	40			X	X	X	X	X	X	X	X	4/1	none		
304	43			X	X	X		X				4/1	none		
385	30			X				X				4/1	none		
3,314	74			X				X	X	X	X	2/15	4/1		
475	70			X				X					4/1		
													none		
													none		
													none		
102	80	78	100									4/15	8/30		
486	80	320	100					X	X	X		3/1	none		
420	90							X	X	X		3/1	4/15		
486	40											3/15	none		
2,728	40						X	X				3/15	none		
													none		
													none		
538	85			X	X	X	X	X	X	X	X	6/15	none		
4,098	37	962	86	X				X	X	X	X	4/15	none		
													none		
502	31				X	X	X	X				7/1	none		
2,376	46			X				X				5/1	none	X	
1,854	60							X				8/20	none		
254	80	221	100	X				X			X	3/31	none		
													9/1	X	

Institution	Tuition and fees	Add'l out-of-state/district tuition	Books and supplies	Costs for campus residents — Room and board	Trans-portation	Other costs	Costs for students at home — Board only	Trans-portation	Other costs
University of Akron									
Akron	‡ 3,360	4,770/—	550	3,844	840		1,995	1,260	1,155
Wayne College	‡ 2,915	7,145/—	550				1,500	960	720
University of Cincinnati									
Access Colleges	3,732	5,175/—	500	4,697	537	1,195	2,053	930	1,067
Cincinnati	‡ 3,732	5,157/—	500	4,697	537	1,195	2,053	930	1,067
Clermont College	‡ 2,916	4,284/—	520						
Raymond Walters College	‡ 3,168	4,896/—	600				1,600	900	900
University of Dayton	12,810		600	4,360	300	800	1,700	300	500
University of Findlay	12,612		550	5,210	400	650	1,000	300	
University of Rio Grande	·‡ 2,496	4,296/336	700	4,068	400	1,500	2,000	2,025	1,500
University of Toledo	‡ 3,399	4,778/—	690	4,167	1,047	2,727	800	1,047	2,727
Urbana University	9,484		500	4,350	150	508	2,450	150	508
Ursuline College	10,410		450	4,330	450	950	3,000	850	850
Virginia Marti College of Fashion and Art	7,870		650				2,700	400	1,512
Walsh University	9,660		500	4,500	500	950		900	1,500
Washington State Community College	‡ 2,190	2,160/—	506		400	1,019	3,534	400	1,019
West Side Institute of Technology	‡ 4,645		1,000				2,043	936	1,353
Wilberforce University	‡ 7,010		550	3,720	970	1,490	1,760	970	1,800
Wilmington College	11,250		500	4,200	800	1,186	2,210	1,410	1,186
Wittenberg University	17,696		400	4,536		800			
Wright State University									
Dayton	‡ 3,234	6,468/—	650	4,002	600	1,000		1,310	1,000
Lake Campus	‡ 2,895	3,234/—	650					1,200	1,000
Xavier University	12,270		600	5,190	600	650	1,700	600	650
Youngstown State University	3,084	3,168/2,160	500	3,950	375	950	1,800	900	950
Oklahoma									
Bacone College	3,590		600	3,270	500	500	3,500	1,000	1,000
Bartlesville Wesleyan College	7,200		650	3,400	1,000	1,000	2,600	1,000	1,000
Cameron University	‡ 1,650	2,070/—	750	2,400	750	900	1,500	750	800
Carl Albert State College	‡ 1,035	1,680/—	600		500	600		900	1,000
Connors State College	‡ 1,049	1,680/—	750	2,054	900	1,000	1,500	900	1,000
East Central University	‡ 1,529	2,063/—	400	2,274	653	1,148	1,548	930	1,148
Eastern Oklahoma State College	‡ 1,020	1,680/—	500	2,124	250	500	1,250	900	500
Langston University	‡ 1,542	2,070/—	450	2,580					
Mid-America Bible College	4,148		400	3,236	1,250	1,530	2,475	850	1,530
Murray State College	‡ 1,086	1,680/—	600	2,466	806	2,000	1,580	756	2,000
National Education Center: Spartan School of Aeronautics	7,674		660		648	1,330	2,000	639	1,260
Northeastern Oklahoma Agricultural and Mechanical College	‡ 1,049	1,680/—	400	2,214	300	675			675
Northeastern State University	‡ 1,467	2,063/—	350	3,024	540	625			625
Northern Oklahoma College	‡ 1,044	1,680/—	500	2,120	500	1,200	1,500	1,600	1,000
Northwestern Oklahoma State University	‡ 1,460	2,063/—	500	1,956	500	1,000	1,000	600	1,200
Oklahoma Baptist University	6,484		760	3,210	500	1,500	650	1,000	1,350
Oklahoma Christian University of Science and Arts	7,360		500	3,650	1,050	850	1,750	1,050	850
Oklahoma City Community College	‡ 1,098	1,680/—	675					900	600
Oklahoma City University	7,476		350	3,830	106	942	1,286	778	942
Oklahoma Panhandle State University	‡ 1,453	2,070/—		1,940	400	1,000	1,500	1,000	1,000

†Figures are projected for 1995-96. ‡Figures are for 1994-95.

All aid		Need–based aid		Grants and scholarships								Financial aid deadlines		Inst aid form	Notes
				Need–based				Non–need–based							
Total fresh–men	Percent receiving aid	Freshmen judged to have need	Percent offered aid	Acad	Music/ drama	Art	Athl	Acad	Music/ drama	Art	Athl	Priority	Closing		
3,075	56	1,682	100	X				X	X	X	X	4/1	none	X	
				X				X							
													none		
2,362	65	1,169	98	X	X			X	X	X	X	3/1	none		
				X	X			X	X	X		3/1	none		
472	40			X				X				3/1	5/1		
1,709	90	1,000	100	X				X	X	X	X	3/31	none	X	
510	80	350	97	X	X		X	X	X		X	4/1	8/1		
				X	X	X	X	X	X		X	3/15	none		
3,168	42	1,930	94	X	X	X	X	X	X	X	X	4/1	none		
218	100	194	100	X				X	X		X	5/1	none		
				X		X		X				3/15	none		
													none		
446	92	250	100	X			X	X			X	3/1	8/1		
865	72			X				X					none		
													none		
360	95	190	100	X				X				4/30	6/1		
234	92	180	100	X	X			X	X			3/1	6/1		
585	60	357	100	X	X	X		X	X	X		3/1	none	X	
1,873	58	1,790	100	X				X	X	X	X	4/1	none		
190	45			X				X				3/1	none		
762	81							X	X	X	X	2/15	none		
2,007	65	1,204	100	X	X	X	X	X	X	X	X	4/1	none	X	
													none		
21	90			X	X		X	X	X		X	3/1	none		
2,004	72	671	97	X	X	X	X	X	X	X	X	5/15	none		
													none		
670	60	1,080	100	X			X	X	X		X	3/31	5/1	X	
587	59			X	X	X	X	X	X	X	X	4/15	none		
628	70			X				X	X		X	3/1	none		
1,002	70							X	X		X	3/1	5/1		
102	99	92	100					X	X			5/1	none		
				X	X	X	X	X	X	X	X	4/15	none		
													none		
								X	X	X	X		3/1		
1,712	72			X	X	X	X	X	X	X	X	4/1	5/1		
536	35	450	100	X	X	X	X	X	X	X	X	3/1	none		
260	65	175	100	X	X	X	X	X	X	X	X	6/1	none		
493	74			X	X	X	X	X	X	X	X	3/1	none		
308	82	207	100					X	X	X	X	4/15	7/31		
2,076	50							X				7/1	none		
293	95	225	100	X	X	X	X	X	X		X	3/1	none		
263	39	182	100	X	X		X	X	X		X	8/25	none		

Institution	Tuition and fees	Add'l out-of-state/ district tuition	Books and supplies	Costs for campus residents			Costs for students at home		
				Room and board	Trans-portation	Other costs	Board only	Trans-portation	Other costs
Oklahoma State University									
Oklahoma City	‡ 1,373	2,040/—	450				3,500	850	1,800
Okmulgee	‡ 1,319	2,040/—	517	2,258	800	800	400	800	800
Stillwater	‡ 1,892	3,204/—	720	3,344	200	1,250	1,750	1,100	1,250
Oral Roberts University	8,730		600	4,150	1,175	1,400	1,700	1,175	1,400
Phillips University	6,550		650	3,904			2,204	480	640
Redlands Community College	‡ 1,147	1,680/—	400					700	1,200
Rogers State College	‡ 1,179	1,680/—	600					1,000	1,200
Rose State College	‡ 1,005	1,680/—	625					225	125
St. Gregory's College	† 5,380		567	3,440	340	958	1,690	546	958
Seminole Junior College	‡ 936	1,590/—	324	1,880	90	175	1,500	510	855
Southeastern Oklahoma State University	‡ 1,531	2,171/—	450	2,619	850	1,124	1,752	971	1,355
Southern Nazarene University	7,128		400	3,790	400	1,200	2,400	800	1,200
Southwestern College of Christian Ministries	3,850		400	2,700	600	1,000	800	600	1,000
Southwestern Oklahoma State University	‡ 1,422	2,063/—	500	2,016	800	900	1,650	800	900
Tulsa Junior College	‡ 975	1,710/—	468			722	1,743	813	722
University of Central Oklahoma	‡ 1,497	2,063/—	500	2,311	600	1,400		600	1,400
University of Oklahoma									
Health Sciences Center	‡ 1,757	3,240/—	875				1,650	882	1,566
Norman	‡ 1,910	3,435/—	765	4,253	1,287	1,889	2,133	1,287	1,889
University of Science and Arts of Oklahoma	‡ 1,440	2,070/—	600	1,920	250	1,200		350	1,200
University of Tulsa	12,300		1,200	4,074	1,000	1,350	1,800	1,650	850
Western Oklahoma State College	‡ 960	1,680/—	450					900	400
Oregon									
Bassist College	8,660		1,300	4,000	600	900	1,500	650	900
Blue Mountain Community College	1,080	2,160/—	450					600	900
Central Oregon Community College	† 1,562	4,500/450	750	3,750	900	800	1,800	900	800
Chemeketa Community College	1,200	4,464/—	1,200					840	840
Clackamas Community College	‡ 1,344	3,360/—	600				2,061	840	720
Clatsop Community College	1,080	2,592/—	660				2,000	1,000	1,000
Concordia College	10,500		500	3,500	400	900	1,500	400	900
Eastern Oregon State College	‡ 2,766		450	3,600	600	900	1,600	600	900
Eugene Bible College	4,728		600	2,766	1,000	600	1,800	750	1,000
George Fox College	13,640		400	4,400	350	800	2,100	350	800
Lane Community College	954	2,250/—	795				1,600	396	1,800
Lewis & Clark College	16,820		500	5,070	300	1,000	2,000		1,000
Linfield College	14,380		600	4,380	200	900	1,500	75	900
Linn-Benton Community College	† 1,440	3,915/—	600		990	855	1,665	700	600
Marylhurst College	‡ 8,550		500				1,760	600	1,688
Mount Angel Seminary	7,700		400	3,750	1,000	1,000			
Mount Hood Community College	‡ 1,485	4,995/—	621				1,038	816	540
Multnomah Bible College	6,700		440	3,260	700	900		900	900
Northwest Christian College	9,535		540	4,105		1,530	1,800		1,530
Oregon Health Sciences University	‡ 4,406	5,955/—	500		1,250	1,000	2,050	1,250	1,000
Oregon Institute of Technology	‡ 3,150	6,186/—	810	3,804	600	2,130	1,800	200	2,130
Oregon Polytechnic Institute	6,100		1,100				2,000	500	700
Oregon State University	‡ 3,048	6,048/—	780	3,814	470	2,388	2,056	300	1,746
Pacific Northwest College of Art	‡ 9,336		900					600	4,500
Pacific University	15,140		550	4,276	500	1,174	1,500	500	1,174
Portland Community College	† 1,506	3,240/—	800				1,775	8,205	760

†Figures are projected for 1995-96. ‡Figures are for 1994-95.

| All aid | | Need-based aid | | Grants and scholarships | | | | | | | | Financial aid deadlines | | Inst aid form | Notes |
| Total freshmen | Percent receiving aid | Freshmen judged to have need | Percent offered aid | Need-based | | | | Non-need-based | | | | | | | |
				Acad	Music/drama	Art	Athl	Acad	Music/drama	Art	Athl	Priority	Closing		
2,500	30	1,000	100	X				X				7/1	none		
858	60			X								3/1	none	X	
2,177	67			X	X	X	X	X	X	X	X	3/1	none		
511	85			X				X	X	X	X	4/1	none		
319	76	210	100	X	X		X	X	X	X	X	3/1	none		
521	22			X				X			X	3/30	none		
1,727	46	350	100	X				X	X	X		4/15	none		
6,262	30			X	X	X	X	X	X	X	X	5/1	none		
93	90	60	100	X	X	X	X	X	X	X	X	6/1	none		
													none		
513	60	287	100	X	X	X	X	X	X	X	X	4/1	11/1		
371	82	209	100					X	X	X	X	3/1	none		
								X	X			8/1	7/15		
859	52							X	X	X	X	3/1	none		
3,937	28			X				X				4/1	none		
1,431	30			X	X	X	X	X	X	X	X	6/1	none		
				X				X				3/1	none		
2,464	71	998	96	X				X	X	X	X	3/1	none		
289	83	163	100					X	X	X	X	3/15	none		
568	87	496	100					X	X	X	X	4/1	none	X	
961	60			X	X	X	X					3/30	none		
32	76	10	100	X				X				6/1	none	X	
													none		
748	33	409	100	X				X	X	X		2/28	none		
4,415	60			X							X	4/1	9/4		
3,517	45							X	X	X	X	3/1	none		
													none		
105	95	74	100				X	X	X		X	5/1	none		
643	80	303	100	X	X			X	X			2/15	none		
74	80	68	100	X	X			X	X			5/1	none	X	
337	86	276	100					X	X		X	3/1	8/1		
4,467	22	1,670	100					X	X		X	3/15	none		
515	69	321	100	X	X	X		X	X			2/15	none	X	
378	92	281	100	X	X	X		X	X			2/1	none	X	
622	50			X				X	X	X	X	4/1	none	X	
196	65			X	X	X			X	X		6/1	none	X	
4	75			X				X					none		
				X	X	X	X	X	X	X	X	4/1	none		
224	75			X	X			X	X			3/1	none	X	
53	93			X				X				4/15	none		
												3/1	none		
256	80			X			X	X				3/1	none		
													none		
1,922	65			X	X			X	X		X	3/1	5/1		
22	74	10	100					X		X		4/1	none		
300	87	249	100	X	X	X		X	X	X		3/15	none		
				X			X				X	3/1	none		

Institution	Tuition and fees	Add'l out-of-state/ district tuition	Books and supplies	Costs for campus residents			Costs for students at home		
				Room and board	Trans- portation	Other costs	Board only	Trans- portation	Other costs
Portland State University	‡ 3,060	6,048/—	750		657	1,098	1,800	657	846
Reed College	20,760		500	5,750	720	450	1,500		450
Rogue Community College	1,146	2,592/648	450				1,800	925	825
Southern Oregon State College	‡ 2,835	4,989/—	600	3,772	405	1,610	1,800	690	520
Southwestern Oregon Community College	† 1,212	2,376/—	600				1,800	840	510
Treasure Valley Community College	‡ 1,845	3,420/2,205	420	3,468	750	750		750	750
Umpqua Community College	1,473	4,230/—	600				1,125	900	1,170
University of Oregon									
Eugene	‡ 3,258	7,512/—	600	3,710	262	1,202	1,654	262	1,202
Robert Donald Clark Honors College	‡ 3,099	7,512/—	570	3,660	275	1,550	1,600	275	1,550
University of Portland	13,300		600	4,240	500	600	1,800	500	600
Warner Pacific College	9,082		450	4,232	370	1,250	1,600	370	1,250
Western Baptist College	10,030		600	4,260	800	1,100		1,100	1,100
Western Oregon State College	2,820	4,989/—	720	3,631	1,000	1,240	1,980	800	1,240
Willamette University	16,490		400	4,800	200	510	1,800	1,200	710
Pennsylvania									
Academy of the New Church	‡ 4,230			3,552		1,400			
Albright College	16,575		500	4,620	200	900	2,000	280	900
Allegheny College	18,020		400	4,550	200	320	1,500	200	320
Allentown College of St. Francis de Sales	10,440		500	5,070		800	2,210		800
Alvernia College	9,850		600	4,400	500	600	1,700	700	600
American Institute of Design	‡ 15,315		815						
Antonelli Institute of Art and Photography	9,300		1,200					1,225	1,320
Art Institute of Pittsburgh	† 11,500		490	7,940			2,315	360	1,220
Baptist Bible College of Pennsylvania	6,686		500	4,070	500	600	2,320	1,766	600
Beaver College	13,970		400	5,750	250	550	1,500	450	550
Berean Institute	‡ 3,125		400				1,500	600	500
Bloomsburg University of Pennsylvania	‡ 3,694	4,758/—	500	2,948	385	1,350	500	788	1,350
Bradley Academy for the Visual Arts	8,640		700						
Bryn Mawr College	19,810		550	7,085	300	800	2,700	400	800
Bucknell University	19,730		600	4,925	200	1,350	2,285	2,650	1,350
Bucks County Community College	1,998	6,540/4,260	500				750	2,100	1,350
Butler County Community College	‡ 1,500	3,000/1,500	558				1,500	1,060	900
Cabrini College	11,600		685	6,500	310	1,110	1,585	2,000	1,415
California University of Pennsylvania	† 4,718	4,758/—	600	3,730	400	1,500	1,000	1,227	1,030
Cambria-Rowe Business College	4,735		600						
Carlow College	10,588		500	4,512		1,200	1,500	240	760
Carnegie Mellon University	18,700		450	5,850	700	1,000	2,140	500	1,840
Cedar Crest College	14,770		550	5,365	550	550	1,600	550	550
Central Pennsylvania Business School	† 5,690		800		700	800	1,650	950	800
Chatham College	‡ 13,650		400	5,230		850	952	582	850
Chestnut Hill College	11,825		700	5,445	450	350	1,600	700	350
Cheyney University of Pennsylvania	‡ 3,591	4,758/—	400	3,906	675	1,000	1,500	675	700
CHI Institute	7,285								
Churchman Business School	5,140		750					725	
Clarion University of Pennsylvania	‡ 3,879	4,758/—	575	2,924	660	834	1,450	660	850
College Misericordia	12,190		550	5,990	500	400	1,500	600	400
Community College of Allegheny County									
Allegheny Campus	‡ 1,602	2,976/1,488	500				1,500	722	950
Boyce Campus	‡ 1,602	2,976/1,488	500				1,550	700	1,000

†Figures are projected for 1995-96. ‡Figures are for 1994-95.

| All aid | | Need–based aid | | Grants and scholarships | | | | | | | | Financial aid deadlines | | Inst aid form | Notes |
| Total freshmen | Percent receiving aid | Freshmen judged to have need | Percent offered aid | Need–based | | | | Non–need–based | | | | | | | |
				Acad	Music/ drama	Art	Athl	Acad	Music/ drama	Art	Athl	Priority	Closing		
812	34			X				X	X	X	X	3/1	none		
302	43	157	82									2/1	3/1	X	
													none		
763	53	674	98	X			X	X	X	X		3/1	none		
				X				X	X	X	X	2/8	none		
1,800	80			X				X	X	X	X	4/1	none		
1,371	60	420	93	X	X	X	X	X	X	X	X	3/1	none		
3,579	45			X				X	X	X	X	3/1	none		
				X				X	X	X	X		2/1		
430	78	294	100	X				X	X		X	3/1	none		
110	71							X	X			6/1	8/15		
116	92			X	X			X	X		X	2/15	none		
658	73	447	97	X	X		X	X	X	X		3/1	none		
478	75	327	100	X	X	X	X	X	X	X		2/1	6/1		
38	64	13	100									3/1	8/15		
295	92	210	100	X				X	X			3/1	4/1		
478	93	385	100	X	X	X		X	X	X		2/15	none		
261	90	189	99	X	X			X	X			2/15	none		
154	85			X				X				4/1	8/30		
													none		
80	84	67	100	X		X						8/1	none		
722	85			X				X		X			none		
202	85			X				X					4/1		
472	76			X				X	X	X	X	3/15	4/15		
													none		
1,122	80			X	X		X	X				3/15	5/1		
174	75									X		8/1	none		
329	51	171	100	X									1/15	X	
899	60	438	100	X	X	X	X						2/1		
				X	X	X		X	X	X		5/1	none		
1,840	55			X			X	X				4/16	5/1		
192	74	138	100	X				X				4/1	none		
967	69			X				X	X	-	X	4/1	none		
166	94			X			X	X		X	X	5/1	none		
1,164	75	839	100	X	X	X		X	X	X		2/15	none		
208	96	183	100					X				5/1	none		
299	47			X				X					5/1		
106	83	86	100					X	X			3/15	5/1	X	
115	70	81	100	X				X				3/15	none		
222	85			X				X	X		X	4/1	none		
325	88												9/20		
121	67	91	99	X									8/1		
1,070	82	874	98					X	X	X	X	3/15	5/1		
299	95	266	100	X				X				3/1	4/1	X	
1,100	24			X				X			X	5/1	none		
640	24	572	100	X				X	X	X	X	5/1	none		

Institution	Tuition and fees	Add'l out-of-state/district tuition	Books and supplies	Costs for campus residents			Costs for students at home		
				Room and board	Transportation	Other costs	Board only	Transportation	Other costs
North Campus	‡ 1,602	2,976/1,488	500				1,500	722	950
South Campus	‡ 1,602	2,976/1,488	500				1,500	722	950
Community College of Beaver County	‡ 1,760	4,320/2,310	500				1,500	700	900
Community College of Philadelphia	‡ 1,905	3,660/1,830					1,975		1,145
Curtis Institute of Music	600		250				1,100	540	1,795
Dean Institute of Technology	‡ 8,960		500					1,000	
Delaware County Community College	‡ 1,545	3,300/1,650	400				875	650	1,580
Delaware Valley College	13,200		500	5,290	500	1,000	1,700	900	1,050
Dickinson College	19,750		600	5,270	250	1,000	1,620	250	1,000
Drexel University	13,844		500	6,474	350	1,500		780	1,500
DuBois Business College	‡ 5,125		450	4,500					
Duquesne University	12,578		400	5,580	553	450	1,500	553	450
East Stroudsburg University of Pennsylvania	‡ 4,034	4,758/—	500	3,456	250	750		900	1,350
Eastern College	‡ 11,190		400	4,800	200	970	1,400	900	800
Edinboro University of Pennsylvania	† 3,720	4,124/—	500	3,440	300	1,174		1,500	1,680
Electronic Institutes									
Middletown	5,430		225				2,400	1,450	1,232
Pittsburgh	8,070		600						
Elizabethtown College	15,490		500	4,550	150	600	1,500	350	600
Franklin and Marshall College			590		200	880			2,680
Gannon University	11,780		600	4,520	700	500	1,634	700	500
Geneva College	10,044		600	4,400	750	1,100			1,100
Gettysburg College	20,834		300	4,522	200	500	1,900	500	300
Gratz College	5,920		600					370	
Grove City College	6,174		525	3,474	225	350	1,832	800	350
Gwynedd-Mercy College	11,500		500	5,800	250	600	900	600	600
Hahnemann University School of Health Sciences and Humanities	‡ 8,868		650	8,526	500	2,000	1,200	750	4,200
Harcum College	8,615		400	4,884		1,500			1,500
Harrisburg Area Community College	‡ 1,650	3,210/1,590	500				1,800	885	790
Haverford College	20,215		720	6,550		1,030			
Holy Family College	‡ 9,000		675				2,400	800	1,500
Hussian School of Art	‡ 6,650		800				2,400	900	1,600
Immaculata College	† 10,880		525	5,678	620	1,030		2,215	775
Indiana University of Pennsylvania	‡ 3,725	4,758/—	500	3,136			1,200		1,400
Johnson Technical Institute	‡ 5,754		450		100	1,386	2,358	952	1,386
Juniata College	15,850		450	4,620	250	420	1,650	600	420
Keystone College	‡ 8,960		600	5,240	350	1,226	1,650	1,588	726
King's College	12,260		550	5,680	350	1,795	1,810	725	1,430
Kutztown University of Pennsylvania	‡ 3,699	4,758/—	550	3,230		1,750		900	1,750
La Roche College	9,286		600	5,022	100	1,000	1,500	300	1,000
La Salle University	13,150		500	5,800		3,160	1,015		5,400
Lackawanna Junior College	‡ 5,920		516				2,750	402	2,400
Lafayette College	19,621		600	6,000	100	900		750	850
Lancaster Bible College	‡ 7,620		475	3,400	500	1,500	1,800	800	1,500
Lansdale School of Business	‡ 6,000		425						
Lebanon Valley College of Pennsylvania	14,785		450	4,755	100	770	1,500	800	770
Lehigh Carbon Community College	† 1,890	4,140/2,070	800				1,500	1,280	640
Lehigh University	19,650		750	5,810	150	1,130	3,060	450	1,130
Lincoln Technical Institute	8,920		750						
Lincoln University	‡ 3,395	1,798/—	350	3,400	500	915	750	500	900

†Figures are projected for 1995-96. ‡Figures are for 1994-95.

All aid		Need-based aid		Grants and scholarships								Financial aid deadlines		Inst aid form	Notes
				Need-based				Non-need-based							
Total fresh-men	Percent receiving aid	Freshmen judged to have need	Percent offered aid	Acad	Music/drama	Art	Athl	Acad	Music/drama	Art	Athl	Priority	Closing		
650	24							X			X	5/1	none		
850	24			X				X	X	X	X	5/1	none	X	
				X			X	X				5/1	none		
				X				X	X	X			5/1	X	
23	100							X					2/15		
3,485	30			X								5/1	none		
384	82	298	100	X				X				3/1	4/1		
518	60	315	100	X	X	X		X				2/15	none		
366	76							X	X	X	X	5/1	none		
1,140	80	803	100	X				X	X		X		5/1		
842	67							X			X		3/15		
191	80	171	100	X	X			X	X				none		
1,396	80	1,262	100	X			X	X			X		5/1		
												8/1	none		
53	90											8/1	none		
473	86	366	100	X	X	X		X	X			3/1	4/1		
500	68	274	100	X				X				2/1			
573	91	398	100	X			X	X			X	3/1	none		
295	91	265	100	X			X	X	X			4/15	none		
609	51	327	98	X	X							2/15			
16	38			X	X							9/15	none		
607	57	243	99	X	X			X				5/1			
74	82	52	100	X				X				3/15	none		
				X				X				5/1	5/31		
138	82			X				X				4/15	none		
				X		X		X			X	5/15	none		
314	45	127	100										1/31		
176	89			X			X	X			X	2/15	5/1		
30	80					X					X	8/1	none		
77	96	65	100	X	X			X	X			3/1	4/1	X	
1,748	79			X	X			X	X	X	X	5/1	none		
264	80			X				X				4/15	8/1		
258	85	222	100	X	X	X		X	X			3/1	none		
362	80	204	98	X		X		X				5/1	none		
396	86	324	98	X				X				3/1	none		
1,505	85	970	72	X	X	X	X	X		X	X		3/15		
158	90	136	100					X				5/1	none		
536	82	389	100	X				X			X	2/15	none		
365	80	342	91	X			X	X			X	5/1	none		
557	53	272	95	X	X	X	X					2/15	none		
109	80	81	89					X	X			6/1	none		
356	91	264	100	X	X			X				3/1	none		
897	40			X				X				5/1	none		
1,105	58	609	100	X	X		X	X					2/15	X	
													none		
354	91			X	X			X	X			3/15	none		

Institution	Tuition and fees	Add'l out-of-state/ district tuition	Books and supplies	Costs for campus residents			Costs for students at home		
				Room and board	Trans-portation	Other costs	Board only	Trans-portation	Other costs
Lock Haven University of Pennsylvania	‡ 3,662	4,758/—	450	3,716	200	1,000		400	1,000
Luzerne County Community College	‡ 1,590	2,880/1,440	400				725	500	625
Lycoming College	14,760		500	4,400	300	600	2,000	300	600
Manor Junior College	7,015		600	3,600	700	1,975	1,700	1,100	1,500
Mansfield University of Pennsylvania	‡ 3,624	4,758/—	650	3,324	800	800	1,700	800	800
Marywood College	12,240		600	4,800	300	700	750	600	700
Mercyhurst College	11,010		465	4,251	275	800		475	
Messiah College	10,954		475	5,040	400	800	1,000	400	800
Millersville University of Pennsylvania	‡ 3,920	4,758/—	450	3,830	300	958	1,056	600	989
Montgomery County Community College	‡ 2,010	3,900/1,950	565					1,045	1,000
Moore College of Art and Design	14,422		800	5,143	500	1,000	1,500	600	700
Moravian College	15,880		550	4,950	300	1,020	2,230	1,320	1,250
Mount Aloysius College	† 8,390		750	3,853		1,500			1,500
Muhlenberg College	17,550		560	4,720	150	800	2,060	150	800
National Education Center: Vale Tech Campus	6,215		850	2,774	499	1,060	1,814	499	1,066
Neumann College	‡ 10,480		650					800	500
Northampton County Area Community College	† 1,950	4,260/2,130	600	3,660	400	1,000	300	400	1,000
Peirce College	6,804		650		550	3,200			
Penn State									
Allentown Campus	‡ 4,878	2,592/—	512				1,800	990	1,854
Altoona Campus	‡ 4,878	2,592/—	512	4,060	378	2,016	1,800	990	1,854
Beaver Campus	‡ 4,878	2,592/—	512	4,060	378	2,016	1,800	990	1,854
Berks Campus	‡ 4,878	2,592/—	512	4,060	378	2,016	1,800	990	1,854
Delaware County Campus	‡ 4,878	2,592/—	512				1,800	990	1,854
Du Bois Campus	‡ 4,878	2,592/—	512				1,800	990	1,854
Erie Behrend College	‡ 5,036	5,688/—	512	4,060	378	2,016	1,800	990	1,854
Fayette Campus	‡ 4,878	2,592/—	512				1,800	990	1,854
Harrisburg Capital College	‡ 5,036	5,688/—	512	4,060	378	2,016	1,800	990	1,854
Hazleton Campus	‡ 4,878	2,592/—	512	4,060	378	2,016	1,800	990	1,854
McKeesport Campus	‡ 4,878	2,592/—	512	4,060	378	2,016	1,800	990	1,854
Mont Alto Campus	‡ 4,878	2,592/—	512	4,060	378	2,016	1,800	990	1,854
New Kensington Campus	‡ 4,878	2,592/—	512				1,800	990	1,854
Ogontz Campus	‡ 4,878	2,592/—	512				1,800	990	1,854
Schuylkill Campus	‡ 4,878	2,592/—	512	4,060	378	2,016	1,800	990	1,854
Shenango Campus	‡ 4,878	2,592/—	512				1,800	990	1,854
University Park Campus	‡ 5,036	5,688/—	512	4,060	378	2,016	1,800	990	1,854
Wilkes-Barre Campus	‡ 4,878	2,592/—	512				1,800	990	1,854
Worthington-Scranton Campus	‡ 4,878	2,592/—	512				1,800	990	1,854
York Campus	‡ 4,878	2,592/—	512				1,800	990	1,854
Penn Technical Institute	7,070		360					1,000	
Pennco Tech	‡ 7,075		800						
Pennsylvania College of Technology	† 6,060	1,200/—	800				1,800	150	1,800
Pennsylvania Institute of Culinary Arts	8,630			6,749					
Pennsylvania Institute of Technology	‡ 7,308		700						
Philadelphia College of Bible	8,060		585	4,444	550	870	2,384	960	870
Philadelphia College of Pharmacy and Science	11,950		500	4,800	400	800	1,800	1,050	800
Philadelphia College of Textiles and Science	12,450		500	5,676	500	1,038		700	1,038

†Figures are projected for 1995-96. ‡Figures are for 1994-95.

| All aid | | Need-based aid | | Grants and scholarships | | | | | | | | Financial aid deadlines | | Inst aid form | Notes |
Total fresh-men	Percent receiving aid	Freshmen judged to have need	Percent offered aid	Need-based Acad	Music/drama	Art	Athl	Non-need-based Acad	Music/drama	Art	Athl	Priority	Closing		
859	90			X	X		X	X	X		X	4/15	5/1		
2,109	80	940	94	X				X				4/15	none		
383	88	310	100					X	X	X		4/15	none	X	
285	90			X			X	X			X	3/15	8/15		
576	75	338	95	X				X	X	X	X	3/15	4/1		
318	90	253	100	X	X	X		X	X	X		2/15	none		
378	92	345	100	X	X			X	X	X	X	3/15	none	X	
595	84	459	100	X				X				4/1	none		
1,095	70	576	93					X	X	X	X		5/1		
3,013	12	1,150	100	X				X				5/1	none		
89	80					X					X	4/1	none		
311	87	258	100	X	X	X		X				2/15	3/15		
536	89			X				X			X	5/1	8/1		
468	62			X	X			X	X			2/15			
													none		
121	79			X				X				3/15	none		
1,804	65			X		X		X				3/31	none		
330	85			X				X				4/15	6/1		
												2/15	none		
												2/15	none		
												2/15	none		
												2/15	none		
												2/15	none		
												2/15	none		
614	67			X	X	X		X	X	X		3/15	none		
												2/15	none		
				X	X	X		X	X	X		2/15	none		
												2/15	none		
												2/15	none		
												2/15	none		
												2/15	none		
												2/15	none		
												2/15	none		
												2/15	none		
3,687	67			X	X	X	X	X	X	X	X	2/15	none		
												2/15	none		
												2/15	none		
												2/15	none		
													none		
													none		
1,345	75			X				X				3/1	none		
		227	100										none		
141	92			X	X			X	X			5/1	none		
374	68	292	94	X				X			X	3/15	4/15		
473	75							X			X	4/15	none		

189

Institution	Tuition and fees	Add'l out-of-state/district tuition	Books and supplies	Costs for campus residents			Costs for students at home		
				Room and board	Transportation	Other costs	Board only	Transportation	Other costs
Pittsburgh Institute of Mortuary Science	‡ 7,660								
Pittsburgh Technical Institute	† 9,105		800		675	1,386			
Point Park College	10,552		400	5,072		450		350	200
Reading Area Community College	‡ 1,800	3,480/1,740	450					600	1,200
Robert Morris College	7,350		500	4,554	400	600	1,500	400	600
Rosemont College	12,405		700	6,100	300	700		650	700
St. Charles Borromeo Seminary-Overbrook	6,000		1,000	3,900	1,100	3,000			
St. Francis College	11,860		475	5,350	435	800	1,500	435	800
St. Joseph's University	13,950		550	6,150	560	1,190	2,000	1,100	2,030
St. Vincent College	11,805		500	4,200		800	1,800		800
Seton Hill College	‡ 11,370		550	4,180	500	1,500	1,600	1,300	1,900
Shippensburg University of Pennsylvania	‡ 3,856	4,758/—	400	3,504	200	1,100		800	1,300
Slippery Rock University of Pennsylvania	‡ 3,776	4,758/—	600	3,374		725		400	725
South Hills Business School	‡ 6,775		551		850	2,330	2,124	850	
Susquehanna University	17,080		600	4,900	200	600	1,500	200	600
Swarthmore College	† 20,186		700	6,880	420	738		1,200	738
Talmudical Yeshiva of Philadelphia	5,006			4,174					
Temple University	5,464	4,782/—	600	5,282		1,000			2,953
Thaddeus Stevens State School of Technology	4,370		275	3,910	600	300	1,000	1,000	300
Thiel College	11,972		600	4,958		1,390	2,000	1,285	575
Thomas Jefferson University: College of Allied Health Sciences	14,350		1,050		900	600	1,900	1,300	600
Triangle Tech: Pittsburgh Campus	† 6,350		500	4,842			1,500	1,754	1,440
University of the Arts	13,670		1,700	5,880	500	1,245	800	800	1,830
University of Pennsylvania	‡ 19,898		550	7,500		1,242	1,350		1,262
University of Pittsburgh									
Bradford	‡ 5,336	5,824/—	500	4,030	600	500		1,200	500
Greensburg	‡ 5,328	5,824/—	550	3,710	550	900	1,900	1,100	900
Johnstown	‡ 5,432	5,824/—	600	3,966		1,500			1,500
Pittsburgh	‡ 5,416	5,824/—	400	4,560	400	900	1,500	600	900
Titusville	‡ 5,200	5,592/—	600	4,170	400	550	1,500	950	550
University of Scranton	12,705		650	5,986	350	900	1,900	800	900
Ursinus College	15,840		500	5,330	135	800	900	450	800
Valley Forge Christian College	5,032		500	3,188	350	1,200	300	1,600	1,200
Valley Forge Military College	‡ 10,900		450	6,630		250			
Villanova University	‡ 15,790		800	6,400		1,200	2,000	500	800
Washington and Jefferson College	16,840		200	4,205	140	500	1,780	1,100	500
Waynesburg College	‡ 9,060		500	3,620	350	751	1,864	1,000	1,101
West Chester University of Pennsylvania	‡ 3,646	4,758/—	450	4,108	514	1,000	1,200	870	1,000
Westminster College	13,515		430	3,980		685	1,980		685
Westmoreland County Community College	1,313	2,580/1,440	400				1,000	500	100
Widener University	12,350		500	5,400	500	900	1,500	900	900
Wilkes University	12,373		550	5,410	500	760	1,500	800	700
Williamson Free School of Mechanical Trades	‡ 185				450	400			
Wilson College	† 12,117		450	5,338	125	350	1,500	300	350
Yeshivath Beth Moshe	‡								
York College of Pennsylvania	5,490		500	3,810	400	850		750	850

†Figures are projected for 1995-96. ‡Figures are for 1994-95.

| All aid | | Need–based aid | | Grants and scholarships | | | | | | | | Financial aid deadlines | | Inst aid form | Notes |
Total freshmen	Percent receiving aid	Freshmen judged to have need	Percent offered aid	Need–based Acad	Music/drama	Art	Athl	Non–need–based Acad	Music/drama	Art	Athl	Priority	Closing		
318	99	317	100	X				X					none	X	
													none		
206	94	189	100	X	X			X	X	X	X	5/1	none		
500	45			X				X				7/15	none		
535	75	391	95	X			X	X			X	3/1	5/1		
120	60	113	100	X	X	X		X		X		2/15	none	X	
12	100	9	100									4/1	none		
290	94	462	100	X			X	X			X	5/1	none		
772	83	501	100	X				X			X		3/1		
276	83	205	100					X	X		X	3/1	5/1		
168	90	160	100	X	X	X	X	X	X	X	X	5/1	8/1	X	
1,252	81	1,076	92	X			X	X			X	5/1	none	X	
1,239	78	890	90	X	X		X	X		X	X	5/1	none		
224	95	220	100	X				X					none		
385	80	298	100					X	X			3/15	5/1	X	
328	44			X								2/1	4/1		
													none		
2,650	63	1,580	100	X				X	X		X		3/31		
288	20	121	90									3/15	none		
291	94	235	100	X				X				4/1	none		
				X				X					5/1		
				X	X	X		X	X	X		3/15	none	X	
2,346	56	1,026	100									2/15	none		
378	60							X				3/1	none		
329	87	221	100	X				X					4/1		
714	84	470	90	X				X			X	4/1	none		
2,435	70	1,600	100	X				X			X	3/1	none		
129	87	130	100					X				5/1	none		
956	76	657	89	X				X				2/15	none	X	
314	90	247	100	X				X	X	X			2/15		
108	51	116	100	X				X	X			5/1	none	X	
96	80			X	X		X		X		X	5/1	none		
1,729	63	1,030	100	X			X	X			X	2/15	3/15		
307	86	255	92	X				X				3/15	none		
271	89			X				X				3/15	none		
1,369	65							X	X		X	3/15	none		
446	81	291	100	X	X		X	X	X		X	5/1	6/30		
1,358	56	480	100	X				X				5/1	none		
492	92			X	X			X	X			3/1	none		
517	90			X	X	X	X	X	X	X	X		none		
100	100														
77	78	52	100	X	X	X		X					4/30	X	
													none		
812	67	318	100	X	X	X		X	X	X		4/15	none		

Institution	Tuition and fees	Add'l out-of-state/district tuition	Books and supplies	Costs for campus residents			Costs for students at home		
				Room and board	Trans-portation	Other costs	Board only	Trans-portation	Other costs
Puerto Rico									
American University of Puerto Rico	† 2,570		400					780	
Bayamon Central University	† 2,814		414				1,500	471	790
Caribbean University	2,750		640				1,200	955	1,950
Colegio Universitario del Este	‡ 2,620		300				1,080	720	1,045
Columbia College	3,825		468						331
Conservatory of Music of Puerto Rico	560		400				2,268	650	450
Electronic Data Processing College of Puerto Rico	2,509		465				600	900	1,455
Escuela de Artes Plasticas de Puerto Rico	‡ 1,584		2,250				1,250	500	1,750
Huertas Junior College	3,235		600				500	600	600
ICPR Junior College	2,700		528				2,280	1,075	1,848
Inter American University of Puerto Rico									
Aguadilla Campus	3,292								
Arecibo Campus	‡ 3,213		640				1,200	540	880
Barranquitas Campus	† 3,213		640		540	880	800	540	880
Bayamon Campus	3,213								
Fajardo Campus	3,213								
Guayama Campus	3,213		640				540	880	
Metropolitan Campus	3,213		590				1,200	540	880
Ponce Campus	3,213								
San German Campus	3,213		700	2,060	100	800	1,000	500	1,000
Pontifical Catholic University of Puerto Rico	2,971		450		408	1,050	957	408	1,050
Technological College of the Municipality of San Juan	1,550		540				900	490	800
Turabo University	‡ 2,620		300				1,080	720	1,045
Universidad Adventista de las Antillas	‡ 3,180		500	2,280	500	500	1,400	500	500
Universidad Metropolitana	‡ 2,620		300				1,080	720	1,045
Universidad Politecnica de Puerto Rico	‡ 4,290		1,000				1,500	984	1,848
University of Puerto Rico									
Aguadilla	970		800				1,000	700	600
Arecibo Campus	970		1,000				1,100	1,000	3,200
Bayamon Technological University College	970		800				2,160	700	600
Carolina Regional College	970		800				2,160	700	600
Cayey University College	1,242		1,000				1,000		800
Humacao University College	970		1,000				2,400	1,000	800
La Montana Regional College	970		900				1,350	700	600
Mayaguez Campus	970		1,000		500	800		1,000	800
Medical Sciences Campus	970		350				1,800	700	663
Ponce Technological University College	970		800				2,160	700	600
Rio Piedras Campus	‡ 970		800	2,890	700	600	1,890	700	600
University of the Sacred Heart	3,190		560		1,350	1,350	1,350	1,400	1,400
Rhode Island									
Brown University	21,277		760	6,212		1,051	2,448		1,051
Bryant College	13,100		500	6,500	200	700	1,500	950	700
Community College of Rhode Island	‡ 1,686	2,960/—	600				2,700	704	1,000
Johnson & Wales University	10,884		500	5,430	600	500	1,800	600	500
New England Institute of Technology	9,735		600				2,317	1,008	1,872

†Figures are projected for 1995-96. ‡Figures are for 1994-95.

All aid		Need-based aid		Grants and scholarships								Financial aid deadlines		Inst aid form	Notes
				Need-based				Non-need-based							
Total freshmen	Percent receiving aid	Freshmen judged to have need	Percent offered aid	Acad	Music/ drama	Art	Athl	Acad	Music/ drama	Art	Athl	Priority	Closing		
899	72			X			X					5/31	6/30		
736	89			X			X	X			X	4/30	8/1	X	
													none		
1,352	90											3/30	5/30	X	
													none		
40	54	15	100	X									none		
													none		
782	94	573	100	X							X		4/28		
1,040	85	905	100				X					4/29	none		
424	95			X	X		X						4/30		
1,529	85												4/30		
1,179	90	1,028	100				X						4/28	X	
1,944	88			X			X		X	X	X	4/29	none	X	
1,386	80												none		
152	89	125	100	X				X					none		
				X									6/30		
921	96	851	100	X				X				3/31	6/30	X	
692	61			X	X		X						6/16		
914	87	815	97	X				X				5/26	6/16		
874	75			X				X			X		6/15		
757	80			X	X	X	X						6/15		
				X									6/30		
400	86			X			X		X		X	5/31	none		
2,008	75	1,344	100					X	X		X		6/30		
				X								4/30	none		
979	90	881	100	X				X	X		X		6/2		
				X	X	X	X	X	X	X	X		5/31		
													6/30		
1,428	44	576	100										1/1	X	
622	72	380	100	X				X			X		2/15		
2,602	40											3/1	none		
1,803	69							X				3/1	none	X	
903	85											6/1	none		

Institution		Tuition and fees	Add'l out–of–state/ district tuition	Books and supplies	Costs for campus residents			Costs for students at home		
					Room and board	Trans–portation	Other costs	Board only	Trans–portation	Other costs
Providence College		15,590		500	6,475		1,200	1,400	1,600	1,200
Rhode Island College	‡	2,838	4,324/—	600	5,237	400	1,000	1,800	1,000	1,000
Rhode Island School of Design		17,780		1,300	6,618	470	1,100	2,750	2,485	1,100
Roger Williams University		14,155		500	6,660	720	735	1,500	720	735
Salve Regina University		14,650		500	6,700	600	900	2,250	800	1,100
University of Rhode Island	‡	4,242	7,326/—	600	5,613	131	1,332	1,728	2,160	1,332
South Carolina										
Aiken Technical College	‡	720	300/—	450				1,875	1,125	900
Allen University		4,950		500	3,910					
Anderson College		8,821		600	4,145	800	1,450	2,000	1,050	950
Benedict College		6,196		700	3,294	833	1,070		833	1,070
Central Carolina Technical College	‡	820	630/220	600				3,700	1,500	1,200
Charleston Southern University		8,192		750	3,178	1,000	1,125	2,000	1,260	1,000
Chesterfield-Marlboro Technical College	‡	800	350/50	600				2,000	1,694	1,884
The Citadel		3,176	3,994/—	800	3,239		1,100			
Claflin College	†	4,412		600	2,460	1,100	1,125	900		660
Clemson University	‡	3,276	5,080/—	800	3,744	1,078	1,618	1,780	2,156	1,184
Coastal Carolina University	‡	2,710	4,290/—	485	2,640	1,323	823	1,748	1,323	823
Coker College		11,131		750	4,516		500	750		500
College of Charleston	†	3,152	3,152/—	666	3,633	254		1,660	1,848	2,316
Columbia Bible College		7,075		800	3,828		1,800	1,800	2,210	1,800
Columbia College		10,995		700	4,160	850	1,600	2,100	1,050	1,500
Columbia Junior College of Business	‡	3,615		675		900	2,250		900	2,250
Converse College		13,150		500	3,825	300	700	750	400	750
Denmark Technical College	‡	1,160	1,080/—	500	2,682	1,200	1,200	1,500	1,200	1,600
Erskine College		11,908		475	4,086	500	746	1,500	650	1,301
Florence-Darlington Technical College	‡	1,010	376/150	700				1,200		700
Francis Marion University	‡	2,920	2,920/—	400	3,138	1,550	900	1,500	1,550	900
Furman University		14,576		600	4,168	600	757		760	2,425
Greenville Technical College	‡	1,006	600/80	500				3,000	1,700	1,250
Horry-Georgetown Technical College	‡	1,000	1,000/—	400						
Lander University	‡	3,340	1,598/—	485	3,280	465	1,150	1,500	800	550
Limestone College		8,000		840	3,600	1,755	900	3,825	2,025	
Medical University of South Carolina	‡	2,970	4,880/—	825						250
Midlands Technical College	‡	990	990/248	400					772	676
Morris College		4,867		850	2,601	1,050	1,050	2,500	1,550	1,300
Newberry College		10,950		450	2,600	400	1,000		700	1,000
Nielsen Electronics Institute		3,000								
North Greenville College		6,500		500	3,600	350	500	1,600	500	1,000
Orangeburg-Calhoun Technical College	‡	840	420/210	400				1,000	300	500
Piedmont Technical College	‡	1,100	530/200	600					800	800
Presbyterian College		13,454		554	4,184	499	916	1,598	796	1,004
South Carolina State University		2,500	2,480/—	400	2,986	100	700		300	700
Southern Wesleyan University		9,081		800	3,233	750	500	2,163	800	600
Spartanburg Methodist College		6,300		500	3,850	700	500		700	500
Spartanburg Technical College	‡	850	850/220	500					1,200	600
Technical College of the Lowcountry	‡	1,000	500/—	425					1,050	1,600
Tri-County Technical College	‡	912	828/—	504				1,575	947	1,014
Trident Technical College	‡	984	708/160	650					1,275	1,000
University of South Carolina										
Aiken	‡	2,500	3,750/—	600		1,500	1,500	2,100	1,500	1,500
Beaufort	‡	1,740	2,604/—	485				1,665	1,176	975

†Figures are projected for 1995-96. ‡Figures are for 1994-95.

All aid		Need-based aid		Grants and scholarships								Financial aid deadlines		Inst aid form	Notes
				Need-based				Non-need-based							
Total fresh-men	Percent receiving aid	Freshmen judged to have need	Percent offered aid	Acad	Music/drama	Art	Athl	Acad	Music/drama	Art	Athl	Priority	Closing		
863	58			X			X	X			X		2/15		
948	61	592	99	X				X	X	X			3/1	X	
375	57	121	60	X		X		X		X			2/15		
683	78			X				X				3/1	none		
395	75	314	100	X				X				3/1	none	X	
1,996	62			X	X	X	X	X	X		X	3/1	none		
555	39			X				X				5/1	none		
145	100	116	95									1/31	4/15		
203	94			X	X	X	X	X	X	X	X	4/1	none		
429	80			X	X		X	X			X	4/15	none		
540	50			X								8/1	none		
470	90				X			X		X	X	3/1	none		
550	53	100	100	X				X					none		
482	60			X				X			X	3/15	none		
284	93			X	X	X	X						6/1		
2,371	59	1,004	100	X				X	X		X	4/1			
746	52			X	X	X		X	X	X	X	4/1			
134	83			X	X	X	X	X	X	X	X	4/1	8/1		
1,357	64	1,020	91	X	X	X	X	X	X	X	X	3/15	none		
78	37	59	100	X	X			X	X			2/15	none		
235	93	180	100	X				X	X	X	X	4/1	none		
													none		
192	94	122	100	X	X		X	X	X		X	5/1			
544	96			X				X				5/1	6/1		
163	97	127	100	X	X		X	X	X		X	3/15	none	X	
355	52			X				X				5/1	none		
				X	X	X	X	X	X	X	X	3/1	none		
647	53	350	100	X				X	X	X	X		2/1	X	
2,665	30			X				X		X		5/1	none		
				X				X				4/1	5/1		
494	45			X				X	X	X	X	4/15	none		
390	98	382	98	X	X	X	X	X	X	X	X	3/31	6/30		
													none		
1,853	30			X				X				5/30	none		
249	98			X	X		X	X				3/30	none	X	
171	90			X				X	X		X	4/1	5/1		
273	94			X	X	X	X	X	X	X	X	6/1	none		
1,154	70							X					none		
567	70							X				5/1	none		
281	75	184	99	X	X		X	X	X		X	3/1	none		
				X				X	X		X	6/1	none		
91	98	80	100				X	X	X		X	4/15	none	X	
388	83	330	100	X	X		X	X	X		X	6/1	none		
													5/1		
				X				X				6/1	none		
				X				X				5/1	none		
403	43	186	80	X				X	X	X	X	3/15	none	X	
155	80			X				X				4/15	none		

Institution	Tuition and fees	Add'l out-of-state/district tuition	Books and supplies	Costs for campus residents			Costs for students at home		
				Room and board	Trans-portation	Other costs	Board only	Trans-portation	Other costs
Columbia	‡ 3,196	4,878/—	495	3,530	735	2,206	1,500	2,207	2,206
Lancaster	‡ 1,840	2,504/—	500				1,700	1,176	938
Salkehatchie Regional Campus	‡ 1,740	2,604/—	450				1,665	1,176	950
Spartanburg	‡ 2,500	3,750/—	450				1,665	1,176	950
Sumter	‡ 1,740	2,604/—	500				1,700	1,176	938
Union	‡ 1,740	2,604/—	450				1,665	1,176	950
Voorhees College	‡ 4,450		500	2,522	1,200	1,500	1,700	1,200	1,500
Williamsburg Technical College	‡ 720		520					1,600	
Winthrop University	† 3,821	2,800/—	609	3,780	800	1,400	2,410	800	1,440
Wofford College	13,795		605	4,185	515	940	725	675	940
York Technical College	‡ 816	816/164	600					1,155	

South Dakota

Institution	Tuition and fees	Add'l out-of-state/district tuition	Books and supplies	Room and board	Trans-portation	Other costs	Board only	Trans-portation	Other costs
Augustana College	11,780		600	3,372	200	800		400	400
Black Hills State University	‡ 2,257	1,899/—	500	2,714	850	1,250	1,800	850	625
Dakota State University	‡ 2,398	1,899/—	600	2,604	500	750	1,500	500	750
Dakota Wesleyan University	7,992		600	2,925	480	920	1,825	480	1,054
Huron University	7,878		600	3,298	720		1,500	720	960
Kilian Community College	† 4,340		480				2,272	1,440	2,000
Lake Area Technical Institute	1,850		400				1,800	450	675
Mitchell Technical Institute	2,500		800				4,000	900	750
Mount Marty College	8,196		500	3,320	540	950	1,800	540	720
National College	7,970		828	3,405	897	1,053	1,800	1,092	
Nettleton Junior College	5,520		450						
Northern State University	‡ 2,121	1,899/—	550	2,514	735	1,100	1,800	735	1,100
Oglala Lakota College	1,620		260				945	320	450
Presentation College	† 7,015		500	3,046	950	600	1,500	950	600
Sinte Gleska University	‡ 1,880		400					900	400
Sisseton-Wahpeton Community College	† 2,540		440					480	
South Dakota School of Mines and Technology	‡ 2,422	2,210/—	500	2,700	555	1,152	1,140	642	1,152
South Dakota State University	† 2,478	2,356/—	500	2,190					
Southeast Vo-Tech Institute	1,910		500				1,800	900	1,350
University of Sioux Falls	9,490		600	3,230	800	950	2,100	675	650
University of South Dakota	‡ 2,448		695	2,672	664	1,151	875	587	824
Western Dakota Technical Institute	2,500		600				1,800	500	

Tennessee

Institution	Tuition and fees	Add'l out-of-state/district tuition	Books and supplies	Room and board	Trans-portation	Other costs	Board only	Trans-portation	Other costs
American Baptist College of ABT Seminary	2,250		440	2,512					
American Technical Institute	5,250								
Aquinas College	4,760		500				1,750	850	650
Austin Peay State University	‡ 1,864	3,934/—	700	2,930	760	1,500	1,500	1,382	1,500
Belmont University	8,750		720	3,832	980	1,100	2,120	980	1,100
Bethel College	7,000		500	3,200		1,000	650	700	
Bryan College	9,500		450	3,950	600	800	1,125	800	400
Carson-Newman College	9,000		400	3,320	1,000	700	1,710	1,200	750
Chattanooga State Technical Community College	‡ 1,010	2,786/—	450				1,900	1,600	1,700
Christian Brothers University	10,120		800	3,400					2,200
Cleveland State Community College	‡ 982	2,786/—	475				1,600	600	800
Columbia State Community College	‡ 1,006	2,786/—	450				1,200	820	625
Crichton College	5,640		664			2,170	1,500	300	2,170
Cumberland University	7,150		600	3,220					

†Figures are projected for 1995-96. ‡Figures are for 1994-95.

| All aid | | Need–based aid | | Grants and scholarships | | | | | | | | Financial aid deadlines | | Inst aid form | Notes |
| Total freshmen | Percent receiving aid | Freshmen judged to have need | Percent offered aid | Need–based | | | | Non–need–based | | | | | | | |
				Acad	Music/drama	Art	Athl	Acad	Music/drama	Art	Athl	Priority	Closing		
3,229	25	846	76	X				X	X	X	X	4/15	none		
218	35	54	100					X				4/15	none		
186	43			X				X			X	4/15	none		
412	47	174	95	X			X	X	X		X	4/15	7/1		
740	71			X				X					4/15		
165	70							X				4/15	none		
212	96	160	100	X			X	X					none		
127	43	53	100	X									5/1		
744	68							X	X	X	X	5/1	none		
310	80	169	100	X	X		X	X	X		X	3/15	none		
805	40			X				X				3/31	none		
402	90			X			X	X	X	X	X	3/4	none		
557	76	389	94	X	X	X		X	X	X	X	4/1	none		
				X			X	X	X		X	3/1	none		
146	95	130	100	X	X	X	X	X	X	X	X	3/15	none		
155	97	99	100	X			X	X			X		none		
46	80	32	100	X				X					none		
568	80	320	100					X				4/15	none		
													none		
143	97	121	100	X	X		X	X	X		X	3/1	none		
88	94			X			X	X			X	3/1	none	X	
693	79	527	98	X	X			X	X	X	X	3/1	none		
													none		
83	98	57	100	X				X				4/1	none		
													none		
90	98	60	100	X									none		
436	52	303	100					X			X	4/1	none		
1,728	82							X	X	X	X	3/15	none		
													none		
139	95			X	X		X	X	X		X	4/1	none		
1,179	79			X	X	X	X	X	X	X	X	3/1	none		
309	80											7/1	none		
													none		
280	5			X				X				3/15	none		
781	70	620	100					X	X	X	X	4/1	none		
997	70			X				X	X		X	3/15	none	X	
128	90							X	X		X	5/1	none		
													none		
673	91	344	100	X	X	X	X	X	X	X	X	3/1	none	X	
				X	X	X	X	X	X	X	X	6/1	none		
310	97			X	X		X	X	X		X	4/1	none		
495	48	350	100	X			X	X				6/1	none		
													none	X	
70	89			X	X			X	X			7/15	none		
299	70			X				X			X	3/1	none		

Institution	Tuition and fees	Add'l out-of-state/district tuition	Books and supplies	Costs for campus residents			Costs for students at home		
				Room and board	Trans-portation	Other costs	Board only	Trans-portation	Other costs
David Lipscomb University	7,792		500	3,450	500	700	1,800	500	700
Draughons Junior College of Business:									
Nashville	3,340		500						
Dyersburg State Community College	‡ 1,012	2,786/—	450				1,500	1,250	500
East Tennessee State University	‡ 1,624	3,934/—	600	3,134	800	1,800		1,000	1,800
Fisk University	‡ 6,305		600	3,690	1,050	1,750		950	1,600
Free Will Baptist Bible College	4,490		427	3,188	667	783	1,800	668	757
Freed-Hardeman University	6,620		650	3,470	700	1,050	1,840	1,050	1,050
Hiwassee College	5,030		400	3,360	300	900			
Jackson State Community College	‡ 982	2,786/—	425				1,800	1,030	700
John A. Gupton College	6,856		650						
Johnson Bible College	4,475		700	3,125	600	1,000	1,800	1,100	1,400
King College	9,624		600	3,350	1,000	1,200	1,500	350	3,600
Knoxville Business College	5,100		750					1,200	1,200
Knoxville College	‡ 5,892		600	3,150	1,000	1,280	1,500	600	1,280
Lambuth University	5,600		600	4,570		1,200	1,872		1,000
Lane College	‡ 4,916		550	2,862	405	675	2,250	630	675
Lee College	5,132		550	3,420	900	900	1,095	1,050	448
LeMoyne-Owen College	6,000		425	3,790				515	1,000
Lincoln Memorial University	6,550		550	2,980	500	1,200	900	1,280	1,200
Martin Methodist College	5,950		400	2,950					
Maryville College	12,246		500	4,378	642	1,000	1,875	500	750
Memphis College of Art	9,900		1,200	4,300	700	470	1,350	1,000	1,100
Middle Tennessee State University	‡ 1,992	3,934/—	600	2,728	750	1,046	1,500	2,350	1,046
Milligan College	9,100		550	3,400	1,250	1,000	1,000	840	1,950
Motlow State Community College	‡ 1,018	2,786/—	600						3,200
Nashville State Technical Institute	‡ 974	2,786/—	550				1,800	1,162	500
Northeast State Technical Community									
College	‡ 1,010	2,786/—	500					750	890
O'More College of Design	7,300		750					1,500	
Pellissippi State Technical Community									
College	‡ 1,040	2,924/—	400				1,800	1,900	1,300
Rhodes College	15,920		550	4,912	600	900	2,072	500	900
Roane State Community College	‡ 982	2,786/—	500				1,500	1,320	750
Shelby State Community College	‡ 972	2,786/—	400				1,500	540	675
Southern College of Seventh-day									
Adventist	8,880		530	3,642	208	728		208	728
State Technical Institute at Memphis	‡ 968	2,786/—	600				1,918	792	675
Tennessee Institute of Electronics	3,816		425				2,000		1,200
Tennessee State University	‡ 1,798	3,934/—	400	2,720	450	700	1,500	450	700
Tennessee Technological University	‡ 1,802	3,934/—	700	3,698	700	700		700	700
Tennessee Temple University	‡ 4,640		600	3,980	880	850		765	680
Tennessee Wesleyan College	6,200		400	3,600	1,000	1,000	2,168	1,200	900
Trevecca Nazarene College	‡ 6,620		550	3,450	799	800	1,800	599	640
Tusculum College	8,400		550	3,500	400	800	1,700	700	900
Union University	6,350		600	2,860		500		500	500
University of Memphis	‡ 1,972	3,934/—	850	3,430	500	715	1,800	825	715
University of the South	16,315		450	4,280	325	850	2,170		850
University of Tennessee									
Chattanooga	‡ 1,850	3,934/—	550		500	900	1,457	1,200	900
Knoxville	‡ 2,052	3,934/—	760	3,398	494	1,432		1,760	1,432
Martin	‡ 1,900	3,934/—	750	3,490	465	1,545	975	575	1,545

†Figures are projected for 1995-96. ‡Figures are for 1994-95.

198

All aid		Need–based aid		Grants and scholarships								Financial aid deadlines		Inst aid form	Notes
				Need–based				Non–need–based							
Total fresh–men	Percent receiving aid	Freshmen judged to have need	Percent offered aid	Acad	Music/ drama	Art	Athl	Acad	Music/ drama	Art	Athl	Priority	Closing		
		217	100					X	X	X	X	4/15	none		
													none		
441	75			X	X		X	X	X		X	3/15	none	X	
1,428	40							X	X	X	X	4/15	none		
242	80			X				X				4/20	none		
													none	X	
286	93	232	100	X				X	X	X	X	4/1	none		
215	80			X	X		X	X	X		X	5/1	none		
1,416	54							X			X	4/1	none		
													none		
		38	100					X	X			7/1	none		
151	90	126	100	X	X		X	X	X		X	3/1	none	X	
													none		
265	99	220	100	X	X			X	X			5/31	none		
351	75			X	X	X	X	X	X	X	X	3/15	none		
193	97	184	98	X			X	X			X	4/1			
453	90			X	X		X	X	X		X	4/15	none		
410	88											4/15	none		
381	70			X	X		X	X	X		X		4/1		
285	87							X	X	X		3/1	none		
43	84					X		X		X		4/1	none		
1,886	60	995	100	X	X	X	X	X	X		X	3/15	5/15		
275	75	176	100	X	X	X	X	X	X	X	X	3/1	none	X	
742	62			X	X		X	X	X		X	5/1	none		
634	19			X				X				5/1	none	X	
720	36			X				X				8/1	none		
47	30			X		X						2/1	7/30	X	
				X	X			X	X	X		5/1	none		
424	79	171	99	X	X	X		X	X	X		3/1	none		
773	35							X	X	X	X	5/1	none		
986	46							X	X	X	X	4/1	none		
276	86	201	96	X	X			X	X			3/1	none	X	
1,041	25			X				X				3/15	none		
													none		
				X	X		X	X	X		X	4/1	none		
1,475	65			X				X	X		X	3/15	none		
130	60							X	X		X	3/31	none		
99	78	77	100					X	X		X	4/30	7/1		
172	95	101	100	X	X		X					4/15			
118	95			X			X	X			X	4/1	none		
519	78	301	88					X	X	X	X	5/15	8/1		
1,777	50							X	X	X	X	4/1	none		
371	58	182	100	X				X				3/1	none		
966	75	623	90	X	X			X	X	X	X	3/1	none		
2,916	50	1,414	75	X	X	X	X	X	X	X	X	2/15	none		
1,132	65	701	98	X				X	X		X	3/1	none		

Institution	Tuition and fees	Add'l out-of-state/district tuition	Books and supplies	Costs for campus residents			Costs for students at home		
				Room and board	Transportation	Other costs	Board only	Transportation	Other costs
Memphis	‡ 1,840	3,934/—	1,097	3,610	1,370	1,527		1,305	1,455
Vanderbilt University	19,422		600	6,786		600			600
Volunteer State Community College	‡ 976	2,786/—	500				1,370	1,444	400
Walters State Community College	‡ 976	2,786/—	500				1,500	1,200	900
Texas									
Abilene Christian University	8,050		500	3,700	960	1,350	1,500	960	1,350
Alvin Community College	567	780/—	550				1,751	800	1,200
Amarillo College	531	1,230/270	540				1,180	1,136	900
Ambassador University	3,410		300	2,300					
Amber University	4,000		350						
Angelina College	† 588	300/158	600	2,600	300	600	900	1,400	600
Angelo State University	‡ 1,694	4,290/—	500	3,732	590	2,000	1,324	1,320	2,000
Arlington Baptist College	2,300		700		600	720	1,100	600	800
Austin College	12,195		412	4,524	210	1,000	2,574	210	1,000
Austin Community College	† 862	2,970/510	452				1,851	968	1,273
Baptist Missionary Association Theological Seminary	1,620		500		600	1,200	4,000	600	1,200
Bauder Fashion College	6,590		750	3,380	582	1,386	2,358	1,155	1,386
Baylor College of Dentistry	2,200		2,100					1,700	2,600
Baylor University	8,444		634	4,140	874	1,426	2,132	1,712	1,486
Bee County College	† 540	750/360	600	2,310	176	605	1,500	396	605
Blinn College	‡ 804	1,650/240	526	2,462	404	1,036		290	1,036
Brazosport College	470	1,650/150	540				2,090	720	880
Brookhaven College	‡ 510	1,390/380	390					1,560	1,245
Cedar Valley College	‡ 510	1,490/380	600				1,500	1,330	1,045
Central Texas College	‡ 648	1,400/—	900	3,158	545	1,577	1,664	593	1,266
Cisco Junior College	† 690	426/120	500	2,150	200	600	1,100	500	800
Clarendon College	† 730	80/60	400	1,760		150	700	400	800
College of the Mainland	† 477	837/408	450					1,225	1,035
Collin County Community College District	660	1,260/210	450				1,893	1,436	1,129
Commonwealth Institute of Funeral Service	6,075						1,500	2,185	2,529
Concordia Lutheran College	7,980		500	4,080	775	1,050	1,500	650	1,050
Criswell College	‡ 2,915		200						
Dallas Baptist University	‡ 6,850		630	3,270	130	1,230	1,400	1,369	1,230
Dallas Christian College	3,568		850	2,790	250	1,000	2,500	800	1,000
Del Mar College	750	780/240	500				1,500	630	810
DeVry Institute of Technology: Irving	6,335		550				2,097	2,015	2,045
East Texas Baptist University	5,960		545	2,790	530	1,015	1,800	575	960
East Texas State University									
Commerce	‡ 1,736	4,290/—	600	3,600	990	1,080	1,500	990	1,080
Texarkana	1,500	4,290/—	650				1,590	875	970
Eastfield College	‡ 510	1,490/380	400				1,100	1,170	935
El Centro College	570	1,490/380	675					400	600
El Paso Community College	952	2,170/—	530				1,500	1,462	1,188
Frank Phillips College	610	120/60	475	1,600	600	900	1,500	1,150	865
Galveston College	640	360/—	600		1,250	1,500	2,000	1,250	1,150
Grayson County College	785	1,122/—	457	2,191	483	1,003	1,845	1,230	1,504
Hardin-Simmons University	7,115		700	2,980	818	1,322	1,196	818	1,322
Hill College	720	580/180	526	2,500	723	937		1,202	965
Houston Baptist University	11,138		525	2,450	1,260	1,400	1,700	1,260	1,370

†Figures are projected for 1995-96. ‡Figures are for 1994-95.

All aid		Need–based aid		Grants and scholarships								Financial aid deadlines		Inst aid form	Notes
Total freshmen	Percent receiving aid	Freshmen judged to have need	Percent offered aid	Need–based Acad	Music/drama	Art	Athl	Non–need–based Acad	Music/drama	Art	Athl	Priority	Closing		
				X				X				2/15	none	X	
1,483	56	610	100	X	X			X	X		X	2/1	none	X	
								X			X	4/15	none		
970	50			X				X	X		X	3/31	none		
822	87	528	98					X	X	X	X	3/15	none	X	
625	20							X	X	X	X	6/15	none		
													none		
244	88	216	100					X	X		X	4/15	none		
1,100	27			X	X	X	X	X	X	X	X	6/15	none		
				X				X				6/1	none		
97	95	15	100	X	X							8/15	none		
271	91	167	99	X				X	X	X		3/15	none	X	
6,418	30							X				2/15	4/1		
												8/1	8/16		
				X				X				6/1	none		
2,351	66	1,377	95	X	X	X	X	X	X	X	X	5/1	none		
808	50	454	89	X				X	X	X		4/1	none		
				X	X		X	X	X		X	7/1	none		
2,000	21							X				8/1	none		
5,605	68			X		X		X				6/1	none		
2,100	35			X	X	X		X	X	X			none		
2,044	28			X				X				7/1	8/1		
1,507	50							X	X		X	8/15	none		
													none		
				X	X	X		X	X	X			none		
1,654	10	840	100	X	X	X	X	X	X	X	X	6/1	none	X	
131	50	53	100					X				7/16	none		
101	80	83	100	X	X		X	X	X		X	4/15	none		
117	90			X	X			X	X			7/1	none		
163	55							X	X	X	X	5/1	none		
39	73			X	X			X	X				4/15		
1,987	40			X	X	X		X	X	X		5/1	none		
								X					none		
								X	X		X	6/1	none		
				X	X	X	X	X	X	X	X	5/1	10/1	X	
												5/1	none		
2,593	24			X	X	X		X	X	X		5/1	none		
3,492	65							X					6/1		
250	42							X	X		X	7/1	none		
477	21			X	X		X	X	X		X	5/15	none		
													none		
444	72	308	100	X				X	X	X		3/15	none	X	
													none		
206	70							X	X	X	X	5/1	none		

Institution	Tuition and fees	Add'l out-of-state/district tuition	Books and supplies	Costs for campus residents			Costs for students at home		
				Room and board	Trans-portation	Other costs	Board only	Trans-portation	Other costs
Houston Community College	‡ 840	1,380/360	1,000				2,657	443	1,328
Howard College	‡ 800	400/50	350	2,100	800	1,175	750	800	1,175
Howard Payne University	5,940		460	3,550	638	1,250	1,500	765	1,085
Huston-Tillotson College	5,544		557	3,878	723	1,190	2,208	1,190	1,190
Incarnate Word College	9,570		750	4,190	950	1,980	1,920	1,442	1,980
Institute for Christian Studies	910		400			1,540			600
Jacksonville College	† 2,590		400	2,496				500	
Jarvis Christian College	† 6,085		550	3,485	750	900		750	900
Kilgore College	† 450	900/410	575	2,200		1,200			1,200
Lamar University—Beaumontt	‡ 1,616	4,290/—	538	3,000	1,606	1,506	1,798	2,601	1,387
Laredo Community College	‡ 786	2,080/1,040	485					1,702	1,818
Lee College	† 422	672/288	500				2,121	789	1,100
LeTourneau University	9,550		600	4,430	500	900	1,700	843	1,021
Lon Morris College	6,400		450	3,690	1,000	1,500	1,150	200	400
Lubbock Christian University	7,748		350	3,220	1,360	1,379	1,477	1,360	1,379
McLennan Community College	750	1,890/150	512				1,713	1,732	1,481
McMurry University	‡ 6,930		415	3,452	545	1,525	1,100	755	1,525
Microcomputer Technology Institute	14,500								
Midland College	† 688	192/48	510				1,136	1,050	1,281
Midwestern State University	‡ 1,736	4,290/—	630	3,436	900	938	856	670	540
Miss Wade's Fashion Merchandising College	5,985		780		1,160	936	1,440	1,160	936
Mountain View College	‡ 510	1,490/380	800				1,500	1,330	1,045
Navarro College	990	232/182	450	3,282	780	835	1,500	833	835
North Central Texas College	† 630	300/—	450	2,400	800	1,075	1,620	950	1,075
North Harris Montgomery Community College District	† 702	1,200/900	530				1,560	1,238	964
North Lake College	‡ 510	1,490/380	600						
Northeast Texas Community College	762	400/240	580	2,700	1,230	1,475	1,500	1,233	1,475
Northwood University: Texas Campus	10,328		600	4,634	500	750	1,500	750	650
Odessa College	1,100	210/130	500	2,983	555	850	1,545	750	850
Our Lady of the Lake University of San Antonio	9,328		630	3,766	740	1,580	1,590	920	1,400
Palo Alto College	‡ 678	1,380/—							
Panola College	570	490/240	650	2,080	920	1,150	1,650	920	1,100
Paris Junior College	‡ 2,790	5,760/810	400	3,600					
Paul Quinn College	4,110		800	3,015	700	500	1,500	400	350
Prairie View A&M University	‡ 1,684	4,290/—	598	3,500	2,250	1,517	1,500	2,663	2,673
Ranger College	830	140/40	450	2,515	1,000	810	1,834	1,200	810
Rice University	12,025		525	5,900	300	1,350	1,500	700	825
Richland College	‡ 510	1,490/380	350						935
St. Edward's University	9,950		600	4,280	650	1,672	1,500	824	1,750
St. Mary's University	9,698		750	4,270	300	1,258	1,700	1,300	1,258
St. Philip's College	840	1,950/570							
Sam Houston State University	‡ 1,606	4,290/—	498	3,380	1,176	1,282	1,370	2,482	1,214
San Antonio College	‡ 692	2,037/1,245	720				1,600	1,270	1,627
San Jacinto College									
Central Campus	430	990/300	400					1,000	1,209
North	460	990/300	500				3,058	1,212	1,630
Schreiner College	9,355		500	6,130	372	1,116	1,500	478	1,066
South Plains College	676	480/—	400	2,600	700	1,100		700	1,100
Southern Methodist University	15,228		576	5,206	326	1,100	1,500	842	1,000

†Figures are projected for 1995-96. ‡Figures are for 1994-95.

| All aid | | Need-based aid | | Need-based | | | | Non-need-based | | | | Financial aid deadlines | | Inst aid form | Notes |
Total freshmen	Percent receiving aid	Freshmen judged to have need	Percent offered aid	Acad	Music/drama	Art	Athl	Acad	Music/drama	Art	Athl	Priority	Closing		
5,059	21	1,011	100	X				X				5/15	none		
653	60			X	X	X	X	X	X	X	X	4/1	none		
309	75			X				X	X	X		5/1	none	X	
142	95	125	96	X	X		X	X					5/1		
707	73	218	100					X	X	X	X	4/1	none		
														X	
107	94			X	X		X	X	X		X	6/10	none		
85	95	75	100	X	X			X	X			7/30	none		
2,300	65							X				8/1	none		
1,248	31	611	100					X	X	X	X	4/1	none	X	
1,248	61			X	X		X	X	X		X	5/1	none		
								X	X	X	X	6/1	none		
256	78	146	100	X			X	X			X	2/15	none		
													none	X	
														X	
1,120	34			X	X		X	X			X	6/1	none		
224	98	181	99					X	X	X		3/15	none		
3,139	45							X	X	X	X		5/1		
789	44			X				X	X	X	X	4/1	none		
135	85	95	100										none		
4,587	10								X	X		6/1	8/10		
950	50							X	X	X	X	6/1	none		
1,750	30							X	X		X		5/1		
4,106	12	928	100					X	X	X		4/15	none		
				X				X				5/1	none		
				X				X	X	X	X	5/1	none		
182	80			X			X	X			X	3/31	none		
954	35	475	100	X				X	X	X	X	6/1	none		
272	85							X	X			4/15	7/15		
													6/1		
456	60	280	80	X	X	X	X	X	X	X	X	6/1	none	X	
880	44			X	X	X	X	X	X	X	X	6/1	none		
													none	X	
1,271	90	822	100	X				X	X	X		4/16	none	X	
620	75			X				X	X		X		none		
7,907	10			X				X				5/2	none		
384	80							X	X		X	3/1	6/30		
521	85			X				X	X		X	3/31	none		
				X				X	X				6/1		
2,625	31	678	100					X	X	X	X	3/31	5/31		
2,473	40			X	X	X		X	X	X		5/1	none		
													none		
													none		
170	65	87	100					X	X		X	4/1	none		
2,784	30							X	X	X	X	6/10	none		
1,164	80	508	100	X	X	X	X	X	X	X	X	2/1	none	X	

Institution	Tuition and fees	Add'l out-of-state/district tuition	Books and supplies	Costs for campus residents			Costs for students at home		
				Room and board	Trans-portation	Other costs	Board only	Trans-portation	Other costs
Southwest Texas Junior College	818	1,380/240	350	1,980	634	411	900	430	773
Southwest Texas State University	‡ 1,724	4,290/—	500	3,675	980	1,710	2,290	1,020	1,260
Southwestern Adventist College	‡ 7,616		430	3,736	923	728	1,500	671	874
Southwestern Assemblies of God College	2,900		495	2,762	996	1,310		785	1,310
Southwestern Christian College	‡ 4,688		460	2,990	800	400	1,700	800	400
Southwestern University	12,700		600	4,868	200	850	1,500	600	800
Stephen F. Austin State University	‡ 1,706	4,290/—	515	3,776	1,197	1,150	1,984	1,197	1,150
Sul Ross State University	‡ 1,536	4,290/—	600	3,050	623	1,112	1,660	890	1,112
Tarleton State University	‡ 1,579	4,290/—	425	3,100	404	1,266	1,500	506	1,094
Tarrant County Junior College	‡ 531	2,808/240	560					1,548	1,230
Temple Junior College	† 720	1,410/390	536	3,500	794	1,093	1,884	1,088	1,061
Texarkana College	‡ 620	500/210	700					750	1,200
Texas A&M International University	‡ 1,322	4,290/—	565	3,503	1,544	1,714	1,946	1,911	1,215
Texas A&M University									
College Station	† 1,813	4,380/—	616	3,441	750	1,460	1,500	1,000	1,460
Galveston	‡ 1,566	4,290/—	680	3,394	750	900	1,000	750	900
Texas A&M University-Corpus Christi	† 1,588	4,320/—	500		700	1,100	1,600	1,200	1,100
Texas A&M University-Kingsville	‡ 1,628	4,290/—	515	3,372	1,236	1,765	1,545	1,541	1,335
Texas Christian University	10,040		650	3,400	554	1,850	1,800	554	1,286
Texas College	4,485		400	2,430	586	1,095	2,500	674	1,095
Texas Lutheran College	8,626		500	3,606	750	1,000	1,300	900	1,000
Texas Southern University	‡ 1,334	4,290/—	500	3,320	1,400	1,700	1,500	1,400	1,700
Texas Southmost College	1,188	4,410/600	400				1,633	824	412
Texas State Technical College									
Amarillo	† 1,206	2,970/—	900	2,956	360	810	1,125	900	630
Harlingen	‡ 1,122	2,970/—	900	3,546	995	1,380	2,500	1,493	1,380
Sweetwater	† 1,206	2,970/—	924	2,994	1,380	650	825	1,380	650
Waco	† 1,122	2,970/—	560		664	1,122		1,196	1,156
Texas Tech University	‡ 1,690	4,290/—	600	3,815					
Texas Wesleyan University	7,300		450	3,484	675	1,284	1,650	675	1,284
Texas Woman's University	‡ 1,588	4,290/—	730	3,102	684	1,566	1,629	963	1,782
Trinity University	13,044		500	5,150	540	490	2,050		
Trinity Valley Community College	† 420	1,560/300	400	2,618	780	850	1,000	870	850
Tyler Junior College	800	750/450	600	2,300	470	590		470	825
University of Central Texas	† 3,880		554	4,698	888	878			
University of Dallas	11,430		600	4,830	700	600	1,500	500	600
University of Houston									
Clear Lake	‡ 1,568	4,290/—	600					1,779	1,669
Downtown	‡ 1,568	4,290/—	500				1,200	1,755	830
Houston	‡ 1,600	4,290/—	500	4,435	1,250	1,600	500	1,250	1,600
Victoria	‡ 1,698	4,290/—	600				1,900	1,175	1,600
University of Mary Hardin-Baylor	6,210		600	3,214	762	1,224	1,545	930	1,398
University of North Texas	‡ 1,600	4,100/—	500	3,500	600	1,100		1,000	1,200
University of St. Thomas	9,400		515	4,170	726	1,138	1,776	1,128	1,138
University of Texas									
Arlington	‡ 1,434	4,290/—	500	4,100	1,770	1,080	1,100	1,770	1,080
Austin	‡ 1,815	4,290/—	650	3,672	750	1,648	1,500	750	1,648
Brownsville	‡ 1,578	4,290/—	487				1,894	917	458
Dallas	‡ 1,618	4,290/—	645		1,579	1,400	1,666	1,579	571
El Paso	‡ 1,573	4,290/—	374	3,200	1,350	1,142	1,750	1,350	1,142
Health Science Center at San Antonio	‡ 985	4,290/—	830				4,260	1,025	1,050
Medical Branch at Galveston	† 1,439	4,230/—	1,185	4,795	2,436	4,556	5,988	2,880	7,700

†Figures are projected for 1995-96. ‡Figures are for 1994-95.

All aid		Need–based aid		Grants and scholarships								Financial aid deadlines		Inst	
Total fresh-men	Percent receiving aid	Freshmen judged to have need	Percent offered aid	Need–based				Non–need–based				Priority	Closing	aid form	Notes
				Acad	Music/ drama	Art	Athl	Acad	Music/ drama	Art	Athl				
2,489	50	1,219	100	X	X			X	X		X	4/1	none none		
184	85	144	100	X				X	X			3/15	none		
336	70	212	100	X				X	X	X			3/15	X	
2,033	50	383	100					X	X		X	6/1	11/1		
365	78	202	100	X				X	X			5/1	none		
970	30			X			X	X	X		X	6/1	none		
4,705	14			X				X	X			4/15	none		
1,384	52			X	X	X	X	X	X		X	8/1	none		
												6/1	7/15		
				X				X				6/30	none		
6,047	45	2,413	94	X				X				4/1	none		
199	48	152	100	X				X				4/1	none		
								X	X	X			3/15		
1,076	85			X				X	X	X	X		4/15		
1,168	65	574	100	X				X	X	X	X	5/1	none		
													none		
262	85	121	100	X	X	X	X	X	X	X	X	5/1	none		
2,557	80	1,845	100									5/1	none		
188	51			X				X				6/1	none		
840	80			X				X				4/28	none		
438	75	421	100	X				X				7/15	none		
1,491	68			X				X				6/1	none	X	
3,189	41			X	X	X		X	X	X	X	4/1	none		
278	93	231	100	X				X	X	X	X	3/15	none		
387	47			X				X	X	X	X	4/1	none	X	
637	75			X	X	X		X	X	X			2/1		
1,317	65	960	100					X	X	X	X	7/1	none		
2,807	16			X	X	X	X	X	X	X	X	7/1	none		
				X								7/1	9/1		
249	92	184	100					X	X	X		3/1	none		
								X				4/1	none		
1,106	70	684	100	X		X		X		X		6/1	none	X	
2,047	35			X	X	X		X	X	X	X	4/1	none	X	
				X				X				4/15	5/1		
258	80	193	100	X				X	X	X	X	5/1	none		
3,461	30			X			X	X			X	6/1	none		
229	86							X	X			3/1	none		
1,582	27	505	84					X	X	X	X	6/1	none	X	
5,547	51	1,700	100	X	X	X	X	X	X	X	X	4/1	none		
												4/1	8/15		
				X				X				3/1	11/1		
2,156	55			X	X		X	X	X		X	3/15	none		
				X				X				3/12	none		
				X				X				3/15	none		

Institution		Tuition and fees	Add'l out-of-state/district tuition	Books and supplies	Costs for campus residents			Costs for students at home		
					Room and board	Trans-portation	Other costs	Board only	Trans-portation	Other costs
Pan American	‡	1,470	4,290/—	507	2,950	492	2,390	1,946	2,039	2,431
Permian Basin		1,558	4,290/—	555		1,452	1,375	1,000	1,452	1,375
San Antonio	‡	1,672	4,290/—	452		2,080	1,700	1,844	2,080	1,652
Southwestern Medical Center at Dallas		1,350	4,380/—	549				3,355	1,501	4,156
Tyler		1,522	4,290/—	400				1,620	580	934
Houston Health Science Center	‡	1,073	4,290/—	450		1,449	168	2,340	1,449	1,728
Vernon Regional Junior College		780	500/196	600	1,999	2,500	3,000		2,500	3,000
Victoria College		743	1,950/—	425				2,500	485	1,170
Wayland Baptist University		5,750		480	3,118	672	1,030	1,772	688	925
Weatherford College	‡	480	1,920/210	300	2,626	100	1,000	1,000	100	1,000
West Texas A&M University	‡	1,526	4,290/—	500	2,714	580	1,040	1,560	1,100	770
Western Texas College	‡	620	300/150	350	2,050	512	720	1,500	704	720
Wharton County Junior College		720	1,740/570	575	2,100	1,200	1,090	1,340	1,200	1,090
Wiley College		4,156		210	2,872	314	556	1,500	314	556
Utah										
Brigham Young University		2,450		900	3,740	1,130	1,270	3,580	1,270	1,270
College of Eastern Utah	‡	1,190	2,799/—	528	2,865	901	1,161	1,500	854	1,351
Dixie College	‡	1,332	3,449/—	675	3,372		300	1,500	225	300
LDS Business College		1,950		600		614	932	1,800	586	825
Phillips Junior College: Salt Lake City Campus		5,100								
Salt Lake Community College	‡	1,410	2,892/—	650				1,590	450	1,080
Snow College	‡	1,173	3,762/—	530	2,100	525	900	1,500	600	700
Southern Utah University	‡	1,686	3,930/—	1,035	2,874	924	1,500		924	1,500
Stevens-Henager College of Business	‡	11,915				960	2,046	2,844	769	2,123
University of Utah	‡	2,381	4,904/—	858	3,865	720	3,273	1,944	720	2,292
Utah State University	‡	2,013	4,125/—	715	3,165	1,050	1,490	2,100	1,055	1,530
Utah Valley State College	‡	1,420	3,002/—	670				1,500	650	650
Weber State University	‡	1,743	3,771/—	600	4,575	1,005	2,073	1,800	1,005	963
Westminster College of Salt Lake City	‡	8,880		600	4,050	950	1,650	1,500	675	1,070
Vermont										
Bennington College				500			600			4,100
Burlington College		7,950		750				2,115	1,150	2,475
Castleton State College	‡	3,897	4,344/—	400	4,690	300	600	2,100	800	600
Champlain College	‡	8,295		450	5,920		600	1,500	650	600
College of St. Joseph in Vermont		9,070		600	5,100	550	900	1,500	750	900
Community College of Vermont	‡	2,724	2,640/—	375					640	
Goddard College				508		470	911	2,500	795	911
Green Mountain College		13,015		400	2,895	500	375	1,500	500	375
Johnson State College	‡	3,897	4,344/—	500	4,690	312	624	750	312	624
Landmark College	‡	23,850		500	5,400	1,200	1,500		300	1,500
Lyndon State College	‡	3,897	4,344/—	500	4,690	300	600	1,000	300	600
Marlboro College	‡	18,935		400	6,075	200	320	2,020	50	320
Middlebury College				550			1,000			
New England Culinary Institute		15,580		500	2,715	1,683	3,996		1,683	3,996
Norwich University		14,346		500	5,310		800			800
St. Michael's College		13,950		350	6,010	250	400	2,245	250	400
School for International Training		12,409		450	5,163	450	960	2,500	450	960
Southern Vermont College		10,060		500	4,648	600	550	1,000	600	550
Sterling College	‡			600		350	350			
Trinity College of Vermont	‡	11,262		550	5,416	250	500	200	500	500

†Figures are projected for 1995-96. ‡Figures are for 1994-95.

All aid — Total freshmen	Percent receiving aid	Need-based aid — Freshmen judged to have need	Percent offered aid	Need-based Acad	Need-based Music/drama	Need-based Art	Need-based Athl	Non-need-based Acad	Non-need-based Music/drama	Non-need-based Art	Non-need-based Athl	Priority	Closing	Inst aid form	Notes
5,127	77	1,594	98	X	X	X	X	X	X	X	X		4/15		
													none		
1,828	46			X				X			X	3/31	none		
				X				X					none		
				X				X				2/1		X	
1,041	35	240	100	X	X		X	X	X	X	X	7/15	none		
995	35			X	X	X		X	X	X		4/15	none		
200	85											5/15	none		
2,086	20	425	75	X	X	X	X	X	X		X	6/1			
974	55	322	100	X				X	X	X	X	4/1	none	X	
664	70							X	X	X	X	7/1	none		
								X	X		X	6/1	none		
													none		
				X	X	X	X	X	X	X	X	6/1	none		
		389	100	X	X	X		X	X	X	X	4/15	none	X	
892	45							X	X	X	X	5/1	none		
													none		
155	85			X				X					none		
4,004	44			X				X		X	X	4/1	none		
1,666	59							X	X	X	X		7/15		
962	55							X	X		X		none		
240	98			X				X				9/10	none		
2,498	56	2,104	100	X	X	X	X	X	X	X	X	2/15	5/30		
				X	X	X	X	X	X	X	X	2/10	5/15		
											X	7/1	none		
								X	X	X	X	5/1	none		
191	80			X				X	X		X	4/30	none		
93	89	82	100	X				X				3/1	none	X	
				X								6/1	none		
355	74	248	100	X	X	X		X	X			3/15	none		
760	88										X	5/1	none	X	
59	92	51	100	X		X		X			X	3/1	none		
759	86							X					none		
												4/1	6/15		
178	63	51	98	X				X		X	X	2/15	none		
236	65							X	X	X		3/1	none		
		35	100	X									none	X	
298	84			X				X				3/15	none		
91	80	76	100	X				X	X	X		3/1	none		
493	36	202	100										none		
224	80												none		
				X				X				5/1	none		
439	62	352	100	X	X	X	X	X			X	3/15	none		
				X				X				6/1	8/15	X	
149	92	116	100	X								5/1	none		
39	70	37	100	X				X				3/15	none	X	
93	94	82	100	X				X				3/1	none	X	

Institution	Tuition and fees	Add'l out-of-state/ district tuition	Books and supplies	Costs for campus residents			Costs for students at home		
				Room and board	Transportation	Other costs	Board only	Transportation	Other costs
University of Vermont	‡ 6,652	9,306/—	510	4,885		1,035	1,500	910	1,035
Vermont Technical College	‡ 4,593	4,008/2,004	700	4,690	350	650	2,050	600	650
Virginia									
Averett College	11,150		750	4,150	600	1,350		600	1,350
Blue Ridge Community College	1,412	3,281/—	600				1,750	1,050	500
Bluefield College	7,770		500	4,430	900	900	3,800	1,065	1,065
Bridgewater College	11,925		600	4,975	200	900	2,475	600	900
Central Virginia Community College	1,420	3,281/—	500				600	500	3,000
Christendom College	‡ 8,880		450	3,600	400	300	1,456		300
Christopher Newport University	‡ 3,236	4,664/—	524	4,750			960	1,000	1,040
Clinch Valley College of the University of Virginia	3,200	4,324/—	600	3,902	660	800	1,500	1,100	850
College of Health Sciences	4,200		750		900	2,100	2,400	1,900	2,100
College of William and Mary	‡ 4,592	8,812/—	600	4,298	350	800	1,800	600	800
Commonwealth College	‡ 6,052		750	2,475	350	300		350	300
Dabney S. Lancaster Community College	1,423	3,281/—	500				1,500	975	1,655
Danville Community College	1,410	3,281/—	500				1,984	900	2,176
Eastern Mennonite University	10,400		600	4,000	200	450	2,500	200	450
Eastern Shore Community College	1,445	3,281/—	450						2,790
Emory and Henry College	9,990		700	4,502	600	1,000	1,500	1,100	800
Ferrum College	9,950		500	4,550	400	1,200	2,100	600	1,000
George Mason University	4,212	7,392/—	634	5,100	1,092	1,144	3,000	1,331	1,144
Germanna Community College	1,433	3,281/—	300				1,000	1,440	1,274
Hampden-Sydney College	14,322		660	4,942		600	2,700		
Hampton University	‡ 7,764		600	3,518	1,200	1,000	1,500	856	1,000
Hollins College	14,234		500	5,745	350	550		300	1,500
J. Sargeant Reynolds Community College	‡ 1,427	3,281/—	600				1,500	900	900
James Madison University	4,014	4,280/—	500	4,680	600	800	2,200	600	800
John Tyler Community College	1,420	3,281/—	500				1,500	900	900
Liberty University	7,350		650	4,800	825	825	1,600	1,050	825
Longwood College	‡ 4,246	5,314/—	550	3,962	1,000	1,200	4,080	1,000	1,200
Lord Fairfax Community College	1,426	3,281/—	450				1,500	1,152	990
Lynchburg College	13,980		450	4,400	430	440	1,500	390	
Mary Baldwin College	11,700		600	7,400	400	900	1,500	700	900
Mary Washington College	‡ 3,206	4,464/—	650	4,942	704	1,398	2,310	1,624	1,760
Marymount University	11,900		500	5,470	470	900	1,500	750	900
Mountain Empire Community College	1,418	3,281/—	500				500	1,000	
National Business College	‡ 4,935		500	3,450	960	500		1,060	500
New River Community College	1,418	3,281/—	350					1,200	950
Norfolk State University	‡ 2,782	3,494/—	500	3,570	700	1,200	1,700	1,300	1,200
Northern Virginia Community College	‡ 1,399	3,099/—	550				736	1,096	1,920
Old Dominion University	‡ 3,706	5,628/—	500	4,585	745	1,170	1,500	1,006	1,170
Patrick Henry Community College	1,410	3,281/—	425				1,500	1,040	840
Paul D. Camp Community College	1,400	3,281/—	450				1,500	900	900
Piedmont Virginia Community College	1,416	3,281/—	500				1,500	920	1,200
Radford University	‡ 3,040	4,128/—	500	4,210	400	900		600	900
Randolph-Macon College	14,955		400	3,835	400	550	750	650	550
Randolph-Macon Woman's College	15,090		400	6,330	265	600	1,500	225	600
Rappahannock Community College	1,431	3,281/—	500				1,100	1,000	600
Richard Bland College	‡ 1,958	3,752/—	500				1,500	750	1,000
Roanoke College	‡ 13,425		450	4,425	600	600	1,500	600	600

†Figures are projected for 1995-96. ‡Figures are for 1994-95.

All aid		Need–based aid		Grants and scholarships								Financial aid deadlines		Inst aid form	Notes
				Need–based				Non–need–based							
Total freshmen	Percent receiving aid	Freshmen judged to have need	Percent offered aid	Acad	Music/ drama	Art	Athl	Acad	Music/ drama	Art	Athl	Priority	Closing		
1,732	42			X	X	X	X	X	X	X	X	3/1	none		
251	78			X				X				3/1	none		
154	82			X	X	X		X	X	X		4/1	none		
354	15			X									none		
165	87			X	X	X	X	X	X	X	X	3/10	none		
264	99	186	100					X	X				3/15		
				X				X				5/1	none		
65	72							X				4/1	6/1		
494	37			X				X	X			4/1	none		
				X			X	X			X	4/1	none		
21	59			X				X				7/1	none		
1,253	32			X	X	X	X	X			X	2/15	none	X	
								X					none		
408	60	246	100	X				X				3/15	none	X	
													none		
197	98	151	99	X	X			X	X			5/1	none	X	
133	66							X				6/1	none		
210	91	151	100					X					4/1		
322	92	271	100	X				X				4/1	none	X	
1,790	49							X	X		X	3/1	none		
661	30			X				X				5/1	none		
299	88	166	100	X				X				3/1	none		
1,219	70							X	X		X	3/31	6/1		
270	66			X	X			X	X	X		2/15	3/1		
1,700	40											6/30	none		
2,289	62			X	X	X		X	X	X	X	2/15	none		
				X				X				6/30	none		
1,783	80			X			X	X	X		X	4/15	none		
664	65	366	98	X				X	X	X	X	2/15	none		
679	40			X				X				5/1	none		
321	74	184	99	X				X	X			4/1	none	X	
227	74			X	X	X		X	X	X		3/15	4/15		
710	50	330	100	X				X	X				3/1		
254	72	164	100	X		X		X				3/1	none	X	
1,565	81	550	99	X				X				5/15	none		
				X				X					none		
650	42			X				X				4/15	none		
1,154	85							X				3/15	none	X	
4,817	14							X				3/1	none	X	
1,501	63	1,134	100	X	X	X	X	X	X	X	X	2/15	5/1		
				X				X					none		
				X				X				7/30	8/16		
												4/15	none		
1,532	61	637	94					X	X	X	X	3/1	none	X	
307	86	153	100	X				X				3/1	none	X	
198	88	151	100					X	X			3/15	none	X	
450	25			X				X				6/1	none		
368	48			X				X				4/1	5/1		
402	85	236	100	X	X	X		X	X	X		3/1	none		

| | | Add'l out-of-state/ | | Costs for campus residents | | | Costs for students at home | | |
Institution	Tuition and fees	district tuition	Books and supplies	Room and board	Trans-portation	Other costs	Board only	Trans-portation	Other costs
St. Paul's College	6,158		400	3,834	360	500	1,500	500	500
Shenandoah University	† 11,470		450	4,800	900	900	1,500	900	900
Southern Virginia College	† 11,250		500	5,400	400	1,030	1,700	950	1,030
Southside Virginia Community College	1,421	3,281/—	523				1,500	1,440	1,602
Southwest Virginia Community College	1,415	3,281/—	500				1,500	1,200	1,258
Sweet Briar College	‡ 14,625		500	6,000	500	750		500	750
Thomas Nelson Community College	1,413	3,281/—	500				1,550	700	650
Tidewater Community College	1,531	3,281/—	400				1,500	750	810
University of Richmond	† 15,500		700	3,625		1,025	1,500		810
University of Virginia	4,614	9,386/—	600	3,846		1,000			
Virginia Commonwealth University	4,030	7,603/—	500	4,306	1,650	1,980	1,500	1,650	1,980
Virginia Highlands Community College	1,400	3,281/—	420				1,575	850	850
Virginia Intermont College	9,600		800	4,250	350	990	2,300	1,650	1,440
Virginia Military Institute	‡ 4,390	6,040/—	600	3,800	300	1,000			
Virginia Polytechnic Institute and State University	‡ 3,951	6,453/—	740	3,165	600	1,600	1,450	600	1,600
Virginia State University	‡ 3,199	3,893/—	500	4,845	500	500	1,350	600	525
Virginia Union University	8,219		500	3,638	450	1,000	1,866	450	1,000
Virginia Wesleyan College	11,800		650	5,200	1,250	1,500	750	1,550	1,500
Virginia Western Community College	1,404	3,281/—	550				1,600	800	1,200
Washington and Lee University	14,655		680	5,310	400	1,115		500	1,115
Wytheville Community College	1,430	3,281/—	550				2,500	620	550
Washington									
Antioch University Seattle	‡ 8,415		750					939	1,164
Art Institute of Seattle	‡ 8,875		937	4,686	1,767	1,305	2,322	1,017	1,305
Bastyr University	7,260		720				2,099	978	690
Bellevue Community College	‡ 1,297	3,798/—	678				1,974	1,008	714
Big Bend Community College	‡ 1,297	3,798/—	678	3,600	1,008	1,416	1,974	1,008	714
Central Washington University	‡ 2,257	5,719/—	678	3,778	1,008	1,416		1,008	714
Centralia College	‡ 1,297	3,798/—	702		1,044		1,674	1,044	600
City University	‡ 2,655		800				1,050	850	1,200
Clark College	‡ 1,297	3,798/—	702				2,040	1,044	
Cogswell College North	7,995		550						
Columbia Basin College	‡ 1,297	3,798/—	678				974	1,008	714
Cornish College of the Arts	‡ 9,950		1,400				2,167	996	700
Eastern Washington University	‡ 2,257	5,719/—	702	3,914	1,044	1,464	1,908	978	1,464
Edmonds Community College	‡ 1,297	3,798/—	678				1,974	1,008	1,416
Everett Community College	‡ 1,297	3,798/—	500					900	1,000
Evergreen State College	‡ 2,257	5,719/—	710		950	1,440	2,100	950	1,440
Gonzaga University	‡ 13,100		650	4,260	950	1,450	1,850	950	750
Grays Harbor College	‡ 1,297	3,798/—	702		1,044	1,464	2,040	1,044	738
Green River Community College	‡ 1,297	3,798/—	677				1,975	1,012	714
Heritage College	6,350		870				2,947	1,392	1,066
Highline Community College	‡ 1,297	3,798/—	560				1,740	880	630
Lake Washington Technical College	‡ 1,742								
Lower Columbia College	‡ 1,297	3,798/—	720		900	1,470	2,040	900	735
Lutheran Bible Institute of Seattle	4,160		500	3,900	1,000	1,200		1,000	800
North Seattle Community College	‡ 1,297	3,798/—	500				1,570	800	1,000
Northwest College	7,800		700	3,660	250	1,500	2,000	1,100	750
Northwest College of Art	† 7,000		1,000		250			250	
Northwest Indian College	1,602	1,440/—	640				4,461	973	1,114
Olympic College	‡ 1,297	3,798/—	653				1,908	978	690

†Figures are projected for 1995-96. ‡Figures are for 1994-95.

Total freshmen	Percent receiving aid	Freshmen judged to have need	Percent offered aid	Acad	Music/drama	Art	Athl	Acad	Music/drama	Art	Athl	Priority	Closing	Inst aid form	Notes
	All aid		**Need–based aid**	**Grants and scholarships**								**Financial aid deadlines**		**Inst aid form**	**Notes**
				Need–based				**Non–need–based**							
228	85							X				3/30	8/12		
242	85			X	X			X	X			3/15	none	X	
								X					none		
300	53			X				X				6/1	8/1		
								X				5/30	none		
183	64	118	100	X	X			X	X			3/1	none		
1,284	20	250	80	X				X				5/1	none		
												8/1	none		
822	55	211	100					X	X		X		2/25	X	
2,761	47	1,062	100								X	3/1	none		
1,658	70	1,011	100					X	X	X	X	4/15	none		
435	42			X				X					none		
111	62			X			X	X			X	3/1	none		
406	66	174	92	X				X			X	3/1	4/1	X	
4,258	70	1,952	100					X	X	X	X	2/15	none		
820	88			X			X	X				3/31	5/1		
407	87							X	X		X	5/15	none		
321	81	250	100	X	X	X		X	X	X		3/1	none		
1,349	20			X				X					none		
443	50	138	100	X	X			X				2/1	none		
687	50	350	86	X				X				4/1	none		
													none		
391	86			X		X							none		
								X				4/15	none		
2,500	26			X			X	X			X	4/14	none	X	
578	50							X	X		X	4/1	7/1		
1,013	60	680	100	X				X	X			3/1	none		
97	50	350	100					X	X		X	5/15	none		
1,725	25							X	X		X	5/1	none		
				X				X					7/1		
600	41							X	X	X	X	4/1	none		
239	81	344	100	X	X	X		X	X	X		2/28	none	X	
747	60	438	91	X			X	X	X	X	X	2/15	none		
3,336	22			X	X		X	X	X	X	X	5/1	none		
				X	X	X	X	X	X	X	X	5/1	7/1	X	
402	15							X	X	X	X	3/15	none	X	
600	85	386	100	X	X		X	X	X		X	2/1	none		
650	80			X	X	X	X	X	X	X	X	5/15	none		
2,400	25							X	X	X	X	3/1	none		
				X				X					none		
3,056	7											4/1	none		
				X				X					none		
755	35	146	100	X	X	X	X	X	X		X	6/1	none	X	
48	73			X	X			X	X			5/1	none	X	
				X	X	X		X	X	X		4/3	9/1		
176	92	162	100	X				X	X	X	X	3/1	none		
36	72	67	100	X		X							7/31		
													none		
				X			X	X	X	X	X	4/30	4/1		

Institution	Tuition and fees	Add'l out-of-state/district tuition	Books and supplies	Costs for campus residents			Costs for students at home		
				Room and board	Trans-portation	Other costs	Board only	Trans-portation	Other costs
Pacific Lutheran University	13,856		702	4,644	550	1,464	2,040	1,044	738
Peninsula College	‡ 1,297	3,798/—	600	3,600	945	1,350			
Pierce College	‡ 1,297	3,798/—	678				1,920	1,008	714
Puget Sound Christian College	† 5,620		750	3,420	360	2,250	2,400	924	1,800
Renton Technical College	† 1,575		730				1,974	1,008	714
St. Martin's College	12,520		700	4,590	934	1,304	1,920	934	647
Seattle Central Community College	‡ 1,297	3,798/—	594				1,908	978	690
Seattle Pacific University	13,479		600	5,169	300	1,250	1,500	300	600
Seattle University	13,635		702	5,091	1,044	1,464	2,040	1,044	1,464
Shoreline Community College	1,297	3,798/—	712				1,908	1,142	750
Skagit Valley College	‡ 1,297	3,798/—	690				1,005	1,050	1,500
South Puget Sound Community College	‡ 1,297	3,798/—	810		951	1,464	1,857	951	738
South Seattle Community College	‡ 1,297	3,798/—	645		945	666	1,845	945	1,320
Spokane Community College	‡ 1,297	3,798/—	654				1,650	840	510
Spokane Falls Community College	‡ 1,297	3,798/—	540				1,620	840	500
Tacoma Community College	1,297	3,798/—	702		1,044	1,044	2,040	1,044	738
University of Puget Sound	17,450		650	4,720	500	1,300	1,800	500	1,300
University of Washington	‡ 2,907	5,292/—	687	5,000	396	1,725	1,770	396	1,473
Walla Walla College	11,475		740	3,483	400	1,320	1,812	1,000	1,320
Walla Walla Community College	‡ 1,297	3,798/—	535				1,800	100	450
Washington State University	‡ 2,907	5,292/—	850	4,210	850	1,288	2,085	850	1,288
Wenatchee Valley College	‡ 1,297	3,798/—	678	3,519	1,008	1,416	1,974	1,008	714
Western Washington University	‡ 2,257	5,719/—	639	4,281	978	1,407	1,920	978	714
Whatcom Community College	‡ 1,311	3,798/—	594				1,845	933	669
Whitman College	17,630		750	5,160		500	2,800	700	1,290
Whitworth College	13,620		702	4,900	1,044	1,464	2,040	1,044	738
Yakima Valley Community College	‡ 1,297	3,798/—	600	3,570	900	1,300	1,800	900	1,100
West Virginia									
Alderson-Broaddus College	‡ 10,560		660	3,380	600	1,200	1,400	800	1,200
Appalachian Bible College	4,800		520	2,700	740	720	1,500	990	630
Bethany College	16,060		450	5,385	600	800	1,744	1,135	1,000
Bluefield State College	‡ 1,856	2,642/—	500				1,700	850	1,500
College of West Virginia	3,240		550				550	1,000	900
Concord College	‡ 2,052	2,374/—	400	3,236	408	978	750	896	978
Davis and Elkins College	10,330		400	4,670			1,500		
Fairmont State College	‡ 1,800	2,438/—	500	3,040		500		600	500
Glenville State College	‡ 1,782	2,298/—	350	3,264	200	1,000		900	1,000
Huntington Junior College of Business	3,600								
Marshall University	‡ 1,990	3,434/1,654	630	4,210	525	1,050	1,575	491	212
Mountain State College	‡ 9,200		380						
National Education Center: National Institute of Technology Campus	11,750								
Ohio Valley College	‡ 5,660		425	3,180	400	800	1,500	800	600
Potomac State College of West Virginia University	‡ 1,760	3,584/—	450	3,530		1,120	1,300		1,120
Salem-Teikyo University	11,103		550	3,952	320	300	1,600	320	300
Shepherd College	‡ 2,064	2,630/—	700	3,820	270	925	1,600	1,210	925
Southern West Virginia Community College	‡ 1,030	1,870/—	450				1,500		900
University of Charleston	10,550		400	3,870	250	500			1,800
West Liberty State College	‡ 1,900	2,570/—	600	2,890	310	900	1,500	800	650
West Virginia Institute of Technology	‡ 2,100	2,670/—	500	3,940	400	700	1,200	700	700

†Figures are projected for 1995-96. ‡Figures are for 1994-95.

| All aid | | Need–based aid | | Grants and scholarships | | | | | | | | Financial aid deadlines | | Inst aid form | Notes |
| Total fresh-men | Percent receiving aid | Freshmen judged to have need | Percent offered aid | Need–based | | | | Non–need–based | | | | | | | |
				Acad	Music/ drama	Art	Athl	Acad	Music/ drama	Art	Athl	Priority	Closing		
566	86	423	100	X	X	X	X	X	X	X		1/31	none		
821	60			X				X	X	X		6/1	none		
2,534	18							X	X		X	4/1	none		
18	90	20	100	X				X	X			5/1	none	X	
				X				X					none		
116	66	36	100	X			X	X			X	3/1	none		
2,438	41			X				X				4/29	7/1		
494	92	300	100	X	X	X		X	X	X	X	1/31	none		
497	70	391	100	X	X		X	X	X	X	X	2/1	5/1		
1,100	18							X			X	4/1	none		
3,365	31	680	96	X	X	X	X	X	X	X	X	4/1	none		
1,783	45			X				X			X	6/28	none	X	
961	27			X				X	X			5/15	none		
2,100	70			X			X				X	3/15	none		
2,000	85	1,100	100	X			X				X	4/1	none		
400	20			X				X	X	X	X	4/13	7/22		
695	75	450	100	X	X	X	X	X	X	X		2/1	none		
3,489	30	1,345	88	X	X		X	X			X	2/28	none		
				X					X	X		4/1	none	X	
				X					X	X	X	5/1	none		
2,766	43			X	X	X	X	X	X	X	X	3/1	none		
									X	X	X	4/1	none		
1,513	63	1,115	98	X	X	X	X	X	X	X	X	2/15	none		
								X				4/15	none		
370	80	251	100	X	X	X		X	X	X			2/15	X	
452	88			X	X	X	X	X	X	X		3/1	none	X	
				X	X		X					6/1	none		
176	94	150	100	X	X		X	X	X		X	5/1	none	X	
													none		
221	75	154	100	X				X	X			4/1	none		
438	75			X			X	X			X	3/1	none	X	
272	91			X			X	X				5/1	none		
969	77			X	X	X	X	X	X	X	X	4/15	none		
187	75	150	100	X	X	X	X	X	X	X	X	3/1	none		
2,116	60	1,968	100	X	X		X	X	X		X		3/1		
													none		
2,093	55							X	X	X	X	3/1	none		
				X				X					none		
													none		
178	93			X	X	X	X	X	X	X	X	6/1	none		
				X	X		X	X				3/1	none		
215	59	144	100	X			X	X			X	4/15	none		
584	22							X	X	X	X	3/1	none		
													none		
247	85	151	100	X	X	X	X	X	X	X	X	3/1	8/1		
510	75	350	100	X	X	X	X	X	X	X	X	3/1	none		
549	80			X	X		X	X	X		X	1/31	4/1		

Institution	Tuition and fees	Add'l out-of-state/district tuition	Books and supplies	Costs for campus residents			Costs for students at home		
				Room and board	Trans-portation	Other costs	Board only	Trans-portation	Other costs
West Virginia Northern Community College	‡ 1,438	2,448/—	450				1,610	896	1,114
West Virginia State College	‡ 1,988	2,628/—	500	3,200	375	940	1,400	940	1,000
West Virginia University									
Morgantown	‡ 2,128	4,242/—	560	4,310	310	1,190	1,595	1,045	1,195
Parkersburg	‡ 1,128	2,400/—	470				1,730	1,100	1,270
West Virginia Wesleyan College	14,750		450	3,850	750	1,100	2,500	750	1,100
Wheeling Jesuit College	12,000		600	4,670	500	600	750	500	750
Wisconsin									
Alverno College	‡ 8,352		550	3,640	200	1,800	1,200	500	1,280
Bellin College of Nursing	‡ 7,175		500				990	747	1,377
Beloit College	17,744		350	3,846	400	700	1,500	600	700
Blackhawk Technical College	‡ 1,517	9,248/—	465				1,856	625	1,025
Cardinal Stritch College	8,424		500	3,726	350	1,200	1,700	800	1,200
Carroll College	12,880		480	4,000	200	900		900	
Carthage College	13,850		500	3,980	900	1,250	810	900	1,250
Chippewa Valley Technical College	‡ 1,517	9,248/—	400				1,852	450	800
Columbia College of Nursing	12,510		490	3,390	210	960		970	810
Concordia University Wisconsin	10,340		600	3,600	120	1,260	2,020	550	1,260
Edgewood College	9,100		625	3,800	265	1,400	950	400	1,400
Fox Valley Technical College	‡ 1,517	9,248/—	663				1,852	673	800
Gateway Technical College	‡ 1,517	9,248/—	500				1,852	673	691
Lac Courte Oreilles Ojibwa Community College	2,425		300		500				
Lakeland College	10,270		500	4,020	700	800	1,000	700	750
Lakeshore Technical College	‡ 1,517	9,248/—	704				1,945	715	1,195
Lawrence University	18,057		500	4,038	300	700			700
Madison Area Technical College	‡ 1,517	9,248/—	663				1,852	673	1,124
Madison Junior College of Business	‡ 5,400			4,200	260	1,160	1,200	260	1,160
Maranatha Baptist Bible College	5,063		460	3,050	345	920	1,080	345	920
Marian College of Fond du Lac	‡ 9,550		550	4,040	1,100	1,100	1,500	1,100	1,100
Marquette University	13,230		600	5,100	1,000	1,350	800	1,000	1,350
Mid-State Technical College	‡ 1,517	9,248/—	663				1,852	1,324	473
Milwaukee Area Technical College	‡ 1,517	9,248/—	663				1,852	673	1,124
Milwaukee Institute of Art & Design	† 12,900		1,250	6,000		1,200	2,430	720	1,200
Milwaukee School of Engineering	12,375		1,025	3,765	910	1,225	1,575	910	1,225
Moraine Park Technical College	‡ 1,517	9,248/—	663				1,852	673	1,124
Mount Mary College	9,750		550	3,322	400	1,289	1,920	800	1,289
Mount Senario College	8,550		600	3,250	580	1,350	1,825	530	1,350
Nicolet Area Technical College	‡ 1,517	9,248/—	663				1,852	673	1,124
Northcentral Technical College	‡ 1,517	9,248/—	663	3,890			1,852	673	1,124
Northeast Wisconsin Technical College	‡ 1,517	9,248/—	663				1,852	673	1,124
Northland College	10,870		450	3,900	600	1,000	2,190	500	1,000
Ripon College	16,320		350	4,280		650	2,330		650
St. Norbert College	13,015		425	4,655	350	910	900	450	910
Silver Lake College	8,950		520	3,900			1,800	1,000	1,026
Southwest Wisconsin Technical College	‡ 1,517	9,248/—	663				1,852	673	1,124
Stratton College	5,700		850				2,320	520	1,542
University of Wisconsin									
Eau Claire	‡ 2,208	4,788/—	175	2,705	780	1,260	1,060	915	965
Green Bay	‡ 2,284	4,788/—	500	2,440	405	1,377	990	747	594
La Crosse	‡ 2,278	4,788/—	160	2,270	350	1,800	920	159	1,600

†Figures are projected for 1995-96. ‡Figures are for 1994-95.

| All aid | | Need–based aid | | Grants and scholarships | | | | | | | | Financial aid deadlines | | Inst aid form | Notes |
| Total freshmen | Percent receiving aid | Freshmen judged to have need | Percent offered aid | Need–based | | | | Non–need–based | | | | | | | |
				Acad	Music/ drama	Art	Athl	Acad	Music/ drama	Art	Athl	Priority	Closing		
614	50			X				X				3/15	none		
795	55			X	X	X	X	X	X	X	X	3/1	6/15		
3,084	57			X				X	X	X	X	2/1	3/1		
				X				X				5/1	none		
454	91	445	100	X	X	X	X	X	X	X	X	3/1	none		
267	93	210	100					X	X		X	3/1	none		
277	81			X	X	X		X	X	X		3/15	none		
												3/1	none		
300	84	209	100	X	X			X	X			4/15	none		
2,707	30											4/1	6/15		
434	83	128	100	X				X	X	X	X	4/1	none		
530	93	367	100	X	X	X		X	X	X		4/15	none		
395	94	363	100	X				X	X	X		2/15	none		
1,710	76			X				X				3/15	none		
56	96			X				X				4/15	none		
320	90							X	X		X	5/1	6/1		
392	85	136	100	X	X	X		X	X	X		3/15	none		
1,400	75			X				X					none		
												5/1	none	X	
													none		
217	95			X	X		X	X				5/1	8/1		
1,067	77	605	100										none		
284	87	200	100	X	X			X	X			3/15	none		
								X				4/15	none		
57	48							X					none		
197	90			X	X	X		X	X	X		3/1	none	X	
1,592	96	1,014	100	X				X	X		X	3/1	none	X	
997	65			X			X	X				5/1	none		
10,000	70							X				3/15	none		
151	74	110	100	X		X		X		X		3/1	none	X	
482	85	371	100	X				X				3/15	none		
962	40	387	100					X				5/1	none	X	
135	98	90	100	X	X	X		X	X	X		3/15	none	X	
153	99	80	84	X				X				6/15	none		
500	75			X				X				4/15	none		
815	66											4/1	none		
								X					none		
226	87	205	100	X	X		X	X	X		X	5/1	8/1		
215	80	182	100	X	X			X	X			3/1	none		
502	92	320	100	X	X	X		X	X	X		3/1	none	X	
35	88			X	X	X	X	X	X	X		3/15	none		
700	80	508	100	X								4/15	none		
298	76	185	100					X					none		
2,084	50	1,042	100	X	X			X	X			4/15	none		
				X			X	X	X	X	X	4/15	none		
1,503	45	750	100	X				X	X			3/15	none	X	

Institution		Tuition and fees	Add'l out-of-state/district tuition	Books and supplies	Costs for campus residents			Costs for students at home		
					Room and board	Transportation	Other costs	Board only	Transportation	Other costs
Madison	‡	2,735	6,359/—	535	3,757	295	1,230	1,500	285	1,230
Milwaukee	‡	2,771	6,015/—	570	3,120	826	4,194	1,751	826	1,154
Oshkosh	‡	2,160	4,788/—	518	2,256	360	1,530	1,000	920	1,390
Parkside	‡	2,280	4,788/—	600	3,416	670	1,130		670	980
Platteville	‡	2,242	4,788/—	300	2,728	400	1,100	1,780	690	930
River Falls	‡	2,228	4,788/—	191	2,634	500	1,370	1,900	1,500	1,370
Stevens Point	‡	2,281	4,788/—	300	3,006	360	1,190	1,500	280	1,190
Stout	‡	2,231	4,788/—	342	2,618	394	1,340		510	1,104
Superior	‡	2,181	4,788/—	525	2,780	575	1,350		575	1,350
Whitewater	‡	2,250	4,788/—	450	2,528	650	1,300	2,800	650	1,300
University of Wisconsin Center										
Baraboo/Sauk County	‡	1,706	3,983/—	455				1,315	705	810
Barron County	‡	1,711	3,983/—	455				1,315	705	2,645
Fond du Lac	‡	1,747	3,983/—	455				1,315	705	810
Fox Valley	‡	1,754	3,983/—	455				1,315	705	810
Manitowoc County	‡	1,688	3,983/—	455				1,315	705	810
Marathon County	‡	1,724	3,983/—	455	2,424	550	900	1,315	705	810
Marinette County	‡	1,686	3,983/—	455				1,315	705	810
Marshfield/Wood County	‡	1,709	3,983/—	455				1,315	705	810
Richland	‡	1,738	3,983/—	455		670	1,170	1,315	705	810
Rock County	‡	1,710	3,983/—	455				1,315	705	810
Sheboygan County	‡	1,710	3,983/—	455				1,315	705	810
Washington County	‡	1,729	3,983/—	455				1,315	705	810
Waukesha	‡	1,691	3,983/—	455				1,315	705	810
Viterbo College		9,850		600	3,750	640	1,500	1,500	640	1,000
Waukesha County Technical College	‡	1,517	9,248/—	663				1,852	673	1,124
Western Wisconsin Technical College	‡	1,517	9,248/—	663		673	1,124	1,852	673	1,124
Wisconsin Indianhead Technical College	‡	1,517	9,864/—	663				1,852	673	1,124
Wisconsin Lutheran College		9,940		500	3,900	300	1,125	1,500	600	990
Wisconsin School of Electronics		4,661		500						
Wyoming										
Casper College		880	1,520/—	500	2,330	450	900	1,500	450	450
Central Wyoming College	‡	976	1,400/—	500	2,812	500	1,000	1,800	400	750
Eastern Wyoming College		1,048	1,520/—	500	2,500	525	1,300	1,750	325	1,300
Laramie County Community College		928	1,520/—	500	3,298	300	500		750	600
Northwest College		944	1,400/—	500	2,690	866	1,000	1,500	600	800
Sheridan College		940	1,520/—	500	2,730	540	800	1,600	540	800
University of Wyoming		2,005		600	3,520	500	1,500	1,960	302	780
Western Wyoming Community College	‡	832	1,400/—	400	2,510	500	950	1,522	250	950
American Samoa, Caroline Islands, Guam, Marianas, Virgin Islands										
American Samoa Community College		154	144/—	500					360	1,100
Guam Community College		475		550			1,548	4,902	900	1,548
Northern Marianas College		1,550	1,500/—	350				900	540	1,200
University of Guam		1,548	2,340/—	671	2,905	900	1,743	1,090	900	1,743
University of the Virgin Islands		1,942	3,632/—	425	4,510	650	800	2,400	600	800
Arab Republic of Egypt										
American University in Cairo		9,064		600		1,400	4,400	2,700	100	

†Figures are projected for 1995-96. ‡Figures are for 1994-95.

| All aid | | Need–based aid | | Grants and scholarships | | | | | | | | Financial aid deadlines | | Inst aid form | Notes |
| Total fresh-men | Percent receiving aid | Freshmen judged to have need | Percent offered aid | Need–based | | | | Non–need–based | | | | Priority | Closing | | |
				Acad	Music/ drama	Art	Athl	Acad	Music/ drama	Art	Athl				
4,681	36			X	X	X	X	X	X	X	X	3/1	none	X	
1,829	59			X			X					3/1	none		
1,396	55	713	100	X				X	X	X		3/15	none		
767	40			X	X	X	X	X	X	X	X	4/1	6/15		
937	75	449	100	X				X	X	X		3/15	none		
1,004	72	665	100					X	X	X		3/15	none	X	
1,378	60							X	X	X		3/15	7/15		
1,073	65			X				X	X	X		4/1	none		
279	67	179	100	X	X	X		X				4/15	5/1		
				X	X			X	X			4/15	none		
260	48	90	100	X	X	X		X	X	X		4/15	none	X	
				X	X	X		X	X	X		3/1	none		
405	35			X	X			X	X			4/15	none		
				X				X				4/15	none		
167	30	90	100	X				X				3/1	none		
322	56	180	100	X	X	X		X	X	X		4/15	none	X	
				X				X				3/1	none		
192	46			X				X				4/15	none	X	
298	65			X	X	X		X	X	X		4/15	8/1		
217	50			X	X			X	X			4/15	none	X	
179	24			X				X				4/15	none	X	
231	23			X	X		X	X	X			4/15	none	X	
527	16							X	X	X		3/1	none	X	
357	88			X	X	X		X	X	X		3/1	none		
1,300	15			X				X					none		
1,095	60											3/1	none	X	
1,897	75			X				X					none		
101	92	83	100	X				X				3/1	none	X	
													none		
688	75			X	X	X	X	X	X	X	X	3/15	8/10		
228	31			X	X	X	X	X	X	X	X	4/15	none		
350	85	131	88	X	X	X	X	X	X	X	X	3/15	none		
817	75			X	X	X	X	X	X	X	X	4/1	none		
													none		
324	38							X	X	X	X	3/1	none	X	
1,347	59			X				X	X	X	X	3/1	none	X	
2,067	50							X	X	X	X	4/1	none	X	
													none		
172	6	41	98	X				X				5/1	none		
													none		
1,912	16			X		X							6/15		
780	80							X	X	X	X				

Institution	Tuition and fees	Add'l out–of–state/ district tuition	Books and supplies	Costs for campus residents			Costs for students at home		
				Room and board	Trans–portation	Other costs	Board only	Trans–portation	Other costs
Bermuda									
Bermuda College	† 1,500								
Canada									
Humber College	1,345			4,050					
Lethbridge Community College	1,139		1,550	1,855		2,440		280	2,400
McGill University	1,980	6,274/—	1,000	7,180	348	2,040		348	2,040
Memorial University of Newfoundland	‡ 2,255	2,150/—	700	3,520					
Simon Fraser University	‡ 2,348		1,065	8,372	910	950			950
University of British Columbia	2,510								
France									
American University of Paris	† 14,756		750				4,030	300	1,000
Mexico									
Sistema Instituto Tecnologico y de Estudios Superiores de Monterrey	7,374		500		250				
Switzerland									
American College of Switzerland	24,148		776	5,876					
Franklin College: Switzerland	‡ 16,820		400		1,000	3,600			
United Kingdom									
Richmond College, The American International University in London	11,520		650	5,850	1,000	1,960		1,000	1,960

†Figures are projected for 1995-96. ‡Figures are for 1994-95.

All aid		Need-based aid		Grants and scholarships								Financial aid deadlines		Inst aid form	Notes
Total fresh-men	Percent receiving aid	Freshmen judged to have need	Percent offered aid	Need-based				Non-need-based				Priority	Closing		
				Acad	Music/drama	Art	Athl	Acad	Music/drama	Art	Athl				
				X			X						none	X	
145	26	88	47	X								3/1	5/1	X	
				X				X			X	4/15	4/22		
16	13							X				4/1	none		
				X									none		
												5/1	none		

219

Sources of information about state grant programs and the Federal Stafford Loan Program

State scholarships and grants

The major state scholarship and grant programs are described in the following list. Included in the description of each program are eligibility requirements, average awards, and the address of the administrative agency. **Unless otherwise indicated, funds are available to state residents who are enrolled for full-time study at eligible postsecondary institutions in their state of residence.**

Alabama

Alabama Student Assistance Program—Variable grants at in-state postsecondary institutions.

Alabama Student Grant Program—Non-need-based grants of up to $1,200 at private nonprofit colleges and universities.

National Guard Educational Assistance Program—Available to members of the Alabama National Guard for college study. Pays for tuition, fees, books, and supplies up to $500 per term or $1,000 per year.

For more information, contact the Alabama Commission on Higher Education, P.O. Box 302000, Montgomery, AL 36130-2000.

Alaska

Alaska State Educational Incentive Grant—Need-based grants of up to $1,500 for use by Alaska residents at eligible in-state and out-of-state postsecondary institutions.

For more information, contact the Alaska Commission on Postsecondary Education, P.O. Box 110505, Juneau, AK 99811-0505.

Arizona

Arizona State Student Incentive Grant Program—Need-based grants of up to $1,500 for use by Arizona residents at eligible in-state and out-of state postsecondary institutions.

For more information, contact the financial aid office at the institution you wish to attend.

Arkansas

Arkansas Student Assistance Grant Program—Need-based grants of $200 to $624 at colleges and universities.

Governor's Scholars Program—100 merit-based $2,000 scholarships for attendance at colleges and universities in Arkansas, renewable for four years, awarded to high school seniors.

Emergency Secondary Education Loan Program—Available to secondary school education majors in shortage areas. Must pursue secondary teacher certification in state. Loans up to $2,500.

Paul Douglas Teacher Scholarship Program—Loans up to $5,000 available to education majors. Must pursue teacher certification in state.

For more information, contact the Department of Higher Education, 114 East Capitol, Little Rock, AR 72201.

California

As of June 1995: Three state student aid programs: Cal Grant A—Grants of $700 to $5,250 at independent colleges, $700 to $3,799 at the University of California, and $700 to $1,584 at California State University. Cal Grant B—Subsistence grants of $700 to $1,410 and in some cases tuition. Cal Grant C—Grants of up to $2,360 for tuition plus $530 for training-related expenses at vocational and technical schools.

For more information, contact the California Student Aid Commission, P.O. Box 510845, Sacramento, CA 94245-0845.

Colorado

Student Grant—Need-based grants of up to $2,000 at eligible postsecondary institutions.

Scholarship Program for Undergraduate Students—Scholarships of up to the amount of resident tuition and mandatory student fees at in-state institutions.

For more information, contact the financial aid office at the institution you wish to attend.

Connecticut

State Scholastic Achievement Grant Program—Grants of up to $2,000 may be taken to Connecticut colleges. Grants of up to $500 may be taken to colleges located in reciprocal states. Based on academic performance and financial need. February 15 application deadline.

For more information, contact the Department of Higher Education, 61 Woodland Street, Hartford, CT 06105.

Delaware

Delaware Postsecondary Scholarship Fund—Need-based grants of $600 to $1,000 at approved Delaware or Pennsylvania colleges and at colleges in other states if the program of study is not offered at Delaware tax-supported colleges.

For more information, contact the Delaware Higher Education Commission, 820 North French Street, Fourth Floor, Wilmington, DE 19801.

Florida

Florida Student Assistance Grant Program—Grants of $200 to $1,500 at eligible Florida colleges. One-year state residency required.

Florida Resident Access Grant—Non-need grants of up to $2,000 at eligible private Florida colleges and universities. One-year state residency required.

Florida Undergraduate Scholars' Fund—Scholarships of up to $2,500 at eligible Florida colleges and universities. One-year state residency required.

For more information, contact the Florida Department of Education, Office of Student Financial Assistance, 1344 Florida Education Center, Tallahassee, FL 32399-0400.

Georgia

Georgia Student Incentive Grant Program—Grants of $300 to $5,000 at nonprofit postsecondary institutions.

Georgia Tuition Equalization Grant Program—Grants of $1,000 at private colleges. Does not require financial need.

Law Enforcement Personnel Dependents Grant—$2,000 a year for dependents of Georgia Law Enforcement Personnel who have been killed or rendered disabled in the line of duty.

For more information, contact the Georgia Student Finance Authority, 2082 East Exchange Place, Suite 200, Tucker, GA 30084

Hawaii

Tuition Waivers and Pacific-Asian Scholarships—provide for tuition expenses at campuses of the University of Hawaii.

Hawaii Student Incentive Grant Program—Grants covering tuition expenses at nonprofit postsecondary institutions.

For more information, contact the financial aid office at the institution you wish to attend.

Idaho

State of Idaho Scholarship—Grants of up to $2,700 per year at Idaho public and private postsecondary institutions. Based on academic ability.

Paul Douglas Teacher Scholarship Program—Federally funded scholarships of $5,000 per year for students pursuing teacher certification.

Paul L. Fowler Scholarship Program—Memorial one-time grant of $2,830 to Idaho high school graduates. Based on academic ability.

For more information, contact the Office of the State Board of Education, P.O. Box 83720, Boise, ID 83720-0037.

Illinois

General Assembly Scholarships—Waivers of tuition and fees at public postsecondary institutions. Selection by general assembly members from residents of their districts.

For more information on this program contact your district legislator directly.

Illinois Monetary Award Program—Need-based grants of up to $3,500 at approved postsecondary institutions for half-time (6 hours minimum) and full-time study.

Illinois Merit Recognition Scholarship—$1,000 scholarships to Illinois students who rank in the top 5 percent of their high school class at the end of the seventh semester. Financial need is not a factor. Not renewable.

Paul Douglas Teacher Scholarship—A federally funded program administered by the Illinois Student Assistance Commission providing scholarships of up to $5,000 per year to outstanding Illinois students who plan to become teachers at the elementary or high school level. Students must rank in the top 10 percent of their high school class and may receive the award for four years.

For more information, contact the Illinois Student Assistance Commission, 1755 Lake Cook Road, Deerfield, IL 60015.

Indiana

Byrd Scholarship Program—Federally funded grants of $1,500 to promote student excellence and achievement. One scholarship per congressional district awarded to the highest scoring graduates of GED programs.

Higher Education Awards—Grants of $200 to $3,500 for full-time students at private, nonprofit in-state postsecondary institutions and of $200 to $1,500 at state-supported universities. Based on need. Awarded to Indiana residents working on their first undergraduate degree.

Hoosier Scholar Awards—One-time grants of $500 to residents in the top 20 percent of their graduating class who are nominated by their high schools. Financial need is not considered.

Paul Douglas Teacher Scholarship—Federally funded program providing renewable scholarships of up to $5,000 per year for students committed to a career in teaching who graduated in the top 10 percent of their high school class. Obligation to teach two years for every year scholarship is received.

Minority Teacher Scholarship—Grants of up to $4,000 for black or Hispanic students who want to be teachers. Renewable for up to four out of six years. Obligation to teach in Indiana for three out of five years following certification.

Special Education Services Scholarship—Grants of up to $1,000 for students who desire to teach in the field of special education. Renewable for up to four out of six years at eligible nonprofit and public postsecondary institutions. Obligation to teach in Indiana for three out of five years after certification.

Nursing Scholarship—Need-based grants for tuition of up to $5,000 for students who attend eligible nonprofit and public postsecondary institutions with nursing programs. Award is renewable.

State Work-Study Program—Summer work available to students who receive the Higher Education Grant or Lilly Grant during the preceding academic year. Funds awarded statewide to employers to reimburse 50 percent of student earnings.

For more information, contact the State Student Assistance Commission of Indiana, 150 W. Market Street, Suite 500, Indianapolis, IN 46204.

Iowa

Iowa Grants—Grants of $1,000 based on financial need for Iowa residents attending Iowa public, independent, and community colleges. Grants may be prorated for less than full-time study.

Iowa Tuition Grant program—Grants of up to $2,650 at private institutions (including nursing and business schools) for part-time and full-time study.

Iowa Vocational-Technical Tuition Grant Program—Grants of up to $600 at two-year public vocational and technical institutions for full-time study.

State of Iowa Scholarship Program—Grants of $410 to Iowa residents who rank in the top 15 percent of senior class. Based on academic ability. Award to freshmen only.

Paul Douglas Teacher Scholarship Program—Federally funded grants of up to $5,000 a year for Iowa students who plan to become teachers. Must rank in the top 10 percent of class and be a State of Iowa Scholarship applicant. Award is renewable for up to four years.

Robert C. Byrd Honors Scholarship Program—Federally funded grants of $1,500 to promote student excellence and achievement and to recognize exceptionally able students who show promise of continued excellence. Applicants must be Iowa residents and accepted at an approved postsecondary school. Award is renewable for up to four years.

For more information, contact the Iowa College Student Aid Commission, 914 Grand Avenue, Suite 201, Des Moines, IA 50309-2824.

Kansas

Kansas Tuition Grant Program—Grants for Kansas residents of up to $1,700 at private, nonprofit postsecondary institutions.

State Scholarship Program—Stipends of up to $1,000 for Kansas residents. Based on academic ability and financial need.

Kansas Minority Scholarship—Stipends of up to $1,500 a year for Kansas resident minority students attending in-state two- or four-year colleges. Based on academic ability and need.

Kansas Teacher Scholarship—Up to $5,000 a year for Kansas residents who will teach in Kansas one year for each year of funding.

Regents Supplemental Grant Program—Grants of up to $900 at Regents institutions for Kansas residents.

Kansas Nursing Scholarship—Up to $2,500 a year for Kansas residents pursuing LPN degrees; $3,500 a year for those pursuing RPN degrees.

For more information, contact the Board of Regents, 700 SW Harrison, Suite 1410, Topeka, KS 66603-3760.

Kentucky

College Access Program Grant—Need-based grants from $500 to $980 per year for full-time undergraduates who attend public and private colleges and universities, proprietary schools, and vocational-technical schools. Smaller awards for half-time stu-dents.

Kentucky Tuition Grant Program—Need-based grants of up to $1,500 per year at eligible private, nonprofit postsecondary institutions.

Paul Douglas Teacher Scholarship Program—Federally funded awards of up to $5,000 per year for students who rank in the top 10 percent of class or on the GED and sign an intent to become a certified teacher and to render teaching service in any state.

Teacher Scholarship Program—Awards up to $5,000 per year to Kentucky residents who intend to become teachers or teachers who wish to pursue certification in a critical shortage area. One year of teaching in a Kentucky-accredited school required for each year of award or one semester of teaching in a critical shortage area required for every two semesters of award.

KHEAA Work-Study Program—Career-related job opportunities for eligible Kentucky resident students attending approved in-state postsecondary institutions. Must be enrolled at least half time.

For more information, contact KHEAA Student Aid Program, 1050 U.S. 127 South, Suite 102, Frankfort, KY 40601.

Louisiana

State Student Incentive Grant Program—Grants of $200 to $2,000 at eligible postsecondary institutions.

Louisiana Honors Scholarship Program—Tuition waivers for students who graduate in top 5% of graduating class from Louisiana public or state-approved nonpublic high schools. Must be enrolled as full-time undergraduates.

Louisiana Tuition Assistance Plan—Tuition exemption for Louisiana residents who attend public colleges full time and meet specific academic and financial need criteria.

T.H. Harris State Academic Scholarship—Awards based on academic achievement for Louisiana high school graduates attending public colleges within the state. 3.0 GPA required. $400 per year with 5-year maximum of $2,000.

Rockefeller Scholarship for Wildlife Programs—Up to $1,000 per year for students in forestry, wildlife management, fisheries, and marine science programs. A 2.5 overall grade-point average is required. Does not require financial need.

Paul Douglas Teacher Scholarship Program—$5,000 per year for students with a high school average of 3.0 and ACT composite score of 23 and who rank in the top 10 percent of their high school graduating class or who have a college average of 3.0 with 24 or more hours of college credit and graduated in the top 10 percent of their high school class.

For more information, contact the Office of Student Financial Assistance for Louisiana, P.O. Box 91202, Baton Rouge, LA 70821-9202.

Maine

Maine Student Incentive Scholarship Program—Need-based grants of $500 to $1,000 for Maine Students attending eligible postsecondary institutions in New England, Pennsylvania, Maryland, District of Columbia, Alaska, and Delaware.

For more information, contact the Finance Authority of Maine, Maine Education Assistance Division, State House Station 119, Augusta ME 04333.

Maryland

Educational Assistance Grant Program—Grants of $200 to $3,000 at public or private postsecondary institutions. Undergraduate awards based on need.

Delegates Scholarship Program—Variable amounts, $200 minimum, to assist with tuition and fees at public and private postsecondary institutions for half-time and full-time study. Undergraduate and graduate students eligible.

Senatorial Scholarship Program—Grants of $200 to $2,000 at postsecondary institutions for half-time and full-time study. Undergraduate, graduate, and non-degree seeking students eligible.

Distinguished Scholar Program—$3,000 undergraduate annual awards based on merit or artistic talent for students nominated by their high schools or who are Merit/Achievement finalists.

For more information, contact the Maryland Higher Education Commission/State Scholarship Administration, 16 Francis Street, Annapolis, MD 21401-1781.

Massachusetts

General Scholarship Program—Grants of $200 to $2,500 for Massachusetts residents attending eligible in-state (and reciprocal state) postsecondary institutions on a full-time basis.

Tuition-Waiver Program—Up to the full cost of tuition waived for students attending a state-supported college or university. Amount of waiver determined by the financial aid office.

For more information, contact the Higher Education Coordinating Council, Office of Student Financial Assistance, 330 Stuart Street, Boston, MA 02116

Michigan

Tuition Grant Program—Need-based grants of up to $2,000 at independent nonprofit colleges and universities.

Competitive Scholarship Program—Awards based on ACT scores and financial need.

For more information, contact Michigan Higher Education Assistance Authority, Office of Scholarships and Grants, P.O. Box 30462, Lansing, MI 48909.

Minnesota

Minnesota State Grant Program—Grants from $100 to $5,889.

Interstate Tuition Reciprocity Programs—Under these programs Minnesota residents pay a tuition rate that is less than the normal out-of-state charge at public colleges and vocational institutions in Wisconsin, North Dakota, South Dakota, some Iowa institutions, and the Canadian province of Manitoba.

For more information, contact the Minnesota Higher Education Coordinating Board, 550 Cedar Street, Suite 400, St. Paul, MN 55101.

Mississippi

State Student Incentive Grant—Grants of $100 to $1,500.

For more information, contact your college financial aid office or the Mississippi Postsecondary Education Financial Assistance Board, 3825 Ridgewood Road, Jackson, MS 39211-6453.

Missouri

Student Grant Program—Grants of up to $1,500 (averaging $1,200) for study at undergraduate nonprofit Missouri postsecondary institutions. Divinity, theology, or religion majors are not eligible. Based on need; renewable.

Missouri Higher Education Academic Scholarship Program—Grants of up to $2,000 for full-time undergraduate students at eligible Missouri institutions. Students must have ACT composite scores or SAT combined scores in top 3 percent of all Missouri students taking those tests. Theology or divinity majors are not eligible. State residency required.

For more information, contact the Missouri Coordinating Board for Higher Education, P.O. Box 6730, Jefferson City, MO 65102.

Montana

Montana Student Incentive Grant Program—Grants of up to $900 at public postsecondary institutions and the three private colleges.

Honor Scholarships—Tuition and fee waivers at public postsecondary institutions for high school graduates.

For more information, contact the Montana University System, 2500 East Broadway, Helena, MT 59620-3101.

Nebraska

For more information about the Scholarship Assistance Program and State Scholarship Award Program, contact a Nebraska postsecondary education institution.

Nevada

Nevada Student Incentive Grant Program—Grants of up to $5,000 for half-time and full-time study.

For more information, contact Nevada Department of Education, Financial Aid, 400 West King Street, Carson City, NV 89710.

New Hampshire

New Hampshire Incentive Program—Need-based grants of $100 to $1,000 for undergraduate, full-time day students. Grants portable by New Hampshire residents to five other New England states. Rank in upper three-fifths of high school graduating class required of first-time freshmen, 2.0 college average required of those with sophomore standing and above.

For more information, contact the New Hampshire Postsecondary Education Commission, 2 Industrial Park Drive, Concord, NH 03301-8512.

New Jersey

Tuition Aid Grant Program—Grants of $600 to $5,210 at in-state colleges only.

Educational Opportunity Fund Grant Program—Grants of $200 to $1,950 at in-state colleges only.

Edward J. Bloustein Distinguished Scholars Program—Grants of $1,000 per year at in-state colleges only. Based on academic ability.

Garden State Scholar Program—Grants of $500 per year at in-state colleges only. Based on academic ability.

For more information, contact the New Jersey Office of Student Assistance, CN 540, Trenton, NJ 08625.

New Mexico

New Mexico Scholars Program—Scholarships provide tuition, required student fees, and books for an academic year for outstanding high school students attending eligible postsecondary institutions as full-time students. Renewable up to four times. Student must have combined family income of less than $30,000 per year.

New Mexico Student Choice Grant Program—For undergraduates attending an eligible private postsecondary institution who are enrolled at least half time.

New Mexico Student Incentive Grant Program—Need-based grants of $200 to $2,500 per year at public and private postsecondary institutions.

New Mexico Vietnam Veterans' Scholarship Program—Scholarships for Vietnam veterans who are New Mexico residents providing tuition and fee grants and book allowances for study at the undergraduate and graduate levels.

For more information, contact the Commission on Higher Education, 1068 Cerrillos Road, Santa Fe, New Mexico 87501-4295.

New York

New York Tuition Assistance Program—Grants of $100 to $3,900 depending on type of institution and need. Annual; available to undergraduate or graduate students.

Vietnam Veterans Tuition Awards—Grants of up to $1,000 per semester for full-time study and $500 per semester for part-time study for eligible applicants who served in the U.S. Armed Forces between December 22, 1961, and May 7, 1975.

Paul Douglas Teacher Scholarship Program—Federally funded program providing renewable scholarships of up to $5,000 per year for students in the top 10 percent of their high school class or with comparable GED scores, who enroll full time in a program leading to teacher certification and agree to teach for 2 years for each year of scholarship assistance.

For more information, contact the Higher Education Services Corporation, Student Information, 99 Washington Avenue, 14th Floor, Albany, NY 12255.

North Carolina

North Carolina Legislative Tuition Grant Program—Grants of up to $1,250 annually for North Carolina residents at private colleges and universities in North Carolina. Does not require financial need.

North Carolina Student Incentive Grant Program—Need-based grants of up to $1,500 or one-half of unmet need, whichever is less, at colleges, universities, and technical and vocational schools.

North Carolina Student Loan Program for Health, Science, and Mathematics—Scholarships/loans ranging from $2,500 to $7,500 annually depending on degree level, to be repaid through practice/service in the state. Available to legal residents in accredited associate, baccalaureate, master's or doctoral programs.

North Carolina Teaching Fellows Program—Grants of up to $5,000 for North Carolina residents to encourage entry into the elementary and secondary teaching profession. May be used to attend 15 designated institutions in North Carolina (13 public, 2 private). Does not require financial need.

State Contractual Scholarship Fund—Grants for North Carolina residents at eligible North Carolina private colleges and universities, based on need.

For more information, contact the North Carolina State Education Assistance Authority, Box 2688, Chapel Hill, NC 27515-2688.

North Dakota

Student Financial Assistance Program—Grants of up to $600 for attendance at public and nonprofit postsecondary institutions.

North Dakota Scholars Program—Tuition scholarships available to students who score at the 95th percentile or above on the ACT, and who rank in the top 20 percent of their graduating class.

For more information, contact the Student Financial Assistance Program, State Capitol, Tenth Floor, 600 East Boulevard, Bismarck, ND 58505.

Ohio

Ohio Instructional Grant Program—Grants of up to $3,750 at Ohio and Pennsylvania approved private postsecondary institutions, up to $1,512 at Ohio and Pennsylvania approved public postsecondary institutions, and up to $3,180 at Ohio and Pennsylvania approved proprietary institutions. For full-time undergraduates enrolled in eligible associate or bachelor's degree or nursing diploma programs.

Ohio Academic Scholarship Program—Scholarships of $1,000 per year at eligible public, private, and proprietary postsecondary Ohio institutions. Based on high school academic ability and ACT scores.

Ohio Student Choice Grant Program—Grants in varying amounts at eligible private postsecondary Ohio institutions. For full-time undergraduates enrolled in a bachelor's degree program who did not attend any institution full time before July 1, 1984.

For more information, contact the Ohio Student Aid Commission, P.O. Box 16610, Columbus, OH 43216-6610.

Oklahoma

Tuition Aid Grant Program—Grants of up to $1,000 or 75 percent of tuition and fees, whichever is less, at eligible colleges, universities, and vocational-technical schools. Based on financial need. Available to undergraduate and graduate students, full time and part time.

For more information, contact the Oklahoma State Regents for Higher Education, Tuition Aid Grant Program, P.O. Box 3020, Oklahoma City, OK 73101-3020.

Oregon

Need Grant Program—Need-based grants of up to $3,180 at accredited nonprofit postsecondary institutions.

For more information, contact the Oregon State Scholarship Commission, Valley River Office Park, 1500 Valley River Drive, Suite 100, Eugene, OR 97401.

Pennsylvania

State Higher Education Grant Program—Grants of up to $2,700, pending passage of state budget, or 80 percent of tuition and fees, whichever is less, at in-state postsecondary institutions; up to $600 at approved out-of-state postsecondary institutions.

POW/MIA Grant Program—Grants of $100 to $1,200 for dependents of U.S. Armed Forces veterans who were taken prisoner or declared missing-in-action; for use at in-state postsecondary institutions. Lower limits at eligible out-of-state institutions.

Veterans Grant Program—Grants of up to $2,400 or 80 percent of tuition and fees, whichever is less, at in-state postsecondary institutions; up to $800 at approved out-of-state postsecondary institutions for applicants who served in the U.S. Armed Forces.

Paul Douglas Teacher Scholarship Program—Scholarships to outstanding high school graduates to enable and encourage them to pursue teaching careers at the preschool, elementary, or secondary level. Grants of up to $5,000 for a maximum of four years.

For more information, contact the Pennsylvania Higher Education Assistance Agency, 1200 N. Seventh St., Harrisburg, PA 17102.

Puerto Rico

Legislative Scholarship Program—Grants for attendance at the University of Puerto Rico.

Supplemental Aid Program—University of Puerto Rico institutional program for supplemental aid that provides additional aid to needy students.

Legislative Scholarship Program—Grants for attendance at private accredited institutions of higher education.

Educational Fund—Grants for attendance at private accredited institutions of higher education.

Paul Douglas Teacher Scholarship Program—Scholarships to outstanding high school graduates to enable and encourage them to pursue teaching careers at the preschool, elementary, or secondary level. Grants of up to $5,000 for a maximum of four years.

Robert C. Byrd Honor Scholarship program—Scholarships to promote student excellence and to recognize exceptionally able students. Grants are $1,500 for one academic year.

Rosa A. Axtmayer Scholarship Program—Grants to needy students for attendance at the University of Puerto Rico.

For more information, contact the Council on Higher Education, Box 23305-UPR Station, Rio Piedras, PR 00931.

Rhode Island

State Grant or Scholarship Program—Scholarships and grants of up to $900 at eligible in-state and out-of-state postsecondary institutions. Scholarships based on SAT scores and financial need; grants based on financial need.

For more information, contact the Rhode Island Higher Education Assistance Authority, 560 Jefferson Boulevard, Warwick, RI 02886.

South Carolina

Tuition Grants Program—Need-based grants of up to $3,260 at in-state private postsecondary institutions.

For more information, contact the Tuition Grants Commission, 811 Keenan Building, P.O. Box 12159, Columbia, SC 29211.

South Dakota

South Dakota Student Incentive Grant Program—Grants of up to $600 for South Dakota residents at participating postsecondary institutions.

South Dakota Tuition Equalization Grant—Grants for South Dakota residents of up to $300 at participating in-state private colleges.

National Guard Tuition Program—Members of the Army or Air National Guard of the state of South Dakota attending any undergraduate-level institution under the control of the Board of Regents or a state vocational institution are entitled to a 50 percent reduction of tuition charges. There is a four-year limit.

Paul Douglas Teacher Scholarship Program—Scholarships to outstanding South Dakota high school graduates to enable and encourage them to pursue teaching careers at the preschool, elementary, or secondary level. Grants of up to $5,000 for a maximum of four years.

Robert C. Byrd Honors Scholarship Program—$1,500 scholarships for South Dakota residents to promote student excellence and achievement and to recognize exceptionally able students who show promise of continued excellence.

For more information, contact the Department of Education and Cultural Affairs, Office of the Secretary, 700 Governors Drive, Pierre, SD 57501-2291.

Tennessee

Tennessee Student Assistance Award Program—Maximum grants of $1,482.

Dependent Children Scholarship—For dependent children of a law enforcement officer, firefighter, or emergency medical service technician in Tennessee who was killed or totally and permanently disabled while performing duties within the scope of his or her employment.

Paul Douglas Teacher Scholarship Program—Federally funded program for students entering the teaching field at the K-12 level. Grants of up to $5,000 for a maximum of four years.

Ned McWherter Scholars Program—Awards of up to $5,000 per academic year for academically superior high school graduates.

Tennessee Teacher Loan/Scholarship Program—For outstanding students who plan to become public school teachers in an academic shortage area designated by the State Board of Education (currently mathematics or science for grades 7-12, art or music for grades K-8, elementary education, and special education). Awards up to the maximum tuition at the highest-cost public institution. Awards may be renewed for four years.

Teacher Loan Program for Disadvantaged Areas of Tennessee—For students who plan to become public school teachers at the K-12 level in a geographic area designated by the State Board of Education as disadvantaged at the time the student completes the requirements for teacher certification. Awards of up to $1,500 per year, for a maximum of $6,000.

Robert C. Byrd Honors Scholarship—Federal scholarships to promote student excellence through awards of $1,500 per academic year.

For more information, contact the Tennessee Student Assistance Corporation, Suite 1950, Parkway Towers, 404 James Robertson Parkway, Nashville, TN 37243-0820.

Texas

Texas Tuition Equalization Grant Program—Grants of up to $1,900 at private, nonprofit postsecondary institutions.

Texas Public Grant Program—Grants of up to $2,500 at public postsecondary institutions.

State Scholarship for Ethnic Recruitment—Scholarships of $500 to $1,000 for eligible minority students attending general academic teaching institutions.

Robert C. Byrd Honors Scholarship Program—Scholarships to promote student excellence and achievement and to recognize exceptionally able students who show promise of continued excellence. Grants are $1,500 for one academic year.

Paul Douglas Teacher Scholarship Program—Loans to outstanding high school graduates to enable and encourage them to pursue teaching careers at the preschool, elementary, or secondary level. Loans of up to $5,000 per year for a maximum of four years.

For more information, contact the financial aid office at the institution you wish to attend.

Utah

State Student Incentive Grant Program—Grants of up to $2,500 based on need.

Utah Educational Career Teaching Scholarship—Available to students who plan a career teaching in the public educational institutions of Utah. Tuition and fees waived, with additional stipends in some instances awarded on merit. Recipient must teach in the public educational institutions of Utah one year for each year they received the scholarship, for a maximum of five years. This must begin no later than two years after certification.

National Guard State Tuition Assistance—Members of the National Guard may receive up to $1,000 per year, not to exceed a $4,000 maximum. Extended service period required.

For more information, contact the financial aid office at the institution you wish to attend.

Vermont

Vermont Incentive Grant Program—Grants of $500 to $5,200 at in-state postsecondary institutions, and grants of $500 to $4,000 at out-of-state postsecondary institutions.

Part-Time Student Grant Program—Grants of $250 to $3,900 for students going less than full time to in-state postsecondary institutions, and grants of $250 to $3,000 for study at out-of-state postsecondary institutions.

For more information, contact the Vermont Student Assistance Corporation, Champlain Mill, P.O. Box 2000, Winooski, VT 05404-2601.

Virginia

College Scholarship Assistance Program—Grants of $400 to $5,000 at public and private colleges.

Virginia Tuition Assistance Grant Program—Non-need-based grants of up to $1,500 for Virginia residents who attend private colleges in Virginia.

Virginia Transfer Grant Program—Full tuition and mandatory fees or remaining need, whichever is lower, awarded to "other race" students who are enrolled in a traditionally white or black four-year public college or university in Virginia. Applicants must meet minimum merit criteria and be first-time transfer students.

Last Dollar Program—Need-based grants for minority undergraduates enrolled for the first time in a state-supported college or university.

Virginia Student Financial Assistance Program—For undergraduate students who have financial need, are enrolled at least half time, and are domiciliary residents of Virginia. Also open to graduate students; however, they do not have to demonstrate financial need. Awards up to full tuition and required fees. An additional component of the program is open to first-time freshmen who demonstrate academic achievement in high school.

For more information, contact the Virginia Council of Higher Education, James Monroe Building, 101 North 14th Street, Richmond, VA 23219.

Washington

State Need Grant Program—Variable grants for low-income state residents attending in-state postsecondary institutions.

Educational Opportunity Grant—A $2,500 grant to needy students who choose to attend a college with existing unused capacity.

Future Teacher Conditional Scholarship Program—Renewable $3,000 conditional loans requiring a 10-year in-state public school teaching commitment to qualify for a 100 percent loan forgiveness.

Paul Douglas Teacher Scholarship Program—Renewable $5,000 conditional loans to those graduating in the top 10 percent of their high school class and intending to pursue a teaching career. Recipients must teach two years for each year of loan forgiveness.

Health Professional Scholarship Program—Renewable conditional loans of up to $15,000. Recipients agree to provide primary care services in state-defined shortage areas for a minimum of three years to qualify for a 100 percent loan forgiveness.

Scholars Tuition Waiver and Grant Program—Four-year tuition waivers at public institutions and grants for those attending private institutions for high school seniors in the top 1 percent of their class, nominated for academic excellence, leadership, and community service by principals.

For more information, contact the Higher Education Coordinating Board, 917 Lakeridge Way, P.O. Box 43430, Olympia WA 98504-3430.

West Virginia

Higher Education Grant Program—Grants of up to $1,944 at approved in-state higher education institutions, and up to $600 at approved Pennsylvania institutions for full-time students.

Robert C. Byrd Honors Scholarship Program—Merit scholarships of $1,500 awarded for study at a degree-granting institution of higher education.

Paul Douglas Teacher Scholarship Program—Grants of up to $5,000 for state residents who graduated in the top 10 percent of their high school class; who are enrolled full time at an in-state college or university in a course of study leading to teacher certification; and who agree to teach in any state for two years for each year of scholarship assistance.

Underwood-Smith Teacher Scholarship Program—Grants of up to

$5,000 for state residents who graduated in the top 10 percent of their high school class or scored in the top 10 percent statewide of those students taking the ACT, who are enrolled in a West Virginia state college or university in a course of study leading to certification as a teacher, and who agree to teach in the state's public school system for two years for each year of scholarship assistance.

For more information, contact the State Colleges and University Systems of West Virginia Central Office, Higher Education Grant Program, P.O. Box 4007, Charleston, WV 25364.

Wisconsin

Wisconsin Higher Education Grants Program—Grants of up to $1,800 at eligible public postsecondary institutions for half-time and full-time study.

Tuition Grant Program—Grants of up to $2,172 at eligible private colleges, universities, and nursing schools for half-time and full-time study.

Interstate Program (Minnesota-Wisconsin)—A reciprocal arrangement paying for Wisconsin resident tuition at public colleges and vocational institutions in Minnesota.

Wisconsin Indian Student Grant Program—Grants of up to $2,200 at any eligible public or private institution of higher education in Wisconsin for half time or full time students who are of at least 25 percent native American heritage.

For more information, contact the Wisconsin Higher Educational Aids Board, P.O. Box 7885, Madison WI 53707.

Wyoming

State Student Incentive Grants Program—Grants at public non-profit postsecondary institutions averaging $300.

For more information, contact the college you plan to attend.

Guam

Government-sponsored scholarships for Teaching and Nursing programs for attendance at the University of Guam. Program covers tuition, fees, book allowance, and monthly stipends ranging from $100 to $450.

Government-sponsored loan programs for undergraduate and graduate students for attendance at the University of Guam and off-island U.S. accredited institutions if the degree programs are not offered at the University of Guam. Programs range from $3,000 to $12,000 per academic year.

Government-sponsored Merit Program for graduating high school seniors from Guam for attendance at the University of Guam. Program covers tuition, fees, and monthly stipends of approximately $600.

For more information, contact the Financial Aid Office, UOG Station, Mangilao, GU 96923.

Virgin Islands

Student Incentive Grant Program—Grants of up to $5,000 at accredited, eligible institutions.

Territorial Scholarship Program—Grants of $500 to $3,000 and loans of $1,000 to $4,000 for students at the College of the Virgin Islands and United States nonprofit accredited postsecondary institutions.

For more information, contact the Financial Aid Office, Virgin Islands Board of Education, P.O. Box 11900, St. Thomas, VI 00801.

Sources of information about the Federal Stafford Loan Program

Alabama

Alabama Commission on
    Higher Education
P.O. Box 302000
Montgomery, AL 36130-2000
(334) 242-1998

Alaska

United Student Aid Funds, Inc.
Loan Information Services, M372
P.O. Box 6180
Indianapolis, IN 46206
(317) 849-6510
(800) LOAN USA (562-6872)

Arizona

Arizona Education Loan Program
25 S. Arizona Place, Suite 530
Chandler, AZ 85225
(800) 352-3033

Arkansas

Student Loan Guarantee
    Foundation of Arkansas
219 South Victory
Little Rock, AR 72201
(501) 372-1491
(800) 622-3446

California

California Student Aid Commission
P.O. Box 510845
Sacramento, CA 94245-0845
(916) 445-0880

Colorado

Colorado Student Loan Program
Denver Place
999 Eighteenth Street, Suite 425
Denver, CO 80202-2440
(303) 294-5050

Connecticut

Connecticut Student Loan
    Foundation
P.O. Box 1009
Rocky Hill, CT 06067
(203) 257-4001

Delaware

Higher Education Loan Program
Delaware Higher Education
    Commission
820 North French Street
Wilmington, DE 19801
(302) 577-6055

Florida

Office of Student Financial Assistance
Federal Programs
1344 Florida Education Center
Florida Department of Education
Tallahassee, FL 32399-0400
(904) 488-4095

Georgia

Georgia Higher Education Assistance
    Corporation
2082 East Exchange Place, Suite 200
Tucker, GA 30084
(404) 414-3000

Hawaii

Hawaii Education Loan Program
United Student Aid Funds, Inc.
P.O. Box 22187
Honolulu, HI 96823-2187
(808) 593-2262

Idaho

Student Loan Fund of Idaho, Inc.
6905 Highway 95
P.O. Box 730
Fruitland, ID 83619-0730
(208) 452-4058

Illinois

Illinois Student Assistance Commission
1755 Lake Cook Road
Deerfield, IL 60015
(708) 948-8550

Indiana

State Student Assistance Commission of
    Indiana
150 W. Market Street, Suite 500
Indianapolis, IN 46204
(317) 232-2350

Iowa

Iowa College Student Aid Commission
914 Grand Avenue, Suite 201
Des Moines, IA 50309-2824
(515) 281-4890

Kansas

Higher Education Loan Program of Kansas
6800 College Boulevard, Suite 600
Overland Park, KS 66211
(913) 345-1300

Kentucky

Kentucky Higher Education Assistance
    Authority
1050 U.S. 127 South, Suite 102
Frankfort, KY 40601-4323
(502) 564-7990

Louisiana

Office of Student Financial Assistance
    for Louisiana Student Financial
    Assistance Commission
P.O. Box 91202
Baton Rouge, LA 70821-9202
(800) 259-5626

Maine

Maine Education Assistance Division
    Finance Authority of Maine
State House Station 119
Augusta, ME 04333
(207) 287-2183

Maryland

Maryland Higher Education
    Loan Corporation
2100 Guilford Avenue
Baltimore, MD 21218
(410) 333-6555

Massachusetts

Massachusetts Higher Education
    Assistance Corporation
330 Stuart Street
Boston, MA 02116
(617) 426-9434

Michigan

Michigan Higher Education
    Assistance Authority
Michigan Guaranty Agency
P.O. Box 30047
Lansing, MI 48909
(517) 373-0760
(800) 642-5626

Minnesota

Northstar Guarantee Inc.
444 Cedar Street, Suite 1910
St. Paul, MN 55101-2133
(612) 290-8795

Mississippi

Mississippi Guarantee Student Loan
    Agency
3825 Ridgewood Road
Jackson, MS 39211-6453
(601) 982-6663

Missouri

Missouri Coordinating Board
    for Higher Education
P.O. Box 6730
Jefferson City, MO 65102
(314) 751-3940

Montana

Montana Guaranteed Student
    Loan Program
2500 Broadway, P.O. Box 203101
Helena, MT 59620-3101
(406) 444-6594

Nebraska

Nebraska Student Loan Program
1300 O Street
P.O. Box 82507
Lincoln, NE 68501-2507
(402) 475-8686

Nevada

United Student Aid Funds, Inc.
Western Regional Center
25 South Arizona Place, Suite 530
Chandler, AZ 85225
(800) 824-7044

New Hampshire

New Hampshire Higher Education
    Assistance Foundation
44 Warren Street
P.O. Box 877
Concord, NH 03302
(603) 225-6612
(800) 525-2577

New Jersey

New Jersey Higher Education
    Assistance Authority
4 Quaker Bridge Plaza
CN 543
Trenton, NJ 08625
(609) 588-3200
(800) 356-5562

New Mexico

New Mexico Student Loan Guarantee
    Corporation
P.O. Box 27020
Albuquerque, NM 87125-7020
(505) 345-8821

New York

New York State Higher Education
    Services Corporation
99 Washington Avenue
Albany, NY 12255
(518) 473-7087

North Carolina

North Carolina State Education
    Assistance Authority
P.O. Box 2688
Chapel Hill, NC 27515-2688
(919) 549-8614
    or
College Foundation
P.O. Box 12100
Raleigh, NC 27605-2100
(919) 821-4771

North Dakota

Student Loans of North Dakota
    —Guarantor
Box 5524
Bismarck, ND 58506-5524
(701) 328-5753
(800) 472-2166

Ohio

Ohio Student Aid Commission
309 South Fourth Street
P.O. Box 16610
Columbus, OH 43216-0610
(614) 466-3091

Oklahoma

Oklahoma State Regents for
    Higher Education
P.O. Box 3000
Oklahoma City, OK 73101-3000
(405) 552-4300
(800) 442-8642

Oregon

Oregon State Scholarship
    Commission
Valley River Office Park
1500 Valley River Drive, Suite 100
Eugene, OR 97401
(503) 687-7400

Pennsylvania

Pennsylvania Higher Education
    Assistance Agency
1200 N. Seventh Street
Harrisburg, PA 17102
(717) 257-2860
(800) 692-7392 (Pennsylvania)

Puerto Rico

Great Lakes Higher Education
    Corporation
2401 International Lane
Madison, WI 53704

Rhode Island

Rhode Island Higher Education
    Assistance Authority
560 Jefferson Boulevard
Warwick, RI 02886
(401) 736-1170

South Carolina

South Carolina Student Loan Corporation
Interstate Center, Suite 210
P.O. Box 21487
Columbia, SC 29221
(803) 798-0916

South Dakota

Education Assistance Corporation
115 First Avenue, S.W.
Aberdeen, SD 57401-4174
(605) 225-6423

Tennessee

Tennessee Student Assistance Corporation
404 James Robertson Parkway
Parkway Towers, Suite 1950
Nashville, TN 37243-0820
(615) 741-1346

Texas

Texas Guaranteed Student Loan
    Corporation
P.O. Box 201725
Austin, TX 78720-1725
(800) 252-9743

Utah

Utah State Board of Regents
3 Triad, Suite 550
355 W. North Temple
Salt Lake City, UT 84180-1205
(801) 321-7207

Vermont

Vermont Student Assistance
    Corporation
Champlain Mill
P.O. Box 2000
Winooski, VT 05404-2601
(802) 655-9602
(800) 642-3177 (Vermont)

Virginia

State Education Assistance Authority
One Franklin Square
411 East Franklin Street
Richmond, VA 23219-2243
(804) 775-4000
(800) 792-LOAN

Washington

Northwest Education Loan Association
500 Colman Building
811 First Avenue
Seattle, WA 98104
(206) 461-5300

West Virginia

West Virginia Education Loan Services
PHEAA Regional Office
20 Kenton Drive
Charleston, WV 25311
(304) 345-7211
(800) 437-3692

Wisconsin

Great Lakes Higher Education
    Corporation
2401 International Lane
Madison, WI 53704
(608) 246-1800

Wyoming

United Student Aid Funds
1912 Capitol Avenue, Suite 320
Cheyenne, WY 82001
(307) 635-3259

Virgin Islands

Virgin Islands Board of Education
P.O. Box 11900
Charlotte Amalie
St. Thomas, VI 00801
(809) 774-4546

Guam, American Samoa, Northern Marianas, Palau

Hawaii Education Loan Program
United Student Aid Funds, Inc.
P.O. Box 22187
Honolulu, HI 96823-2187
(808) 593-2262

United Student Aid Funds, Inc.

United Student Aid Funds, Inc.
Loan Information Services, M372
P.O. Box 6180
Indianapolis, IN 46206
(800) LOAN USA (562-6872)
(317) 849-6510

Colleges that offer academic, music or drama, and art scholarships

Academic scholarships

Alabama

Alabama Agricultural and
  Mechanical University
Alabama Aviation and Technical
  College
Alabama Southern Community
  College
Alabama State University
Athens State College
Auburn University
  Auburn
  Montgomery
Bessemer State Technical College
Bevill State Community College
Birmingham-Southern College
Bishop State Community College
Central Alabama Community
  College
Chattahoochee Valley Community
  College
Douglas MacArthur State Technical
  College
Enterprise State Junior College
Faulkner University
Gadsden State Community College
Harry M. Ayers State Technical
  College
Huntingdon College
J. F. Drake State Technical College
Jacksonville State University
James H. Faulkner State
  Community College
Jefferson State Community College
John C. Calhoun State Community
  College
Lurleen B. Wallace State Junior
  College
Marion Military Institute
Miles College
Northeast Alabama Community
  College
Northwest-Shoals Community
  College
Oakwood College
Samford University
Shelton State Community College
Snead State Community College
Southeastern Bible College
Southern Christian University
Sparks State Technical College
Spring Hill College
Stillman College
Talladega College
Troy State University
  Dothan
  Troy

Tuskegee University
UAB: Walker College
University of Alabama
  Birmingham
  Huntsville
  Tuscaloosa
University of Mobile
University of Montevallo
University of North Alabama
University of South Alabama
University of West Alabama
Wallace State College at Hanceville

Alaska

Alaska Bible College
Alaska Pacific University
Prince William Sound Community
  College
Sheldon Jackson College
University of Alaska
  Anchorage
  Southeast

Arizona

American Indian College of the
  Assemblies of God
Arizona College of the Bible
Arizona State University
Arizona Western College
Cochise College
DeVry Institute of Technology:
  Phoenix
Eastern Arizona College
Embry-Riddle Aeronautical
  University: Prescott Campus
Gateway Community College
Glendale Community College
Mesa Community College
Mohave Community College
Navajo Community College
Northern Arizona University
Northland Pioneer College
Paradise Valley Community College
Phoenix College
Pima Community College
Prescott College
Scottsdale Community College
South Mountain Community
  College
University of Arizona

Arkansas

Arkansas State University
  Beebe Branch
  Jonesboro
Arkansas Tech University
Central Baptist College
Garland County Community
  College
Harding University

Henderson State University
Hendrix College
John Brown University
Lyon College
Mississippi County Community
  College
North Arkansas Community/
  Technical College
Ouachita Baptist University
Philander Smith College
Phillips County Community College
Rich Mountain Community College
South Arkansas Community College
Southern Arkansas University
  Magnolia
  Tech
University of Arkansas
  Fayetteville
  Little Rock
  Monticello
University of Central Arkansas
University of the Ozarks
Williams Baptist College

California

Academy of Art College
Allan Hancock College
American Academy of Dramatic
  Arts: West
American River College
Antelope Valley College
Art Institute of Southern California
Azusa Pacific University
Bakersfield College
Bethany College
Biola University
Brooks Institute of Photography
Butte College
California Baptist College
California College of Arts and
  Crafts
California Institute of Technology
California Lutheran University
California Maritime Academy
California Polytechnic State
  University: San Luis Obispo
California State Polytechnic
  University: Pomona

California State University
  Bakersfield
  Chico
  Dominguez Hills
  Fresno
  Fullerton
  Hayward
  Long Beach
  Los Angeles
  Northridge
  San Bernardino
  San Marcos
  Stanislaus
Cerritos Community College
Cerro Coso Community College
Chabot College
Chaffey Community College
Chapman University
Charles R. Drew University: College
  of Allied Health
Christian Heritage College
Citrus College
City College of San Francisco
Claremont McKenna College
Cogswell Polytechnical College
Coleman College
College of the Desert
College of Marin: Kentfield
College of Notre Dame
College of the Redwoods
College of the Sequoias
College of the Siskiyous
Columbia College
Compton Community College
Concordia University
Cosumnes River College
Crafton Hills College
Cuesta College
De Anza College
DeVry Institute of Technology:
  Pomona
Diablo Valley College
Dominican College of San Rafael
El Camino College
Evergreen Valley College
Feather River College
Foothill College
Fresno City College
Fresno Pacific College
Fullerton College
Gavilan Community College
Golden Gate University
Grossmont Community College
Harvey Mudd College
Holy Names College
Humboldt State University
Imperial Valley College
Irvine Valley College
John F. Kennedy University
Kings River Community College

La Sierra University
Lake Tahoe Community College
LIFE Bible College
Long Beach City College
Los Angeles Harbor College
Los Angeles Mission College
Los Angeles Pierce College
Los Angeles Southwest College
Los Medanos College
Loyola Marymount University
Marymount College
Master's College
Menlo College
Merced College
Mills College
MiraCosta College
Mission College
Modesto Junior College
Monterey Institute of International
    Studies
Monterey Peninsula College
Mount St. Mary's College
Mount San Jacinto College
Napa Valley College
New School of Art and
    Architecture
Occidental College
Ohlone College
Orange Coast College
Pacific Christian College
Pacific Oaks College
Pacific Union College
Palomar College
Pasadena City College
Patten College
Pepperdine University
Point Loma Nazarene College
Porterville College
Rio Hondo College
Riverside Community College
Saddleback College
St. Mary's College of California
Samuel Merritt College
San Diego City College
San Diego Mesa College
San Diego State University
San Francisco State University
San Joaquin Delta College
San Jose Christian College
Santa Barbara City College
Santa Clara University
Santa Monica College
Santa Rosa Junior College
Scripps College
Simpson College
Sonoma State University
Southern California College
Southern California Institute of
    Architecture
Taft College
United States International
    University
University of California
    Berkeley
    Davis
    Irvine
    Los Angeles
    Riverside
    San Diego
    San Francisco
    Santa Barbara
    Santa Cruz
University of Judaism
University of the Pacific
University of Redlands
University of San Diego
University of San Francisco
University of Southern California
Victor Valley College
Westmont College
Whittier College
Woodbury University

Yuba College

Colorado

Adams State College
Aims Community College
Arapahoe Community College
Bel-Rea Institute of Animal
    Technology
Colorado Christian University
Colorado College
Colorado Institute of Art
Colorado Mountain College
    Alpine Campus
    Spring Valley Campus
    Timberline Campus
Colorado Northwestern Community
    College
Colorado School of Mines
Colorado State University
Colorado Technical College
Community College of Aurora
Community College of Denver
Fort Lewis College
Front Range Community College
Lamar Community College
Mesa State College
Metropolitan State College of
    Denver
Morgan Community College
Naropa Institute
Northeastern Junior College
Pikes Peak Community College
Pueblo Community College
Regis University
Rocky Mountain College of Art &
    Design
Trinidad State Junior College
University of Colorado
    Boulder
    Colorado Springs
    Denver
    Health Sciences Center
University of Denver
University of Northern Colorado
University of Southern Colorado
Western State College of Colorado

Connecticut

Albertus Magnus College
Briarwood College
Capital Community-Technical
    College
Central Connecticut State
    University
Eastern Connecticut State
    University
Fairfield University
Gateway Community-Technical
    College
Naugatuck Valley Community-
    Technical College
Northwestern Connecticut
    Community-Technical College
Quinebaug Valley Community-
    Technical College
Quinnipiac College
Sacred Heart University
St. Joseph College
Southern Connecticut State
    University
Teikyo-Post University
Tunxis Community-Technical
    College
University of Bridgeport
University of Connecticut
University of Hartford
University of New Haven
Western Connecticut State
    University

Delaware

Delaware State University

Delaware Technical and
    Community College
    Southern Campus
    Stanton/Wilmington Campus
    Terry Campus
Goldey-Beacom College
University of Delaware
Wesley College
Wilmington College

District of Columbia

American University
Catholic University of America
Corcoran School of Art
Gallaudet University
George Washington University
Howard University
Mount Vernon College
Southeastern University
Strayer College
Trinity College
University of the District of
    Columbia

Florida

Barry University
Bethune-Cookman College
Brevard Community College
Broward Community College
Central Florida Community College
Chipola Junior College
Daytona Beach Community College
Eckerd College
Edison Community College
Embry-Riddle Aeronautical
    University
Flagler College
Florida Agricultural and Mechanical
    University
Florida Atlantic University
Florida Bible College
Florida Christian College
Florida College
Florida Community College at
    Jacksonville
Florida Institute of Technology
Florida International University
Florida Keys Community College
Florida Memorial College
Florida Southern College
Florida State University
Fort Lauderdale College
Gulf Coast Community College
Hillsborough Community College
Indian River Community College
International Fine Arts College
Jacksonville University
Jones College
Lake City Community College
Lake-Sumter Community College
Lynn University
Manatee Community College
Miami-Dade Community College
New College of the University of
    South Florida
North Florida Junior College
Nova Southeastern University
Okaloosa-Walton Community
    College
Palm Beach Atlantic College
Palm Beach Community College
Pasco-Hernando Community
    College
Pensacola Junior College
Polk Community College
Rollins College
St. Johns River Community College
St. Leo College
St. Petersburg Junior College
St. Thomas University
Santa Fe Community College
Schiller International University

Seminole Community College
South Florida Community College
Southeastern College of the
    Assemblies of God
Stetson University
Tallahassee Community College
Talmudic College of Florida
Tampa College
Trinity International University
University of Central Florida
University of Florida
University of Miami
University of North Florida
University of South Florida
University of Tampa
University of West Florida
Valencia Community College
Warner Southern College
Webber College

Georgia

Abraham Baldwin Agricultural
    College
Agnes Scott College
Albany State College
American College for the Applied
    Arts
Armstrong State College
Atlanta Christian College
Atlanta College of Art
Augusta College
Augusta Technical Institute
Bainbridge College
Berry College
Brenau University
Brewton-Parker College
Brunswick College
Chattahoochee Technical Institute
Clark Atlanta University
Clayton State College
Columbus College
Covenant College
Dalton College
Darton College
DeKalb Technical Institute
DeVry Institute of Technology:
    Atlanta
East Georgia College
Emmanuel College
Emory University
Floyd College
Fort Valley State College
Gainesville College
Georgia Baptist College of Nursing
Georgia College
Georgia Institute of Technology
Georgia Southern University
Georgia Southwestern College
Georgia State University
Gordon College
Gwinnett Technical Institute
Kennesaw State College
LaGrange College
Macon College
Medical College of Georgia
Mercer University
    Atlanta
    Macon
Middle Georgia College
Morehouse College
Morris Brown College
North Georgia College
Oglethorpe University
Oxford College of Emory University
Paine College
Piedmont College
Reinhardt College
Savannah College of Art and
    Design
Savannah State College
School of Visual Arts: Savannah
Shorter College

South College
South Georgia College
Southern College of Technology
Spelman College
Thomas College
Toccoa Falls College
Truett-McConnell College
University of Georgia
Valdosta State University
Waycross College
Wesleyan College
West Georgia College
Young Harris College

Hawaii

Brigham Young University-Hawaii
Chaminade University of Honolulu
Hawaii Pacific University
University of Hawaii
    Hawaii Community College
    Hilo
    Honolulu Community College
    Kauai Community College
    Leeward Community College
    Manoa

Idaho

Albertson College
Boise Bible College
Boise State University
College of Southern Idaho
Eastern Idaho Technical College
Idaho State University
Lewis Clark State College
North Idaho College
Northwest Nazarene College
Ricks College
University of Idaho

Illinois

Augustana College
Aurora University
Barat College
Belleville Area College
Black Hawk College
Blackburn College
Blessing-Reiman College of Nursing
Bradley University
Carl Sandburg College
Chicago State University
City Colleges of Chicago
    Kennedy-King College
    Olive-Harvey College
College of DuPage
College of Lake County
College of St. Francis
Columbia College
Concordia University
Danville Area Community College
De Paul University
DeVry Institute of Technology
    Addison
    Chicago
Eastern Illinois University
Elgin Community College
Elmhurst College
Eureka College
Governors State University
Greenville College
Highland Community College
Illinois Benedictine College
Illinois College
Illinois Eastern Community
  Colleges
    Frontier Community College
    Lincoln Trail College
    Olney Central College
    Wabash Valley College
Illinois Institute of Technology
Illinois State University
Illinois Valley Community College
Illinois Wesleyan University

John A. Logan College
John Wood Community College
Joliet Junior College
Judson College
Kaskaskia College
Kendall College
Knox College
Lake Land College
Lewis and Clark Community
  College
Lewis University
Lexington Institute of Hospitality
  Careers
Lincoln Christian College and
  Seminary
Lincoln Land Community College
Loyola University of Chicago
MacCormac Junior College
MacMurray College
McHenry County College
McKendree College
Millikin University
Monmouth College
Moraine Valley Community College
Morrison Institute of Technology
Morton College
National-Louis University
North Central College
North Park College
Northeastern Illinois University
Northern Illinois University
Oakton Community College
Olivet Nazarene University
Parkland College
Principia College
Quincy University
Ray College of Design
Rend Lake College
Richland Community College
Robert Morris College: Chicago
Rock Valley College
Rockford College
Roosevelt University
Rosary College
St. Xavier University
Sangamon State University
Shimer College
Southeastern Illinois College
Southern Illinois University
    Carbondale
    Edwardsville
Spoon River College
Trinity Christian College
Trinity College
Triton College
University of Chicago
University of Illinois
    Chicago
    Urbana-Champaign
Western Illinois University
Wheaton College
William Rainey Harper College

Indiana

Ancilla College
Anderson University
Ball State University
Bethel College
Butler University
Calumet College of St. Joseph
DePauw University
Earlham College
Franklin College
Goshen College
Grace College
Hanover College
Huntington College
Indiana Institute of Technology
Indiana State University

Indiana University
    Bloomington
    East
    Kokomo
    Northwest
    South Bend
    Southeast
Indiana University—Purdue
  University
    Fort Wayne
    Indianapolis
Indiana Vocational Technical
  College
    Central Indiana
    Columbus
    Eastcentral
    Kokomo
    Lafayette
    Northcentral
    Northeast
    Northwest
    Southcentral
    Southeast
    Southwest
    Wabash Valley
    Whitewater
Indiana Wesleyan University
Lutheran College of Health
  Professions
Manchester College
Marian College
Martin University
Oakland City College
Purdue University
    Calumet
    North Central Campus
    West Lafayette
Rose-Hulman Institute of
  Technology
St. Francis College
St. Joseph's College
St. Mary-of-the-Woods College
St. Mary's College
St. Meinrad College
Taylor University
Tri-State University
University of Evansville
University of Indianapolis
University of Southern Indiana
Valparaiso University
Vincennes University
Wabash College

Iowa

American Institute of Business
Briar Cliff College
Buena Vista College
Central College
Clarke College
Coe College
Cornell College
Des Moines Area Community
  College
Dordt College
Drake University
Faith Baptist Bible College and
  Theological Seminary
Graceland College
Grand View College
Grinnell College
Hawkeye Community College
Indian Hills Community College
Iowa Central Community College
Iowa Lakes Community College
Iowa State University
Iowa Wesleyan College
Iowa Western Community College
Loras College
Luther College
Maharishi International University
Marshalltown Community College
Morningside College

Mount Mercy College
North Iowa Area Community
  College
Northeast Iowa Community College
Northwest Iowa Community
  College
Northwestern College
St. Ambrose University
Simpson College
Southeastern Community College:
  North Campus
Southwestern Community College
Teikyo Marycrest University
Teikyo Westmar University
University of Dubuque
University of Iowa
University of Northern Iowa
Upper Iowa University
Waldorf College
Wartburg College

Kansas

Allen County Community College
Baker University
Barclay College
Barton County Community College
Benedictine College
Bethany College
Bethel College
Butler County Community College
Central College
Coffeyville Community College
Colby Community College
Cowley County Community College
Dodge City Community College
Donnelly College
Emporia State University
Fort Hays State University
Friends University
Garden City Community College
Hesston College
Hutchinson Community College
Independence Community College
Johnson County Community
  College
Kansas City Kansas Community
  College
Kansas State University
Kansas Wesleyan University
Manhattan Christian College
McPherson College
MidAmerica Nazarene College
Neosho County Community College
Ottawa University
Pittsburg State University
Pratt Community College
St. Mary College
Seward County Community College
Southwestern College
Sterling College
Tabor College
University of Kansas
    Lawrence
    Medical Center
Washburn University of Topeka
Wichita State University

Kentucky

Alice Lloyd College
Asbury College
Ashland Community College
Bellarmine College
Brescia College
Campbellsville College
Centre College
Clear Creek Baptist Bible College
Cumberland College
Eastern Kentucky University
Elizabethtown Community College
Georgetown College
Hazard Community College
Henderson Community College

Hopkinsville Community College
Jefferson Community College
Kentucky Christian College
Kentucky State University
Kentucky Wesleyan College
Lexington Community College
Lindsey Wilson College
Madisonville Community College
Maysville Community College
Mid-Continent Baptist Bible College
Midway College
Morehead State University
Murray State University
Northern Kentucky University
Paducah Community College
Pikeville College
Prestonsburg Community College
Somerset Community College
Southeast Community College
Spalding University
Sue Bennett College
Thomas More College
Transylvania University
Union College
University of Kentucky
University of Louisville
Western Kentucky University

Louisiana

Bossier Parish Community College
Centenary College of Louisiana
Dillard University
Grambling State University
Louisiana College
Louisiana State University
    Agricultural and Mechanical
        College
    Alexandria
    Eunice
    Shreveport
Louisiana Tech University
Loyola University
McNeese State University
Nicholls State University
Northeast Louisiana University
Northwestern State University
Nunez Community College
Our Lady of Holy Cross College
St. Joseph Seminary College
Southeastern Louisiana University
Southern University in Shreveport
Tulane University
University of New Orleans
University of Southwestern
    Louisiana
Xavier University of Louisiana

Maine

Andover College
Beal College
Eastern Maine Technical College
Husson College
Maine College of Art
Maine Maritime Academy
Northern Maine Technical College
St. Joseph's College
Thomas College
Unity College
University of Maine
    Augusta
    Farmington
    Fort Kent
    Orono
    Presque Isle
University of New England
University of Southern Maine

Maryland

Allegany Community College
Anne Arundel Community College
Baltimore City Community College

Baltimore International Culinary
    College
Bowie State University
Capitol College
Carroll Community College
Catonsville Community College
Cecil Community College
Charles County Community College
Chesapeake College
College of Notre Dame of
    Maryland
Columbia Union College
Coppin State College
Dundalk Community College
Essex Community College
Frederick Community College
Frostburg State University
Garrett Community College
Goucher College
Hagerstown Business College
Hagerstown Junior College
Harford Community College
Hood College
Johns Hopkins University
Loyola College in Maryland
Maryland College of Art and
    Design
Maryland Institute College of Art
Morgan State University
Mount St. Mary's College
Prince George's Community College
St. Mary's College of Maryland
Salisbury State University
Towson State University
University of Baltimore
University of Maryland
    Baltimore County
    College Park
    Eastern Shore
    University College
Villa Julie College
Washington Bible College
Washington College
Western Maryland College

Massachusetts

American International College
Anna Maria College
Aquinas College at Newton
Atlantic Union College
Babson College
Bay Path College
Bay State College
Becker College
    Leicester Campus
    Worcester Campus
Bentley College
Berklee College of Music
Boston Architectural Center
Boston College
Boston University
Bradford College
Brandeis University
Bridgewater State College
Bristol Community College
Clark University
College of the Holy Cross
Eastern Nazarene College
Elms College
Emerson College
Emmanuel College
Fisher College
Fitchburg State College
Forsyth School for Dental
    Hygienists
Framingham State College
Gordon College
Hampshire College
Hellenic College
Holyoke Community College
Lasell College
Lesley College

Massachusetts Bay Community
    College
Massachusetts College of Pharmacy
    and Allied Health Sciences
Massachusetts Maritime Academy
Massasoit Community College
Newbury College
Nichols College
North Adams State College
Northeastern University
Pine Manor College
Quincy College
Quinsigamond Community College
Regis College
St. Hyacinth College and Seminary
Salem State College
Simmons College
Springfield Technical Community
    College
Stonehill College
Suffolk University
Tufts University
University of Massachusetts
    Amherst
    Boston
Wentworth Institute of Technology
Westfield State College
Worcester State College

Michigan

Adrian College
Albion College
Alma College
Alpena Community College
Andrews University
Aquinas College
Baker College
    Auburn Hills
    Cadillac
    Flint
    Jackson
    Mount Clemens
    Muskegon
    Owosso
    Port Huron
Bay de Noc Community College
Calvin College
Central Michigan University
Concordia College
Cornerstone College and Grand
    Rapids Baptist Seminary
Davenport College of Business
Delta College
Detroit College of Business
Eastern Michigan University
Ferris State University
Glen Oaks Community College
GMI Engineering & Management
    Institute
Gogebic Community College
Grace Bible College
Grand Rapids Community College
Grand Valley State University
Great Lakes Christian College
Henry Ford Community College
Hillsdale College
Hope College
Jackson Community College
Kalamazoo College
Kalamazoo Valley Community
    College
Kellogg Community College
Kendall College of Art and Design
Kirtland Community College
Lake Superior State University
Lansing Community College
Lawrence Technological University
Madonna University
Michigan Christian College
Michigan State University
Michigan Technological University
Mid Michigan Community College

Monroe County Community
    College
Montcalm Community College
Mott Community College
Muskegon Community College
Northern Michigan University
Northwestern Michigan College
Northwood University
Oakland Community College
Oakland University
Olivet College
Reformed Bible College
Saginaw Valley State University
St. Clair County Community
    College
St. Mary's College
Schoolcraft College
Siena Heights College
Southwestern Michigan College
Spring Arbor College
Suomi College
University of Detroit Mercy
University of Michigan
    Ann Arbor
    Dearborn
    Flint
Walsh College of Accountancy and
    Business Administration
Washtenaw Community College
Wayne State University
West Shore Community College
Western Michigan University
William Tyndale College

Minnesota

Alexandria Technical College
Anoka-Ramsey Community College
Augsburg College
Austin Community College
Bemidji State University
Bethany Lutheran College
Bethel College
Carleton College
Central Lakes College
College of Associated Arts
College of St. Benedict
College of St. Catherine: St.
    Catherine Campus
College of St. Catherine-
    Minneapolis
College of St. Scholastica
Concordia College: Moorhead
Concordia College: St. Paul
Crown College
Dunwoody Industrial Institute
Fergus Falls Community College
Gustavus Adolphus College
Hamline University
Hibbing Community College
Inver Hills Community College
Itasca Community College:
    Arrowhead Region
Lakewood Community College
Macalester College
Mankato State University
Martin Luther College
Mesabi Community College:
    Arrowhead Region
Minneapolis College of Art and
    Design
Minneapolis Community College
Minnesota Bible College
Moorhead State University
National College
NEI College of Technology
Normandale Community College
North Central Bible College
Northland Community College
Northwestern College
Oak Hills Bible College
Pillsbury Baptist Bible College
Rainy River Community College

Rasmussen College-Minnetonka
Rochester Community College
St. Cloud State University
St. John's University
St. Mary's College of Minnesota
St. Olaf College
Southwest State University
University of Minnesota
   Crookston
   Duluth
   Morris
   Twin Cities
University of St. Thomas
Vermilion Community College
Willmar Community College
Winona State University
Worthington Community College

Mississippi

Alcorn State University
Belhaven College
Blue Mountain College
Copiah-Lincoln Community College
Delta State University
East Central Community College
Hinds Community College
Holmes Community College
Jackson State University
Magnolia Bible College
Meridian Community College
Millsaps College
Mississippi College
Mississippi Delta Community
   College
Mississippi Gulf Coast Community
   College
    Jackson County Campus
    Jefferson Davis Campus
    Perkinston
Mississippi State University
Mississippi University for Women
Mississippi Valley State University
Pearl River Community College
Rust College
Tougaloo College
University of Mississippi
   Medical Center
   University
University of Southern Mississippi
Wesley College
William Carey College

Missouri

Avila College
Baptist Bible College
Calvary Bible College
Central Bible College
Central Christian College of the
   Bible
Central Methodist College
Central Missouri State University
College of the Ozarks
Columbia College
Cottey College
Crowder College
Culver-Stockton College
DeVry Institute of Technology:
   Kansas City
Drury College
East Central College
Evangel College
Fontbonne College
Harris Stowe State College
Jefferson College
Lincoln University
Lindenwood College
Longview Community College
Maryville University of St. Louis
Mineral Area College
Missouri Baptist College
Missouri Southern State College
Missouri Valley College

Missouri Western State College
Moberly Area Community College
North Central Missouri College
Northeast Missouri State University
Northwest Missouri State
   University
Ozark Christian College
Park College
Ranken Technical College
Research College of Nursing
Rockhurst College
St. Charles County Community
   College
St. Louis Christian College
St. Louis College of Pharmacy
St. Louis Community College
   Florissant Valley
   Forest Park
   Meramec
St. Louis University
Southeast Missouri State University
Southwest Baptist University
Southwest Missouri State University
State Fair Community College
Stephens College
Three Rivers Community College
University of Missouri
   Columbia
   Kansas City
   Rolla
   St. Louis
Washington University
Webster University
Wentworth Military Academy
Westminster College
William Jewell College

Montana

Carroll College
College of Great Falls
Dawson Community College
Helena College of Technology of
   the University of Montana
Miles Community College
Montana State University
   Billings
   Bozeman
   Northern
Montana Tech of The University of
   Montana
Montana Tech of the University of
   Montana: Division of Technology
Rocky Mountain College
Stone Child College
University of Montana-Missoula
Western Montana College of the
   University of Montana

Nebraska

Bellevue University
Central Community College
Clarkson College
College of St. Mary
Concordia College
Creighton University
Dana College
Doane College
Grace University
Hastings College
Lincoln School of Commerce
McCook Community College
Metropolitan Community College
Mid Plains Community College
Midland Lutheran College
Nebraska Christian College
Nebraska College of Technical
   Agriculture
Nebraska Methodist College of
   Nursing and Allied Health
Nebraska Wesleyan University
Northeast Community College
Peru State College

Southeast Community College
   Beatrice Campus
   Lincoln Campus
   Milford Campus
Union College
University of Nebraska
   Medical Center
   Kearney
   Lincoln
   Omaha
Wayne State College
Western Nebraska Community
   College: Scottsbluff Campus
York College

Nevada

Morrison College: Reno
Northern Nevada Community
   College
Sierra Nevada College
University of Nevada
   Las Vegas
   Reno
Western Nevada Community
   College

New Hampshire

Castle College
Colby-Sawyer College
Daniel Webster College
Franklin Pierce College
Hesser College
Keene State College
McIntosh College
New England College
New Hampshire College
New Hampshire Technical College
   Claremont
   Laconia
New Hampshire Technical Institute
Notre Dame College
Plymouth State College of the
   University System of New
   Hampshire
Rivier College
St. Anselm College
University of New Hampshire
   Durham
   Manchester
White Pines College

New Jersey

Bergen Community College
Berkeley College of Business
Bloomfield College
Brookdale Community College
Burlington County College
Caldwell College
Camden County College
Centenary College
College of St. Elizabeth
County College of Morris
DeVry Technical Institute
Drew University
Fairleigh Dickinson University
   Edward Williams College
   Teaneck
Felician College
Georgian Court College
Gloucester County College
Hudson County Community College
Jersey City State College
Kean College of New Jersey
Mercer County Community College
Monmouth College
Montclair State University
New Jersey Institute of Technology
Passaic County Community College
Ramapo College of New Jersey
Richard Stockton College of New
   Jersey
Rider University

Rowan College of New Jersey
Rutgers, The State University of
   New Jersey
   Camden College of Arts and
    Sciences
   College of Engineering
   College of Nursing
   College of Pharmacy
   Cook College
   Douglass College
   Livingston College
   Mason Gross School of the
    Arts
   Newark College of Arts and
    Sciences
   Rutgers College
St. Peter's College
Salem Community College
Seton Hall University
Stevens Institute of Technology
Sussex County Community College
Trenton State College
Union County College
Warren County Community College
Westminster Choir College of Rider
   University
William Paterson College of New
   Jersey

New Mexico

Clovis Community College
College of Santa Fe
College of the Southwest
Eastern New Mexico University
   Portales
   Roswell Campus
National College
New Mexico Highlands University
New Mexico Institute of Mining
   and Technology
New Mexico Junior College
New Mexico Military Institute
New Mexico State University
   Carlsbad
   Las Cruces
San Juan College
University of New Mexico

New York

Adelphi University
Adirondack Community College
Alfred University
Bard College
Berkeley College of New York City
Boricua College
Bramson ORT Technical Institute
Briarcliffe: The College for Business
   and Technology
Broome Community College
Bryant & Stratton Business
   Institute: Syracuse
Canisius College
Cayuga County Community College
Cazenovia College
Central City Business Institute
City University of New York
   Baruch College
   Brooklyn College
   City College
   Hostos Community College
   Hunter College
   John Jay College of Criminal
    Justice
   Lehman College
   Queens College
   Queensborough Community
    College
Clarkson University
Clinton Community College
Cochran School of Nursing-St.
   John's Riverside Hospital
College of Aeronautics

College of Insurance
College of Mount St. Vincent
College of New Rochelle
College of St. Rose
Columbia University: School of
  Nursing
Columbia-Greene Community
  College
Concordia College
Cooper Union
Corning Community College
Culinary Institute of America
Daemen College
Dominican College of Blauvelt
Dowling College
Dutchess Community College
D'Youville College
Eastman School of Music of the
  University of Rochester
Elmira College
Eugene Lang College/New School
  for Social Research
Fashion Institute of Technology
Finger Lakes Community College
Five Towns College
Fordham University
Fulton-Montgomery Community
  College
Genesee Community College
Hartwick College
Helene Fuld School of Nursing
Herkimer County Community
  College
Hilbert College
Hofstra University
Houghton College
Iona College
Jamestown Business College
Jamestown Community College
Jefferson Community College
Jewish Theological Seminary of
  America
Juilliard School
Keuka College
Le Moyne College
Long Island University
  Brooklyn Campus
  C. W. Post Campus
  Southampton College
Manhattan College
Manhattan School of Music
Manhattanville College
Marist College
Marymount College
Marymount Manhattan College
Mater Dei College
Medaille College
Mercy College
Mohawk Valley Community College
Molloy College
Monroe Community College
Mount St. Mary College
Nassau Community College
Nazareth College of Rochester
New York Institute of Technology
New York School of Interior
  Design
New York University
Niagara County Community College
Niagara University
Nyack College
Olean Business Institute
Onondaga Community College
Orange County Community College
Pace University
Paul Smith's College
Phillips Beth Israel School of
  Nursing
Plaza Business Institute
Polytechnic University
  Brooklyn
  Long Island Campus

Pratt Institute
Rensselaer Polytechnic Institute
Roberts Wesleyan College
Rochester Institute of Technology
Rockland Community College
Russell Sage College
Sage Junior College of Albany
St. Bonaventure University
St. Francis College
St. John Fisher College
St. John's University
St. Joseph's College
  Brooklyn
  Suffolk Campus
St. Joseph's Hospital Health Center
  School of Nursing
St. Lawrence University
St. Thomas Aquinas College
Schenectady County Community
  College
School of Visual Arts
Siena College
State University of New York
  Albany
  Binghamton
  Buffalo
  Oswego
  Purchase
  Stony Brook
  College of Agriculture and
    Technology at Cobleskill
  College of Agriculture and
    Technology at Morrisville
  College at Brockport
  College at Buffalo
  College at Cortland
  College of Environmental
    Science and Forestry
  College at Geneseo
  College at Old Westbury
  College at Oneonta
  College at Plattsburgh
  College at Potsdam
  College of Technology at
    Alfred
  College of Technology at
    Canton
  College of Technology at
    Farmingdale
  Health Sciences Center at
    Stony Brook
  Institute of Technology at
    Utica/Rome
  Maritime College
Suffolk County Community College
  Eastern Campus
  Selden
  Western Campus
Sullivan County Community
  College
Syracuse University
Tompkins-Cortland Community
  College
Touro College
Trocaire College
Ulster County Community College
University of Rochester
University of the State of New
  York: Regents College
Utica College of Syracuse
  University
Utica School of Commerce
Villa Maria College of Buffalo
Wadhams Hall Seminary-College
Wagner College
Webb Institute
Wells College
Westchester Business Institute
Westchester Community College
Wood Tobe-Coburn School
Yeshiva University

North Carolina
Alamance Community College
Appalachian State University
Barber-Scotia College
Barton College
Beaufort County Community
  College
Belmont Abbey College
Bennett College
Blue Ridge Community College
Brevard College
Brunswick Community College
Caldwell Community College and
  Technical Institute
Campbell University
Cape Fear Community College
Catawba College
Chowan College
Cleveland Community College
College of the Albemarle
Craven Community College
Davidson College
Davidson County Community
  College
Duke University
Durham Technical Community
  College
East Carolina University
Edgecombe Community College
Elizabeth City State University
Elon College
Fayetteville State University
Fayetteville Technical Community
  College
Forsyth Technical Community
  College
Gardner-Webb University
Gaston College
Greensboro College
Guilford College
Halifax Community College
Haywood Community College
High Point University
James Sprunt Community College
John Wesley College
Johnson C. Smith University
Johnston Community College
Lees-McRae College
Lenoir-Rhyne College
Livingstone College
Louisburg College
Mars Hill College
Mayland Community College
McDowell Technical Community
  College
Meredith College
Methodist College
Mitchell Community College
Montreat-Anderson College
Mount Olive College
Nash Community College
North Carolina Agricultural and
  Technical State University
North Carolina Central University
North Carolina School of the Arts
North Carolina State University
North Carolina Wesleyan College
Peace College
Pembroke State University
Pfeiffer College
Pitt Community College
Queens College
Randolph Community College
Richmond Community College
Roanoke Bible College
Roanoke-Chowan Community
  College
St. Andrews Presbyterian College
St. Augustine's College
St. Mary's College
Salem College
Sampson Community College

Sandhills Community College
Southeastern Community College
Stanly Community College
Surry Community College
University of North Carolina
  Asheville
  Chapel Hill
  Charlotte
  Greensboro
  Wilmington
Vance-Granville Community
  College
Wake Forest University
Wake Technical Community
  College
Warren Wilson College
Western Carolina University
Western Piedmont Community
  College
Wilkes Community College
Wingate College
Winston-Salem State University

North Dakota
Bismarck State College
Dickinson State University
Jamestown College
Minot State University
North Dakota State College of
  Science
North Dakota State University
  Bottineau
  Fargo
Trinity Bible College
University of Mary
University of North Dakota
  Grand Forks
  Lake Region
  Williston
Valley City State University

Ohio
Antioch College
Art Academy of Cincinnati
Ashland University
Baldwin-Wallace College
Belmont Technical College
Bluffton College
Bowling Green State University
  Bowling Green
  Firelands College
Bryant & Stratton Business
  Institute: Cleveland West
Capital University
Case Western Reserve University
Cedarville College
Central Ohio Technical College
Cincinnati State Technical and
  Community College
Clark State Community College
Cleveland Institute of Art
Cleveland Institute of Music
Cleveland State University
College of Mount St. Joseph
College of Wooster
Columbus State Community College
Cuyahoga Community College
  Eastern Campus
  Metropolitan Campus
  Western Campus
Davis College
Denison University
DeVry Institute of Technology:
  Columbus
Dyke College
Edison State Community College
Franciscan University of
  Steubenville
Franklin University
God's Bible School and College
Heidelberg College
Hiram College

Hocking Technical College
Jefferson Technical College
John Carroll University
Kent State University
　Ashtabula Regional Campus
　East Liverpool Regional
　　Campus
　Kent
　Salem Regional Campus
　Stark Campus
　Trumbull Campus
　Tuscarawas Campus
Kenyon College
Kettering College of Medical Arts
Lake Erie College
Lakeland Community College
Lorain County Community College
Malone College
Marietta College
Marion Technical College
Miami University
　Hamilton Campus
　Middletown Campus
　Oxford Campus
Mount Union College
Mount Vernon Nazarene College
Muskingum Area Technical College
Muskingum College
North Central Technical College
Northwest State Community
　College
Northwestern College
Notre Dame College of Ohio
Oberlin College
Ohio Dominican College
Ohio Northern University
Ohio State University
　Agricultural Technical Institute
　Columbus Campus
　Lima Campus
　Mansfield Campus
　Marion Campus
　Newark Campus
Ohio University
　Athens
　Chillicothe Campus
Ohio Wesleyan University
Otterbein College
Owens Community College: Toledo
Shawnee State University
Sinclair Community College
Southern State Community College
Stark Technical College
Terra Community College
Tiffin University
University of Akron
　Akron
　Wayne College
University of Cincinnati
　Cincinnati
　Clermont College
　Raymond Walters College
University of Dayton
University of Findlay
University of Rio Grande
University of Toledo
Urbana University
Ursuline College
Walsh University
Washington State Community
　College
Wilberforce University
Wilmington College
Wittenberg University
Wright State University
　Dayton
　Lake Campus
Xavier University
Youngstown State University

Oklahoma

Bartlesville Wesleyan College

Cameron University
Connors State College
East Central University
Eastern Oklahoma State College
Langston University
Mid-America Bible College
Murray State College
Northeastern Oklahoma
　Agricultural and Mechanical
　College
Northeastern State University
Northern Oklahoma College
Northwestern Oklahoma State
　University
Oklahoma Baptist University
Oklahoma Christian University of
　Science and Arts
Oklahoma City Community College
Oklahoma City University
Oklahoma Panhandle State
　University
Oklahoma State University
　Oklahoma City
　Stillwater
Oral Roberts University
Phillips University
Redlands Community College
Rogers State College
Rose State College
St. Gregory's College
Southeastern Oklahoma State
　University
Southern Nazarene University
Southwestern College of Christian
　Ministries
Southwestern Oklahoma State
　University
Tulsa Junior College
University of Central Oklahoma
University of Oklahoma
　Health Sciences Center
　Norman
University of Science and Arts of
　Oklahoma
University of Tulsa

Oregon

Bassist College
Central Oregon Community College
Clackamas Community College
Concordia College
Eastern Oregon State College
Eugene Bible College
George Fox College
Lane Community College
Lewis & Clark College
Linfield College
Linn-Benton Community College
Mount Angel Seminary
Mount Hood Community College
Multnomah Bible College
Northwest Christian College
Oregon Institute of Technology
Oregon State University
Pacific Northwest College of Art
Pacific University
Portland State University
Southern Oregon State College
Southwestern Oregon Community
　College
Treasure Valley Community College
Umpqua Community College
University of Oregon
　Eugene
　Robert Donald Clark Honors
　　College
University of Portland
Warner Pacific College
Western Baptist College
Western Oregon State College
Willamette University

Pennsylvania

Albright College
Allegheny College
Allentown College of St. Francis de
　Sales
Alvernia College
Art Institute of Pittsburgh
Baptist Bible College of
　Pennsylvania
Beaver College
Bloomsburg University of
　Pennsylvania
Bucks County Community College
Butler County Community College
Cabrini College
California University of
　Pennsylvania
Carlow College
Carnegie Mellon University
Cedar Crest College
Central Pennsylvania Business
　School
Chatham College
Chestnut Hill College
Cheyney University of Pennsylvania
Clarion University of Pennsylvania
College Misericordia
Community College of Allegheny
　County
　Allegheny Campus
　Boyce Campus
　North Campus
　South Campus
Community College of Beaver
　County
Community College of Philadelphia
Delaware Valley College
Dickinson College
Drexel University
Duquesne University
East Stroudsburg University of
　Pennsylvania
Eastern College
Edinboro University of
　Pennsylvania
Elizabethtown College
Franklin and Marshall College
Gannon University
Geneva College
Grove City College
Gwynedd-Mercy College
Hahnemann University School of
　Health Sciences and Humanities
Harcum College
Harrisburg Area Community
　College
Holy Family College
Immaculata College
Indiana University of Pennsylvania
Johnson Technical Institute
Juniata College
Keystone College
King's College
Kutztown University of
　Pennsylvania
La Roche College
La Salle University
Lackawanna Junior College
Lancaster Bible College
Lebanon Valley College of
　Pennsylvania
Lehigh Carbon Community College
Lehigh University
Lincoln University
Lock Haven University of
　Pennsylvania
Luzerne County Community
　College
Lycoming College
Manor Junior College
Mansfield University of
　Pennsylvania

Marywood College
Mercyhurst College
Messiah College
Millersville University of
　Pennsylvania
Montgomery County Community
　College
Moravian College
Mount Aloysius College
Muhlenberg College
Neumann College
Northampton County Area
　Community College
Peirce College
Penn State
　Erie Behrend College
　Harrisburg Capital College
　University Park Campus
Pennsylvania College of Technology
Philadelphia College of Bible
Philadelphia College of Pharmacy
　and Science
Philadelphia College of Textiles and
　Science
Pittsburgh Technical Institute
Point Park College
Reading Area Community College
Robert Morris College
Rosemont College
St. Francis College
St. Joseph's University
St. Vincent College
Seton Hill College
Shippensburg University of
　Pennsylvania
Slippery Rock University of
　Pennsylvania
Susquehanna University
Temple University
Thiel College
Thomas Jefferson University:
　College of Allied Health Sciences
University of the Arts
University of Pittsburgh
　Bradford
　Greensburg
　Johnstown
　Pittsburgh
　Titusville
University of Scranton
Ursinus College
Valley Forge Christian College
Villanova University
Washington and Jefferson College
Waynesburg College
West Chester University of
　Pennsylvania
Westminster College
Widener University
Wilkes University
Wilson College
York College of Pennsylvania

Puerto Rico

Bayamon Central University
Universidad Adventista de las
　Antillas
Universidad Politecnica de Puerto
　Rico
University of Puerto Rico
　Arecibo Campus
　Bayamon Technological
　　University College
　Mayaguez Campus
　Ponce Technological
　　University College
　Rio Piedras Campus

Rhode Island

Bryant College
Johnson & Wales University
Providence College

Rhode Island College
Rhode Island School of Design
Roger Williams University
Salve Regina University
University of Rhode Island

South Carolina

Aiken Technical College
Anderson College
Benedict College
Charleston Southern University
Chesterfield-Marlboro Technical
  College
The Citadel
Clemson University
Coastal Carolina University
Coker College
College of Charleston
Columbia Bible College
Columbia College
Converse College
Denmark Technical College
Erskine College
Francis Marion University
Furman University
Greenville Technical College
Horry-Georgetown Technical
  College
Lander University
Limestone College
Midlands Technical College
Morris College
Newberry College
North Greenville College
Orangeburg-Calhoun Technical
  College
Piedmont Technical College
Presbyterian College
South Carolina State University
Southern Wesleyan University
Spartanburg Methodist College
Tri-County Technical College
Trident Technical College
University of South Carolina
  Aiken
  Beaufort
  Columbia
  Lancaster
  Salkehatchie Regional Campus
  Spartanburg
  Sumter
  Union
Voorhees College
Williamsburg Technical College
Winthrop University
Wofford College
York Technical College

South Dakota

Augustana College
Black Hills State University
Dakota State University
Dakota Wesleyan University
Huron University
Kilian Community College
Lake Area Technical Institute
Mount Marty College
National College
Northern State University
Presentation College
South Dakota School of Mines and
  Technology
South Dakota State University
University of Sioux Falls
University of South Dakota

Tennessee

Aquinas College
Austin Peay State University
Belmont University
Bethel College
Carson-Newman College

Chattanooga State Technical
  Community College
Christian Brothers University
Cleveland State Community College
Crichton College
Cumberland University
David Lipscomb University
Dyersburg State Community
  College
East Tennessee State University
Fisk University
Freed-Hardeman University
Hiwassee College
Jackson State Community College
Johnson Bible College
King College
Knoxville College
Lambuth University
Lane College
Lee College
Lincoln Memorial University
Maryville College
Memphis College of Art
Middle Tennessee State University
Milligan College
Motlow State Community College
Nashville State Technical Institute
Northeast State Technical
  Community College
Pellissippi State Technical
  Community College
Rhodes College
Roane State Community College
Shelby State Community College
Southern College of Seventh-day
  Adventist
State Technical Institute at
  Memphis
Tennessee State University
Tennessee Technological University
Tennessee Temple University
Tennessee Wesleyan College
Tusculum College
Union University
University of Memphis
University of the South
University of Tennessee
  Chattanooga
  Knoxville
  Martin
  Memphis
Vanderbilt University
Volunteer State Community College
Walters State Community College

Texas

Abilene Christian University
Alvin Community College
Ambassador University
Angelina College
Angelo State University
Austin College
Austin Community College
Baylor College of Dentistry
Baylor University
Bee County College
Blinn College
Brazosport College
Brookhaven College
Cedar Valley College
Central Texas College
Cisco Junior College
College of the Mainland
Collin County Community College
  District
Commonwealth Institute of Funeral
  Service
Concordia Lutheran College
Criswell College
Dallas Baptist University
Dallas Christian College
Del Mar College

DeVry Institute of Technology:
  Irving
East Texas Baptist University
East Texas State University
El Centro College
El Paso Community College
Frank Phillips College
Galveston College
Hardin-Simmons University
Houston Baptist University
Houston Community College
Howard College
Howard Payne University
Huston-Tillotson College
Incarnate Word College
Jacksonville College
Jarvis Christian College
Kilgore College
Lamar University—Beaumont
Laredo Community College
Lee College
LeTourneau University
McLennan Community College
McMurry University
Midland College
Midwestern State University
Navarro College
North Central Texas College
North Harris Montgomery
  Community College District
North Lake College
Northeast Texas Community
  College
Northwood University: Texas
  Campus
Odessa College
Our Lady of the Lake University of
  San Antonio
Panola College
Paris Junior College
Prairie View A&M University
Rice University
Richland College
St. Edward's University
St. Mary's University
St. Philip's College
Sam Houston State University
San Antonio College
Schreiner College
South Plains College
Southern Methodist University
Southwest Texas State University
Southwestern Adventist College
Southwestern University
Stephen F. Austin State University
Sul Ross State University
Tarleton State University
Tarrant County Junior College
Temple Junior College
Texas A&M International
  University
Texas A&M University
  College Station
  Galveston
Texas A&M University-Corpus
  Christi
Texas A&M University-Kingsville
Texas Christian University
Texas Lutheran College
Texas State Technical College
  Amarillo
  Harlingen
  Waco
Texas Tech University
Texas Wesleyan University
Texas Woman's University
Trinity University
Trinity Valley Community College
Tyler Junior College
University of Dallas

University of Houston
  Clear Lake
  Downtown
  Houston
  Victoria
University of Mary Hardin-Baylor
University of North Texas
University of St. Thomas
University of Texas
  Arlington
  Austin
  Dallas
  El Paso
  Health Science Center at San
    Antonio
  Medical Branch at Galveston
  Pan American
  San Antonio
  Southwestern Medical Center
    at Dallas
  Houston Health Science
    Center
Vernon Regional Junior College
Victoria College
Weatherford College
West Texas A&M University
Western Texas College
Wharton County Junior College

Utah

Brigham Young University
College of Eastern Utah
Dixie College
Phillips Junior College: Salt Lake
  City Campus
Salt Lake Community College
Snow College
Southern Utah University
Stevens-Henager College of
  Business
University of Utah
Utah State University
Utah Valley State College
Weber State University
Westminster College of Salt Lake
  City

Vermont

Bennington College
Castleton State College
College of St. Joseph in Vermont
Community College of Vermont
Green Mountain College
Johnson State College
Lyndon State College
Marlboro College
Norwich University
St. Michael's College
School for International Training
Sterling College
Trinity College of Vermont
University of Vermont
Vermont Technical College

Virginia

Averett College
Bluefield College
Bridgewater College
Central Virginia Community College
Christendom College
Christopher Newport University
Clinch Valley College of the
  University of Virginia
College of Health Sciences
College of William and Mary
Commonwealth College
Dabney S. Lancaster Community
  College
Eastern Mennonite University
Eastern Shore Community College
Emory and Henry College
Ferrum College

George Mason University
Germanna Community College
Hampden-Sydney College
Hampton University
Hollins College
James Madison University
John Tyler Community College
Liberty University
Longwood College
Lord Fairfax Community College
Lynchburg College
Mary Baldwin College
Mary Washington College
Marymount University
Mountain Empire Community
    College
National Business College
New River Community College
Norfolk State University
Northern Virginia Community
    College
Old Dominion University
Patrick Henry Community College
Paul D. Camp Community College
Radford University
Randolph-Macon College
Randolph-Macon Woman's College
Rappahannock Community College
Richard Bland College
Roanoke College
St. Paul's College
Shenandoah University
Southern Virginia College
Southside Virginia Community
    College
Southwest Virginia Community
    College
Sweet Briar College
Thomas Nelson Community College
University of Richmond
Virginia Commonwealth University
Virginia Highlands Community
    College
Virginia Intermont College
Virginia Military Institute
Virginia Polytechnic Institute and
    State University
Virginia State University
Virginia Union University
Virginia Wesleyan College
Virginia Western Community
    College
Washington and Lee University
Wytheville Community College

Washington

Bastyr University
Bellevue Community College
Big Bend Community College
Central Washington University
Centralia College
Clark College
Cogswell College North
Columbia Basin College
Cornish College of the Arts
Eastern Washington University
Edmonds Community College
Everett Community College
Evergreen State College
Gonzaga University
Grays Harbor College
Green River Community College
Heritage College
Lake Washington Technical College
Lower Columbia College
Lutheran Bible Institute of Seattle
North Seattle Community College
Northwest College
Olympic College
Pacific Lutheran University
Peninsula College
Pierce College

Puget Sound Christian College
Renton Technical College
St. Martin's College
Seattle Central Community College
Seattle Pacific University
Seattle University
Shoreline Community College
Skagit Valley College
South Puget Sound Community
    College
South Seattle Community College
Tacoma Community College
University of Puget Sound
University of Washington
Walla Walla College
Walla Walla Community College
Washington State University
Wenatchee Valley College
Western Washington University
Whatcom Community College
Whitman College
Whitworth College

West Virginia

Alderson-Broaddus College
Bethany College
Bluefield State College
College of West Virginia
Concord College
Davis and Elkins College
Fairmont State College
Marshall University
Mountain State College
Ohio Valley College
Potomac State College of West
    Virginia University
Salem-Teikyo University
Shepherd College
University of Charleston
West Liberty State College
West Virginia Institute of
    Technology
West Virginia Northern Community
    College
West Virginia State College
West Virginia University
    Morgantown
    Parkersburg
West Virginia Wesleyan College
Wheeling Jesuit College

Wisconsin

Alverno College
Beloit College
Cardinal Stritch College
Carroll College
Carthage College
Chippewa Valley Technical College
Columbia College of Nursing
Concordia University Wisconsin
Edgewood College
Fox Valley Technical College
Lakeland College
Lawrence University
Madison Area Technical College
Madison Junior College of Business
Marian College of Fond du Lac
Marquette University
Mid-State Technical College
Milwaukee Area Technical College
Milwaukee Institute of Art &
    Design
Milwaukee School of Engineering
Moraine Park Technical College
Mount Mary College
Mount Senario College
Nicolet Area Technical College
Northeast Wisconsin Technical
    College
Northland College
Ripon College
St. Norbert College

Silver Lake College
Stratton College
University of Wisconsin
    Eau Claire
    Green Bay
    La Crosse
    Madison
    Oshkosh
    Parkside
    Platteville
    River Falls
    Stevens Point
    Stout
    Superior
    Whitewater
University of Wisconsin Center
    Baraboo/Sauk County
    Barron County
    Fond du Lac
    Fox Valley
    Manitowoc County
    Marathon County
    Marinette County
    Marshfield/Wood County
    Richland
    Rock County
    Sheboygan County
    Washington County
    Waukesha
Viterbo College
Waukesha County Technical
    College
Wisconsin Indianhead Technical
    College
Wisconsin Lutheran College

Wyoming

Casper College
Central Wyoming College
Eastern Wyoming College
Laramie County Community
    College
Sheridan College
University of Wyoming
Western Wyoming Community
    College

**American Samoa, Caroline
Islands, Guam, Marianas,
Virgin Islands**

Guam Community College

Arab Republic of Egypt

American University in Cairo

Mexico

Sistema Instituto Tecnologico y de
    Estudios Superiores de
    Monterrey

Switzerland

American College of Switzerland

Music or drama
scholarships

Alabama

Alabama Agricultural and
    Mechanical University
Alabama Southern Community
    College
Alabama State University
Athens State College
Auburn University
    Auburn
    Montgomery
Bevill State Community College
Birmingham-Southern College
Bishop State Community College

Central Alabama Community
    College
Chattahoochee Valley Community
    College
Enterprise State Junior College
Gadsden State Community College
Huntingdon College
Jacksonville State University
James H. Faulkner State
    Community College
Jefferson State Community College
John C. Calhoun State Community
    College
Lurleen B. Wallace State Junior
    College
Marion Military Institute
Northeast Alabama Community
    College
Northwest-Shoals Community
    College
Samford University
Shelton State Community College
Snead State Community College
Southeastern Bible College
Stillman College
Troy State University
Tuskegee University
University of Alabama
    Birmingham
    Huntsville
    Tuscaloosa
University of Mobile
University of Montevallo
University of North Alabama
University of South Alabama
University of West Alabama
Wallace State College at Hanceville

Alaska

Alaska Bible College
Sheldon Jackson College
University of Alaska
    Anchorage
    Fairbanks
    Southeast

Arizona

Arizona College of the Bible
Arizona State University
Arizona Western College
Eastern Arizona College
Glendale Community College
Mesa Community College
Mohave Community College
Northern Arizona University
Northland Pioneer College
Phoenix College
Scottsdale Community College
South Mountain Community
    College
University of Arizona

Arkansas

Arkansas State University
    Beebe Branch
    Jonesboro
Arkansas Tech University
Central Baptist College
Garland County Community
    College
Harding University
Henderson State University
Hendrix College
John Brown University
Lyon College
Mississippi County Community
    College
North Arkansas Community/
    Technical College
Ouachita Baptist University
Phillips County Community College
South Arkansas Community College

Southern Arkansas University
  Magnolia
  Tech
University of Arkansas
  Fayetteville
  Little Rock
  Monticello
University of Central Arkansas
University of the Ozarks
Williams Baptist College

California

Allan Hancock College
American Academy of Dramatic
  Arts: West
Antelope Valley College
Azusa Pacific University
Bethany College
Biola University
Butte College
California Baptist College
California Institute of the Arts
California Lutheran University
California State University
  Bakersfield
  Dominguez Hills
  Fresno
  Fullerton
  Long Beach
  Los Angeles
  Northridge
  Stanislaus
Cerro Coso Community College
Chapman University
Christian Heritage College
Citrus College
College of the Desert
College of Notre Dame
Columbia College
Compton Community College
Concordia University
Cypress College
De Anza College
Dominican College of San Rafael
El Camino College
Evergreen Valley College
Foothill College
Fresno City College
Fresno Pacific College
Fullerton College
Gavilan Community College
Grossmont Community College
Holy Names College
Humboldt State University
Imperial Valley College
Irvine Valley College
Kings River Community College
La Sierra University
Lake Tahoe Community College
LIFE Bible College
Long Beach City College
Los Medanos College
Loyola Marymount University
Master's College
Mills College
MiraCosta College
Modesto Junior College
Monterey Peninsula College
Mount San Jacinto College
Napa Valley College
Occidental College
Ohlone College
Orange Coast College
Pacific Christian College
Pacific Union College
Pasadena City College
Patten College
Pepperdine University
Rio Hondo College
Riverside Community College
Saddleback College
San Diego City College

San Diego State University
San Francisco Conservatory of
  Music
San Francisco State University
San Joaquin Delta College
San Jose Christian College
Santa Clara University
Santa Monica College
Santa Rosa Junior College
Simpson College
Sonoma State University
University of California
  Irvine
  Los Angeles
  Riverside
  Santa Barbara
  Santa Cruz
University of the Pacific
University of Redlands
University of Southern California
Ventura College
Westmont College
Whittier College

Colorado

Adams State College
Colorado Christian University
Colorado Institute of Art
Colorado School of Mines
Colorado State University
Community College of Denver
Fort Lewis College
Mesa State College
Metropolitan State College of
  Denver
Northeastern Junior College
Trinidad State Junior College
University of Colorado
  Boulder
  Denver
University of Denver
University of Northern Colorado
University of Southern Colorado
Western State College of Colorado

Connecticut

Fairfield University
University of Bridgeport
University of Connecticut
University of Hartford

Delaware

Delaware State University
University of Delaware

District of Columbia

Catholic University of America
George Washington University
Howard University
University of the District of
  Columbia

Florida

Barry University
Bethune-Cookman College
Brevard Community College
Broward Community College
Central Florida Community College
Chipola Junior College
Daytona Beach Community College
Eckerd College
Edison Community College
Flagler College
Florida Agricultural and Mechanical
  University
Florida Atlantic University
Florida Bible College
Florida Christian College
Florida College
Florida Community College at
  Jacksonville
Florida International University

Florida Memorial College
Florida Southern College
Florida State University
Gulf Coast Community College
Hillsborough Community College
Indian River Community College
Jacksonville University
Lake-Sumter Community College
Manatee Community College
Miami-Dade Community College
North Florida Junior College
Okaloosa-Walton Community
  College
Palm Beach Atlantic College
Palm Beach Community College
Pensacola Junior College
Polk Community College
Rollins College
St. Johns River Community College
St. Leo College
St. Petersburg Junior College
Santa Fe Community College
Seminole Community College
South Florida Community College
Southeastern College of the
  Assemblies of God
Stetson University
Tallahassee Community College
University of Central Florida
University of Florida
University of Miami
University of North Florida
University of South Florida
University of Tampa
University of West Florida
Valencia Community College

Georgia

Abraham Baldwin Agricultural
  College
Agnes Scott College
Armstrong State College
Augusta College
Berry College
Brenau University
Brewton-Parker College
Clark Atlanta University
Clayton State College
Columbus College
Covenant College
Darton College
Emmanuel College
Emory University
Fort Valley State College
Gainesville College
Georgia College
Georgia Southern University
Georgia Southwestern College
Georgia State University
Gordon College
Kennesaw State College
LaGrange College
Macon College
Mercer University
Middle Georgia College
Morehouse College
Morris Brown College
North Georgia College
Oglethorpe University
Paine College
Piedmont College
Reinhardt College
Savannah State College
Shorter College
Spelman College
Toccoa Falls College
Truett-McConnell College
University of Georgia
Valdosta State University
Wesleyan College
West Georgia College
Young Harris College

Hawaii

Brigham Young University-Hawaii
Hawaii Pacific University
University of Hawaii
  Hilo
  Kauai Community College
  Manoa

Idaho

Albertson College
Boise State University
College of Southern Idaho
Idaho State University
Lewis Clark State College
North Idaho College
Northwest Nazarene College
Ricks College
University of Idaho

Illinois

American Conservatory of Music
Augustana College
Barat College
Belleville Area College
Black Hawk College
Bradley University
Carl Sandburg College
Chicago State University
College of DuPage
College of Lake County
Concordia University
De Paul University
Eastern Illinois University
Elgin Community College
Elmhurst College
Eureka College
Governors State University
Highland Community College
Illinois Benedictine College
Illinois College
Illinois State University
Illinois Valley Community College
Illinois Wesleyan University
John A. Logan College
John Wood Community College
Joliet Junior College
Judson College
Kaskaskia College
Knox College
Lake Land College
Lewis and Clark Community
  College
Lewis University
Lincoln Land Community College
Loyola University of Chicago
MacMurray College
McHenry County College
McKendree College
Millikin University
Monmouth College
Morton College
North Central College
North Park College
Northeastern Illinois University
Northern Illinois University
Northwestern University
Oakton Community College
Olivet Nazarene University
Parkland College
Quincy University
Rock Valley College
Roosevelt University
St. Xavier University
Shimer College
Southeastern Illinois College
Southern Illinois University
  Carbondale
  Edwardsville
Spoon River College
Trinity Christian College
Trinity College
University of Chicago

University of Illinois
  Chicago
  Urbana-Champaign
VanderCook College of Music
Western Illinois University
Wheaton College
William Rainey Harper College

Indiana

Anderson University
Ball State University
Bethel College
Butler University
DePauw University
Franklin College
Goshen College
Grace College
Huntington College
Indiana State University
Indiana University
  Bloomington
  South Bend
  Southeast
Indiana University-Purdue
  University Fort Wayne
Indiana Wesleyan University
Manchester College
Marian College
Oakland City College
St. Joseph's College
St. Mary-of-the-Woods College
Taylor University
University of Evansville
University of Indianapolis
University of Southern Indiana
Valparaiso University
Vincennes University
Wabash College

Iowa

Briar Cliff College
Buena Vista College
Central College
Clarke College
Coe College
Cornell College
Dordt College
Drake University
Graceland College
Grand View College
Indian Hills Community College
Iowa Central Community College
Iowa Lakes Community College
Iowa State University
Iowa Wesleyan College
Loras College
Luther College
Morningside College
Mount Mercy College
North Iowa Area Community
  College
Northwestern College
St. Ambrose University
Simpson College
Southwestern Community College
Teikyo Marycrest University
Teikyo Westmar University
University of Dubuque
University of Iowa
University of Northern Iowa
Upper Iowa University
Waldorf College
Wartburg College

Kansas

Allen County Community College
Baker University
Barclay College
Barton County Community College
Benedictine College
Bethany College
Bethel College

Butler County Community College
Central College
Coffeyville Community College
Colby Community College
Cowley County Community College
Dodge City Community College
Emporia State University
Fort Hays State University
Friends University
Garden City Community College
Hutchinson Community College
Independence Community College
Johnson County Community
  College
Kansas City Kansas Community
  College
Kansas State University
Kansas Wesleyan University
McPherson College
MidAmerica Nazarene College
Neosho County Community College
Ottawa University
Pittsburg State University
Pratt Community College
St. Mary College
Seward County Community College
Southwestern College
Sterling College
Tabor College
University of Kansas
Washburn University of Topeka
Wichita State University

Kentucky

Asbury College
Bellarmine College
Brescia College
Campbellsville College
Clear Creek Baptist Bible College
Cumberland College
Eastern Kentucky University
Georgetown College
Kentucky Christian College
Kentucky State University
Kentucky Wesleyan College
Lindsey Wilson College
Midway College
Morehead State University
Murray State University
Northern Kentucky University
Somerset Community College
Spalding University
Thomas More College
Transylvania University
Union College
University of Kentucky
University of Louisville
Western Kentucky University

Louisiana

Bossier Parish Community College
Centenary College of Louisiana
Grambling State University
Louisiana College
Louisiana State University and
  Agricultural and Mechanical
  College
Louisiana Tech University
Loyola University
McNeese State University
Nicholls State University
Northeast Louisiana University
Northwestern State University
Southeastern Louisiana University
University of New Orleans
University of Southwestern
  Louisiana
Xavier University of Louisiana

Maine

University of Maine
  Augusta
  Orono
  Presque Isle
University of Southern Maine

Maryland

Bowie State University
Cecil Community College
Charles County Community College
College of Notre Dame of
  Maryland
Columbia Union College
Essex Community College
Frederick Community College
Frostburg State University
Goucher College
Harford Community College
Johns Hopkins University
Johns Hopkins University: Peabody
  Conservatory of Music
Prince George's Community College
St. Mary's College of Maryland
Towson State University
University of Maryland
  Baltimore County
  College Park
  Eastern Shore
Washington Bible College
Washington College

Massachusetts

Anna Maria College
Atlantic Union College
Bay Path College
Berklee College of Music
Boston Conservatory
Boston University
Eastern Nazarene College
Emerson College
Fitchburg State College
Gordon College
Holyoke Community College
New England Conservatory of
  Music
Quinsigamond Community College
Salem State College
Springfield Technical Community
  College
Stonehill College
University of Massachusetts
  Amherst

Michigan

Adrian College
Albion College
Alma College
Andrews University
Aquinas College
Calvin College
Central Michigan University
Concordia College
Cornerstone College and Grand
  Rapids Baptist Seminary
Eastern Michigan University
Ferris State University
Glen Oaks Community College
Grace Bible College
Grand Rapids Community College
Grand Valley State University
Great Lakes Christian College
Henry Ford Community College
Hillsdale College
Hope College
Jackson Community College
Kalamazoo College
Kellogg Community College
Lansing Community College
Madonna University
Michigan Christian College
Michigan State University

Monroe County Community
  College
Montcalm Community College
Mott Community College
Muskegon Community College
Northwestern Michigan College
Oakland University
Olivet College
Saginaw Valley State University
St. Clair County Community
  College
Schoolcraft College
Siena Heights College
Southwestern Michigan College
Spring Arbor College
Suomi College
University of Michigan
  Ann Arbor
  Flint
Wayne State University
West Shore Community College
Western Michigan University
William Tyndale College

Minnesota

Anoka-Ramsey Community College
Augsburg College
Austin Community College
Bemidji State University
Bethany Lutheran College
Bethel College
Central Lakes College
College of St. Benedict
College of St. Catherine: St.
  Catherine Campus
College of St. Scholastica
Concordia College: Moorhead
Concordia College: St. Paul
Crown College
Fergus Falls Community College
Gustavus Adolphus College
Inver Hills Community College
Mankato State University
Martin Luther College
Minnesota Bible College
Moorhead State University
North Central Bible College
North Hennepin Community
  College
Northland Community College
Northwestern College
Pillsbury Baptist Bible College
Rainy River Community College
St. Cloud State University
St. John's University
St. Mary's College of Minnesota
St. Olaf College
Southwest State University
University of Minnesota
  Duluth
  Morris
  Twin Cities
University of St. Thomas
Willmar Community College
Winona State University
Worthington Community College

Mississippi

Alcorn State University
Belhaven College
Blue Mountain College
Copiah-Lincoln Community College
Delta State University
East Central Community College
Hinds Community College
Holmes Community College
Jackson State University
Meridian Community College
Millsaps College
Mississippi College
Mississippi Delta Community
  College

Mississippi Gulf Coast Community
 College
  Jackson County Campus
  Jefferson Davis Campus
  Perkinston
Mississippi State University
Mississippi University for Women
Mississippi Valley State University
Pearl River Community College
Rust College
Tougaloo College
University of Mississippi
University of Southern Mississippi
Wesley College
William Carey College

Missouri

Avila College
Central Bible College
Central Christian College of the
 Bible
Central Methodist College
Central Missouri State University
College of the Ozarks
Columbia College
Cottey College
Crowder College
Culver-Stockton College
Drury College
East Central College
Evangel College
Fontbonne College
Harris Stowe State College
Jefferson College
Lincoln University
Lindenwood College
Longview Community College
Mineral Area College
Missouri Baptist College
Missouri Southern State College
Missouri Valley College
Missouri Western State College
Moberly Area Community College
Northeast Missouri State University
Northwest Missouri State
 University
Ozark Christian College
Park College
St. Charles County Community
 College
St. Louis Christian College
St. Louis Community College
 Florissant Valley
 Forest Park
 Meramec
St. Louis University
Southeast Missouri State University
Southwest Baptist University
Southwest Missouri State University
State Fair Community College
Stephens College
Three Rivers Community College
University of Missouri
 Columbia
 Kansas City
 Rolla
Webster University
Westminster College
William Jewell College

Montana

Carroll College
Dawson Community College
Miles Community College
Montana State University
 Billings
 Bozeman
 Northern
Rocky Mountain College
University of Montana-Missoula
Western Montana College of the
 University of Montana

Nebraska

Central Community College
College of St. Mary
Concordia College
Doane College
Grace University
Hastings College
McCook Community College
Mid Plains Community College
Midland Lutheran College
Nebraska Wesleyan University
Northeast Community College
Peru State College
Southeast Community College:
 Beatrice Campus
Union College
University of Nebraska
 Kearney
 Lincoln
 Omaha
Wayne State College
Western Nebraska Community
 College: Scottsbluff Campus
York College

Nevada

Sierra Nevada College
University of Nevada
 Las Vegas
 Reno

New Hampshire

Colby-Sawyer College
Keene State College
Plymouth State College of the
 University System of New
 Hampshire
University of New Hampshire

New Jersey

Georgian Court College
Jersey City State College
Mercer County Community College
Richard Stockton College of New
 Jersey
Rider University
Rowan College of New Jersey
Rutgers, The State University of
 New Jersey
 Douglass College
 Livingston College
 Mason Gross School of the
  Arts
 Rutgers College
Trenton State College
Westminster Choir College of Rider
 University
William Paterson College of New
 Jersey

New Mexico

College of Santa Fe
College of the Southwest
Eastern New Mexico University
New Mexico Highlands University
New Mexico Junior College
New Mexico Military Institute
New Mexico State University
San Juan College
University of New Mexico

New York

Adelphi University
Bard College
City University of New York:
 Brooklyn College
Clarkson University
College of New Rochelle
College of St. Rose
Concordia College
Eastman School of Music of the
 University of Rochester

Elmira College
Finger Lakes Community College
Five Towns College
Fordham University
Genesee Community College
Hartwick College
Hofstra University
Houghton College
Ithaca College
Jamestown Community College
Juilliard School
Long Island University
 Brooklyn Campus
 C. W. Post Campus
Manhattan School of Music
Manhattanville College
Mannes College of Music
Marist College
Marymount College
Marymount Manhattan College
Molloy College
Nassau Community College
Nazareth College of Rochester
New York University
Niagara University
Orange County Community College
Pace University
Roberts Wesleyan College
St. Bonaventure University
St. John's University
Skidmore College
State University of New York
 Binghamton
 Buffalo
 Oswego
 Purchase
 College at Brockport
 College at Buffalo
 College at Cortland
 College at Geneseo
 College at Plattsburgh
 College at Potsdam
 College of Technology at
  Alfred
Syracuse University
University of Rochester
Villa Maria College of Buffalo
Wagner College
Westchester Community College

North Carolina

Appalachian State University
Barton College
Bennett College
Brevard College
Campbell University
Catawba College
College of the Albemarle
Davidson College
Duke University
East Carolina University
Elizabeth City State University
Elon College
Fayetteville State University
Gardner-Webb University
Greensboro College
Guilford College
John Wesley College
Johnson C. Smith University
Lees-McRae College
Lenoir-Rhyne College
Livingstone College
Louisburg College
Mars Hill College
Meredith College
Methodist College
Mitchell Community College
Mount Olive College
North Carolina Agricultural and
 Technical State University
North Carolina School of the Arts
Peace College

Pembroke State University
Pfeiffer College
Queens College
Roanoke Bible College
St. Andrews Presbyterian College
St. Augustine's College
St. Mary's College
Salem College
Sandhills Community College
University of North Carolina
 Asheville
 Chapel Hill
 Greensboro
 Wilmington
Wake Forest University
Western Carolina University
Wilkes Community College
Wingate College
Winston-Salem State University

North Dakota

Bismarck State College
Dickinson State University
Jamestown College
Minot State University
North Dakota State College of
 Science
Trinity Bible College
University of Mary
University of North Dakota
Valley City State University

Ohio

Ashland University
Baldwin-Wallace College
Bluffton College
Bowling Green State University
 Bowling Green
 Firelands Campus
Capital University
Case Western Reserve University
Cedarville College
Cleveland Institute of Music
Cleveland State University
College of Mount St. Joseph
College of Wooster
Cuyahoga Community College
 Metropolitan Campus
 Western Campus
Denison University
God's Bible School and College
Heidelberg College
Hiram College
Kent State University
 Kent
 Trumbull Campus
Lake Erie College
Lakeland Community College
Malone College
Marietta College
Miami University: Oxford Campus
Mount Union College
Mount Vernon Nazarene College
Muskingum College
Oberlin College
Ohio Northern University
Ohio State University
 Columbus Campus
 Lima Campus
 Mansfield Campus
Ohio University
Ohio Wesleyan University
Otterbein College
Shawnee State University
Sinclair Community College
University of Akron
University of Cincinnati
 Cincinnati
 Clermont College
University of Dayton
University of Findlay
University of Rio Grande

Colleges that offer academic, music or drama, or art scholarships

University of Toledo
Urbana University
Wilmington College
Wittenberg University
Wright State University
Xavier University
Youngstown State University

Oklahoma

Bartlesville Wesleyan College
Cameron University
Connors State College
East Central University
Eastern Oklahoma State College
Langston University
Mid-America Bible College
Murray State College
Northeastern Oklahoma
 Agricultural and Mechanical
 College
Northeastern State University
Northern Oklahoma College
Northwestern Oklahoma State
 University
Oklahoma Baptist University
Oklahoma Christian University of
 Science and Arts
Oklahoma City University
Oklahoma Panhandle State
 University
Oklahoma State University
Oral Roberts University
Phillips University
Rogers State College
Rose State College
St. Gregory's College
Southeastern Oklahoma State
 University
Southern Nazarene University
Southwestern College of Christian
 Ministries
Southwestern Oklahoma State
 University
University of Central Oklahoma
University of Oklahoma
University of Science and Arts of
 Oklahoma
University of Tulsa

Oregon

Central Oregon Community College
Clackamas Community College
Concordia College
Eastern Oregon State College
Eugene Bible College
George Fox College
Lane Community College
Lewis & Clark College
Linfield College
Linn-Benton Community College
Marylhurst College
Mount Hood Community College
Multnomah Bible College
Oregon State University
Pacific University
Portland State University
Southern Oregon State College
Southwestern Oregon Community
 College
Treasure Valley Community College
Umpqua Community College
University of Oregon
 Eugene
 Robert Donald Clark Honors
 College
University of Portland
Warner Pacific College
Western Baptist College
Western Oregon State College
Willamette University

Pennsylvania

Albright College
Allegheny College
Allentown College of St. Francis de
 Sales
Beaver College
Bucks County Community College
California University of
 Pennsylvania
Carnegie Mellon University
Chatham College
Cheyney University of Pennsylvania
Clarion University of Pennsylvania
Community College of Allegheny
 County
 Boyce Campus
 South Campus
Community College of Philadelphia
Curtis Institute of Music
Drexel University
Duquesne University
Eastern College
Elizabethtown College
Geneva College
Immaculata College
Indiana University of Pennsylvania
Juniata College
Lancaster Bible College
Lincoln University
Lock Haven University of
 Pennsylvania
Lycoming College
Mansfield University of
 Pennsylvania
Marywood College
Mercyhurst College
Millersville University of
 Pennsylvania
Muhlenberg College
Penn State
 Erie Behrend College
 Harrisburg Capital College
 University Park Campus
Philadelphia College of Bible
Point Park College
St. Vincent College
Seton Hill College
Slippery Rock University of
 Pennsylvania
Susquehanna University
Temple University
University of the Arts
Ursinus College
Valley Forge Christian College
Valley Forge Military College
West Chester University of
 Pennsylvania
Westminster College
Widener University
Wilkes University
York College of Pennsylvania

Puerto Rico

Pontifical Catholic University of
 Puerto Rico
University of Puerto Rico
 La Montana Regional College
 Mayaguez Campus
 Ponce Technological
 University College
 Rio Piedras Campus

Rhode Island

Rhode Island College
University of Rhode Island

South Carolina

Anderson College
Clemson University
Coastal Carolina University
Coker College
College of Charleston

Columbia Bible College
Columbia College
Converse College
Erskine College
Francis Marion University
Furman University
Lander University
Limestone College
Newberry College
North Greenville College
Presbyterian College
South Carolina State University
Southern Wesleyan University
Spartanburg Methodist College
University of South Carolina
 Aiken
 Columbia
 Spartanburg
Winthrop University
Wofford College

South Dakota

Augustana College
Black Hills State University
Dakota State University
Dakota Wesleyan University
Mount Marty College
Northern State University
South Dakota State University
University of Sioux Falls
University of South Dakota

Tennessee

Austin Peay State University
Belmont University
Bethel College
Carson-Newman College
Chattanooga State Technical
 Community College
Christian Brothers University
Crichton College
David Lipscomb University
Dyersburg State Community
 College
East Tennessee State University
Freed-Hardeman University
Hiwassee College
Johnson Bible College
King College
Knoxville College
Lambuth University
Lee College
Lincoln Memorial University
Maryville College
Middle Tennessee State University
Milligan College
Motlow State Community College
Pellissippi State Technical
 Community College
Rhodes College
Roane State Community College
Shelby State Community College
Southern College of Seventh-day
 Adventist
Tennessee State University
Tennessee Technological University
Tennessee Temple University
Tennessee Wesleyan College
Union University
University of Memphis
University of Tennessee
 Chattanooga
 Knoxville
 Martin
Vanderbilt University
Walters State Community College

Texas

Abilene Christian University
Alvin Community College
Ambassador University
Angelina College

Austin College
Baylor University
Bee County College
Blinn College
Cedar Valley College
Cisco Junior College
College of the Mainland
Collin County Community College
 District
Concordia Lutheran College
Criswell College
Dallas Baptist University
Dallas Christian College
Del Mar College
East Texas Baptist University
East Texas State University
El Centro College
Frank Phillips College
Galveston College
Hardin-Simmons University
Houston Baptist University
Howard College
Howard Payne University
Incarnate Word College
Jacksonville College
Jarvis Christian College
Lamar University—Beaumont
Laredo Community College
Lee College
McMurry University
Midland College
Midwestern State University
Mountain View College
Navarro College
North Central Texas College
North Harris Montgomery
 Community College District
Northeast Texas Community
 College
Odessa College
Our Lady of the Lake University of
 San Antonio
Panola College
Paris Junior College
Prairie View A&M University
Rice University
St. Edward's University
St. Mary's University
St. Philip's College
Sam Houston State University
San Antonio College
Schreiner College
South Plains College
Southern Methodist University
Southwest Texas State University
Southwestern Adventist College
Southwestern University
Stephen F. Austin State University
Sul Ross State University
Tarleton State University
Tarrant County Junior College
Temple Junior College
Texas A&M University-Corpus
 Christi
Texas A&M University-Kingsville
Texas Christian University
Texas Lutheran College
Texas Tech University
Texas Wesleyan University
Texas Woman's University
Trinity University
Trinity Valley Community College
Tyler Junior College
University of Dallas
University of Houston
University of Mary Hardin-Baylor
University of St. Thomas
University of Texas
 Arlington
 Austin
 El Paso
 Pan American

Vernon Regional Junior College
Victoria College
Weatherford College
West Texas A&M University
Western Texas College
Wharton County Junior College

Utah

Brigham Young University
College of Eastern Utah
Dixie College
Snow College
Southern Utah University
University of Utah
Utah State University
Weber State University
Westminster College of Salt Lake City

Vermont

Castleton State College
Johnson State College
Marlboro College
University of Vermont

Virginia

Averett College
Bluefield College
Bridgewater College
Christopher Newport University
Eastern Mennonite University
George Mason University
Hampton University
Hollins College
James Madison University
Liberty University
Longwood College
Lynchburg College
Mary Baldwin College
Mary Washington College
Old Dominion University
Radford University
Randolph-Macon Woman's College
Roanoke College
Shenandoah University
Sweet Briar College
University of Richmond
Virginia Commonwealth University
Virginia Polytechnic Institute and State University
Virginia Union University
Virginia Wesleyan College

Washington

Big Bend Community College
Central Washington University
Centralia College
Clark College
Columbia Basin College
Cornish College of the Arts
Eastern Washington University
Edmonds Community College
Everett Community College
Evergreen State College
Gonzaga University
Grays Harbor College
Green River Community College
Lower Columbia College
Lutheran Bible Institute of Seattle
North Seattle Community College
Northwest College
Olympic College
Pacific Lutheran University
Peninsula College
Pierce College
Puget Sound Christian College
Seattle Pacific University
Seattle University
Skagit Valley College
South Seattle Community College
Tacoma Community College
University of Puget Sound

Walla Walla College
Walla Walla Community College
Washington State University
Wenatchee Valley College
Western Washington University
Whitman College
Whitworth College

West Virginia

Alderson-Broaddus College
Bethany College
Concord College
Davis and Elkins College
Fairmont State College
Marshall University
Ohio Valley College
Shepherd College
University of Charleston
West Liberty State College
West Virginia Institute of Technology
West Virginia State College
West Virginia University
West Virginia Wesleyan College
Wheeling Jesuit College

Wisconsin

Alverno College
Beloit College
Cardinal Stritch College
Carroll College
Carthage College
Concordia University Wisconsin
Edgewood College
Lawrence University
Marian College of Fond du Lac
Marquette University
Mount Mary College
Northland College
Ripon College
St. Norbert College
Silver Lake College
University of Wisconsin
    Eau Claire
    Green Bay
    La Crosse
    Madison
    Oshkosh
    Parkside
    Platteville
    River Falls
    Stevens Point
    Stout
    Whitewater
University of Wisconsin Center
    Baraboo/Sauk County
    Barron County
    Fond du Lac
    Marathon County
    Richland
    Rock County
    Washington County
    Waukesha
Viterbo College

Wyoming

Casper College
Central Wyoming College
Eastern Wyoming College
Laramie County Community College
Sheridan College
University of Wyoming
Western Wyoming Community College

Arab Republic of Egypt

American University in Cairo

Art scholarships

Alabama

Alabama Southern Community College
Alabama State University
Athens State College
Auburn University
Birmingham-Southern College
Central Alabama Community College
Chattahoochee Valley Community College
Enterprise State Junior College
Huntingdon College
Jacksonville State University
James H. Faulkner State Community College
John C. Calhoun State Community College
Lawson State Community College
Lurleen B. Wallace State Junior College
Northeast Alabama Community College
Northwest-Shoals Community College
Samford University
Shelton State Community College
Snead State Community College
Troy State University
UAB: Walker College
University of Alabama
    Birmingham
    Huntsville
    Tuscaloosa
University of Mobile
University of North Alabama
University of West Alabama
Wallace State College at Hanceville

Alaska

University of Alaska
    Anchorage
    Fairbanks
    Southeast

Arizona

Arizona State University
Arizona Western College
Eastern Arizona College
Glendale Community College
Mesa Community College
Mohave Community College
Northern Arizona University
Northland Pioneer College
Phoenix College
Scottsdale Community College
South Mountain Community College
University of Arizona

Arkansas

Arkansas State University
Garland County Community College
Harding University
Henderson State University
Hendrix College
John Brown University
Lyon College
Mississippi County Community College
North Arkansas Community/Technical College
Southern Arkansas University Tech
University of Arkansas
    Fayetteville
    Little Rock
University of Central Arkansas

Williams Baptist College

California

Academy of Art College
Allan Hancock College
Antelope Valley College
Art Institute of Southern California
Bethany College
Biola University
Brooks Institute of Photography
Butte College
California College of Arts and Crafts
California Institute of the Arts
California Lutheran University
California Polytechnic State University: San Luis Obispo
California State University
    Bakersfield
    Dominguez Hills
    Fresno
    Fullerton
    Long Beach
    Los Angeles
    Northridge
    Stanislaus
Cerro Coso Community College
Chapman University
Citrus College
College of the Desert
College of Notre Dame
College of the Redwoods
Columbia College
Compton Community College
De Anza College
Dominican College of San Rafael
El Camino College
Evergreen Valley College
Foothill College
Fresno City College
Fresno Pacific College
Fullerton College
Gavilan Community College
Grossmont Community College
Holy Names College
Humboldt State University
Imperial Valley College
Irvine Valley College
La Sierra University
Lake Tahoe Community College
LIFE Bible College
Long Beach City College
Mills College
MiraCosta College
Modesto Junior College
Monterey Peninsula College
Mount San Jacinto College
Napa Valley College
New School of Art and Architecture
Ohlone College
Pasadena City College
Pepperdine University
Rio Hondo College
Riverside Community College
Saddleback College
San Diego City College
San Diego State University
San Francisco Art Institute
San Joaquin Delta College
Santa Monica College
Santa Rosa Junior College
Southern California Institute of Architecture
University of California
    Irvine
    Los Angeles
    Riverside
    Santa Barbara
    Santa Cruz
University of the Pacific
University of Redlands

University of Southern California
Ventura College
Westmont College
Whittier College

Colorado

Adams State College
Colorado Institute of Art
Colorado State University
Community College of Denver
Fort Lewis College
Lamar Community College
Mesa State College
Northeastern Junior College
Rocky Mountain College of Art &
    Design
Trinidad State Junior College
University of Colorado
    Boulder
    Denver
University of Denver
University of Northern Colorado
University of Southern Colorado
Western State College of Colorado

Connecticut

Quinebaug Valley Community-
    Technical College
Sacred Heart University
University of Connecticut
University of Hartford

District of Columbia

Corcoran School of Art
George Washington University
Howard University

Florida

Brevard Community College
Broward Community College
Central Florida Community College
Chipola Junior College
Daytona Beach Community College
Eckerd College
Edison Community College
Flagler College
Florida Atlantic University
Florida Community College at
    Jacksonville
Florida International University
Florida Keys Community College
Florida Southern College
Florida State University
Gulf Coast Community College
Hillsborough Community College
Indian River Community College
International Fine Arts College
Jacksonville University
Lake-Sumter Community College
Manatee Community College
Miami-Dade Community College
North Florida Junior College
Okaloosa-Walton Community
    College
Pensacola Junior College
Polk Community College
Ringling School of Art and Design
Rollins College
St. Johns River Community College
St. Leo College
St. Petersburg Junior College
Santa Fe Community College
Seminole Community College
University of Central Florida
University of South Florida
University of Tampa
University of West Florida
Valencia Community College

Georgia

Abraham Baldwin Agricultural
    College

Armstrong State College
Atlanta College of Art
Augusta College
Berry College
Brenau University
Brewton-Parker College
Clayton State College
Columbus College
Darton College
Gainesville College
Georgia Southwestern College
Georgia State University
Gordon College
Kennesaw State College
LaGrange College
Macon College
Mercer University
Morris Brown College
North Georgia College
Piedmont College
Reinhardt College
Savannah College of Art and
    Design
School of Visual Arts: Savannah
Shorter College
Valdosta State University
Wesleyan College
West Georgia College
Young Harris College

Hawaii

Brigham Young University-Hawaii
University of Hawaii at Hilo

Idaho

Albertson College
Boise State University
College of Southern Idaho
Idaho State University
North Idaho College
Northwest Nazarene College
Ricks College
University of Idaho

Illinois

American Academy of Art
Augustana College
Barat College
Belleville Area College
Black Hawk College
Bradley University
Carl Sandburg College
Chicago State University
College of DuPage
College of Lake County
De Paul University
Eastern Illinois University
Elgin Community College
Eureka College
Governors State University
Highland Community College
Illinois Benedictine College
Illinois State University
Illinois Valley Community College
Illinois Wesleyan University
John A. Logan College
John Wood Community College
Joliet Junior College
Judson College
Knox College
Lake Land College
Lewis University
Lincoln Land Community College
Loyola University of Chicago
MacMurray College
McHenry County College
McKendree College
Millikin University
Monmouth College
Morton College
North Central College
North Park College

Northeastern Illinois University
Northern Illinois University
Oakton Community College
Olivet Nazarene University
Parkland College
Quincy University
Ray College of Design
Roosevelt University
School of the Art Institute of
    Chicago
Shimer College
Southeastern Illinois College
Southern Illinois University
    Carbondale
    Edwardsville
Spoon River College
Trinity Christian College
University of Chicago
University of Illinois at Urbana-
    Champaign
Western Illinois University
William Rainey Harper College

Indiana

Anderson University
DePauw University
Franklin College
Grace College
Huntington College
Indiana State University
Indiana University
    Bloomington
    South Bend
    Southeast
Indiana University—Purdue
    University
    Fort Wayne
    Indianapolis
Indiana Wesleyan University
Manchester College
Marian College
Oakland City College
St. Francis College
St. Mary-of-the-Woods College
Taylor University
University of Evansville
University of Indianapolis
University of Southern Indiana
Vincennes University
Wabash College

Iowa

Briar Cliff College
Buena Vista College
Central College
Clarke College
Coe College
Cornell College
Dordt College
Drake University
Graceland College
Grand View College
Indian Hills Community College
Iowa Lakes Community College
Iowa State University
Iowa Wesleyan College
Loras College
Luther College
Marshalltown Community College
Morningside College
Mount Mercy College
North Iowa Area Community
    College
Northwestern College
St. Ambrose University
Simpson College
Teikyo Marycrest University
University of Iowa
University of Northern Iowa
Upper Iowa University
Waldorf College
Wartburg College

Kansas

Baker University
Barton County Community College
Bethany College
Bethel College
Butler County Community College
Coffeyville Community College
Colby Community College
Cowley County Community College
Emporia State University
Fort Hays State University
Friends University
Garden City Community College
Hutchinson Community College
Independence Community College
Johnson County Community
    College
Kansas State University
Kansas Wesleyan University
McPherson College
Neosho County Community College
Ottawa University
Pittsburg State University
Pratt Community College
St. Mary College
Seward County Community College
Southwestern College
Sterling College
University of Kansas
Washburn University of Topeka
Wichita State University

Kentucky

Asbury College
Bellarmine College
Brescia College
Campbellsville College
Cumberland College
Eastern Kentucky University
Georgetown College
Kentucky Wesleyan College
Lindsey Wilson College
Midway College
Morehead State University
Murray State University
Northern Kentucky University
Spalding University
Thomas More College
Transylvania University
University of Kentucky
University of Louisville
Western Kentucky University

Louisiana

Centenary College of Louisiana
Louisiana State University
    Agricultural and Mechanical
        College
    Alexandria
Louisiana Tech University
Loyola University
McNeese State University
Northeast Louisiana University
Northwestern State University
University of Southwestern
    Louisiana
Xavier University of Louisiana

Maine

Maine College of Art
University of Maine
    Augusta
    Orono
    Presque Isle

Maryland

Cecil Community College
Charles County Community College
College of Notre Dame of
    Maryland
Frederick Community College
Frostburg State University

Garrett Community College
Goucher College
Maryland College of Art and
Design
Maryland Institute College of Art
Towson State University
University of Maryland
Baltimore County
College Park
Eastern Shore
Washington College

Massachusetts

Boston Architectural Center
Boston University
Bradford College
Bristol Community College
Fitchburg State College
Holyoke Community College
Montserrat College of Art
Quinsigamond Community College
Salem State College
Springfield Technical Community
College
University of Massachusetts
Amherst

Michigan

Adrian College
Albion College
Alma College
Aquinas College
Calvin College
Center for Creative Studies: College
of Art and Design
Central Michigan University
Concordia College
Eastern Michigan University
Glen Oaks Community College
Grand Rapids Community College
Grand Valley State University
Henry Ford Community College
Hillsdale College
Hope College
Kalamazoo College
Kellogg Community College
Kendall College of Art and Design
Lansing Community College
Madonna University
Michigan State University
Monroe County Community
College
Mott Community College
Muskegon Community College
Northwestern Michigan College
Saginaw Valley State University
St. Clair County Community
College
Schoolcraft College
Siena Heights College
Southwestern Michigan College
Spring Arbor College
Suomi College
University of Michigan
Washtenaw Community College
Wayne State University
Western Michigan University

Minnesota

Bemidji State University
Bethany Lutheran College
Bethel College
Central Lakes College
College of Associated Arts
College of St. Benedict
Fergus Falls Community College
Inver Hills Community College
Mankato State University
Minneapolis College of Art and
Design
Moorhead State University
North Central Bible College

North Hennepin Community
College
Northland Community College
Northwestern College
Rainy River Community College
St. Cloud State University
St. John's University
St. Mary's College of Minnesota
University of Minnesota
Duluth
Twin Cities
Willmar Community College
Winona State University
Worthington Community College

Mississippi

Belhaven College
Copiah-Lincoln Community College
Delta State University
East Central Community College
Hinds Community College
Holmes Community College
Jackson State University
Meridian Community College
Millsaps College
Mississippi College
Mississippi Delta Community
College
Mississippi Gulf Coast Community
College: Perkinston
Mississippi University for Women
University of Mississippi
University of Southern Mississippi

Missouri

Avila College
Central Missouri State University
College of the Ozarks
Columbia College
Cottey College
Crowder College
Culver-Stockton College
Drury College
East Central College
Evangel College
Fontbonne College
Jefferson College
Kansas City Art Institute
Lincoln University
Lindenwood College
Longview Community College
Mineral Area College
Missouri Southern State College
Missouri Valley College
Northeast Missouri State University
Northwest Missouri State
University
Park College
St. Louis Community College
Florissant Valley
Forest Park
Meramec
St. Louis University
Southeast Missouri State University
Southwest Missouri State University
State Fair Community College
Three Rivers Community College
University of Missouri
Columbia
Kansas City
Washington University
Webster University
Westminster College
William Jewell College

Montana

Dawson Community College
Montana State University
Billings
Bozeman
Rocky Mountain College
University of Montana-Missoula

Western Montana College of the
University of Montana

Nebraska

Central Community College
College of St. Mary
Concordia College
Doane College
Hastings College
McCook Community College
Mid Plains Community College
Midland Lutheran College
Nebraska Wesleyan University
Northeast Community College
Peru State College
Southeast Community College:
Beatrice Campus
University of Nebraska
Kearney
Omaha
Wayne State College
Western Nebraska Community
College: Scottsbluff Campus
York College

Nevada

Sierra Nevada College
University of Nevada: Las Vegas

New Hampshire

Colby-Sawyer College
Keene State College
University of New Hampshire

New Jersey

Caldwell College
College of St. Elizabeth
Georgian Court College
Richard Stockton College of New
Jersey
Rowan College of New Jersey
Rutgers, The State University of
New Jersey: Mason Gross School
of the Arts
Union County College

New Mexico

College of Santa Fe
Eastern New Mexico University
New Mexico Highlands University

New York

Adelphi University
Alfred University
Bard College
Cazenovia College
City University of New York:
Brooklyn College
Clarkson University
College of New Rochelle
College of St. Rose
Elmira College
Finger Lakes Community College
Genesee Community College
Hofstra University
Houghton College
Iona College
Long Island University
Brooklyn Campus
C. W. Post Campus
Southampton College
Manhattanville College
Marymount College
Marymount Manhattan College
Molloy College
Nassau Community College
Nazareth College of Rochester
New York School of Interior
Design
Orange County Community College
Pratt Institute
Roberts Wesleyan College

Rochester Institute of Technology
Sage Junior College of Albany
St. John's University
St. Thomas Aquinas College
School of Visual Arts
State University of New York
Binghamton
Buffalo
Purchase
College at Brockport
College at Buffalo
College at Cortland
College at Plattsburgh
Sullivan County Community
College
Syracuse University
University of Rochester
Villa Maria College of Buffalo
Westchester Community College

North Carolina

Appalachian State University
Barton College
Brevard College
College of the Albemarle
Davidson College
Duke University
East Carolina University
Greensboro College
Guilford College
Meredith College
Mitchell Community College
Mount Olive College
North Carolina Agricultural and
Technical State University
North Carolina School of the Arts
Peace College
Pembroke State University
Queens College
St. Andrews Presbyterian College
St. Mary's College
Sandhills Community College
University of North Carolina
Asheville
Wilmington
Wake Forest University
Western Carolina University
Wilkes Community College
Winston-Salem State University

North Dakota

Dickinson State University
University of North Dakota
Valley City State University

Ohio

Art Academy of Cincinnati
Ashland University
Baldwin-Wallace College
Bluffton College
Bowling Green State University
Case Western Reserve University
Cleveland Institute of Art
Cleveland State University
College of Mount St. Joseph
Columbus College of Art and
Design
Cuyahoga Community College
Metropolitan Campus
Western Campus
Denison University
Kent State University
Kent
Trumbull Campus
Lake Erie College
Lakeland Community College
Marietta College
Miami University: Oxford Campus
Mount Union College
Muskingum College
Ohio Northern University

Ohio State University
   Columbus Campus
   Lima Campus
   Mansfield Campus
Ohio University
Ohio Wesleyan University
Otterbein College
Shawnee State University
Sinclair Community College
University of Akron
University of Cincinnati
   Cincinnati
   Clermont College
University of Dayton
University of Toledo
Wittenberg University
Wright State University
Xavier University
Youngstown State University

Oklahoma

Cameron University
East Central University
Murray State College
Northeastern Oklahoma
   Agricultural and Mechanical
   College
Northeastern State University
Northern Oklahoma College
Northwestern Oklahoma State
   University
Oklahoma Baptist University
Oklahoma Christian University of
   Science and Arts
Oklahoma City University
Oklahoma State University
Oral Roberts University
Phillips University
Rogers State College
Rose State College
St. Gregory's College
Southeastern Oklahoma State
   University
Southern Nazarene University
Southwestern Oklahoma State
   University
University of Central Oklahoma
University of Oklahoma
University of Science and Arts of
   Oklahoma
University of Tulsa

Oregon

Central Oregon Community College
Clackamas Community College
Linn-Benton Community College
Marylhurst College
Mount Hood Community College
Pacific Northwest College of Art
Pacific University
Portland State University
Southern Oregon State College
Southwestern Oregon Community
   College
Treasure Valley Community College
Umpqua Community College
University of Oregon
   Eugene
   Robert Donald Clark Honors
     College
Western Oregon State College
Willamette University

Pennsylvania

Allegheny College
Art Institute of Pittsburgh
Beaver College
Bradley Academy for the Visual
   Arts
Bucks County Community College
Carlow College
Carnegie Mellon University

Clarion University of Pennsylvania
Community College of Allegheny
   County
     Boyce Campus
     South Campus
Community College of Philadelphia
Drexel University
Harrisburg Area Community
   College
Hussian School of Art
Indiana University of Pennsylvania
Juniata College
Kutztown University of
   Pennsylvania
Lycoming College
Mansfield University of
   Pennsylvania
Marywood College
Mercyhurst College
Millersville University of
   Pennsylvania
Moore College of Art and Design
Penn State
   Erie Behrend College
   Harrisburg Capital College
   University Park Campus
Point Park College
Rosemont College
Seton Hill College
Slippery Rock University of
   Pennsylvania
University of the Arts
Ursinus College
Wilkes University
York College of Pennsylvania

Puerto Rico

Pontifical Catholic University of
   Puerto Rico
University of Puerto Rico: Rio
   Piedras Campus

Rhode Island

Rhode Island College
Rhode Island School of Design

South Carolina

Anderson College
Charleston Southern University
Coastal Carolina University
Coker College
College of Charleston
Columbia College
Francis Marion University
Furman University
Greenville Technical College
Lander University
Limestone College
North Greenville College
University of South Carolina
   Aiken
   Columbia
Winthrop University

South Dakota

Augustana College
Black Hills State University
Dakota Wesleyan University
Northern State University
South Dakota State University
University of South Dakota

Tennessee

Austin Peay State University
Carson-Newman College
Chattanooga State Technical
   Community College
David Lipscomb University
East Tennessee State University
Freed-Hardeman University
Lambuth University
Maryville College

Memphis College of Art
Milligan College
Pellissippi State Technical
   Community College
Rhodes College
Roane State Community College
Shelby State Community College
Union University
University of Memphis
University of Tennessee
   Chattanooga
   Knoxville

Texas

Abilene Christian University
Alvin Community College
Angelina College
Austin College
Baylor University
Bee County College
Cedar Valley College
College of the Mainland
Collin County Community College
   District
Dallas Baptist University
Del Mar College
East Texas State University
El Centro College
Hardin-Simmons University
Houston Baptist University
Howard College
Howard Payne University
Incarnate Word College
Lamar University—Beaumont
Lee College
McMurry University
Midland College
Midwestern State University
Mountain View College
Navarro College
North Harris Montgomery
   Community College District
Northeast Texas Community
   College
Odessa College
Panola College
Paris Junior College
Prairie View A&M University
Sam Houston State University
San Antonio College
South Plains College
Southern Methodist University
Southwestern University
Texas A&M University-Corpus
   Christi
Texas A&M University-Kingsville
Texas Christian University
Texas Lutheran College
Texas Tech University
Texas Wesleyan University
Texas Woman's University
Trinity University
Trinity Valley Community College
Tyler Junior College
University of Dallas
University of Houston
   Downtown
   Houston
University of Mary Hardin-Baylor
University of Texas
   Arlington
   Austin
   Pan American
Vernon Regional Junior College
Victoria College
West Texas A&M University
Western Texas College

Utah

Brigham Young University
College of Eastern Utah
Dixie College

Salt Lake Community College
Snow College
University of Utah
Utah State University
Weber State University
Westminster College of Salt Lake
   City

Vermont

Green Mountain College
Johnson State College
Marlboro College
University of Vermont

Virginia

Averett College
Bluefield College
Hollins College
James Madison University
Longwood College
Mary Baldwin College
Old Dominion University
Radford University
Roanoke College
Virginia Commonwealth University
Virginia Polytechnic Institute and
   State University
Virginia Wesleyan College

Washington

Columbia Basin College
Cornish College of the Arts
Eastern Washington University
Edmonds Community College
Everett Community College
Evergreen State College
Grays Harbor College
Green River Community College
North Seattle Community College
Northwest College
Olympic College
Pacific Lutheran University
Peninsula College
Seattle Pacific University
Seattle University
Skagit Valley College
Tacoma Community College
University of Puget Sound
Washington State University
Wenatchee Valley College
Western Washington University
Whitman College
Whitworth College

West Virginia

Concord College
Davis and Elkins College
Marshall University
Ohio Valley College
Shepherd College
University of Charleston
West Liberty State College
West Virginia State College
West Virginia University
West Virginia Wesleyan College

Wisconsin

Alverno College
Cardinal Stritch College
Carroll College
Carthage College
Edgewood College
Marian College of Fond du Lac
Milwaukee Institute of Art &
   Design
Mount Mary College
St. Norbert College
Silver Lake College

University of Wisconsin
    Green Bay
    Madison
    Oshkosh
    Parkside
    Platteville
    River Falls
    Stevens Point
    Stout
University of Wisconsin Center
    Baraboo/Sauk County
    Barron County
    Marathon County
    Richland
    Waukesha
Viterbo College

Wyoming

Casper College
Central Wyoming College
Eastern Wyoming College
Laramie County Community
    College
Sheridan College
University of Wyoming
Western Wyoming Community
    College

Arab Republic of Egypt

American University in Cairo

Colleges that offer athletic scholarships

Archery

Arizona
Glendale Community College W
Navajo Community College M, W

Badminton

Missouri
Central Methodist College M

Texas
University of Texas at Austin M

Baseball

Alabama
Alabama Agricultural and
    Mechanical University M
Alabama State University M
Auburn University M
Bevill State Community College M
Birmingham-Southern College M
Chattahoochee Valley Community
    College M
Enterprise State Junior College M
Gadsden State Community College
    M
Huntingdon College M
Jacksonville State University M
James H. Faulkner State
    Community College M
Jefferson State Community College
    M
Lurleen B. Wallace State Junior
    College M
Miles College M
Northwest-Shoals Community
    College M
Samford University M
Snead State Community College M
Spring Hill College M
Troy State University M
Tuskegee University M
University of Alabama
    Birmingham M
    Tuscaloosa M
University of Mobile M
University of Montevallo M
University of North Alabama M
University of South Alabama M

Arizona
Arizona State University M
Arizona Western College M
Cochise College M
Glendale Community College M
Pima Community College M
Scottsdale Community College M
South Mountain Community
    College M
University of Arizona M

Arkansas
Arkansas State University M
Harding University M
University of Arkansas
    Fayetteville M
    Little Rock M

California
Azusa Pacific University M
Biola University M
California Baptist College M
California Polytechnic State
    University: San Luis Obispo M
California State University
    Fresno M
    Fullerton M
    Long Beach M
    Los Angeles M
    Northridge M
    Sacramento M
    San Bernardino M
Concordia University M
Loyola Marymount University M
Master's College M
Pepperdine University M
Point Loma Nazarene College M
St. Mary's College of California M
San Diego State University M
San Jose State University M
Santa Clara University M
Southern California College M
Stanford University M
University of California
    Berkeley M
    Los Angeles M
    Riverside M
University of the Pacific M
University of San Diego M
University of San Francisco M
University of Southern California M
Westmont College M

Colorado
Colorado Northwestern Community
    College M
Colorado School of Mines M
Lamar Community College M
Mesa State College M

Metropolitan State College of
    Denver M
Otero Junior College M
Regis University M
Trinidad State Junior College M
University of Denver M
University of Northern Colorado M

Connecticut
Central Connecticut State
    University M
Fairfield University M
Quinnipiac College M
Teikyo-Post University M
University of Bridgeport M
University of Connecticut M
University of Hartford M
University of New Haven M

Delaware
Delaware State University M
Delaware Technical and
    Community College
    Southern Campus M
    Stanton/Wilmington Campus
    M
University of Delaware M

District of Columbia
George Washington University M
Howard University M

Florida
Bethune-Cookman College M
Brevard Community College M
Central Florida Community College
    M
Eckerd College M
Embry-Riddle Aeronautical
    University M
Flagler College M
Florida Atlantic University M
Florida Community College at
    Jacksonville M
Florida Institute of Technology M
Florida International University M
Florida Memorial College M
Florida Southern College M
Florida State University M
Gulf Coast Community College M
Hillsborough Community College M
Lake City Community College M
Lynn University M
Manatee Community College M
North Florida Junior College M
Nova Southeastern University M
Okaloosa-Walton Community
    College M
Palm Beach Atlantic College M
Palm Beach Community College M

Pasco-Hernando Community
    College M
Rollins College M
St. Johns River Community College
    M
St. Leo College M
St. Petersburg Junior College M
St. Thomas University M
Stetson University M
Tallahassee Community College M
University of Florida M
University of Miami M
University of North Florida M
University of South Florida M
University of Tampa M
University of West Florida M
Valencia Community College M
Warner Southern College M

Georgia
Abraham Baldwin Agricultural
    College M
Augusta College M
Brewton-Parker College M
Columbus College M
Emmanuel College M
Georgia College M
Georgia Institute of Technology M
Georgia Southern University M
Georgia Southwestern College M
Gordon College M
Kennesaw State College M
Mercer University M
Middle Georgia College M
Paine College M
Piedmont College M
Savannah State College M
Shorter College M
Southern College of Technology M
Thomas College M
Truett-McConnell College M
University of Georgia M
Valdosta State University M
West Georgia College M
Young Harris College M

Hawaii
Hawaii Pacific University M
University of Hawaii at Manoa M

Idaho
Albertson College M
College of Southern Idaho M
Lewis Clark State College M
North Idaho College M
Northwest Nazarene College M
Ricks College M

Illinois
Belleville Area College M

Bradley University M
Carl Sandburg College M
Chicago State University M
College of St. Francis M
Danville Area Community College M
Eastern Illinois University M
Highland Community College M
Illinois Eastern Community Colleges
  Olney Central College M
  Wabash Valley College M
Illinois Institute of Technology M
Illinois State University M
John A. Logan College M
Judson College M
Kaskaskia College M
Lake Land College M
Lewis University M
McHenry County College M
McKendree College M
Moraine Valley Community College M
Morton College M
Northeastern Illinois University M
Northwestern University M
Olivet Nazarene University M
Quincy University M
Rend Lake College M, W
Rosary College M
St. Xavier University M
Southeastern Illinois College M
Southern Illinois University
  Carbondale M
  Edwardsville M
Trinity College M
University of Illinois
  Chicago M
  Urbana-Champaign M
Western Illinois University M

Indiana

Ball State University M
Bethel College M
Butler University M
Goshen College M
Grace College M
Huntington College M
Indiana State University M
Indiana University
  Bloomington M
  Southeast M
Indiana University-Purdue University Indianapolis M
Indiana Wesleyan University M
Marian College M
Oakland City College M
Purdue University M
St. Francis College M
St. Joseph's College M
Taylor University M
Tri-State University M
University of Evansville M
University of Indianapolis M
University of Notre Dame M
University of Southern Indiana M
Valparaiso University M
Vincennes University M

Iowa

Briar Cliff College M
Graceland College M
Grand View College M
Indian Hills Community College M
Iowa Central Community College M
Iowa Lakes Community College M
Iowa State University M
Iowa Wesleyan College M
Marshalltown Community College M
Morningside College M

North Iowa Area Community College M
Northwestern College M
St. Ambrose University M
Teikyo Marycrest University M
Teikyo Westmar University M
University of Iowa M
University of Northern Iowa M
Waldorf College M

Kansas

Allen County Community College M
Baker University M
Benedictine College M
Bethany College M
Butler County Community College M
Central College M
Coffeyville Community College M
Colby Community College M
Dodge City Community College M
Emporia State University M
Fort Scott Community College M
Friends University M
Garden City Community College M
Hesston College M
Hutchinson Community College M
Independence Community College M
Johnson County Community College M
Kansas City Kansas Community College M
Kansas Newman College M
Kansas State University M
MidAmerica Nazarene College M
Neosho County Community College M
Ottawa University M
Sterling College M
University of Kansas M
Wichita State University M

Kentucky

Alice Lloyd College M
Bellarmine College M
Campbellsville College M
Cumberland College M
Eastern Kentucky University M
Kentucky State University M
Kentucky Wesleyan College M
Lindsey Wilson College M
Morehead State University M
Murray State University M
Northern Kentucky University M
Union College M
University of Kentucky M
University of Louisville M
Western Kentucky University M

Louisiana

Bossier Parish Community College M
Centenary College of Louisiana M
Grambling State University M
Louisiana State University and Agricultural and Mechanical College M
Louisiana Tech University M
Nicholls State University M
Northeast Louisiana University M
Northwestern State University M
Southeastern Louisiana University M
Tulane University M
University of New Orleans M
University of Southwestern Louisiana M

Maine

Husson College M

University of Maine M

Maryland

Bowie State University M
Charles County Community College M
Chesapeake College M
Dundalk Community College M
Garrett Community College M
Hagerstown Junior College M
Mount St. Mary's College M
Towson State University M
University of Maryland
  Baltimore County M
  College Park M
  Eastern Shore M

Massachusetts

American International College M
Becker College: Leicester Campus M
Boston University M
Dean College M
Northeastern University M
University of Massachusetts Amherst M

Michigan

Aquinas College M
Central Michigan University M
Cornerstone College and Grand Rapids Baptist Seminary M
Eastern Michigan University M
Glen Oaks Community College M
Henry Ford Community College M
Highland Park Community College M
Hillsdale College M
Kellogg Community College M
Michigan Christian College M
Michigan State University M
Northwood University M
Oakland University M
Saginaw Valley State University M
Southwestern Michigan College M
University of Detroit Mercy M
University of Michigan M
Wayne State University M

Minnesota

Mankato State University M
St. Cloud State University M
University of Minnesota
  Crookston M
  Duluth M
  Twin Cities M
Winona State University M

Mississippi

Alcorn State University M
Belhaven College M
Copiah-Lincoln Community College M
Delta State University M
Hinds Community College M
Holmes Community College M
Mississippi College M
Mississippi State University M
Mississippi Valley State University M
University of Mississippi M
William Carey College M

Missouri

Avila College M
Central Methodist College M
Central Missouri State University M
College of the Ozarks M
Crowder College M
Culver-Stockton College M
Harris Stowe State College M
Jefferson College M

Lincoln University M
Lindenwood College M
Longview Community College M
Mineral Area College M
Missouri Southern State College M
Missouri Western State College M
North Central Missouri College M
Northeast Missouri State University M
Research College of Nursing M
Rockhurst College M
St. Louis Community College at Forest Park M
St. Louis University M
Southeast Missouri State University M
Southwest Baptist University M
Southwest Missouri State University M
University of Missouri
  Columbia M
  Rolla M
  St. Louis M
William Jewell College M

Nebraska

Bellevue University M
Concordia College M
Creighton University M
Dana College M
Doane College M
Hastings College M
Midland Lutheran College M
Peru State College M
University of Nebraska
  Kearney M
  Lincoln M
  Omaha M
Wayne State College M
York College M

Nevada

University of Nevada: Reno M

New Hampshire

Franklin Pierce College M
University of New Hampshire M

New Jersey

Bloomfield College M
Burlington County College M
Caldwell College M
Fairleigh Dickinson University
  Edward Williams College M
  Teaneck M
Monmouth College M
Rider University M
Rutgers, The State University of New Jersey
  College of Engineering M
  College of Pharmacy M
  Cook College M
  Livingston College M
  Mason Gross School of the Arts M
  Rutgers College M
St. Peter's College M
Salem Community College M
Seton Hall University M

New Mexico

College of the Southwest M
Eastern New Mexico University M
New Mexico Highlands University M
New Mexico Junior College M
New Mexico Military Institute M
New Mexico State University M
University of New Mexico M

New York

Adelphi University M

Canisius College M
College of St. Rose M
Concordia College M
Dominican College of Blauvelt M
Dowling College M
Fordham University M
Genesee Community College M
Hofstra University M
Iona College M
Le Moyne College M
Long Island University
    Brooklyn Campus M
    C. W. Post Campus M
Manhattan College M
Marist College M
Mercy College M
Molloy College M
Monroe Community College M
New York Institute of Technology
    M
Niagara University M
Onondaga Community College M
Pace University M
St. Bonaventure University M
St. Francis College M
St. John's University M
St. Thomas Aquinas College M
Siena College M
Wagner College M

North Carolina

Appalachian State University M
Barton College M
Belmont Abbey College M
Brevard College M
Campbell University M
Catawba College M
Duke University M
East Carolina University M
Elon College M
Gardner-Webb University M
High Point University M
Lees-McRae College M
Lenoir-Rhyne College M
Louisburg College M
Mars Hill College M
Montreat-Anderson College M
Mount Olive College M
North Carolina Agricultural and
    Technical State University M
North Carolina State University M
Pembroke State University M
Pfeiffer College M
St. Andrews Presbyterian College M
St. Augustine's College M
Southeastern Community College M
University of North Carolina
    Asheville M
    Chapel Hill M
    Charlotte M
    Greensboro M
    Wilmington M
Wake Forest University M
Western Carolina University M
Wingate College M

North Dakota

Dickinson State University M
Mayville State University M
North Dakota State University
    Bottineau M
    Fargo M
University of Mary M
University of North Dakota
    Grand Forks M
    Williston M

Ohio

Ashland University M
Bowling Green State University M
Cedarville College M
Cleveland State University M

Cuyahoga Community College:
    Western Campus M
Kent State University M
Malone College M
Miami University: Oxford Campus
    M
Mount Vernon Nazarene College M
Ohio Dominican College M
Ohio State University: Columbus
    Campus M
Ohio University M
Shawnee State University M
Sinclair Community College M
Tiffin University M
University of Akron M
University of Cincinnati M
University of Dayton M
University of Findlay M
University of Rio Grande M
University of Toledo M
Urbana University M
Walsh University M
Wright State University M
Xavier University M
Youngstown State University M

Oklahoma

Cameron University M
Eastern Oklahoma State College M
Northwestern Oklahoma State
    University M
Oklahoma Baptist University M
Oklahoma Christian University of
    Science and Arts M
Oklahoma City University M
Oral Roberts University M
Redlands Community College M
Rose State College M
Southwestern Oklahoma State
    University M
University of Central Oklahoma M
University of Oklahoma M
Western Oklahoma State College M

Oregon

Clackamas Community College M
Concordia College M
George Fox College M
Linn-Benton Community College M
Mount Hood Community College
    M
Oregon State University M
Portland State University M
Treasure Valley Community College
    M
University of Portland M
Western Baptist College M

Pennsylvania

California University of
    Pennsylvania M
Drexel University M
Duquesne University M
Edinboro University of
    Pennsylvania M
Gannon University M
Geneva College M
Kutztown University of
    Pennsylvania M
Lock Haven University of
    Pennsylvania M
Mercyhurst College M
Millersville University of
    Pennsylvania M
Penn State University Park Campus
    M
Philadelphia College of Pharmacy
    and Science M
Point Park College M
St. Joseph's University M
St. Vincent College M

Shippensburg University of
    Pennsylvania M
Temple University M
University of Pittsburgh M
Villanova University M
West Chester University of
    Pennsylvania M

Puerto Rico

Inter American University of Puerto
    Rico: San German Campus M
University of Puerto Rico:
    Mayaguez Campus M

Rhode Island

Providence College M
University of Rhode Island M

South Carolina

Anderson College M
Charleston Southern University M
Clemson University M
Coastal Carolina University M
Coker College M
College of Charleston M
Erskine College M
Francis Marion University M
Furman University M
Limestone College M
Morris College M
North Greenville College M
Presbyterian College M
Southern Wesleyan University M
Spartanburg Methodist College M
University of South Carolina
    Aiken M
    Columbia M
    Spartanburg M
Voorhees College M
Winthrop University M
Wofford College M

South Dakota

Dakota Wesleyan University M
Huron University M
Mount Marty College M
South Dakota State University M
University of Sioux Falls M

Tennessee

Austin Peay State University M
Belmont University M
Bethel College M
Carson-Newman College M
Chattanooga State Technical
    Community College M
Christian Brothers University M
Cleveland State Community College
    M
David Lipscomb University M
Dyersburg State Community
    College M
East Tennessee State University M
Freed-Hardeman University M
Jackson State Community College
    M
King College M
Lambuth University M
Lane College M
Lincoln Memorial University M
Middle Tennessee State University
    M
Milligan College M
Roane State Community College M
Shelby State Community College M
Tennessee Technological University
    M
Trevecca Nazarene College M
Tusculum College M
Union University M
University of Memphis M

University of Tennessee
    Knoxville M
    Martin M
Vanderbilt University M
Volunteer State Community College
    M

Texas

Angelina College M
Baylor University M
Blinn College M
Concordia Lutheran College M
Dallas Baptist University M
East Texas Baptist University M
Galveston College M
Houston Baptist University M
Incarnate Word College M
Lamar University—Beaumont M
Laredo Community College M
Lee College M
LeTourneau University M
North Central Texas College M
Northwood University: Texas
    Campus M
Odessa College M
Rice University M
St. Edward's University M
St. Mary's University M
Schreiner College M
Southwest Texas State University M
Tarleton State University M
Texas A&M University M
Texas Christian University M
Texas Lutheran College M
Texas Tech University M
Texas Wesleyan University M
University of Houston M
University of Mary Hardin-Baylor
    M
University of Texas
    Arlington M
    Austin M
Vernon Regional Junior College M
Wharton County Junior College M

Utah

Brigham Young University M
College of Eastern Utah M
Dixie College M
Snow College M
University of Utah M
Utah Valley State College M

Vermont

University of Vermont M

Virginia

Bluefield College M
Clinch Valley College of the
    University of Virginia M
College of William and Mary M
George Mason University M
James Madison University M
Liberty University M
Longwood College M
Norfolk State University M
Old Dominion University M
Radford University M
St. Paul's College M
University of Richmond M
University of Virginia M
Virginia Commonwealth University
    M
Virginia Intermont College M
Virginia Military Institute M
Virginia Polytechnic Institute and
    State University M

Washington

Big Bend Community College M
Central Washington University M
Centralia College M

Edmonds Community College M
Gonzaga University M
Green River Community College M
Lower Columbia College M
Olympic College M
Pacific Lutheran University M
Pierce College M
Shoreline Community College M
Spokane Community College M
Tacoma Community College M
University of Puget Sound M
University of Washington M
Walla Walla Community College M
Washington State University M
Wenatchee Valley College M
Yakima Valley Community College
  M

West Virginia

Alderson-Broaddus College M
Bluefield State College M
Concord College M
Davis and Elkins College M
Marshall University M
Ohio Valley College M
Potomac State College of West
  Virginia University M
Salem-Teikyo University M
University of Charleston M
West Liberty State College M
West Virginia Institute of
  Technology M
West Virginia State College M
West Virginia University M
West Virginia Wesleyan College M

Wyoming

University of Wyoming M

Basketball

Alabama

Alabama Agricultural and
  Mechanical University M, W
Alabama State University M, W
Athens State College M
Auburn University M, W
Bevill State Community College M,
  W
Birmingham-Southern College M
Chattahoochee Valley Community
  College M, W
Enterprise State Junior College M
Faulkner University M
Gadsden State Community College
  M, W
Jacksonville State University M, W
James H. Faulkner State
  Community College M, W
John C. Calhoun State Community
  College M, W
Lawson State Community College
  M, W
Lurleen B. Wallace State Junior
  College M, W
Miles College M, W
Northwest-Shoals Community
  College M, W
Samford University M
Snead State Community College M,
  W
Spring Hill College M, W
Troy State University M, W
Tuskegee University M, W
UAB: Walker College M
University of Alabama
  Birmingham M, W
  Huntsville M, W
  Tuscaloosa M, W

University of Mobile M, W
University of Montevallo M, W
University of North Alabama M, W
University of South Alabama M, W

Alaska

University of Alaska
  Anchorage M, W
  Fairbanks M, W

Arizona

Arizona State University M, W
Arizona Western College M
Cochise College M, W
Eastern Arizona College M, W
Glendale Community College M, W
Mesa Community College M, W
Northern Arizona University M, W
Pima Community College M, W
Scottsdale Community College M,
  W
South Mountain Community
  College M, W
University of Arizona M, W

Arkansas

Arkansas State University M, W
Harding University M, W
Henderson State University M, W
John Brown University M, W
Lyon College M, W
North Arkansas Community/
  Technical College M, W
Ouachita Baptist University M, W
Shorter College W
University of Arkansas
  Fayetteville M, W
  Little Rock M
  Pine Bluff M, W
University of Central Arkansas M,
  W
Williams Baptist College M, W

California

Azusa Pacific University M, W
Biola University M, W
California Baptist College M, W
California Polytechnic State
  University: San Luis Obispo M,
  W
California State University
  Bakersfield M
  Fresno M, W
  Fullerton M, W
  Long Beach M, W
  Los Angeles M, W
  Northridge M, W
  Sacramento M, W
  San Bernardino M, W
Christian Heritage College M, W
Concordia University M, W
Dominican College of San Rafael
  M, W
Fresno Pacific College M, W
Holy Names College M, W
Loyola Marymount University M,
  W
Master's College M, W
Patten College M
Pepperdine University M, W
Point Loma Nazarene College M,
  W
St. Mary's College of California M,
  W
San Diego State University M, W
San Jose State University M, W
Santa Clara University M, W
Southern California College M, W
Stanford University M, W

University of California
  Berkeley M, W
  Irvine M, W
  Los Angeles M, W
  Riverside M, W
  Santa Barbara M, W
University of the Pacific M, W
University of San Diego M, W
University of San Francisco M, W
University of Southern California
  M, W
Westmont College M

Colorado

Adams State College M, W
Colorado Christian University M,
  W
Colorado Northwestern Community
  College M, W
Colorado School of Mines M, W
Colorado State University M, W
Fort Lewis College M, W
Lamar Community College M
Mesa State College M, W
Metropolitan State College of
  Denver M, W
Northeastern Junior College M, W
Otero Junior College M, W
Regis University M, W
Trinidad State Junior College M
University of Colorado
  Boulder M, W
  Colorado Springs M, W
University of Denver M, W
University of Northern Colorado M,
  W
University of Southern Colorado M,
  W
Western State College of Colorado
  M, W

Connecticut

Central Connecticut State
  University M, W
Fairfield University M, W
Quinnipiac College M, W
Teikyo-Post University M, W
University of Bridgeport M, W
University of Connecticut M, W
University of Hartford M, W
University of New Haven M, W

Delaware

Delaware State University M, W
Delaware Technical and
  Community College: Stanton/
  Wilmington Campus M, W
University of Delaware M, W

District of Columbia

American University M, W
George Washington University M,
  W
Georgetown University M, W
Howard University M, W
University of the District of
  Columbia M, W

Florida

Bethune-Cookman College M, W
Brevard Community College M, W
Central Florida Community College
  M
Daytona Beach Community College
  M
Eckerd College M, W
Embry-Riddle Aeronautical
  University M
Flagler College M, W
Florida Agricultural and Mechanical
  University M
Florida Atlantic University M, W

Florida College M
Florida Community College at
  Jacksonville M, W
Florida Institute of Technology M,
  W
Florida International University M,
  W
Florida Memorial College M, W
Florida Southern College M, W
Florida State University M, W
Gulf Coast Community College M
Hillsborough Community College
  M, W
Lake City Community College M,
  W
Lynn University M, W
Manatee Community College M, W
North Florida Junior College M, W
Nova Southeastern University M
Okaloosa-Walton Community
  College M, W
Palm Beach Atlantic College M
Palm Beach Community College M,
  W
Pasco-Hernando Community
  College M
Rollins College M, W
St. Johns River Community College
  M
St. Leo College M, W
St. Petersburg Junior College M, W
St. Thomas University M
Stetson University M, W
Tallahassee Community College M,
  W
University of Central Florida M
University of Florida M, W
University of Miami M, W
University of North Florida M, W
University of South Florida M, W
University of Tampa M, W
University of West Florida M, W
Valencia Community College M, W
Warner Southern College M, W
Webber College M, W

Georgia

Abraham Baldwin Agricultural
  College M
Augusta College M, W
Augusta Technical Institute M
Brewton-Parker College M, W
Clark Atlanta University M, W
Clayton State College M, W
Columbus College M, W
Covenant College M, W
Emmanuel College M, W
Fort Valley State College M, W
Georgia College M, W
Georgia Institute of Technology M,
  W
Georgia Southern University M, W
Georgia Southwestern College M,
  W
Kennesaw State College M, W
Macon College M
Mercer University M, W
Middle Georgia College M
Morehouse College M
North Georgia College M, W
Paine College M, W
Piedmont College M, W
Reinhardt College M, W
Savannah State College M, W
Shorter College M, W
Southern College of Technology M
Truett-McConnell College M, W
University of Georgia M, W
Valdosta State University M, W
West Georgia College M, W

Hawaii

Hawaii Pacific University M
University of Hawaii
   Hilo M
   Manoa M, W

Idaho

Albertson College M
Boise State University M, W
College of Southern Idaho M, W
Idaho State University M, W
Lewis Clark State College M, W
North Idaho College M, W
Northwest Nazarene College M, W
Ricks College M, W
University of Idaho M, W

Illinois

Barat College M
Belleville Area College M, W
Bradley University M, W
Carl Sandburg College M, W
Chicago State University M, W
City Colleges of Chicago: Kennedy-
   King College M
College of St. Francis M, W
Danville Area Community College
   M, W
De Paul University M, W
Eastern Illinois University M, W
Highland Community College M, W
Illinois Eastern Community
   Colleges
      Lincoln Trail College M, W
      Olney Central College M, W
      Wabash Valley College M, W
Illinois Institute of Technology M,
   W
Illinois State University M, W
John A. Logan College M, W
Judson College M, W
Kaskaskia College M, W
Lake Land College M, W
Lewis University M, W
Lincoln Land Community College
   M, W
Loyola University of Chicago M, W
McHenry County College M, W
McKendree College M, W
Moraine Valley Community College
   M, W
Morton College M, W
Northeastern Illinois University M,
   W
Northwestern University M, W
Olivet Nazarene University M, W
Quincy University M, W
Rend Lake College M, W
Rosary College M, W
St. Xavier University M
Southeastern Illinois College M, W
Southern Illinois University
   Carbondale M, W
   Edwardsville M, W
Trinity College M, W
University of Illinois
   Chicago M, W
   Urbana-Champaign M, W
Western Illinois University M, W

Indiana

Ball State University M, W
Bethel College M, W
Butler University M, W
Goshen College M, W
Grace College M, W
Huntington College M, W
Indiana State University M, W
Indiana University
   Bloomington M, W
   Southeast M, W

Indiana University-Purdue
   University Indianapolis M, W
Indiana Wesleyan University M, W
Marian College M, W
Oakland City College M, W
Purdue University M, W
St. Francis College M, W
St. Joseph's College M, W
St. Mary-of-the-Woods College W
Taylor University M, W
Tri-State University M, W
University of Evansville M, W
University of Indianapolis M, W
University of Notre Dame M, W
University of Southern Indiana M,
   W
Valparaiso University M, W
Vincennes University M, W

Iowa

Briar Cliff College M, W
Drake University M, W
Graceland College M, W
Grand View College M, W
Indian Hills Community College M
Iowa Central Community College
   M, W
Iowa Lakes Community College M,
   W
Iowa State University M, W
Iowa Wesleyan College M, W
Marshalltown Community College
   M, W
Morningside College M, W
North Iowa Area Community
   College M, W
Northwestern College M, W
St. Ambrose University M, W
Teikyo Marycrest University M, W
Teikyo Westmar University M, W
University of Iowa M, W
University of Northern Iowa M, W
Waldorf College M, W

Kansas

Allen County Community College
   M, W
Baker University M, W
Benedictine College M, W
Bethany College M, W
Bethel College M, W
Butler County Community College
   M, W
Central College M, W
Coffeyville Community College M,
   W
Colby Community College M, W
Cowley County Community College
   M, W
Dodge City Community College M,
   W
Emporia State University M, W
Fort Hays State University M
Fort Scott Community College M,
   W
Friends University M, W
Garden City Community College
   M, W
Hesston College M, W
Hutchinson Community College M,
   W
Independence Community College
   M
Johnson County Community
   College M, W
Kansas City Kansas Community
   College M, W
Kansas Newman College W
Kansas State University M, W
McPherson College M, W
MidAmerica Nazarene College M,
   W

Neosho County Community College
   M, W
Ottawa University M, W
Pratt Community College M, W
St. Mary College M, W
Seward County Community College
   M, W
Southwestern College M, W
Sterling College M, W
University of Kansas M, W
Wichita State University M, W

Kentucky

Alice Lloyd College M, W
Bellarmine College M, W
Campbellsville College M, W
Cumberland College M, W
Eastern Kentucky University M, W
Georgetown College M, W
Kentucky State University M, W
Kentucky Wesleyan College M, W
Lindsey Wilson College M, W
Midway College W
Morehead State University M, W
Murray State University M, W
Northern Kentucky University M,
   W
Spalding University M, W
Transylvania University M, W
Union College M, W
University of Kentucky M, W
University of Louisville M, W
Western Kentucky University M, W

Louisiana

Bossier Parish Community College
   M
Centenary College of Louisiana M
Dillard University M, W
Grambling State University M, W
Louisiana State University and
   Agricultural and Mechanical
   College M, W
Louisiana Tech University M, W
Nicholls State University M, W
Northeast Louisiana University M,
   W
Northwestern State University M,
   W
Southeastern Louisiana University
   M, W
Tulane University M, W
University of New Orleans M, W
University of Southwestern
   Louisiana M, W
Xavier University of Louisiana M,
   W

Maine

Husson College M, W
Unity College M
University of Maine M, W

Maryland

Bowie State University M, W
Charles County Community College
   M
Chesapeake College M, W
Dundalk Community College M, W
Garrett Community College M, W
Hagerstown Junior College M, W
Loyola College in Maryland M, W
Morgan State University M, W
Mount St. Mary's College M, W
Prince George's Community College
   M, W
Towson State University M, W
University of Maryland
   Baltimore County M, W
   College Park M, W
   Eastern Shore M, W

Massachusetts

American International College M,
   W
Assumption College M, W
Becker College
   Leicester Campus M
   Worcester Campus M
Bentley College M, W
Boston College M, W
Boston University M, W
Dean College M
Merrimack College M, W
Mount Ida College M
North Shore Community College M
Northeastern University M, W
Roxbury Community College M
Stonehill College M, W
University of Massachusetts
   Amherst M, W
   Lowell M, W

Michigan

Alpena Community College M, W
Aquinas College M, W
Central Michigan University M, W
Cornerstone College and Grand
   Rapids Baptist Seminary M, W
Delta College M, W
Eastern Michigan University M, W
Glen Oaks Community College M,
   W
Gogebic Community College M, W
Henry Ford Community College M,
   W
Highland Park Community College
   M, W
Hillsdale College M, W
Kellogg Community College M, W
Lansing Community College M, W
Michigan Christian College M, W
Michigan State University M, W
Michigan Technological University
   M, W
Northern Michigan University M,
   W
Northwood University M, W
Oakland University M, W
Saginaw Valley State University M,
   W
Southwestern Michigan College M,
   W
Spring Arbor College M, W
University of Detroit Mercy M
University of Michigan
   Ann Arbor M, W
   Dearborn M, W
Wayne State University M, W
Western Michigan University M, W

Minnesota

Bemidji State University M, W
Mankato State University M, W
Moorhead State University M, W
St. Cloud State University M, W
Southwest State University M, W
University of Minnesota
   Crookston M, W
   Duluth M, W
   Twin Cities M, W
Winona State University M, W

Mississippi

Alcorn State University M, W
Belhaven College M, W
Blue Mountain College W
Copiah-Lincoln Community College
   M, W
Delta State University M, W
East Central Community College
   M, W
Hinds Community College M, W
Holmes Community College M, W

Mary Holmes College M, W
Mississippi College M
Mississippi State University M, W
Mississippi University for Women W
University of Mississippi M, W
William Carey College M, W

Missouri

Avila College M, W
Central Missouri State University M, W
College of the Ozarks M, W
Columbia College M
Crowder College W
Culver-Stockton College M, W
Drury College M
Harris Stowe State College M, W
Jefferson College W
Lincoln University M, W
Lindenwood College M, W
Mineral Area College M, W
Missouri Southern State College M, W
Missouri Western State College M, W
Northeast Missouri State University M, W
Park College M, W
Research College of Nursing M, W
Rockhurst College M, W
St. Louis Community College
    Forest Park M, W
    Meramec M, W
St. Louis University M, W
Southeast Missouri State University M, W
Southwest Baptist University M, W
Southwest Missouri State University M, W
State Fair Community College M, W
University of Missouri
    Columbia M, W
    Kansas City M, W
    Rolla M, W
    St. Louis M, W
William Jewell College M, W
William Woods University W

Montana

Carroll College M, W
Dawson Community College M, W
Miles Community College M, W
Montana State University
    Billings M, W
    Bozeman M, W
    Northern M, W
Montana Tech of The University of Montana M, W
Rocky Mountain College M, W
University of Montana-Missoula M, W
Western Montana College of the University of Montana M, W

Nebraska

Bellevue University M
Central Community College M, W
Concordia College M, W
Creighton University M, W
Dana College M, W
Doane College M, W
Hastings College M, W
McCook Community College M, W
Midland Lutheran College M, W
Northeast Community College M, W
Peru State College M, W
Southeast Community College:
    Beatrice Campus M, W

University of Nebraska
    Kearney M, W
    Lincoln M, W
    Omaha M, W
Wayne State College M, W
Western Nebraska Community College: Scottsbluff Campus M, W
York College M, W

Nevada

Sierra Nevada College M
University of Nevada: Reno M, W

New Hampshire

Franklin Pierce College M, W
Hesser College M, W
New Hampshire College M, W
Notre Dame College M, W
St. Anselm College M, W
University of New Hampshire M, W

New Jersey

Bloomfield College M, W
Burlington County College M
Caldwell College M, W
Fairleigh Dickinson University
    Edward Williams College M, W
    Teaneck M, W
Georgian Court College W
Monmouth College M, W
Rider University M, W
Rutgers, The State University of New Jersey
    College of Engineering M, W
    College of Pharmacy M, W
    Cook College M, W
    Douglass College W
    Livingston College M, W
    Mason Gross School of the Arts M, W
    Rutgers College M, W
St. Peter's College M, W
Salem Community College W
Seton Hall University M, W
Union County College W

New Mexico

Eastern New Mexico University M, W
New Mexico Highlands University M, W
New Mexico Junior College M, W
New Mexico Military Institute M
New Mexico State University M, W
University of New Mexico M, W

New York

Adelphi University M, W
Canisius College M, W
Cazenovia College M, W
City University of New York:
    Queens College M, W
College of St. Rose M, W
Concordia College M, W
Daemen College M, W
Dominican College of Blauvelt M, W
Dowling College M
D'Youville College M, W
Fordham University M, W
Genesee Community College M, W
Hofstra University M, W
Houghton College M, W
Iona College M, W
Le Moyne College M, W
Long Island University
    Brooklyn Campus M, W
    C. W. Post Campus M, W
    Southampton College M, W

Manhattan College M, W
Marist College M, W
Mater Dei College W
Mercy College M, W
Molloy College M, W
Monroe Community College M
New York Institute of Technology M, W
Niagara County Community College M
Niagara University M, W
Nyack College M, W
Pace University M, W
Paul Smith's College M, W
Roberts Wesleyan College M, W
Sage Junior College of Albany M
St. Bonaventure University M, W
St. Francis College M, W
St. John's University M, W
St. Thomas Aquinas College M, W
Siena College M, W
State University of New York at Buffalo M, W
Syracuse University M, W
Wagner College M, W

North Carolina

Appalachian State University M, W
Barber-Scotia College M, W
Barton College M, W
Belmont Abbey College M, W
Brevard College M, W
Campbell University M, W
Catawba College M, W
Craven Community College M
Davidson College M, W
Duke University M, W
East Carolina University M, W
Elizabeth City State University M, W
Elon College M, W
Fayetteville State University M, W
Gardner-Webb University M, W
High Point University M, W
Johnson C. Smith University M, W
Lees-McRae College M, W
Lenoir-Rhyne College M, W
Livingstone College M, W
Louisburg College M, W
Mars Hill College M, W
Montreat-Anderson College M, W
Mount Olive College M, W
North Carolina Agricultural and Technical State University M, W
North Carolina Central University M, W
North Carolina State University M, W
Pembroke State University M, W
Pfeiffer College M, W
Pitt Community College M
Queens College M, W
St. Andrews Presbyterian College M, W
St. Augustine's College M, W
University of North Carolina
    Asheville M, W
    Chapel Hill M, W
    Charlotte M, W
    Greensboro M, W
    Wilmington M, W
Wake Forest University M, W
Western Carolina University M, W
Wingate College M, W
Winston-Salem State University M, W

North Dakota

Dickinson State University M, W
Mayville State University M, W
North Dakota State College of Science M, W

North Dakota State University
    Bottineau M, W
    Fargo M, W
University of Mary M, W
University of North Dakota
    Grand Forks M, W
    Williston M, W

Ohio

Ashland University M
Bowling Green State University M, W
Cedarville College M, W
Cincinnati State Technical and Community College M, W
Clark State Community College M, W
Cleveland State University M, W
Kent State University M, W
Malone College M, W
Miami University. Oxford Campus M, W
Mount Vernon Nazarene College M, W
Ohio Dominican College M, W
Ohio State University: Columbus Campus M, W
Ohio University M, W
Owens Technical College
    Findlay Campus M, W
    Toledo M, W
Shawnee State University M, W
Sinclair Community College M, W
Tiffin University M, W
University of Akron M, W
University of Cincinnati M, W
University of Dayton M, W
University of Findlay M, W
University of Rio Grande M, W
University of Toledo M, W
Urbana University M, W
Walsh University M, W
Wright State University M, W
Xavier University M, W
Youngstown State University M, W

Oklahoma

Bartlesville Wesleyan College M, W
Cameron University M, W
East Central University M, W
Eastern Oklahoma State College M, W
Northwestern Oklahoma State University M, W
Oklahoma Baptist University M, W
Oklahoma Christian University of Science and Arts M, W
Oklahoma City University M, W
Oklahoma Panhandle State University M, W
Oral Roberts University M, W
Phillips University M, W
Redlands Community College M, W
Rose State College M, W
St. Gregory's College M, W
Southern Nazarene University M, W
Southwestern Oklahoma State University M, W
University of Central Oklahoma M, W
University of Oklahoma M, W
University of Tulsa M
Western Oklahoma State College M, W

Oregon

Chemeketa Community College M, W
Clackamas Community College M, W
Concordia College M, W

George Fox College M, W
Linn-Benton Community College
M, W
Mount Hood Community College
M, W
Oregon State University M, W
Portland State University W
Treasure Valley Community College
M, W
University of Oregon M, W
University of Portland M, W
Western Baptist College M, W

Pennsylvania

Bloomsburg University of
Pennsylvania M, W
California University of
Pennsylvania M, W
Carlow College M, W
Cheyney University of Pennsylvania
M, W
Community College of Beaver
County M
Drexel University M, W
Duquesne University M, W
Edinboro University of
Pennsylvania M, W
Gannon University M, W
Geneva College M, W
Indiana University of Pennsylvania
M, W
Kutztown University of
Pennsylvania M, W
Lock Haven University of
Pennsylvania M, W
Manor Junior College M, W
Mercyhurst College M, W
Millersville University of
Pennsylvania M, W
Mount Aloysius College M, W
Penn State University Park Campus
M, W
Philadelphia College of Pharmacy
and Science M, W
Point Park College M, W
Robert Morris College M, W
St. Francis College M, W
St. Joseph's University M, W
St. Vincent College M, W
Seton Hill College W
Shippensburg University of
Pennsylvania M, W
Temple University M, W
University of Pittsburgh
Johnstown M, W
Pittsburgh M, W
Villanova University M, W
West Chester University of
Pennsylvania M, W
Westminster College M, W

Puerto Rico

Inter American University of Puerto
Rico: San German Campus M, W
University of Puerto Rico
Bayamon Technological
University College M, W
La Montana Regional College
M, W
Mayaguez Campus M, W
University of the Sacred Heart M

Rhode Island

Bryant College M, W
Providence College M, W
University of Rhode Island M, W

South Carolina

Anderson College M, W
Charleston Southern University M,
W
Claflin College M, W

Clemson University M, W
Coastal Carolina University M, W
Coker College M, W
College of Charleston M, W
Erskine College M, W
Francis Marion University M, W
Furman University M, W
Lander University M, W
Limestone College M, W
Morris College M, W
North Greenville College M, W
Presbyterian College M, W
South Carolina State University M,
W
Southern Wesleyan University M,
W
Spartanburg Methodist College M,
W
University of South Carolina
Aiken M, W
Columbia M, W
Spartanburg M, W
Voorhees College M, W
Winthrop University M, W
Wofford College M, W

South Dakota

Augustana College M, W
Black Hills State University M, W
Dakota State University M, W
Dakota Wesleyan University M, W
Huron University M, W
Mount Marty College M, W
Northern State University M, W
South Dakota State University M,
W
University of Sioux Falls M, W

Tennessee

Austin Peay State University M, W
Belmont University M, W
Bethel College M, W
Carson-Newman College M, W
Chattanooga State Technical
Community College M, W
Christian Brothers University M, W
Cleveland State Community College
M, W
David Lipscomb University M, W
Dyersburg State Community
College M, W
East Tennessee State University M,
W
Freed-Hardeman University M, W
Jackson State Community College
M, W
King College M, W
Lambuth University M, W
Lane College M, W
Lee College M, W
LeMoyne-Owen College M, W
Lincoln Memorial University M, W
Middle Tennessee State University
M, W
Milligan College M, W
Roane State Community College M,
W
Shelby State Community College
M, W
Tennessee Technological University
M, W
Tennessee Temple University M, W
Tennessee Wesleyan College M, W
Trevecca Nazarene College M
Tusculum College M, W
Union University M, W
University of Memphis M, W
University of Tennessee
Chattanooga M, W
Knoxville M, W
Martin M, W
Vanderbilt University M, W

Volunteer State Community College
M, W

Texas

Abilene Christian University M, W
Ambassador University M, W
Angelina College M, W
Angelo State University M, W
Baylor University M, W
Blinn College M, W
Concordia Lutheran College M, W
East Texas Baptist University M, W
East Texas State University M, W
Houston Baptist University M
Incarnate Word College M, W
Jacksonville College M
Kilgore College M, W
Lamar University—Beaumont M, W
Lee College M
LeTourneau University M, W
Odessa College M, W
Rice University M, W
St. Edward's University M, W
St. Mary's University M, W
Sam Houston State University M,
W
Schreiner College M, W
South Plains College M, W
Southern Methodist University M,
W
Southwest Texas State University
M, W
Stephen F. Austin State University
M, W
Tarleton State University M, W
Texas A&M University M, W
Texas A&M University-Kingsville
M, W
Texas Christian University M, W
Texas Lutheran College M, W
Texas Tech University M, W
Texas Wesleyan University M, W
Texas Woman's University W
University of Houston M, W
University of Mary Hardin-Baylor
M, W
University of North Texas M, W
University of Texas
Arlington M, W
Austin M, W
San Antonio M, W
Wayland Baptist University M, W
Weatherford College M, W
West Texas A&M University M, W
Western Texas College W

Utah

Brigham Young University M, W
College of Eastern Utah M, W
Dixie College M, W
Salt Lake Community College M,
W
Snow College M, W
Southern Utah University M, W
University of Utah M, W
Utah State University M
Utah Valley State College M, W
Weber State University M, W

Vermont

Champlain College M
College of St. Joseph in Vermont
M, W
Green Mountain College M, W
St. Michael's College M, W
University of Vermont M, W

Virginia

Bluefield College M, W
Clinch Valley College of the
University of Virginia M, W
College of William and Mary M, W

George Mason University M, W
Hampton University M, W
James Madison University M, W
Liberty University M, W
Longwood College M, W
Norfolk State University M, W
Old Dominion University M, W
Radford University M, W
St. Paul's College M, W
University of Richmond M, W
University of Virginia M, W
Virginia Commonwealth University
M, W
Virginia Intermont College M, W
Virginia Military Institute M
Virginia Polytechnic Institute and
State University M, W
Virginia State University M, W
Virginia Union University M, W

Washington

Big Bend Community College M, W
Central Washington University M,
W
Centralia College M, W
Eastern Washington University M,
W
Edmonds Community College M,
W
Gonzaga University M, W
Green River Community College
M, W
Highline Community College M, W
Lower Columbia College M, W
Northwest College M, W
Olympic College M, W
Pacific Lutheran University M, W
Pierce College M, W
St. Martin's College M, W
Seattle Pacific University M, W
Seattle University M, W
Shoreline Community College M,
W
Spokane Community College M, W
Tacoma Community College M, W
University of Puget Sound M, W
University of Washington M, W
Walla Walla Community College M,
W
Washington State University M, W
Wenatchee Valley College M, W
Western Washington University M,
W
Yakima Valley Community College
M, W

West Virginia

Alderson-Broaddus College M, W
Bluefield State College M, W
Concord College M, W
Davis and Elkins College M, W
Fairmont State College M, W
Marshall University M, W
Ohio Valley College M, W
Potomac State College of West
Virginia University M, W
Salem-Teikyo University M, W
Shepherd College M, W
University of Charleston M, W
West Liberty State College M, W
West Virginia Institute of
Technology M, W
West Virginia State College M, W
West Virginia University M, W
West Virginia Wesleyan College M,
W
Wheeling Jesuit College M, W

Wisconsin

Marquette University M, W
Northland College M, W

University of Wisconsin
  Green Bay M, W
  Madison M, W

Wyoming

Casper College M, W
Eastern Wyoming College M
Sheridan College M, W
University of Wyoming M, W
Western Wyoming Community
  College M, W

Arab Republic of Egypt

American University in Cairo M, W

Canada

Simon Fraser University M, W

Bowling

Florida

Florida Agricultural and Mechanical
  University M, W

Indiana

Vincennes University M, W

Kansas

Fort Hays State University M, W

Maryland

Dundalk Community College M, W
Prince George's Community College
  M, W

Michigan

Aquinas College M, W
Saginaw Valley State University M

Mississippi

Mississippi Valley State University
  M, W

Missouri

Avila College M

New York

Niagara County Community College
  M, W

North Carolina

North Carolina Central University
  M, W

Pennsylvania

Community College of Beaver
  County M

Utah

Weber State University W

Cross-country

Alabama

Alabama Agricultural and
  Mechanical University M, W
Alabama State University M, W
Auburn University M, W
Jacksonville State University M, W
Lurleen B. Wallace State Junior
  College M, W
Miles College M, W
Samford University M, W
Spring Hill College W
Troy State University M, W

University of Alabama
  Birmingham M, W
  Huntsville M, W
  Tuscaloosa M, W
University of Mobile M, W
University of North Alabama M, W
University of South Alabama M, W

Alaska

University of Alaska
  Anchorage M
  Fairbanks M, W

Arizona

Arizona State University M, W
Glendale Community College M, W
Mesa Community College M, W
Navajo Community College M, W
Northern Arizona University M, W
Pima Community College M, W
Scottsdale Community College M,
  W
South Mountain Community
  College M, W
University of Arizona M, W

Arkansas

Arkansas State University M, W
Harding University M, W
University of Arkansas
  Fayetteville M, W
  Little Rock M, W

California

Azusa Pacific University M, W
Biola University M, W
California Baptist College M, W
California Polytechnic State
  University: San Luis Obispo M,
  W
California State University
  Bakersfield M, W
  Fresno M
  Fullerton M, W
  Long Beach M, W
  Los Angeles M, W
  Northridge M, W
  Sacramento M, W
Concordia University M, W
Dominican College of San Rafael
  M, W
Fresno Pacific College M, W
MiraCosta College W
Mount St. Mary's College W
Point Loma Nazarene College M,
  W
St. Mary's College of California M,
  W
San Diego State University W
San Jose State University W
Southern California College M, W
University of California
  Berkeley M, W
  Irvine M, W
  Los Angeles M, W
  Riverside M, W
  Santa Barbara M, W
University of San Diego M, W
University of San Francisco M, W
Westmont College M, W

Colorado

Adams State College M, W
Colorado School of Mines M, W
Colorado State University M, W
Fort Lewis College M, W
Mesa State College W
University of Colorado at Boulder
  M, W
Western State College of Colorado
  M, W

Connecticut

Central Connecticut State
  University M, W
Fairfield University M, W
Quinnipiac College M, W
Teikyo-Post University M, W
University of Connecticut M, W
University of Hartford M, W
University of New Haven M

District of Columbia

American University M, W
George Washington University M,
  W
Howard University M, W

Florida

Bethune-Cookman College M, W
Brevard Community College M, W
Eckerd College M, W
Flagler College M, W
Florida Atlantic University M, W
Florida Community College at
  Jacksonville M, W
Florida Institute of Technology M,
  W
Florida State University M, W
Nova Southeastern University M,
  W
Stetson University M, W
University of Central Florida M, W
University of Florida M, W
University of Miami M, W
University of Tampa M, W
Warner Southern College M, W
Webber College M, W

Georgia

Augusta College M, W
Columbus College M, W
Covenant College M, W
Georgia College M, W
Georgia Institute of Technology M,
  W
Kennesaw State College M, W
Mercer University M, W
Morehouse College M
Paine College M, W
Piedmont College M, W
Savannah State College W
Shorter College M, W
University of Georgia M, W
Valdosta State University M, W
West Georgia College M, W

Hawaii

Hawaii Pacific University M, W
University of Hawaii
  Hilo M, W
  Manoa W

Idaho

Boise State University M, W
College of Southern Idaho M, W
Idaho State University M, W
North Idaho College M, W
University of Idaho M, W

Illinois

Bradley University M, W
Chicago State University M, W
College of St. Francis W
Danville Area Community College
  M, W
De Paul University M, W
Eastern Illinois University M, W
Illinois Institute of Technology M,
  W
Illinois State University M, W
Judson College M, W
Lewis University M, W
Loyola University of Chicago M, W

Morton College M, W
Northeastern Illinois University M,
  W
Olivet Nazarene University M, W
St. Xavier University W
Southern Illinois University
  Carbondale M, W
  Edwardsville M, W
University of Illinois
  Chicago M, W
  Urbana-Champaign M, W
Western Illinois University M, W

Indiana

Ball State University M, W
Bethel College M, W
Butler University M, W
Goshen College M, W
Huntington College M, W
Indiana State University M, W
Indiana University Bloomington M,
  W
Indiana Wesleyan University M, W
Marian College M, W
Oakland City College M, W
Purdue University M, W
St. Francis College M, W
St. Joseph's College M, W
Taylor University M, W
Tri-State University M, W
University of Evansville M, W
University of Indianapolis M, W
University of Notre Dame M, W
University of Southern Indiana M,
  W
Valparaiso University M, W
Vincennes University M, W

Iowa

Drake University M, W
Graceland College M, W
Iowa State University M, W
Iowa Wesleyan College M, W
Morningside College M, W
Northwestern College M, W
St. Ambrose University M, W
University of Iowa M, W
University of Northern Iowa M, W

Kansas

Allen County Community College
  M, W
Baker University M, W
Benedictine College M, W
Bethany College M, W
Butler County Community College
  M, W
Central College M, W
Coffeyville Community College M,
  W
Colby Community College M, W
Emporia State University M, W
Fort Hays State University M, W
Garden City Community College
  M, W
Hutchinson Community College M,
  W
Independence Community College
  M, W
Johnson County Community
  College M, W
Kansas City Kansas Community
  College M, W
Kansas State University M, W
McPherson College M, W
Neosho County Community College
  M, W
Ottawa University M, W
Pratt Community College M, W
Southwestern College M, W
Sterling College M, W
University of Kansas M, W

Wichita State University M, W

Kentucky

Alice Lloyd College M, W
Bellarmine College M, W
Campbellsville College M, W
Cumberland College M, W
Eastern Kentucky University M, W
Georgetown College M, W
Kentucky State University M, W
Lindsey Wilson College M
Midway College W
Murray State University M, W
Northern Kentucky University M, W
Sue Bennett College M, W
Union College M, W
University of Kentucky M, W
University of Louisville M, W
Western Kentucky University M, W

Louisiana

Centenary College of Louisiana M, W
Louisiana State University and Agricultural and Mechanical College M, W
Louisiana Tech University M, W
Nicholls State University M, W
Northeast Louisiana University M, W
Northwestern State University M, W
Southeastern Louisiana University M
Tulane University M, W
University of New Orleans M, W
University of Southwestern Louisiana M, W

Maine

Unity College M, W
University of Maine M, W

Maryland

Bowie State University M, W
Hagerstown Junior College M, W
Morgan State University M, W
Mount St. Mary's College M, W
Towson State University M, W
University of Maryland
    Baltimore County M, W
    College Park M, W
    Eastern Shore M, W

Massachusetts

Boston College W
Boston University M, W
Northeastern University M, W
University of Massachusetts
    Amherst M, W
    Lowell M, W

Michigan

Aquinas College M, W
Central Michigan University M, W
Cornerstone College and Grand Rapids Baptist Seminary M, W
Eastern Michigan University M, W
Highland Park Community College M, W
Hillsdale College M, W
Lansing Community College M, W
Michigan Christian College M, W
Michigan State University M, W
Northern Michigan University M, W
Northwood University M, W
Oakland University M, W
Saginaw Valley State University M, W

Southwestern Michigan College M, W
Spring Arbor College M, W
University of Detroit Mercy M, W
University of Michigan M, W
Wayne State University M
Western Michigan University M, W

Minnesota

Mankato State University M, W
Moorhead State University M, W
St. Cloud State University M, W
University of Minnesota
    Duluth M, W
    Twin Cities M, W
Winona State University W

Mississippi

Alcorn State University M, W
Delta State University W
Mississippi State University M, W
Mississippi Valley State University M, W

Missouri

Central Methodist College M, W
Central Missouri State University M, W
Lindenwood College M, W
Missouri Southern State College M, W
Northeast Missouri State University M, W
Park College M, W
St. Louis University M, W
Southeast Missouri State University M, W
Southwest Baptist University M, W
Southwest Missouri State University M, W
University of Missouri
    Columbia M, W
    Kansas City M, W
    Rolla M, W
William Jewell College M, W

Montana

Montana State University
    Billings M, W
    Bozeman M, W
University of Montana-Missoula M, W

Nebraska

Concordia College M, W
Creighton University M, W
Dana College M, W
Doane College M, W
Hastings College M, W
Midland Lutheran College M, W
University of Nebraska
    Kearney M, W
    Lincoln M, W
    Omaha W
Wayne State College M, W

Nevada

University of Nevada: Reno W

New Hampshire

University of New Hampshire W

New Jersey

Fairleigh Dickinson University
    Edward Williams College M, W
    Teaneck M, W
Georgian Court College W
Monmouth College M, W
Rider University M, W

Rutgers, The State University of New Jersey
    College of Engineering M, W
    College of Pharmacy M, W
    Cook College M, W
    Douglass College W
    Livingston College M, W
    Mason Gross School of the Arts M, W
    Rutgers College M, W
St. Peter's College M, W
Seton Hall University M, W

New Mexico

New Mexico Highlands University M, W
New Mexico State University M, W
University of New Mexico M, W

New York

Adelphi University M, W
Canisius College M, W
College of St. Rose M, W
Concordia College M, W
Fordham University M, W
Hofstra University M, W
Houghton College M, W
Iona College M
Le Moyne College M, W
Long Island University: C. W. Post Campus M, W
Manhattan College M, W
Marist College M, W
Mercy College M, W
New York Institute of Technology M, W
Niagara University M, W
Pace University M, W
Roberts Wesleyan College M, W
St. Bonaventure University M, W
St. Francis College M, W
St. John's University M, W
St. Thomas Aquinas College M, W
State University of New York at Buffalo M, W
Syracuse University M, W

North Carolina

Appalachian State University M, W
Brevard College M, W
Campbell University M, W
Davidson College W
East Carolina University M, W
Elon College M, W
Fayetteville State University M, W
High Point University M, W
Johnson C. Smith University M, W
Lees-McRae College M, W
Lenoir-Rhyne College M, W
Livingstone College M, W
Mars Hill College M, W
North Carolina Agricultural and Technical State University M, W
North Carolina Central University M, W
North Carolina State University M, W
Pembroke State University M, W
Pfeiffer College M, W
St. Andrews Presbyterian College M, W
St. Augustine's College M, W
University of North Carolina
    Asheville M, W
    Chapel Hill M, W
    Charlotte M, W
    Greensboro M
    Wilmington M, W
Wake Forest University M, W
Western Carolina University M, W
Winston-Salem State University M, W

North Dakota

Dickinson State University M, W
North Dakota State College of Science M, W
North Dakota State University M, W
University of Mary M, W

Ohio

Ashland University M, W
Bowling Green State University M, W
Cedarville College M, W
Cleveland State University W
Kent State University M, W
Malone College M, W
Miami University: Oxford Campus M, W
Ohio State University: Columbus Campus M, W
Ohio University M, W
Tiffin University M, W
University of Akron M, W
University of Dayton M, W
University of Findlay M, W
University of Rio Grande M, W
University of Toledo M, W
Walsh University M, W
Wright State University M, W
Xavier University M, W
Youngstown State University M, W

Oklahoma

Oklahoma Baptist University M, W
Oklahoma Christian University of Science and Arts M, W
Oral Roberts University M, W
Southern Nazarene University M, W
University of Central Oklahoma M, W
University of Oklahoma M, W
University of Tulsa M, W

Oregon

Clackamas Community College M, W
George Fox College M, W
Mount Hood Community College M, W
Portland State University M, W
University of Portland M, W

Pennsylvania

Bloomsburg University of Pennsylvania W
Carlow College M, W
Cheyney University of Pennsylvania M, W
Drexel University M
Duquesne University M, W
Edinboro University of Pennsylvania M, W
Gannon University M, W
Geneva College M, W
Indiana University of Pennsylvania M, W
Kutztown University of Pennsylvania M, W
Lock Haven University of Pennsylvania M, W
Mercyhurst College M, W
Millersville University of Pennsylvania M, W
Penn State University Park Campus M, W
Robert Morris College M, W
St. Francis College M, W
St. Joseph's University M, W
St. Vincent College M, W
Seton Hill College W

Shippensburg University of
Pennsylvania M, W
University of Pittsburgh M, W
Villanova University M, W
Westminster College W

Puerto Rico

Inter American University of Puerto
Rico: San German Campus M, W
University of Puerto Rico
La Montana Regional College
M, W
Mayaguez Campus M, W
University of the Sacred Heart M,
W

Rhode Island

Providence College M, W
University of Rhode Island M, W

South Carolina

Anderson College M, W
Charleston Southern University M,
W
Clemson University M, W
Coastal Carolina University M, W
College of Charleston M, W
Erskine College M, W
Francis Marion University M, W
Furman University M, W
Lander University M, W
South Carolina State University M,
W
Southern Wesleyan University M,
W
University of South Carolina
Aiken M, W
Columbia M, W
Spartanburg M
Voorhees College M, W
Winthrop University M, W
Wofford College M, W

South Dakota

Augustana College M, W
Black Hills State University M, W
Dakota State University M, W
Dakota Wesleyan University M, W
Mount Marty College M, W
South Dakota State University M,
W
University of Sioux Falls M, W

Tennessee

Austin Peay State University M, W
Belmont University M, W
Carson-Newman College M, W
David Lipscomb University M, W
East Tennessee State University M,
W
Lincoln Memorial University M, W
Middle Tennessee State University
M, W
Tennessee Technological University
M, W
University of Memphis M
University of Tennessee
Chattanooga M, W
Knoxville M, W
Martin M, W
Vanderbilt University M, W

Texas

Abilene Christian University M, W
Ambassador University M, W
Angelo State University M, W
Baylor University M, W
East Texas State University M, W
Incarnate Word College M, W
Lamar University—Beaumont M, W
LeTourneau University W

Northwood University: Texas
Campus M, W
Prairie View A&M University W
Sam Houston State University M,
W
South Plains College M
Southern Methodist University M,
W
Southwest Texas State University
M, W
Stephen F. Austin State University
M, W
Texas A&M University M, W
Texas Christian University M, W
Texas Tech University M, W
University of Houston M, W
University of North Texas M, W
University of Texas
Arlington M, W
Austin M, W
San Antonio M, W
Wayland Baptist University M, W

Utah

Brigham Young University M, W
University of Utah M, W
Utah State University M, W
Weber State University M, W

Virginia

College of William and Mary M, W
George Mason University M, W
Hampton University M, W
James Madison University M, W
Liberty University M, W
Norfolk State University M, W
Old Dominion University W
Radford University M, W
St. Paul's College M, W
University of Virginia M, W
Virginia Commonwealth University
M, W
Virginia Military Institute M
Virginia Polytechnic Institute and
State University M, W
Virginia State University M, W

Washington

Central Washington University M,
W
Eastern Washington University M,
W
Gonzaga University M, W
Highline Community College M
Lower Columbia College M, W
Northwest College M, W
Pacific Lutheran University M, W
Seattle Pacific University M, W
Seattle University M, W
Spokane Community College M, W
University of Puget Sound M, W
University of Washington M, W
Washington State University M, W
Western Washington University M,
W

West Virginia

Alderson-Broaddus College M, W
Bluefield State College M, W
Concord College M
Davis and Elkins College M, W
West Virginia University M, W
West Virginia Wesleyan College M,
W
Wheeling Jesuit College M, W

Wisconsin

Marquette University M, W
University of Wisconsin
Green Bay M, W
Madison M, W

Wyoming

University of Wyoming M, W

Canada

Simon Fraser University M, W

Diving

Alabama

Auburn University M, W
University of Alabama M, W

Arizona

Northern Arizona University M, W
University of Arizona M, W

Arkansas

University of Arkansas M, W

California

California State University:
Northridge M, W
Pepperdine University W
University of California: Irvine M,
W
University of San Diego W
University of Southern California
M, W

Colorado

Colorado State University W
University of Denver M, W

Connecticut

Central Connecticut State
University M, W
University of Connecticut M, W

District of Columbia

American University M, W
George Washington University M,
W
Howard University M, W

Florida

Florida State University M, W
University of Florida M, W
University of Miami M, W

Georgia

University of Georgia M, W

Hawaii

University of Hawaii at Manoa M,
W

Illinois

Bradley University M
Illinois Institute of Technology M,
W
Illinois State University W
Northeastern Illinois University M,
W
Northwestern University M, W
Southern Illinois University at
Carbondale M, W
University of Illinois
Chicago M, W
Urbana-Champaign W
Western Illinois University M, W

Indiana

Butler University M, W
Indiana University Bloomington M,
W
Purdue University M, W
University of Evansville M, W
University of Indianapolis M, W
University of Notre Dame M, W

Valparaiso University M, W

Iowa

University of Iowa M, W

Kansas

University of Kansas M, W

Kentucky

Campbellsville College M, W
Union College M, W
University of Kentucky M, W
University of Louisville M, W
Western Kentucky University M, W

Maine

University of Maine M, W

Maryland

Towson State University M, W
University of Maryland: Baltimore
County M, W

Massachusetts

Boston College W
Boston University M, W
Northeastern University M, W
University of Massachusetts
Amherst M, W

Michigan

Eastern Michigan University M, W
Hillsdale College W
Northern Michigan University W
Oakland University M, W
Southwestern Michigan College M,
W
University of Michigan M, W
Wayne State University M, W

Minnesota

Mankato State University M, W
University of Minnesota: Twin
Cities M, W

Mississippi

Delta State University M, W

Missouri

Drury College M, W
Northeast Missouri State University
W
St. Louis University M, W
Southwest Missouri State University
M
University of Missouri
Columbia M, W
Rolla M

Nebraska

University of Nebraska
Kearney W
Lincoln M, W

Nevada

University of Nevada: Reno W

New Jersey

Rider University M, W
Rutgers, The State University of
New Jersey
College of Engineering M, W
College of Pharmacy M, W
Cook College M, W
Douglass College W
Livingston College M, W
Mason Gross School of the
Arts M, W
Rutgers College M, W
St. Peter's College M, W

New Mexico

University of New Mexico M, W

New York

Canisius College M, W
Fordham University M, W
Iona College M, W
Marist College M, W
Niagara University M, W
St. Bonaventure University M, W
State University of New York at
Buffalo M, W
Syracuse University M, W

North Carolina

Davidson College W
East Carolina University M, W
North Carolina State University M,
W
University of North Carolina at
Wilmington M, W

Ohio

Bowling Green State University M,
W
Cleveland State University M, W
Miami University: Oxford Campus
M, W
Ohio State University: Columbus
Campus M, W
Ohio University M, W
University of Toledo M, W
Wright State University M, W
Xavier University M, W

Pennsylvania

Duquesne University M
Gannon University M, W
Indiana University of Pennsylvania
M, W
Lock Haven University of
Pennsylvania W
University of Pittsburgh M, W
Villanova University M, W

Rhode Island

University of Rhode Island M, W

South Carolina

Clemson University M, W
College of Charleston M, W

South Dakota

South Dakota State University M,
W

Tennessee

University of Tennessee: Knoxville
M, W

Texas

Southern Methodist University M,
W
Texas A&M University M, W
Texas Christian University M, W
University of Houston W
University of Texas at Austin M, W

Utah

Brigham Young University M, W
University of Utah M, W

Virginia

James Madison University M, W
Old Dominion University M, W
University of Virginia M, W
Virginia Military Institute M
Virginia Polytechnic Institute and
State University M, W

Wisconsin

University of Wisconsin
Green Bay M, W
Madison M, W

Canada

Simon Fraser University M, W

Fencing

California

California State University:
Fullerton M, W

Florida

Florida Institute of Technology M,
W

Indiana

Tri-State University M, W
University of Notre Dame M, W

Michigan

University of Detroit Mercy M, W
Wayne State University M, W

New Jersey

Fairleigh Dickinson University
Edward Williams College W
Teaneck W
Rutgers, The State University of
New Jersey
College of Engineering M, W
College of Pharmacy M, W
Cook College M, W
Douglass College W
Livingston College M, W
Mason Gross School of the
Arts M, W
Rutgers College M, W

New York

St. John's University M, W

North Carolina

North Carolina State University M,
W
University of North Carolina at
Chapel Hill M, W

Ohio

Cleveland State University M, W
Ohio State University: Columbus
Campus W

Oklahoma

St. Gregory's College M, W

Pennsylvania

Penn State University Park Campus
M, W
Temple University W

Arab Republic of Egypt

American University in Cairo M, W

Field hockey

California

University of the Pacific W

Connecticut

Fairfield University W
University of Connecticut W

Delaware

University of Delaware W

District of Columbia

American University W

Illinois

Northwestern University W

Iowa

University of Iowa W

Kentucky

Bellarmine College W
Transylvania University W
University of Louisville W

Maine

University of Maine W

Maryland

Towson State University W
University of Maryland: College
Park W

Massachusetts

Becker College
Leicester Campus W
Worcester Campus W
Boston College W
Boston University W
Dean College W
Northeastern University W
University of Massachusetts
Amherst W

Michigan

Central Michigan University W
Michigan State University W
University of Michigan W

Minnesota

Winona State University W

Missouri

St. Louis University W
Southwest Missouri State University
W

New Hampshire

University of New Hampshire W

New Jersey

Rider University W
Rutgers, The State University of
New Jersey
College of Engineering W
College of Pharmacy W
Cook College W
Douglass College W
Livingston College W
Rutgers College W

New Mexico

New Mexico State University W

New York

Hofstra University W
Houghton College W
Long Island University: C. W. Post
Campus W
Syracuse University W

North Carolina

Appalachian State University W
Catawba College W
Davidson College W
Duke University W
University of North Carolina at
Chapel Hill W

Ohio

Kent State University W
Ohio State University: Columbus
Campus W
Ohio University W

Pennsylvania

Bloomsburg University of
Pennsylvania W
Drexel University W
Indiana University of Pennsylvania
W
Kutztown University of
Pennsylvania W
Lock Haven University of
Pennsylvania W
Millersville University of
Pennsylvania W
Penn State University Park Campus
W
Shippensburg University of
Pennsylvania W
Temple University W
Villanova University W
West Chester University of
Pennsylvania W

Rhode Island

Providence College W
University of Rhode Island W

Virginia

College of William and Mary W
James Madison University W
Longwood College W
Radford University W
University of Richmond W
University of Virginia W
Virginia Commonwealth University
W

West Virginia

Davis and Elkins College W

Canada

Simon Fraser University W

Football (tackle)

Alabama

Alabama Agricultural and
Mechanical University M
Alabama State University M
Auburn University M
Jacksonville State University M
Miles College M
Samford University M
Troy State University M
Tuskegee University M
University of Alabama
Birmingham M
Tuscaloosa M
University of North Alabama M

Arizona

Arizona State University M
Arizona Western College M
Eastern Arizona College M
Glendale Community College M
Mesa Community College M
Northern Arizona University M
Scottsdale Community College M
University of Arizona M

Arkansas

Arkansas State University M
Harding University M
Henderson State University M
Ouachita Baptist University M

University of Arkansas
  Fayetteville M
  Pine Bluff M
University of Central Arkansas M

California

Azusa Pacific University M
California Polytechnic State
  University: San Luis Obispo M
California State University
  Fresno M
  Northridge M
  Sacramento M
St. Mary's College of California M
San Diego State University M
San Jose State University M
Stanford University M
University of California: Los
  Angeles M
University of the Pacific M
University of Southern California M

Colorado

Adams State College M
Colorado School of Mines M
Colorado State University M
Fort Lewis College M
Mesa State College M
University of Northern Colorado M
Western State College of Colorado
  M

Connecticut

Central Connecticut State
  University M
University of Connecticut M
University of New Haven M

Delaware

Delaware State University M
University of Delaware M

District of Columbia

Howard University M

Florida

Bethune-Cookman College M
Florida Agricultural and Mechanical
  University M
Florida State University M
University of Central Florida M
University of Florida M
University of Miami M

Georgia

Clark Atlanta University M
Fort Valley State College M
Georgia Institute of Technology M
Georgia Military College M
Georgia Southern University M
Middle Georgia College M
Morehouse College M
Savannah State College M
University of Georgia M
Valdosta State University M
West Georgia College M

Hawaii

University of Hawaii at Manoa M

Idaho

Boise State University M
Idaho State University M
Ricks College M
University of Idaho M

Illinois

College of St. Francis M
Eastern Illinois University M
Illinois State University M
Northwestern University M
Olivet Nazarene University M

St. Xavier University M
Southern Illinois University at
  Carbondale M
Trinity College M
Western Illinois University M

Indiana

Ball State University M
Butler University M
Indiana State University M
Indiana University Bloomington M
Purdue University M, W
St. Joseph's College M
Taylor University M
Tri-State University M
University of Indianapolis M
University of Notre Dame M
Valparaiso University M

Iowa

Graceland College M
Iowa Central Community College
  M
Iowa Lakes Community College M
Iowa State University M
Iowa Wesleyan College M
Morningside College M
North Iowa Area Community
  College M
Northwestern College M
St. Ambrose University M
Teikyo Westmar University M
University of Iowa M
University of Northern Iowa M
Waldorf College M

Kansas

Baker University M
Benedictine College M
Bethany College M, W
Bethel College M
Butler County Community College
  M
Coffeyville Community College M
Dodge City Community College M
Emporia State University M
Fort Hays State University M
Fort Scott Community College M
Friends University M
Garden City Community College M
Hutchinson Community College M
Kansas State University M
McPherson College M
MidAmerica Nazarene College M
Ottawa University M
Southwestern College M
Sterling College M
University of Kansas M

Kentucky

Campbellsville College M
Eastern Kentucky University M
Kentucky State University M
Morehead State University M
Murray State University M
Union College M
University of Kentucky M
University of Louisville M
Western Kentucky University M

Louisiana

Grambling State University M
Louisiana State University and
  Agricultural and Mechanical
  College M
Louisiana Tech University M
Nicholls State University M
Northeast Louisiana University M
Northwestern State University M
Tulane University M
University of Southwestern
  Louisiana M

Maine

University of Maine M

Maryland

Bowie State University M
Morgan State University M
Towson State University M
University of Maryland: College
  Park M

Massachusetts

American International College M
Boston College M
Boston University M
Dean College M
Northeastern University M
University of Massachusetts
  Amherst M

Michigan

Central Michigan University M
Eastern Michigan University M
Hillsdale College M
Michigan State University M
Michigan Technological University
  M
Northern Michigan University M
Northwood University M
Saginaw Valley State University M
University of Michigan M
Wayne State University M
Western Michigan University M

Minnesota

Bemidji State University M
Mankato State University M
Moorhead State University M
St. Cloud State University M
Southwest State University M
University of Minnesota
  Crookston M
  Duluth M
  Twin Cities M
Winona State University M

Mississippi

Alcorn State University M
Copiah-Lincoln Community College
  M
Delta State University M
East Central Community College M
Hinds Community College M
Holmes Community College M
Mississippi College M
Mississippi State University M
Mississippi Valley State University
  M
University of Mississippi M

Missouri

Central Missouri State University M
Culver-Stockton College M
Lindenwood College M
Missouri Southern State College M
Missouri Western State College M
Northeast Missouri State University
  M
Southeast Missouri State University
  M
Southwest Baptist University M
Southwest Missouri State University
  M
University of Missouri
  Columbia M
  Rolla M
  St. Louis M
William Jewell College M

Montana

Carroll College M
Montana State University-Bozeman
  M

Montana Tech of The University of
  Montana M
Rocky Mountain College M
Western Montana College of the
  University of Montana M

Nebraska

Concordia College M
Dana College M
Doane College M
Hastings College M
McCook Community College M
Midland Lutheran College M
Peru State College M
University of Nebraska
  Kearney M
  Omaha M
Wayne State College M

Nevada

University of Nevada: Reno M

New Hampshire

University of New Hampshire M

New Jersey

Rutgers, The State University of
  New Jersey
  College of Engineering M
  College of Pharmacy M
  Cook College M
  Livingston College M
  Mason Gross School of the
    Arts M
  Rutgers College M

New Mexico

Eastern New Mexico University M
New Mexico Highlands University
  M
New Mexico Military Institute M
New Mexico State University M
University of New Mexico M

New York

Fordham University M
Hofstra University M
State University of New York at
  Buffalo M
Syracuse University M

North Carolina

Appalachian State University M
Catawba College M
Duke University M
East Carolina University M
Elizabeth City State University M
Elon College M
Fayetteville State University M
Gardner-Webb University M
Johnson C. Smith University M
Lenoir-Rhyne College M
Livingstone College M
Mars Hill College M
North Carolina Agricultural and
  Technical State University M
North Carolina Central University
  M
North Carolina State University M
University of North Carolina at
  Chapel Hill M
Wake Forest University M
Western Carolina University M
Wingate College M
Winston-Salem State University M

North Dakota

Dickinson State University M
Mayville State University M
North Dakota State College of
  Science M
North Dakota State University M

University of Mary M
University of North Dakota M

Ohio

Ashland University M
Bowling Green State University M
Kent State University M
Malone College M
Miami University: Oxford Campus M
Ohio State University: Columbus Campus M
Ohio University M
Tiffin University M
University of Akron M
University of Cincinnati M
University of Findlay M
University of Toledo M
Urbana University M
Walsh University M
Youngstown State University M

Oklahoma

East Central University M
Northwestern Oklahoma State University M
Oklahoma Panhandle State University M
Southwestern Oklahoma State University M
University of Central Oklahoma M
University of Oklahoma M
University of Tulsa M

Oregon

Oregon State University M
Portland State University M
University of Oregon M

Pennsylvania

Bloomsburg University of Pennsylvania M
California University of Pennsylvania M
Cheyney University of Pennsylvania M
Duquesne University M
Edinboro University of Pennsylvania M
Geneva College M
Indiana University of Pennsylvania M
Kutztown University of Pennsylvania M
Lock Haven University of Pennsylvania M
Millersville University of Pennsylvania M
Penn State University Park Campus M
Shippensburg University of Pennsylvania M
Temple University M
University of Pittsburgh M
Villanova University M
West Chester University of Pennsylvania M
Westminster College M

Rhode Island

University of Rhode Island M

South Carolina

Clemson University M
Francis Marion University M
Furman University M
North Greenville College M
Presbyterian College M
South Carolina State University M
University of South Carolina M
Wofford College M

South Dakota

Augustana College M
Black Hills State University M
Dakota State University M
Dakota Wesleyan University M
Huron University M
Northern State University M
South Dakota State University M
University of Sioux Falls M

Tennessee

Austin Peay State University M
Carson-Newman College M
East Tennessee State University M
Lane College M
Tennessee Technological University M
University of Memphis M
University of Tennessee
  Chattanooga M
  Knoxville M
  Martin M
Vanderbilt University M

Texas

Abilene Christian University M
Angelo State University M
Baylor University M
Blinn College M
East Texas State University M
Kilgore College M
Prairie View A&M University M
Rice University M
Sam Houston State University M
Southern Methodist University M
Southwest Texas State University M
Stephen F. Austin State University M
Tarleton State University M
Texas A&M University M
Texas A&M University-Kingsville M
Texas Christian University M
Texas Tech University M
University of Houston M
University of North Texas M
University of Texas at Austin M
West Texas A&M University M

Utah

Brigham Young University M
Dixie College M
Snow College M
Southern Utah University M
University of Utah M
Utah State University M
Weber State University M

Virginia

College of William and Mary M
Hampton University M
James Madison University M
Liberty University M
Norfolk State University M
University of Richmond M
University of Virginia M
Virginia Military Institute M
Virginia Polytechnic Institute and State University M
Virginia State University M
Virginia Union University M

Washington

Central Washington University M
Eastern Washington University M
Pacific Lutheran University M
University of Puget Sound M
University of Washington M
Walla Walla Community College M
Washington State University M
Western Washington University M

West Virginia

Concord College M
Fairmont State College M
Marshall University M
Potomac State College of West Virginia University M
Shepherd College M
West Liberty State College M
West Virginia Institute of Technology M
West Virginia State College M
West Virginia University M
West Virginia Wesleyan College M

Wisconsin

University of Wisconsin-Madison M

Wyoming

University of Wyoming M

Canada

Simon Fraser University M

Golf

Alabama

Alabama State University M
Auburn University M, W
Enterprise State Junior College M
Gadsden State Community College M
Huntingdon College M
Jacksonville State University M, W
James H. Faulkner State Community College M, W
Northwest-Shoals Community College M, W
Samford University M, W
Snead State Community College M
Spring Hill College M, W
Troy State University M, W
University of Alabama
  Birmingham M, W
  Tuscaloosa M, W
University of Mobile M, W
University of Montevallo M, W
University of North Alabama M
University of South Alabama M, W

Arizona

Arizona State University M, W
Glendale Community College M
Mesa Community College M
Pima Community College M
Scottsdale Community College M
University of Arizona M, W

Arkansas

Arkansas State University M, W
University of Arkansas
  Fayetteville M, W
  Little Rock M, W

California

California Baptist College M
California State University
  Fresno M
  Long Beach M, W
  Northridge M
  Sacramento M
  San Bernardino M
Loyola Marymount University M
Pepperdine University M, W
Point Loma Nazarene College M
St. Mary's College of California M
San Diego State University M, W
San Jose State University M, W

University of California
  Berkeley M
  Irvine M
  Los Angeles M, W
University of the Pacific M
University of San Diego M
University of San Francisco M, W
University of Southern California M, W

Colorado

Colorado Christian University M, W
Colorado School of Mines M
Colorado State University M, W
Fort Lewis College M
Mesa State College W
Northeastern Junior College M
Regis University M
University of Colorado
  Boulder M, W
  Colorado Springs M
University of Northern Colorado M
University of Southern Colorado M, W

Connecticut

Central Connecticut State University M
Fairfield University M
Quinnipiac College M
University of Connecticut M
University of Hartford M, W

District of Columbia

American University M
George Washington University M
Georgetown University M

Florida

Bethune-Cookman College M
Brevard Community College M
Eckerd College M
Embry-Riddle Aeronautical University M
Flagler College M
Florida Atlantic University M, W
Florida Community College at Jacksonville M
Florida International University M, W
Florida Southern College M, W
Florida State University M, W
Lynn University M, W
Manatee Community College M
Nova Southeastern University M
Palm Beach Community College W
Rollins College M, W
St. Petersburg Junior College W
St. Thomas University M, W
Stetson University M, W
University of Central Florida M, W
University of Florida M, W
University of Miami W
University of North Florida M, W
University of West Florida M, W
Webber College M

Georgia

Abraham Baldwin Agricultural College M
Augusta College M
Augusta Technical Institute M
Brewton-Parker College M
Clayton State College W
Columbus College M
Georgia College M, W
Georgia Institute of Technology M
Georgia Southern University M
Georgia Southwestern College M
Kennesaw State College M
Mercer University M

Piedmont College M, W
Reinhardt College M
Shorter College M
Thomas College M, W
University of Georgia M, W
Valdosta State University M
West Georgia College M

Hawaii

University of Hawaii
    Hilo M
    Manoa M, W

Idaho

Boise State University M, W
University of Idaho M

Illinois

Bradley University M, W
College of St. Francis M
Danville Area Community College
    M, W
De Paul University M
Highland Community College M, W
Illinois State University M, W
John A. Logan College M
Lewis University M, W
Loyola University of Chicago M, W
McKendree College M, W
Moraine Valley Community College
    M
Morton College M, W
Northeastern Illinois University M,
    W
Northwestern University M, W
Olivet Nazarene University M
Rend Lake College M
Southern Illinois University at
    Carbondale M, W
University of Illinois at Urbana-
    Champaign M, W
Western Illinois University M

Indiana

Bethel College M
Butler University M
Goshen College M
Grace College M
Huntington College M, W
Indiana University Bloomington M,
    W
Indiana Wesleyan University M
Marian College M, W
Oakland City College M, W
Purdue University M, W
St. Francis College M
St. Joseph's College M, W
Taylor University M
Tri-State University M, W
University of Evansville M
University of Indianapolis M, W
University of Notre Dame M, W
University of Southern Indiana M
Vincennes University M, W

Iowa

Briar Cliff College M, W
Drake University M
Grand View College W
Indian Hills Community College M
Iowa Central Community College
    M, W
Iowa Lakes Community College M,
    W
Iowa State University M, W
Iowa Wesleyan College M, W
Marshalltown Community College
    M, W
North Iowa Area Community
    College M
Northwestern College M, W
St. Ambrose University M, W

Teikyo Westmar University M, W
University of Iowa M, W
University of Northern Iowa W
Waldorf College M, W

Kansas

Allen County Community College
    M
Baker University M
Benedictine College M, W
Butler County Community College
    M
Coffeyville Community College M
Dodge City Community College M,
    W
Friends University M
Garden City Community College M
Hutchinson Community College M
Johnson County Community
    College M
Kansas Newman College M
Kansas State University M, W
McPherson College M, W
Ottawa University M
Southwestern College M
University of Kansas M, W
Wichita State University M, W

Kentucky

Bellarmine College M, W
Campbellsville College M, W
Cumberland College M, W
Eastern Kentucky University M
Georgetown College M
Kentucky State University M
Kentucky Wesleyan College M
Lindsey Wilson College M
Morehead State University M
Murray State University M, W
Northern Kentucky University M
Transylvania University M
Union College M
University of Kentucky M, W
University of Louisville M
Western Kentucky University M, W

Louisiana

Bossier Parish Community College
    M
Centenary College of Louisiana M
Grambling State University M
Louisiana State University and
    Agricultural and Mechanical
    College M, W
Louisiana Tech University M
Nicholls State University M
Northeast Louisiana University M
Northwestern State University M
Southeastern Louisiana University
    M
Tulane University M, W
University of New Orleans M
University of Southwestern
    Louisiana M

Maryland

Charles County Community College
    M, W
Loyola College in Maryland M
University of Maryland
    Baltimore County M
    College Park M

Michigan

Aquinas College M
Cornerstone College and Grand
    Rapids Baptist Seminary M
Detroit College of Business M
Eastern Michigan University M
Glen Oaks Community College M
Hillsdale College M
Kellogg Community College W

Lansing Community College M
Michigan State University M, W
Northern Michigan University M
Northwood University M
Oakland University M, W
Saginaw Valley State University M
Spring Arbor College M
University of Michigan M, W
Wayne State University M

Minnesota

Mankato State University M, W
Moorhead State University M, W
University of Minnesota: Twin
    Cities M, W
Winona State University M, W

Mississippi

Alcorn State University M, W
Belhaven College M
Delta State University M
Mississippi State University M, W
Mississippi Valley State University
    M, W
University of Mississippi M, W

Missouri

Columbia College M, W
Culver-Stockton College M
Drury College M
Lincoln University M
Lindenwood College M, W
Missouri Southern State College M
Missouri Western State College M
Northeast Missouri State University
    W
St. Louis University M
Southeast Missouri State University
    M
Southwest Baptist University M
Southwest Missouri State University
    M, W
University of Missouri
    Columbia M, W
    Kansas City M, W
    Rolla M
    St. Louis M

Montana

Montana State University-Bozeman
    W

Nebraska

Central Community College W
College of St. Mary W
Concordia College M, W
Creighton University M, W
Hastings College M, W
McCook Community College M, W
Midland Lutheran College M, W
Northeast Community College M,
    W
Southeast Community College:
    Beatrice Campus M
University of Nebraska
    Kearney M, W
    Lincoln M
Wayne State College M, W
Western Nebraska Community
    College: Scottsbluff Campus M

Nevada

University of Nevada: Reno M

New Jersey

Caldwell College M, W
Fairleigh Dickinson University
    Edward Williams College M
    Teaneck M
Rider University M

Rutgers, The State University of
    New Jersey
    College of Engineering M, W
    College of Pharmacy M, W
    Cook College M, W
    Douglass College W
    Livingston College M, W
    Mason Gross School of the
        Arts M, W
    Rutgers College M, W
Seton Hall University M

New Mexico

New Mexico Junior College M
New Mexico Military Institute M
New Mexico State University M, W
University of New Mexico M, W

New York

Adelphi University M
Canisius College M, W
Dominican College of Blauvelt M
Fordham University M
Hofstra University M
Iona College M
Le Moyne College M
Long Island University: Brooklyn
    Campus M
Manhattan College M
Mercy College M
Monroe Community College M
Niagara University M
St. Bonaventure University M
St. John's University M
St. Thomas Aquinas College M
Wagner College M, W

North Carolina

Appalachian State University M, W
Barton College M
Belmont Abbey College M
Brevard College M
Campbell University M, W
Craven Community College M, W
Duke University M, W
East Carolina University M
Edgecombe Community College M
Elon College M
Fayetteville State University M
Gardner-Webb University M
High Point University M
Johnson C. Smith University M
Lenoir-Rhyne College M
Livingstone College M
Louisburg College M
Mars Hill College M
Mount Olive College M
North Carolina State University M,
    W
Pembroke State University M
Pfeiffer College M
Queens College M
St. Andrews Presbyterian College
    M, W
St. Augustine's College M, W
University of North Carolina
    Asheville W
    Chapel Hill M, W
    Charlotte M
    Greensboro M, W
    Wilmington M, W
Wake Forest University M, W
Western Carolina University M, W
Wingate College M

North Dakota

Dickinson State University M

Ohio

Bowling Green State University M,
    W
Cedarville College M

Clark State Community College M
Cleveland State University M
Kent State University M
Malone College M
Miami University: Oxford Campus M
Mount Vernon Nazarene College M
Ohio State University: Columbus Campus M, W
Ohio University M
Shawnee State University M
Sinclair Community College M
Southern State Community College M
Tiffin University M, W
University of Akron M
University of Dayton M, W
University of Findlay M, W
University of Toledo M, W
Urbana University M, W
Walsh University M
Wright State University M
Xavier University M, W
Youngstown State University M

Oklahoma

Cameron University M
Oklahoma City University M
Oklahoma Panhandle State University M, W
Oral Roberts University M, W
Phillips University M
St. Gregory's College M, W
Southwestern Oklahoma State University M
University of Central Oklahoma M
University of Oklahoma M, W
University of Tulsa M, W

Oregon

Oregon State University M, W
Portland State University M
University of Oregon M, W
University of Portland M

Pennsylvania

Duquesne University M
Edinboro University of Pennsylvania M
Gannon University M
Indiana University of Pennsylvania M
Mercyhurst College M, W
Millersville University of Pennsylvania M
Penn State University Park Campus M, W
Robert Morris College M
St. Francis College M, W
St. Joseph's University M
Temple University M
Villanova University M
West Chester University of Pennsylvania M

Rhode Island

University of Rhode Island M

South Carolina

Anderson College M
Charleston Southern University M, W
Clemson University M
Coastal Carolina University M, W
Coker College M
College of Charleston M, W
Erskine College M
Francis Marion University M
Furman University M, W
Limestone College M
North Greenville College M
Presbyterian College M, W

South Carolina State University M
Southern Wesleyan University M
Spartanburg Methodist College M
University of South Carolina at Aiken M
Winthrop University M, W
Wofford College M, W

South Dakota

Northern State University W
South Dakota State University M, W

Tennessee

Bethel College M
Carson-Newman College M
David Lipscomb University M
East Tennessee State University M, W
Freed-Hardeman University M
King College M
Lambuth University M
Lee College M
Lincoln Memorial University M
Middle Tennessee State University M
Milligan College M
Shelby State Community College M
Tennessee Technological University M, W
Tennessee Wesleyan College W
Tusculum College M
Union University M
University of Memphis M, W
University of Tennessee
Knoxville M, W
Martin M, W
Vanderbilt University M, W

Texas

Abilene Christian University M
Ambassador University M
Baylor University M, W
Concordia Lutheran College M
East Texas State University M
Incarnate Word College M, W
Lamar University—Beaumont M, W
Odessa College M
St. Edward's University M
St. Mary's University M
Sam Houston State University M
Southern Methodist University M, W
Southwest Texas State University M
Stephen F. Austin State University M
Texas A&M University M, W
Texas Christian University M, W
Texas Lutheran College M
Texas Tech University M, W
Texas Wesleyan University M
University of Houston M
University of Mary Hardin-Baylor M
University of North Texas M, W
University of Texas
Arlington M
Austin M, W
San Antonio M
Weatherford College M
West Texas A&M University M
Western Texas College M

Utah

Brigham Young University M, W
University of Utah M
Utah State University M
Weber State University M, W

Virginia

Bluefield College M
College of William and Mary W

George Mason University M
Hampton University M
James Madison University M, W
Liberty University M
Longwood College M, W
Old Dominion University M
Radford University M, W
St. Paul's College M
University of Richmond M
University of Virginia M
Virginia Commonwealth University M, W
Virginia Military Institute M
Virginia Polytechnic Institute and State University M
Virginia Union University M, W

Washington

Eastern Washington University M, W
Edmonds Community College M, W
Green River Community College M
Lower Columbia College M, W
Pacific Lutheran University M, W
St. Martin's College M, W
Spokane Community College M
Tacoma Community College M, W
University of Puget Sound M, W
University of Washington M, W
Walla Walla Community College M, W
Washington State University M, W
Western Washington University M

West Virginia

Bluefield State College M
Concord College M
Davis and Elkins College M
Marshall University M
University of Charleston M
West Liberty State College M
West Virginia Wesleyan College M

Wisconsin

University of Wisconsin
Green Bay M
Madison M, W

Wyoming

Eastern Wyoming College M, W
University of Wyoming M, W

Canada

Simon Fraser University M

Gymnastics

Alabama

Auburn University W
University of Alabama W

Alaska

University of Alaska Anchorage W

Arizona

Arizona State University W
University of Arizona W

California

California Polytechnic State University: San Luis Obispo W
California State University: Fullerton W
San Jose State University M, W
University of California
Berkeley M, W
Los Angeles W
Santa Barbara M, W

Colorado

University of Denver W

Connecticut

University of Bridgeport W

District of Columbia

George Washington University W
Howard University M, W

Florida

University of Florida W

Georgia

University of Georgia W

Idaho

Boise State University W

Illinois

Illinois State University W
University of Illinois
Chicago M, W
Urbana-Champaign M, W

Indiana

Ball State University W

Iowa

Iowa State University W
University of Iowa M, W

Kansas

Fort Hays State University M

Louisiana

Centenary College of Louisiana W
Louisiana State University and Agricultural and Mechanical College W

Maryland

Towson State University W
University of Maryland: College Park W

Massachusetts

Northeastern University W
University of Massachusetts Amherst M, W

Michigan

Eastern Michigan University W
Michigan State University M, W
University of Michigan M, W
Western Michigan University M, W

Minnesota

University of Minnesota: Twin Cities M, W
Winona State University W

Missouri

Southeast Missouri State University W
University of Missouri: Columbia W

Nebraska

University of Nebraska—Lincoln M, W

New Hampshire

University of New Hampshire W

New Jersey

Rutgers, The State University of
New Jersey
College of Engineering W
College of Pharmacy W
Cook College W
Douglass College W
Livingston College W
Mason Gross School of the
Arts W
Rutgers College W

New Mexico

University of New Mexico M, W

New York

Syracuse University M

North Carolina

North Carolina State University M,
W
University of North Carolina at
Chapel Hill W

Ohio

Bowling Green State University W
Kent State University M, W
Ohio State University: Columbus
Campus M, W

Oklahoma

University of Oklahoma M, W

Oregon

Oregon State University W

Pennsylvania

Indiana University of Pennsylvania
W
Penn State University Park Campus
M, W
Temple University M, W
University of Pittsburgh M, W
West Chester University of
Pennsylvania W

Puerto Rico

University of Puerto Rico: La
Montana Regional College M

Rhode Island

University of Rhode Island W

Tennessee

Southern College of Seventh-day
Adventist M, W

Texas

Texas Woman's University W

Utah

Brigham Young University M, W
Southern Utah University W
University of Utah W
Utah State University W

Virginia

College of William and Mary M, W
James Madison University M, W
Radford University M, W

Washington

Seattle Pacific University W

West Virginia

West Virginia University W

Arab Republic of Egypt

American University in Cairo M, W

Horseback riding

Kentucky

Midway College W
Murray State University M, W

Michigan

Hillsdale College M

Missouri

Park College M, W
William Woods University W

New York

Cazenovia College M, W
Molloy College M, W

North Carolina

St. Andrews Presbyterian College
M, W

Ice hockey

Alabama

University of Alabama in Huntsville
M

Alaska

University of Alaska
Anchorage M
Fairbanks M

Colorado

Colorado College M
University of Denver M

Connecticut

Fairfield University M
University of Connecticut M

Illinois

University of Illinois at Chicago M

Indiana

University of Notre Dame M

Maine

University of Maine M

Massachusetts

Boston College M
Boston University M
Merrimack College M
Northeastern University M
University of Massachusetts Lowell
M

Michigan

Michigan State University M
Michigan Technological University
M
Northern Michigan University M
University of Michigan M

Minnesota

Mankato State University M
St. Cloud State University M
University of Minnesota
Duluth M
Twin Cities M

New Hampshire

University of New Hampshire M

New York

Canisius College M
Clarkson University M

Rensselaer Polytechnic Institute M

North Dakota

North Dakota State University:
Bottineau M
University of North Dakota M

Ohio

Bowling Green State University M
Kent State University M
Ohio State University: Columbus
Campus M

Pennsylvania

Villanova University M

Rhode Island

Providence College M, W

Vermont

University of Vermont M

Wisconsin

University of Wisconsin-Madison M

Lacrosse

Colorado

Colorado School of Mines M

Connecticut

Fairfield University M
University of Hartford M

Delaware

University of Delaware M, W

District of Columbia

Georgetown University M

Indiana

Butler University M

Louisiana

Bossier Parish Community College
W

Maryland

Johns Hopkins University M
Loyola College in Maryland M, W
Mount St. Mary's College M
Towson State University M, W
University of Maryland
Baltimore County M, W
College Park M, W

Massachusetts

Boston College W
Boston University W
Dean College M
Mount Ida College M
University of Massachusetts
Amherst M, W
Lowell M

Michigan

Michigan State University M
Northwood University M

New Jersey

Monmouth College W

Rutgers, The State University of
New Jersey
College of Engineering M, W
College of Pharmacy M, W
Cook College M, W
Douglass College W
Livingston College M, W
Mason Gross School of the
Arts M, W
Rutgers College M, W

New York

Adelphi University M
Canisius College M
Hofstra University M, W
Long Island University
C. W. Post Campus M
Southampton College M
Manhattan College M
New York Institute of Technology
M
St. John's University M
Syracuse University M
Wagner College W

North Carolina

Duke University M
St. Andrews Presbyterian College M
University of North Carolina at
Chapel Hill M

Pennsylvania

Drexel University M
Lock Haven University of
Pennsylvania W
Millersville University of
Pennsylvania W
Penn State University Park Campus
M, W
St. Joseph's University M, W
St. Vincent College M
Shippensburg University of
Pennsylvania W
Temple University W
Villanova University M, W
West Chester University of
Pennsylvania M, W

South Carolina

Limestone College M

Tennessee

Vanderbilt University W

Virginia

College of William and Mary W
James Madison University W
Old Dominion University W
Radford University M
University of Richmond W
University of Virginia M, W
Virginia Military Institute M
Virginia Polytechnic Institute and
State University W

Rifle

Alabama

Jacksonville State University M, W
University of North Alabama M

Alaska

University of Alaska Fairbanks M,
W

California

University of San Francisco M, W

Georgia
Mercer University M, W
North Georgia College M, W

Illinois
De Paul University M, W

Kentucky
Murray State University M, W

Louisiana
Centenary College of Louisiana M, W

Missouri
University of Missouri: Kansas City M, W

Nevada
University of Nevada: Reno M, W

New Mexico
Eastern New Mexico University M, W

New York
Canisius College M, W
St. John's University M, W

Ohio
University of Akron M, W
Xavier University M, W

Pennsylvania
Duquesne University M, W

Tennessee
Austin Peay State University W
University of Memphis M
University of Tennessee: Martin M

Virginia
George Mason University M, W
Virginia Military Institute M

West Virginia
West Virginia University M, W

Wyoming
University of Wyoming M, W

Rowing (crew)

California
California State University:
Sacramento M, W

District of Columbia
George Washington University M, W

Florida
Florida Institute of Technology M, W
Stetson University M, W
University of Central Florida W

Iowa
University of Iowa W

Massachusetts
Boston University M, W
Northeastern University M, W

Nebraska
Creighton University M, W

New Jersey
Rutgers, The State University of New Jersey
College of Engineering M, W
College of Pharmacy M, W
Cook College M, W
Douglass College W
Livingston College M, W
Mason Gross School of the Arts M, W
Rutgers College M, W

New York
Syracuse University M, W

Pennsylvania
Drexel University M
Mercyhurst College M, W
Temple University M, W

Tennessee
University of Tennessee: Knoxville W

Virginia
University of Virginia W

Washington
Washington State University W

West Virginia
University of Charleston M, W

Wisconsin
University of Wisconsin-Madison M, W

Arab Republic of Egypt
American University in Cairo M, W

Canada
Simon Fraser University M, W

Rugby

Canada
Simon Fraser University M

Sailing

Virginia
Old Dominion University M, W

Skiing

Alaska
University of Alaska
Anchorage M, W
Fairbanks M, W

Colorado
University of Colorado at Boulder M, W
University of Denver M, W
Western State College of Colorado M, W

Florida
Florida Southern College M, W

Idaho
Albertson College M, W

Massachusetts
University of Massachusetts
Amherst M

Michigan
Northern Michigan University M, W

Minnesota
University of Minnesota: Twin Cities M, W

Montana
Montana State University-Bozeman W
Rocky Mountain College M, W

Nevada
Sierra Nevada College M, W
University of Nevada: Reno M, W

New Hampshire
University of New Hampshire M, W

New Mexico
University of New Mexico M, W

New York
Paul Smith's College M, W

North Carolina
Lees-McRae College M, W

Utah
Brigham Young University M, W
University of Utah M, W

Vermont
Green Mountain College M, W
University of Vermont M, W

Washington
Seattle University M, W

Skin diving

South Dakota
National College M

Soccer

Alabama
Alabama Agricultural and Mechanical University M
Auburn University W
Birmingham-Southern College M, W
Huntingdon College M, W
Spring Hill College M
University of Alabama
Birmingham M
Huntsville M
Tuscaloosa W
University of Mobile M, W
University of Montevallo M
University of South Alabama M, W

Arizona
Arizona Western College M
Glendale Community College M
Mesa Community College M
Pima Community College M
Scottsdale Community College M
South Mountain Community College M

University of Arizona W

Arkansas
John Brown University M
University of Arkansas
Fayetteville W
Little Rock M, W

California
Azusa Pacific University M, W
Biola University M
California Baptist College M, W
California Polytechnic State University: San Luis Obispo M
California State University
Bakersfield M
Fresno M
Fullerton M, W
Los Angeles M, W
Northridge M
Sacramento M, W
San Bernardino M, W
Christian Heritage College M
Concordia University M
Dominican College of San Rafael M, W
Fresno Pacific College M
Loyola Marymount University M, W
Master's College M, W
Pepperdine University W
Point Loma Nazarene College M
St. Mary's College of California M, W
San Diego State University M, W
San Jose State University M
Santa Clara University M, W
Southern California College M
United States International University M, W
University of California
Berkeley M, W
Los Angeles M, W
Santa Barbara M, W
University of San Diego M, W
University of San Francisco M, W
University of Southern California W
Westmont College M, W

Colorado
Colorado Christian University M, W
Colorado College W
Colorado School of Mines M
Fort Lewis College M, W
Mesa State College W
Metropolitan State College of Denver M, W
Regis University M, W
University of Colorado at Colorado Springs M
University of Denver M, W
University of Northern Colorado W
University of Southern Colorado M, W

Connecticut
Central Connecticut State University M, W
Fairfield University M, W
Quinnipiac College M, W
Teikyo-Post University M, W
University of Bridgeport M, W
University of Connecticut M, W
University of Hartford M, W
University of New Haven M, W

Delaware
Goldey-Beacom College M
University of Delaware M, W

District of Columbia
American University M, W
George Washington University M, W
Howard University M

Florida
Eckerd College M, W
Embry-Riddle Aeronautical University M
Flagler College M
Florida Atlantic University M, W
Florida Institute of Technology M, W
Florida International University M, W
Florida Southern College M
Florida State University W
Lynn University M, W
Nova Southeastern University M, W
Palm Beach Atlantic College M
Rollins College M
St. Leo College M
St. Thomas University M, W
Stetson University M, W
University of Central Florida M, W
University of North Florida M, W
University of South Florida M
University of Tampa M
University of West Florida M
Warner Southern College M
Webber College M

Georgia
Augusta College M
Brewton-Parker College M, W
Clayton State College M
Covenant College M, W
Georgia Southern University M, W
Mercer University M, W
North Georgia College M, W
Piedmont College M, W
Reinhardt College M
Thomas College M
Truett-McConnell College M
Young Harris College M

Hawaii
Hawaii Pacific University M, W
University of Hawaii at Manoa W

Idaho
Albertson College M, W
Northwest Nazarene College M

Illinois
Belleville Area College M
Bradley University M
College of St. Francis M, W
De Paul University M
Eastern Illinois University M, W
Illinois State University M
Judson College M, W
Lewis University M, W
Lincoln Land Community College M
Loyola University of Chicago M, W
McHenry County College M
McKendree College M, W
Moraine Valley Community College M
Northeastern Illinois University M
Olivet Nazarene University M
Quincy University M, W
Rosary College M
St. Xavier University M
Southern Illinois University at Edwardsville M, W
Trinity College M, W
University of Illinois at Chicago M
Western Illinois University M

Indiana
Bethel College M
Butler University M
Goshen College M, W
Grace College M, W
Huntington College M
Indiana University Bloomington M, W
Indiana University-Purdue University Indianapolis M
Indiana Wesleyan University M, W
St. Francis College M, W
St. Joseph's College M, W
Tri-State University M, W
University of Evansville M, W
University of Indianapolis M, W
University of Notre Dame M, W
University of Southern Indiana M
Valparaiso University M, W

Iowa
Briar Cliff College M, W
Drake University M
Graceland College M, W
Grand View College M
Iowa State University W
St. Ambrose University M, W
Teikyo Marycrest University M, W
Teikyo Westmar University M, W
Waldorf College M

Kansas
Allen County Community College M
Baker University M, W
Benedictine College M, W
Bethany College M, W
Bethel College M, W
Central College M, W
Coffeyville Community College M
Friends University M, W
Hesston College M
Johnson County Community College M
Kansas Newman College M, W
McPherson College M, W
Ottawa University W
St. Mary College M, W
Sterling College M, W

Kentucky
Bellarmine College M, W
Campbellsville College M
Cumberland College W
Georgetown College M
Kentucky Wesleyan College M, W
Lindsey Wilson College M, W
Midway College W
Northern Kentucky University M
Sue Bennett College M
Transylvania University M
Union College M, W
University of Kentucky M, W
University of Louisville M, W

Louisiana
Centenary College of Louisiana M, W

Maine
Husson College M
Unity College M
University of Maine M, W

Maryland
Charles County Community College M
Chesapeake College M
Dundalk Community College M, W
Hagerstown Junior College M
Loyola College in Maryland M, W
Mount St. Mary's College M, W
Towson State University M, W
University of Maryland
    Baltimore County M, W
    College Park M, W
    Eastern Shore M

Massachusetts
Becker College
    Leicester Campus M, W
    Worcester Campus M, W
Boston College M, W
Boston University M, W
Dean College M, W
Mount Ida College M, W
Northeastern University M
University of Massachusetts
    Amherst M, W
    Lowell M, W

Michigan
Aquinas College M, W
Detroit College of Business M
Eastern Michigan University M, W
Kellogg Community College M
Michigan Christian College M
Michigan State University M, W
Northwood University W
Oakland University M, W
Spring Arbor College M, W
University of Detroit Mercy M
Western Michigan University M

Minnesota
University of Minnesota
    Duluth W
    Twin Cities W

Mississippi
Belhaven College M
Hinds Community College M
Mary Holmes College M
Mississippi College M
Mississippi State University W
William Carey College M, W

Missouri
Avila College M, W
Central Methodist College M, W
Columbia College M
Culver-Stockton College M
Drury College M, W
Harris Stowe State College M, W
Lincoln University M
Lindenwood College M, W
Missouri Southern State College M
Northeast Missouri State University M, W
Park College M, W
Research College of Nursing M, W
Rockhurst College M, W
St. Louis Community College
    Forest Park M
    Meramec M
St. Louis University M
Southwest Baptist University M, W
Southwest Missouri State University M
State Fair Community College M
University of Missouri
    Kansas City M
    Rolla M
    St. Louis M, W
William Woods University W

Montana
University of Montana-Missoula W

Nebraska
Central Community College M
College of St. Mary W
Concordia College M
Creighton University M, W

York College M, W

New Hampshire
Franklin Pierce College M, W
Hesser College M, W
New Hampshire College M, W
Notre Dame College M, W
University of New Hampshire M, W

New Jersey
Bloomfield College M
Burlington County College M, W
Caldwell College M
Fairleigh Dickinson University
    Edward Williams College M
    Teaneck M
Georgian Court College W
Monmouth College M, W
Rider University M
Rutgers, The State University of New Jersey
    College of Engineering M, W
    College of Pharmacy M, W
    Cook College M, W
    Douglass College W
    Livingston College M, W
    Mason Gross School of the Arts M, W
    Rutgers College M, W
St. Peter's College M, W
Seton Hall University M, W

New Mexico
College of the Southwest W
University of New Mexico M, W

New York
Adelphi University M, W
Canisius College M, W
Cazenovia College M, W
City University of New York:
    Queens College M
College of St. Rose M, W
Concordia College M, W
Dominican College of Blauvelt M, W
Dowling College M
Fordham University M, W
Genesee Community College M, W
Hartwick College M
Hofstra University M
Houghton College M, W
Iona College M
Le Moyne College M, W
Long Island University
    Brooklyn Campus M
    C. W. Post Campus M, W
    Southampton College M, W
Manhattan College M, W
Marist College M, W
Mercy College M
Monroe Community College M, W
New York Institute of Technology M, W
Niagara County Community College M, W
Niagara University M, W
Nyack College M, W
Paul Smith's College M, W
Roberts Wesleyan College M, W
St. Bonaventure University M, W
St. Francis College M
St. John's University M, W
Siena College M, W
State University of New York at Buffalo M, W
Syracuse University M
Wagner College W

North Carolina
Appalachian State University M

Barton College M, W
Belmont Abbey College M
Brevard College M, W
Campbell University M, W
Catawba College M, W
Davidson College W
Duke University M, W
East Carolina University M, W
Elon College M, W
Gardner-Webb University M
High Point University M, W
Lees-McRae College M, W
Lenoir-Rhyne College M, W
Louisburg College M, W
Mars Hill College M, W
Montreat-Anderson College M, W
Mount Olive College M
North Carolina State University M, W
Pembroke State University M
Pfeiffer College M, W
Queens College M, W
St. Andrews Presbyterian College M, W
University of North Carolina
   Asheville M, W
   Chapel Hill M, W
   Charlotte M
   Greensboro M, W
   Wilmington M, W
Wake Forest University M, W
Wingate College M, W

North Dakota

University of Mary M, W

Ohio

Bowling Green State University M
Cedarville College M
Cleveland State University M
Malone College M
Mount Vernon Nazarene College M
Ohio Dominican College M
Ohio State University: Columbus Campus M, W
Shawnee State University M
Southern State Community College M
Tiffin University M, W
University of Akron M
University of Dayton M, W
University of Findlay M, W
University of Rio Grande M
University of Toledo W
Walsh University M, W
Wright State University M, W
Xavier University M, W

Oklahoma

Bartlesville Wesleyan College M, W
Oklahoma Christian University of Science and Arts M, W
Oklahoma City University M, W
Oral Roberts University M, W
Phillips University M
Southern Nazarene University M, W
University of Tulsa M, W

Oregon

Concordia College M
George Fox College M, W
Oregon State University M, W
Portland State University M
University of Portland M, W
Western Baptist College M, W

Pennsylvania

Bloomsburg University of Pennsylvania M, W
California University of Pennsylvania M, W

Drexel University M
Duquesne University M, W
Gannon University M, W
Geneva College M, W
Kutztown University of Pennsylvania M, W
Lock Haven University of Pennsylvania M, W
Manor Junior College M, W
Mercyhurst College M, W
Millersville University of Pennsylvania M
Penn State University Park Campus M, W
Point Park College M
Robert Morris College M, W
St. Francis College M, W
St. Joseph's University M
St. Vincent College M, W
Seton Hill College W
Shippensburg University of Pennsylvania M, W
Temple University M, W
University of Pittsburgh M
Villanova University M, W
West Chester University of Pennsylvania M, W

Puerto Rico

Inter American University of Puerto Rico: San German Campus M
University of Puerto Rico: Mayaguez Campus M

Rhode Island

Providence College M, W
University of Rhode Island M, W

South Carolina

Anderson College M, W
Charleston Southern University M, W
Clemson University M, W
Coastal Carolina University M
Coker College M, W
College of Charleston M, W
Erskine College M, W
Francis Marion University M, W
Furman University M, W
Lander University M
Limestone College M, W
Presbyterian College M, W
Southern Wesleyan University M
Spartanburg Methodist College M, W
University of South Carolina
   Aiken M
   Spartanburg M
Winthrop University M
Wofford College M, W

South Dakota

Dakota Wesleyan University W
University of Sioux Falls W

Tennessee

Belmont University M
Carson-Newman College M, W
Christian Brothers University M
David Lipscomb University M
King College M
Lambuth University M, W
Lee College M, W
Lincoln Memorial University M, W
Middle Tennessee State University M
Milligan College M
Tennessee Temple University M
Tennessee Wesleyan College M, W
Tusculum College M, W
University of Memphis M
University of Tennessee: Martin M

Vanderbilt University M, W

Texas

Ambassador University M, W
Angelo State University W
Incarnate Word College M, W
LeTourneau University M, W
St. Edward's University M, W
St. Mary's University M, W
Schreiner College M
Southern Methodist University M, W
Stephen F. Austin State University W
Texas A&M University W
Texas Lutheran College M, W
Texas Wesleyan University M
University of Mary Hardin-Baylor M
University of North Texas M
University of Texas at Austin M
West Texas A&M University M

Utah

Westminster College of Salt Lake City M

Vermont

Champlain College M, W
College of St. Joseph in Vermont M, W
Green Mountain College M, W
University of Vermont M

Virginia

Bluefield College M
College of William and Mary M, W
George Mason University M, W
James Madison University M, W
Liberty University M, W
Longwood College M
Old Dominion University M, W
Radford University M, W
University of Richmond M, W
University of Virginia M, W
Virginia Commonwealth University M
Virginia Military Institute M
Virginia Polytechnic Institute and State University M, W

Washington

Central Washington University M, W
Edmonds Community College M
Evergreen State College M, W
Gonzaga University M, W
Green River Community College M
Highline Community College M
Northwest College M
Pacific Lutheran University M, W
Pierce College M
Seattle Pacific University M
Seattle University M, W
Shoreline Community College M
Spokane Community College M, W
Tacoma Community College M
University of Puget Sound M, W
University of Washington M, W
Washington State University W
Western Washington University M, W

West Virginia

Alderson-Broaddus College M
Davis and Elkins College M
Marshall University M
Salem-Teikyo University M
University of Charleston M, W
West Virginia University M
West Virginia Wesleyan College M, W

Wheeling Jesuit College M, W

Wisconsin

Marquette University M, W
Northland College M
University of Wisconsin
   Green Bay M, W
   Madison M, W

Arab Republic of Egypt

American University in Cairo M

Canada

Simon Fraser University M, W

Softball

Alabama

Athens State College W
Auburn University W
Bevill State Community College W
Chattahoochee Valley Community College W
Enterprise State Junior College W
Faulkner University W
Gadsden State Community College W
Huntingdon College W
Jacksonville State University W
James H. Faulkner State Community College W
John C. Calhoun State Community College W
Lurleen B. Wallace State Junior College W
Miles College W
Northwest-Shoals Community College W
Samford University W
Snead State Community College W
Troy State University W
University of Mobile W

Arizona

Arizona State University W
Arizona Western College W
Eastern Arizona College W
Glendale Community College W
Mesa Community College W
Pima Community College W
Scottsdale Community College W
South Mountain Community College W
University of Arizona W

California

Azusa Pacific University W
California Baptist College W
California Polytechnic State University: San Luis Obispo W
California State University
   Bakersfield W
   Fresno W
   Fullerton W
   Long Beach W
   Northridge W
   San Bernardino W
Concordia University W
Point Loma Nazarene College W
St. Mary's College of California W
San Diego State University W
San Jose State University W
Southern California College W
University of California
   Berkeley W
   Los Angeles W
   Riverside W
University of the Pacific W

Colorado

Adams State College W
Colorado Northwestern Community
 College W
Colorado School of Mines W
Colorado State University W
Fort Lewis College W
Mesa State College W
Northeastern Junior College W
Regis University W
University of Colorado at Colorado
 Springs W

Connecticut

Central Connecticut State
 University W
Fairfield University W
Quinnipiac College W
Teikyo-Post University W
University of Bridgeport W
University of Connecticut W
University of New Haven W

Delaware

Goldey-Beacom College W
University of Delaware W

Florida

Bethune-Cookman College W
Brevard Community College W
Central Florida Community College
 W
Daytona Beach Community College
 W
Eckerd College W
Florida Atlantic University W
Florida Community College at
 Jacksonville W
Florida Institute of Technology W
Florida Southern College W
Florida State University W
Gulf Coast Community College W
Hillsborough Community College W
Lake City Community College W
Nova Southeastern University W
Okaloosa-Walton Community
 College W
Palm Beach Community College W
Pasco-Hernando Community
 College W
Rollins College W
St. Johns River Community College
 W
St. Leo College W
St. Petersburg Junior College W
St. Thomas University W
Stetson University W
Tallahassee Community College W
University of North Florida W
University of South Florida W
University of Tampa W
Valencia Community College W
Webber College W

Georgia

Abraham Baldwin Agricultural
 College W
Augusta College W
Brewton-Parker College W
Columbus College W
Emmanuel College W
Georgia College W
Georgia Southern University W
Gordon College W
Kennesaw State College W
Macon College W
Mercer University W
Middle Georgia College W
Paine College W
Piedmont College W
Reinhardt College W
Shorter College W

Thomas College W
Truett-McConnell College W
Valdosta State University W
West Georgia College W
Young Harris College W

Hawaii

Hawaii Pacific University W
University of Hawaii
 Hilo W
 Manoa W

Illinois

Belleville Area College W
Bradley University W
Carl Sandburg College W
College of St. Francis W
Danville Area Community College
 W
De Paul University W
Eastern Illinois University W
Highland Community College W
Illinois Eastern Community
 Colleges
  Lincoln Trail College M, W
  Olney Central College W
  Wabash Valley College W
Illinois Institute of Technology W
Illinois State University W
John A. Logan College W
Judson College W
Kaskaskia College W
Lake Land College W
Lewis University W
Lincoln Land Community College
 W
Loyola University of Chicago M, W
McHenry County College W
McKendree College W
Moraine Valley Community College
 W
Morton College W
Northeastern Illinois University W
Northwestern University W
Olivet Nazarene University W
Quincy University W
Rend Lake College W
St. Xavier University W
Southeastern Illinois College W
Southern Illinois University
  Carbondale W
  Edwardsville W
Trinity College W
University of Illinois at Chicago W
Western Illinois University W

Indiana

Ball State University W
Bethel College W
Butler University W
Goshen College W
Grace College W
Huntington College W
Indiana State University W
Indiana University Bloomington W
Indiana University-Purdue
 University Indianapolis W
Indiana Wesleyan University W
Marian College W
Oakland City College M, W
Purdue University W
St. Francis College W
St. Joseph's College W
St. Mary-of-the-Woods College W
Tri-State University W
University of Evansville W
University of Indianapolis W
University of Notre Dame W
University of Southern Indiana W
Valparaiso University W

Iowa

Briar Cliff College W
Drake University W
Graceland College W
Grand View College W
Indian Hills Community College W
Iowa Central Community College
 W
Iowa Lakes Community College W
Iowa State University W
Iowa Wesleyan College W
Marshalltown Community College
 W
Morningside College W
North Iowa Area Community
 College W
Northwestern College W
St. Ambrose University W
Teikyo Marycrest University W
Teikyo Westmar University W
University of Iowa W
University of Northern Iowa W
Waldorf College W

Kansas

Allen County Community College
 W
Baker University W
Benedictine College W
Bethany College W
Butler County Community College
 W
Central College W
Coffeyville Community College W
Colby Community College W
Cowley County Community College
 W
Dodge City Community College W
Emporia State University W
Fort Scott Community College W
Friends University W
Hutchinson Community College W
Johnson County Community
 College W
Kansas City Kansas Community
 College W
Kansas Newman College W
Neosho County Community College
 W
St. Mary College W
Sterling College W
University of Kansas W
Wichita State University W

Kentucky

Bellarmine College W
Campbellsville College W
Cumberland College W
Eastern Kentucky University W
Georgetown College W
Kentucky State University W
Kentucky Wesleyan College W
Midway College W
Northern Kentucky University W
Union College W

Louisiana

Centenary College of Louisiana W
Louisiana Tech University W
Nicholls State University W
Northeast Louisiana University W
Northwestern State University W
University of Southwestern
 Louisiana W

Maine

Husson College W
University of Maine W

Maryland

Bowie State University W

Charles County Community College
 W
Chesapeake College W
Dundalk Community College W
Hagerstown Junior College W
Mount St. Mary's College W
Prince George's Community College
 W
Towson State University W
University of Maryland
 Baltimore County W
 Eastern Shore W

Massachusetts

American International College W
Becker College
 Leicester Campus W
 Worcester Campus W
Boston College W
Boston University W
Dean College W
Mount Ida College W
University of Massachusetts
 Amherst W

Michigan

Aquinas College W
Central Michigan University W
Cornerstone College and Grand
 Rapids Baptist Seminary W
Eastern Michigan University W
Henry Ford Community College W
Hillsdale College W
Kellogg Community College W
Michigan Christian College W
Michigan State University W
Northwood University W
Saginaw Valley State University W
Southwestern Michigan College W
Spring Arbor College W
University of Detroit Mercy W
University of Michigan W
Wayne State University W
Western Michigan University W

Minnesota

Mankato State University W
Moorhead State University W
St. Cloud State University W
Southwest State University W
University of Minnesota
 Crookston W
 Duluth W
Winona State University W

Mississippi

Delta State University W
East Central Community College W
Hinds Community College W
Mary Holmes College W
Mississippi State University W
Mississippi University for Women
 W

Missouri

Avila College W
Central Methodist College W
Central Missouri State University W
Columbia College W
Culver-Stockton College W
Lincoln University W
Lindenwood College W
Missouri Southern State College W
Missouri Western State College W
North Central Missouri College W
Northeast Missouri State University
 W
Park College W
St. Louis Community College
 Forest Park W
 Meramec W
St. Louis University W

Southeast Missouri State University W
Southwest Baptist University W
Southwest Missouri State University W
University of Missouri
    Columbia W
    Kansas City W
    Rolla W
    St. Louis W
William Jewell College W
William Woods University W

Nebraska

College of St. Mary W
Concordia College W
Creighton University W
Dana College W
Doane College W
Hastings College W
Midland Lutheran College W
Peru State College W
University of Nebraska
    Kearney W
    Lincoln W
    Omaha W
Wayne State College W

New Hampshire

Franklin Pierce College W
Hesser College W

New Jersey

Bloomfield College W
Burlington County College W
Caldwell College W
Georgian Court College W
Rider University W
Rutgers, The State University of New Jersey
    College of Engineering W
    College of Pharmacy W
    Cook College W
    Douglass College W
    Livingston College W
    Mason Gross School of the Arts W
    Rutgers College W
St. Peter's College W
Seton Hall University W

New Mexico

New Mexico Highlands University W
New Mexico State University W
University of New Mexico W

New York

Adelphi University W
Canisius College W
Cazenovia College W
City University of New York:
    Queens College W
College of St. Rose W
Concordia College W
Dominican College of Blauvelt W
Fordham University W
Genesee Community College W
Hofstra University W
Iona College W
Le Moyne College W
Long Island University
    Brooklyn Campus W
    C. W. Post Campus W
    Southampton College W
Manhattan College W
Marist College W
Mercy College W
Molloy College W
Monroe Community College W
New York Institute of Technology W

Niagara County Community College W
Niagara University W
Pace University W
St. Bonaventure University W
St. Francis College W
St. John's University W
St. Thomas Aquinas College W
Siena College W
Wagner College W

North Carolina

Barber-Scotia College W
Barton College W
Campbell University W
East Carolina University W
Elon College W
Fayetteville State University W
Gardner-Webb University W
Johnson C. Smith University W
Lenoir-Rhyne College W
Livingstone College W
Louisburg College W
Mars Hill College W
Montreat-Anderson College W
Mount Olive College W
North Carolina Central University W
Pembroke State University W
Pfeiffer College W
Queens College W
St. Andrews Presbyterian College W
St. Augustine's College W
University of North Carolina
    Chapel Hill W
    Charlotte W
    Greensboro W
    Wilmington W
Wingate College W
Winston-Salem State University W

North Dakota

Mayville State University W
North Dakota State University W
University of Mary W
University of North Dakota W

Ohio

Ashland University W
Bowling Green State University W
Cedarville College W
Cleveland State University W
Kent State University W
Malone College W
Miami University: Oxford Campus W
Mount Vernon Nazarene College W
Ohio Dominican College W
Ohio State University: Columbus Campus W
Ohio University W
Shawnee State University W
Southern State Community College W
Tiffin University W
University of Akron W
University of Dayton W
University of Findlay W
University of Rio Grande W
University of Toledo W
Urbana University W
Walsh University W
Wright State University W
Youngstown State University W

Oklahoma

Cameron University M
Eastern Oklahoma State College W
Oklahoma Baptist University W
Oklahoma Christian University of Science and Arts W
Oklahoma City University W

Southern Nazarene University W
University of Central Oklahoma W
University of Oklahoma W
University of Tulsa W

Oregon

Clackamas Community College W
Concordia College W
George Fox College W
Oregon State University W
Portland State University W
University of Oregon W

Pennsylvania

Bloomsburg University of Pennsylvania W
California University of Pennsylvania W
Community College of Beaver County W
Drexel University W
Edinboro University of Pennsylvania W
Gannon University W
Geneva College W
Indiana University of Pennsylvania W
Kutztown University of Pennsylvania W
Lock Haven University of Pennsylvania W
Mercyhurst College W
Millersville University of Pennsylvania W
Penn State University Park Campus W
Philadelphia College of Pharmacy and Science W
Point Park College W
Robert Morris College W
St. Francis College W
St. Joseph's University W
St. Vincent College W
Seton Hill College W
Shippensburg University of Pennsylvania W
Temple University W
Villanova University W
West Chester University of Pennsylvania W
Westminster College W

Puerto Rico

University of Puerto Rico:
    Mayaguez Campus W

Rhode Island

Providence College W
University of Rhode Island W

South Carolina

Anderson College W
Charleston Southern University W
Claflin College W
Coastal Carolina University W
Coker College W
College of Charleston W
Erskine College W
Francis Marion University W
Furman University W
Lander University W
Limestone College W
Morris College W
North Greenville College W
South Carolina State University W
Southern Wesleyan University W
Spartanburg Methodist College W
University of South Carolina
    Aiken W
    Spartanburg W
Voorhees College W
Winthrop University W

South Dakota

Augustana College W
Dakota Wesleyan University W
Northern State University W
South Dakota State University W

Tennessee

Austin Peay State University W
Belmont University W
Bethel College W
Carson-Newman College W
Cleveland State Community College W
Freed-Hardeman University W
King College W
Lambuth University W
Lincoln Memorial University W
Milligan College W
Roane State Community College W
Tennessee Technological University W
Tennessee Wesleyan College W
Trevecca Nazarene College W
Tusculum College W
Union University W
University of Tennessee
    Chattanooga W
    Knoxville W
    Martin W

Texas

Abilene Christian University W
Baylor University W
Houston Baptist University W
Incarnate Word College W
Northwood University: Texas Campus W
St. Edward's University W
St. Mary's University W
Southwest Texas State University W
Stephen F. Austin State University W
Texas A&M University W
Texas Lutheran College W
Texas Wesleyan University W
University of Mary Hardin-Baylor W
University of Texas
    Arlington W
    Austin W
Vernon Regional Junior College W

Utah

College of Eastern Utah W
Dixie College W
Snow College W
Southern Utah University W
University of Utah W
Utah State University W
Utah Valley State College W

Vermont

Champlain College W
College of St. Joseph in Vermont W
Green Mountain College W

Virginia

Bluefield College W
George Mason University W
Hampton University W
Longwood College W
Norfolk State University W
Radford University W
St. Paul's College W
University of Virginia W
Virginia Union University W

Washington

Central Washington University W
Edmonds Community College W
Green River Community College W
Lower Columbia College W

Olympic College W
Pacific Lutheran University W
Pierce College W
St. Martin's College W
Shoreline Community College W
Spokane Community College W
University of Puget Sound W
University of Washington W
Walla Walla Community College W
Wenatchee Valley College W
Western Washington University W
Yakima Valley Community College
W

West Virginia

Alderson-Broaddus College W
Bluefield State College W
Concord College W
Davis and Elkins College W
Marshall University W
Shepherd College W
University of Charleston W
West Liberty State College W
West Virginia Institute of
Technology W
West Virginia State College W
West Virginia Wesleyan College W

Wisconsin

University of Wisconsin
Green Bay W
Madison W

Canada

Simon Fraser University W

Squash

New York

Nyack College M, W

West Virginia

Salem-Teikyo University W

Arab Republic of Egypt

American University in Cairo M, W

Swimming

Alabama

Auburn University M, W
University of Alabama M, W

Alaska

University of Alaska Anchorage M

Arizona

Arizona State University M, W
Northern Arizona University M, W
University of Arizona M, W

Arkansas

John Brown University M, W
University of Arkansas
Fayetteville M, W
Little Rock M, W

California

California State University
Bakersfield M, W
Fresno M
Northridge M, W
San Bernardino M, W
Pepperdine University W
San Jose State University W
Stanford University M, W

University of California
Berkeley M, W
Irvine M, W
Los Angeles W
Santa Barbara M, W
University of the Pacific M, W
University of San Diego W
University of Southern California
M, W

Colorado

Colorado School of Mines M, W
Colorado State University W
Metropolitan State College of
Denver M, W
University of Denver M, W
University of Northern Colorado W

Connecticut

Central Connecticut State
University M, W
Fairfield University M, W
University of Connecticut M, W

District of Columbia

American University M, W
George Washington University M,
W
Howard University M, W

Florida

Brevard Community College M, W
Eckerd College M, W
Florida Atlantic University M, W
Florida State University M, W
University of Florida M, W
University of Miami M, W
University of Tampa M, W

Georgia

Georgia Institute of Technology M
Georgia Southern University M, W
Mercer University M, W
Morehouse College M
University of Georgia M, W

Hawaii

University of Hawaii at Manoa M,
W

Illinois

Bradley University M, W
Illinois Institute of Technology M,
W
Loyola University of Chicago M
Northeastern Illinois University M,
W
Northwestern University M, W
Southern Illinois University at
Carbondale M, W
University of Illinois
Chicago M, W
Urbana-Champaign W
Western Illinois University M, W

Indiana

Ball State University M, W
Butler University M, W
Indiana University Bloomington M,
W
Purdue University M, W
University of Evansville M, W
University of Indianapolis M, W
University of Notre Dame M, W
Valparaiso University M, W
Vincennes University M, W

Iowa

Iowa State University M, W
University of Iowa M, W
University of Northern Iowa W

Kansas

University of Kansas M, W

Kentucky

Campbellsville College M, W
Transylvania University M, W
Union College M, W
University of Kentucky M, W
University of Louisville M, W
Western Kentucky University M

Louisiana

Louisiana State University and
Agricultural and Mechanical
College M, W
Northeast Louisiana University M,
W

Maine

University of Maine M, W

Maryland

Towson State University M, W
University of Maryland
Baltimore County M, W
College Park M, W

Massachusetts

Boston College W
Boston University M, W
Northeastern University M, W
University of Massachusetts
Amherst M, W
Lowell M

Michigan

Eastern Michigan University M, W
Hillsdale College W
Michigan State University M, W
Northern Michigan University W
Oakland University M, W
University of Michigan M, W
Wayne State University M, W

Minnesota

Mankato State University M, W
St. Cloud State University M, W
University of Minnesota: Twin
Cities M, W

Mississippi

Delta State University M, W
Mississippi University for Women
W

Missouri

Drury College M, W
Lindenwood College M, W
St. Louis University M, W
Southwest Missouri State University
M
University of Missouri
Columbia M, W
Rolla M
St. Louis M, W
William Woods University W

Nebraska

University of Nebraska
Kearney W
Lincoln M, W

Nevada

University of Nevada: Reno W

New Hampshire

University of New Hampshire W

New Jersey

Rider University M, W

Rutgers, The State University of
New Jersey
College of Engineering M, W
College of Pharmacy M, W
Cook College M, W
Douglass College W
Livingston College M, W
Mason Gross School of the
Arts M, W
Rutgers College M, W
St. Peter's College M, W
Seton Hall University M, W

New Mexico

New Mexico State University M, W
University of New Mexico M, W

New York

Adelphi University M, W
Canisius College M, W
City University of New York:
Queens College M, W
College of St. Rose M, W
Fordham University M, W
Iona College M
Manhattan College W
Marist College M, W
Monroe Community College M, W
Niagara University M, W
St. Bonaventure University M, W
St. Francis College M, W
St. John's University M, W
State University of New York at
Buffalo M, W
Syracuse University M, W

North Carolina

Davidson College W
East Carolina University M, W
North Carolina State University M,
W
Pfeiffer College W
University of North Carolina
Chapel Hill M, W
Wilmington M, W

North Dakota

University of North Dakota M, W

Ohio

Ashland University M, W
Bowling Green State University M,
W
Cleveland State University M, W
Miami University: Oxford Campus
M, W
Ohio State University: Columbus
Campus M, W
Ohio University M, W
University of Findlay M, W
University of Toledo M, W
Walsh University W
Wright State University M, W
Xavier University M, W

Oregon

Oregon State University W

Pennsylvania

Bloomsburg University of
Pennsylvania M, W
Drexel University M, W
Duquesne University M, W
Edinboro University of
Pennsylvania M, W
Gannon University M, W
Indiana University of Pennsylvania
M, W
Kutztown University of
Pennsylvania M, W
Lock Haven University of
Pennsylvania W

Millersville University of
  Pennsylvania W
Penn State University Park Campus
  M, W
St. Francis College W
Shippensburg University of
  Pennsylvania M, W
University of Pittsburgh M, W
Villanova University M, W
West Chester University of
  Pennsylvania M, W
Westminster College W

Puerto Rico

University of Puerto Rico
     La Montana Regional College
       M, W
     Mayaguez Campus M, W
University of the Sacred Heart M,
  W

Rhode Island

Providence College M, W
University of Rhode Island M, W

South Carolina

Clemson University M, W
College of Charleston M, W

South Dakota

South Dakota State University M,
  W

Tennessee

University of Tennessee: Knoxville
  M, W

Texas

Rice University W
Southern Methodist University M,
  W
Texas A&M University M, W
Texas Christian University M, W
University of Houston W
University of Texas at Austin M, W

Utah

Brigham Young University M, W
University of Utah M, W

Virginia

James Madison University M, W
Old Dominion University M, W
University of Richmond W
University of Virginia M, W
Virginia Military Institute M
Virginia Polytechnic Institute and
  State University M, W

Washington

Central Washington University M,
  W
Evergreen State College M, W
Pacific Lutheran University M, W
University of Puget Sound M, W
University of Washington M, W
Washington State University W

West Virginia

Salem-Teikyo University M, W
West Virginia University M, W
West Virginia Wesleyan College M,
  W
Wheeling Jesuit College M, W

Wisconsin

University of Wisconsin
     Green Bay M, W
     Madison M, W

Wyoming

University of Wyoming M, W

Arab Republic of Egypt

American University in Cairo M, W

Canada

Simon Fraser University M, W

Table tennis

Alabama

Snead State Community College M,
  W

Arizona

South Mountain Community
  College M, W

Maryland

Chesapeake College M

Ohio

Ohio State University: Columbus
  Campus M, W

Puerto Rico

University of Puerto Rico:
  Mayaguez Campus M, W

South Carolina

Anderson College M, W
South Carolina State University M

Texas

Rice University M, W

Washington

Central Washington University M,
  W

West Virginia

Salem-Teikyo University M, W

Arab Republic of Egypt

American University in Cairo M, W

Tennis

Alabama

Alabama Agricultural and
  Mechanical University M
Auburn University M, W
Birmingham-Southern College M,
  W
Chattahoochee Valley Community
  College M, W
Enterprise State Junior College M,
  W
Huntingdon College M, W
Jacksonville State University M, W
James H. Faulkner State
  Community College M, W
Jefferson State Community College
  M, W
Lurleen B. Wallace State Junior
  College M
Miles College M, W
Northwest-Shoals Community
  College M, W
Samford University M, W
Spring Hill College M, W
Troy State University M, W
University of Alabama
     Birmingham M, W
     Huntsville M, W
     Tuscaloosa M, W
University of Mobile M, W
University of Montevallo W

University of North Alabama M, W
University of South Alabama M, W

Arizona

Arizona State University M, W
Glendale Community College M, W
Northern Arizona University M, W
Pima Community College M, W
Scottsdale Community College M,
  W
South Mountain Community
  College M, W
University of Arizona M, W

Arkansas

Arkansas State University W
Harding University M, W
John Brown University M, W
University of Arkansas
     Fayetteville M, W
     Little Rock M, W

California

Azusa Pacific University M
Biola University W
California Baptist College M
California Polytechnic State
  University: San Luis Obispo M,
  W
California State University
     Bakersfield M, W
     Fresno M
     Fullerton W
     Long Beach W
     Los Angeles M, W
     Northridge W
     Sacramento M, W
Dominican College of San Rafael
  M, W
Loyola Marymount University W
Marymount College M, W
Mount St. Mary's College W
Pepperdine University M, W
Point Loma Nazarene College M,
  W
St. Mary's College of California M,
  W
San Diego State University M, W
San Jose State University M, W
Southern California College M, W
Stanford University M, W
United States International
  University M, W
University of California
     Berkeley M, W
     Irvine M, W
     Los Angeles M, W
     Riverside M, W
     Santa Barbara M, W
University of the Pacific M, W
University of San Diego M, W
University of San Francisco M, W
University of Southern California
  M, W
Westmont College M, W

Colorado

Colorado School of Mines M
Colorado State University M, W
Mesa State College M, W
Metropolitan State College of
  Denver M, W
Northeastern Junior College M, W
Regis University M, W
University of Colorado
     Boulder M, W
     Colorado Springs M, W
University of Denver M, W
University of Northern Colorado M,
  W
University of Southern Colorado M,
  W

Connecticut

Central Connecticut State
  University M, W
Fairfield University M, W
Quinnipiac College M, W
University of Connecticut M, W
University of Hartford M, W
University of New Haven M

Delaware

Delaware State University M, W

District of Columbia

American University M, W
George Washington University M,
  W
Georgetown University W
Howard University M, W

Florida

Bethune-Cookman College M, W
Eckerd College M, W
Embry-Riddle Aeronautical
  University M
Flagler College M, W
Florida Atlantic University M, W
Florida Community College at
  Jacksonville M, W
Florida Institute of Technology M
Florida International University M,
  W
Florida Southern College W
Florida State University M, W
Hillsborough Community College W
Lynn University M, W
Nova Southeastern University W
Palm Beach Community College M,
  W
Rollins College M, W
St. Leo College M, W
St. Thomas University M, W
Stetson University M, W
University of Central Florida M, W
University of Florida M, W
University of Miami M, W
University of North Florida M, W
University of South Florida M, W
University of Tampa M, W
University of West Florida M, W
Webber College M, W

Georgia

Abraham Baldwin Agricultural
  College M
Augusta College M, W
Brenau University W
Brewton-Parker College M, W
Clark Atlanta University M, W
Columbus College M, W
Fort Valley State College M, W
Georgia College M, W
Georgia Southern University M, W
Gordon College W
Kennesaw State College W
Mercer University M, W
Morehouse College M
North Georgia College M, W
Piedmont College M, W
Savannah State College W
Shorter College M, W
Southern College of Technology M
Thomas College M, W
Truett-McConnell College M, W
University of Georgia M, W
Valdosta State University M, W
West Georgia College M, W
Young Harris College M, W

Hawaii

Hawaii Pacific University M, W

University of Hawaii
  Hilo M, W
  Manoa M, W

Idaho

Albertson College W
Boise State University M, W
Idaho State University M, W
Lewis Clark State College M, W
Northwest Nazarene College W
University of Idaho M, W

Illinois

Belleville Area College M, W
Bradley University M, W
Chicago State University M, W
College of St. Francis M, W
De Paul University M, W
Illinois Eastern Community
  Colleges: Olney Central College
  M
Illinois State University M, W
John A. Logan College M, W
Judson College M, W
Lake Land College M
Lewis University M, W
McHenry County College M, W
McKendree College M, W
Moraine Valley Community College
  W
Northeastern Illinois University M,
  W
Northwestern University M, W
Olivet Nazarene University M, W
Quincy University W
Rosary College M, W
Southern Illinois University
  Carbondale M, W
  Edwardsville M, W
Trinity College M, W
University of Illinois
  Chicago M, W
  Urbana-Champaign M, W
Western Illinois University M, W

Indiana

Ball State University M, W
Bethel College M, W
Butler University M, W
Goshen College M, W
Grace College M
Huntington College M, W
Indiana State University M, W
Indiana University Bloomington M,
  W
Indiana University-Purdue
  University Indianapolis M, W
Indiana Wesleyan University M, W
Marian College M, W
Purdue University M, W
St. Francis College W
Tri-State University M, W
University of Evansville M, W
University of Indianapolis M, W
University of Notre Dame M, W
University of Southern Indiana M,
  W
Valparaiso University M, W
Vincennes University M, W

Iowa

Drake University M, W
Graceland College M, W
Grand View College M, W
Iowa State University W
Northwestern College M, W
St. Ambrose University M, W
Teikyo Westmar University M, W
University of Iowa M, W
University of Northern Iowa W

Kansas

Baker University M, W
Benedictine College M, W
Bethany College M, W
Bethel College M, W
Butler County Community College
  M, W
Central College M, W
Coffeyville Community College M,
  W
Cowley County Community College
  M, W
Emporia State University M, W
Fort Hays State University W
Friends University M, W
Hesston College M, W
Hutchinson Community College M,
  W
Independence Community College
  M, W
Johnson County Community
  College M, W
Kansas State University M
McPherson College M, W
Ottawa University M, W
Pratt Community College M, W
Seward County Community College
  M, W
Southwestern College M, W
University of Kansas M, W
Wichita State University M, W

Kentucky

Bellarmine College M, W
Campbellsville College M, W
Cumberland College M, W
Eastern Kentucky University M, W
Georgetown College M, W
Kentucky State University M, W
Kentucky Wesleyan College M, W
Morehead State University M, W
Murray State University M, W
Northern Kentucky University M,
  W
Transylvania University M, W
Union College M, W
University of Kentucky M, W
University of Louisville M, W
Western Kentucky University M, W

Louisiana

Bossier Parish Community College
  M, W
Centenary College of Louisiana M,
  W
Grambling State University M, W
Louisiana State University and
  Agricultural and Mechanical
  College M, W
Louisiana Tech University W
Nicholls State University W
Northeast Louisiana University M,
  W
Northwestern State University W
Southeastern Louisiana University
  M, W
Tulane University M, W
University of New Orleans M, W
University of Southwestern
  Louisiana M, W

Maryland

Charles County Community College
  M, W
Dundalk Community College M, W
Morgan State University M, W
Mount St. Mary's College M, W
Towson State University M, W
University of Maryland
  Baltimore County M, W
  College Park M, W
  Eastern Shore M, W

Massachusetts

Becker College
  Leicester Campus M
  Worcester Campus M
Boston College W
Boston University W
Dean College M
University of Massachusetts
  Amherst M, W
  Lowell M, W

Michigan

Aquinas College M, W
Eastern Michigan University M, W
Henry Ford Community College M,
  W
Hillsdale College M, W
Michigan State University M, W
Michigan Technological University
  W
Northern Michigan University W
Northwood University M, W
Oakland University W
Saginaw Valley State University W
Spring Arbor College M, W
University of Detroit Mercy M
University of Michigan M, W
Wayne State University M, W
Western Michigan University M, W

Minnesota

Bemidji State University W
Mankato State University M, W
Moorhead State University M, W
St. Cloud State University M, W
Southwest State University W
University of Minnesota
  Duluth M, W
  Twin Cities M, W
Winona State University M, W

Mississippi

Alcorn State University M, W
Belhaven College M, W
Blue Mountain College W
Delta State University M, W
Hinds Community College M, W
Holmes Community College M, W
Mississippi State University M, W
Mississippi University for Women
  W
University of Mississippi M, W
William Carey College M, W

Missouri

Central Methodist College M, W
Culver-Stockton College M, W
Drury College M, W
Jefferson College M
Lincoln University M, W
Missouri Southern State College W
Missouri Western State College W
Northeast Missouri State University
  M, W
Research College of Nursing M, W
Rockhurst College M, W
St. Louis Community College at
  Forest Park M
St. Louis University M, W
Southeast Missouri State University
  W
Southwest Baptist University M, W
Southwest Missouri State University
  M, W
University of Missouri
  Kansas City M, W
  St. Louis M, W
William Woods University W

Montana

Montana State University
  Billings M, W
  Bozeman M, W
University of Montana-Missoula M,
  W

Nebraska

College of St. Mary W
Concordia College M, W
Creighton University M, W
Hastings College M, W
Midland Lutheran College M, W
University of Nebraska
  Kearney M, W
  Lincoln M, W
York College M, W

Nevada

University of Nevada: Reno M, W

New Hampshire

Franklin Pierce College M, W

New Jersey

Burlington County College M, W
Caldwell College M, W
Fairleigh Dickinson University
  Edward Williams College M,
  W
  Teaneck M, W
Monmouth College M, W
Rider University M, W
Rutgers, The State University of
  New Jersey
  College of Engineering M, W
  College of Pharmacy M, W
  Cook College M, W
  Douglass College W
  Livingston College M, W
  Mason Gross School of the
  Arts M, W
  Rutgers College M, W
St. Peter's College M, W
Seton Hall University M, W

New Mexico

Eastern New Mexico University W
New Mexico Military Institute M
New Mexico State University M, W
University of New Mexico M, W

New York

Adelphi University M, W
Canisius College M, W
Cazenovia College M, W
City University of New York:
  Queens College M, W
College of St. Rose M, W
Concordia College M, W
Dowling College M, W
Fordham University M, W
Hofstra University M, W
Iona College M, W
Le Moyne College M, W
Manhattan College M, W
Marist College M, W
Mercy College M
Molloy College W
Monroe Community College M, W
Niagara University M, W
Pace University M, W
St. Bonaventure University M, W
St. Francis College M, W
St. John's University M, W
State University of New York at
  Buffalo M, W
Syracuse University W
Wagner College M, W

North Carolina

Appalachian State University M, W

Barber-Scotia College M, W
Barton College M, W
Belmont Abbey College M, W
Campbell University M, W
Catawba College M, W
Craven Community College M, W
Davidson College W
Duke University M, W
East Carolina University M, W
Elon College M, W
Fayetteville State University W
Gardner-Webb University M, W
High Point University M, W
Johnson C. Smith University M
Lees-McRae College M, W
Lenoir-Rhyne College M, W
Livingstone College M
Louisburg College M, W
Mars Hill College M, W
Mount Olive College M, W
North Carolina Central University M, W
North Carolina State University M, W
Peace College W
Pfeiffer College M, W
Queens College M, W
St. Andrews Presbyterian College M, W
St. Augustine's College M
University of North Carolina
    Asheville M, W
    Chapel Hill M, W
    Charlotte M, W
    Greensboro M, W
    Wilmington M, W
Wake Forest University M, W
Western Carolina University W
Wingate College M, W
Winston-Salem State University M, W

North Dakota

Dickinson State University M, W
University of Mary M, W

Ohio

Bowling Green State University M, W
Cedarville College M, W
Cleveland State University W
Lake Erie College W
Malone College M, W
Miami University: Oxford Campus M, W
Mount Vernon Nazarene College M, W
Ohio State University: Columbus Campus M, W
Shawnee State University W
Sinclair Community College M, W
Tiffin University M, W
University of Akron M, W
University of Dayton M, W
University of Findlay M, W
University of Toledo M, W
Walsh University M, W
Wright State University M, W
Xavier University M, W
Youngstown State University M, W

Oklahoma

Cameron University M
East Central University W
Oklahoma Baptist University M
Oklahoma Christian University of Science and Arts M
Oklahoma City University M, W
Oral Roberts University M, W
St. Gregory's College M, W
Southwestern Oklahoma State University M, W

University of Central Oklahoma M, W
University of Oklahoma M, W
University of Tulsa M, W

Oregon

Portland State University W
University of Oregon M, W
University of Portland M, W

Pennsylvania

Bloomsburg University of Pennsylvania W
California University of Pennsylvania W
Cheyney University of Pennsylvania M, W
Drexel University M
Duquesne University M, W
Edinboro University of Pennsylvania M, W
Gannon University M, W
Geneva College M, W
Indiana University of Pennsylvania W
Kutztown University of Pennsylvania M, W
Mercyhurst College M, W
Millersville University of Pennsylvania M, W
Penn State University Park Campus M, W
Robert Morris College M, W
St. Francis College M, W
St. Joseph's University M, W
St. Vincent College M
Seton Hill College W
Shippensburg University of Pennsylvania W
Temple University M, W
University of Pittsburgh M, W
Villanova University M, W
West Chester University of Pennsylvania M, W
Westminster College W

Puerto Rico

Inter American University of Puerto Rico: San German Campus M, W
University of Puerto Rico
    Bayamon Technological University College M, W
    Mayaguez Campus M, W
University of the Sacred Heart M, W

Rhode Island

Providence College M, W

South Carolina

Anderson College M, W
Charleston Southern University M, W
Claflin College M, W
Clemson University M, W
Coastal Carolina University M, W
Coker College M, W
College of Charleston M, W
Erskine College M, W
Francis Marion University M, W
Furman University M, W
Lander University M, W
Limestone College M, W
North Greenville College M
Presbyterian College M, W
South Carolina State University M, W
Spartanburg Methodist College W
University of South Carolina
    Columbia M, W
    Spartanburg M, W
Winthrop University M, W

Wofford College M, W

South Dakota

Augustana College M, W
Northern State University W
University of Sioux Falls M, W

Tennessee

Austin Peay State University M, W
Belmont University M, W
Bethel College W
Carson-Newman College M, W
Christian Brothers University M, W
David Lipscomb University M, W
East Tennessee State University M, W
Freed-Hardeman University M, W
Lambuth University M, W
Lee College M, W
Lincoln Memorial University M, W
Middle Tennessee State University M, W
Milligan College M, W
Tennessee Technological University M, W
Tennessee Wesleyan College W
Union University M, W
University of Memphis M, W
University of Tennessee
    Chattanooga M, W
    Knoxville M, W
    Martin M, W
Vanderbilt University M, W

Texas

Ambassador University M, W
Baylor University M, W
Collin County Community College District M
Concordia Lutheran College M, W
Incarnate Word College M, W
Lamar University—Beaumont M, W
Laredo Community College M, W
Lee College W
North Central Texas College W
Rice University M, W
St. Edward's University M, W
St. Mary's University M, W
Sam Houston State University W
Schreiner College M, W
Southern Methodist University M, W
Southwest Texas State University M, W
Stephen F. Austin State University W
Texas A&M University M, W
Texas A&M University-Kingsville M, W
Texas Christian University M, W
Texas Lutheran College M, W
Texas Tech University M, W
Texas Wesleyan University M, W
Texas Woman's University W
University of Houston W
University of Mary Hardin-Baylor M, W
University of North Texas M, W
University of Texas
    Arlington M, W
    Austin M, W
    San Antonio M, W
Weatherford College M
West Texas A&M University M, W
Wharton County Junior College M, W

Utah

Brigham Young University M, W
Southern Utah University W
University of Utah M, W
Utah State University M, W

Weber State University M, W

Virginia

Bluefield College M
Clinch Valley College of the University of Virginia M, W
College of William and Mary M, W
George Mason University M, W
Hampton University M
James Madison University M, W
Liberty University M
Longwood College W
Old Dominion University M, W
Radford University M, W
St. Paul's College M, W
University of Richmond M, W
University of Virginia M, W
Virginia Commonwealth University M, W
Virginia Intermont College M, W
Virginia Military Institute M
Virginia Polytechnic Institute and State University M, W
Virginia Union University M, W

Washington

Eastern Washington University M, W
Green River Community College M, W
Lower Columbia College W
Pacific Lutheran University M, W
Seattle University M, W
Shoreline Community College M, W
Spokane Community College M, W
University of Puget Sound M, W
University of Washington M, W
Walla Walla Community College M, W
Washington State University M, W
Western Washington University M, W
Yakima Valley Community College M, W

West Virginia

Bluefield State College M, W
Concord College M, W
Davis and Elkins College M, W
Marshall University W
University of Charleston M, W
West Liberty State College M, W
West Virginia Institute of Technology M, W
West Virginia University M, W
West Virginia Wesleyan College M, W

Wisconsin

Marquette University M, W
University of Wisconsin
    Green Bay M, W
    Madison M, W

Arab Republic of Egypt

American University in Cairo M, W

Track and field

Alabama

Alabama Agricultural and Mechanical University M, W
Alabama State University M, W
Auburn University M, W
Chattahoochee Valley Community College M, W
Gadsden State Community College M, W

274

Lawson State Community College M
Miles College M, W
Troy State University M, W
University of Alabama
Birmingham M, W
Tuscaloosa M, W
University of South Alabama M, W

Arizona

Arizona State University M, W
Glendale Community College M, W
Mesa Community College M, W
Northern Arizona University M, W
Pima Community College M, W
Scottsdale Community College M, W
South Mountain Community College W
University of Arizona M, W

Arkansas

Arkansas State University M, W
University of Arkansas
Fayetteville M, W
Little Rock M, W
Pine Bluff M, W

California

Azusa Pacific University M, W
Biola University M, W
California Baptist College M, W
California Polytechnic State University: San Luis Obispo M, W
California State University
Bakersfield M, W
Fresno M
Fullerton M, W
Long Beach M, W
Los Angeles M, W
Northridge M, W
Sacramento M, W
Fresno Pacific College M, W
Point Loma Nazarene College M, W
San Diego State University W
Southern California College M, W
University of California
Berkeley M, W
Irvine M, W
Los Angeles M, W
Riverside M, W
Santa Barbara M, W
University of Southern California M, W
Westmont College M, W

Colorado

Adams State College M, W
Colorado School of Mines M, W
Colorado State University M, W
University of Colorado at Boulder M, W
University of Northern Colorado M, W
Western State College of Colorado M, W

Connecticut

Central Connecticut State University M, W
University of Connecticut M, W
University of New Haven M

Delaware

Delaware State University M, W

District of Columbia

Georgetown University M, W
Howard University M, W

Florida

Bethune-Cookman College M, W
Brevard Community College M, W
Florida Agricultural and Mechanical University M, W
Florida Community College at Jacksonville M, W
Florida International University M, W
Florida Memorial College M
Florida State University M, W
University of Central Florida M, W
University of Florida M, W
University of Miami M, W

Georgia

Fort Valley State College M, W
Georgia Institute of Technology M, W
Morehouse College M
Paine College M, W
Savannah State College M, W
Shorter College M
University of Georgia M, W

Idaho

Boise State University M, W
College of Southern Idaho M, W
Idaho State University M, W
North Idaho College M, W
Northwest Nazarene College M, W
Ricks College M, W
University of Idaho M, W

Illinois

Chicago State University M, W
Danville Area Community College M, W
De Paul University M, W
Eastern Illinois University M, W
Illinois State University M, W
Lewis University M, W
Loyola University of Chicago M, W
Olivet Nazarene University M, W
Southern Illinois University
Carbondale M, W
Edwardsville M, W
University of Illinois at Urbana-Champaign M, W
Western Illinois University M, W

Indiana

Ball State University M, W
Butler University M
Goshen College M, W
Grace College M, W
Huntington College M, W
Indiana State University M, W
Indiana University Bloomington M, W
Indiana Wesleyan University M, W
Marian College M, W
Purdue University M, W
St. Joseph's College M, W
Tri-State University M, W
University of Indianapolis M, W
University of Notre Dame M, W
Vincennes University M, W

Iowa

Drake University M, W
Graceland College M, W
Iowa State University M, W
Iowa Wesleyan College M, W
Morningside College M, W
Northwestern College M, W
St. Ambrose University M, W
Teikyo Westmar University M, W
University of Iowa M, W
University of Northern Iowa M, W

Kansas

Allen County Community College M, W
Baker University M, W
Benedictine College M, W
Bethany College M, W
Bethel College M, W
Butler County Community College M, W
Coffeyville Community College M, W
Colby Community College M, W
Emporia State University M, W
Fort Hays State University M, W
Garden City Community College M, W
Hesston College W
Hutchinson Community College M, W
Johnson County Community College M, W
Kansas City Kansas Community College W
Kansas State University M, W
McPherson College M, W
MidAmerica Nazarene College M, W
Neosho County Community College M, W
Ottawa University M, W
Pratt Community College M, W
Southwestern College M, W
Sterling College M, W
University of Kansas M, W
Wichita State University M, W

Kentucky

Cumberland College M, W
Eastern Kentucky University M, W
Kentucky State University M, W
Midway College W
Murray State University M, W
University of Louisville M, W
Western Kentucky University M, W

Louisiana

Grambling State University M, W
Louisiana State University and Agricultural and Mechanical College M, W
Louisiana Tech University M, W
Nicholls State University M, W
Northeast Louisiana University M, W
Northwestern State University M, W
Southeastern Louisiana University M, W
Tulane University M, W
University of New Orleans M, W
University of Southwestern Louisiana M, W

Maine

University of Maine M, W

Maryland

Bowie State University M, W
Hagerstown Junior College M, W
Morgan State University M, W
Mount St. Mary's College M, W
Towson State University M, W
University of Maryland
Baltimore County M, W
College Park M, W
Eastern Shore M, W

Massachusetts

Boston College M, W
Boston University M, W
Northeastern University M, W

University of Massachusetts
Amherst M, W
Lowell M, W

Michigan

Aquinas College M, W
Central Michigan University M, W
Eastern Michigan University M, W
Hillsdale College M, W
Michigan Christian College M, W
Michigan State University M, W
Northwood University M, W
Saginaw Valley State University M, W
Southwestern Michigan College M, W
University of Michigan M, W
Western Michigan University M, W

Minnesota

Bemidji State University M, W
Mankato State University M, W
Moorhead State University M, W
St. Cloud State University M, W
University of Minnesota
Duluth M, W
Twin Cities M, W
Winona State University W

Mississippi

Alcorn State University M, W
Hinds Community College M
Mississippi State University M, W
University of Mississippi M, W

Missouri

Central Methodist College M, W
Central Missouri State University M, W
Harris Stowe State College W
Lincoln University M, W
Lindenwood College M, W
Missouri Southern State College M, W
Northeast Missouri State University M, W
Park College M, W
Southeast Missouri State University M, W
Southwest Baptist University M, W
Southwest Missouri State University M, W
University of Missouri
Columbia M, W
Kansas City M, W
Rolla M, W
William Jewell College M, W

Montana

Montana State University-Bozeman M, W
University of Montana-Missoula M, W

Nebraska

Concordia College M, W
Dana College M, W
Doane College M, W
Hastings College M, W
Midland Lutheran College M, W
University of Nebraska
Kearney M, W
Lincoln M, W
Wayne State College M, W

Nevada

University of Nevada: Reno W

New Jersey

Fairleigh Dickinson University
    Edward Williams College M, W
    Teaneck M, W
Monmouth College M, W
Rider University M, W
Rutgers, The State University of New Jersey
    College of Engineering M, W
    College of Pharmacy M, W
    Cook College M, W
    Douglass College W
    Livingston College M, W
    Mason Gross School of the Arts M, W
    Rutgers College M, W
St. Peter's College M, W
Seton Hall University M, W

New Mexico

New Mexico Military Institute M
New Mexico State University M, W
University of New Mexico M, W

New York

Canisius College M, W
City University of New York:
    Queens College M, W
College of St. Rose M
Fordham University M, W
Houghton College M, W
Iona College M
Long Island University
    Brooklyn Campus M, W
    C. W. Post Campus M, W
Manhattan College M, W
Marist College M, W
New York Institute of Technology M, W
Roberts Wesleyan College M, W
St. Francis College M, W
St. John's University M, W
Syracuse University M, W
Wagner College M, W

North Carolina

Appalachian State University M, W
Barber-Scotia College M, W
Brevard College M, W
Campbell University M, W
Davidson College W
East Carolina University M, W
Elon College M
Fayetteville State University W
High Point University M
Johnson C. Smith University M, W
Lees-McRae College W
Livingstone College M, W
North Carolina Agricultural and Technical State University M, W
North Carolina Central University M, W
North Carolina State University M, W
Pembroke State University M
St. Augustine's College M, W
University of North Carolina
    Chapel Hill M, W
    Charlotte M, W
    Wilmington M
Wake Forest University M, W
Western Carolina University M, W
Winston-Salem State University M, W

North Dakota

Dickinson State University M, W
North Dakota State College of Science M, W
North Dakota State University M, W

University of Mary M, W
University of North Dakota M, W

Ohio

Ashland University M, W
Bowling Green State University M, W
Cedarville College M, W
Kent State University M, W
Malone College M, W
Miami University: Oxford Campus M, W
Ohio State University: Columbus Campus M, W
Ohio University M, W
University of Akron M, W
University of Findlay M, W
University of Rio Grande M, W
University of Toledo M, W
Urbana University M, W
Walsh University M, W
Youngstown State University M, W

Oklahoma

Oklahoma Baptist University M, W
Oklahoma Christian University of Science and Arts M, W
Oral Roberts University M, W
Southern Nazarene University M, W
Southwestern Oklahoma State University M, W
University of Central Oklahoma M, W
University of Oklahoma M, W
University of Tulsa M, W

Oregon

Chemeketa Community College M, W
Clackamas Community College M, W
George Fox College M, W
Linn-Benton Community College M, W
Mount Hood Community College M, W
Portland State University M, W
Treasure Valley Community College M, W
University of Oregon M, W
University of Portland M, W

Pennsylvania

Cheyney University of Pennsylvania M, W
Drexel University M
Duquesne University M, W
Edinboro University of Pennsylvania M, W
Geneva College M, W
Indiana University of Pennsylvania M, W
Kutztown University of Pennsylvania M, W
Lock Haven University of Pennsylvania M, W
Millersville University of Pennsylvania M, W
Penn State University Park Campus M, W
Robert Morris College M, W
St. Francis College M, W
St. Joseph's University M, W
Shippensburg University of Pennsylvania M, W
Temple University M, W
University of Pittsburgh M, W
Villanova University M, W
West Chester University of Pennsylvania M, W

Puerto Rico

Inter American University of Puerto Rico
    Metropolitan Campus M, W
    San German Campus M, W
University of Puerto Rico
    Bayamon Technological University College M, W
    La Montana Regional College M, W
    Mayaguez Campus M, W
University of the Sacred Heart M, W

Rhode Island

Providence College M, W
University of Rhode Island M, W

South Carolina

Anderson College M, W
Charleston Southern University M, W
Claflin College M, W
Clemson University M, W
Coastal Carolina University M, W
Francis Marion University M, W
Furman University M, W
Morris College M, W
South Carolina State University M, W
Voorhees College M, W
Winthrop University M, W
Wofford College W

South Dakota

Black Hills State University M, W
Dakota State University M, W
Dakota Wesleyan University M, W
Huron University M, W
Mount Marty College M, W
Northern State University M, W
South Dakota State University M, W
University of Sioux Falls M, W

Tennessee

Austin Peay State University W
Belmont University M, W
David Lipscomb University M
East Tennessee State University M, W
Middle Tennessee State University M, W
University of Tennessee
    Chattanooga M, W
    Knoxville M, W
    Martin M, W
Vanderbilt University M, W

Texas

Abilene Christian University M, W
Ambassador University M, W
Angelo State University M, W
Baylor University M, W
East Texas State University M, W
Lamar University—Beaumont M, W
Odessa College W
Prairie View A&M University W
Rice University M, W
Sam Houston State University M, W
South Plains College M
Southern Methodist University M, W
Southwest Texas State University M, W
Stephen F. Austin State University M, W
Tarleton State University M, W
Texas A&M University M, W
Texas Christian University M, W
Texas Tech University M, W

University of Houston M, W
University of North Texas M, W
University of Texas
    Arlington M, W
    Austin M, W
    San Antonio M, W
Wayland Baptist University M, W

Utah

Brigham Young University M, W
University of Utah M, W
Utah State University M, W
Weber State University M, W

Virginia

College of William and Mary M, W
George Mason University M, W
Hampton University M, W
James Madison University M, W
Liberty University M, W
Norfolk State University M, W
St. Paul's College M, W
University of Virginia M, W
Virginia Commonwealth University M, W
Virginia Military Institute M
Virginia Polytechnic Institute and State University M, W
Virginia Union University M, W

Washington

Central Washington University M, W
Eastern Washington University M, W
Highline Community College M
Lower Columbia College M, W
Northwest College M, W
Pacific Lutheran University M, W
Seattle Pacific University M, W
Spokane Community College M, W
University of Puget Sound M, W
University of Washington M, W
Washington State University M, W
Western Washington University M, W
Yakima Valley Community College M, W

West Virginia

Marshall University M, W
West Virginia State College M, W
West Virginia University M, W
West Virginia Wesleyan College M, W
Wheeling Jesuit College M, W

Wisconsin

Marquette University M, W
University of Wisconsin-Madison M, W

Wyoming

University of Wyoming M, W

Arab Republic of Egypt

American University in Cairo M, W

Canada

Simon Fraser University M, W

Volleyball

Alabama

Alabama Agricultural and Mechanical University W
Alabama State University W
Auburn University W
Bevill State Community College W

Enterprise State Junior College W
Gadsden State Community College W
Huntingdon College W
Jacksonville State University W
James H. Faulkner State Community College M, W
Lawson State Community College W
Miles College W
Northwest-Shoals Community College W
Samford University W
Snead State Community College W
Tuskegee University W
University of Alabama
    Birmingham W
    Huntsville W
    Tuscaloosa W
University of Montevallo W
University of North Alabama W
University of South Alabama W

Alaska

University of Alaska
    Anchorage W
    Fairbanks W

Arizona

Arizona State University W
Arizona Western College W
Eastern Arizona College W
Glendale Community College W
Northern Arizona University W
Pima Community College W
Scottsdale Community College W
University of Arizona W

Arkansas

Arkansas State University W
Harding University W
Henderson State University W
John Brown University W
Ouachita Baptist University W
University of Arkansas
    Fayetteville W
    Little Rock W
University of Central Arkansas W
Williams Baptist College W

California

Azusa Pacific University W
California Baptist College W
California Polytechnic State University: San Luis Obispo W
California State University
    Bakersfield W
    Fresno W
    Fullerton W
    Long Beach M, W
    Los Angeles W
    Northridge M, W
    Sacramento W
    San Bernardino W
Christian Heritage College W
Concordia University W
Dominican College of San Rafael M, W
Fresno Pacific College W
Holy Names College W
Loyola Marymount University M, W
Master's College W
Mount St. Mary's College W
Pepperdine University M, W
Point Loma Nazarene College W
St. Mary's College of California W
San Diego State University M, W
San Jose State University W
Santa Clara University W
Southern California College W

University of California
    Berkeley W
    Irvine W
    Los Angeles M, W
    Riverside W
    Santa Barbara M, W
University of the Pacific M, W
University of San Diego W
University of San Francisco W
University of Southern California M, W
Westmont College W

Colorado

Adams State College W
Colorado Christian University W
Colorado Northwestern Community College W
Colorado School of Mines W
Colorado State University W
Fort Lewis College W
Lamar Community College W
Mesa State College W
Metropolitan State College of Denver W
Northeastern Junior College W
Otero Junior College W
Regis University W
Trinidad State Junior College W
University of Colorado
    Boulder W
    Colorado Springs W
University of Denver W
University of Northern Colorado W
University of Southern Colorado W
Western State College of Colorado W

Connecticut

Central Connecticut State University W
Fairfield University M, W
Quinnipiac College W
University of Connecticut W
University of Hartford W
University of New Haven W

Delaware

Delaware State University W
University of Delaware W

District of Columbia

American University W
George Washington University W
Georgetown University W
Howard University W

Florida

Bethune-Cookman College W
Brevard Community College W
Eckerd College M, W
Embry-Riddle Aeronautical University M
Flagler College W
Florida Agricultural and Mechanical University M
Florida Atlantic University W
Florida Community College at Jacksonville W
Florida Institute of Technology W
Florida International University W
Florida Memorial College W
Florida Southern College W
Florida State University W
Hillsborough Community College W
Manatee Community College W
Nova Southeastern University W
Palm Beach Atlantic College W
Pasco-Hernando Community College W
Rollins College W
St. Leo College W

St. Thomas University W
Stetson University W
University of Florida W
University of North Florida W
University of South Florida W
University of Tampa W
Warner Southern College W
Webber College M, W

Georgia

Augusta College W
Covenant College W
Fort Valley State College W
Georgia Institute of Technology W
Georgia Southern University W
Mercer University W
Paine College W
University of Georgia M, W
Valdosta State University W
West Georgia College W

Hawaii

Hawaii Pacific University W
University of Hawaii
    Hilo W
    Manoa M, W

Idaho

Albertson College W
Boise State University W
College of Southern Idaho W
Idaho State University W
Lewis Clark State College W
North Idaho College W
Northwest Nazarene College W
Ricks College W
University of Idaho W

Illinois

Barat College W
Belleville Area College W
Bradley University W
Carl Sandburg College W
Chicago State University W
College of St. Francis W
Danville Area Community College W
De Paul University W
Eastern Illinois University W
Highland Community College W
Illinois Eastern Community Colleges
    Lincoln Trail College W
    Olney Central College W
    Wabash Valley College W
Illinois Institute of Technology M, W
Illinois State University W
John A. Logan College W
Judson College W
Kaskaskia College W
Lake Land College W
Lewis University M, W
Loyola University of Chicago M, W
McHenry County College W
McKendree College W
Moraine Valley Community College W
Morton College W
Northeastern Illinois University W
Northwestern University W
Olivet Nazarene University W
Quincy University M, W
Rosary College W
St. Xavier University W
Southern Illinois University
    Carbondale W
    Edwardsville W
Trinity College M, W
University of Illinois
    Chicago W
    Urbana-Champaign W

Western Illinois University W

Indiana

Ball State University M, W
Bethel College W
Butler University W
Goshen College W
Grace College M
Huntington College W
Indiana State University W
Indiana University
    Bloomington W
    Southeast W
Indiana University-Purdue University Indianapolis W
Indiana Wesleyan University M, W
Marian College W
Oakland City College M
Purdue University W
St. Francis College W
St. Joseph's College M, W
Tri-State University M, W
University of Evansville W
University of Indianapolis W
University of Notre Dame W
University of Southern Indiana W
Valparaiso University W
Vincennes University M, W

Iowa

Briar Cliff College W
Drake University W
Graceland College M, W
Grand View College W
Iowa Central Community College W
Iowa Lakes Community College M, W
Iowa State University W
Iowa Wesleyan College W
Morningside College W
North Iowa Area Community College W
Northwestern College W
St. Ambrose University W
Teikyo Marycrest University M, W
Teikyo Westmar University W
University of Iowa W
University of Northern Iowa W
Waldorf College W

Kansas

Allen County Community College W
Baker University W
Benedictine College W
Bethany College W
Bethel College W
Butler County Community College W
Central College W
Coffeyville Community College W
Colby Community College W
Cowley County Community College W
Dodge City Community College W
Emporia State University W
Fort Scott Community College W
Friends University W
Garden City Community College W
Hutchinson Community College W
Independence Community College W
Johnson County Community College W
Kansas City Kansas Community College W
Kansas Newman College W
Kansas State University W
McPherson College W
MidAmerica Nazarene College W

Neosho County Community College W
Ottawa University W
Pratt Community College W
St. Mary College W
Seward County Community College W
Sterling College W
University of Kansas W
Wichita State University W

Kentucky

Bellarmine College W
Campbellsville College W
Eastern Kentucky University W
Georgetown College W
Kentucky State University W
Kentucky Wesleyan College W
Midway College W
Morehead State University W
Murray State University W
Northern Kentucky University W
Sue Bennett College W
Union College W
University of Kentucky W
University of Louisville W
Western Kentucky University W

Louisiana

Centenary College of Louisiana W
Louisiana State University and Agricultural and Mechanical College W
Louisiana Tech University W
Nicholls State University W
Northeast Louisiana University W
Northwestern State University W
Southeastern Louisiana University W
Tulane University W
University of New Orleans W

Maine

Unity College W

Maryland

Bowie State University W
Charles County Community College W
Chesapeake College W
Dundalk Community College W
Garrett Community College W
Hagerstown Junior College W
Loyola College in Maryland W
Morgan State University W
Prince George's Community College W
Towson State University M, W
University of Maryland
 Baltimore County W
 College Park W
 Eastern Shore W

Massachusetts

American International College W
Becker College
 Leicester Campus W
 Worcester Campus W
Boston College W
Dean College W
Mount Ida College M
Northeastern University W
University of Massachusetts
 Amherst W
 Lowell W

Michigan

Aquinas College W
Central Michigan University M, W
Cornerstone College and Grand Rapids Baptist Seminary W
Eastern Michigan University W

Glen Oaks Community College W
Hillsdale College W
Kellogg Community College W
Lansing Community College W
Michigan Christian College W
Michigan State University W
Michigan Technological University W
Northwood University W
Oakland University W
Saginaw Valley State University W
Southwestern Michigan College W
Spring Arbor College W
University of Michigan
 Ann Arbor W
 Dearborn W
Wayne State University W
Western Michigan University W

Minnesota

Bemidji State University W
Mankato State University W
Moorhead State University W
St. Cloud State University W
Southwest State University W
University of Minnesota
 Crookston W
 Duluth W
 Twin Cities W
Winona State University W

Mississippi

Alcorn State University W
Mississippi State University W
Mississippi University for Women W
Mississippi Valley State University W
University of Mississippi W

Missouri

Avila College W
Central Methodist College W
Central Missouri State University W
College of the Ozarks W
Columbia College W
Culver-Stockton College W
Drury College W
Harris Stowe State College W
Jefferson College W
Lindenwood College M, W
Longview Community College W
Mineral Area College W
Missouri Southern State College W
Missouri Western State College W
Northeast Missouri State University W
Park College M, W
Research College of Nursing W
Rockhurst College M, W
St. Louis Community College at Forest Park W
St. Louis University W
Southeast Missouri State University W
Southwest Baptist University W
Southwest Missouri State University W
University of Missouri
 Columbia W
 Kansas City W
 St. Louis W
William Jewell College W
William Woods University W

Montana

Carroll College W
Montana State University
 Billings W
 Bozeman W
 Northern W

Montana Tech of The University of Montana W
Rocky Mountain College W
University of Montana-Missoula W
Western Montana College of the University of Montana W

Nebraska

Bellevue University W
Central Community College W
College of St. Mary W
Concordia College W
Creighton University W
Dana College W
Doane College M, W
Hastings College W
McCook Community College W
Midland Lutheran College W
Northeast Community College W
Peru State College W
Southeast Community College: Beatrice Campus W
University of Nebraska
 Kearney W
 Lincoln W
 Omaha W
Wayne State College W
Western Nebraska Community College: Scottsbluff Campus W
York College W

Nevada

Sierra Nevada College M
University of Nevada: Reno W

New Hampshire

Franklin Pierce College W
Hesser College M, W
University of New Hampshire W

New Jersey

Bloomfield College W
Fairleigh Dickinson University
 Edward Williams College W
 Teaneck W
Rider University W
Rutgers, The State University of New Jersey
 College of Engineering W
 College of Nursing M
 College of Pharmacy W
 Cook College W
 Douglass College W
 Livingston College W
 Mason Gross School of the Arts W
 Newark College of Arts and Sciences M
 Rutgers College W
St. Peter's College W
Seton Hall University W

New Mexico

College of the Southwest W
Eastern New Mexico University W
New Mexico Highlands University W
New Mexico State University W
University of New Mexico W

New York

Adelphi University W
Canisius College W
Cazenovia College W
City University of New York: Queens College W
College of St. Rose W
Concordia College M, W
Dominican College of Blauvelt W
D'Youville College M
Fordham University W
Genesee Community College M, W

Hofstra University W
Houghton College W
Iona College W
Le Moyne College W
Long Island University
 Brooklyn Campus W
 C. W. Post Campus W
 Southampton College M, W
Manhattan College W
Marist College M, W
Mercy College W
Molloy College W
New York Institute of Technology W
Niagara County Community College W
Niagara University W
Nyack College W
Pace University W
Sage Junior College of Albany W
St. Bonaventure University W
St. Francis College W
St. Thomas Aquinas College W
Siena College W
State University of New York at Buffalo W
Syracuse University W
Wagner College W

North Carolina

Appalachian State University W
Barber-Scotia College W
Barton College W
Belmont Abbey College W
Campbell University W
Catawba College W
Davidson College W
Duke University W
East Carolina University W
Elon College W
Fayetteville State University W
Gardner-Webb University W
High Point University W
Johnson C. Smith University W
Lees-McRae College W
Lenoir-Rhyne College W
Livingstone College W
Mars Hill College W
Montreat-Anderson College W
Mount Olive College W
North Carolina Agricultural and Technical State University W
North Carolina Central University W
North Carolina State University W
Pembroke State University W
Pfeiffer College W
Queens College W
St. Andrews Presbyterian College W
St. Augustine's College W
University of North Carolina
 Asheville W
 Chapel Hill W
 Charlotte W
 Greensboro W
 Wilmington W
Western Carolina University W
Wingate College W
Winston-Salem State University W

North Dakota

Dickinson State University W
North Dakota State College of Science W
North Dakota State University
 Bottineau W
 Fargo W
University of Mary W
University of North Dakota
 Grand Forks W
 Williston W

Ohio

Ashland University W
Bowling Green State University W
Cedarville College W
Clark State Community College W
Cleveland State University W
Kent State University W
Malone College W
Miami University: Oxford Campus W
Mount Vernon Nazarene College W
Ohio Dominican College W
Ohio State University: Columbus Campus M, W
Ohio University W
Shawnee State University W
Sinclair Community College M, W
Southern State Community College W
Tiffin University W
University of Akron W
University of Dayton W
University of Findlay W
University of Rio Grande W
University of Toledo W
Urbana University W
Walsh University W
Wright State University W
Xavier University W
Youngstown State University W

Oklahoma

Bartlesville Wesleyan College W
Cameron University M
Oral Roberts University W
Southern Nazarene University M, W
University of Central Oklahoma W
University of Oklahoma W
University of Tulsa W

Oregon

Clackamas Community College W
Concordia College W
George Fox College W
Linn-Benton Community College W
Mount Hood Community College W
Oregon State University W
Portland State University W
Treasure Valley Community College W
University of Oregon W
University of Portland W
Western Baptist College W

Pennsylvania

California University of Pennsylvania W
Carlow College M, W
Cheyney University of Pennsylvania W
Community College of Beaver County W
Duquesne University W
Edinboro University of Pennsylvania W
Gannon University W
Geneva College W
Indiana University of Pennsylvania W
Kutztown University of Pennsylvania W
Lock Haven University of Pennsylvania W
Manor Junior College W
Mercyhurst College W
Millersville University of Pennsylvania W
Penn State University Park Campus M, W
Point Park College W

Robert Morris College W
St. Francis College M, W
St. Vincent College W
Seton Hill College W
Shippensburg University of Pennsylvania W
University of Pittsburgh W
Villanova University W
West Chester University of Pennsylvania W
Westminster College W

Puerto Rico

Inter American University of Puerto Rico: San German Campus M, W
University of Puerto Rico
  Bayamon Technological University College M, W
  La Montana Regional College M, W
  Mayaguez Campus M, W
University of the Sacred Heart M, W

Rhode Island

Providence College W
University of Rhode Island W

South Carolina

Anderson College W
Charleston Southern University W
Claflin College M, W
Clemson University W
Coastal Carolina University W
Coker College W
College of Charleston W
Erskine College W
Francis Marion University W
Furman University W
Limestone College W
North Greenville College W
Presbyterian College W
South Carolina State University W
Southern Wesleyan University W
Spartanburg Methodist College W
University of South Carolina
  Aiken W
  Spartanburg W
Voorhees College W
Winthrop University W
Wofford College W

South Dakota

Augustana College W
Black Hills State University W
Dakota State University W
Dakota Wesleyan University W
Huron University W
National College W
South Dakota State University W
University of Sioux Falls W

Tennessee

Austin Peay State University W
Belmont University W
Carson-Newman College W
Christian Brothers University W
David Lipscomb University W
East Tennessee State University W
Freed-Hardeman University W
King College W
Lambuth University M, W
Lane College W
Lee College W
Lincoln Memorial University W
Middle Tennessee State University W
Milligan College W
Tennessee Technological University W
Trevecca Nazarene College W
Tusculum College W

University of Memphis M
University of Tennessee
  Chattanooga W
  Knoxville W
  Martin M, W

Texas

Abilene Christian University M, W
Ambassador University M, W
Angelo State University W
Baylor University W
Concordia Lutheran College W
Dallas Baptist University W
East Texas State University W
Houston Baptist University W
Incarnate Word College W
Jacksonville College W
Lamar University—Beaumont W
Laredo Community College W
Lee College W
LeTourneau University W
North Central Texas College W
Rice University W
St. Edward's University W
St. Mary's University W
Schreiner College W
Southwest Texas State University W
Stephen F. Austin State University W
Tarleton State University W
Texas A&M University W
Texas A&M University-Kingsville W
Texas Lutheran College W
Texas Tech University W
Texas Wesleyan University W
Texas Woman's University W
University of Houston W
University of Mary Hardin-Baylor W
University of North Texas W
University of Texas
  Arlington W
  Austin W
  San Antonio W
Vernon Regional Junior College W
West Texas A&M University W
Wharton County Junior College W

Utah

Brigham Young University M, W
College of Eastern Utah W
Dixie College W
Snow College W
University of Utah W
Utah State University W
Utah Valley State College W
Weber State University W

Virginia

Bluefield College W
Clinch Valley College of the University of Virginia W
College of William and Mary W
George Mason University M, W
Hampton University W
James Madison University W
Liberty University W
Norfolk State University W
Radford University W
St. Paul's College W
University of Virginia W
Virginia Commonwealth University W
Virginia Polytechnic Institute and State University W
Virginia Union University W

Washington

Big Bend Community College W
Central Washington University W
Centralia College W

Eastern Washington University W
Edmonds Community College W
Gonzaga University W
Green River Community College W
Highline Community College W
Lower Columbia College W
Northwest College W
Olympic College W
Pacific Lutheran University W
Pierce College W
St. Martin's College W
Seattle Pacific University W
Shoreline Community College W
Spokane Community College W
Tacoma Community College W
University of Puget Sound W
University of Washington W
Walla Walla Community College W
Washington State University W
Western Washington University W
Yakima Valley Community College W

West Virginia

Alderson-Broaddus College W
Concord College W
Marshall University W
Ohio Valley College W
Potomac State College of West Virginia University W
Salem-Teikyo University W
Shepherd College W
University of Charleston W
West Virginia Institute of Technology W
West Virginia University W
West Virginia Wesleyan College W
Wheeling Jesuit College W

Wisconsin

Cardinal Stritch College W
Marquette University W
Northland College W
University of Wisconsin-Green Bay W

Wyoming

Casper College W
Eastern Wyoming College W
Sheridan College W
University of Wyoming W

Arab Republic of Egypt

American University in Cairo M, W

Canada

Simon Fraser University W

Water polo

California

California State University
  Fresno M
  Long Beach M
Pepperdine University M
Stanford University M
University of California
  Berkeley M
  Irvine M
  Los Angeles M
  Santa Barbara M
University of the Pacific M
University of Southern California M

District of Columbia

George Washington University M

Kansas

Wichita State University W

Massachusetts

University of Massachusetts
Amherst M

Nebraska

University of Nebraska—Kearney
W

New York

City University of New York:
Queens College M
Fordham University M
Manhattan College M
St. Francis College M

Ohio

Bowling Green State University W

Pennsylvania

Villanova University M

Puerto Rico

University of Puerto Rico:
Mayaguez Campus M

Texas

Abilene Christian University W

Washington

Central Washington University W

Wyoming

Western Wyoming Community
College M

Arab Republic of Egypt

American University in Cairo M

Canada

Simon Fraser University M

Wrestling

Arizona

Arizona State University M
Embry-Riddle Aeronautical
University: Prescott Campus M

California

California Polytechnic State
University: San Luis Obispo M
California State University
Bakersfield M
Fresno M
Fullerton M

Colorado

Adams State College M
Colorado Northwestern Community
College M
Colorado School of Mines M
Fort Lewis College M
University of Northern Colorado M
University of Southern Colorado M
Western State College of Colorado
M

Connecticut

Central Connecticut State
University M

Delaware

Delaware State University M

District of Columbia

American University M
Howard University M

Idaho

Boise State University M
North Idaho College M
Ricks College M

Illinois

Belleville Area College M
Chicago State University M
Illinois State University M
Northwestern University M
Southern Illinois University at
Edwardsville M
University of Illinois at Urbana-
Champaign M

Indiana

Indiana University Bloomington M
Purdue University M
University of Indianapolis M
Valparaiso University M

Iowa

Drake University M
Iowa Central Community College
M
Iowa State University M
Northwestern College M
Teikyo Westmar University M
University of Iowa M
University of Northern Iowa M
Waldorf College M

Kansas

Colby Community College M
Fort Hays State University M
Garden City Community College M

Maryland

Morgan State University M
University of Maryland: College
Park M

Massachusetts

Boston University M
University of Massachusetts Lowell
M

Michigan

Central Michigan University M
Eastern Michigan University M
Michigan State University M
University of Michigan M

Minnesota

Mankato State University M
Moorhead State University M
St. Cloud State University M
Southwest State University M
University of Minnesota
Duluth M
Twin Cities M

Missouri

Central Missouri State University M
Lindenwood College M
St. Louis Community College at
Meramec M
Southwest Missouri State University
M
University of Missouri: Columbia M

Montana

Montana State University-Northern
M
Western Montana College of the
University of Montana M

Nebraska

Dana College M

University of Nebraska
Kearney M
Lincoln M
Omaha M

New Jersey

Rider University M
Rutgers, The State University of
New Jersey
College of Engineering M
College of Pharmacy M
Cook College M
Livingston College M
Mason Gross School of the
Arts M
Rutgers College M
Seton Hall University M

New Mexico

University of New Mexico M

New York

Hofstra University M
Niagara County Community College
M
State University of New York at
Buffalo M
Syracuse University M
Wagner College M

North Carolina

Appalachian State University M
Campbell University M
Duke University M
Gardner-Webb University M
North Carolina State University M
Pembroke State University M
University of North Carolina at
Chapel Hill M

North Dakota

Dickinson State University M
Mayville State University M
North Dakota State College of
Science M
North Dakota State University M
University of Mary M
University of North Dakota M

Ohio

Ashland University M
Cleveland State University M
Cuyahoga Community College:
Western Campus M
Kent State University M
Miami University: Oxford Campus
M
Ohio State University: Columbus
Campus M
Ohio University M
University of Findlay M

Oklahoma

University of Central Oklahoma M
University of Oklahoma M

Oregon

Clackamas Community College M
Oregon State University M
Portland State University M
University of Oregon M

Pennsylvania

Bloomsburg University of
Pennsylvania M
California University of
Pennsylvania M
Cheyney University of Pennsylvania
M
Drexel University M
Duquesne University M

Edinboro University of
Pennsylvania M
Gannon University M
Kutztown University of
Pennsylvania M
Lehigh University M
Lock Haven University of
Pennsylvania M
Millersville University of
Pennsylvania M
Penn State University Park Campus
M
Shippensburg University of
Pennsylvania M
University of Pittsburgh
Johnstown M
Pittsburgh M
Wilkes University M

Puerto Rico

University of Puerto Rico
Bayamon Technological
University College M
Mayaguez Campus M

South Carolina

Anderson College M
Clemson University M

South Dakota

Augustana College M
Dakota Wesleyan University M
Northern State University M
South Dakota State University M

Tennessee

Carson-Newman College M
University of Tennessee:
Chattanooga M

Utah

Brigham Young University M

Virginia

George Mason University M
James Madison University M
Liberty University M
Longwood College M
Norfolk State University M
Old Dominion University M
University of Virginia M
Virginia Military Institute M
Virginia Polytechnic Institute and
State University M

Washington

Big Bend Community College M
Central Washington University M
Pacific Lutheran University M
Yakima Valley Community College
M

West Virginia

West Liberty State College M
West Virginia University M

Wisconsin

Marquette University M
University of Wisconsin-Madison M

Wyoming

University of Wyoming M

Arab Republic of Egypt

American University in Cairo M

Canada

Simon Fraser University M

Colleges that offer tuition and/or fee waivers and special tuition payment plans

Tuition and/or fee waiver for adult students

Alabama
Community College of the Air Force
Faulkner University

Arizona
Northern Arizona University
Western International University

Arkansas
John Brown University
Southern Arkansas University Tech

California
Butte College
California State University: Dominguez Hills
Cerritos Community College
City College of San Francisco
Compton Community College
Contra Costa College
Cosumnes River College
Feather River College
Fresno City College
Fullerton College
Irvine Valley College
Mission College
Napa Valley College
Orange Coast College
Riverside Community College
Saddleback College

Colorado
Aims Community College
Northeastern Junior College
Regis University

Connecticut
Trinity College

District of Columbia
Mount Vernon College

Florida
Webber College

Georgia
Berry College
Emmanuel College
Wesleyan College

Idaho
Albertson College

Illinois
Lewis University
Northeastern Illinois University
Shimer College

Indiana
Anderson University
Bethel College
St. Francis College

Iowa
Coe College
Northwestern College
Simpson College

Kansas
Fort Hays State University
Kansas Newman College
Kansas Wesleyan University
Sterling College
Tabor College

Kentucky
Brescia College
Campbellsville College
Kentucky State University
University of Kentucky

Louisiana
University of New Orleans

Maryland
Harford Community College
Western Maryland College

Massachusetts
Atlantic Union College
Bay Path College
Berkshire Community College
Marian Court College
Massasoit Community College
Middlesex Community College
Pine Manor College
Simmons College

Michigan
Aquinas College
Mid Michigan Community College

Minnesota
Fergus Falls Community College
North Hennepin Community College
St. Olaf College
University of Minnesota: Crookston
Willmar Community College

Mississippi
Millsaps College
Mississippi College

University of Mississippi

Missouri
Culver-Stockton College
North Central Missouri College
St. Louis University
William Jewell College

Montana
Montana State University-Northern

Nebraska
College of St. Mary
Hastings College
Nebraska Wesleyan University

New Jersey
Felician College

New Mexico
College of Santa Fe

New York
Medaille College
Nyack College

North Carolina
Campbell University
Greensboro College
Salem College

North Dakota
University of North Dakota: Lake Region

Ohio
Cleveland College of Jewish Studies
Denison University

Oklahoma
Northern Oklahoma College
Oklahoma State University: Oklahoma City
Redlands Community College
Southeastern Oklahoma State University
University of Central Oklahoma

Oregon
Central Oregon Community College
Concordia College
Southwestern Oregon Community College

Pennsylvania
Immaculata College
Juniata College
Keystone College
Mercyhurst College
Rosemont College

St. Francis College
Seton Hill College
Thiel College

Puerto Rico
Inter American University of Puerto Rico: Barranquitas Campus

South Carolina
Anderson College
Coker College
Spartanburg Methodist College

South Dakota
South Dakota School of Mines and Technology

Tennessee
Carson-Newman College
Hiwassee College
Jackson State Community College
Lambuth University

Texas
Abilene Christian University
Concordia Lutheran College
Texas Christian University

Utah
Utah State University

Virginia
Bluefield College
Lynchburg College
Randolph-Macon Woman's College

Washington
Grays Harbor College
Lower Columbia College

West Virginia
Alderson-Broaddus College
Fairmont State College

Wisconsin
Beloit College
Blackhawk Technical College
Viterbo College

Wyoming
Eastern Wyoming College

Tuition and/or fee waiver for children of alumni

Alabama
Lawson State Community College

Alaska
University of Alaska Fairbanks

Arizona
Arizona College of the Bible

Arkansas
Arkansas State University
Southern Arkansas University

California
California Baptist College
Compton Community College
Irvine Valley College
LIFE Bible College
Mission College
Mount St. Mary's College
Patten College
Saddleback College
Santa Clara University

Colorado
Colorado Christian University

Florida
Florida Bible College
Florida Southern College
Webber College

Georgia
Oglethorpe University
Wesleyan College

Idaho
Albertson College

Illinois
Augustana College
Chicago State University
College of St. Francis
Eureka College
Illinois Benedictine College
Lewis University
MacCormac Junior College
MacMurray College

Indiana
Goshen College
Indiana State University
Manchester College
Marian College
St. Francis College
St. Joseph's College
St. Mary-of-the-Woods College
University of Evansville

Iowa
Clarke College
Dordt College
Iowa Wesleyan College
Loras College
Morningside College
Northwestern College
St. Ambrose University
Teikyo Marycrest University
Upper Iowa University

Kansas
Kansas Newman College
Kansas Wesleyan University
Tabor College

Kentucky
Asbury College
Bellarmine College
Brescia College
Morehead State University
Sue Bennett College
Thomas More College
Union College
Western Kentucky University

Louisiana
Grambling State University
Louisiana State University
    Agricultural and Mechanical
        College
    Shreveport
Louisiana Tech University
McNeese State University
University of New Orleans

Maine
University of New England

Massachusetts
Anna Maria College
Boston University
Curry College
Eastern Nazarene College
Hellenic College
Pine Manor College
Springfield College

Michigan
Aquinas College
Concordia College
Detroit College of Business
Lake Superior State University
Michigan Christian College
Michigan Technological University
Northwood University
University of Detroit Mercy
Wayne State University

Mississippi
Delta State University
Millsaps College
Mississippi State University
Mississippi University for Women
University of Mississippi
University of Southern Mississippi

Missouri
Avila College
Central Christian College of the
    Bible
Columbia College
Culver-Stockton College
Missouri Baptist College
Missouri Valley College
Northwest Missouri State
    University
Rockhurst College
University of Missouri: Rolla
Westminster College
William Jewell College

Nebraska
College of St. Mary
Dana College
Grace University
York College

Nevada
University of Nevada
    Las Vegas
    Reno

New Hampshire
Notre Dame College
Rivier College

New Jersey
Bloomfield College

New Mexico
College of the Southwest

New York
Adelphi University
Boricua College
Daemen College
Dowling College
Hartwick College
Iona College
Long Island University: Brooklyn
    Campus
Manhattan College
Plaza Business Institute
St. Joseph's College
University of Rochester

North Carolina
Greensboro College
Montreat-Anderson College

Ohio
Ashland University
Cedarville College
Kent State University
Malone College
Mount Union College
Muskingum College
University of Findlay
Walsh University

Oklahoma
Oklahoma Baptist University
Oklahoma Christian University of
    Science and Arts
Oklahoma State University
Oral Roberts University
Southeastern Oklahoma State
    University
Southwestern Oklahoma State
    University
University of Central Oklahoma
University of Oklahoma
    Health Sciences Center
    Norman

Oregon
Bassist College
Warner Pacific College

Pennsylvania
Albright College
Baptist Bible College of
    Pennsylvania
Cabrini College
Chatham College
Keystone College
Lancaster Bible College
Mercyhurst College
Peirce College
Philadelphia College of Bible
Point Park College
University of the Arts
Wilkes University
Wilson College

South Carolina
Anderson College
Coker College
Erskine College
North Greenville College
Spartanburg Methodist College

South Dakota
Augustana College
Black Hills State University
Northern State University
South Dakota School of Mines and
    Technology

South Dakota State University

Tennessee
Christian Brothers University
Crichton College
Tennessee Wesleyan College

Texas
Dallas Baptist University
University of Mary Hardin-Baylor
University of St. Thomas

Utah
Utah State University

Vermont
College of St. Joseph in Vermont

Virginia
Marymount University

Washington
Pacific Lutheran University
Seattle Pacific University

West Virginia
Bethany College
Fairmont State College

Wisconsin
Blackhawk Technical College
Carroll College
Concordia University Wisconsin
Viterbo College

Wyoming
Eastern Wyoming College
University of Wyoming

Arab Republic of Egy
American University in Cairo

Tuition and/or fee waiver for senior citizens

Alabama
Alabama Aviation and Technical
    College
Alabama Southern Community
    College
Athens State College
Bessemer State Technical College
Bevill State Community College
Bishop State Community College
Central Alabama Community
    College
Chattahoochee Valley Community
    College
Douglas MacArthur State Technical
    College
Enterprise State Junior College
Faulkner University
Gadsden State Community College
Harry M. Ayers State Technical
    College
J. F. Drake State Technical College
James H. Faulkner State
    Community College
Jefferson State Community College
John C. Calhoun State Community
    College
John M. Patterson State Technical
    College
Lawson State Community College
Lurleen B. Wallace State Junior
    College
Northeast Alabama Community
    College

Northwest-Shoals Community
College
Reid State Technical College
Shelton State Community College
Snead State Community College
Sparks State Technical College
University of Montevallo
Wallace State College at Hanceville

Alaska

Alaska Pacific University
Prince William Sound Community
College
Sheldon Jackson College
University of Alaska
Anchorage
Fairbanks
Southeast

Arizona

Arizona Western College
Cochise College
Gateway Community College
Mohave Community College
Southwestern College

Arkansas

Arkansas State University
Beebe Branch
Jonesboro
Arkansas Tech University
East Arkansas Community College
Garland County Community
College
Harding University
Henderson State University
John Brown University
Mississippi County Community
College
North Arkansas Community/
Technical College
Phillips County Community College
Rich Mountain Community College
South Arkansas Community College
Southern Arkansas University
Magnolia
Tech
University of Arkansas
Fayetteville
Little Rock
Medical Sciences
Monticello
Pine Bluff
University of Central Arkansas

California

Azusa Pacific University
California Polytechnic State
University: San Luis Obispo
California State Polytechnic
University: Pomona
California State University
Bakersfield
Chico
Dominguez Hills
Fresno
Fullerton
Hayward
Long Beach
Los Angeles
Northridge
Sacramento
San Bernardino
San Marcos
Stanislaus
Cerritos Community College
Citrus College
City College of San Francisco
College of the Desert
College of Notre Dame
Compton Community College
Foothill College

Fullerton College
Humboldt State University
Irvine Valley College
Los Angeles Harbor College
Mission College
Pacific Christian College
Point Loma Nazarene College
Porterville College
Saddleback College
San Diego State University
San Francisco State University
San Jose State University

Colorado

Adams State College
Arapahoe Community College
Colorado Mountain College
Alpine Campus
Spring Valley Campus
Timberline Campus
Colorado Northwestern Community
College
Community College of Aurora
Community College of Denver
Front Range Community College
Lamar Community College
Mesa State College
Metropolitan State College of
Denver
Morgan Community College
Naropa Institute
Northeastern Junior College
Pikes Peak Community College
Pueblo Community College
University of Colorado
Boulder
Denver
University of Northern Colorado
University of Southern Colorado
Western State College of Colorado

Connecticut

Asnuntuck Community-Technical
College
Capital Community-Technical
College
Central Connecticut State
University
Eastern Connecticut State
University
Gateway Community-Technical
College
Housatonic Community-Technical
College
Middlesex Community-Technical
College
Naugatuck Valley Community-
Technical College
Northwestern Connecticut
Community-Technical College
Norwalk Community-Technical
College
Quinebaug Valley Community-
Technical College
Quinnipiac College
Southern Connecticut State
University
Teikyo-Post University
Three Rivers Community-Technical
College
Tunxis Community-Technical
College
University of Connecticut
University of New Haven
Western Connecticut State
University

Delaware

Delaware State University
Delaware Technical and
Community College
Southern Campus
Stanton/Wilmington Campus
Terry Campus
University of Delaware

Florida

Brevard Community College
Broward Community College
Daytona Beach Community College
Edison Community College
Florida Agricultural and Mechanical
University
Florida Atlantic University
Florida Institute of Technology
Florida International University
Florida State University
Hillsborough Community College
Lake City Community College
Lake-Sumter Community College
North Florida Junior College
Palm Beach Atlantic College
Pensacola Junior College
St. Petersburg Junior College
Santa Fe Community College
Seminole Community College
Tallahassee Community College
University of Central Florida
University of Florida
University of North Florida
University of South Florida
Valencia Community College
Webber College

Georgia

Abraham Baldwin Agricultural
College
Albany State College
Armstrong State College
Atlanta Metropolitan College
Augusta College
Bainbridge College
Berry College
Brunswick College
Chattahoochee Technical Institute
Clayton State College
Columbus College
Columbus Technical Institute
Darton College
DeKalb College
DeKalb Technical Institute
Emmanuel College
Floyd College
Fort Valley State College
Georgia College
Georgia Southern University
Georgia Southwestern College
Georgia State University
Gordon College
Kennesaw State College
Macon College
Middle Georgia College
North Georgia College
Savannah State College
Shorter College
South Georgia College
Southern College of Technology
Thomas College
Toccoa Falls College
University of Georgia
Valdosta State University
Waycross College
Wesleyan College
West Georgia College

Hawaii

University of Hawaii
Hawaii Community College
Hilo
Honolulu Community College
Kauai Community College
Leeward Community College
Manoa

Idaho

Albertson College
Boise Bible College
Boise State University
College of Southern Idaho
Idaho State University
Lewis Clark State College
North Idaho College
Northwest Nazarene College

Illinois

Aurora University
Belleville Area College
Black Hawk College
Bradley University
Carl Sandburg College
Chicago State University
City Colleges of Chicago
Harold Washington College
Kennedy-King College
Olive-Harvey College
College of DuPage
College of Lake County
Danville Area Community College
Eastern Illinois University
Elgin Community College
Elmhurst College
Governors State University
Greenville College
Highland Community College
Illinois College
Illinois Eastern Community
Colleges
Frontier Community College
Lincoln Trail College
Olney Central College
Wabash Valley College
Illinois State University
Illinois Valley Community College
John A. Logan College
John Wood Community College
Joliet Junior College
Judson College
Kaskaskia College
Kendall College
Lake Land College
Lewis and Clark Community
College
Lincoln Land Community College
Loyola University of Chicago
MacMurray College
McHenry County College
Moraine Valley Community College
Morton College
Northeastern Illinois University
Northern Illinois University
Oakton Community College
Parkland College
Rend Lake College
Richland Community College
Rock Valley College
Roosevelt University
St. Xavier University
Sangamon State University
Southeastern Illinois College
Southern Illinois University
Carbondale
Edwardsville
Spoon River College
State Community College
Trinity Christian College
Triton College

University of Illinois
  Chicago
  Urbana-Champaign
Western Illinois University
William Rainey Harper College

Indiana

Anderson University
Ball State University
Calumet College of St. Joseph
Franklin College
Huntington College
Indiana State University
Indiana University
  Bloomington
  Southeast
Indiana University-Purdue
  University Fort Wayne
Indiana Vocational Technical
  College: Northwest
Indiana Wesleyan University
Marian College
Oakland City College
Purdue University: North Central
  Campus
St. Francis College
Taylor University
University of Evansville
University of Indianapolis
University of Southern Indiana
Vincennes University

Iowa

Briar Cliff College
Clarke College
Des Moines Area Community
  College
Drake University
Graceland College
Grand View College
Indian Hills Community College
Iowa Wesleyan College
Iowa Western Community College
Kirkwood Community College
Morningside College
St. Ambrose University
Simpson College
Southeastern Community College:
  North Campus
Teikyo Westmar University

Kansas

Barton County Community College
Butler County Community College
Coffeyville Community College
Cowley County Community College
Dodge City Community College
Donnelly College
Emporia State University
Garden City Community College
Hesston College
Hutchinson Community College
Independence Community College
Johnson County Community
  College
Kansas Newman College
Kansas Wesleyan University
Manhattan Christian College
MidAmerica Nazarene College
Neosho County Community College
St. Mary College
Southwestern College
Sterling College
Tabor College
Washburn University of Topeka
Wichita State University

Kentucky

Asbury College
Ashland Community College
Bellarmine College
Brescia College

Campbellsville College
Cumberland College
Eastern Kentucky University
Elizabethtown Community College
Hazard Community College
Hopkinsville Community College
Jefferson Community College
Kentucky State University
Kentucky Wesleyan College
Lexington Community College
Madisonville Community College
Maysville Community College
Mid-Continent Baptist Bible College
Midway College
Morehead State University
Murray State University
Northern Kentucky University
Paducah Community College
Pikeville College
Prestonsburg Community College
Somerset Community College
Southeast Community College
Spalding University
Sue Bennett College
Union College
University of Kentucky
University of Louisville
Western Kentucky University

Louisiana

Bossier Parish Community College
Grambling State University
Louisiana College
Louisiana State University
  Agricultural and Mechanical
    College
  Alexandria
  Eunice
  Shreveport
Louisiana Tech University
McNeese State University
Nicholls State University
Northeast Louisiana University
Northwestern State University
Nunez Community College
Our Lady of Holy Cross College
Southeastern Louisiana University
Southern University in Shreveport
University of New Orleans
University of Southwestern
  Louisiana
Xavier University of Louisiana

Maine

Colby College
Eastern Maine Technical College
Husson College
Unity College
University of Maine
  Augusta
  Farmington
  Fort Kent
  Machias
  Orono
  Presque Isle
University of Southern Maine

Maryland

Allegany Community College
Anne Arundel Community College
Baltimore City Community College
Baltimore Hebrew University
Bowie State University
Catonsville Community College
Cecil Community College
Charles County Community College
Chesapeake College
Coppin State College
Dundalk Community College
Essex Community College
Frederick Community College
Frostburg State University

Garrett Community College
Hagerstown Junior College
Harford Community College
Hood College
Howard Community College
Maryland Institute College of Art
Montgomery College
  Germantown Campus
  Rockville Campus
  Takoma Park Campus
Morgan State University
Prince George's Community College
St. Mary's College of Maryland
Salisbury State University
Towson State University
University of Baltimore
University of Maryland
  Baltimore County
  College Park
  Eastern Shore
  University College

Massachusetts

American International College
Anna Maria College
Atlantic Union College
Bay Path College
Becker College
  Leicester Campus
  Worcester Campus
Bentley College
Berkshire Community College
Boston University
Bridgewater State College
Bristol Community College
Bunker Hill Community College
Cape Cod Community College
Eastern Nazarene College
Elms College
Fitchburg State College
Framingham State College
Greenfield Community College
Holyoke Community College
Marian Court College
Massachusetts Bay Community
  College
Massachusetts College of Art
Massasoit Community College
Merrimack College
Middlesex Community College
Mount Wachusett Community
  College
Nichols College
North Adams State College
North Shore Community College
Northeastern University
Northern Essex Community College
Quincy College
Quinsigamond Community College
Roxbury Community College
Salem State College
Springfield Technical Community
  College
Stonehill College
Suffolk University
University of Massachusetts
  Amherst
  Boston
  Lowell
Western New England College
Westfield State College
Worcester State College

Michigan

Alpena Community College
Andrews University
Aquinas College
Bay de Noc Community College
Delta College
Glen Oaks Community College
Gogebic Community College
Henry Ford Community College

Highland Park Community College
Jackson Community College
Kalamazoo Valley Community
  College
Kellogg Community College
Kirtland Community College
Lake Superior State University
Madonna University
Michigan Christian College
Michigan Technological University
Mid Michigan Community College
Monroe County Community
  College
Montcalm Community College
Mott Community College
Muskegon Community College
Northern Michigan University
Reformed Bible College
Saginaw Valley State University
St. Clair County Community
  College
Schoolcraft College
Southwestern Michigan College
University of Michigan
  Dearborn
  Flint
Washtenaw Community College
Wayne State University
West Shore Community College
Western Michigan University
William Tyndale College

Minnesota

Alexandria Technical College
Anoka-Ramsey Community College
Augsburg College
Austin Community College
Bemidji State University
Bethel College
Central Lakes College
College of St. Catherine: St.
  Catherine Campus
College of St. Scholastica
Concordia College: St. Paul
Fergus Falls Community College
Gustavus Adolphus College
Itasca Community College:
  Arrowhead Region
Lakewood Community College
Mankato State University
Mesabi Community College:
  Arrowhead Region
Metropolitan State University
Minneapolis Community College
Minnesota Bible College
Normandale Community College
North Central Bible College
North Hennepin Community
  College
Northwestern College
Rainy River Community College
Rochester Community College
St. Cloud State University
St. Olaf College
St. Paul Technical College
Southwest State University
University of Minnesota
  Crookston
  Duluth
University of St. Thomas
Willmar Community College
Willmar Technical College
Winona State University

Mississippi

Belhaven College
Copiah-Lincoln Community College
Delta State University
East Central Community College
Hinds Community College
Holmes Community College
Meridian Community College

Millsaps College
Mississippi Gulf Coast Community
College
   Jackson County Campus
   Jefferson Davis Campus
   Perkinston
Mississippi State University
Northwest Mississippi Community
College
Pearl River Community College
Southeastern Baptist College
Southwest Mississippi Community
College
University of Mississippi
University of Southern Mississippi

Missouri

Avila College
Calvary Bible College
Central Methodist College
Columbia College
Crowder College
Culver-Stockton College
Drury College
East Central College
Fontbonne College
Lincoln University
Lindenwood College
Longview Community College
Maryville University of St. Louis
Missouri Baptist College
Missouri Southern State College
Missouri Valley College
Missouri Western State College
Moberly Area Community College
North Central Missouri College
Northeast Missouri State University
Northwest Missouri State
University
Ozark Christian College
Park College
Rockhurst College
St. Charles County Community
College
St. Louis Community College
   Forest Park
   Meramec
Southeast Missouri State University
Southwest Missouri State University
State Fair Community College
Three Rivers Community College
William Jewell College

Montana

Carroll College
College of Great Falls
Dawson Community College
Miles Community College
Montana State University
   Billings
   Bozeman
   Northern
Montana Tech of The University of
Montana
Stone Child College
University of Montana-Missoula
Western Montana College of the
University of Montana

Nebraska

Doane College
Grace University
Hastings College
McCook Community College
Metropolitan Community College
Mid Plains Community College
Midland Lutheran College
Nebraska Indian Community
College
Nebraska Wesleyan University

Southeast Community College
   Beatrice Campus
   Lincoln Campus
Western Nebraska Community
College: Scottsbluff Campus

Nevada

Community College of Southern
Nevada
Northern Nevada Community
College
Truckee Meadows Community
College
University of Nevada
   Las Vegas
   Reno
Western Nevada Community
College

New Hampshire

Franklin Pierce College
Keene State College
New England College
New Hampshire Technical College
   Claremont
   Laconia
   Manchester
New Hampshire Technical Institute
Notre Dame College
Plymouth State College of the
University System of New
Hampshire
Rivier College
St. Anselm College
University of New Hampshire
   Durham
   Manchester

New Jersey

Atlantic Community College
Bergen Community College
Bloomfield College
Brookdale Community College
Burlington County College
Caldwell College
Camden County College
Centenary College
College of St. Elizabeth
County College of Morris
Cumberland County College
Drew University
Fairleigh Dickinson University
   Edward Williams College
   Teaneck
Felician College
Georgian Court College
Gloucester County College
Hudson County Community College
Jersey City State College
Kean College of New Jersey
Monmouth College
Montclair State University
Passaic County Community College
Ramapo College of New Jersey
Richard Stockton College of New
Jersey
Rutgers, The State University of
New Jersey
   Camden College of Arts and
   Sciences
   College of Engineering
   College of Nursing
   College of Pharmacy
   Cook College
   Douglass College
   Livingston College
   Mason Gross School of the
   Arts
   Newark College of Arts and
   Sciences
   Rutgers College
Salem Community College

Seton Hall University
Sussex County Community College
Trenton State College
Union County College
Warren County Community College
William Paterson College of New
Jersey

New Mexico

Clovis Community College
College of Santa Fe
Dona Ana Branch Community
College of New Mexico State
University
Eastern New Mexico University:
Roswell Campus
National College
New Mexico Institute of Mining
and Technology
New Mexico State University
   Carlsbad
   Las Cruces
San Juan College

New York

Adelphi University
Adirondack Community College
Broome Community College
Cayuga County Community College
City University of New York
   Baruch College
   Borough of Manhattan
   Community College
   Bronx Community College
   Brooklyn College
   City College
   College of Staten Island
   Hostos Community College
   Hunter College
   John Jay College of Criminal
   Justice
   Lehman College
   Medgar Evers College
   New York City Technical
   College
   Queens College
   York College
Clinton Community College
College of Mount St. Vincent
College of St. Rose
Columbia-Greene Community
College
Concordia College
Daemen College
Dominican College of Blauvelt
Dowling College
Dutchess Community College
D'Youville College
Erie Community College
   North Campus
   South Campus
Finger Lakes Community College
Five Towns College
Fordham University
Fulton-Montgomery Community
College
Hofstra University
Houghton College
Iona College
Jamestown Community College
Jefferson Community College
Jewish Theological Seminary of
America
Maria College
Mercy College
Mohawk Valley Community College
Nassau Community College
New York Institute of Technology
Niagara County Community College
North Country Community College
Nyack College
Orange County Community College

Pace University
Roberts Wesleyan College
Rockland Community College
Russell Sage College
Sage Junior College of Albany
St. Bonaventure University
St. John Fisher College
St. John's University
St. Joseph's College: Suffolk
Campus
St. Thomas Aquinas College
Schenectady County Community
College
State University of New York
   Albany
   Purchase
   College of Agriculture and
   Technology at Cobleskill
   College at Cortland
   College at Old Westbury
   Institute of Technology at
   Utica/Rome
Suffolk County Community College
   Eastern Campus
   Selden
   Western Campus
Sullivan County Community
College
Tompkins-Cortland Community
College
Trocaire College
Ulster County Community College
Utica College of Syracuse
University
Villa Maria College of Buffalo
Wagner College
Wells College
Westchester Business Institute

North Carolina

Alamance Community College
Anson Community College
Appalachian State University
Beaufort County Community
College
Belmont Abbey College
Bladen Community College
Blue Ridge Community College
Brunswick Community College
Caldwell Community College and
Technical Institute
Cape Fear Community College
Carteret Community College
Central Carolina Community
College
Central Piedmont Community
College
Chowan College
Cleveland Community College
College of the Albemarle
Craven Community College
Davidson County Community
College
Durham Technical Community
College
East Carolina University
Edgecombe Community College
Fayetteville State University
Fayetteville Technical Community
College
Forsyth Technical Community
College
Gaston College
Halifax Community College
Haywood Community College
Johnston Community College
Lenoir Community College
Lenoir-Rhyne College
Mayland Community College
McDowell Technical Community
College
Methodist College

Mitchell Community College
Montgomery Community College
Montreat-Anderson College
Nash Community College
North Carolina Agricultural and
    Technical State University
North Carolina State University
Pamlico Community College
Pembroke State University
Pitt Community College
Randolph Community College
Richmond Community College
Roanoke Bible College
Roanoke-Chowan Community
    College
Sampson Community College
Sandhills Community College
Southeastern Community College
Southwestern Community College
Stanly Community College
Surry Community College
Tri-County Community College
University of North Carolina
    Asheville
    Chapel Hill
    Charlotte
    Greensboro
    Wilmington
Vance-Granville Community
    College
Wake Technical Community
    College
Wayne Community College
Western Carolina University
Western Piedmont Community
    College
Wilkes Community College
Wilson Technical Community
    College
Winston-Salem State University

North Dakota

Mayville State University
North Dakota State University:
    Bottineau
University of Mary
University of North Dakota
    Grand Forks
    Lake Region
    Williston
Valley City State University

Ohio

Belmont Technical College
Bowling Green State University
    Bowling Green
    Firelands College
Cedarville College
Central Ohio Technical College
Chatfield College
Cincinnati State Technical and
    Community College
Clark State Community College
Cleveland College of Jewish Studies
Cleveland State University
Columbus College of Art and
    Design
Columbus State Community College
Cuyahoga Community College
    Eastern Campus
    Metropolitan Campus
    Western Campus
Denison University
Edison State Community College
Hocking Technical College
Jefferson Technical College
Kent State University
    East Liverpool Regional
        Campus
    Trumbull Campus
    Tuscarawas Campus
Lake Erie College

Lakeland Community College
Lourdes College
Malone College
Marion Technical College
Miami University: Hamilton
    Campus
Mount Union College
Mount Vernon Nazarene College
Muskingum Area Technical College
North Central Technical College
Northwest State Community
    College
Ohio Dominican College
Ohio Northern University
Ohio State University
    Mansfield Campus
    Marion Campus
    Newark Campus
Ohio University: Chillicothe
    Campus
Owens Technical College
    Findlay Campus
    Toledo
Shawnee State University
Sinclair Community College
Southern State Community College
Stark Technical College
Terra Community College
Tiffin University
University of Akron
University of Cincinnati: Raymond
    Walters College
University of Dayton
University of Findlay
University of Rio Grande
University of Toledo
Urbana University
Walsh University
Washington State Community
    College
Wittenberg University
Wright State University
    Dayton
    Lake Campus
Xavier University
Youngstown State University

Oklahoma

Bartlesville Wesleyan College
Cameron University
Connors State College
East Central University
Murray State College
Northeastern State University
Northwestern Oklahoma State
    University
Oklahoma Baptist University
Oklahoma City Community College
Oklahoma City University
Oklahoma Panhandle State
    University
Oklahoma State University
    Oklahoma City
    Stillwater
Phillips University
Redlands Community College
Rogers State College
Rose State College
Southeastern Oklahoma State
    University
Southern Nazarene University
Southwestern Oklahoma State
    University
Tulsa Junior College
University of Central Oklahoma
University of Oklahoma
    Health Sciences Center
    Norman
University of Science and Arts of
    Oklahoma
Western Oklahoma State College

Oregon

Central Oregon Community College
Chemeketa Community College
Clackamas Community College
Concordia College
George Fox College
Lane Community College
Linfield College
Linn-Benton Community College
Portland Community College
Portland State University
Southwestern Oregon Community
    College
Treasure Valley Community College
Umpqua Community College
Warner Pacific College
Western Oregon State College

Pennsylvania

Academy of the New Church
Albright College
Alvernia College
Beaver College
Bryn Mawr College
Bucks County Community College
Butler County Community College
California University of
    Pennsylvania
Chestnut Hill College
Clarion University of Pennsylvania
College Misericordia
Community College of Beaver
    County
Community College of Philadelphia
Delaware County Community
    College
Delaware Valley College
Duquesne University
East Stroudsburg University of
    Pennsylvania
Edinboro University of
    Pennsylvania
Gannon University
Gratz College
Gwynedd-Mercy College
Holy Family College
Immaculata College
Indiana University of Pennsylvania
Juniata College
Keystone College
King's College
Lackawanna Junior College
Lancaster Bible College
Lehigh Carbon Community College
Lock Haven University of
    Pennsylvania
Luzerne County Community
    College
Manor Junior College
Marywood College
Messiah College
Millersville University of
    Pennsylvania
Montgomery County Community
    College
Northampton County Area
    Community College

Penn State
    Allentown Campus
    Altoona Campus
    Beaver Campus
    Berks Campus
    Delaware County Campus
    Du Bois Campus
    Erie Behrend College
    Fayette Campus
    Harrisburg Capital College
    Hazleton Campus
    McKeesport Campus
    Mont Alto Campus
    New Kensington Campus
    Ogontz Campus
    Schuylkill Campus
    Shenango Campus
    University Park Campus
    Wilkes-Barre Campus
    Worthington-Scranton Campus
    York Campus
Point Park College
Reading Area Community College
Rosemont College
Seton Hill College
Shippensburg University of
    Pennsylvania
Temple University
University of Pittsburgh at Bradford
University of Scranton
Ursinus College
Villanova University
West Chester University of
    Pennsylvania
Westmoreland County Community
    College
Wilkes University

Rhode Island

Community College of Rhode
    Island
Rhode Island College
University of Rhode Island

South Carolina

Aiken Technical College
Anderson College
Benedict College
Central Carolina Technical College
Chesterfield-Marlboro Technical
    College
The Citadel
Clemson University
Coastal Carolina University
College of Charleston
Denmark Technical College
Florence-Darlington Technical
    College
Francis Marion University
Greenville Technical College
Horry-Georgetown Technical
    College
Lander University
Limestone College
Midlands Technical College
Orangeburg-Calhoun Technical
    College
Piedmont Technical College
South Carolina State University
Southern Wesleyan University
Spartanburg Methodist College
Technical College of the
    Lowcountry
Tri-County Technical College
Trident Technical College

University of South Carolina
  Aiken
  Beaufort
  Columbia
  Lancaster
  Salkehatchie Regional Campus
  Spartanburg
  Sumter
  Union
Williamsburg Technical College
Winthrop University
York Technical College

South Dakota

Augustana College
Black Hills State University
Dakota State University
Kilian Community College
Mount Marty College
Northern State University
Sisseton-Wahpeton Community
  College
South Dakota School of Mines and
  Technology
South Dakota State University
University of Sioux Falls

Tennessee

Austin Peay State University
Belmont University
Bethel College
Carson-Newman College
Chattanooga State Technical
  Community College
Cleveland State Community College
Dyersburg State Community
  College
East Tennessee State University
Freed-Hardeman University
Hiwassee College
Jackson State Community College
King College
Lambuth University
Lee College
Lincoln Memorial University
Middle Tennessee State University
Motlow State Community College
Nashville State Technical Institute
Pellissippi State Technical
  Community College
Roane State Community College
Shelby State Community College
Southern College of Seventh-day
  Adventist
State Technical Institute at
  Memphis
Tennessee State University
Tennessee Technological University
University of Memphis
University of Tennessee
  Chattanooga
  Knoxville
  Martin
Volunteer State Community College
Walters State Community College

Texas

Alvin Community College
Angelina College
Bee County College
College of the Mainland
Del Mar College
East Texas State University
El Paso Community College
Frank Phillips College
Galveston College
Hardin-Simmons University
Houston Baptist University
Houston Community College
Howard College
Howard Payne University
Incarnate Word College

Laredo Community College
Lee College
McMurry University
Northeast Texas Community
  College
Paris Junior College
St. Philip's College
Southwestern Adventist College
Tarleton State University
Temple Junior College
Texarkana College
Texas A&M University
Texas A&M University-Corpus
  Christi
Texas A&M University-Kingsville
Texas Christian University
Trinity Valley Community College
Vernon Regional Junior College
Wayland Baptist University
Weatherford College
Western Texas College

Utah

College of Eastern Utah
Dixie College
Salt Lake Community College
University of Utah
Utah Valley State College
Weber State University

Vermont

Burlington College
Castleton State College
Champlain College
College of St. Joseph in Vermont
Community College of Vermont
Johnson State College
Lyndon State College
Southern Vermont College
Trinity College of Vermont
University of Vermont

Virginia

Averett College
Blue Ridge Community College
Bluefield College
Bridgewater College
Central Virginia Community College
Christopher Newport University
Clinch Valley College of the
  University of Virginia
College of William and Mary
Dabney S. Lancaster Community
  College
Danville Community College
Eastern Shore Community College
Ferrum College
George Mason University
Germanna Community College
J. Sargeant Reynolds Community
  College
John Tyler Community College
Longwood College
Lord Fairfax Community College
Mary Washington College
Marymount University
Mountain Empire Community
  College
New River Community College
Norfolk State University
Northern Virginia Community
  College
Old Dominion University
Patrick Henry Community College
Paul D. Camp Community College
Piedmont Virginia Community
  College
Radford University
Rappahannock Community College
Richard Bland College
Roanoke College

Southside Virginia Community
  College
Southwest Virginia Community
  College
Thomas Nelson Community College
Tidewater Community College
University of Virginia
Virginia Commonwealth University
Virginia Highlands Community
  College
Virginia Western Community
  College
Wytheville Community College

Washington

Big Bend Community College
Central Washington University
Centralia College
Clark College
Columbia Basin College
Edmonds Community College
Everett Community College
Gonzaga University
Grays Harbor College
Green River Community College
Heritage College
Lake Washington Technical College
Lower Columbia College
North Seattle Community College
Northwest College
Olympic College
Peninsula College
Pierce College
Puget Sound Christian College
Seattle Central Community College
Seattle Pacific University
Shoreline Community College
South Seattle Community College
Spokane Falls Community College
Tacoma Community College
University of Washington
Walla Walla College
Walla Walla Community College
Washington State University
Western Washington University
Whatcom Community College
Whitworth College
Yakima Valley Community College

West Virginia

Fairmont State College
Wheeling Jesuit College

Wisconsin

Blackhawk Technical College
Lakeland College
Marian College of Fond du Lac
Milwaukee Area Technical College
Mount Mary College
Mount Senario College
Northland College
Silver Lake College
University of Wisconsin
  Eau Claire
  Green Bay
  La Crosse
  Milwaukee
  River Falls
  Stout
  Whitewater
University of Wisconsin Center
  Fond du Lac
  Fox Valley
  Waukesha
Viterbo College

Wyoming

Casper College
Central Wyoming College
Eastern Wyoming College
Laramie County Community
  College

Sheridan College
University of Wyoming
Western Wyoming Community
  College

American Samoa, Caroline Islands, Guam, Marianas, Virgin Islands

Guam Community College
University of Guam

Tuition and/or fee waiver for minority students

Alabama

Alabama State University
Faulkner University

Alaska

Prince William Sound Community
  College
University of Alaska Southeast

Arizona

Arizona State University
Northern Arizona University
University of Arizona

California

American River College
Antioch Southern California at Los
  Angeles
California Baptist College
Cerritos Community College
City College of San Francisco
College of the Desert
Compton Community College
Fresno City College
Fullerton College
Irvine Valley College
Mission College
Napa Valley College
Orange Coast College
Porterville College
Saddleback College
Westmont College

Colorado

Colorado Technical College
Fort Lewis College
Northeastern Junior College

Connecticut

Albertus Magnus College
Sacred Heart University
University of Hartford

Florida

Brevard Community College
Broward Community College
Central Florida Community College
Florida Atlantic University
Florida International University
Florida Southern College
Lake City Community College
Okaloosa-Walton Community
  College
Santa Fe Community College
University of Florida

Hawaii

University of Hawaii at Manoa

Idaho

University of Idaho

Illinois

Eureka College
Governors State University
Illinois Benedictine College
Northern Illinois University
Parkland College

Indiana

Anderson University
Indiana University at Kokomo
Indiana Wesleyan University
Oakland City College
Purdue University: North Central
Campus
St. Joseph's College
St. Mary-of-the-Woods College

Iowa

Iowa Wesleyan College
St. Ambrose University

Kansas

Ottawa University
Pittsburg State University

Kentucky

Bellarmine College
Madisonville Community College
Murray State University
Thomas More College
Transylvania University
University of Kentucky

Louisiana

Bossier Parish Community College
Grambling State University
Louisiana State University and
Agricultural and Mechanical
College

Maine

Central Maine Technical College
Eastern Maine Technical College
University of Maine
Augusta
Farmington
Machias
Orono
Presque Isle

Maryland

Morgan State University
University of Maryland: Eastern
Shore

Massachusetts

Eastern Nazarene College
Greenfield Community College
Hellenic College
Merrimack College
St. John's Seminary College
Stonehill College
University of Massachusetts Boston

Michigan

Concordia College
Michigan Technological University
Northern Michigan University
Northwestern Michigan College

Minnesota

Bemidji State University
University of Minnesota
Crookston
Morris
Twin Cities

Mississippi

Mississippi University for Women
University of Mississippi

Missouri

North Central Missouri College
Northwest Missouri State
University
Rockhurst College
St. Louis University
University of Missouri: Rolla
Westminster College
William Woods University

Montana

Montana State University
Billings
Bozeman
Northern
Montana Tech of The University of
Montana
University of Montana-Missoula
Western Montana College of the
University of Montana

Nebraska

College of St. Mary
Midland Lutheran College
Peru State College
Southeast Community College:
Beatrice Campus

Nevada

University of Nevada: Reno

New Hampshire

St. Anselm College

New York

Canisius College
Iona College
Parsons School of Design
St. Bonaventure University
State University of New York
College at Buffalo

North Carolina

Lenoir-Rhyne College
Western Carolina University

North Dakota

Bismarck State College
Dickinson State University
Minot State University
North Dakota State College of
Science
North Dakota State University:
Bottineau
University of North Dakota
Lake Region
Williston

Ohio

Northwestern College
Walsh University

Oklahoma

Northern Oklahoma College
Oklahoma State University
Oklahoma City
Stillwater
Southeastern Oklahoma State
University
University of Central Oklahoma
University of Oklahoma Health
Sciences Center

Oregon

Eastern Oregon State College
George Fox College
Oregon Health Sciences University
Oregon Institute of Technology
Portland State University
Southern Oregon State College

University of Oregon
Eugene
Robert Donald Clark Honors
College
Warner Pacific College
Western Oregon State College

Pennsylvania

Albright College
Bloomsburg University of
Pennsylvania
California University of
Pennsylvania
Cheyney University of Pennsylvania
Clarion University of Pennsylvania
Edinboro University of
Pennsylvania
King's College
Kutztown University of
Pennsylvania
Lock Haven University of
Pennsylvania
Lycoming College
Manor Junior College
Mansfield University of
Pennsylvania
Millersville University of
Pennsylvania
St. Charles Borromeo Seminary-
Overbrook
West Chester University of
Pennsylvania

Puerto Rico

American University of Puerto Rico
Inter American University of Puerto
Rico: Barranquitas Campus

Rhode Island

Providence College

South Carolina

Spartanburg Methodist College
University of South Carolina at
Lancaster

Tennessee

Carson-Newman College
Hiwassee College
Jackson State Community College
Northeast State Technical
Community College
Tennessee Wesleyan College
University of Tennessee: Memphis
Volunteer State Community College
Walters State Community College

Texas

Dallas Baptist University
El Centro College
McMurry University
Texas Southern University
University of Mary Hardin-Baylor

Utah

Utah State University

Virginia

Blue Ridge Community College
Norfolk State University
Randolph-Macon Woman's College
St. Paul's College
Virginia State University

Washington

Edmonds Community College
Grays Harbor College
Skagit Valley College

West Virginia

Bethany College
Fairmont State College

West Virginia University

Wisconsin

Blackhawk Technical College
University of Wisconsin-Superior

Tuition and/or fee waiver for family members enrolled simultaneously

Alabama

International Bible College
Marion Military Institute
Spring Hill College
Tuskegee University

Arizona

Arizona College of the Bible
Western International University

Arkansas

Philander Smith College

California

Azusa Pacific University
California Baptist College
California Lutheran University
Cerritos Community College
City College of San Francisco
Compton Community College
LIFE Bible College
New School of Art and
Architecture
Pacific Christian College
Patten College
Riverside Community College
St. Mary's College of California
San Jose Christian College
Santa Clara University
Solano Community College
University of San Francisco

Colorado

Colorado Christian University

Connecticut

Albertus Magnus College
Briarwood College
Fairfield University
Sacred Heart University
Teikyo-Post University
University of Bridgeport
University of Hartford
University of New Haven

Delaware

Goldey-Beacom College

District of Columbia

Catholic University of America
George Washington University
Trinity College

Florida

Barry University
Florida Christian College
Florida Southern College
Jacksonville University
St. Leo College
Santa Fe Community College
Schiller International University
Trinity International University
Warner Southern College

Georgia

Berry College
Brenau University
Morris Brown College

Oglethorpe University
Paine College
Shorter College
Toccoa Falls College
Truett-McConnell College
Wesleyan College

Hawaii

Chaminade University of Honolulu

Idaho

Northwest Nazarene College

Illinois

Augustana College
College of St. Francis
Eureka College
Illinois Benedictine College
Judson College
Kendall College
Lewis University
Lincoln Christian College and
 Seminary
MacCormac Junior College
Olivet Nazarene University
Quincy University
Rockford College
Rosary College

Indiana

Bethel College
Huntington College
Indiana Institute of Technology
Indiana State University
Indiana Wesleyan University
Manchester College
Marian College
St. Francis College
St. Joseph's College
St. Mary's College
Vincennes University

Iowa

American Institute of Business
Clarke College
Faith Baptist Bible College and
 Theological Seminary
Loras College
Northwestern College
Simpson College
Teikyo Marycrest University
University of Dubuque
Upper Iowa University

Kansas

Colby Community College
Kansas Newman College
Kansas Wesleyan University
St. Mary College
Southwestern College
Tabor College

Kentucky

Asbury College
Clear Creek Baptist Bible College
Spalding University
Sue Bennett College

Louisiana

Nunez Community College
Xavier University of Louisiana

Maine

St. Joseph's College
University of New England

Maryland

College of Notre Dame of
 Maryland
Coppin State College
Hood College
Loyola College in Maryland

Mount St. Mary's College
Western Maryland College

Massachusetts

American International College
Anna Maria College
Assumption College
Atlantic Union College
Bay Path College
Becker College: Worcester Campus
Curry College
Eastern Nazarene College
Elms College
Lasell College
Merrimack College
Nichols College
Pine Manor College
Springfield College
Stonehill College
Suffolk University
Western New England College

Michigan

Andrews University
Great Lakes Christian College
Michigan Christian College
Northwood University
Reformed Bible College
Saginaw Valley State University
Siena Heights College
Yeshiva Beth Yehuda-Yeshiva
 Gedolah of Greater Detroit

Minnesota

Minnesota Bible College
North Central Bible College
Northwestern College
Oak Hills Bible College
University of St. Thomas
Willmar Community College

Mississippi

Blue Mountain College
Holmes Community College
Magnolia Bible College
Rust College

Missouri

Avila College
Calvary Bible College
Central Bible College
Central Christian College of the
 Bible
Central Methodist College
Columbia College
Fontbonne College
Maryville University of St. Louis
Missouri Baptist College
Missouri Valley College
Research College of Nursing
Rockhurst College
St. Louis University
Stephens College
Wentworth Military Academy
William Woods University

Montana

Carroll College
College of Great Falls

Nebraska

College of St. Mary
Creighton University
Dana College
Grace University
Hastings College
Midland Lutheran College
Nebraska Christian College

Nevada

Sierra Nevada College
Western Nevada Community
 College

New Hampshire

Franklin Pierce College
Hesser College
McIntosh College
New England College
Notre Dame College
Rivier College
St. Anselm College

New Jersey

Bloomfield College
Burlington County College
Caldwell College
Centenary College
College of St. Elizabeth
Fairleigh Dickinson University
 Edward Williams College
 Teaneck
Felician College
Georgian Court College
Monmouth College
Seton Hall University

New Mexico

National College

New York

Canisius College
College of Mount St. Vincent
College of New Rochelle
 New Rochelle
 School of New Resources
Daemen College
D'Youville College
Elmira College
Hartwick College
Houghton College
Iona College
Long Island University: Brooklyn
 Campus
Marymount College
Molloy College
Nazareth College of Rochester
Nyack College
Russell Sage College
Sage Junior College of Albany
St. Bonaventure University
St. John's University
St. Joseph's College
 Brooklyn
 Suffolk Campus
St. Thomas Aquinas College
Villa Maria College of Buffalo
Wagner College

North Carolina

Alamance Community College
East Coast Bible College
Greensboro College
John Wesley College
Lenoir-Rhyne College
Livingstone College
Peace College
Pfeiffer College
Queens College
Roanoke Bible College

North Dakota

Trinity Bible College
University of Mary

Ohio

Antioch College
Ashland University
Capital University
Franciscan University of
 Steubenville

Lake Erie College
Malone College
Mount Union College
Mount Vernon Nazarene College
Muskingum College
Ohio Northern University
Otterbein College
Terra Community College
University of Dayton
University of Findlay
Ursuline College
Walsh University
Wilmington College
Xavier University

Oklahoma

Northeastern Oklahoma
 Agricultural and Mechanical
 College
Oklahoma Christian University of
 Science and Arts
Oral Roberts University
Southeastern Oklahoma State
 University
University of Central Oklahoma

Oregon

Bassist College
Eugene Bible College
George Fox College
Lewis & Clark College
Linn-Benton Community College
Multnomah Bible College
Southwestern Oregon Community
 College

Pennsylvania

Albright College
Allentown College of St. Francis de
 Sales
Baptist Bible College of
 Pennsylvania
Cabrini College
Carlow College
Cedar Crest College
Elizabethtown College
Gratz College
Immaculata College
King's College
La Roche College
Lackawanna Junior College
Lancaster Bible College
Lycoming College
Marywood College
Mercyhurst College
Messiah College
Moore College of Art and Design
Peirce College
Philadelphia College of Bible
Rosemont College
St. Francis College
Seton Hill College
Thiel College
University of the Arts
University of Scranton
Ursinus College
Valley Forge Christian College
Valley Forge Military College
Waynesburg College
Wilkes University

Puerto Rico

Universidad Adventista de las
 Antillas

Rhode Island

Bryant College
Johnson & Wales University
Providence College

South Carolina

Erskine College
Limestone College
North Greenville College
Southern Wesleyan University
Spartanburg Methodist College

South Dakota

Augustana College
Huron University
Mount Marty College
National College

Tennessee

Belmont University
Carson-Newman College
Hiwassee College
Knoxville College
Lee College
Southern College of Seventh-day
  Adventist
Tennessee Temple University
Tennessee Wesleyan College
Union University

Texas

Arlington Baptist College
Dallas Baptist University
Northwood University: Texas
  Campus
Southwestern Adventist College
Stephen F. Austin State University
University of Dallas

Utah

Westminster College of Salt Lake
  City

Vermont

Champlain College
College of St. Joseph in Vermont
Green Mountain College
Johnson State College
Lyndon State College
St. Michael's College

Virginia

Averett College
Christendom College
Ferrum College
Mary Baldwin College
Marymount University
Randolph-Macon College
Southern Virginia College
Virginia Intermont College

Washington

Gonzaga University
Northwest College
Puget Sound Christian College
St. Martin's College

West Virginia

Alderson-Broaddus College

Wisconsin

Alverno College
Beloit College
Blackhawk Technical College
Cardinal Stritch College
Carroll College
Marian College of Fond du Lac
Marquette University
Mount Mary College
St. Norbert College
Viterbo College
Wisconsin Lutheran College

Mexico

Sistema Instituto Tecnologico y de
  Estudios Superiores de
  Monterrey

Tuition and/or fee waiver for unemployed or children of unemployed workers

Alabama

Bessemer State Technical College
Faulkner University

Arizona

Mohave Community College

Arkansas

Southern Arkansas University Tech

California

Cerritos Community College
City College of San Francisco
Coastline Community College
College of the Desert
Compton Community College
Contra Costa College
Feather River College
Fresno City College
Fullerton College
Irvine Valley College
Laney College
Las Positas College
Long Beach City College
Merritt College
Mission College
Orange Coast College
Pasadena City College
Porterville College
Queen of the Holy Rosary College
Riverside Community College
Saddleback College
San Diego City College
San Diego Miramar College
Santa Barbara City College
Santa Monica College
West Hills Community College

Georgia

Brewton-Parker College

Hawaii

University of Hawaii: Kauai
  Community College

Idaho

Northwest Nazarene College

Iowa

Drake University

Kansas

Butler County Community College
Cowley County Community College
Neosho County Community College

Massachusetts

Atlantic Union College
Berkshire Community College
Bridgewater State College
Bristol Community College
Massachusetts Bay Community
  College
Massachusetts College of Art
Massasoit Community College
Mount Wachusett Community
  College
North Adams State College
Salem State College

Michigan

Olivet College
St. Mary's College
Wayne State University

Minnesota

Rainy River Community College

Missouri

Calvary Bible College
St. Louis University

Nebraska

Western Nebraska Community
  College: Scottsbluff Campus

Nevada

Western Nevada Community
  College

New Jersey

Brookdale Community College
Camden County College
County College of Morris
Cumberland County College
Mercer County Community College
Passaic County Community College
Sussex County Community College
Trenton State College
Warren County Community College
William Paterson College of New
  Jersey

New York

Bramson ORT Technical Institute
Bryant & Stratton Business
  Institute: Albany
Herkimer County Community
  College
Mannes College of Music
New York Institute of Technology
Plaza Business Institute
Villa Maria College of Buffalo

Ohio

Belmont Technical College

Oklahoma

Northern Oklahoma College

Oregon

Linn-Benton Community College
Marylhurst College
Southwestern Oregon Community
  College
Warner Pacific College

Pennsylvania

Bucks County Community College
Gratz College
King's College
Manor Junior College
Mercyhurst College
Point Park College
St. Charles Borromeo Seminary-
  Overbrook
Thaddeus Stevens State School of
  Technology
University of the Arts

Rhode Island

Rhode Island College
University of Rhode Island

South Carolina

Greenville Technical College
Spartanburg Methodist College
York Technical College

Texas

El Centro College

Utah

Utah State University

Washington

Big Bend Community College
Centralia College
Columbia Basin College
Edmonds Community College
Everett Community College
Grays Harbor College
Lower Columbia College
North Seattle Community College
Peninsula College
Pierce College
Seattle Central Community College
Skagit Valley College
South Puget Sound Community
  College
South Seattle Community College
Tacoma Community College
Walla Walla Community College
Whatcom Community College
Yakima Valley Community College

Wisconsin

Blackhawk Technical College

Tuition payment by credit card

Alabama

Alabama Agricultural and
  Mechanical University
Alabama Southern Community
  College
Alabama State University
Bessemer State Technical College
Bevill State Community College
Birmingham-Southern College
Bishop State Community College
Central Alabama Community
  College
Draughons Junior College
Enterprise State Junior College
Faulkner University
Gadsden State Community College
Huntingdon College
International Bible College
J. F. Drake State Technical College
Jacksonville State University
Jefferson State Community College
John C. Calhoun State Community
  College
John M. Patterson State Technical
  College
Lawson State Community College
Lurleen B. Wallace State Junior
  College
Northwest-Shoals Community
  College
Oakwood College
Reid State Technical College
Samford University
Shelton State Community College
Southeastern Bible College
Southern Christian University
Talladega College
Troy State University
  Dothan
  Montgomery
  Troy
UAB: Walker College
University of Alabama
  Birmingham
  Huntsville
  Tuscaloosa
University of Mobile
University of Montevallo
University of South Alabama
Wallace State College at Hanceville

Alaska

Alaska Pacific University
Prince William Sound Community
  College
Sheldon Jackson College
University of Alaska
  Anchorage
  Fairbanks
  Southeast

Arizona

Arizona College of the Bible
Arizona State University
Arizona Western College
Cochise College
DeVry Institute of Technology:
  Phoenix
Eastern Arizona College
Embry-Riddle Aeronautical
  University: Prescott Campus
Gateway Community College
Glendale Community College
Mesa Community College
Mohave Community College
Northern Arizona University
Paradise Valley Community College
Phoenix College
Pima Community College
Prescott College
Rio Salado Community College
Scottsdale Community College
University of Arizona
University of Phoenix
Western International University

Arkansas

Arkansas Tech University
East Arkansas Community College
Garland County Community
  College
Harding University
Henderson State University
Mississippi County Community
  College
North Arkansas Community/
  Technical College
Ouachita Baptist University
South Arkansas Community College
Southern Arkansas University
  Magnolia
  Tech
University of Arkansas
  Fayetteville
  Little Rock
  Medical Sciences
  Monticello
  Pine Bluff
University of Central Arkansas
Williams Baptist College

California

Academy of Art College
Allan Hancock College
American College for the Applied
  Arts: Los Angeles
Antioch Southern California at Los
  Angeles
Armstrong University
Art Center College of Design
Art Institute of Southern California
Azusa Pacific University
Bethany College
Biola University
Brooks Institute of Photography
Cabrillo College
California Baptist College
California College of Arts and
  Crafts
California Lutheran University

California State University
  Bakersfield
  Dominguez Hills
  Fresno
  Hayward
  Long Beach
  Los Angeles
  Sacramento
  San Bernardino
  San Marcos
  Stanislaus
Chapman University
Christian Heritage College
Citrus College
Claremont McKenna College
Coastline Community College
Cogswell Polytechnical College
Coleman College
College of Alameda
College of Marin: Kentfield
College of Notre Dame
College of San Mateo
College of the Sequoias
Columbia College: Hollywood
Compton Community College
Contra Costa College
Cosumnes River College
Crafton Hills College
De Anza College
DeVry Institute of Technology:
  Pomona
Diablo Valley College
Dominican College of San Rafael
Evergreen Valley College
Fashion Institute of Design and
  Merchandising
Foothill College
Fresno Pacific College
Gavilan Community College
Golden Gate University
Holy Names College
Humboldt State University
Humphreys College
Irvine Valley College
John F. Kennedy University
Kings River Community College
La Sierra University
Lake Tahoe Community College
Lincoln University
Long Beach City College
Los Angeles Pierce College
Los Medanos College
Marymount College
Master's College
Menlo College
MiraCosta College
Mission College
Modesto Junior College
Monterey Institute of International
  Studies
Mount St. Mary's College
National University
New School of Art and
  Architecture
Occidental College
Otis College of Art and Design
Pacific Christian College
Pacific Oaks College
Patten College
Pepperdine University
Phillips Junior College: San
  Fernando Valley Campus
Point Loma Nazarene College
Riverside Community College
Sacramento City College
Saddleback College
St. Mary's College of California
Samuel Merritt College
San Diego City College
San Diego Mesa College
San Diego Miramar College

San Francisco Conservatory of
  Music
San Francisco State University
San Jose City College
Santa Clara University
Santa Monica College
Santa Rosa Junior College
Scripps College
Simpson College
Skyline College
Solano Community College
Sonoma State University
Southern California College
Southern California Institute of
  Architecture
Southwestern College
Taft College
University of California: Los
  Angeles
University of Judaism
University of La Verne
University of the Pacific
University of Redlands
University of San Francisco
University of Southern California
University of West Los Angeles
Whittier College
Woodbury University

Colorado

Adams State College
Aims Community College
Arapahoe Community College
Beth-El College of Nursing
Colorado Christian University
Colorado Institute of Art
Colorado Mountain College
  Alpine Campus
  Spring Valley Campus
  Timberline Campus
Colorado Northwestern Community
  College
Colorado School of Mines
Colorado State University
Colorado Technical College
Community College of Aurora
Fort Lewis College
Front Range Community College
Lamar Community College
Mesa State College
Metropolitan State College of
  Denver
Morgan Community College
Naropa Institute
Northeastern Junior College
Otero Junior College
Pikes Peak Community College
Pueblo Community College
Regis University
Rocky Mountain College of Art &
  Design
Technical Trades Institute
Trinidad State Junior College
University of Colorado
  Colorado Springs
  Denver
University of Denver
University of Northern Colorado
University of Southern Colorado
Western State College of Colorado

Connecticut

Albertus Magnus College
Asnuntuck Community-Technical
  College
Briarwood College
Capital Community-Technical
  College
Central Connecticut State
  University
Eastern Connecticut State
  University

Gateway Community-Technical
  College
Housatonic Community-Technical
  College
Middlesex Community-Technical
  College
Mitchell College
Naugatuck Valley Community-
  Technical College
Northwestern Connecticut
  Community-Technical College
Quinebaug Valley Community-
  Technical College
Quinnipiac College
Sacred Heart University
St. Joseph College
Southern Connecticut State
  University
Teikyo-Post University
Three Rivers Community-Technical
  College
Tunxis Community-Technical
  College
University of Bridgeport
University of Hartford
University of New Haven
Western Connecticut State
  University
Yale University

Delaware

Delaware State University
Delaware Technical and
  Community College
  Southern Campus
  Stanton/Wilmington Campus
  Terry Campus
Goldey-Beacom College
Wesley College
Wilmington College

District of Columbia

American University
Catholic University of America
Corcoran School of Art
Gallaudet University
Howard University
Mount Vernon College
Southeastern University
Strayer College
Trinity College
University of the District of
  Columbia

Florida

Barry University
Bethune-Cookman College
Brevard Community College
Broward Community College
Central Florida Community College
Daytona Beach Community College
Eckerd College
Edison Community College
Embry-Riddle Aeronautical
  University
Florida Agricultural and Mechanical
  University
Florida College
Florida Community College at
  Jacksonville
Florida Institute of Technology
Florida Keys Community College
Florida Memorial College
Fort Lauderdale College
Gulf Coast Community College
Hillsborough Community College
Hobe Sound Bible College
Indian River Community College
International Fine Arts College
Jacksonville University
Jones College
Lake-Sumter Community College

291

Lynn University
Manatee Community College
Miami-Dade Community College
Nova Southeastern University
Okaloosa-Walton Community
    College
Palm Beach Atlantic College
Palm Beach Community College
Pensacola Junior College
Polk Community College
Ringling School of Art and Design
Rollins College
St. Johns River Community College
St. Leo College
St. Petersburg Junior College
St. Thomas University
Santa Fe Community College
Seminole Community College
South Florida Community College
Southeastern College of the
    Assemblies of God
Southern College
Tallahassee Community College
Talmudic College of Florida
Tampa College
Trinity International University
University of Central Florida
University of Miami
University of North Florida
University of Tampa
University of West Florida
Valencia Community College
Warner Southern College
Webber College

Georgia

Abraham Baldwin Agricultural
    College
Albany State College
Atlanta Christian College
Augusta College
Augusta Technical Institute
Berry College
Brenau University
Brunswick College
Chattahoochee Technical Institute
Clark Atlanta University
Columbus College
Columbus Technical Institute
Covenant College
Darton College
DeKalb College
DeKalb Technical Institute
DeVry Institute of Technology:
    Atlanta
Emmanuel College
Floyd College
Fort Valley State College
Gainesville College
Georgia College
Georgia Institute of Technology
Georgia Southern University
Georgia Southwestern College
Georgia State University
Gordon College
Gwinnett Technical Institute
Kennesaw State College
LaGrange College
Macon College
Meadows College of Business
Mercer University
    Atlanta
    Macon
Middle Georgia College
Morris Brown College
North Georgia College
Oglethorpe University
Piedmont College
Savannah College of Art and
    Design
School of Visual Arts: Savannah
Shorter College

South College
South Georgia College
Southern College of Technology
Thomas College
Waycross College
Wesleyan College
West Georgia College

Hawaii

Chaminade University of Honolulu
Hawaii Pacific University
University of Hawaii
    Hawaii Community College
    Hilo
    Honolulu Community College
    Kauai Community College
    Leeward Community College
    Manoa

Idaho

Albertson College
Boise Bible College
Boise State University
College of Southern Idaho
Eastern Idaho Technical College
Lewis Clark State College
North Idaho College
Ricks College

Illinois

American Academy of Art
American Conservatory of Music
Aurora University
Barat College
Belleville Area College
Black Hawk College
Blackburn College
Bradley University
Carl Sandburg College
Chicago College of Commerce
Chicago State University
City Colleges of Chicago
    Harold Washington College
    Kennedy-King College
    Olive-Harvey College
College of DuPage
College of Lake County
College of St. Francis
Columbia College
Concordia University
Danville Area Community College
De Paul University
DeVry Institute of Technology
    Addison
    Chicago
Elgin Community College
Elmhurst College
Eureka College
Gem City College
Governors State University
Greenville College
Harrington Institute of Interior
    Design
Highland Community College
Illinois Benedictine College
Illinois Institute of Technology
Illinois Wesleyan University
John Wood Community College
Joliet Junior College
Judson College
Kendall College
Lake Land College
Lewis and Clark Community
    College
Lewis University
Lincoln Land Community College
Loyola University of Chicago
MacMurray College
McHenry County College
McKendree College
Millikin University
Moraine Valley Community College

Morrison Institute of Technology
Morton College
National-Louis University
North Central College
North Park College
Northeastern Illinois University
Oakton Community College
Olivet Nazarene University
Parkland College
Principia College
Quincy University
Ray College of Design
Richland Community College
Rock Valley College
Rockford College
Roosevelt University
Rosary College
St. Xavier University
Sangamon State University
School of the Art Institute of
    Chicago
Shimer College
Southern Illinois University at
    Edwardsville
Spoon River College
Trinity College
Triton College
University of Chicago
VanderCook College of Music
William Rainey Harper College

Indiana

Butler University
Calumet College of St. Joseph
DePauw University
Goshen College
Huntington College
Indiana Institute of Technology
Indiana State University
Indiana University
    Bloomington
    East
    Kokomo
    Northwest
    South Bend
    Southeast
Indiana University—Purdue
    University
    Fort Wayne
    Indianapolis
Indiana Vocational Technical
    College
    Central Indiana
    Columbus
    Eastcentral
    Kokomo
    Lafayette
    Northcentral
    Northeast
    Northwest
    Southcentral
    Southeast
    Southwest
    Wabash Valley
    Whitewater
Indiana Wesleyan University
Lutheran College of Health
    Professions
Marian College
Martin University
Oakland City College
Purdue University
    Calumet
    North Central Campus
Rose-Hulman Institute of
    Technology
St. Francis College
St. Mary-of-the-Woods College
Tri-State University
University of Evansville
University of Indianapolis
University of Southern Indiana

Valparaiso University
Vincennes University

Iowa

American Institute of Business
American Institute of Commerce
Briar Cliff College
Central College
Clarke College
Coe College
Des Moines Area Community
    College
Drake University
Grand View College
Hawkeye Community College
Indian Hills Community College
Iowa Lakes Community College
Iowa Wesleyan College
Iowa Western Community College
Kirkwood Community College
Luther College
Maharishi International University
Marshalltown Community College
Morningside College
North Iowa Area Community
    College
Northeast Iowa Community College
Northwest Iowa Community
    College
St. Ambrose University
Simpson College
Southeastern Community College:
    North Campus
Southwestern Community College
Teikyo Marycrest University
Teikyo Westmar University
University of Dubuque

Kansas

Allen County Community College
Baker University
Barton County Community College
Benedictine College
Bethany College
Bethel College
Butler County Community College
Central College
Coffeyville Community College
Colby Community College
Cowley County Community College
Dodge City Community College
Emporia State University
Fort Hays State University
Fort Scott Community College
Friends University
Garden City Community College
Hutchinson Community College
Independence Community College
Johnson County Community
    College
Kansas City Kansas Community
    College
Kansas Newman College
Kansas State University
McPherson College
MidAmerica Nazarene College
Neosho County Community College
Ottawa University
Pittsburg State University
Pratt Community College
St. Mary College
Seward County Community College
Southwestern College
Sterling College
Tabor College
University of Kansas
    Lawrence
    Medical Center
Washburn University of Topeka
Wichita State University

Kentucky

Ashland Community College
Bellarmine College
Campbellsville College
Centre College
Eastern Kentucky University
Elizabethtown Community College
Georgetown College
Hopkinsville Community College
Jefferson Community College
Kentucky Christian College
Kentucky State University
Kentucky Wesleyan College
Lexington Community College
Madisonville Community College
Maysville Community College
Midway College
Morehead State University
Murray State University
Northern Kentucky University
Pikeville College
Prestonsburg Community College
Southeast Community College
Spalding University
Thomas More College
Union College
University of Louisville
Western Kentucky University

Louisiana

Bossier Parish Community College
Dillard University
Grambling State University
Grantham College of Engineering
Louisiana State University in
   Shreveport
Louisiana Tech University
Loyola University
McNeese State University
Nicholls State University
Northeast Louisiana University
Nunez Community College
Our Lady of Holy Cross College
Southeastern Louisiana University
Southern University in Shreveport
University of New Orleans
University of Southwestern
   Louisiana
Xavier University of Louisiana

Maine

Andover College
Beal College
Casco Bay College
Central Maine Technical College
Eastern Maine Technical College
Husson College
Maine College of Art
St. Joseph's College
Southern Maine Technical College
Thomas College
Unity College
University of Maine
   Augusta
   Fort Kent
   Machias
   Orono
   Presque Isle
University of New England
University of Southern Maine
Westbrook College

Maryland

Allegany Community College
Anne Arundel Community College
Baltimore City Community College
Baltimore Hebrew University
Baltimore International Culinary
   College
Bowie State University
Capitol College
Carroll Community College

Catonsville Community College
Cecil Community College
Charles County Community College
Chesapeake College
College of Notre Dame of
   Maryland
Coppin State College
Dundalk Community College
Essex Community College
Frederick Community College
Frostburg State University
Hagerstown Business College
Hagerstown Junior College
Harford Community College
Hood College
Howard Community College
Johns Hopkins University: Peabody
   Conservatory of Music
Loyola College in Maryland
Maryland College of Art and
   Design
Maryland Institute College of Art
Montgomery College
   Germantown Campus
   Rockville Campus
   Takoma Park Campus
Morgan State University
Mount St. Mary's College
Prince George's Community College
St. Mary's College of Maryland
Towson State University
University of Baltimore
University of Maryland
   Baltimore
   Baltimore County
   College Park
   Eastern Shore
   University College
Villa Julie College
Washington College
Western Maryland College

Massachusetts

American International College
Anna Maria College
Atlantic Union College
Babson College
Bay Path College
Bentley College
Berklee College of Music
Berkshire Community College
Boston Architectural Center
Boston University
Bradford College
Brandeis University
Bridgewater State College
Bristol Community College
Bunker Hill Community College
Cape Cod Community College
Clark University
Curry College
Eastern Nazarene College
Elms College
Emerson College
Emmanuel College
Endicott College
Fisher College
Framingham State College
Franklin Institute of Boston
Greenfield Community College
Hebrew College
Hellenic College
Holyoke Community College
Lasell College
Marian Court College
Massachusetts Bay Community
   College
Massasoit Community College
Merrimack College
Middlesex Community College
Montserrat College of Art
Mount Holyoke College

Mount Ida College
Mount Wachusett Community
   College
New England Conservatory of
   Music
Newbury College
Nichols College
North Shore Community College
Northeastern University
Northern Essex Community College
Pine Manor College
Quincy College
Quinsigamond Community College
Roxbury Community College
School of the Museum of Fine Arts
Springfield College
Springfield Technical Community
   College
Suffolk University
Tufts University
University of Massachusetts
   Amherst
   Dartmouth
Wentworth Institute of Technology
Western New England College
Westfield State College
Worcester State College

Michigan

Alma College
Alpena Community College
Andrews University
Aquinas College
Baker College
   Auburn Hills
   Cadillac
   Flint
   Jackson
   Mount Clemens
   Muskegon
   Owosso
   Port Huron
Center for Creative Studies: College
   of Art and Design
Central Michigan University
Concordia College
Cornerstone College and Grand
   Rapids Baptist Seminary
Davenport College of Business
Delta College
Detroit College of Business
Eastern Michigan University
Glen Oaks Community College
GMI Engineering & Management
   Institute
Grace Bible College
Grand Rapids Community College
Grand Valley State University
Henry Ford Community College
Highland Park Community College
Jackson Community College
Kalamazoo Valley Community
   College
Kellogg Community College
Kendall College of Art and Design
Kirtland Community College
Madonna University
Michigan Christian College
Mid Michigan Community College
Monroe County Community
   College
Montcalm Community College
Mott Community College
Muskegon Community College
Northwestern Michigan College
Oakland Community College
Oakland University
Olivet College
Reformed Bible College
Sacred Heart Major Seminary
Saginaw Valley State University

St. Clair County Community
   College
St. Mary's College
Schoolcraft College
Southwestern Michigan College
Spring Arbor College
Suomi College
University of Detroit Mercy
University of Michigan
   Dearborn
   Flint
Walsh College of Accountancy and
   Business Administration
Washtenaw Community College
Wayne State University
West Shore Community College
Western Michigan University

Minnesota

Augsburg College
Austin Community College
Bethany Lutheran College
Bethel College
College of St. Benedict
College of St. Catherine: St.
   Catherine Campus
College of St. Catherine-
   Minneapolis
College of St. Scholastica
Concordia College: St. Paul
Dunwoody Industrial Institute
Hamline University
Inver Hills Community College
Lakewood Community College
Mankato State University
Metropolitan State University
Minneapolis Community College
National College
Normandale Community College
North Central Bible College
North Hennepin Community
   College
Northwestern College
Pillsbury Baptist Bible College
Rainy River Community College
Rasmussen College-Minnetonka
Rochester Community College
St. Paul Technical College
Willmar Technical College

Mississippi

Alcorn State University
Belhaven College
Blue Mountain College
Delta State University
Hinds Community College
Jackson State University
Magnolia Bible College
Mary Holmes College
Millsaps College
Mississippi Gulf Coast Community
   College
   Jackson County Campus
   Jefferson Davis Campus
   Perkinston
Mississippi State University
Mississippi University for Women
Northwest Mississippi Community
   College
Pearl River Community College
Rust College
Tougaloo College
University of Mississippi
University of Southern Mississippi
William Carey College

Missouri

Avila College
Baptist Bible College
Calvary Bible College
Central Methodist College
Central Missouri State University

Columbia College
Crowder College
DeVry Institute of Technology:
Kansas City
East Central College
Evangel College
Fontbonne College
Harris Stowe State College
Jefferson College
Lincoln University
Lindenwood College
Longview Community College
Maryville University of St. Louis
Missouri Baptist College
Missouri Southern State College
Missouri Valley College
Missouri Western State College
Moberly Area Community College
North Central Missouri College
Northeast Missouri State University
Northwest Missouri State
University
Ozark Christian College
Park College
Ranken Technical College
Research College of Nursing
Rockhurst College
St. Charles County Community
College
St. Louis Christian College
St. Louis Community College
Florissant Valley
Forest Park
Meramec
St. Louis University
Southeast Missouri State University
Southwest Baptist University
Southwest Missouri State University
State Fair Community College
Stephens College
Three Rivers Community College
University of Missouri
Columbia
Kansas City
Rolla
St. Louis
Webster University
Westminster College
William Jewell College
William Woods University

Montana

College of Great Falls
Montana State University
College of Technology-Great
Falls
Bozeman
University of Montana-Missoula
University of Montana College of
Technology

Nebraska

Bellevue University
Central Community College
Clarkson College
College of St. Mary
Concordia College
Creighton University
Dana College
Doane College
Grace University
Lincoln School of Commerce
Metropolitan Community College
Midland Lutheran College
Nebraska Christian College
Nebraska Methodist College of
Nursing and Allied Health
Nebraska Wesleyan University
Northeast Community College
Peru State College

Southeast Community College
Beatrice Campus
Lincoln Campus
Milford Campus
Union College
University of Nebraska Medical
Center
Wayne State College
Western Nebraska Community
College: Scottsbluff Campus
York College

Nevada

Community College of Southern
Nevada
Morrison College: Reno
Northern Nevada Community
College
Sierra Nevada College
Truckee Meadows Community
College
University of Nevada
Las Vegas
Reno
Western Nevada Community
College

New Hampshire

Colby-Sawyer College
Daniel Webster College
Franklin Pierce College
Hesser College
Keene State College
McIntosh College
New England College
New Hampshire College
New Hampshire Technical College
Claremont
Laconia
Manchester
Nashua
New Hampshire Technical Institute
Notre Dame College
Rivier College
University of New Hampshire at
Manchester

New Jersey

Atlantic Community College
Bergen Community College
Berkeley College of Business
Bloomfield College
Brookdale Community College
Burlington County College
Caldwell College
Camden County College
Centenary College
Cumberland County College
DeVry Technical Institute
Drew University
Fairleigh Dickinson University
Edward Williams College
Teaneck
Felician College
Georgian Court College
Gloucester County College
Hudson County Community College
Kean College of New Jersey
Mercer County Community College
Monmouth College
Montclair State University
New Jersey Institute of Technology
Passaic County Community College
Ramapo College of New Jersey
Richard Stockton College of New
Jersey
Rider University
Rowan College of New Jersey
St. Peter's College
Salem Community College
Seton Hall University
Union County College

Westminster Choir College of Rider
University
William Paterson College of New
Jersey

New Mexico

Albuquerque Technical-Vocational
Institute
Clovis Community College
College of Santa Fe
College of the Southwest
Dona Ana Branch Community
College of New Mexico State
University
Eastern New Mexico University
Portales
Roswell Campus
National College
New Mexico Highlands University
New Mexico Institute of Mining
and Technology
New Mexico Junior College
New Mexico Military Institute
New Mexico State University
San Juan College
University of New Mexico

New York

Adelphi University
Adirondack Community College
American Academy of Dramatic
Arts
Audrey Cohen College
Barnard College
Bramson ORT Technical Institute
Briarcliffe: The College for Business
and Technology
Broome Community College
Bryant & Stratton Business Institute
Albany
Syracuse
Canisius College
Cayuga County Community College
Cazenovia College
Central City Business Institute
City University of New York
City College
Hunter College
John Jay College of Criminal
Justice
Queens College
Queensborough Community
College
Clarkson University
Clinton Community College
Cochran School of Nursing-St.
John's Riverside Hospital
College of Aeronautics
College of Insurance
College of Mount St. Vincent
College of New Rochelle
New Rochelle
School of New Resources
College of St. Rose
Columbia University
Columbia College
School of Engineering and
Applied Science
School of General Studies
School of Nursing
Columbia-Greene Community
College
Corning Community College
Daemen College
Darkei Noam Rabbinical College
Dominican College of Blauvelt
Dowling College
Dutchess Community College
D'Youville College
Eastman School of Music of the
University of Rochester
Elmira College

Erie Community College
North Campus
South Campus
Eugene Lang College/New School
for Social Research
Fashion Institute of Technology
Finger Lakes Community College
Fordham University
Fulton-Montgomery Community
College
Genesee Community College
Herkimer County Community
College
Hilbert College
Hofstra University
Hudson Valley Community College
Iona College
Ithaca College
Jamestown Community College
Jefferson Community College
Katharine Gibbs School: Melville
Keuka College
Le Moyne College
Long Island University
Brooklyn Campus
C. W. Post Campus
Southampton College
Manhattan College
Manhattanville College
Maria College
Marist College
Marymount College
Marymount Manhattan College
Mater Dei College
Medaille College
Mercy College
Mohawk Valley Community College
Molloy College
Monroe Community College
Mount St. Mary College
Nazareth College of Rochester
New York Institute of Technology
New York School of Interior
Design
New York University
Niagara County Community College
Niagara University
North Country Community College
Nyack College
Olean Business Institute
Onondaga Community College
Orange County Community College
Pace University
Parsons School of Design
Paul Smith's College
Phillips Beth Israel School of
Nursing
Plaza Business Institute
Polytechnic University
Brooklyn
Long Island Campus
Pratt Institute
Rensselaer Polytechnic Institute
Roberts Wesleyan College
Rochester Business Institute
Rochester Institute of Technology
Rockland Community College
Russell Sage College
Sage Junior College of Albany
St. Francis College
St. John Fisher College
St. John's University
St. Joseph's College
Brooklyn
Suffolk Campus
St. Thomas Aquinas College
Schenectady County Community
College
School of Visual Arts
Siena College

State University of New York
Albany
Binghamton
Buffalo
Oswego
Purchase
Stony Brook
College of Agriculture and
Technology at Cobleskill
College of Agriculture and
Technology at Morrisville
College at Brockport
College at Buffalo
College at Cortland
College at Fredonia
College at Geneseo
College at New Paltz
College at Old Westbury
College at Oneonta
College at Plattsburgh
College at Potsdam
College of Technology at
Alfred
College of Technology at
Canton
College of Technology at Delhi
College of Technology at
Farmingdale
Institute of Technology at
Utica/Rome
Suffolk County Community College
Selden
Western Campus
Sullivan County Community
College
Tompkins-Cortland Community
College
Touro College
Trocaire College
Ulster County Community College
University of Rochester
University of the State of New
York: Regents College
Utica College of Syracuse
University
Utica School of Commerce
Villa Maria College of Buffalo
Wagner College
Wells College
Westchester Business Institute
Westchester Community College

North Carolina

Alamance Community College
Anson Community College
Appalachian State University
Barton College
Belmont Abbey College
Bennett College
Brevard College
Brunswick Community College
Campbell University
Cape Fear Community College
Catawba College
Central Piedmont Community
College
Davidson County Community
College
East Carolina University
East Coast Bible College
Elon College
Fayetteville State University
Fayetteville Technical Community
College
Gardner-Webb University
Gaston College
Greensboro College
Guilford College
James Sprunt Community College
John Wesley College
Johnson C. Smith University
Lenoir-Rhyne College

Louisburg College
Methodist College
Montreat-Anderson College
Mount Olive College
Nash Community College
North Carolina Agricultural and
Technical State University
North Carolina Central University
Pembroke State University
Pfeiffer College
Pitt Community College
Queens College
Randolph Community College
Roanoke-Chowan Community
College
Sampson Community College
Sandhills Community College
Shaw University
University of North Carolina
Chapel Hill
Charlotte
Greensboro
Wilmington
Warren Wilson College

North Dakota

Trinity Bible College
University of North Dakota

Ohio

Antonelli Institute of Art and
Photography
Art Academy of Cincinnati
Ashland University
Baldwin-Wallace College
Belmont Technical College
Bluffton College
Bowling Green State University
Bowling Green
Firelands College
Bryant & Stratton Business
Institute: Cleveland West
Capital University
Central Ohio Technical College
Chatfield College
Cincinnati State Technical and
Community College
Circleville Bible College
Clark State Community College
Cleveland College of Jewish Studies
Cleveland Institute of Art
Cleveland Institute of Music
Cleveland State University
College of Mount St. Joseph
Columbus College of Art and
Design
Columbus State Community College
Cuyahoga Community College
Eastern Campus
Metropolitan Campus
Western Campus
Davis College
DeVry Institute of Technology:
Columbus
Dyke College
Edison State Community College
Franciscan University of
Steubenville
Franklin University
God's Bible School and College
Heidelberg College
Hiram College
Hocking Technical College
ITT Technical Institute:
Youngstown
John Carroll University

Kent State University
Ashtabula Regional Campus
East Liverpool Regional
Campus
Kent
Salem Regional Campus
Stark Campus
Trumbull Campus
Tuscarawas Campus
Kenyon College
Kettering College of Medical Arts
Lake Erie College
Lakeland Community College
Lorain County Community College
Lourdes College
Malone College
Marietta College
Marion Technical College
Miami University
Hamilton Campus
Middletown Campus
Miami-Jacobs College
Mount Union College
Muskingum Area Technical College
Muskingum College
North Central Technical College
Northwest State Community
College
Northwestern College
Ohio Dominican College
Ohio Northern University
Ohio State University
Columbus Campus
Lima Campus
Mansfield Campus
Marion Campus
Newark Campus
Ohio University
Athens
Chillicothe Campus
Ohio Valley Business College
Ohio Wesleyan University
Otterbein College
Owens Technical College
Findlay Campus
Toledo
Shawnee State University
Sinclair Community College
Southern State Community College
Stark Technical College
Terra Community College
Tiffin University
Union Institute
University of Akron
University of Cincinnati
Cincinnati
Clermont College
Raymond Walters College
University of Dayton
University of Toledo
Urbana University
Ursuline College
Washington State Community
College
Wilberforce University
Wilmington College
Wright State University
Dayton
Lake Campus
Xavier University
Youngstown State University

Oklahoma

Bartlesville Wesleyan College
Cameron University
Connors State College
East Central University
Langston University
Northeastern Oklahoma
Agricultural and Mechanical
College
Northeastern State University

Northern Oklahoma College
Northwestern Oklahoma State
University
Oklahoma Baptist University
Oklahoma Christian University of
Science and Arts
Oklahoma City Community College
Oklahoma City University
Oklahoma Panhandle State
University
Oklahoma State University
Oklahoma City
Stillwater
Oral Roberts University
Phillips University
Redlands Community College
Rogers State College
Rose State College
Southeastern Oklahoma State
University
Southern Nazarene University
Southwestern Oklahoma State
University
Tulsa Junior College
University of Central Oklahoma
University of Oklahoma
Health Sciences Center
Norman
University of Science and Arts of
Oklahoma
University of Tulsa
Western Oklahoma State College

Oregon

Bassist College
Central Oregon Community College
Chemeketa Community College
Clackamas Community College
Concordia College
Eastern Oregon State College
Lane Community College
Lewis & Clark College
Linfield College
Linn-Benton Community College
Marylhurst College
Multnomah Bible College
Oregon Health Sciences University
Oregon Institute of Technology
Pacific Northwest College of Art
Portland Community College
Portland State University
Southern Oregon State College
Southwestern Oregon Community
College
Treasure Valley Community College
University of Portland
Warner Pacific College
Western Baptist College
Willamette University

Pennsylvania

Albright College
Allentown College of St. Francis de
Sales
Alvernia College
Antonelli Institute of Art and
Photography
Art Institute of Pittsburgh
Baptist Bible College of
Pennsylvania
Beaver College
Bradley Academy for the Visual
Arts
Bryn Mawr College
Bucks County Community College
Butler County Community College
Cabrini College
Carlow College
Cedar Crest College
Central Pennsylvania Business
School
Chatham College

Chestnut Hill College
Cheyney University of Pennsylvania
CHI Institute
Clarion University of Pennsylvania
Community College of Allegheny
County
    Allegheny Campus
    Boyce Campus
    North Campus
    South Campus
Community College of Beaver
County
Community College of Philadelphia
Delaware County Community
College
Delaware Valley College
Drexel University
Duquesne University
East Stroudsburg University of
Pennsylvania
Eastern College
Elizabethtown College
Gannon University
Gratz College
Gwynedd-Mercy College
Harrisburg Area Community
College
Holy Family College
Hussian School of Art
Johnson Technical Institute
King's College
Kutztown University of
Pennsylvania
La Roche College
La Salle University
Lackawanna Junior College
Lebanon Valley College of
Pennsylvania
Lehigh Carbon Community College
Lincoln Technical Institute
Lincoln University
Luzerne County Community
College
Manor Junior College
Mansfield University of
Pennsylvania
Marywood College
Mercyhurst College
Millersville University of
Pennsylvania
Montgomery County Community
College
Moore College of Art and Design
Mount Aloysius College
National Education Center: Vale
Tech Campus
Neumann College
Northampton County Area
Community College
Peirce College
Philadelphia College of Textiles and
Science
Pittsburgh Technical Institute
Point Park College
Reading Area Community College
Robert Morris College
Rosemont College
St. Joseph's University
Seton Hill College
Slippery Rock University of
Pennsylvania
Temple University
Thiel College
Thomas Jefferson University:
College of Allied Health Sciences
University of the Arts
University of Pittsburgh
    Bradford
    Greensburg
    Pittsburgh
University of Scranton
Valley Forge Christian College

Villanova University
West Chester University of
Pennsylvania
Westmoreland County Community
College
Widener University
Wilkes University
Wilson College

Puerto Rico

American University of Puerto Rico
Colegio Universitario del Este
Inter American University of Puerto
Rico
    Arecibo Campus
    Barranquitas Campus
    San German Campus
Pontifical Catholic University of
Puerto Rico
Turabo University
Universidad Metropolitana
Universidad Politecnica de Puerto
Rico
University of Puerto Rico: Ponce
Technological University College
University of the Sacred Heart

Rhode Island

Bryant College
Community College of Rhode
Island
Johnson & Wales University
New England Institute of
Technology
Rhode Island College
Rhode Island School of Design
Roger Williams University
Salve Regina University

South Carolina

Aiken Technical College
Central Carolina Technical College
Chesterfield-Marlboro Technical
College
The Citadel
Claflin College
Clemson University
Coastal Carolina University
Coker College
College of Charleston
Columbia Bible College
Converse College
Florence-Darlington Technical
College
Francis Marion University
Greenville Technical College
Horry-Georgetown Technical
College
Lander University
Limestone College
Newberry College
North Greenville College
Orangeburg-Calhoun Technical
College
Piedmont Technical College
Presbyterian College
Southern Wesleyan University
Technical College of the
Lowcountry
Tri-County Technical College
Trident Technical College
University of South Carolina
    Aiken
    Beaufort
    Columbia
    Lancaster
    Salkehatchie Regional Campus
    Spartanburg
    Sumter
    Union
Winthrop University
York Technical College

South Dakota

Augustana College
Black Hills State University
Dakota State University
Dakota Wesleyan University
Huron University
Kilian Community College
National College
Northern State University
Presentation College
South Dakota School of Mines and
Technology
South Dakota State University
University of Sioux Falls
University of South Dakota

Tennessee

Aquinas College
Austin Peay State University
Belmont University
Carson-Newman College
Chattanooga State Technical
Community College
Christian Brothers University
Cleveland State Community College
Crichton College
Dyersburg State Community
College
East Tennessee State University
Fisk University
Freed-Hardeman University
Hiwassee College
Jackson State Community College
King College
Knoxville College
Lane College
Lee College
LeMoyne-Owen College
Lincoln Memorial University
Maryville College
Memphis College of Art
Middle Tennessee State University
Milligan College
Nashville State Technical Institute
Northeast State Technical
Community College
Pellissippi State Technical
Community College
Rhodes College
Roane State Community College
Shelby State Community College
Southern College of Seventh-day
Adventist
State Technical Institute at
Memphis
Tennessee State University
Tennessee Technological University
Tennessee Wesleyan College
Tusculum College
University of Memphis
University of the South
University of Tennessee
    Chattanooga
    Knoxville
    Martin
    Memphis
Volunteer State Community College
Walters State Community College

Texas

Abilene Christian University
Ambassador University
Angelina College
Arlington Baptist College
Bee County College
Brazosport College
Brookhaven College
Cedar Valley College
Central Texas College
Cisco Junior College
Collin County Community College
District

Concordia Lutheran College
Dallas Baptist University
Dallas Christian College
Del Mar College
DeVry Institute of Technology:
Irving
East Texas Baptist University
Eastfield College
El Centro College
El Paso Community College
Galveston College
Hardin-Simmons University
Houston Baptist University
Houston Community College
Howard College
Howard Payne University
Huston-Tillotson College
Incarnate Word College
Jarvis Christian College
Lamar University—Beaumont
Lee College
McLennan Community College
McMurry University
Midwestern State University
Mountain View College
Navarro College
North Central Texas College
North Harris Montgomery
Community College District
North Lake College
Northeast Texas Community
College
Odessa College
Our Lady of the Lake University of
San Antonio
Panola College
Prairie View A&M University
Richland College
St. Edward's University
St. Mary's University
St. Philip's College
Sam Houston State University
San Antonio College
South Plains College
Southwest Texas State University
Tarleton State University
Tarrant County Junior College
Temple Junior College
Texas A&M International
University
Texas A&M University-Corpus
Christi
Texas A&M University-Kingsville
Texas Southern University
Texas State Technical College
    Harlingen
    Waco
Texas Tech University
Texas Wesleyan University
Texas Woman's University
Tyler Junior College
University of Dallas
University of Houston: Downtown
University of Mary Hardin-Baylor
University of North Texas
University of St. Thomas
University of Texas
    Arlington
    Dallas
    El Paso
    Medical Branch at Galveston
    Pan American
    San Antonio
Wayland Baptist University
Weatherford College
West Texas A&M University
Western Texas College

Utah

Phillips Junior College: Salt Lake
City Campus
Salt Lake Community College

Stevens-Henager College of
Business
University of Utah
Utah State University
Utah Valley State College
Weber State University

Vermont

Burlington College
Castleton State College
Champlain College
College of St. Joseph in Vermont
Community College of Vermont
Goddard College
Johnson State College
Lyndon State College
Marlboro College
Norwich University
St. Michael's College
School for International Training
Southern Vermont College
Trinity College of Vermont
University of Vermont

Virginia

Averett College
Blue Ridge Community College
Bluefield College
Central Virginia Community College
Christopher Newport University
Clinch Valley College of the
University of Virginia
College of Health Sciences
Commonwealth College
Dabney S. Lancaster Community
College
Danville Community College
Eastern Shore Community College
Ferrum College
George Mason University
Germanna Community College
Hampton University
J. Sargeant Reynolds Community
College
James Madison University
John Tyler Community College
Liberty University
Longwood College
Lord Fairfax Community College
Lynchburg College
Mary Baldwin College
Mary Washington College
Marymount University
Mountain Empire Community
College
New River Community College
Norfolk State University
Northern Virginia Community
College
Old Dominion University
Patrick Henry Community College
Paul D. Camp Community College
Piedmont Virginia Community
College
Randolph-Macon College
Rappahannock Community College
Richard Bland College
St. Paul's College
Shenandoah University
Southern Virginia College
Southside Virginia Community
College
Southwest Virginia Community
College
Thomas Nelson Community College
Tidewater Community College
Virginia Commonwealth University
Virginia Highlands Community
College
Virginia Intermont College
Virginia Polytechnic Institute and
State University

Virginia State University
Virginia Union University
Virginia Wesleyan College
Virginia Western Community
College ·
Wytheville Community College

Washington

Art Institute of Seattle
Bellevue Community College
Big Bend Community College
Central Washington University
Centralia College
City University
Clark College
Cogswell College North
Columbia Basin College
Cornish College of the Arts
Eastern Washington University
Edmonds Community College
Everett Community College
Evergreen State College
Gonzaga University
Grays Harbor College
Green River Community College
Heritage College
Highline Community College
Lower Columbia College
North Seattle Community College
Northwest College
Olympic College
Pacific Lutheran University
Peninsula College
Pierce College
Puget Sound Christian College
Renton Technical College
St. Martin's College
Seattle Central Community College
Seattle Pacific University
Seattle University
Shoreline Community College
Skagit Valley College
South Puget Sound Community
College
South Seattle Community College
Spokane Community College
Spokane Falls Community College
Tacoma Community College
Walla Walla College
Walla Walla Community College
Wenatchee Valley College
Western Washington University
Whatcom Community College
Whitworth College
Yakima Valley Community College

West Virginia

Alderson-Broaddus College
Bluefield State College
College of West Virginia
Davis and Elkins College
Mountain State College
Shepherd College
University of Charleston
West Liberty State College
West Virginia Northern Community
College
West Virginia State College
West Virginia University
Wheeling Jesuit College

Wisconsin

Alverno College
Carroll College
Fox Valley Technical College
Gateway Technical College
Lakeland College
Lakeshore Technical College
Madison Area Technical College
Madison Junior College of Business
Marian College of Fond du Lac
Marquette University

Moraine Park Technical College
Mount Senario College
Northeast Wisconsin Technical
College
Northland College
St. Norbert College
Stratton College
Viterbo College
Waukesha County Technical
College
Wisconsin Lutheran College

Wyoming

Casper College
Central Wyoming College
Laramie County Community
College

American Samoa, Caroline Islands, Guam, Marianas, Virgin Islands

Guam Community College
University of Guam

Canada

Memorial University of
Newfoundland

France

American University of Paris

Mexico

Sistema Instituto Tecnologico y de
Estudios Superiores de
Monterrey

Tuition payment by installments

Alabama

Alabama State University
Auburn University at Montgomery
Birmingham-Southern College
Draughons Junior College
Faulkner University
Huntingdon College
Lawson State Community College
Marion Military Institute
Miles College
Southeastern Bible College
Stillman College
Talladega College
Tuskegee University
UAB: Walker College
University of Alabama
University of Montevallo
University of West Alabama

Alaska

Alaska Bible College
Alaska Pacific University
University of Alaska
Fairbanks
Southeast

Arizona

American Indian College of the
Assemblies of God
Arizona College of the Bible
DeVry Institute of Technology:
Phoenix
Gateway Community College
Navajo Community College
Northland Pioneer College
Prescott College
South Mountain Community
College
Southwestern College

Western International University

Arkansas

Arkansas State University
Arkansas Tech University
Central Baptist College
Garland County Community
College
Harding University
Hendrix College
John Brown University
Lyon College
Mississippi County Community
College
North Arkansas Community/
Technical College
Philander Smith College
Phillips County Community College
Rich Mountain Community College
Shorter College
South Arkansas Community College
Southern Arkansas University
Magnolia
Tech
University of Arkansas
Fayetteville
Little Rock
Pine Bluff
University of the Ozarks
Williams Baptist College

California

Academy of Art College
American College for the Applied
Arts: Los Angeles
Antelope Valley College
Antioch Southern California
Los Angeles
Santa Barbara
Armstrong University
Art Center College of Design
Art Institute of Southern California
Azusa Pacific University
Bethany College
Biola University
Brooks Institute of Photography
California Baptist College
California College of Arts and
Crafts
California Institute of Technology
California Lutheran University
California Polytechnic State
University: San Luis Obispo
California State Polytechnic
University: Pomona
California State University
Bakersfield
Chico
Hayward
Long Beach
Sacramento
Stanislaus
Cerro Coso Community College
Chabot College
Chapman University
Charles R. Drew University: College
of Allied Health
Christian Heritage College
Claremont McKenna College
Cogswell Polytechnical College
College of Alameda
College of the Desert
College of Notre Dame
College of San Mateo
College of the Sequoias
Columbia College: Hollywood
Compton Community College
Cosumnes River College
De Anza College
DeVry Institute of Technology:
Pomona
Dominican College of San Rafael

Dominican School of Philosophy
and Theology
Fashion Institute of Design and
Merchandising
Feather River College
Fresno Pacific College
Golden Gate University
Harvey Mudd College
Heald Business College: Fresno
Hebrew Union College: Jewish
Institute of Religion
Holy Names College
Humphreys College
John F. Kennedy University
Kings River Community College
La Sierra University
Lassen College
LIFE Bible College
Lincoln University
Loyola Marymount University
Marymount College
Master's College
Menlo College
Mills College
Mission College
Monterey Peninsula College
Mount St. Mary's College
Mount San Jacinto College
Napa Valley College
New College of California
New School of Art and
Architecture
Occidental College
Otis College of Art and Design
Pacific Christian College
Pacific Oaks College
Pacific Union College
Patten College
Pepperdine University
Phillips Junior College
Fresno Campus
San Fernando Valley Campus
Pitzer College
Point Loma Nazarene College
Pomona College
Porterville College
Sacramento City College
St. John's Seminary College
St. Mary's College of California
Samuel Merritt College
San Diego State University
San Francisco Art Institute
San Francisco Conservatory of
Music
San Francisco State University
San Jose Christian College
San Jose State University
Santa Clara University
Santa Rosa Junior College
Scripps College
Simpson College
Southern California College
Stanford University
Taft College
Thomas Aquinas College
United States International
University
University of California
Berkeley
Riverside
Santa Cruz
University of Judaism
University of La Verne
University of the Pacific
University of Redlands
University of San Diego
University of San Francisco
University of Southern California
University of West Los Angeles
Victor Valley College
Westmont College
Whittier College

Woodbury University
Yuba College

Colorado

Adams State College
Arapahoe Community College
Bel-Rea Institute of Animal
Technology
Beth-El College of Nursing
Colorado Christian University
Colorado College
Colorado Institute of Art
Colorado Northwestern Community
College
Colorado School of Mines
Colorado State University
Colorado Technical College
Community College of Aurora
Fort Lewis College
Lamar Community College
Northeastern Junior College
Otero Junior College
Regis University
Rocky Mountain College of Art &
Design
Technical Trades Institute
Trinidad State Junior College
University of Colorado
Colorado Springs
Denver
University of Denver
University of Northern Colorado
University of Southern Colorado
Western State College of Colorado

Connecticut

Albertus Magnus College
Briarwood College
Connecticut College
Eastern Connecticut State
University
Fairfield University
Mitchell College
Norwalk Community-Technical
College
Paier College of Art
Quinnipiac College
Sacred Heart University
St. Joseph College
Teikyo-Post University
Trinity College
University of Bridgeport
University of Hartford
University of New Haven
Wesleyan University
Yale University

Delaware

Delaware State University
Delaware Technical and
Community College
Southern Campus
Stanton/Wilmington Campus
Terry Campus
Goldey-Beacom College
University of Delaware
Wesley College
Wilmington College

District of Columbia

American University
Catholic University of America
Corcoran School of Art
Gallaudet University
George Washington University
Georgetown University
Mount Vernon College
Oblate College
Southeastern University
Strayer College
Trinity College

University of the District of
Columbia

Florida

Barry University
Brevard Community College
Embry-Riddle Aeronautical
University
Florida Atlantic University
Florida Baptist Theological College
Florida Bible College
Florida Christian College
Florida College
Florida Memorial College
Florida Southern College
Florida State University
Fort Lauderdale College
Hobe Sound Bible College
International Fine Arts College
Jacksonville University
Jones College
North Florida Junior College
Nova Southeastern University
Okaloosa-Walton Community
College
Palm Beach Atlantic College
Rollins College
St. John Vianney College Seminary
Southeastern College of the
Assemblies of God
Southern College
Stetson University
Talmudic College of Florida
Tampa College
Trinity International University
University of Miami
University of South Florida
University of Tampa
University of West Florida
Warner Southern College
Webber College

Georgia

Agnes Scott College
Atlanta Christian College
Atlanta College of Art
Augusta Technical Institute
Berry College
Brenau University
Brewton-Parker College
Clark Atlanta University
Covenant College
DeVry Institute of Technology:
Atlanta
Emory University
Georgia Institute of Technology
LaGrange College
Meadows College of Business
Morris Brown College
Oglethorpe University
Paine College
Piedmont College
Reinhardt College
Savannah College of Art and
Design
School of Visual Arts: Savannah
Shorter College
South College
Thomas College
Toccoa Falls College
Truett-McConnell College
Wesleyan College
Young Harris College

Hawaii

Chaminade University of Honolulu
Hawaii Pacific University

Idaho

Albertson College
Boise Bible College

Illinois

American Conservatory of Music
Augustana College
Aurora University
Barat College
Belleville Area College
Black Hawk College
Blackburn College
Blessing-Reiman College of Nursing
Bradley University
Carl Sandburg College
Chicago College of Commerce
City Colleges of Chicago
Harold Washington College
Kennedy-King College
College of DuPage
College of Lake County
College of St. Francis
Columbia College
Concordia University
Danville Area Community College
De Paul University
DeVry Institute of Technology
Addison
Chicago
Eastern Illinois University
Elgin Community College
Elmhurst College
Governors State University
Greenville College
Harrington Institute of Interior
Design
Illinois Benedictine College
Illinois College
Illinois Institute of Technology
Illinois State University
Illinois Wesleyan University
Kaskaskia College
Kendall College
Knox College
Lake Forest College
Lakeview College of Nursing
Lewis and Clark Community
College
Lewis University
Lexington Institute of Hospitality
Careers
Lincoln Christian College and
Seminary
Loyola University of Chicago
MacCormac Junior College
MacMurray College
McHenry County College
Millikin University
Monmouth College
Moraine Valley Community College
Morrison Institute of Technology
National-Louis University
North Central College
North Park College
Northeastern Illinois University
Northern Illinois University
Northwestern University
Olivet Nazarene University
Parkland College
Principia College
Quincy University
Ray College of Design
Richland Community College
Robert Morris College: Chicago
Rockford College
Roosevelt University
Rosary College
St. Xavier University
Sangamon State University
School of the Art Institute of
Chicago
Shimer College
Southeastern Illinois College
Southern Illinois University
Carbondale
Edwardsville

Spoon River College
State Community College
Trinity Christian College
Trinity College
University of Chicago
University of Illinois
    Chicago
    Urbana-Champaign
VanderCook College of Music
Western Illinois University
Wheaton College
William Rainey Harper College

Indiana

Anderson University
Ball State University
Bethel College
Butler University
Calumet College of St. Joseph
Earlham College
Franklin College
Goshen College
Grace College
Hanover College
Huntington College
Indiana Institute of Technology
Indiana University
    Kokomo
    Southeast
Indiana University-Purdue
    University Indianapolis
Indiana Vocational Technical
    College
        Central Indiana
        Columbus
        Eastcentral
        Kokomo
        Lafayette
        Northcentral
        Northeast
        Southcentral
        Southeast
        Southwest
        Wabash Valley
        Whitewater
Indiana Wesleyan University
Lutheran College of Health
    Professions
Manchester College
Marian College
Martin University
Oakland City College
Purdue University
    Calumet
    West Lafayette
St. Francis College
St. Mary-of-the-Woods College
St. Meinrad College
Taylor University
University of Evansville
University of Indianapolis
University of Notre Dame
University of Southern Indiana
Vincennes University
Wabash College

Iowa

American Institute of Business
American Institute of Commerce
Briar Cliff College
Buena Vista College
Central College
Clarke College
Coe College
Cornell College
Des Moines Area Community
    College
Drake University
Faith Baptist Bible College and
    Theological Seminary
Graceland College
Grand View College

Grinnell College
Hamilton Technical College
Hawkeye Community College
Indian Hills Community College
Iowa Central Community College
Iowa Lakes Community College
Iowa State University
Iowa Western Community College
Kirkwood Community College
Loras College
Luther College
Maharishi International University
Marshalltown Community College
Morningside College
Mount Mercy College
North Iowa Area Community
    College
Northeast Iowa Community College
Northwestern College
St. Ambrose University
Simpson College
Teikyo Marycrest University
Teikyo Westmar University
University of Dubuque
University of Iowa
University of Northern Iowa
Upper Iowa University
Waldorf College
Wartburg College

Kansas

Baker University
Barclay College
Benedictine College
Bethany College
Bethel College
Butler County Community College
Central College
Coffeyville Community College
Cowley County Community College
Dodge City Community College
Donnelly College
Emporia State University
Fort Scott Community College
Friends University
Garden City Community College
Hesston College
Independence Community College
Kansas Newman College
Kansas Wesleyan University
Manhattan Christian College
MidAmerica Nazarene College
Neosho County Community College
Pratt Community College
St. Mary College
Seward County Community College
Southwestern College
Sterling College
Tabor College
Washburn University of Topeka
Wichita State University

Kentucky

Alice Lloyd College
Asbury College
Bellarmine College
Brescia College
Campbellsville College
Centre College
Clear Creek Baptist Bible College
Cumberland College
Eastern Kentucky University
Georgetown College
Institute of Electronic Technology
Kentucky Christian College
Kentucky State University
Kentucky Wesleyan College
Lindsey Wilson College
Midway College
Morehead State University
Murray State University
Pikeville College

RETS Electronic Institute
Southeast Community College
Spalding University
Transylvania University
Union College
University of Louisville

Louisiana

Centenary College of Louisiana
Dillard University
Grantham College of Engineering
Louisiana College
Louisiana State University and
    Agricultural and Mechanical
    College
Northwestern State University
Nunez Community College
St. Joseph Seminary College
Southeastern Louisiana University
Southern University in Shreveport
Xavier University of Louisiana

Maine

Beal College
Bowdoin College
Casco Bay College
Central Maine Technical College
Colby College
College of the Atlantic
Eastern Maine Technical College
Husson College
Maine College of Art
Maine Maritime Academy
Southern Maine Technical College
Thomas College
Unity College
University of Maine
    Augusta
    Farmington
    Fort Kent
    Machias
    Orono
    Presque Isle
University of New England
University of Southern Maine

Maryland

Baltimore City Community College
Baltimore International Culinary
    College
Bowie State University
Capitol College
Cecil Community College
Columbia Union College
Dundalk Community College
Garrett Community College
Goucher College
Hagerstown Business College
Hood College
Howard Community College
Johns Hopkins University
Maryland Institute College of Art
Montgomery College
    Germantown Campus
    Rockville Campus
    Takoma Park Campus
Morgan State University
Mount St. Mary's College
St. John's College
University of Maryland
    Baltimore
    College Park
Villa Julie College
Washington Bible College
Washington College
Western Maryland College

Massachusetts

American International College
Anna Maria College
Aquinas College at Newton
Assumption College

Atlantic Union College
Babson College
Bay Path College
Bay State College
Bentley College
Berklee College of Music
Berkshire Community College
Boston Architectural Center
Boston College
Boston Conservatory
Boston University
Brandeis University
Bridgewater State College
Clark University
Dean College
Elms College
Emerson College
Emmanuel College
Endicott College
Essex Agricultural and Technical
    Institute
Fisher College
Framingham State College
Franklin Institute of Boston
Gordon College
Hampshire College
Harvard and Radcliffe Colleges
Hebrew College
Hellenic College
Katharine Gibbs School
Marian Court College
Massachusetts Institute of
    Technology
Massasoit Community College
Merrimack College
Middlesex Community College
Montserrat College of Art
Mount Holyoke College
Mount Ida College
Newbury College
Nichols College
North Adams State College
Northeastern University
Pine Manor College
Regis College
St. Hyacinth College and Seminary
Salem State College
School of the Museum of Fine Arts
Simon's Rock College of Bard
Smith College
Springfield College
Suffolk University
Tufts University
University of Massachusetts
    Amherst
    Dartmouth
    Lowell
Wellesley College
Wentworth Institute of Technology
Western New England College
Westfield State College
Wheaton College
Williams College
Worcester Polytechnic Institute

Michigan

Adrian College
Albion College
Alma College
Andrews University
Aquinas College
Baker College
    Auburn Hills
    Cadillac
    Flint
    Jackson
    Mount Clemens
    Muskegon
    Owosso
    Port Huron
Calvin College

Center for Creative Studies: College of Art and Design
Concordia College
Cornerstone College and Grand Rapids Baptist Seminary
Davenport College of Business
Detroit College of Business
Eastern Michigan University
GMI Engineering & Management Institute
Grace Bible College
Grand Valley State University
Great Lakes Christian College
Highland Park Community College
Hillsdale College
Hope College
Kalamazoo College
Kellogg Community College
Kendall College of Art and Design
Lawrence Technological University
Madonna University
Michigan Christian College
Mid Michigan Community College
Montcalm Community College
Northern Michigan University
Oakland University
Olivet College
Reformed Bible College
Sacred Heart Major Seminary
Saginaw Valley State University
St. Mary's College
Siena Heights College
Southwestern Michigan College
Spring Arbor College
Suomi College
University of Detroit Mercy
University of Michigan
    Ann Arbor
    Dearborn
    Flint
Walsh College of Accountancy and Business Administration
William Tyndale College

Minnesota

Augsburg College
Bemidji State University
Bethany Lutheran College
Bethel College
Carleton College
College of St. Benedict
College of St. Catherine: St. Catherine Campus
College of St. Catherine-Minneapolis
College of St. Scholastica
Concordia College: Moorhead
Concordia College: St. Paul
Dunwoody Industrial Institute
Gustavus Adolphus College
Hamline University
Macalester College
Martin Luther College
Minneapolis College of Art and Design
Minnesota Bible College
National College
NEI College of Technology
North Central Bible College
Northwestern College
Oak Hills Bible College
Pillsbury Baptist Bible College
St. John's University
St. Mary's College of Minnesota
St. Olaf College
Southwest State University
University of Minnesota
    Crookston
    Duluth
    Morris
    Twin Cities
University of St. Thomas

Mississippi

Blue Mountain College
Delta State University
Jackson State University
Magnolia Bible College
Mary Holmes College
Millsaps College
Mississippi College
Mississippi Gulf Coast Community College: Perkinston
Mississippi State University
Mississippi University for Women
Mississippi Valley State University
Northwest Mississippi Community College
Pearl River Community College
Rust College
Southeastern Baptist College
Tougaloo College
University of Mississippi Medical Center University
University of Southern Mississippi
Wesley College

Missouri

Avila College
Baptist Bible College
Calvary Bible College
Central Bible College
Central Christian College of the Bible
Central Methodist College
Central Missouri State University
Columbia College
Crowder College
Culver-Stockton College
DeVry Institute of Technology: Kansas City
Drury College
East Central College
Evangel College
Fontbonne College
Harris Stowe State College
Jefferson College
Kansas City Art Institute
Lincoln University
Lindenwood College
Maryville University of St. Louis
Missouri Baptist College
Missouri Southern State College
Missouri Valley College
Missouri Western State College
Moberly Area Community College
North Central Missouri College
Northeast Missouri State University
Northwest Missouri State University
Ozark Christian College
Park College
Ranken Technical College
Research College of Nursing
Rockhurst College
St. Louis Christian College
St. Louis College of Pharmacy
St. Louis University
Southeast Missouri State University
Stephens College
University of Missouri
    Columbia
    Rolla
    St. Louis
Washington University
Webster University
Wentworth Military Academy
Westminster College
William Jewell College
William Woods University

Montana

Carroll College
College of Great Falls

Dawson Community College
Miles Community College
Montana State University
    Billings
    Bozeman
Rocky Mountain College
Stone Child College
University of Montana-Missoula
Western Montana College of the University of Montana

Nebraska

Bellevue University
Central Community College
Clarkson College
College of St. Mary
Concordia College
Creighton University
Dana College
Doane College
Hastings College
Lincoln School of Commerce
McCook Community College
Mid Plains Community College
Midland Lutheran College
Nebraska Christian College
Nebraska Indian Community College
Nebraska Methodist College of Nursing and Allied Health
Nebraska Wesleyan University
Southeast Community College: Beatrice Campus
Union College
Wayne State College
Western Nebraska Community College: Scottsbluff Campus
York College

Nevada

Community College of Southern Nevada
Morrison College: Reno
University of Nevada: Las Vegas

New Hampshire

Daniel Webster College
Dartmouth College
Franklin Pierce College
Hesser College
McIntosh College
New England College
New Hampshire College
New Hampshire Technical College
    Laconia
    Manchester
    Nashua
New Hampshire Technical Institute
Notre Dame College
White Pines College

New Jersey

Berkeley College of Business
Bloomfield College
Burlington County College
Caldwell College
Camden County College
Centenary College
College of St. Elizabeth
DeVry Technical Institute
Drew University
Fairleigh Dickinson University
    Edward Williams College
    Teaneck
Felician College
Georgian Court College
Jersey City State College
Monmouth College
Montclair State University
New Jersey Institute of Technology
Passaic County Community College
Princeton University

Ramapo College of New Jersey
Richard Stockton College of New Jersey
Rider University
Rowan College of New Jersey
Rutgers, The State University of New Jersey
    Camden College of Arts and Sciences
    College of Engineering
    College of Nursing
    College of Pharmacy
    Cook College
    Douglass College
    Livingston College
    Mason Gross School of the Arts
    Newark College of Arts and Sciences
    Rutgers College
St. Peter's College
Salem Community College
Seton Hall University
Trenton State College
Westminster Choir College of Rider University
William Paterson College of New Jersey

New Mexico

College of Santa Fe
College of the Southwest
Dona Ana Branch Community College of New Mexico State University
Eastern New Mexico University
National College
New Mexico Highlands University
New Mexico State University
St. John's College

New York

Adelphi University
Adirondack Community College
Albany College of Pharmacy
Alfred University
American Academy of Dramatic Arts
Audrey Cohen College
Bard College
Barnard College
Berkeley College of New York City
Boricua College
Bramson ORT Technical Institute
Briarcliffe: The College for Business and Technology
Bryant & Stratton Business Institute
    Albany
    Syracuse
Canisius College
Catholic Medical Center of Brooklyn and Queens School of Nursing
Cazenovia College
Central City Business Institute
City University of New York
    Borough of Manhattan Community College
    Hostos Community College
    John Jay College of Criminal Justice
Clarkson University
Cochran School of Nursing-St. John's Riverside Hospital
Colgate University
College of Aeronautics
College of Insurance
College of Mount St. Vincent
College of New Rochelle
    New Rochelle
    School of New Resources
College of St. Rose

Columbia University
    Columbia College
    School of Engineering and
        Applied Science
Columbia-Greene Community
    College
Concordia College
Cornell University
Daemen College
Darkei Noam Rabbinical College
Dominican College of Blauvelt
Dowling College
D'Youville College
Eastman School of Music of the
    University of Rochester
Elmira College
Eugene Lang College/New School
    for Social Research
Fashion Institute of Technology
Fordham University
Hamilton College
Hartwick College
Helene Fuld School of Nursing
Herkimer County Community
    College
Hilbert College
Hobart and William Smith Colleges
Houghton College
Hudson Valley Community College
Interboro Institute
Iona College
Ithaca College
Jamestown Community College
Jewish Theological Seminary of
    America
Juilliard School
Katharine Gibbs School: Melville
Keuka College
Laboratory Institute of
    Merchandising
Le Moyne College
Long Island University
    Brooklyn Campus
    C. W. Post Campus
    Southampton College
Manhattan College
Manhattan School of Music
Manhattanville College
Mannes College of Music
Maria College
Marist College
Marymount College
Marymount Manhattan College
Mater Dei College
Medaille College
Mercy College
Molloy College
Monroe College
Monroe Community College
Nazareth College of Rochester
New York Institute of Technology
New York School of Interior
    Design
New York University
Niagara University
Olean Business Institute
Pace University
Parsons School of Design
Paul Smith's College
Phillips Beth Israel School of
    Nursing
Plaza Business Institute
Polytechnic University
Pratt Institute
Rensselaer Polytechnic Institute
Roberts Wesleyan College
Rochester Business Institute
Rochester Institute of Technology
Sage Junior College of Albany
St. John Fisher College

St. Joseph's College
    Brooklyn
    Suffolk Campus
St. Joseph's Hospital Health Center
    School of Nursing
St. Lawrence University
St. Thomas Aquinas College
Sarah Lawrence College
School of Visual Arts
Skidmore College
State University of New York
    Albany
    Binghamton
    Buffalo
    Oswego
    Purchase
    Stony Brook
    College at Brockport
    College at Buffalo
    College at Cortland
    College at Fredonia
    College at New Paltz
    College at Oneonta
    College at Plattsburgh
    College at Potsdam
    College of Technology at
        Alfred
    College of Technology at Delhi
    College of Technology at
        Farmingdale
    Institute of Technology at
        Utica/Rome
Sullivan County Community
    College
Syracuse University
Talmudical Institute of Upstate New
    York
Talmudical Seminary Oholei Torah
Tompkins-Cortland Community
    College
Touro College
Trocaire College
Ulster County Community College
University of Rochester
University of the State of New
    York: Regents College
Utica College of Syracuse
    University
Utica School of Commerce
Vassar College
Villa Maria College of Buffalo
Wadhams Hall Seminary-College
Wagner College
Wells College
Westchester Business Institute
Wood Tobe-Coburn School
Yeshiva University

North Carolina
Barber-Scotia College
Barton College
Belmont Abbey College
Bennett College
Campbell University
Catawba College
Chowan College
Davidson College
Duke University
Elon College
Fayetteville State University
Gardner-Webb University
Greensboro College
Guilford College
High Point University
John Wesley College
Johnson C. Smith University
Lees-McRae College
Lenoir-Rhyne College
Livingstone College
Louisburg College
Mars Hill College

McDowell Technical Community
    College
Meredith College
Methodist College
Montreat-Anderson College
Mount Olive College
North Carolina Agricultural and
    Technical State University
North Carolina Wesleyan College
Peace College
Pembroke State University
Pfeiffer College
Queens College
Roanoke Bible College
St. Andrews Presbyterian College
St. Augustine's College
St. Mary's College
Salem College
Shaw University
University of North Carolina at
    Wilmington
Wake Forest University
Warren Wilson College
Wingate College
Winston-Salem State University

North Dakota
Bismarck State College
Jamestown College
Mayville State University
University of Mary

Ohio
Antonelli Institute of Art and
    Photography
Art Academy of Cincinnati
Ashland University
Baldwin-Wallace College
Belmont Technical College
Bluffton College
Bowling Green State University
    Bowling Green
    Firelands College
Bryant & Stratton Business
    Institute: Cleveland West
Capital University
Case Western Reserve University
Cedarville College
Chatfield College
Cincinnati State Technical and
    Community College
Circleville Bible College
Cleveland College of Jewish Studies
Cleveland Institute of Art
Cleveland State University
College of Mount St. Joseph
College of Wooster
Columbus College of Art and
    Design
Davis College
Denison University
DeVry Institute of Technology:
    Columbus
Dyke College
Edison State Community College
Franciscan University of
    Steubenville
Franklin University
God's Bible School and College
Heidelberg College
Hiram College
Hocking Technical College
ITT Technical Institute:
    Youngstown
Jefferson Technical College
John Carroll University

Kent State University
    Ashtabula Regional Campus
    East Liverpool Regional
        Campus
    Kent
    Salem Regional Campus
    Stark Campus
    Trumbull Campus
    Tuscarawas Campus
Kettering College of Medical Arts
Lake Erie College
Lakeland Community College
Lourdes College
Malone College
Marion Technical College
Miami University
    Hamilton Campus
    Middletown Campus
    Oxford Campus
Miami-Jacobs College
Mount Union College
Mount Vernon Nazarene College
MTI Business College
Muskingum College
North Central Technical College
Northwestern College
Notre Dame College of Ohio
Oberlin College
Ohio Dominican College
Ohio Northern University
Ohio State University
    Agricultural Technical Institute
    Marion Campus
Ohio University
Ohio Valley Business College
Ohio Wesleyan University
Otterbein College
Owens Technical College
    Findlay Campus
    Toledo
Shawnee State University
Stark Technical College
Terra Community College
Tiffin University
Union Institute
University of Akron
University of Cincinnati
    Cincinnati
    Clermont College
University of Findlay
University of Rio Grande
University of Toledo
Urbana University
Ursuline College
Walsh University
Washington State Community
    College
Wilmington College
Wittenberg University
Wright State University
    Dayton
    Lake Campus
Xavier University
Youngstown State University

Oklahoma
Bartlesville Wesleyan College
Connors State College
Mid-America Bible College
Northeastern Oklahoma
    Agricultural and Mechanical
    College
Oklahoma Baptist University
Oklahoma Christian University of
    Science and Arts
Oklahoma City Community College
Oklahoma City University
Oklahoma Panhandle State
    University
Oklahoma State University
Oral Roberts University
Phillips University

Redlands Community College
Rogers State College
Rose State College
St. Gregory's College
Southern Nazarene University
Southwestern College of Christian
    Ministries
Southwestern Oklahoma State
    University
University of Oklahoma
University of Tulsa

Oregon

Bassist College
Central Oregon Community College
Clackamas Community College
Concordia College
George Fox College
Lane Community College
Linfield College
Linn-Benton Community College
Northwest Christian College
Oregon Institute of Technology
Oregon State University
Pacific Northwest College of Art
Pacific University
Portland Community College
Portland State University
Reed College
Southern Oregon State College
Southwestern Oregon Community
    College
University of Oregon
    Eugene
    Robert Donald Clark Honors
        College
University of Portland
Warner Pacific College
Western Baptist College
Western Oregon State College
Willamette University

Pennsylvania

Academy of the New Church
Albright College
Allegheny College
Allentown College of St. Francis de
    Sales
Alvernia College
Antonelli Institute of Art and
    Photography
Art Institute of Pittsburgh
Baptist Bible College of
    Pennsylvania
Beaver College
Bradley Academy for the Visual
    Arts
Bryn Mawr College
Bucknell University
Bucks County Community College
Cabrini College
Cambria-Rowe Business College
Carlow College
Carnegie Mellon University
Cedar Crest College
Central Pennsylvania Business
    School
Chatham College
Cheyney University of Pennsylvania
CHI Institute
Churchman Business School
Clarion University of Pennsylvania
College Misericordia
Community College of Beaver
    County
Delaware Valley College
Dickinson College
Drexel University
East Stroudsburg University of
    Pennsylvania
Eastern College
Elizabethtown College

Franklin and Marshall College
Gannon University
Geneva College
Gettysburg College
Gratz College
Gwynedd-Mercy College
Hahnemann University School of
    Health Sciences and Humanities
Harcum College
Harrisburg Area Community
    College
Haverford College
Holy Family College
Hussian School of Art
Immaculata College
Indiana University of Pennsylvania
Johnson Technical Institute
Juniata College
Keystone College
King's College
Kutztown University of
    Pennsylvania
La Roche College
La Salle University
Lackawanna Junior College
Lafayette College
Lancaster Bible College
Lebanon Valley College of
    Pennsylvania
Lehigh University
Lincoln Technical Institute
Lincoln University
Lock Haven University of
    Pennsylvania
Manor Junior College
Mansfield University of
    Pennsylvania
Marywood College
Mercyhurst College
Messiah College
Millersville University of
    Pennsylvania
Moore College of Art and Design
National Education Center: Vale
    Tech Campus
Neumann College
Northampton County Area
    Community College
Peirce College
Philadelphia College of Bible
Philadelphia College of Pharmacy
    and Science
Philadelphia College of Textiles and
    Science
Pittsburgh Technical Institute
Point Park College
Reading Area Community College
Robert Morris College
St. Charles Borromeo Seminary-
    Overbrook
St. Francis College
St. Joseph's University
St. Vincent College
Seton Hill College
Shippensburg University of
    Pennsylvania
Slippery Rock University of
    Pennsylvania
South Hills Business School
Swarthmore College
Thaddeus Stevens State School of
    Technology
Thomas Jefferson University:
    College of Allied Health Sciences
University of the Arts
University of Pennsylvania
University of Pittsburgh
    Bradford
    Greensburg
    Pittsburgh
    Titusville
Ursinus College

Valley Forge Christian College
Valley Forge Military College
Waynesburg College
West Chester University of
    Pennsylvania
Widener University
Wilkes University
Wilson College

Puerto Rico

American University of Puerto Rico
Colegio Universitario del Este
Inter American University of Puerto
    Rico: San German Campus
Pontifical Catholic University of
    Puerto Rico
Turabo University
Universidad Adventista de las
    Antillas
Universidad Politecnica de Puerto
    Rico
University of Puerto Rico
    Cayey University College
    Mayaguez Campus
    Ponce Technological
        University College
    Rio Piedras Campus

Rhode Island

Brown University
Bryant College
Johnson & Wales University
New England Institute of
    Technology
Providence College
Rhode Island College
Rhode Island School of Design

South Carolina

Anderson College
Benedict College
Charleston Southern University
Claflin College
Coker College
College of Charleston
Columbia College
Erskine College
Furman University
Greenville Technical College
Lander University
Limestone College
Morris College
Newberry College
North Greenville College
Presbyterian College
Southern Wesleyan University
Spartanburg Methodist College
University of South Carolina
    Spartanburg
    Union
Voorhees College

South Dakota

Augustana College
Black Hills State University
Dakota Wesleyan University
Huron University
Kilian Community College
Mount Marty College
National College
Oglala Lakota College
Presentation College
Sisseton-Wahpeton Community
    College
South Dakota School of Mines and
    Technology
University of Sioux Falls
University of South Dakota

Tennessee

Aquinas College
Bethel College

Carson-Newman College
Christian Brothers University
David Lipscomb University
Freed-Hardeman University
Hiwassee College
King College
Knoxville College
Lambuth University
Lane College
Lee College
LeMoyne-Owen College
Lincoln Memorial University
Maryville College
Memphis College of Art
Milligan College
O'More College of Design
Rhodes College
Tennessee Temple University
Tennessee Wesleyan College
Trevecca Nazarene College
Union University
University of the South
University of Tennessee
    Chattanooga
    Knoxville
    Memphis
Vanderbilt University

Texas

Ambassador University
Angelo State University
Arlington Baptist College
Austin College
Baptist Missionary Association
    Theological Seminary
Central Texas College
Cisco Junior College
Commonwealth Institute of Funeral
    Service
Concordia Lutheran College
Criswell College
Dallas Baptist University
Dallas Christian College
DeVry Institute of Technology:
    Irving
East Texas Baptist University
East Texas State University
Hardin-Simmons University
Houston Baptist University
Howard Payne University
Huston-Tillotson College
Incarnate Word College
Jacksonville College
Jarvis Christian College
Lamar University—Beaumont
LeTourneau University
McMurry University
Midwestern State University
Miss Wade's Fashion
    Merchandising College
North Harris Montgomery
    Community College District
Our Lady of the Lake University of
    San Antonio
Prairie View A&M University
Rice University
St. Edward's University
St. Mary's University
Sam Houston State University
Schreiner College
Southern Methodist University
Southwest Texas State University
Southwestern Adventist College
Southwestern University
Stephen F. Austin State University
Sul Ross State University
Tarleton State University
Texas A&M International
    University
Texas A&M University
    College Station
    Galveston

Texas A&M University-Corpus
  Christi
Texas A&M University-Kingsville
Texas Christian University
Texas Lutheran College
Texas Southern University
Texas State Technical College
  Harlingen
  Sweetwater
  Waco
Texas Tech University
Texas Wesleyan University
Texas Woman's University
University of Central Texas
University of Dallas
University of Houston
  Clear Lake
  Downtown
  Houston
  Victoria
University of North Texas
University of Texas
  Arlington
  Austin
  Dallas
  El Paso
  Health Science Center at San
    Antonio
  Medical Branch at Galveston
  Pan American
  San Antonio
  Southwestern Medical Center
    at Dallas
  Houston Health Science
    Center
Wayland Baptist University
West Texas A&M University

Utah

Phillips Junior College: Salt Lake
  City Campus
Salt Lake Community College
Southern Utah University
Stevens-Henager College of
  Business
Westminster College of Salt Lake
  City

Vermont

Bennington College
Burlington College
Castleton State College
Champlain College
College of St. Joseph in Vermont
Green Mountain College
Middlebury College
New England Culinary Institute
Norwich University
Southern Vermont College
Sterling College
Trinity College of Vermont
University of Vermont
Vermont Technical College

Virginia

Averett College
Bluefield College
Christendom College
Christopher Newport University
College of William and Mary
Commonwealth College
Emory and Henry College
Ferrum College
George Mason University
Hampden-Sydney College
Hollins College
James Madison University
Liberty University
Longwood College
Lynchburg College
Mary Baldwin College
Mary Washington College

Norfolk State University
Old Dominion University
Radford University
Randolph-Macon College
Randolph-Macon Woman's College
Roanoke College
St. Paul's College
Shenandoah University
Southern Virginia College
Sweet Briar College
University of Virginia
Virginia Commonwealth University
Virginia Intermont College
Virginia Military Institute
Virginia Polytechnic Institute and
  State University
Virginia State University
Virginia Union University
Virginia Wesleyan College

Washington

Antioch University Seattle
Art Institute of Seattle
Cornish College of the Arts
Eastern Washington University
Evergreen State College
Gonzaga University
Heritage College
Lutheran Bible Institute of Seattle
Northwest College
Northwest College of Art
Pacific Lutheran University
Puget Sound Christian College
St. Martin's College
Seattle Pacific University
Seattle University
University of Puget Sound
Walla Walla College
Whitman College
Whitworth College

West Virginia

Bethany College
Bluefield State College
College of West Virginia
Davis and Elkins College
Fairmont State College
Mountain State College
Ohio Valley College
Shepherd College
University of Charleston
West Liberty State College
West Virginia Institute of
  Technology
West Virginia Northern Community
  College
West Virginia University
West Virginia Wesleyan College
Wheeling Jesuit College

Wisconsin

Alverno College
Bellin College of Nursing
Beloit College
Cardinal Stritch College
Carroll College
Carthage College
Concordia University Wisconsin
Edgewood College
Gateway Technical College
Lakeland College
Lakeshore Technical College
Lawrence University
Marian College of Fond du Lac
Marquette University
Milwaukee Institute of Art &
  Design
Milwaukee School of Engineering
Mount Mary College
Mount Senario College
Northland College
Ripon College

St. Norbert College
Silver Lake College
Southwest Wisconsin Technical
  College
Stratton College
University of Wisconsin
  Eau Claire
  Green Bay
  La Crosse
  Milwaukee
  Oshkosh
  Parkside
  Platteville
  River Falls
  Stevens Point
  Stout
  Superior
  Whitewater
University of Wisconsin Center
  Baraboo/Sauk County
  Barron County
  Fond du Lac
  Fox Valley
  Manitowoc County
  Marathon County
  Marinette County
  Marshfield/Wood County
  Richland
  Rock County
  Sheboygan County
  Washington County
  Waukesha
Viterbo College
Wisconsin Lutheran College

Wyoming

Casper College
Central Wyoming College
Eastern Wyoming College
Sheridan College

**American Samoa, Caroline
Islands, Guam, Marianas,
Virgin Islands**

University of Guam

Canada

McGill University

France

American University of Paris

Switzerland

American College of Switzerland
Franklin College: Switzerland

Tuition discount for
prepayment

Alabama

Faulkner University

Arizona

Arizona College of the Bible

California

American College for the Applied
  Arts: Los Angeles
Azusa Pacific University
Biola University
California Maritime Academy
Christian Heritage College
Compton Community College
Fashion Institute of Design and
  Merchandising
LIFE Bible College
Pacific Christian College
Pacific Union College

St. Mary's College of California
Southern California College
Thomas Aquinas College
University of Redlands
University of San Diego
University of San Francisco
University of Southern California
Westmont College

Colorado

Bel-Rea Institute of Animal
  Technology
Colorado Technical College

Connecticut

Albertus Magnus College

District of Columbia

Mount Vernon College
Southeastern University

Florida

Hobe Sound Bible College
Jones College
Lynn University
New College of the University of
  South Florida
Talmudic College of Florida
University of Miami
Webber College

Georgia

Augusta Technical Institute
Meadows College of Business
Oglethorpe University
Shorter College
Spelman College

Hawaii

Chaminade University of Honolulu

Idaho

Boise Bible College

Illinois

Barat College
Chicago College of Commerce
Columbia College
National-Louis University
State Community College
Trinity College

Indiana

Anderson University
Butler University
Goshen College
Huntington College
Indiana Vocational Technical
  College: Northwest

Iowa

Coe College
Luther College

Kansas

Cowley County Community College
Hesston College
Seward County Community College

Kentucky

Kentucky Christian College

Louisiana

Grantham College of Engineering

Maine

Unity College
University of New England

Maryland

Johns Hopkins University
Mount St. Mary's College

Washington Bible College

Massachusetts

American International College
Atlantic Union College
Boston College
Boston University
Gordon College
Marian Court College
Pine Manor College

Michigan

Alma College
Andrews University
Center for Creative Studies: College
of Art and Design
Ferris State University
Kendall College of Art and Design
Kirtland Community College

Minnesota

Bethel College
College of St. Benedict
Concordia College: Moorhead
Gustavus Adolphus College
Hamline University
North Central Bible College
St. John's University
St. Olaf College

Mississippi

Rust College
Tougaloo College

Missouri

Central Bible College
Evangel College
Lindenwood College
Research College of Nursing
Washington University
Wentworth Military Academy

Nebraska

Union College

New Hampshire

Colby-Sawyer College
Franklin Pierce College
New England College
Notre Dame College

New Jersey

Berkeley College of Business

New Mexico

College of Santa Fe
St. John's College

New York

Alfred University
American Academy of Dramatic
Arts
Barnard College
Berkeley College of New York City
Colgate University
Columbia University
Columbia College
School of Engineering and
Applied Science
Hobart and William Smith Colleges
Medaille College
New York Institute of Technology
New York University
Nyack College
Rochester Institute of Technology
Touro College
Wells College

North Carolina

Duke University
Pfeiffer College
Roanoke Bible College

North Dakota

Trinity Bible College

Ohio

Cedarville College
Circleville Bible College
God's Bible School and College
Heidelberg College
Hiram College
Kent State University Trumbull
Campus
Lake Erie College
Malone College
Ohio Northern University
Ohio Wesleyan University
Wittenberg University

Oklahoma

Oklahoma Christian University of
Science and Arts

Oregon

Bassist College
Eugene Bible College
Linfield College
Pacific University
Western Baptist College

Pennsylvania

Academy of the New Church
Allegheny College
Baptist Bible College of
Pennsylvania
Duquesne University
Gettysburg College
Lafayette College
Mercyhurst College
Muhlenberg College
Philadelphia College of Bible
Susquehanna University
Thomas Jefferson University:
College of Allied Health Sciences
University of Pennsylvania

Rhode Island

Brown University

South Carolina

Midlands Technical College

South Dakota

Dakota Wesleyan University
University of Sioux Falls

Tennessee

Milligan College
Southern College of Seventh-day
Adventist

Texas

Criswell College
Huston-Tillotson College
St. Mary's University
Schreiner College
Southwestern Adventist College

Vermont

Champlain College
Lyndon State College
Middlebury College
Norwich University
Southern Vermont College

Virginia

Christendom College
Clinch Valley College of the
University of Virginia
Liberty University
Lynchburg College
Marymount University
Southern Virginia College

Washington

City University
Lutheran Bible Institute of Seattle
Pacific Lutheran University

Wisconsin

Carthage College
Lakeland College
Lawrence University

France

American University of Paris

Tuition payment by deferred payments

Alabama

Alabama Agricultural and
Mechanical University
Alabama State University
Auburn University at Montgomery
Birmingham-Southern College
Bishop State Community College
Draughons Junior College
Huntingdon College
Marion Military Institute
Spring Hill College
Troy State University
Montgomery
Troy
UAB: Walker College
University of Alabama
Huntsville
Tuscaloosa
University of Mobile
University of West Alabama

Alaska

Prince William Sound Community
College
Sheldon Jackson College
University of Alaska
Fairbanks
Southeast

Arizona

DeVry Institute of Technology:
Phoenix
Embry-Riddle Aeronautical
University: Prescott Campus
Gateway Community College
Mohave Community College
Navajo Community College
Northern Arizona University
Paradise Valley Community College
Phoenix College
Prescott College
Rio Salado Community College
Southwestern College
University of Arizona
Western International University

Arkansas

Garland County Community
College
Mississippi County Community
College
Shorter College
University of Arkansas
University of the Ozarks

California

Academy of Art College
Allan Hancock College
American Academy of Dramatic
Arts: West
Antelope Valley College

Antioch Southern California at Los
Angeles
Armstrong University
Bakersfield College
Biola University
Butte College
California College of Arts and
Crafts
California Lutheran University
California State University
Chico
Northridge
Cerritos Community College
Charles R. Drew University: College
of Allied Health
Christian Heritage College
Cogswell Polytechnical College
College of Alameda
College of the Desert
College of Notre Dame
College of San Mateo
Columbia College: Hollywood
Compton Community College
Cosumnes River College
De Anza College
DeVry Institute of Technology:
Pomona
Dominican College of San Rafael
Evergreen Valley College
Fashion Institute of Design and
Merchandising
Feather River College
Glendale Community College
Golden Gate University
Holy Names College
Kings River Community College
Long Beach City College
Los Angeles City College
Los Angeles Harbor College
Los Angeles Mission College
Los Angeles Southwest College
Los Angeles Trade and Technical
College
Los Medanos College
Loyola Marymount University
Master's College
Merced College
Mills College
MiraCosta College
Mission College
Modesto Junior College
Monterey Peninsula College
Mount St. Mary's College
Napa Valley College
New College of California
Occidental College
Ohlone College
Orange Coast College
Otis College of Art and Design
Pacific Christian College
Pacific Union College
Pasadena City College
Patten College
Pepperdine University
Riverside Community College
Sacramento City College
Samuel Merritt College
San Jose City College
Santa Barbara City College
Santa Clara University
Santa Monica College
Santa Rosa Junior College
Scripps College
Skyline College
Sonoma State University
Stanford University
Taft College
United States International
University
University of California
San Diego
Santa Barbara

University of Judaism
University of La Verne
University of the Pacific
University of San Francisco
University of Southern California
Ventura College
Victor Valley College
West Hills Community College
Woodbury University
Yuba College

Colorado

Adams State College
Aims Community College
Arapahoe Community College
Beth-El College of Nursing
Colorado Christian University
Colorado Institute of Art
Colorado Mountain College
    Alpine Campus
    Spring Valley Campus
    Timberline Campus
Colorado School of Mines
Community College of Denver
Fort Lewis College
Mesa State College
Metropolitan State College of
    Denver
Morgan Community College
Naropa Institute
Northeastern Junior College
Pikes Peak Community College
Pueblo Community College
Regis University
Trinidad State Junior College
University of Colorado at Boulder
University of Denver
University of Southern Colorado
Western State College of Colorado

Connecticut

Capital Community-Technical
    College
Central Connecticut State
    University
Connecticut College
Fairfield University
Quinebaug Valley Community-
    Technical College
Quinnipiac College
Sacred Heart University
Tunxis Community-Technical
    College
University of Bridgeport
Wesleyan University

Delaware

Delaware State University
Delaware Technical and
    Community College
    Stanton/Wilmington Campus
    Terry Campus
Goldey-Beacom College

District of Columbia

American University
George Washington University
Georgetown University
Howard University
Strayer College
Trinity College
University of the District of
    Columbia

Florida

Barry University
Bethune-Cookman College
Brevard Community College
Broward Community College
Central Florida Community College
Chipola Junior College

Embry-Riddle Aeronautical
    University
Florida Atlantic University
Florida Christian College
Florida Community College at
    Jacksonville
Florida International University
Florida State University
International Fine Arts College
Jacksonville University
Lake City Community College
Lake-Sumter Community College
Nova Southeastern University
Okaloosa-Walton Community
    College
Pasco-Hernando Community
    College
St. John Vianney College Seminary
St. Thomas University
Schiller International University
Tallahassee Community College
Tampa College
University of Florida
University of Miami
University of North Florida
Warner Southern College
Webber College

Georgia

Clark Atlanta University
Covenant College
DeKalb Technical Institute
DeVry Institute of Technology:
    Atlanta
Emmanuel College
Fort Valley State College
Georgia Institute of Technology
Georgia Southern University
Gwinnett Technical Institute
LaGrange College
Meadows College of Business
Morris Brown College
Oglethorpe University
Reinhardt College
School of Visual Arts: Savannah
South College
Spelman College
Thomas College
Toccoa Falls College

Idaho

Boise State University
College of Southern Idaho
Idaho State University
Lewis Clark State College
Ricks College
University of Idaho

Illinois

Aurora University
Barat College
Belleville Area College
Black Hawk College
Blackburn College
Bradley University
Carl Sandburg College
Chicago State University
City Colleges of Chicago: Olive-
    Harvey College
College of DuPage
College of Lake County
Danville Area Community College
De Paul University
DeVry Institute of Technology
    Addison
    Chicago
Elgin Community College
Finch University of Health
    Sciences/The Chicago Medical
    School
Governors State University
Greenville College

Joliet Junior College
Judson College
Kaskaskia College
Knox College
Lake Land College
Lakeview College of Nursing
Lewis and Clark Community
    College
Lewis University
Lincoln Christian College and
    Seminary
Lincoln Land Community College
MacMurray College
Moody Bible Institute
Moraine Valley Community College
Morton College
National-Louis University
Olivet Nazarene University
Quincy University
Rend Lake College
Richland Community College
Rockford College
Roosevelt University
Rush University
St. Xavier University
Sangamon State University
Southeastern Illinois College
Southern Illinois University at
    Edwardsville
State Community College
Trinity Christian College
Trinity College
Triton College
VanderCook College of Music
Western Illinois University
Wheaton College
William Rainey Harper College

Indiana

Ancilla College
Anderson University
Bethel College
DePauw University
Earlham College
Goshen College
Indiana Institute of Technology
Indiana State University
Indiana University
    Bloomington
    East
    Northwest
    South Bend
    Southeast
Indiana University-Purdue
    University Indianapolis
Indiana Vocational Technical
    College
    Central Indiana
    Columbus
    Eastcentral
    Kokomo
    Lafayette
    Northcentral
    Northeast
    Northwest
    Southcentral
    Southeast
    Southwest
    Wabash Valley
    Whitewater
Indiana Wesleyan University
Manchester College
Oakland City College
Purdue University
    Calumet
    West Lafayette
St. Mary-of-the-Woods College
St. Meinrad College
University of Indianapolis

Iowa

Briar Cliff College
Cornell College
Drake University
Grand View College
Indian Hills Community College
Iowa Wesleyan College
Iowa Western Community College
Marshalltown Community College
Morningside College
North Iowa Area Community
    College
Northeast Iowa Community College
St. Ambrose University
Southeastern Community College:
    North Campus
Teikyo Marycrest University
University of Dubuque
University of Iowa
University of Northern Iowa
Wartburg College

Kansas

Allen County Community College
Bethel College
Butler County Community College
Coffeyville Community College
Colby Community College
Cowley County Community College
Dodge City Community College
Emporia State University
Fort Hays State University
Fort Scott Community College
Garden City Community College
Kansas City Kansas Community
    College
Manhattan Christian College
Neosho County Community College
Pittsburg State University
Pratt Community College
St. Mary College
Seward County Community College
Southwestern College
University of Kansas
Washburn University of Topeka
Wichita State University

Kentucky

Asbury College
Brescia College
Campbellsville College
Clear Creek Baptist Bible College
Cumberland College
Eastern Kentucky University
Georgetown College
Jefferson Community College
Kentucky State University
Kentucky Wesleyan College
Lindsey Wilson College
Madisonville Community College
Maysville Community College
Mid-Continent Baptist Bible College
Midway College
Morehead State University
Murray State University
Northern Kentucky University
Somerset Community College
Southeast Community College
Transylvania University

Louisiana

Bossier Parish Community College
Dillard University
Grambling State University
Louisiana State University
    Agricultural and Mechanical
        College
    Alexandria
    Eunice
    Shreveport
McNeese State University
Northwestern State University

Nunez Community College
Southeastern Louisiana University
Southern University in Shreveport
University of New Orleans
Xavier University of Louisiana

Maine

Beal College
Bowdoin College
Casco Bay College
Central Maine Medical Center
    School of Nursing
Unity College
University of Maine
    Augusta
    Fort Kent
University of Southern Maine

Maryland

Allegany Community College
Anne Arundel Community College
Baltimore City Community College
Bowie State University
Capitol College
Catonsville Community College
Cecil Community College
Coppin State College
Dundalk Community College
Essex Community College
Frostburg State University
Garrett Community College
Hagerstown Junior College
Hood College
Johns Hopkins University
Maryland College of Art and
    Design
Montgomery College
    Germantown Campus
    Rockville Campus
    Takoma Park Campus
Morgan State University
Mount St. Mary's College
University of Baltimore
University of Maryland
    Baltimore County
    College Park

Massachusetts

Anna Maria College
Atlantic Union College
Boston Conservatory
Boston University
Bristol Community College
Cape Cod Community College
Elms College
Emerson College
Forsyth School for Dental
    Hygienists
Hampshire College
Massachusetts Bay Community
    College
Merrimack College
Middlesex Community College
Mount Holyoke College
Quinsigamond Community College
School of the Museum of Fine Arts
Smith College
Springfield Technical Community
    College
Suffolk University
Wellesley College
Western New England College

Michigan

Albion College
Alma College
Aquinas College
Center for Creative Studies: College
    of Art and Design
Concordia College
Detroit College of Business
Eastern Michigan University

Ferris State University
Glen Oaks Community College
Grand Valley State University
Highland Park Community College
Jackson Community College
Kalamazoo College
Kalamazoo Valley Community
    College
Kellogg Community College
Kendall College of Art and Design
Kirtland Community College
Lawrence Technological University
Michigan State University
Mid Michigan Community College
Monroe County Community
    College
Mott Community College
Northwestern Michigan College
Sacred Heart Major Seminary
St. Clair County Community
    College
St. Mary's College
Siena Heights College
Spring Arbor College
Suomi College
University of Detroit Mercy
University of Michigan: Dearborn
Walsh College of Accountancy and
    Business Administration
Washtenaw Community College
Wayne State University
West Shore Community College
William Tyndale College

Minnesota

Anoka-Ramsey Community College
Bemidji State University
Central Lakes College
College of St. Catherine: St.
    Catherine Campus
Hibbing Community College
Lakewood Community College
Mankato State University
Moorhead State University
NEI College of Technology
Rainy River Community College
Southwest State University
University of Minnesota: Morris
University of St. Thomas
Vermilion Community College
Willmar Community College
Willmar Technical College

Mississippi

Belhaven College
Blue Mountain College
Copiah-Lincoln Community College
East Central Community College
Hinds Community College
Jackson State University
Magnolia Bible College
Mary Holmes College
Meridian Community College
Millsaps College
Mississippi College
Mississippi Gulf Coast Community
    College
    Jackson County Campus
    Jefferson Davis Campus
    Perkinston
Mississippi State University
Mississippi University for Women
Mississippi Valley State University
Northwest Mississippi Community
    College
Pearl River Community College
Tougaloo College
University of Mississippi
    Medical Center
    University
University of Southern Mississippi
William Carey College

Missouri

Avila College
Central Christian College of the
    Bible
Columbia College
DeVry Institute of Technology:
    Kansas City
Drury College
East Central College
Fontbonne College
Harris Stowe State College
Jefferson College
Lincoln University
Lindenwood College
Maryville University of St. Louis
Missouri Baptist College
Missouri Western State College
Research College of Nursing
Rockhurst College
St. Louis University
Southeast Missouri State University
Southwest Baptist University
Southwest Missouri State University
Three Rivers Community College
University of Missouri
    Columbia
    Rolla
Washington University
Webster University
Wentworth Military Academy
William Jewell College

Montana

College of Great Falls
Dawson Community College
Miles Community College
Montana State University
    Billings
    Bozeman
    Northern
Montana Tech of The University of
    Montana
Montana Tech of the University of
    Montana: Division of Technology
University of Montana College of
    Technology
Western Montana College of the
    University of Montana

Nebraska

Bellevue University
Central Community College
College of St. Mary
Dana College
Grace University
Hastings College
Metropolitan Community College
Midland Lutheran College
Nebraska Christian College
Nebraska College of Technical
    Agriculture
Nebraska Indian Community
    College
Nebraska Methodist College of
    Nursing and Allied Health
Nebraska Wesleyan University
University of Nebraska—Omaha
Western Nebraska Community
    College: Scottsbluff Campus
York College

Nevada

Community College of Southern
    Nevada
Northern Nevada Community
    College
Truckee Meadows Community
    College
University of Nevada
    Las Vegas
    Reno

Western Nevada Community
    College

New Hampshire

Dartmouth College
Franklin Pierce College
McIntosh College
New Hampshire College
New Hampshire Technical College
    Laconia
    Manchester
    Nashua
Rivier College

New Jersey

Bloomfield College
Burlington County College
DeVry Technical Institute
Fairleigh Dickinson University
    Edward Williams College
    Teaneck
Hudson County Community College
Jersey City State College
Kean College of New Jersey
Monmouth College
New Jersey Institute of Technology
Passaic County Community College
Princeton University
Richard Stockton College of New
    Jersey
Rutgers, The State University of
    New Jersey
    Camden College of Arts and
        Sciences
    College of Engineering
    College of Nursing
    College of Pharmacy
    Cook College
    Douglass College
    Livingston College
    Mason Gross School of the
        Arts
    Newark College of Arts and
        Sciences
    Rutgers College
St. Peter's College
Salem Community College
Seton Hall University
Stevens Institute of Technology
Trenton State College
Union County College
William Paterson College of New
    Jersey

New Mexico

Albuquerque Technical-Vocational
    Institute
Clovis Community College
College of the Southwest
Dona Ana Branch Community
    College of New Mexico State
    University
Eastern New Mexico University:
    Roswell Campus
National College
New Mexico Highlands University
New Mexico Military Institute
New Mexico State University
    Carlsbad
    Las Cruces

New York

Adelphi University
Adirondack Community College
Albany College of Pharmacy
American Academy of Dramatic
    Arts
Audrey Cohen College
Barnard College
Berkeley College of New York City
Boricua College
Bramson ORT Technical Institute

Broome Community College
Canisius College
Catholic Medical Center of
    Brooklyn and Queens School of
    Nursing
Cayuga County Community College
Cazenovia College
Central City Business Institute
City University of New York
    Baruch College
    Bronx Community College
    City College
    College of Staten Island
    Hostos Community College
    Hunter College
    John Jay College of Criminal
        Justice
    Lehman College
    Medgar Evers College
    New York City Technical
        College
    Queensborough Community
        College
    York College
Clinton Community College
College of Insurance
College of Mount St. Vincent
College of New Rochelle
    New Rochelle
    School of New Resources
College of St. Rose
Columbia University
    Columbia College
    School of Engineering and
        Applied Science
Columbia-Greene Community
    College
Concordia College
Dominican College of Blauvelt
Dowling College
Dutchess Community College
D'Youville College
Elmira College
Erie Community College: North
    Campus
Eugene Lang College/New School
    for Social Research
Finger Lakes Community College
Five Towns College
Fordham University
Fulton-Montgomery Community
    College
Genesee Community College
Hofstra University
Hudson Valley Community College
Ithaca College
Long Island University
    Brooklyn Campus
    C. W. Post Campus
    Southampton College
Manhattan College
Mannes College of Music
Marymount Manhattan College
Mater Dei College
Medaille College
Mercy College
Molloy College
Monroe College
Monroe Community College
Mount St. Mary College
New York Institute of Technology
New York School of Interior
    Design
New York University
Niagara County Community College
Niagara University
Onondaga Community College
Pace University
Paul Smith's College
Plaza Business Institute

Polytechnic University
    Brooklyn
    Long Island Campus
Pratt Institute
Rochester Business Institute
Rochester Institute of Technology
Sage Junior College of Albany
St. Bonaventure University
St. John Fisher College
School of Visual Arts
State University of New York
    Albany
    College at Brockport
    College at Cortland
    College of Environmental
        Science and Forestry
    College at New Paltz
    College at Old Westbury
    College at Potsdam
    College of Technology at
        Alfred
    College of Technology at
        Canton
    College of Technology at Delhi
Tompkins-Cortland Community
    College
Trocaire College
Ulster County Community College
Utica College of Syracuse
    University
Vassar College
Wadhams Hall Seminary-College
Westchester Business Institute
Westchester Community College
Yeshiva University

North Carolina

Alamance Community College
Anson Community College
Bladen Community College
Chowan College
East Coast Bible College
Guilford College
Mayland Community College
McDowell Technical Community
    College
Methodist College
Montgomery Community College
North Carolina Agricultural and
    Technical State University
Peace College
Pfeiffer College
Pitt Community College
Richmond Community College
Roanoke Bible College
St. Andrews Presbyterian College
Southwestern Community College
University of North Carolina at
    Asheville
Wayne Community College
Western Piedmont Community
    College
Wilson Technical Community
    College

North Dakota

North Dakota State University

Ohio

Art Academy of Cincinnati
Bluffton College
Cedarville College
Central Ohio Technical College
Chatfield College
Circleville Bible College
Clark State Community College
Cleveland State University
Cuyahoga Community College
    Eastern Campus
    Metropolitan Campus
    Western Campus
Denison University

DeVry Institute of Technology:
    Columbus
Edison State Community College
Franklin University
God's Bible School and College
Hiram College
Kent State University
    Ashtabula Regional Campus
    East Liverpool Regional
        Campus
    Salem Regional Campus
    Stark Campus
    Trumbull Campus
Lorain County Community College
Lourdes College
Malone College
Marietta College
Marion Technical College
Miami-Jacobs College
Mount Vernon Nazarene College
Muskingum Area Technical College
Muskingum College
North Central Technical College
Northwest State Community
    College
Oberlin College
Ohio Dominican College
Southern State Community College
Terra Community College
Tiffin University
Union Institute
University of Cincinnati
    Cincinnati
    Clermont College
    Raymond Walters College
University of Dayton
University of Toledo
Urbana University
Walsh University
Wilberforce University
Wilmington College
Xavier University

Oklahoma

Bartlesville Wesleyan College
Northeastern State University
Oklahoma Christian University of
    Science and Arts
Oklahoma City Community College
Oklahoma City University
Oklahoma Panhandle State
    University
Rogers State College
Southeastern Oklahoma State
    University
Southwestern Oklahoma State
    University
University of Central Oklahoma

Oregon

Bassist College
Central Oregon Community College
Chemeketa Community College
Clackamas Community College
Concordia College
Eastern Oregon State College
George Fox College
Lane Community College
Linfield College
Marylhurst College
Multnomah Bible College
Northwest Christian College
Oregon Health Sciences University
Oregon Institute of Technology
Pacific Northwest College of Art
Pacific University
Portland Community College
Southwestern Oregon Community
    College
Treasure Valley Community College
University of Portland
Western Baptist College

Western Oregon State College
Willamette University

Pennsylvania

Academy of the New Church
Albright College
Allentown College of St. Francis de
    Sales
Art Institute of Pittsburgh
Baptist Bible College of
    Pennsylvania
Bryn Mawr College
Bucks County Community College
California University of
    Pennsylvania
Carnegie Mellon University
Central Pennsylvania Business
    School
Chestnut Hill College
Churchman Business School
Clarion University of Pennsylvania
College Misericordia
Community College of Allegheny
    County
    Allegheny Campus
    Boyce Campus
    North Campus
    South Campus
Community College of Beaver
    County
Delaware County Community
    College
Delaware Valley College
Drexel University
Duquesne University
East Stroudsburg University of
    Pennsylvania
Elizabethtown College
Gettysburg College
Gratz College
Harcum College
Haverford College
Holy Family College
Hussian School of Art
Immaculata College
Kutztown University of
    Pennsylvania
La Roche College
La Salle University
Lackawanna Junior College
Lafayette College
Lancaster Bible College
Manor Junior College
Mansfield University of
    Pennsylvania
Marywood College
Moravian College
Neumann College
Peirce College
Penn State
    Allentown Campus
    Altoona Campus
    Beaver Campus
    Berks Campus
    Delaware County Campus
    Du Bois Campus
    Erie Behrend College
    Fayette Campus
    Harrisburg Capital College
    Hazleton Campus
    McKeesport Campus
    Mont Alto Campus
    New Kensington Campus
    Ogontz Campus
    Schuylkill Campus
    Shenango Campus
    University Park Campus
    Wilkes-Barre Campus
    Worthington-Scranton Campus
    York Campus
Pennsylvania College of Technology
Pittsburgh Technical Institute

Point Park College
Reading Area Community College
Robert Morris College
St. Charles Borromeo Seminary-
Overbrook
Temple University
University of the Arts
University of Pennsylvania
University of Pittsburgh
Ursinus College
Valley Forge Military College
Wilkes University
York College of Pennsylvania

Puerto Rico

Bayamon Central University
Colegio Universitario del Este
Escuela de Artes Plasticas de
Puerto Rico
Inter American University of Puerto
Rico
Arecibo Campus
Barranquitas Campus
San German Campus
Pontifical Catholic University of
Puerto Rico
Turabo University
Universidad Metropolitana
Universidad Politecnica de Puerto
Rico
University of Puerto Rico
Aguadilla
Arecibo Campus
Bayamon Technological
University College
Humacao University College
La Montana Regional College
Mayaguez Campus
Ponce Technological
University College
Rio Piedras Campus
University of the Sacred Heart

Rhode Island

Rhode Island School of Design

South Carolina

The Citadel
Coastal Carolina University
Columbia Bible College
Columbia College
Southern Wesleyan University
Technical College of the
Lowcountry
University of South Carolina
Aiken
Columbia
Spartanburg
Union
Williamsburg Technical College
Winthrop University

South Dakota

Black Hills State University
Dakota State University
Dakota Wesleyan University
Huron University
Northern State University
Presentation College
South Dakota School of Mines and
Technology
Western Dakota Technical Institute

Tennessee

Carson-Newman College
Christian Brothers University
Johnson Bible College
Lee College
Lincoln Memorial University
Memphis College of Art
Tennessee Temple University
Tennessee Wesleyan College

Trevecca Nazarene College
Union University
University of Tennessee
Chattanooga
Knoxville
Martin
Vanderbilt University

Texas

Abilene Christian University
Ambassador University
Amber University
Arlington Baptist College
Concordia Lutheran College
Dallas Baptist University
Dallas Christian College
DeVry Institute of Technology:
Irving
East Texas State University
Huston-Tillotson College
Jarvis Christian College
Lee College
LeTourneau University
Midwestern State University
North Lake College
Odessa College
Prairie View A&M University
St. Edward's University
St. Mary's University
Southern Methodist University
Southwestern University
Texas A&M University-Corpus
Christi
Texas Southern University
Texas State Technical College:
Sweetwater
Texas Wesleyan University
University of Houston: Downtown
University of Mary Hardin-Baylor
University of Texas
El Paso
Medical Branch at Galveston
Houston Health Science
Center

Utah

Stevens-Henager College of
Business
University of Utah
Utah State University
Utah Valley State College

Vermont

Champlain College
Goddard College
Southern Vermont College
Trinity College of Vermont
University of Vermont
Vermont Technical College

Virginia

George Mason University
Hampton University
Lord Fairfax Community College
Marymount University
Norfolk State University
Old Dominion University
Randolph-Macon Woman's College
Shenandoah University
Southern Virginia College
Tidewater Community College
Virginia State University
Virginia Union University

Washington

Antioch University Seattle
Art Institute of Seattle
Cogswell College North
Cornish College of the Arts
Eastern Washington University
Gonzaga University
Heritage College

Lower Columbia College
Northwest College
Peninsula College
Pierce College
Puget Sound Christian College
St. Martin's College
Skagit Valley College
Tacoma Community College
University of Puget Sound
Western Washington University

West Virginia

Mountain State College
West Virginia State College
West Virginia University

Wisconsin

Blackhawk Technical College
Carroll College
Fox Valley Technical College
Gateway Technical College
Madison Area Technical College
Marquette University
Mid-State Technical College
Milwaukee Area Technical College
Milwaukee Institute of Art &
Design
Moraine Park Technical College
Northcentral Technical College
St. Norbert College
Silver Lake College
University of Wisconsin Center
Baraboo/Sauk County
Barron County
Fond du Lac
Fox Valley
Manitowoc County
Marathon County
Marinette County
Marshfield/Wood County
Rock County
Sheboygan County
Washington County
Waukesha County Technical
College
Western Wisconsin Technical
College

Wyoming

Central Wyoming College
Sheridan College
Western Wyoming Community
College

**American Samoa, Caroline
Islands, Guam, Marianas,
Virgin Islands**

Guam Community College

Arab Republic of Egy

American University in Cairo

Canada

McGill University

Mexico

Sistema Instituto Tecnologico y de
Estudios Superiores de
Monterrey

Alphabetical list of colleges

Abilene Christian University, Abilene, TX 79699-6000
Abraham Baldwin Agricultural College, Tifton, GA 31794-2693
Academy of Art College, San Francisco, CA 94115-3410
Academy of Business College, Phoenix, AZ 85051
Academy of the New Church, Bryn Athyn, PA 19009
Adams State College, Alamosa, CO 81102
Adelphi University, Garden City, NY 11530
Adirondack Community College, Queensbury, NY 12804-1498
Adrian College, Adrian, MI 49221-2575
Agnes Scott College, Decatur, GA 30030-3797
Aiken Technical College, Aiken, SC 29802-0696
Aims Community College, Greeley, CO 80632
Al Collins Graphic Design School, Tempe, AZ 85281
Alabama Agricultural and Mechanical University, Normal, AL 35762
Alabama Aviation and Technical College, Ozark, AL 36361-1209
Alabama Southern Community College, Monroeville, AL 36461-2000
Alabama State University, Montgomery, AL 36101-0271
Alamance Community College, Graham, NC 27253
Alaska Bible College, Glennallen, AK 99588
Alaska Pacific University, Anchorage, AK 99508-4672
Albany College of Pharmacy, Albany, NY 12208
Albany State College, Albany, GA 31705-2796
Albertson College, Caldwell, ID 83605
Albertus Magnus College, New Haven, CT 06511-1189
Albion College, Albion, MI 49224
Albright College, Reading, PA 19612-5234
Albuquerque Technical-Vocational Institute, Albuquerque, NM 87106
Alcorn State University, Lorman, MS 39096
Alderson-Broaddus College, Philippi, WV 26416
Alexandria Technical College, Alexandria, MN 56308-3799
Alfred University, Alfred, NY 14802-9985
Alice Lloyd College, Pippa Passes, KY 41844
Allan Hancock College, Santa Maria, CA 93454-6399
Allegany Community College, Cumberland, MD 21502
Allegheny College, Meadville, PA 16335-3902
Allen County Community College, Iola, KS 66749
Allen University, Columbia, SC 29204
Allentown College of St. Francis de Sales, Center Valley, PA 18034-9568
Alma College, Alma, MI 48801-1599
Alpena Community College, Alpena, MI 49707
Alvernia College, Reading, PA 19607-1799
Alverno College, Milwaukee, WI 53234-3922
Alvin Community College, Alvin, TX 77511-4898
Amarillo College, Amarillo, TX 79178
Ambassador University, Big Sandy, TX 75755
Amber University, Garland, TX 75041-5595
American Academy of Art, Chicago, IL 60604-4302
American Academy of Dramatic Arts
    New York, New York, NY 10016
    West, Pasadena, CA 91107
American Academy McAllister Institute of Funeral Service, New York, NY 10019-3602
American Baptist College of ABT Seminary, Nashville, TN 37207
American College for the Applied Arts
    Atlanta, Atlanta, GA 30326
    Los Angeles, Los Angeles, CA 90024-5603
American College of Switzerland, Leysin, Switzerland 00000
American Conservatory of Music, Chicago, IL 60602-4792
American Indian College of the Assemblies of God, Phoenix, AZ 85021-2199

American Institute of Business, Des Moines, IA 50321
American Institute of Commerce, Davenport, IA 52807-2095
American Institute of Design, Philadelphia, PA 19124
American International College, Springfield, MA 01109-3184
American River College, Sacramento, CA 95841
American Samoa Community College, Pago Pago, AS 00000
American Technical Institute, Brunswick, TN 38014
American University, Washington, DC 20016-8001
American University in Cairo, Cairo, Arab Republic of 9959 00000
American University of Paris, Paris, France 00000
American University of Puerto Rico, Bayamon, PR 00960-2037
Amherst College, Amherst, MA 01002
Ancilla College, Donaldson, IN 46513
Anderson College, Anderson, SC 29621
Anderson University, Anderson, IN 46012-3462
Andover College, Portland, ME 04103
Andrew College, Cuthbert, GA 31740-1395
Andrews University, Berrien Springs, MI 49104
Angelina College, Lufkin, TX 75902-1768
Angelo State University, San Angelo, TX 76909
Anna Maria College, Paxton, MA 01612-1198
Anne Arundel Community College, Arnold, MD 21012-1895
Anoka-Ramsey Community College, Coon Rapids, MN 55433
Anson Community College, Polkton, NC 28135
Antelope Valley College, Lancaster, CA 93536-5426
Antioch College, Yellow Springs, OH 45387
Antioch Southern California
    Los Angeles, Marina Del Rey, CA 90292-7090
    Santa Barbara, Santa Barbara, CA 93101
Antioch University Seattle, Seattle, WA 98121
Antonelli Institute of Art and Photography, Plymouth Meeting, PA 19462-0570
Antonelli Institute of Art and Photography, Cincinnati, OH 45202
Appalachian Bible College, Bradley, WV 25818-1353
Appalachian State University, Boone, NC 28608
Aquinas College, Grand Rapids, MI 49506-1799
Aquinas College, Nashville, TN 37205
Aquinas College at Milton, Milton, MA 02186
Aquinas College at Newton, Newton, MA 02158-9990
Arapahoe Community College, Littleton, CO 80160-9002
Arizona College of the Bible, Phoenix, AZ 85021-5197
Arizona State University, Tempe, AZ 85287-0112
Arizona Western College, Yuma, AZ 85366-0929
Arkansas Baptist College, Little Rock, AR 72202
Arkansas State University
    Beebe Branch, Beebe, AR 72012-1008
    Jonesboro, Jonesboro, AR 72467-1630
Arkansas Tech University, Russellville, AR 72801-2222
Arlington Baptist College, Arlington, TX 76012-3425
Armstrong State College, Savannah, GA 31419-1997
Armstrong University, Berkeley, CA 94704
Art Academy of Cincinnati, Cincinnati, OH 45202-1700
Art Center College of Design, Pasadena, CA 91103
Art Institute of Atlanta, Atlanta, GA 30326
Art Institute of Fort Lauderdale, Fort Lauderdale, FL 33316-3000
Art Institute of Pittsburgh, Pittsburgh, PA 15222
Art Institute of Seattle, Seattle, WA 98121
Art Institute of Southern California, Laguna Beach, CA 92651
Asbury College, Wilmore, KY 40390-1198
Asheville Buncombe Technical Community College, Asheville, NC 28801

Ashland Community College, Ashland, KY 41101-3683
Ashland University, Ashland, OH 44805-9981
Asnuntuck Community-Technical College, Enfield, CT 06082
Assumption College, Worcester, MA 01615-0005
Assumption College for Sisters, Mendham, NJ 07945-0800
Athens Area Technical Institute, Athens, GA 30610-0399
Athens State College, Athens, AL 35611
Atlanta Christian College, East Point, GA 30344
Atlanta College of Art, Atlanta, GA 30309
Atlanta Metropolitan College, Atlanta, GA 30310
Atlantic Community College, Mays Landing, NJ 08330-2699
Atlantic Union College, South Lancaster, MA 01561
Auburn University
        Auburn, Auburn, AL 36849-5145
        Montgomery, Montgomery, AL 36117-3596
Audrey Cohen College, New York, NY 10014-9931
Augsburg College, Minneapolis, MN 55454
Augusta College, Augusta, GA 30904-2200
Augusta Technical Institute, Augusta, GA 30906
Augustana College, Rock Island, IL 61201-2296
Augustana College, Sioux Falls, SD 57197-9990
Aurora University, Aurora, IL 60506-4892
Austin College, Sherman, TX 75090-4440
Austin Community College, Austin, MN 55912
Austin Community College, Austin, TX 78752-4390
Austin Peay State University, Clarksville, TN 37044
Averett College, Danville, VA 24541
Avila College, Kansas City, MO 64145-1698
Azusa Pacific University, Azusa, CA 91702-7000
Babson College, Babson Park, MA 02157-0310
Bacone College, Muskogee, OK 74403-1597
Bainbridge College, Bainbridge, GA 31717-0953
Baker College
        Auburn Hills, Auburn Hills, MI 48326
        Cadillac, Cadillac, MI 49601-9169
        Flint, Flint, MI 48507-5508
        Jackson, Jackson, MI 49201-2328
        Mount Clemens, Clinton Township, MI 48035-4701
        Muskegon, Muskegon, MI 49442
        Owosso, Owosso, MI 48867
        Port Huron, Port Huron, MI 48060-2597
Baker University, Baldwin City, KS 66006
Bakersfield College, Bakersfield, CA 93305
Baldwin-Wallace College, Berea, OH 44017-2088
Ball State University, Muncie, IN 47306-0855
Baltimore City Community College, Baltimore, MD 21215
Baltimore Hebrew University, Baltimore, MD 21215-3996
Baltimore International Culinary College, Baltimore, MD 21202-3230
Baptist Bible College, Springfield, MO 65803
Baptist Bible College of Pennsylvania, Clarks Summit, PA 18411
Baptist Missionary Association Theological Seminary, Jacksonville, TX 75766-5414
Barat College, Lake Forest, IL 60045
Barber-Scotia College, Concord, NC 28025
Barclay College, Haviland, KS 67059
Bard College, Annandale-on-Hudson, NY 12504
Barnard College, New York, NY 10027-6598
Barry University, Miami Shores, FL 33161
Barstow College, Barstow, CA 92311-9984
Bartlesville Wesleyan College, Bartlesville, OK 74006
Barton College, Wilson, NC 27893-9910
Barton County Community College, Great Bend, KS 67530-9283
Bassist College, Portland, OR 97201
Bastyr University, Seattle, WA 98105
Bates College, Lewiston, ME 04240-0917
Bauder College, Atlanta, GA 30326-9975
Bauder Fashion College, Arlington, TX 76010
Bay de Noc Community College, Escanaba, MI 49829
Bay Path College, Longmeadow, MA 01106
Bay State College, Boston, MA 02116
Bayamon Central University, Bayamon, PR 00960-1725
Baylor College of Dentistry, Dallas, TX 75266-0677
Baylor University, Waco, TX 76798-7056
Beal College, Bangor, ME 04401
Beaufort County Community College, Washington, NC 27889
Beaver College, Glenside, PA 19038-3295
Becker College
        Leicester Campus, Leicester, MA 01524-1197
        Worcester Campus, Worcester, MA 01615-0071
Bee County College, Beeville, TX 78102
Belhaven College, Jackson, MS 39202-1789
Bellarmine College, Louisville, KY 40205-0671

Belleville Area College, Belleville, IL 62221-9989
Bellevue Community College, Bellevue, WA 98007-6484
Bellevue University, Bellevue, NE 68005-3098
Bellin College of Nursing, Green Bay, WI 54305-3400
Belmont Abbey College, Belmont, NC 28012-2795
Belmont Technical College, St. Clairsville, OH 43950
Belmont University, Nashville, TN 37212-3757
Beloit College, Beloit, WI 53511-5595
Bel-Rea Institute of Animal Technology, Denver, CO 80231
Bemidji State University, Bemidji, MN 56601
Benedict College, Columbia, SC 29204
Benedictine College, Atchison, KS 66002-1499
Bennett College, Greensboro, NC 27401-3239
Bennington College, Bennington, VT 05201
Bentley College, Waltham, MA 02154-4705
Berea College, Berea, KY 40404
Berean College, Springfield, MO 65802
Berean Institute, Philadelphia, PA 19130
Bergen Community College, Paramus, NJ 07652-1595
Berkeley College, White Plains, NY 10604
Berkeley College of Business, West Paterson, NJ 07424-0440
Berkeley College of New York City, New York, NY 10017
Berklee College of Music, Boston, MA 02215
Berkshire Community College, Pittsfield, MA 01201-5786
Bermuda College, Devonshire, Bermuda 00000
Berry College, Mount Berry, GA 30149
Bessemer State Technical College, Bessemer, AL 35021
Beth Hamedrash Shaarei Yosher Institute, Brooklyn, NY 11204
Beth Medrash Govoha, Lakewood, NJ 08701
Bethany College, Scotts Valley, CA 95066-2898
Bethany College, Bethany, WV 26032-0417
Bethany College, Lindsborg, KS 67456-1897
Bethany Lutheran College, Mankato, MN 56001-4490
Bethel College, McKenzie, TN 38201
Bethel College, Mishawaka, IN 46545
Bethel College, North Newton, KS 67117-9899
Bethel College, St. Paul, MN 55112
Beth-El College of Nursing, Colorado Springs, CO 80917-5338
Bethune-Cookman College, Daytona Beach, FL 32114-3099
Bevill State Community College, Sumiton, AL 35148
Big Bend Community College, Moses Lake, WA 98837-3299
Biola University, La Mirada, CA 90639-0001
Birmingham-Southern College, Birmingham, AL 35254
Bishop State Community College, Mobile, AL 36603-5898
Bismarck State College, Bismarck, ND 58501
Black Hawk College
        East Campus, Kewanee, IL 61443-0489
        Moline, Moline, IL 61265
Black Hills State University, Spearfish, SD 57799-9502
Blackburn College, Carlinville, IL 62626
Blackfeet Community College, Browning, MT 59417
Blackhawk Technical College, Janesville, WI 53547
Bladen Community College, Dublin, NC 28332
Blair Junior College, Colorado Springs, CO 80915
Blessing-Reiman College of Nursing, Quincy, IL 62301
Blinn College, Brenham, TX 77833
Bloomfield College, Bloomfield, NJ 07003
Bloomsburg University of Pennsylvania, Bloomsburg, PA 17815
Blue Mountain College, Blue Mountain, MS 38610
Blue Mountain Community College, Pendleton, OR 97801
Blue Ridge Community College, Flat Rock, NC 28731-9624
Blue Ridge Community College, Weyers Cave, VA 24486-9989
Bluefield College, Bluefield, VA 24605-1799
Bluefield State College, Bluefield, WV 24701
Bluffton College, Bluffton, OH 45817-1196
Boise Bible College, Boise, ID 83714-1220
Boise State University, Boise, ID 83725
Boricua College, New York, NY 10032
Bossier Parish Community College, Bossier City, LA 71111
Boston Architectural Center, Boston, MA 02115-2795
Boston College, Chestnut Hill, MA 02167-3809
Boston Conservatory, Boston, MA 02215
Boston University, Boston, MA 02215
Bowdoin College, Brunswick, ME 04011-2595
Bowie State University, Bowie, MD 20715
Bowling Green State University
        Bowling Green, Bowling Green, OH 43403-0085
        Firelands College, Huron, OH 44839-9791
Bradford College, Bradford, MA 01835-7393
Bradford School, Columbus, OH 43229
Bradley Academy for the Visual Arts, York, PA 17403
Bradley University, Peoria, IL 61625

Bramson ORT Technical Institute, Forest Hills, NY 11375
Brandeis University, Waltham, MA 02254-9110
Brazosport College, Lake Jackson, TX 77566
Brenau University, Gainesville, GA 30501-3697
Brescia College, Owensboro, KY 42301-3023
Brevard College, Brevard, NC 28712
Brevard Community College, Cocoa, FL 32922-9987
Brewton-Parker College, Mount Vernon, GA 30445
Briar Cliff College, Sioux City, IA 51104-2100
Briarcliffe: The College for Business and Technology, Woodbury, NY 11797
Briarwood College, Southington, CT 06489
Bridgewater College, Bridgewater, VA 22812-1599
Bridgewater State College, Bridgewater, MA 02325
Brigham Young University
    Provo, Provo, UT 84602
    Hawaii, Laie, HI 96762-1294
Bristol Community College, Fall River, MA 02720
Brookdale Community College, Lincroft, NJ 07738
Brookhaven College, Farmers Branch, TX 75244
Brooks College, Long Beach, CA 90804
Brooks Institute of Photography, Santa Barbara, CA 93108
Broome Community College, Binghamton, NY 13902
Broward Community College, Fort Lauderdale, FL 33301
Brown Mackie College, Salina, KS 67402-1787
Brown University, Providence, RI 02912
Brunswick College, Brunswick, GA 31523
Brunswick Community College, Supply, NC 28462
Bryan College, Dayton, TN 37321-7000
Bryant College, Smithfield, RI 02917-1285
Bryant & Stratton Business Institute
    Albany, Albany, NY 12205
    Buffalo, Buffalo, NY 14202
    Cleveland West, Parma, OH 44130-1013
    Rochester, Rochester, NY 14604-1381
    Syracuse, Syracuse, NY 13203-2502
Bryn Mawr College, Bryn Mawr, PA 19010
Bucknell University, Lewisburg, PA 17837-9988
Bucks County Community College, Newtown, PA 18940
Buena Vista College, Storm Lake, IA 50588-1798
Bunker Hill Community College, Boston, MA 02129-2991
Burlington College, Burlington, VT 05401
Burlington County College, Pemberton, NJ 08068-1599
Butler County Community College, Butler, PA 16003-1203
Butler County Community College, Eldorado, KS 67042-3280
Butler University, Indianapolis, IN 46208
Butte College, Oroville, CA 95965
Cabrillo College, Aptos, CA 95003
Cabrini College, Radnor, PA 19087-3698
Caldwell College, Caldwell, NJ 07006-6195
Caldwell Community College and Technical Institute, Hudson, NC 28638-2397
California Baptist College, Riverside, CA 92504-3297
California College of Arts and Crafts, Oakland, CA 94618-1487
California Culinary Academy, San Francisco, CA 94102
California Institute of the Arts, Valencia, CA 91355
California Institute of Technology, Pasadena, CA 91125
California Lutheran University, Thousand Oaks, CA 91360-2787
California Maritime Academy, Vallejo, CA 94590-0644
California Polytechnic State University: San Luis Obispo, San Luis Obispo, CA 93407
California State Polytechnic University: Pomona, Pomona, CA 91768-4019
California State University
    Bakersfield, Bakersfield, CA 93311-1099
    Chico, Chico, CA 95929-0722
    Dominguez Hills, Carson, CA 90747-9960
    Fresno, Fresno, CA 93740-0057
    Fullerton, Fullerton, CA 92634-9480
    Hayward, Hayward, CA 94542-3035
    Long Beach, Long Beach, CA 90840-0106
    Los Angeles, Los Angeles, CA 90032-8530
    Northridge, Northridge, CA 91328-1286
    Sacramento, Sacramento, CA 95819-6048
    San Bernardino, San Bernardino, CA 92407-2397
    San Marcos, San Marcos, CA 92096-0001
    Stanislaus, Turlock, CA 95382-0283
California University of Pennsylvania, California, PA 15419-1394
Calumet College of St. Joseph, Hammond, IN 46394-2195
Calvary Bible College, Kansas City, MO 64147-1341
Calvin College, Grand Rapids, MI 49546-4388
Cambria-Rowe Business College, Johnstown, PA 15902
Camden County College, Blackwood, NJ 08012
Cameron University, Lawton, OK 73505-6377

Campbell University, Buies Creek, NC 27506
Campbellsville College, Campbellsville, KY 42718-2799
Canada College, Redwood City, CA 94061
Canisius College, Buffalo, NY 14208-9989
Cape Cod Community College, West Barnstable, MA 02668-1599
Cape Fear Community College, Wilmington, NC 28401-3993
Capital Community-Technical College, Hartford, CT 06105-2354
Capital University, Columbus, OH 43209-2394
Capitol College, Laurel, MD 20708
Cardinal Stritch College, Milwaukee, WI 53217-3985
Caribbean Center for Advanced Studies: Miami Institute of Psychology, Miami, FL 33166
Caribbean University, Bayamon, PR 00960-0493
Carl Albert State College, Poteau, OK 74953-5208
Carl Sandburg College, Galesburg, IL 61401
Carleton College, Northfield, MN 55057
Carlow College, Pittsburgh, PA 15213-3165
Carnegie Mellon University, Pittsburgh, PA 15213-3890
Carroll College, Waukesha, WI 53186
Carroll College, Helena, MT 59625
Carroll Community College, Westminster, MD 21157
Carson-Newman College, Jefferson City, TN 37760
Carteret Community College, Morehead City, NC 28557-2989
Carthage College, Kenosha, WI 53140-1994
Casco Bay College, Portland, ME 04101-3483
Case Western Reserve University, Cleveland, OH 44106-7055
Casper College, Casper, WY 82601
Castle College, Windham, NH 03087-1297
Castleton State College, Castleton, VT 05735-9987
Catawba College, Salisbury, NC 28144-2488
Catawba Valley Community College, Hickory, NC 28602
Catholic Medical Center of Brooklyn and Queens School of Nursing, Woodhaven, NY 11421
Catholic University of America, Washington, DC 20064
Catonsville Community College, Catonsville, MD 21228
Cayuga County Community College, Auburn, NY 13021
Cazenovia College, Cazenovia, NY 13035-9989
Cecil Community College, North East, MD 21901-1999
Cecils College, Asheville, NC 28816
Cedar Crest College, Allentown, PA 18104-6196
Cedar Valley College, Lancaster, TX 75134
Cedarville College, Cedarville, OH 45314-0601
Centenary College, Hackettstown, NJ 07840-9989
Centenary College of Louisiana, Shreveport, LA 71134-1188
Center for Creative Studies: College of Art and Design, Detroit, MI 48202-4034
Central Alabama Community College, Alexander City, AL 35011
Central Arizona College, Coolidge, AZ 85228
Central Baptist College, Conway, AR 72032
Central Bible College, Springfield, MO 65803-1069
Central Carolina Community College, Sanford, NC 27330
Central Carolina Technical College, Sumter, SC 29150
Central Christian College of the Bible, Moberly, MO 65270-1997
Central City Business Institute, Syracuse, NY 13202
Central College, Pella, IA 50219-1999
Central College, McPherson, KS 67460-5740
Central Community College, Grand Island, NE 68802-4903
Central Connecticut State University, New Britain, CT 06050
Central Florida Community College, Ocala, FL 34478
Central Lakes College, Brainerd, MN 56401
Central Maine Medical Center School of Nursing, Lewiston, ME 04240-9986
Central Maine Technical College, Auburn, ME 04210-6498
Central Methodist College, Fayette, MO 65248-1198
Central Michigan University, Mount Pleasant, MI 48859
Central Missouri State University, Warrensburg, MO 64093
Central Ohio Technical College, Newark, OH 43055
Central Oregon Community College, Bend, OR 97701-5998
Central Pennsylvania Business School, Summerdale, PA 17093-0309
Central Piedmont Community College, Charlotte, NC 28235-5009
Central State University, Wilberforce, OH 45384-3002
Central Texas College, Killeen, TX 76540-9990
Central Virginia Community College, Lynchburg, VA 24502-2498
Central Washington University, Ellensburg, WA 98926-7463
Central Wyoming College, Riverton, WY 82501
Centralia College, Centralia, WA 98531
Centre College, Danville, KY 40422
Cerritos Community College, Norwalk, CA 90650
Cerro Coso Community College, Ridgecrest, CA 93555-7777
Chabot College, Hayward, CA 94545
Chadron State College, Chadron, NE 69337
Chaffey Community College, Rancho Cucamonga, CA 91701-3002

Chaminade University of Honolulu, Honolulu, HI 96816-1578
Champlain College, Burlington, VT 05402-0670
Chapman University, Orange, CA 92666-1099
Charles County Community College, La Plata, MD 20646
Charles R. Drew University: College of Allied Health, Los Angeles, CA 90059
Charleston Southern University, Charleston, SC 29411
Chatfield College, St. Martin, OH 45118-9705
Chatham College, Pittsburgh, PA 15232-9987
Chattahoochee Technical Institute, Marietta, GA 30060
Chattahoochee Valley Community College, Phenix City, AL 36869
Chattanooga State Technical Community College, Chattanooga, TN 37406
Chemeketa Community College, Salem, OR 97309-7070
Chesapeake College, Wye Mills, MD 21679-0008
Chesterfield-Marlboro Technical College, Cheraw, SC 29520
Chestnut Hill College, Philadelphia, PA 19118-2695
Cheyney University of Pennsylvania, Cheyney, PA 19319-0019
CHI Institute, Southampton, PA 18966
Chicago College of Commerce, Chicago, IL 60603
Chicago State University, Chicago, IL 60628
Chipola Junior College, Marianna, FL 32446
Chippewa Valley Technical College, Eau Claire, WI 54701
Chowan College, Murfreesboro, NC 27855-9901
Christendom College, Front Royal, VA 22630
Christian Brothers University, Memphis, TN 38104-5581
Christian Heritage College, El Cajon, CA 92019-1157
Christopher Newport University, Newport News, VA 23606-2998
Churchman Business School, Easton, PA 18042
Cincinnati Bible College and Seminary, Cincinnati, OH 45204-3200
Cincinnati College of Mortuary Science, Cincinnati, OH 45207-1033
Cincinnati State Technical and Community College, Cincinnati, OH 45223
Circleville Bible College, Circleville, OH 43113
Cisco Junior College, Cisco, TX 76437
The Citadel, Charleston, SC 29409
Citrus College, Glendora, CA 91740-1899
City College of San Francisco, San Francisco, CA 94112
City Colleges of Chicago
    Harold Washington College, Chicago, IL 60601
    Harry S. Truman College, Chicago, IL 60640
    Kennedy-King College, Chicago, IL 60621
    Malcolm X College, Chicago, IL 60612
    Olive-Harvey College, Chicago, IL 60628
    Richard J. Daley College, Chicago, IL 60652
    Wright College, Chicago, IL 60634-4276
City University, Bellevue, WA 98055
City University of New York
    Baruch College, New York, NY 10010-5585
    Borough of Manhattan Community College, New York, NY 10007-1097
    Bronx Community College, New York, NY 10453
    Brooklyn College, Brooklyn, NY 11210
    City College, New York, NY 10031
    College of Staten Island, Staten Island, NY 10314
    Hostos Community College, Bronx, NY 10451
    Hunter College, New York, NY 10021
    John Jay College of Criminal Justice, New York, NY 10019
    Kingsborough Community College, Brooklyn, NY 11235
    La Guardia Community College, Long Island City, NY 11101
    Lehman College, Bronx, NY 10468
    Medgar Evers College, Brooklyn, NY 11225-2201
    New York City Technical College, Brooklyn, NY 11201-2983
    Queens College, Flushing, NY 11367
    Queensborough Community College, Bayside, NY 11364-1497
    York College, Jamaica, NY 11451-9989
Clackamas Community College, Oregon City, OR 97045
Claflin College, Orangeburg, SC 29115
Claremont McKenna College, Claremont, CA 91711-6420
Clarendon College, Clarendon, TX 79226
Clarion University of Pennsylvania, Clarion, PA 16214
Clark Atlanta University, Atlanta, GA 30314
Clark College, Vancouver, WA 98663
Clark State Community College, Springfield, OH 45501
Clark University, Worcester, MA 01610-1477
Clarke College, Dubuque, IA 52001-3198
Clarkson College, Omaha, NE 68131-2739
Clarkson University, Potsdam, NY 13699
Clatsop Community College, Astoria, OR 97103
Clayton State College, Morrow, GA 30260-1221
Clear Creek Baptist Bible College, Pineville, KY 40977
Clearwater Christian College, Clearwater, FL 34619-9997
Cleary College, Ypsilanti, MI 48197
Clemson University, Clemson, SC 29634-5124

Cleveland College of Jewish Studies, Beachwood, OH 44122
Cleveland Community College, Shelby, NC 28150
Cleveland Institute of Art, Cleveland, OH 44106
Cleveland Institute of Music, Cleveland, OH 44106
Cleveland State Community College, Cleveland, TN 37320-3570
Cleveland State University, Cleveland, OH 44115-2403
Clinch Valley College of the University of Virginia, Wise, VA 24293
Clinton Community College, Plattsburgh, NY 12901-4297
Clinton Community College, Clinton, IA 52732-6299
Cloud County Community College, Concordia, KS 66901-1002
Clovis Community College, Clovis, NM 88101-8345
Coahoma Community College, Clarksdale, MS 38614-9799
Coastal Carolina Community College, Jacksonville, NC 28540-6877
Coastal Carolina University, Conway, SC 29526
Coastline Community College, Fountain Valley, CA 92708
Cochise College, Douglas, AZ 85607-9724
Cochran School of Nursing-St. John's Riverside Hospital, Yonkers, NY 10701
Coe College, Cedar Rapids, IA 52402-9983
Coffeyville Community College, Coffeyville, KS 67337
Cogswell College North, Kirkland, WA 98033
Cogswell Polytechnical College, Sunnyvale, CA 94089
Coker College, Hartsville, SC 29550
Colby College, Waterville, ME 04901-8848
Colby Community College, Colby, KS 67701
Colby-Sawyer College, New London, NH 03257
Colegio Universitario del Este, Carolina, PR 00983-2010
Coleman College, La Mesa, CA 91942-1500
Colgate University, Hamilton, NY 13346-1383
College of Aeronautics, Flushing, NY 11371
College of Alameda, Alameda, CA 94501
College of the Albemarle, Elizabeth City, NC 27906-2327
College of Associated Arts, St. Paul, MN 55102-2199
College of the Atlantic, Bar Harbor, ME 04609
College of the Canyons, Valencia, CA 91355
College of Charleston, Charleston, SC 29424
College of the Desert, Palm Desert, CA 92260
College of DuPage, Glen Ellyn, IL 60137-6599
College of Eastern Utah, Price, UT 84501
College of Great Falls, Great Falls, MT 59405
College of Health Sciences, Roanoke, VA 24031-3186
College of the Holy Cross, Worcester, MA 01610-2395
College of Insurance, New York, NY 10007-2132
College of Lake County, Grayslake, IL 60030-1198
College for Lifelong Learning, Concord, NH 03301
College of the Mainland, Texas City, TX 77591
College of Marin: Kentfield, Kentfield, CA 94904
College Misericordia, Dallas, PA 18612-9984
College of Mount St. Joseph, Cincinnati, OH 45233-1672
College of Mount St. Vincent, Riverdale, NY 10471-1093
College of New Rochelle
    New Rochelle, New Rochelle, NY 10805-2308
    School of New Resources, New Rochelle, NY 10805-2308
College of Notre Dame, Belmont, CA 94002-1997
College of Notre Dame of Maryland, Baltimore, MD 21210-2476
College of Oceaneering, Wilmington, CA 90744
College of the Ozarks, Point Lookout, MO 65726-0017
College of the Redwoods, Eureka, CA 95501-9300
College of St. Benedict, St. Joseph, MN 56374-2099
College of St. Catherine: St. Catherine Campus, St. Paul, MN 55105
College of St. Catherine-Minneapolis, Minneapolis, MN 55454
College of St. Elizabeth, Morristown, NJ 07960-6989
College of St. Francis, Joliet, IL 60435-6188
College of St. Joseph in Vermont, Rutland, VT 05701-3899
College of St. Mary, Omaha, NE 68124
College of St. Rose, Albany, NY 12203
College of St. Scholastica, Duluth, MN 55811-4199
College of San Mateo, San Mateo, CA 94402-3784
College of Santa Fe, Santa Fe, NM 87501-5634
College of the Sequoias, Visalia, CA 93277
College of the Siskiyous, Weed, CA 96094
College of Southern Idaho, Twin Falls, ID 83303-1238
College of the Southwest, Hobbs, NM 88240-9987
College of West Virginia, Beckley, WV 25802-2830
College of William and Mary, Williamsburg, VA 23187-8795
College of Wooster, Wooster, OH 44691-2363
Collin County Community College District, McKinney, TX 75070-2906
Colorado Christian University, Denver, CO 80226
Colorado College, Colorado Springs, CO 80903-9854
Colorado Institute of Art, Denver, CO 80203

Colorado Mountain College
    Alpine Campus, Steamboat Springs, CO 80477
    Spring Valley Campus, Glenwood Springs, CO 81601
    Timberline Campus, Leadville, CO 80461
Colorado Northwestern Community College, Rangely, CO 81648-9988
Colorado School of Mines, Golden, CO 80401
Colorado State University, Fort Collins, CO 80523-0015
Colorado Technical College, Colorado Springs, CO 80907-3896
Columbia Basin College, Pasco, WA 99301
Columbia Bible College, Columbia, SC 29230-3122
Columbia College, Chicago, IL 60605-1996
Columbia College, Columbia, CA 95310
Columbia College, Columbia, SC 29203-5998
Columbia College, Columbia, MO 65216
Columbia College, Caguas, PR 00626
Columbia College: Hollywood, Los Angeles, CA 90038
Columbia College of Nursing, Milwaukee, WI 53186
Columbia Junior College of Business, Columbia, SC 29203
Columbia State Community College, Columbia, TN 38401
Columbia Union College, Takoma Park, MD 20912
Columbia University
    Columbia College, New York, NY 10027
    School of Engineering and Applied Science, New York, NY 10027
    School of General Studies, New York, NY 10027
    School of Nursing, New York, NY 10032
Columbia-Greene Community College, Hudson, NY 12534
Columbus College, Columbus, GA 31907-5645
Columbus College of Art and Design, Columbus, OH 43215-3875
Columbus State Community College, Columbus, OH 43216-1609
Columbus Technical Institute, Columbus, GA 31995
Commonwealth College, Virginia Beach, VA 23462-4417
Commonwealth Institute of Funeral Service, Houston, TX 77090-5913
Community College of Allegheny County
    Allegheny Campus, Pittsburgh, PA 15212
    Boyce Campus, Monroeville, PA 15146
    North Campus, Pittsburgh, PA 15237
    South Campus, West Mifflin, PA 15122
Community College of Aurora, Aurora, CO 80011
Community College of Beaver County, Monaca, PA 15061
Community College of Denver, Denver, CO 80217-3363
Community College of Philadelphia, Philadelphia, PA 19130-3991
Community College of Rhode Island, Warwick, RI 02886-1807
Community College of Southern Nevada, North Las Vegas, NV 89030
Community College of Vermont, Waterbury, VT 05676
Compton Community College, Compton, CA 90221
Conception Seminary College, Conception, MO 64433
Concord College, Athens, WV 24712
Concordia College, Ann Arbor, MI 48105
Concordia College, Selma, AL 36701
Concordia College, Bronxville, NY 10708
Concordia College, Portland, OR 97211-6099
Concordia College, Seward, NE 68434-9989
Concordia College: Moorhead, Moorhead, MN 56562-9981
Concordia College: St. Paul, St. Paul, MN 55104-5494
Concordia Lutheran College, Austin, TX 78705-2799
Concordia University, River Forest, IL 60305-1499
Concordia University, Irvine, CA 92715-3299
Concordia University Wisconsin, Mequon, WI 53097-9650
Connecticut College, New London, CT 06320
Connors State College, Warner, OK 74469-9700
Conservatory of Music of Puerto Rico, Santurce, PR 00940
Contra Costa College, San Pablo, CA 94806
Converse College, Spartanburg, SC 29302-0006
Cooper Union, New York, NY 10003-7183
Copiah-Lincoln Community College, Wesson, MS 39191
Coppin State College, Baltimore, MD 21216
Corcoran School of Art, Washington, DC 20006
Cornell College, Mount Vernon, IA 52314-1098
Cornell University, Ithaca, NY 14850
Cornerstone College and Grand Rapids Baptist Seminary, Grand Rapids, MI 49505
Corning Community College, Corning, NY 14830
Cornish College of the Arts, Seattle, WA 98102
Cosumnes River College, Sacramento, CA 95823-5799
Cottey College, Nevada, MO 64772
County College of Morris, Randolph, NJ 07869-2086
Covenant College, Lookout Mountain, GA 30750
Cowley County Community College, Arkansas City, KS 67005
Crafton Hills College, Yucaipa, CA 92399-1799
Craven Community College, New Bern, NC 28562
Creighton University, Omaha, NE 68178
Crichton College, Memphis, TN 38175-7830

Criswell College, Dallas, TX 75246-1537
Crowder College, Neosho, MO 64850
Crown College, St. Bonifacius, MN 55375-9001
Cuesta College, San Luis Obispo, CA 93403-8106
Culinary Institute of America, Hyde Park, NY 12538-1499
Culver-Stockton College, Canton, MO 63435-1299
Cumberland College, Williamsburg, KY 40769-6178
Cumberland County College, Vineland, NJ 08360
Cumberland University, Lebanon, TN 37087
Curry College, Milton, MA 02186-9984
Curtis Institute of Music, Philadelphia, PA 19103
Cuyahoga Community College
    Eastern Campus, Highland Hills, OH 44122
    Metropolitan Campus, Cleveland, OH 44115-2878
    Western Campus, Parma, OH 44130
Cuyamaca College, El Cajon, CA 92019-4304
Cypress College, Cypress, CA 90630-5897
Dabney S. Lancaster Community College, Clifton Forge, VA 24422-1000
Daemen College, Amherst, NY 14226-3592
Dakota State University, Madison, SD 57042
Dakota Wesleyan University, Mitchell, SD 57301-4398
Dallas Baptist University, Dallas, TX 75211-9800
Dallas Christian College, Dallas, TX 75234-7299
Dalton College, Dalton, GA 30720
Dana College, Blair, NE 68008-1099
Daniel Webster College, Nashua, NH 03063-1300
Danville Area Community College, Danville, IL 61832
Danville Community College, Danville, VA 24541
Darkei Noam Rabbinical College, Brooklyn, NY 11210
Dartmouth College, Hanover, NH 03755
Darton College, Albany, GA 31707-3098
Davenport College of Business, Grand Rapids, MI 49503-4499
David Lipscomb University, Nashville, TN 37204-3951
Davidson College, Davidson, NC 28036
Davidson County Community College, Lexington, NC 27293-1287
Davis College, Toledo, OH 43623
Davis and Elkins College, Elkins, WV 26241
Dawson Community College, Glendive, MT 59330
Daytona Beach Community College, Daytona Beach, FL 32120-2811
De Anza College, Cupertino, CA 95014
De Paul University, Chicago, IL 60604-2287
Deaconess College of Nursing, St. Louis, MO 63139
Dean College, Franklin, MA 02038-1994
Dean Institute of Technology, Pittsburgh, PA 15226
Defiance College, Defiance, OH 43512-1695
DeKalb College, Decatur, GA 30021-2396
DeKalb Technical Institute, Clarkston, GA 30021-2397
Del Mar College, Corpus Christi, TX 78404-3897
Delaware County Community College, Media, PA 19063-1094
Delaware State University, Dover, DE 19901
Delaware Technical and Community College
    Southern Campus, Georgetown, DE 19947
    Stanton/Wilmington Campus, Newark, DE 19713
    Terry Campus, Dover, DE 19904
Delaware Valley College, Doylestown, PA 18901-2697
Delgado Community College, New Orleans, LA 70119-4399
Delta College, University Center, MI 48710
Delta State University, Cleveland, MS 38733
Denison University, Granville, OH 43023
Denmark Technical College, Denmark, SC 29042-0327
DePauw University, Greencastle, IN 46135-1611
Des Moines Area Community College, Ankeny, IA 50021
Detroit College of Business, Dearborn, MI 48126-3799
DeVry Institute of Technology
    Addison, Addison, IL 60101-6106
    Atlanta, Decatur, GA 30030-2198
    Chicago, Chicago, IL 60618-5994
    Columbus, Columbus, OH 43209-2705
    Irving, Irving, TX 75063-2440
    Kansas City, Kansas City, MO 64131-3626
    Phoenix, Phoenix, AZ 85021-2995
    Pomona, Pomona, CA 91768-2642
DeVry Technical Institute, Woodbridge, NJ 07095
Diablo Valley College, Pleasant Hill, CA 94523
Dickinson College, Carlisle, PA 17013-2896
Dickinson State University, Dickinson, ND 58601-4896
Dillard University, New Orleans, LA 70122-3097
Divine Word College, Epworth, IA 52045
Dixie College, St. George, UT 84770
Doane College, Crete, NE 68333
Dodge City Community College, Dodge City, KS 67801-2399
Dominican College of Blauvelt, Orangeburg, NY 10962

Dominican College of San Rafael, San Rafael, CA 94901-8008
Dominican School of Philosophy and Theology, Berkeley, CA 94709-1295
Don Bosco Technical Institute, Rosemead, CA 91770-4299
Dona Ana Branch Community College of New Mexico State University, Las Cruces, NM 88003-0001
Donnelly College, Kansas City, KS 66102-4210
Dordt College, Sioux Center, IA 51250
Douglas MacArthur State Technical College, Opp, AL 36467
Dowling College, Oakdale, NY 11769-1999
D-Q University, Davis, CA 95617
Drake University, Des Moines, IA 50311-4505
Draughons Junior College, Montgomery, AL 36104
Draughons Junior College of Business: Nashville, Nashville, TN 37217
Drew University, Madison, NJ 07940
Drexel University, Philadelphia, PA 19104-2875
Drury College, Springfield, MO 65802-9977
DuBois Business College, DuBois, PA 15801
Duke University, Durham, NC 27706
Dull Knife Memorial College, Lame Deer, MT 59043
Dundalk Community College, Baltimore, MD 21222-4692
Dunwoody Industrial Institute, Minneapolis, MN 55403-1192
Duquesne University, Pittsburgh, PA 15282-0201
Durham Technical Community College, Durham, NC 27703
Dutchess Community College, Poughkeepsie, NY 12601-1595
Dyersburg State Community College, Dyersburg, TN 38024
Dyke College, Cleveland, OH 44115-1096
D'Youville College, Buffalo, NY 14201-1084
Earlham College, Richmond, IN 47374
East Arkansas Community College, Forrest City, AR 72335-9598
East Carolina University, Greenville, NC 27858-4353
East Central College, Union, MO 63084-0529
East Central Community College, Decatur, MS 39327
East Central University, Ada, OK 74820-6899
East Coast Bible College, Charlotte, NC 28214
East Georgia College, Swainsboro, GA 30401-2699
East Los Angeles College, Monterey Park, CA 91754
East Mississippi Community College, Scooba, MS 39358
East Stroudsburg University of Pennsylvania, East Stroudsburg, PA 18301
East Tennessee State University, Johnson City, TN 37614-0002
East Texas Baptist University, Marshall, TX 75670-1498
East Texas State University
    Commerce, Commerce, TX 75429-3011
    Texarkana, Texarkana, TX 75505-5518
Eastern Arizona College, Thatcher, AZ 85552-0769
Eastern College, St. Davids, PA 19087-3696
Eastern Connecticut State University, Willimantic, CT 06226-2295
Eastern Idaho Technical College, Idaho Falls, ID 83404
Eastern Illinois University, Charleston, IL 61920-3099
Eastern Kentucky University, Richmond, KY 40475-3101
Eastern Maine Technical College, Bangor, ME 04401
Eastern Mennonite University, Harrisonburg, VA 22801-2462
Eastern Michigan University, Ypsilanti, MI 48197-2260
Eastern Nazarene College, Quincy, MA 02170-2999
Eastern New Mexico University
    Portales, Portales, NM 88130
    Roswell Campus, Roswell, NM 88202-6000
Eastern Oklahoma State College, Wilburton, OK 74578-4999
Eastern Oregon State College, LaGrande, OR 97850-2899
Eastern Shore Community College, Melfa, VA 23410-9755
Eastern Washington University, Cheney, WA 99004-2496
Eastern Wyoming College, Torrington, WY 82240
Eastfield College, Mesquite, TX 75150-1212
Eastman School of Music of the University of Rochester, Rochester, NY 14604-2599
East-West University, Chicago, IL 60605
Eckerd College, St. Petersburg, FL 33711-4700
Edgecombe Community College, Tarboro, NC 27886
Edgewood College, Madison, WI 53711
Edinboro University of Pennsylvania, Edinboro, PA 16444
Edison Community College, Fort Myers, FL 33906-6210
Edison State Community College, Piqua, OH 45356-9253
Edmonds Community College, Lynnwood, WA 98036
Edward Waters College, Jacksonville, FL 32209
El Camino College, Torrance, CA 90506
El Centro College, Dallas, TX 75202
El Paso Community College, El Paso, TX 79998
Electronic Data Processing College of Puerto Rico, Hato Rey, PR 00918
Electronic Institutes
    Middletown, Middletown, PA 17057-4851
    Pittsburgh, Pittsburgh, PA 15217
Elgin Community College, Elgin, IL 60123
Elizabeth City State University, Elizabeth City, NC 27909

Elizabethtown College, Elizabethtown, PA 17022-2298
Elizabethtown Community College, Elizabethtown, KY 42701
Ellsworth Community College, Iowa Falls, IA 50126
Elmhurst College, Elmhurst, IL 60126-3296
Elmira College, Elmira, NY 14901-2345
Elms College, Chicopee, MA 01013-2839
Elon College, Elon College, NC 27244-2010
Embry-Riddle Aeronautical University
    Daytona Beach, Daytona Beach, FL 32114-3900
    Prescott Campus, Prescott, AZ 86301
Emerson College, Boston, MA 02116-1596
Emmanuel College, Boston, MA 02115
Emmanuel College, Franklin Springs, GA 30639-0129
Emmaus Bible College, Dubuque, IA 52001
Emory and Henry College, Emory, VA 24327-0947
Emory University, Atlanta, GA 30322
Emporia State University, Emporia, KS 66801-5087
Endicott College, Beverly, MA 01915-9985
Enterprise State Junior College, Enterprise, AL 36331
Erie Community College
    City Campus, Buffalo, NY 14203-2601
    North Campus, Williamsville, NY 14221
    South Campus, Orchard Park, NY 14127-2199
Erskine College, Due West, SC 29639-0176
Escuela de Artes Plasticas de Puerto Rico, San Juan, PR 00902-1112
Essex Agricultural and Technical Institute, Hathorne, MA 01937
Essex Community College, Baltimore, MD 21237-3899
Essex County College, Newark, NJ 07102
ETI Technical College, Cleveland, OH 44103
Eugene Bible College, Eugene, OR 97405
Eugene Lang College/New School for Social Research, New York, NY 10011
Eureka College, Eureka, IL 61530
Evangel College, Springfield, MO 65802
Everett Community College, Everett, WA 98201
Evergreen State College, Olympia, WA 98505
Evergreen Valley College, San Jose, CA 95135
Fairfield University, Fairfield, CT 06430-5195
Fairleigh Dickinson University
    Edward Williams College, Hackensack, NJ 07666-1914
    Teaneck, Teaneck, NJ 07666-1914
Fairmont State College, Fairmont, WV 26554-2491
Faith Baptist Bible College and Theological Seminary, Ankeny, IA 50021
Fashion Institute of Design and Merchandising
    Los Angeles, Los Angeles, CA 90015
    San Francisco, San Francisco, CA 94108-5805
Fashion Institute of Technology, New York, NY 10001-5992
Faulkner University, Montgomery, AL 36109-3398
Fayetteville State University, Fayetteville, NC 28301-4298
Fayetteville Technical Community College, Fayetteville, NC 28303-0236
Feather River College, Quincy, CA 95971
Felician College, Lodi, NJ 07644-2198
Fergus Falls Community College, Fergus Falls, MN 56537-1000
Ferris State University, Big Rapids, MI 49307-2295
Ferrum College, Ferrum, VA 24088
Finch University of Health Sciences/The Chicago Medical School, North Chicago, IL 60064
Finger Lakes Community College, Canandaigua, NY 14424-8399
Fisher College, Boston, MA 02116
Fisk University, Nashville, TN 37208
Fitchburg State College, Fitchburg, MA 01420-2697
Five Towns College, Dix Hills, NY 11746-6055
Flagler College, St. Augustine, FL 32084
Flathead Valley Community College, Kalispell, MT 59901
Florence-Darlington Technical College, Florence, SC 29501-0548
Florida Agricultural and Mechanical University, Tallahassee, FL 32307
Florida Atlantic University, Boca Raton, FL 33431-0991
Florida Baptist Theological College, Graceville, FL 32440-1830
Florida Bible College, Kissimmee, FL 34758
Florida Christian College, Kissimmee, FL 34744-4402
Florida College, Temple Terrace, FL 33617
Florida Community College at Jacksonville, Jacksonville, FL 32256
Florida Institute of Technology, Melbourne, FL 32901-6988
Florida International University, Miami, FL 33199
Florida Keys Community College, Key West, FL 33040
Florida Memorial College, Miami, FL 33054
Florida Southern College, Lakeland, FL 33801-5698
Florida State University, Tallahassee, FL 32306-1009
Floyd College, Rome, GA 30162-1864
Fontbonne College, St. Louis, MO 63105
Foothill College, Los Altos Hills, CA 94022-4599
Fordham University, Bronx, NY 10458

Forsyth School for Dental Hygienists, Boston, MA 02115
Forsyth Technical Community College, Winston-Salem, NC 27103
Fort Belknap College, Harlem, MT 59526-0159
Fort Bethold Community College, New Town, ND 58763
Fort Hays State University, Hays, KS 67601-4099
Fort Lauderdale College, Fort Lauderdale, FL 33304
Fort Lewis College, Durango, CO 81301-3999
Fort Peck Community College, Poplar, MT 59255-0398
Fort Scott Community College, Fort Scott, KS 66701
Fort Valley State College, Fort Valley, GA 31030
Fox Valley Technical College, Appleton, WI 54913-2277
Framingham State College, Framingham, MA 01701
Francis Marion University, Florence, SC 29501-0547
Franciscan University of Steubenville, Steubenville, OH 43952-6701
Frank Phillips College, Borger, TX 79008-5118
Franklin College, Franklin, IN 46131-2598
Franklin College: Switzerland, Lugano, Switzerland 00000
Franklin Institute of Boston, Boston, MA 02116
Franklin and Marshall College, Lancaster, PA 17604-3003
Franklin Pierce College, Rindge, NH 03461-0060
Franklin University, Columbus, OH 43215-5399
Frederick Community College, Frederick, MD 21702
Free Will Baptist Bible College, Nashville, TN 37205-0117
Freed-Hardeman University, Henderson, TN 38340
Fresno City College, Fresno, CA 93741
Fresno Pacific College, Fresno, CA 93702
Friends University, Wichita, KS 67213
Front Range Community College, Westminster, CO 80030
Frostburg State University, Frostburg, MD 21532-1099
Fullerton College, Fullerton, CA 92632-2095
Fulton-Montgomery Community College, Johnstown, NY 12095-9609
Furman University, Greenville, SC 29613-0645
Gadsden State Community College, Gadsden, AL 35902-0227
Gainesville College, Gainesville, GA 30503
Gallaudet University, Washington, DC 20002
Galveston College, Galveston, TX 77550
Gannon University, Erie, PA 16541-0001
Garden City Community College, Garden City, KS 67846
Gardner-Webb University, Boiling Springs, NC 28017-9980
Garland County Community College, Hot Springs, AR 71914
Garrett Community College, McHenry, MD 21541
Gaston College, Dallas, NC 28034-1499
Gateway Community College, Phoenix, AZ 85034-1795
Gateway Community-Technical College, New Haven, CT 06511-5970
Gateway Technical College, Kenosha, WI 53144-1690
Gavilan Community College, Gilroy, CA 95020
Gem City College, Quincy, IL 62306
Genesee Community College, Batavia, NY 14020-9704
Geneva College, Beaver Falls, PA 15010-3599
George C. Wallace State Community College
    Dothan, Dothan, AL 36303-9234
    Selma, Selma, AL 36702-1049
George Fox College, Newberg, OR 97132-2697
George Mason University, Fairfax, VA 22030-4444
George Washington University, Washington, DC 20052
Georgetown College, Georgetown, KY 40324-1696
Georgetown University, Washington, DC 20057
Georgia Baptist College of Nursing, Atlanta, GA 30312
Georgia College, Milledgeville, GA 31061-0490
Georgia Institute of Technology, Atlanta, GA 30332-0320
Georgia Military College, Milledgeville, GA 31061
Georgia Southern University, Statesboro, GA 30460-8024
Georgia Southwestern College, Americus, GA 31709-4693
Georgia State University, Atlanta, GA 30303-3083
Georgian Court College, Lakewood, NJ 08701-2697
Germanna Community College, Locust Grove, VA 22508
Gettysburg College, Gettysburg, PA 17325-1484
Glen Oaks Community College, Centreville, MI 49032
Glendale Community College, Glendale, CA 91208
Glendale Community College, Glendale, AZ 85302-3090
Glenville State College, Glenville, WV 26351-1292
Gloucester County College, Sewell, NJ 08080
GMI Engineering & Management Institute, Flint, MI 48504-4898
Goddard College, Plainfield, VT 05667
God's Bible School and College, Cincinnati, OH 45210
Gogebic Community College, Ironwood, MI 49938
Golden Gate University, San Francisco, CA 94105-2968
Golden West College, Huntington Beach, CA 92647-2748
Goldey-Beacom College, Wilmington, DE 19808
Gonzaga University, Spokane, WA 99258-0001
Gordon College, Wenham, MA 01984-1899
Gordon College, Barnesville, GA 30204

Goshen College, Goshen, IN 46526-9988
Goucher College, Baltimore, MD 21204
Governors State University, University Park, IL 60466
Grace Bible College, Grand Rapids, MI 49509-0910
Grace College, Winona Lake, IN 46590
Grace University, Omaha, NE 68108
Graceland College, Lamoni, IA 50140
Grambling State University, Grambling, LA 71245
Grand Canyon University, Phoenix, AZ 85061-1097
Grand Rapids Community College, Grand Rapids, MI 49503
Grand Valley State University, Allendale, MI 49401-9403
Grand View College, Des Moines, IA 50316
Grantham College of Engineering, Slidell, LA 70469-5700
Gratz College, Melrose Park, PA 19027
Grays Harbor College, Aberdeen, WA 98520-7599
Grayson County College, Denison, TX 75020
Great Lakes Christian College, Lansing, MI 48917
Great Lakes Junior College of Business, Saginaw, MI 48607-1184
Green Mountain College, Poultney, VT 05764
Green River Community College, Auburn, WA 98092
Greenfield Community College, Greenfield, MA 01301
Greensboro College, Greensboro, NC 27401-1875
Greenville College, Greenville, IL 62246
Greenville Technical College, Greenville, SC 29606-5616
Grinnell College, Grinnell, IA 50112-0807
Grossmont Community College, El Cajon, CA 92020
Grove City College, Grove City, PA 16127-2104
Guam Community College, Barrigada, GU 00000
Guilford College, Greensboro, NC 27410-4171
Guilford Technical Community College, Jamestown, NC 27282
Gulf Coast Community College, Panama City, FL 32401-1041
Gustavus Adolphus College, St. Peter, MN 56082-1498
Gwinnett Technical Institute, Lawrenceville, GA 30246-1505
Gwynedd-Mercy College, Gwynedd Valley, PA 19437
Hagerstown Business College, Hagerstown, MD 21742-2752
Hagerstown Junior College, Hagerstown, MD 21742-6590
Hahnemann University School of Health Sciences and Humanities,
    Philadelphia, PA 19102-1192
Halifax Community College, Weldon, NC 27890
Hamilton College, Clinton, NY 13323-1293
Hamilton Technical College, Davenport, IA 52807
Hamline University, St. Paul, MN 55104-1284
Hampden-Sydney College, Hampden-Sydney, VA 23943
Hampshire College, Amherst, MA 01002-9988
Hampton University, Hampton, VA 23668
Hannibal-LaGrange College, Hannibal, MO 63401
Hanover College, Hanover, IN 47243-0108
Harcum College, Bryn Mawr, PA 19010-3476
Harding University, Searcy, AR 72149
Hardin-Simmons University, Abilene, TX 79698
Harford Community College, Bel Air, MD 21015
Harrington Institute of Interior Design, Chicago, IL 60605
Harris Stowe State College, St. Louis, MO 63103-2199
Harrisburg Area Community College, Harrisburg, PA 17110-2999
Harry M. Ayers State Technical College, Anniston, AL 36202
Hartnell College, Salinas, CA 93901
Hartwick College, Oneonta, NY 13820-9989
Harvard and Radcliffe Colleges, Cambridge, MA 02138
Harvey Mudd College, Claremont, CA 91711-5901
Haskell Indian Junior College, Lawrence, KS 66046-4800
Hastings College, Hastings, NE 68901
Haverford College, Haverford, PA 19041-1392
Hawaii Pacific University, Honolulu, HI 96813
Hawkeye Community College, Waterloo, IA 50704
Haywood Community College, Clyde, NC 28721
Hazard Community College, Hazard, KY 41701
Heald Business College
    Concord, Concord, CA 94520
    Fresno, Fresno, CA 93704-1706
    San Jose, San Jose, CA 95130
Heald Business College: Honolulu, Honolulu, HI 96814-3715
Heald College
    Sacramento, Rancho Cordova, CA 95670
    Santa Rosa, Santa Rosa, CA 95403
Heald Institute of Technology, Martinez, CA 94553-4000
Hebrew College, Brookline, MA 02146
Hebrew Union College: Jewish Institute of Religion, Los Angeles, CA 90007
Heidelberg College, Tiffin, OH 44883-2462
Helena College of Technology of the University of Montana, Helena, MT
    59601-3098
Helene Fuld School of Nursing, New York, NY 10035
Hellenic College, Brookline, MA 02146

Henderson Community College, Henderson, KY 42420
Henderson State University, Arkadelphia, AR 71999-0001
Hendrix College, Conway, AR 72032-3080
Henry Ford Community College, Dearborn, MI 48128
Heritage College, Toppenish, WA 98948-9599
Herkimer County Community College, Herkimer, NY 13350-1598
Hesser College, Manchester, NH 03103-9969
Hesston College, Hesston, KS 67062-2093
Hibbing Community College, Hibbing, MN 55746
High Point University, High Point, NC 27262-3598
Highland Community College, Freeport, IL 61032-9341
Highland Community College, Highland, KS 66035-0068
Highland Park Community College, Highland Park, MI 48203
Highline Community College, Des Moines, WA 98198-9800
Hilbert College, Hamburg, NY 14075
Hill College, Hillsboro, TX 76645
Hillsborough Community College, Tampa, FL 33631-3127
Hillsdale College, Hillsdale, MI 49242
Hinds Community College, Raymond, MS 39154-9799
Hiram College, Hiram, OH 44234
Hiwassee College, Madisonville, TN 37354
Hobart and William Smith Colleges, Geneva, NY 14456-3385
Hobe Sound Bible College, Hobe Sound, FL 33475-1065
Hocking Technical College, Nelsonville, OH 45764-9704
Hofstra University, Hempstead, NY 11550-1090
Hollins College, Roanoke, VA 24020-1707
Holmes Community College, Goodman, MS 39079
Holy Apostles College and Seminary, Cromwell, CT 06416
Holy Cross College, Notre Dame, IN 46556-0308
Holy Family College, Philadelphia, PA 19114-2094
Holy Names College, Oakland, CA 94619-1699
Holy Trinity Orthodox Seminary, Jordanville, NY 13361
Holyoke Community College, Holyoke, MA 01040
Hood College, Frederick, MD 21701-8575
Hope College, Holland, MI 49422-9000
Hopkinsville Community College, Hopkinsville, KY 42241-2100
Horry-Georgetown Technical College, Conway, SC 29526-1966
Houghton College, Houghton, NY 14744-9989
Housatonic Community-Technical College, Bridgeport, CT 06608
Houston Baptist University, Houston, TX 77074-3298
Houston Community College, Houston, TX 77270
Howard College, Big Spring, TX 79720
Howard Community College, Columbia, MD 21044
Howard Payne University, Brownwood, TX 76801-2794
Howard University, Washington, DC 20059
Hudson County Community College, Jersey City, NJ 07306
Hudson Valley Community College, Troy, NY 12180
Huertas Junior College, Caguas, PR 00726
Humber College, Etobicoke, Ontario, Canada 00000
Humboldt State University, Arcata, CA 95521-8299
Humphreys College, Stockton, CA 95207-3896
Huntingdon College, Montgomery, AL 36106-2148
Huntington College, Huntington, IN 46750
Huntington Junior College of Business, Huntington, WV 25701
Huron University, Huron, SD 57350
Hussian School of Art, Philadelphia, PA 19107
Husson College, Bangor, ME 04401
Huston-Tillotson College, Austin, TX 78702
Hutchinson Community College, Hutchinson, KS 67501
ICPR Junior College, Hato Rey, PR 00919-0304
Idaho State University, Pocatello, ID 83209
Illinois Benedictine College, Lisle, IL 60532-0900
Illinois Central College, East Peoria, IL 61635
Illinois College, Jacksonville, IL 62650-9990
Illinois Eastern Community Colleges
    Frontier Community College, Fairfield, IL 62837-9801
    Lincoln Trail College, Robinson, IL 62454-9803
    Olney Central College, Olney, IL 62450
    Wabash Valley College, Mount Carmel, IL 62863-2657
Illinois Institute of Technology, Chicago, IL 60616
Illinois State University, Normal, IL 61790-2200
Illinois Valley Community College, Oglesby, IL 61348-9691
Illinois Wesleyan University, Bloomington, IL 61702-9965
Immaculata College, Immaculata, PA 19345
Imperial Valley College, Imperial, CA 92251-0158
Incarnate Word College, San Antonio, TX 78209-6397
Independence Community College, Independence, KS 67301
Indian Hills Community College, Ottumwa, IA 52501
Indian River Community College, Fort Pierce, FL 34981-5599
Indiana Business College, Indianapolis, IN 46204
Indiana Institute of Technology, Fort Wayne, IN 46803
Indiana State University, Terre Haute, IN 47809

Indiana University
    Bloomington, Bloomington, IN 47405-7700
    East, Richmond, IN 47374-1289
    Kokomo, Kokomo, IN 46904-9003
    Northwest, Gary, IN 46408
    South Bend, South Bend, IN 46634-7111
    Southeast, New Albany, IN 47150-6405
Indiana University of Pennsylvania, Indiana, PA 15705-1088
Indiana University—Purdue University
    Fort Wayne, Fort Wayne, IN 46805-1499
    Indianapolis, Indianapolis, IN 46202-5143
Indiana Vocational Technical College
    Central Indiana, Indianapolis, IN 46206-1763
    Columbus, Columbus, IN 47203
    Eastcentral, Muncie, IN 47307
    Kokomo, Kokomo, IN 46903-1373
    Lafayette, Lafayette, IN 47903
    Northcentral, South Bend, IN 46619
    Northeast, Fort Wayne, IN 46805
    Northwest, Gary, IN 46409-1499
    Southcentral, Sellersburg, IN 47172
    Southeast, Madison, IN 47250
    Southwest, Evansville, IN 47710
    Wabash Valley, Terre Haute, IN 47802
    Whitewater, Richmond, IN 47374
Indiana Wesleyan University, Marion, IN 46953-9980
Institute of American Indian Arts, Santa Fe, NM 87504
Institute for Christian Studies, Austin, TX 78705
Institute of Design and Construction, Brooklyn, NY 11201-5380
Institute of Electronic Technology, Paducah, KY 42001
Inter American University of Puerto Rico
    Aguadilla Campus, Aguadilla, PR 00605
    Arecibo Campus, Arecibo, PR 00614-4050
    Barranquitas Campus, Barranquitas, PR 00794
    Bayamon Campus, Bayamon, PR 00959
    Fajardo Campus, Fajardo, PR 00738
    Guayama Campus, Guayama, PR 00784
    Metropolitan Campus, San Juan, PR 00919
    Ponce Campus, Mercedita, PR 00715
    San German Campus, San German, PR 00683
Interboro Institute, New York, NY 10019
International Academy of Merchandising and Design, Chicago, IL 60602
International Bible College, Florence, AL 35630
International Business College, Fort Wayne, IN 46804
International Fine Arts College, Miami, FL 33132
Inver Hills Community College, Inver Grove Heights, MN 55076-3209
Iona College, New Rochelle, NY 10801-1890
Iowa Central Community College, Fort Dodge, IA 50501
Iowa Lakes Community College, Estherville, IA 51334
Iowa State University, Ames, IA 50011-2010
Iowa Wesleyan College, Mount Pleasant, IA 52641-1398
Iowa Western Community College, Council Bluffs, IA 51502-3004
Irvine Valley College, Irvine, CA 92720
Isothermal Community College, Spindale, NC 28160
Itasca Community College: Arrowhead Region, Grand Rapids, MN 55744
Itawamba Community College, Fulton, MS 38843
Ithaca College, Ithaca, NY 14850-7020
ITT Technical Institute
    Hoffman Estates, Hoffman Estates, IL 60195
    Youngstown, Youngstown, OH 44509
J. F. Drake State Technical College, Huntsville, AL 35811-3421
J. Sargeant Reynolds Community College, Richmond, VA 23285-5622
Jackson Community College, Jackson, MI 49201
Jackson State Community College, Jackson, TN 38301-3797
Jackson State University, Jackson, MS 39217
Jacksonville College, Jacksonville, TX 75766-4759
Jacksonville State University, Jacksonville, AL 36265-9982
Jacksonville University, Jacksonville, FL 32211
James H. Faulkner State Community College, Bay Minette, AL 36507
James Madison University, Harrisonburg, VA 22807
James Sprunt Community College, Kenansville, NC 28349-0398
Jamestown Business College, Jamestown, NY 14702-0429
Jamestown College, Jamestown, ND 58405-0001
Jamestown Community College, Jamestown, NY 14702-0020
Jarvis Christian College, Hawkins, TX 75765
Jefferson College, Hillsboro, MO 63050-2441
Jefferson Community College, Louisville, KY 40202
Jefferson Community College, Watertown, NY 13601
Jefferson Davis Community College, Brewton, AL 36426
Jefferson State Community College, Birmingham, AL 35215-3098
Jefferson Technical College, Steubenville, OH 43952
Jersey City State College, Jersey City, NJ 07305-1597

Jewish Theological Seminary of America, New York, NY 10027
John A. Gupton College, Nashville, TN 37203-2920
John A. Logan College, Carterville, IL 62918
John Brown University, Siloam Springs, AR 72761
John C. Calhoun State Community College, Decatur, AL 35609-2216
John Carroll University, University Heights, OH 44118-4581
John F. Kennedy University, Orinda, CA 94563
John M. Patterson State Technical College, Montgomery, AL 36116
John Tyler Community College, Chester, VA 23831-5399
John Wesley College, High Point, NC 27265-3197
John Wood Community College, Quincy, IL 62301
Johns Hopkins University, Baltimore, MD 21218
Johns Hopkins University: Peabody Conservatory of Music, Baltimore, MD 21202
Johnson Bible College, Knoxville, TN 37998
Johnson C. Smith University, Charlotte, NC 28216-5398
Johnson County Community College, Overland Park, KS 66210-1299
Johnson State College, Johnson, VT 05656
Johnson Technical Institute, Scranton, PA 18508
Johnson & Wales University, Providence, RI 02903-3703
Johnston Community College, Smithfield, NC 27577-2350
Joliet Junior College, Joliet, IL 60436-9352
Jones College, Jacksonville, FL 32211
Jones County Junior College, Ellisville, MS 39437
Judson College, Marion, AL 36756
Judson College, Elgin, IL 60123
Juilliard School, New York, NY 10023-6590
Juniata College, Huntingdon, PA 16652-2119
Kalamazoo College, Kalamazoo, MI 49006-3295
Kalamazoo Valley Community College, Kalamazoo, MI 49009
Kankakee Community College, Kankakee, IL 60901
Kansas City Art Institute, Kansas City, MO 64111
Kansas City Kansas Community College, Kansas City, KS 66112
Kansas Newman College, Wichita, KS 67213-2097
Kansas State University, Manhattan, KS 66506
Kansas Wesleyan University, Salina, KS 67401-6196
Kaskaskia College, Centralia, IL 62801
Katharine Gibbs School
    Boston, Boston, MA 02116
    Melville, Melville, NY 11747
    Montclair, Montclair, NJ 07042
    New York, New York, NY 10166
Kean College of New Jersey, Union, NJ 07083-7131
Keene State College, Keene, NH 03431-4183
Kellogg Community College, Battle Creek, MI 49016-3397
Kelsey-Jenney College, San Diego, CA 92101
Kemper Military School and College, Boonville, MO 65233
Kendall College, Evanston, IL 60201-2899
Kendall College of Art and Design, Grand Rapids, MI 49503-3194
Kennebec Valley Technical College, Fairfield, ME 04937
Kennesaw State College, Marietta, GA 30061
Kent State University
    Ashtabula Regional Campus, Ashtabula, OH 44004
    East Liverpool Regional Campus, East Liverpool, OH 43920
    Kent, Kent, OH 44242-0001
    Salem Regional Campus, Salem, OH 44460
    Stark Campus, Canton, OH 44720-7599
    Trumbull Campus, Warren, OH 44483-1998
    Tuscarawas Campus, New Philadelphia, OH 44663-9447
Kentucky Christian College, Grayson, KY 41143-2205
Kentucky College of Business, Lexington, KY 40508
Kentucky State University, Frankfort, KY 40601
Kentucky Wesleyan College, Owensboro, KY 42302-1039
Kenyon College, Gambier, OH 43022-9623
Kettering College of Medical Arts, Kettering, OH 45429
Keuka College, Keuka Park, NY 14478-0098
Keystone College, La Plume, PA 18440-0200
Kilgore College, Kilgore, TX 75662-3299
Kilian Community College, Sioux Falls, SD 57102-0316
King College, Bristol, TN 37620-2699
King's College, Wilkes-Barre, PA 18711-0801
Kings River Community College, Reedley, CA 93654
Kirkwood Community College, Cedar Rapids, IA 52406
Kirtland Community College, Roscommon, MI 48653
Kishwaukee College, Malta, IL 60150-9699
Knox College, Galesburg, IL 61401-4999
Knoxville Business College, Knoxville, TN 37917
Knoxville College, Knoxville, TN 37921
Kutztown University of Pennsylvania, Kutztown, PA 19530
La Roche College, Pittsburgh, PA 15237
La Salle University, Philadelphia, PA 19141-1199
La Sierra University, Riverside, CA 92515-8247

Labette Community College, Parsons, KS 67357
Laboratory Institute of Merchandising, New York, NY 10022-5268
Laboure College, Boston, MA 02124
Lac Courte Oreilles Ojibwa Community College, Hayward, WI 54843
Lackawanna Junior College, Scranton, PA 18505
Lafayette College, Easton, PA 18042-1770
LaGrange College, LaGrange, GA 30240-2999
Lake Area Technical Institute, Watertown, SD 57201-0730
Lake City Community College, Lake City, FL 32055
Lake Erie College, Painesville, OH 44077-3389
Lake Forest College, Lake Forest, IL 60045-2399
Lake Land College, Mattoon, IL 61938-9366
Lake Michigan College, Benton Harbor, MI 49022-1899
Lake Superior State University, Sault Ste. Marie, MI 49783-1699
Lake Tahoe Community College, South Lake Tahoe, CA 96150-4524
Lake Washington Technical College, Kirkland, WA 98034
Lakeland College, Sheboygan, WI 53082-0359
Lakeland Community College, Kirtland, OH 44094
Lakeshore Technical College, Cleveland, WI 53015-9761
Lake-Sumter Community College, Leesburg, FL 34788-8751
Lakeview College of Nursing, Danville, IL 61832
Lakewood Community College, White Bear Lake, MN 55110
Lamar Community College, Lamar, CO 81052-3999
Lamar University—Beaumont, Beaumont, TX 77710
Lambuth University, Jackson, TN 38301-5296
Lamson Junior College at Mesa, Mesa, AZ 85201
Lancaster Bible College, Lancaster, PA 17601
Lander University, Greenwood, SC 29649
Landmark College, Putney, VT 05346
Lane College, Jackson, TN 38301
Lane Community College, Eugene, OR 97405
Laney College, Oakland, CA 94607
Langston University, Langston, OK 73050
Lansdale School of Business, North Wales, PA 19454
Lansing Community College, Lansing, MI 48901
Laramie County Community College, Cheyenne, WY 82007
Laredo Community College, Laredo, TX 78040-4395
Las Positas College, Livermore, CA 94550
Lasell College, Newton, MA 02166
Lassen College, Susanville, CA 96130
Lawrence Technological University, Southfield, MI 48075-1058
Lawrence University, Appleton, WI 54912-0599
Lawson State Community College, Birmingham, AL 35221-1717
LDS Business College, Salt Lake City, UT 84111-1392
Le Moyne College, Syracuse, NY 13214-1399
Lebanon Valley College of Pennsylvania, Annville, PA 17003-0501
Lee College, Cleveland, TN 37311-3450
Lee College, Baytown, TX 77522-0818
Lees College, Jackson, KY 41339
Lees-McRae College, Banner Elk, NC 28604
Lehigh Carbon Community College, Schnecksville, PA 18078-2598
Lehigh University, Bethlehem, PA 18015-3094
LeMoyne-Owen College, Memphis, TN 38126
Lenoir Community College, Kinston, NC 28501
Lenoir-Rhyne College, Hickory, NC 28603
Lesley College, Cambridge, MA 02138-2790
Lethbridge Community College, Lethbridge, AB, Canada 00000
LeTourneau University, Longview, TX 75607-7001
Lewis & Clark College, Portland, OR 97219-7899
Lewis and Clark Community College, Godfrey, IL 62035-2466
Lewis Clark State College, Lewiston, ID 83501-2698
Lewis College of Business, Detroit, MI 48235
Lewis University, Romeoville, IL 60441-2298
Lexington Community College, Lexington, KY 40506-0235
Lexington Institute of Hospitality Careers, Chicago, IL 60643-3294
Liberty University, Lynchburg, VA 24506-8001
LIFE Bible College, San Dimas, CA 91773-3298
Lima Technical College, Lima, OH 45804
Limestone College, Gaffney, SC 29340
Lincoln Christian College and Seminary, Lincoln, IL 62656-2111
Lincoln College, Lincoln, IL 62656
Lincoln Land Community College, Springfield, IL 62794-9256
Lincoln Memorial University, Harrogate, TN 37752
Lincoln School of Commerce, Lincoln, NE 68501-2826
Lincoln Technical Institute, Allentown, PA 18104
Lincoln University, Lincoln University, PA 19352-0999
Lincoln University, San Francisco, CA 94118
Lincoln University, Jefferson City, MO 65102-0029
Lindenwood College, St. Charles, MO 63301-1695
Lindsey Wilson College, Columbia, KY 42728
Linfield College, McMinnville, OR 97128-6894
Linn-Benton Community College, Albany, OR 97321-3779

Little Big Horn College, Crow Agency, MT 59022
Little Hoop Community College, Fort Totten, ND 58335
Livingstone College, Salisbury, NC 28144-5213
Lock Haven University of Pennsylvania, Lock Haven, PA 17745
Loma Linda University, Loma Linda, CA 92350
Lon Morris College, Jacksonville, TX 75766
Long Beach City College, Long Beach, CA 90808
Long Island College Hospital School of Nursing, Brooklyn, NY 11201
Long Island University
      Brooklyn Campus, Brooklyn, NY 11201
      C. W. Post Campus, Brookville, NY 11548-1300
      Southampton College, Southampton, NY 11968
Longview Community College, Lee's Summit, MO 64081-2105
Longwood College, Farmville, VA 23909-1898
Lorain County Community College, Elyria, OH 44035-1697
Loras College, Dubuque, IA 52001
Lord Fairfax Community College, Middletown, VA 22645
Los Angeles City College, Los Angeles, CA 90029-3589
Los Angeles Harbor College, Wilmington, CA 90744
Los Angeles Mission College, Sylmar, CA 91342
Los Angeles Pierce College, Woodland Hills, CA 91371
Los Angeles Southwest College, Los Angeles, CA 90047
Los Angeles Trade and Technical College, Los Angeles, CA 90015-4181
Los Angeles Valley College, Van Nuys, CA 91401-4096
Los Medanos College, Pittsburg, CA 94565
Louisburg College, Louisburg, NC 27549
Louise Salinger Academy of Fashion, San Francisco, CA 94105
Louisiana College, Pineville, LA 71359-0560
Louisiana State University
      Agricultural and Mechanical College, Baton Rouge, LA 70803-2750
      Alexandria, Alexandria, LA 71302-9633
      Eunice, Eunice, LA 70535
      Medical Center, New Orleans, LA 70112-2223
      Shreveport, Shreveport, LA 71115-2399
Louisiana Tech University, Ruston, LA 71272
Louisville Technical Institute, Louisville, KY 40218-4524
Lourdes College, Sylvania, OH 43560-2898
Lower Columbia College, Longview, WA 98632-0310
Loyola College in Maryland, Baltimore, MD 21210-2699
Loyola Marymount University, Los Angeles, CA 90045-2699
Loyola University, New Orleans, LA 70118-6143
Loyola University of Chicago, Chicago, IL 60611
Lubbock Christian University, Lubbock, TX 79407-2099
Lurleen B. Wallace State Junior College, Andalusia, AL 36420-1418
Luther College, Decorah, IA 52101-1042
Lutheran Bible Institute of Seattle, Issaquah, WA 98027
Lutheran College of Health Professions, Fort Wayne, IN 46807-1698
Luzerne County Community College, Nanticoke, PA 18634-9804
Lycoming College, Williamsport, PA 17701
Lynchburg College, Lynchburg, VA 24501-9986
Lyndon State College, Lyndonville, VT 05851
Lynn University, Boca Raton, FL 33431-5598
Lyon College, Batesville, AR 72503-2317
Macalester College, St. Paul, MN 55105-1899
MacCormac Junior College, Chicago, IL 60605
Machzikei Hadath Rabbinical College, Brooklyn, NY 11204
MacMurray College, Jacksonville, IL 62650-2590
Macomb Community College, Warren, MI 48093-3896
Macon College, Macon, GA 31297
Madison Area Technical College, Madison, WI 53704-2599
Madison Junior College of Business, Madison, WI 53705-1399
Madisonville Community College, Madisonville, KY 42431
Madonna University, Livonia, MI 48150-1173
Magnolia Bible College, Kosciusko, MS 39090
Maharishi International University, Fairfield, IA 52557-1155
Maine College of Art, Portland, ME 04101-3987
Maine Maritime Academy, Castine, ME 04420-5000
Malone College, Canton, OH 44709-3897
Manatee Community College, Bradenton, FL 34206-1849
Manchester College, North Manchester, IN 46962-0365
Manchester Community-Technical College, Manchester, CT 06040
Manhattan Christian College, Manhattan, KS 66502
Manhattan College, Riverdale, NY 10471
Manhattan School of Music, New York, NY 10027-4698
Manhattanville College, Purchase, NY 10577
Mankato State University, Mankato, MN 56002-8400
Mannes College of Music, New York, NY 10024
Manor Junior College, Jenkintown, PA 19046-3399
Mansfield University of Pennsylvania, Mansfield, PA 16933
Maple Woods Community College, Kansas City, MO 64156-1299
Maranatha Baptist Bible College, Watertown, WI 53094
Maria College, Albany, NY 12208

Marian College, Indianapolis, IN 46222
Marian College of Fond du Lac, Fond du Lac, WI 54935-4699
Marian Court College, Swampscott, MA 01907-2896
Marietta College, Marietta, OH 45750-4005
Marion Military Institute, Marion, AL 36756-0420
Marion Technical College, Marion, OH 43302-5694
Marist College, Poughkeepsie, NY 12601-1387
Marlboro College, Marlboro, VT 05344-0300
Marquette University, Milwaukee, WI 53201-1881
Mars Hill College, Mars Hill, NC 28754
Marshall University, Huntington, WV 25755-2020
Marshalltown Community College, Marshalltown, IA 50158
Martin Community College, Williamston, NC 27892-9988
Martin Luther College, New Ulm, MN 56073-3300
Martin Methodist College, Pulaski, TN 38478-2799
Martin University, Indianapolis, IN 46218
Mary Baldwin College, Staunton, VA 24401
Mary Holmes College, West Point, MS 39773-1257
Mary Washington College, Fredericksburg, VA 22401-5358
Marygrove College, Detroit, MI 48221
Maryland College of Art and Design, Silver Spring, MD 20902
Maryland Institute College of Art, Baltimore, MD 21217-9986
Marylhurst College, Marylhurst, OR 97036
Marymount College, Tarrytown, NY 10591-3796
Marymount College, Rancho Palos Verdes, CA 90275-6299
Marymount Manhattan College, New York, NY 10021-4597
Marymount University, Arlington, VA 22207-4299
Maryville College, Maryville, TN 37804-5907
Maryville University of St. Louis, St. Louis, MO 63141-7299
Marywood College, Scranton, PA 18509-9989
Massachusetts Bay Community College, Wellesley Hills, MA 02181
Massachusetts College of Art, Boston, MA 02115-5882
Massachusetts College of Pharmacy and Allied Health Sciences, Boston, MA 02115
Massachusetts Institute of Technology, Cambridge, MA 02139
Massachusetts Maritime Academy, Buzzards Bay, MA 02532-1803
Massasoit Community College, Brockton, MA 02402
Master's College, Santa Clarita, CA 91322-0878
Mater Dei College, Ogdensburg, NY 13669-9699
Mayland Community College, Spruce Pine, NC 28777
Maysville Community College, Maysville, KY 41056
Mayville State University, Mayville, ND 58257
McCook Community College, McCook, NE 69001
McDowell Technical Community College, Marion, NC 28752
McGill University, Montreal, Quebec, Canada 00000
McGregor School of Antioch University, Yellow Springs, OH 45387
McHenry County College, Crystal Lake, IL 60012-2761
McIntosh College, Dover, NH 03820
McKendree College, Lebanon, IL 62254
McLennan Community College, Waco, TX 76708
McMurry University, Abilene, TX 79697-0001
McNeese State University, Lake Charles, LA 70609-2495
McPherson College, McPherson, KS 67460-1402
Meadows College of Business, Columbus, GA 31906
Medaille College, Buffalo, NY 14214
Medcenter One College of Nursing, Bismarck, ND 58501
Medical College of Georgia, Augusta, GA 30912
Medical University of South Carolina, Charleston, SC 29425-2970
Memorial University of Newfoundland, St. John's, Newfoundland, Canada 00000
Memphis College of Art, Memphis, TN 38104-2764
Mendocino College, Ukiah, CA 95482
Menlo College, Atherton, CA 94027-4301
Mennonite College of Nursing, Bloomington, IL 61701
Merced College, Merced, CA 95348-2898
Mercer County Community College, Trenton, NJ 08690-1099
Mercer University
      Atlanta, Atlanta, GA 30341-4115
      Macon, Macon, GA 31207-0001
Mercy College, Dobbs Ferry, NY 10522
Mercyhurst College, Erie, PA 16546-0001
Meredith College, Raleigh, NC 27607-5298
Meridian Community College, Meridian, MS 39307
Merrimack College, North Andover, MA 01845
Merritt College, Oakland, CA 94619
Mesa Community College, Mesa, AZ 85202
Mesa State College, Grand Junction, CO 81502-2647
Mesabi Community College: Arrowhead Region, Virginia, MN 55792-3448
Mesivta Torah Vodaath Seminary, Brooklyn, NY 11218
Messiah College, Grantham, PA 17027-0800
Methodist College, Fayetteville, NC 28311-1420
Metropolitan Community College, Omaha, NE 68103-3777

Metropolitan State College of Denver, Denver, CO 80217-3362
Metropolitan State University, St. Paul, MN 55106-5000
Miami University
    Hamilton Campus, Hamilton, OH 45011
    Middletown Campus, Middletown, OH 45042
    Oxford Campus, Oxford, OH 45056
Miami-Dade Community College, Miami, FL 33132-2297
Miami-Jacobs College, Dayton, OH 45401
Michigan Christian College, Rochester Hills, MI 48307-2764
Michigan State University, East Lansing, MI 48824-1046
Michigan Technological University, Houghton, MI 49931-1295
Microcomputer Technology Institute, Houston, TX 77036
Mid Michigan Community College, Harrison, MI 48625
Mid Plains Community College, North Platte, NE 69101-0001
Mid-America Bible College, Oklahoma City, OK 73170
MidAmerica Nazarene College, Olathe, KS 66062-1899
Mid-Continent Baptist Bible College, Mayfield, KY 42066-0357
Middle Georgia College, Cochran, GA 31014-1599
Middle Tennessee State University, Murfreesboro, TN 37132
Middlebury College, Middlebury, VT 05753-6002
Middlesex Community College, Bedford, MA 01730
Middlesex Community-Technical College, Middletown, CT 06457
Middlesex County College, Edison, NJ 08818-3050
Midland College, Midland, TX 79705
Midland Lutheran College, Fremont, NE 68025
Midlands Technical College, Columbia, SC 29202
Midstate College, Peoria, IL 61602-9990
Mid-State Technical College, Wisconsin Rapids, WI 54494
Midway College, Midway, KY 40347-1120
Midwestern State University, Wichita Falls, TX 76308
Miles College, Fairfield, AL 35064
Miles Community College, Miles City, MT 59301
Millersville University of Pennsylvania, Millersville, PA 17551-0302
Milligan College, Milligan College, TN 37682
Millikin University, Decatur, IL 62522-2084
Mills College, Oakland, CA 94613
Millsaps College, Jackson, MS 39210
Milwaukee Area Technical College, Milwaukee, WI 53233
Milwaukee Institute of Art & Design, Milwaukee, WI 53202
Milwaukee School of Engineering, Milwaukee, WI 53201-0644
Mineral Area College, Park Hills, MO 63601
Minneapolis College of Art and Design, Minneapolis, MN 55404
Minneapolis Community College, Minneapolis, MN 55403-1779
Minnesota Bible College, Rochester, MN 55902
Minot State University, Minot, ND 58707-5002
MiraCosta College, Oceanside, CA 92056-3899
Miss Wade's Fashion Merchandising College, Dallas, TX 75258
Mission College, Santa Clara, CA 95054-1897
Mississippi College, Clinton, MS 39058
Mississippi County Community College, Blytheville, AR 72316-1109
Mississippi Delta Community College, Moorhead, MS 38761
Mississippi Gulf Coast Community College
    Jackson County Campus, Gautier, MS 39553
    Jefferson Davis Campus, Gulfport, MS 39507-3894
    Perkinston, Perkinston, MS 39573
Mississippi State University, Mississippi State, MS 39762-5268
Mississippi University for Women, Columbus, MS 39701
Mississippi Valley State University, Itta Bena, MS 38941-1400
Missouri Baptist College, St. Louis, MO 63141
Missouri Southern State College, Joplin, MO 64801-1595
Missouri Valley College, Marshall, MO 65340
Missouri Western State College, St. Joseph, MO 64507-2294
Mitchell College, New London, CT 06320
Mitchell Community College, Statesville, NC 28677
Mitchell Technical Institute, Mitchell, SD 57301
Moberly Area Community College, Moberly, MO 65270
Modesto Junior College, Modesto, CA 95350
Mohave Community College, Kingman, AZ 86401
Mohawk Valley Community College, Utica, NY 13501-9979
Molloy College, Rockville Center, NY 11570
Monmouth College, Monmouth, IL 61462-9989
Monmouth College, West Long Branch, NJ 07764-1898
Monroe College, Bronx, NY 10468
Monroe Community College, Rochester, NY 14623
Monroe County Community College, Monroe, MI 48161
Montana State University
    Billings College of Technology, Billings, MT 59102
    College of Technology-Great Falls, Great Falls, MT 59405
    Billings, Billings, MT 59101-0298
    Bozeman, Bozeman, MT 59717-0016
    Northern, Havre, MT 59501
Montana Tech of The University of Montana, Butte, MT 59701-8997

Montana Tech of the University of Montana: Division of Technology, Butte, MT 59701
Montay College, Chicago, IL 60659-3115
Montcalm Community College, Sidney, MI 48885-0300
Montclair State University, Upper Montclair, NJ 07043-1624
Monterey Institute of International Studies, Monterey, CA 93940
Monterey Peninsula College, Monterey, CA 93940
Montgomery College
    Germantown Campus, Germantown, MD 20876
    Rockville Campus, Rockville, MD 20850
    Takoma Park Campus, Takoma Park, MD 20912
Montgomery Community College, Troy, NC 27371-0787
Montgomery County Community College, Blue Bell, PA 19422-0758
Montreat-Anderson College, Montreat, NC 28757-9987
Montserrat College of Art, Beverly, MA 01915
Moody Bible Institute, Chicago, IL 60610-3284
Moore College of Art and Design, Philadelphia, PA 19103-1179
Moorhead State University, Moorhead, MN 56563
Moorpark College, Moorpark, CA 93021
Moraine Park Technical College, Fond du Lac, WI 54935
Moraine Valley Community College, Palos Hills, IL 60465-0937
Moravian College, Bethlehem, PA 18018
Morehead State University, Morehead, KY 40351
Morehouse College, Atlanta, GA 30314
Morgan Community College, Fort Morgan, CO 80701
Morgan State University, Baltimore, MD 21239
Morningside College, Sioux City, IA 51106-1751
Morris Brown College, Atlanta, GA 30314
Morris College, Sumter, SC 29150-3599
Morrison College: Reno, Reno, NV 89503
Morrison Institute of Technology, Morrison, IL 61270-2959
Morton College, Cicero, IL 60650
Motlow State Community College, Tullahoma, TN 37388-8100
Mott Community College, Flint, MI 48503
Mount Aloysius College, Cresson, PA 16630
Mount Angel Seminary, St. Benedict, OR 97373
Mount Holyoke College, South Hadley, MA 01075-1488
Mount Hood Community College, Gresham, OR 97030
Mount Ida College, Newton Centre, MA 02159
Mount Marty College, Yankton, SD 57078-3724
Mount Mary College, Milwaukee, WI 53222-4597
Mount Mercy College, Cedar Rapids, IA 52402
Mount Olive College, Mount Olive, NC 28365
Mount St. Clare College, Clinton, IA 52732
Mount St. Mary College, Newburgh, NY 12550
Mount St. Mary's College, Los Angeles, CA 90049-1597
Mount St. Mary's College, Emmitsburg, MD 21727-7796
Mount San Antonio College, Walnut, CA 91789
Mount San Jacinto College, San Jacinto, CA 92583-2399
Mount Senario College, Ladysmith, WI 54848
Mount Union College, Alliance, OH 44601-3993
Mount Vernon College, Washington, DC 20007
Mount Vernon Nazarene College, Mount Vernon, OH 43050
Mount Wachusett Community College, Gardner, MA 01440
Mountain Empire Community College, Big Stone Gap, VA 24219
Mountain State College, Parkersburg, WV 26101-3993
Mountain View College, Dallas, TX 75211-6599
MTI Business College, Cleveland, OH 44115
Muhlenberg College, Allentown, PA 18104-5586
Multnomah Bible College, Portland, OR 97220-5898
Murray State College, Tishomingo, OK 73460
Murray State University, Murray, KY 42071
Muscatine Community College, Muscatine, IA 52761-5396
Muskegon Community College, Muskegon, MI 49442
Muskingum Area Technical College, Zanesville, OH 43701
Muskingum College, New Concord, OH 43762
NAES College, Chicago, IL 60659
Napa Valley College, Napa, CA 94558
Naropa Institute, Boulder, CO 80302
Nash Community College, Rocky Mount, NC 27804-7488
Nashville State Technical Institute, Nashville, TN 37209
Nassau Community College, Garden City, NY 11530-6793
National Business College, Roanoke, VA 24017-0400
National College, Denver, CO 80222
National College, Kansas City, MO 64133-1612
National College, St. Paul, MN 55108
National College, Albuquerque, NM 87110-3156
National College, Rapid City, SD 57709-1780
National College of Chiropractic, Lombard, IL 60148

National Education Center
  Bauder Campus, Fort Lauderdale, FL 33334-3971
  Brown Institute Campus, Minneapolis, MN 55407
  National Institute of Technology Campus, Cross Lanes, WV 25313
  Spartan School of Aeronautics, Tulsa, OK 74158-2833
  Vale Tech Campus, Blairsville, PA 15717
National University, San Diego, CA 92108-4107
National-Louis University, Evanston, IL 60201-1796
Naugatuck Valley Community-Technical College, Waterbury, CT 06708-3089
Navajo Community College, Tsaile, AZ 86556
Navarro College, Corsicana, TX 75110
Nazarene Bible College, Colorado Springs, CO 80935
Nazareth College of Rochester, Rochester, NY 14618-3790
Nebraska Christian College, Norfolk, NE 68701
Nebraska College of Technical Agriculture, Curtis, NE 69025-0069
Nebraska Indian Community College, Winnebago, NE 68071
Nebraska Methodist College of Nursing and Allied Health, Omaha, NE 68114
Nebraska Wesleyan University, Lincoln, NE 68504
NEI College of Technology, Minneapolis, MN 55421-9990
Neosho County Community College, Chanute, KS 66720
Nettleton Junior College, Sioux Falls, SD 57104
Neumann College, Aston, PA 19014-1297
New College of California, San Francisco, CA 94110
New College of the University of South Florida, Sarasota, FL 34243-2197
New England Banking Institute, Boston, MA 02111
New England College, Henniker, NH 03242-0792
New England Conservatory of Music, Boston, MA 02115
New England Culinary Institute, Montpelier, VT 05602
New England Institute of Technology
  Warwick, Warwick, RI 02886
  West Palm Beach, West Palm Beach, FL 33407
New Hampshire College, Manchester, NH 03106-1045
New Hampshire Technical College
  Berlin, Berlin, NH 03570
  Claremont, Claremont, NH 03743-9707
  Laconia, Laconia, NH 03246-9204
  Manchester, Manchester, NH 03102-8518
  Nashua, Nashua, NH 03061-2052
  Stratham, Stratham, NH 03885-2297
New Hampshire Technical Institute, Concord, NH 03301
New Jersey Institute of Technology, Newark, NJ 07102-1982
New Mexico Highlands University, Las Vegas, NM 87701
New Mexico Institute of Mining and Technology, Socorro, NM 87801
New Mexico Junior College, Hobbs, NM 88240
New Mexico Military Institute, Roswell, NM 88201-5173
New Mexico State University
  Alamogordo, Alamogordo, NM 88310
  Carlsbad, Carlsbad, NM 88220
  Grants, Grants, NM 87020
  Las Cruces, Las Cruces, NM 88003-8001
New Orleans Baptist Theological Seminary: School of Christian Education, New Orleans, LA 70126-4858
New River Community College, Dublin, VA 24084
New School of Art and Architecture, San Diego, CA 92101
New York Institute of Technology, Old Westbury, NY 11568-8000
New York School of Interior Design, New York, NY 10021
New York University, New York, NY 10011-9108
Newberry College, Newberry, SC 29108
Newbury College, Brookline, MA 02146
Niagara County Community College, Sanborn, NY 14132
Niagara University, Niagara University, NY 14109-2011
Nicholls State University, Thibodaux, LA 70310
Nichols College, Dudley, MA 01570-5000
Nicolet Area Technical College, Rhinelander, WI 54501
Nielsen Electronics Institute, Charleston, SC 29405
Norfolk State University, Norfolk, VA 23504
Normandale Community College, Bloomington, MN 55431
North Adams State College, North Adams, MA 01247
North Arkansas Community/Technical College, Harrison, AR 72601
North Carolina Agricultural and Technical State University, Greensboro, NC 27411
North Carolina Central University, Durham, NC 27707
North Carolina School of the Arts, Winston-Salem, NC 27117-2189
North Carolina State University, Raleigh, NC 27695-7103
North Carolina Wesleyan College, Rocky Mount, NC 27804
North Central Bible College, Minneapolis, MN 55404
North Central College, Naperville, IL 60566-7065
North Central Michigan College, Petoskey, MI 49770
North Central Missouri College, Trenton, MO 64683
North Central Technical College, Mansfield, OH 44901-0698

North Central Texas College, Gainesville, TX 76240
North Country Community College, Saranac Lake, NY 12983
North Dakota State College of Science, Wahpeton, ND 58076
North Dakota State University
  Bottineau, Bottineau, ND 58318-1198
  Fargo, Fargo, ND 58105
North Florida Junior College, Madison, FL 32340
North Georgia College, Dahlonega, GA 30597
North Greenville College, Tigerville, SC 29688-1892
North Harris Montgomery Community College District, Houston, TX 77060-2000
North Hennepin Community College, Minneapolis, MN 55445
North Idaho College, Coeur d'Alene, ID 83814-2199
North Iowa Area Community College, Mason City, IA 50401
North Lake College, Irving, TX 75038-3899
North Park College, Chicago, IL 60625-4987
North Seattle Community College, Seattle, WA 98103-3599
North Shore Community College, Danvers, MA 01923-0840
Northampton County Area Community College, Bethlehem, PA 18017
Northcentral Technical College, Wausau, WI 54401
Northeast Alabama Community College, Rainsville, AL 35986
Northeast Community College, Norfolk, NE 68702-0469
Northeast Iowa Community College, Calmar, IA 52132
Northeast Louisiana University, Monroe, LA 71209-0730
Northeast Mississippi Community College, Booneville, MS 38829
Northeast Missouri State University, Kirksville, MO 63501-9980
Northeast State Technical Community College, Blountville, TN 37617-0246
Northeast Texas Community College, Mount Pleasant, TX 75455-1307
Northeast Wisconsin Technical College, Green Bay, WI 54307-9042
Northeastern Illinois University, Chicago, IL 60625
Northeastern Junior College, Sterling, CO 80751
Northeastern Oklahoma Agricultural and Mechanical College, Miami, OK 74354-6497
Northeastern State University, Tahlequah, OK 74464
Northeastern University, Boston, MA 02115-9959
Northern Arizona University, Flagstaff, AZ 86011-4084
Northern Essex Community College, Haverhill, MA 01830-2399
Northern Illinois University, DeKalb, IL 60115-2854
Northern Kentucky University, Highland Heights, KY 41099-7010
Northern Maine Technical College, Presque Isle, ME 04769
Northern Marianas College, Saipan, CM 00000
Northern Michigan University, Marquette, MI 49855
Northern Nevada Community College, Elko, NV 89801
Northern New Mexico Community College, Espanola, NM 87532
Northern Oklahoma College, Tonkawa, OK 74653-0310
Northern State University, Aberdeen, SD 57401
Northern Virginia Community College, Annandale, VA 22003-3723
Northland College, Ashland, WI 54806
Northland Community College, Thief River Falls, MN 56701
Northland Pioneer College, Holbrook, AZ 86025
Northwest Christian College, Eugene, OR 97401-9983
Northwest College, Kirkland, WA 98083-0579
Northwest College, Powell, WY 82435
Northwest College of Art, Poulsbo, WA 98370
Northwest Indian College, Bellingham, WA 98226
Northwest Iowa Community College, Sheldon, IA 51201
Northwest Mississippi Community College, Senatobia, MS 38668
Northwest Missouri State University, Maryville, MO 64468-6001
Northwest Nazarene College, Nampa, ID 83686
Northwest State Community College, Archbold, OH 43502
Northwest Technical Institute, Eden Prairie, MN 55344-5351
Northwestern College, Lima, OH 45805
Northwestern College, St. Paul, MN 55113-1598
Northwestern College, Orange City, IA 51041
Northwestern Connecticut Community-Technical College, Winsted, CT 06098-1798
Northwestern Michigan College, Traverse City, MI 49684
Northwestern Oklahoma State University, Alva, OK 73717-2799
Northwestern State University, Natchitoches, LA 71497
Northwestern University, Evanston, IL 60204-3060
Northwest-Shoals Community College, Muscle Shoals, AL 35662
Northwood University, Midland, MI 48640
Northwood University: Texas Campus, Cedar Hill, TX 75104-0058
Norwalk Community-Technical College, Norwalk, CT 06854
Norwich University, Northfield, VT 05663-1097
Notre Dame College, Manchester, NH 03104-2299
Notre Dame College of Ohio, South Euclid, OH 44121-4293
Nova Southeastern University, Fort Lauderdale, FL 33314
Nunez Community College, Chalmette, LA 70043
Nyack College, Nyack, NY 10960
Oak Hills Bible College, Bemidji, MN 56601
Oakland City College, Oakland City, IN 47660

Oakland Community College, Bloomfield Hills, MI 48304-2266
Oakland University, Rochester, MI 48309-4401
Oakton Community College, Des Plaines, IL 60016
Oakwood College, Huntsville, AL 35896
Oberlin College, Oberlin, OH 44074
Oblate College, Washington, DC 20017-1587
Occidental College, Los Angeles, CA 90041-3393
Ocean County College, Toms River, NJ 08753-2001
Odessa College, Odessa, TX 79764-7127
Oglala Lakota College, Kyle, SD 57752
Oglethorpe University, Atlanta, GA 30319-2797
Ohio Dominican College, Columbus, OH 43219-2099
Ohio Institute of Photography and Technology, Dayton, OH 45439
Ohio Northern University, Ada, OH 45810-1599
Ohio State University
    Agricultural Technical Institute, Wooster, OH 44691-4099
    Columbus Campus, Columbus, OH 43210-1200
    Lima Campus, Lima, OH 45804-3596
    Mansfield Campus, Mansfield, OH 44906
    Marion Campus, Marion, OH 43302
    Newark Campus, Newark, OH 43055
Ohio University
    Athens, Athens, OH 45701-2979
    Chillicothe Campus, Chillicothe, OH 45601
    Eastern Campus, St. Clairsville, OH 43950
    Lancaster Campus, Lancaster, OH 43130
    Southern Campus at Ironton, Ironton, OH 45638
    Zanesville Campus, Zanesville, OH 43701
Ohio Valley Business College, East Liverpool, OH 43920
Ohio Valley College, Parkersburg, WV 26101-9975
Ohio Wesleyan University, Delaware, OH 43015-2398
Ohlone College, Fremont, CA 94539-0390
Ohr Somayach Tanenbaum Education Center, Monsey, NY 10952
Okaloosa-Walton Community College, Niceville, FL 32578
Oklahoma Baptist University, Shawnee, OK 74801
Oklahoma Christian University of Science and Arts, Oklahoma City, OK 73136-1100
Oklahoma City Community College, Oklahoma City, OK 73159
Oklahoma City University, Oklahoma City, OK 73106
Oklahoma Panhandle State University, Goodwell, OK 73939-0430
Oklahoma State University
    Oklahoma City, Oklahoma City, OK 73107
    Okmulgee, Okmulgee, OK 74447-3901
    Stillwater, Stillwater, OK 74078
Old Dominion University, Norfolk, VA 23529-0050
Olean Business Institute, Olean, NY 14760-2691
Olivet College, Olivet, MI 49076
Olivet Nazarene University, Kankakee, IL 60901-0592
Olympic College, Bremerton, WA 98337-1699
O'More College of Design, Franklin, TN 37064-0908
Onondaga Community College, Syracuse, NY 13215
Oral Roberts University, Tulsa, OK 74171
Orange Coast College, Costa Mesa, CA 92628-5005
Orange County Community College, Middletown, NY 10940
Orangeburg-Calhoun Technical College, Orangeburg, SC 29115
Oregon Health Sciences University, Portland, OR 97201
Oregon Institute of Technology, Klamath Falls, OR 97601-8801
Oregon Polytechnic Institute, Portland, OR 97214
Oregon State University, Corvallis, OR 97331-2130
Otero Junior College, La Junta, CO 81050
Otis College of Art and Design, Los Angeles, CA 90057
Ottawa University, Ottawa, KS 66067-3399
Otterbein College, Westerville, OH 43081
Ouachita Baptist University, Arkadelphia, AR 71998-0001
Our Lady of Holy Cross College, New Orleans, LA 70131-7399
Our Lady of the Lake University of San Antonio, San Antonio, TX 78207-4689
Owens Technical College
    Findlay Campus, Findlay, OH 45840
    Toledo, Toledo, OH 43699-1947
Owensboro Community College, Owensboro, KY 42303
Owensboro Junior College of Business, Owensboro, KY 42303
Oxford College of Emory University, Oxford, GA 30267-1328
Oxnard College, Oxnard, CA 93033
Ozark Christian College, Joplin, MO 64801
Pace University, New York, NY 10038-1598
Pacific Christian College, Fullerton, CA 92631
Pacific Lutheran University, Tacoma, WA 98447-0003
Pacific Northwest College of Art, Portland, OR 97205-2486
Pacific Oaks College, Pasadena, CA 91103
Pacific Union College, Angwin, CA 94508
Pacific University, Forest Grove, OR 97116-1797

Paducah Community College, Paducah, KY 42002-7380
Paier College of Art, Hamden, CT 06514-3902
Paine College, Augusta, GA 30901-3182
Palm Beach Atlantic College, West Palm Beach, FL 33416-4708
Palm Beach Community College, Lake Worth, FL 33461-4796
Palo Alto College, San Antonio, TX 78224
Palo Verde College, Blythe, CA 92225
Palomar College, San Marcos, CA 92069-1487
Pamlico Community College, Grantsboro, NC 28529
Panola College, Carthage, TX 75633
Paradise Valley Community College, Phoenix, AZ 85032
Paris Junior College, Paris, TX 75460
Park College, Parkville, MO 64152-9970
Parkland College, Champaign, IL 61821-1899
Parks College, Albuquerque, NM 87102
Parsons School of Design, New York, NY 10011
Pasadena City College, Pasadena, CA 91106
Pasco-Hernando Community College, Dade City, FL 34654-5199
Passaic County Community College, Paterson, NJ 07505-1179
Patrick Henry Community College, Martinsville, VA 24115-5311
Patten College, Oakland, CA 94601-2699
Paul D. Camp Community College, Franklin, VA 23851-0737
Paul Quinn College, Dallas, TX 75241
Paul Smith's College, Paul Smiths, NY 12970-0265
Peace College, Raleigh, NC 27604-1194
Pearl River Community College, Poplarville, MS 39470
Peirce College, Philadelphia, PA 19102
Pellissippi State Technical Community College, Knoxville, TN 37933-0990
Pembroke State University, Pembroke, NC 28372
Peninsula College, Port Angeles, WA 98362
Penn State
    Allentown Campus, Fogelsville, PA 18051-9733
    Altoona Campus, Altoona, PA 16601-3760
    Beaver Campus, Monaca, PA 15061
    Berks Campus, Reading, PA 19610-6009
    Delaware County Campus, Media, PA 19063
    Du Bois Campus, Du Bois, PA 15801
    Erie Behrend College, Erie, PA 16563-0195
    Fayette Campus, Uniontown, PA 15401
    Harrisburg Capital College, Middletown, PA 17057-4898
    Hazleton Campus, Hazleton, PA 18201
    McKeesport Campus, McKeesport, PA 15132
    Mont Alto Campus, Mont Alto, PA 17237
    New Kensington Campus, New Kensington, PA 15068
    Ogontz Campus, Abington, PA 19001
    Schuylkill Campus, Schuylkill Haven, PA 17972
    Shenango Campus, Sharon, PA 16146
    University Park Campus, University Park, PA 16802
    Wilkes-Barre Campus, Lehman, PA 18627
    Worthington-Scranton Campus, Dunmore, PA 18512
    York Campus, York, PA 17403
Penn Technical Institute, Pittsburgh, PA 15222
Penn Valley Community College, Kansas City, MO 64111
Pennco Tech, Bristol, PA 19007
Pennsylvania College of Technology, Williamsport, PA 17701-5799
Pennsylvania Institute of Culinary Arts, Pittsburgh, PA 15222
Pennsylvania Institute of Technology, Media, PA 19063-4098
Pensacola Junior College, Pensacola, FL 32504
Pepperdine University, Malibu, CA 90263-4392
Peru State College, Peru, NE 68421
Pfeiffer College, Misenheimer, NC 28109
Philadelphia College of Bible, Langhorne, PA 19047-2992
Philadelphia College of Pharmacy and Science, Philadelphia, PA 19104-4495
Philadelphia College of Textiles and Science, Philadelphia, PA 19144-5497
Philander Smith College, Little Rock, AR 72202
Phillips Beth Israel School of Nursing, New York, NY 10010
Phillips County Community College, Helena, AR 72342
Phillips Junior College
    Fresno Campus, Fresno, CA 93727
    Jackson, Jackson, MS 39216
    Melbourne, Melbourne, FL 32935
    New Orleans, New Orleans, LA 70121
    Salt Lake City Campus, Salt Lake City, UT 84106
    San Fernando Valley Campus, Northridge, CA 91325
    Springfield, Springfield, MO 65807
Phillips Junior College: Birmingham, Birmingham, AL 35223
Phillips University, Enid, OK 73701-6439
Phoenix College, Phoenix, AZ 85013
Piedmont Bible College, Winston-Salem, NC 27101-5197
Piedmont College, Demorest, GA 30535
Piedmont Community College, Roxboro, NC 27573-1197
Piedmont Technical College, Greenwood, SC 29648

Piedmont Virginia Community College, Charlottesville, VA 22902-8714
Pierce College, Tacoma, WA 98498-1999
Pikes Peak Community College, Colorado Springs, CO 80906-5498
Pikeville College, Pikeville, KY 41501-1194
Pillsbury Baptist Bible College, Owatonna, MN 55060
Pima Community College, Tucson, AZ 85709-1120
Pine Manor College, Chestnut Hill, MA 02167
Pitt Community College, Greenville, NC 27835-7007
Pittsburg State University, Pittsburg, KS 66762
Pittsburgh Institute of Mortuary Science, Pittsburgh, PA 15206-3706
Pittsburgh Technical Institute, Pittsburgh, PA 15222
Pitzer College, Claremont, CA 91711-6114
Plaza Business Institute, Jackson Heights, NY 11372
Plymouth State College of the University System of New Hampshire,
   Plymouth, NH 03264
Point Loma Nazarene College, San Diego, CA 92106-2899
Point Park College, Pittsburgh, PA 15222-1984
Polk Community College, Winter Haven, FL 33881-4299
Polytechnic University
      Brooklyn, Brooklyn, NY 11201-2999
      Long Island Campus, Farmingdale, NY 11735-3995
Pomona College, Claremont, CA 91711-6312
Pontifical Catholic University of Puerto Rico, Ponce, PR 00731-6382
Pontifical College Josephinum, Columbus, OH 43085
Porterville College, Porterville, CA 93257
Portland Community College, Portland, OR 97219-0990
Portland State University, Portland, OR 97207-0751
Potomac State College of West Virginia University, Keyser, WV 26726
Prairie State College, Chicago Heights, IL 60411
Prairie View A&M University, Prairie View, TX 77446
Pratt Community College, Pratt, KS 67124
Pratt Institute, Brooklyn, NY 11205
Presbyterian College, Clinton, SC 29325-9989
Prescott College, Prescott, AZ 86301
Presentation College, Aberdeen, SD 57401
Prestonsburg Community College, Prestonsburg, KY 41653
Prince George's Community College, Largo, MD 20772-2199
Prince William Sound Community College, Valdez, AK 99686
Princeton University, Princeton, NJ 08544-0430
Principia College, Elsah, IL 62028-9799
Providence College, Providence, RI 02918-0001
Pueblo Community College, Pueblo, CO 81004
Puget Sound Christian College, Edmonds, WA 98020-3171
Purdue University
      Calumet, Hammond, IN 46323-2094
      North Central Campus, Westville, IN 46391-9528
      West Lafayette, West Lafayette, IN 47907-1080
Queen of the Holy Rosary College, Fremont, CA 94539-0391
Queens College, Charlotte, NC 28274
Quincy College, Quincy, MA 02169
Quincy University, Quincy, IL 62301-2699
Quinebaug Valley Community-Technical College, Danielson, CT 06239-1440
Quinnipiac College, Hamden, CT 06518-1908
Quinsigamond Community College, Worcester, MA 01606
Rabbinical College of America, Morristown, NJ 07960
Rabbinical College Bobover Yeshiva B'nei Zion, Brooklyn, NY 11219
Rabbinical College Ch'san Sofer of New York, Brooklyn, NY 11204
Rabbinical College of Long Island, Long Beach, NY 11561
Rabbinical College of Telshe, Wickliffe, OH 44092-2584
Rabbinical Seminary Adas Yereim, Brooklyn, NY 11211
Radford University, Radford, VA 24142-6903
Rainy River Community College, International Falls, MN 56649
Ramapo College of New Jersey, Mahwah, NJ 07430-1680
Rancho Santiago Community College, Santa Ana, CA 92706
Randolph Community College, Asheboro, NC 27204-1009
Randolph-Macon College, Ashland, VA 23005-5505
Randolph-Macon Woman's College, Lynchburg, VA 24503-1526
Ranger College, Ranger, TX 76470
Ranken Technical College, St. Louis, MO 63113
Rappahannock Community College, Glenns, VA 23149
Raritan Valley Community College, Somerville, NJ 08876-1265
Rasmussen College-Minnetonka, Minnetonka, MN 56001
Ray College of Design, Chicago, IL 60654
Reading Area Community College, Reading, PA 19603-1706
Red Rocks Community College, Lakewood, CO 80401
Redlands Community College, El Reno, OK 73036
Reed College, Portland, OR 97202-8199
Reformed Bible College, Grand Rapids, MI 49505-9749
Regis College, Weston, MA 02193-1571
Regis University, Denver, CO 80221-1099
Reid State Technical College, Evergreen, AL 36401
Reinhardt College, Waleska, GA 30183

Rend Lake College, Ina, IL 62846
Rensselaer Polytechnic Institute, Troy, NY 12180-3590
Renton Technical College, Renton, WA 98056-4195
Research College of Nursing, Kansas City, MO 64110-2508
RETS
      Electronic Institute, Louisville, KY 40219
      Tech Center, Centerville, OH 45459
Rhode Island College, Providence, RI 02908
Rhode Island School of Design, Providence, RI 02903-2791
Rhodes College, Memphis, TN 38112-1690
Rice University, Houston, TX 77251
Rich Mountain Community College, Mena, AR 71953
Richard Bland College, Petersburg, VA 23805
Richard Stockton College of New Jersey, Pomona, NJ 08240-0000
Richland College, Dallas, TX 75243-2199
Richland Community College, Decatur, IL 62521
Richmond College, The American International University in London,
      London, United Kingdom 00000
Richmond Community College, Hamlet, NC 28345
Ricks College, Rexburg, ID 83460-4104
Rider University, Lawrenceville, NJ 08648-3099
Ringling School of Art and Design, Sarasota, FL 34234
Rio Hondo College, Whittier, CA 90608
Rio Salado Community College, Phoenix, AZ 85003
Ripon College, Ripon, WI 54971
Riverside Community College, Riverside, CA 92506-1299
Rivier College, Nashua, NH 03060-5086
Roane State Community College, Harriman, TN 37748
Roanoke Bible College, Elizabeth City, NC 27909
Roanoke College, Salem, VA 24153-3794
Roanoke-Chowan Community College, Ahoskie, NC 27910-9522
Robert Morris College, Coraopolis, PA 15108-1189
Robert Morris College: Chicago, Chicago, IL 60601
Roberts Wesleyan College, Rochester, NY 14624-1997
Robeson Community College, Lumberton, NC 28359
Rochester Business Institute, Rochester, NY 14622
Rochester Community College, Rochester, MN 55904-4999
Rochester Institute of Technology, Rochester, NY 14623-5604
Rock Valley College, Rockford, IL 61114-5699
Rockford Business College, Rockford, IL 61103
Rockford College, Rockford, IL 61108-2393
Rockhurst College, Kansas City, MO 64110-2508
Rockingham Community College, Wentworth, NC 27375-0038
Rockland Community College, Suffern, NY 10901
Rocky Mountain College, Billings, MT 59102-1796
Rocky Mountain College of Art & Design, Denver, CO 80224-2359
Roger Williams University, Bristol, RI 02809-2923
Rogers State College, Claremore, OK 74017-2099
Rogue Community College, Grants Pass, OR 97527
Rollins College, Winter Park, FL 32789-4499
Roosevelt University, Chicago, IL 60605-1394
Rosary College, River Forest, IL 60305-1099
Rose State College, Midwest City, OK 73110-2799
Rose-Hulman Institute of Technology, Terre Haute, IN 47803-3999
Rosemont College, Rosemont, PA 19010
Rowan College of New Jersey, Glassboro, NJ 08028
Rowan-Cabarrus Community College, Salisbury, NC 28145-1595
Roxbury Community College, Roxbury Crossing, MA 02120-3400
Rush University, Chicago, IL 60612
Russell Sage College, Troy, NY 12180
Rust College, Holly Springs, MS 38635-2328
Rutgers, The State University of New Jersey
      Camden College of Arts and Sciences, Camden, NJ 08102
      College of Engineering, New Brunswick, NJ 08903-2101
      College of Nursing, Newark, NJ 07102-1896
      College of Pharmacy, New Brunswick, NJ 08903-2101
      Cook College, New Brunswick, NJ 08903-2101
      Douglass College, New Brunswick, NJ 08903-2101
      Livingston College, New Brunswick, NJ 08903-2101
      Mason Gross School of the Arts, New Brunswick, NJ 08903-2101
      Newark College of Arts and Sciences, Newark, NJ 07102-1896
      Rutgers College, New Brunswick, NJ 08903-2101
Sacramento City College, Sacramento, CA 95822
Sacred Heart Major Seminary, Detroit, MI 48226
Sacred Heart University, Fairfield, CT 06432-1000
Saddleback College, Mission Viejo, CA 92692-4206
Sage Junior College of Albany, Albany, NY 12208
Saginaw Valley State University, University Center, MI 48710-0001
St. Ambrose University, Davenport, IA 52803
St. Andrews Presbyterian College, Laurinburg, NC 28352-9151
St. Anselm College, Manchester, NH 03102-1310
St. Augustine College, Chicago, IL 60640-3501

St. Augustine's College, Raleigh, NC 27610-2298
St. Bonaventure University, St. Bonaventure, NY 14778-2284
St. Catharine College, St. Catharine, KY 40061
St. Charles Borromeo Seminary-Overbrook, Wynnewood, PA 19096-3099
St. Charles County Community College, St. Peters, MO 63376
St. Clair County Community College, Port Huron, MI 48061-5015
St. Cloud State University, St. Cloud, MN 56301-4498
St. Cloud Technical College, St. Cloud, MN 56303
St. Edward's University, Austin, TX 78704-6489
St. Francis College, Fort Wayne, IN 46808
St. Francis College, Brooklyn Heights, NY 11201
St. Francis College, Loretto, PA 15940-0600
St. Francis Medical Center College of Nursing, Peoria, IL 61603
St. Gregory's College, Shawnee, OK 74801
St. Hyacinth College and Seminary, Granby, MA 01033-9742
St. John Fisher College, Rochester, NY 14618-3597
St. John Vianney College Seminary, Miami, FL 33165
St. John's College, Santa Fe, NM 87501-4599
St. John's College, Annapolis, MD 21404-2800
St. Johns River Community College, Palatka, FL 32177-3897
St. John's Seminary College, Brighton, MA 02135
St. John's Seminary College, Camarillo, CA 93012-2599
St. John's University, Jamaica, NY 11439
St. John's University, Collegeville, MN 56321
St. Joseph College, West Hartford, CT 06117-2700
St. Joseph College of Nursing, Joliet, IL 60435
St. Joseph Seminary College, St. Benedict, LA 70457-9990
St. Joseph's College, Rensselaer, IN 47978
St. Joseph's College, Standish, ME 04084-5263
St. Joseph's College
      Brooklyn, Brooklyn, NY 11205-3688
      Suffolk Campus, Patchogue, NY 11772-2603
St. Joseph's Hospital Health Center School of Nursing, Syracuse, NY 13203
St. Joseph's University, Philadelphia, PA 19131
St. Lawrence University, Canton, NY 13617-1447
St. Leo College, St. Leo, FL 33574-2008
St. Louis Christian College, Florissant, MO 63033
St. Louis College of Pharmacy, St. Louis, MO 63110
St. Louis Community College
      Florissant Valley, St. Louis, MO 63135
      Forest Park, St. Louis, MO 63110
      Meramec, St. Louis, MO 63122-5799
St. Louis University, St. Louis, MO 63103-2097
St. Martin's College, Lacey, WA 98503-1297
St. Mary College, Leavenworth, KS 66048-5082
St. Mary-of-the-Woods College, St. Mary-of-the-Woods, IN 47876-0068
St. Mary's College, Notre Dame, IN 46556-5001
St. Mary's College, Orchard Lake, MI 48324-0515
St. Mary's College, Raleigh, NC 27603-1689
St. Mary's College of California, Moraga, CA 94575-4800
St. Mary's College of Maryland, St. Mary's City, MD 20686-9998
St. Mary's College of Minnesota, Winona, MN 55987-1399
St. Mary's University, San Antonio, TX 78228-8503
St. Meinrad College, St. Meinrad, IN 47577-1030
St. Michael's College, Colchester, VT 05439
St. Norbert College, De Pere, WI 54115-2099
St. Olaf College, Northfield, MN 55057-1098
St. Paul Technical College, St. Paul, MN 55102-9913
St. Paul's College, Lawrenceville, VA 23868
St. Peter's College, Jersey City, NJ 07306-5944
St. Petersburg Junior College, St. Petersburg, FL 33733
St. Philip's College, San Antonio, TX 78203-2098
St. Thomas Aquinas College, Sparkill, NY 10976
St. Thomas University, Miami, FL 33054
St. Vincent College, Latrobe, PA 15650-2690
St. Xavier University, Chicago, IL 60655
Salem College, Winston-Salem, NC 27108
Salem Community College, Carneys Point, NJ 08069-2799
Salem State College, Salem, MA 01970
Salem-Teikyo University, Salem, WV 26426
Salisbury State University, Salisbury, MD 21801-6862
Salish Kootenai College, Pablo, MT 59855
Salt Lake Community College, Salt Lake City, UT 84130-0808
Salve Regina University, Newport, RI 02840-4192
Sam Houston State University, Huntsville, TX 77341-2418
Samford University, Birmingham, AL 35229-0000
Sampson Community College, Clinton, NC 28328
Samuel Merritt College, Oakland, CA 94609-9954
San Antonio College, San Antonio, TX 78212-4299
San Bernardino Valley College, San Bernardino, CA 92410
San Diego City College, San Diego, CA 92101
San Diego Mesa College, San Diego, CA 92111

San Diego Miramar College, San Diego, CA 92126-2999
San Diego State University, San Diego, CA 92182
San Francisco Art Institute, San Francisco, CA 94133-2299
San Francisco College of Mortuary Science, San Francisco, CA 94110
San Francisco Conservatory of Music, San Francisco, CA 94122-4498
San Francisco State University, San Francisco, CA 94132
San Jacinto College
      Central Campus, Pasadena, TX 77501-2007
      North, Houston, TX 77049
San Joaquin Delta College, Stockton, CA 95207
San Jose Christian College, San Jose, CA 95108-1090
San Jose City College, San Jose, CA 95128-2798
San Jose State University, San Jose, CA 95192-0009
San Juan College, Farmington, NM 87402
Sandhills Community College, Pinehurst, NC 28374
Sangamon State University, Springfield, IL 62794-9243
Santa Barbara City College, Santa Barbara, CA 93109-2394
Santa Clara University, Santa Clara, CA 95053
Santa Fe Community College, Santa Fe, NM 87502-4187
Santa Fe Community College, Gainesville, FL 32602
Santa Monica College, Santa Monica, CA 90405-1628
Santa Rosa Junior College, Santa Rosa, CA 95401
Sarah Lawrence College, Bronxville, NY 10708
Sauk Valley Community College, Dixon, IL 61021-9110
Savannah College of Art and Design, Savannah, GA 31402-3146
Savannah State College, Savannah, GA 31404
Savannah Technical Institute, Savannah, GA 31499
Schenectady County Community College, Schenectady, NY 12305
Schiller International University, Dunedin, FL 34698-4964
School of the Art Institute of Chicago, Chicago, IL 60603
School for International Training, Brattleboro, VT 05301
School of the Museum of Fine Arts, Boston, MA 02115
School of Visual Arts, New York, NY 10010-3994
School of Visual Arts: Savannah, Savannah, GA 31401
Schoolcraft College, Livonia, MI 48152-2696
Schreiner College, Kerrville, TX 78028
Scott Community College, Bettendorf, IA 52722-6804
Scottsdale Community College, Scottsdale, AZ 85250-2699
Scripps College, Claremont, CA 91711-3948
Seattle Central Community College, Seattle, WA 98122
Seattle Pacific University, Seattle, WA 98119-1997
Seattle University, Seattle, WA 98122-4460
Selma University, Selma, AL 36701
Seminole Community College, Sanford, FL 32773-6199
Seminole Junior College, Seminole, OK 74818-0351
Seton Hall University, South Orange, NJ 07079-2689
Seton Hill College, Greensburg, PA 15601-1599
Seward County Community College, Liberal, KS 67905-1137
Shasta College, Redding, CA 96099
Shaw University, Raleigh, NC 27601
Shawnee Community College, Ullin, IL 62992
Shawnee State University, Portsmouth, OH 45662
Shelby State Community College, Memphis, TN 38174-0568
Sheldon Jackson College, Sitka, AK 99835
Shelton State Community College, Tuscaloosa, AL 35405
Shenandoah University, Winchester, VA 22601-5195
Shepherd College, Shepherdstown, WV 25443-1569
Sheridan College, Sheridan, WY 82801-1500
Shimer College, Waukegan, IL 60079-0500
Shippensburg University of Pennsylvania, Shippensburg, PA 17257
Shoreline Community College, Seattle, WA 98133
Shorter College, Rome, GA 30165-4298
Shorter College, North Little Rock, AR 72114
Siena College, Loudonville, NY 12211-1462
Siena Heights College, Adrian, MI 49221-9937
Sierra College, Rocklin, CA 95677
Sierra Nevada College, Incline Village, NV 89450-4269
Silver Lake College, Manitowoc, WI 54220-9391
Simmons College, Boston, MA 02115-5898
Simon Fraser University, Burnaby, Canada 00000
Simon's Rock College of Bard, Great Barrington, MA 01230
Simpson College, Redding, CA 96003-8606
Simpson College, Indianola, IA 50125-1299
Sinclair Community College, Dayton, OH 45402-1460
Sinte Gleska University, Rosebud, SD 57570
Sisseton-Wahpeton Community College, Sisseton, SD 57262-0689
Sistema Instituto Tecnologico y de Estudios Superiores de Monterrey,
      Monterrey Nuevo Leon, Mexico 00000
Skagit Valley College, Mount Vernon, WA 98273
Skidmore College, Saratoga Springs, NY 12866-1632
Skyline College, San Bruno, CA 94066-1698
Slippery Rock University of Pennsylvania, Slippery Rock, PA 16057

Smith College, Northampton, MA 01063
Snead State Community College, Boaz, AL 35957
Snow College, Ephraim, UT 84627
Sojourner-Douglass College, Baltimore, MD 21205
Solano Community College, Suisun City, CA 94585
Somerset Community College, Somerset, KY 42501
Sonoma State University, Rohnert Park, CA 94928
South Arkansas Community College, El Dorado, AR 71731-7010
South Carolina State University, Orangeburg, SC 29117-0001
South College
    Palm Beach Campus, West Palm Beach, FL 33409
    Savannah, Savannah, GA 31406
South Dakota School of Mines and Technology, Rapid City, SD 57701-3995
South Dakota State University, Brookings, SD 57007-0649
South Florida Community College, Avon Park, FL 33825
South Georgia College, Douglas, GA 31533-5098
South Hills Business School, State College, PA 16801
South Mountain Community College, Phoenix, AZ 85040
South Plains College, Levelland, TX 79336
South Puget Sound Community College, Olympia, WA 98512-6218
South Seattle Community College, Seattle, WA 98106
South Suburban College of Cook County, South Holland, IL 60473
Southeast Community College, Cumberland, KY 40823
Southeast Community College
    Beatrice Campus, Beatrice, NE 68310
    Lincoln Campus, Lincoln, NE 68520
    Milford Campus, Milford, NE 68405
Southeast Missouri State University, Cape Girardeau, MO 63701
Southeast Vo-Tech Institute, Sioux Falls, SD 57107
Southeastern Baptist College, Laurel, MS 39440
Southeastern Baptist Theological Seminary, Wake Forest, NC 27587-1889
Southeastern Bible College, Birmingham, AL 35243-4181
Southeastern Business College, Lorain, OH 44055
Southeastern College of the Assemblies of God, Lakeland, FL 33801
Southeastern Community College, Whiteville, NC 28472
Southeastern Community College
    North Campus, West Burlington, IA 52655-0605
    South Campus, Keokuk, IA 52632-6007
Southeastern Illinois College, Harrisburg, IL 62946
Southeastern Louisiana University, Hammond, LA 70402-0752
Southeastern Oklahoma State University, Durant, OK 74701-0609
Southeastern University, Washington, DC 20024
Southern Arkansas University
    Magnolia, Magnolia, AR 71753-5000
    Tech, Camden, AR 71701
Southern California College, Costa Mesa, CA 92626-9601
Southern California Institute of Architecture, Los Angeles, CA 90066
Southern Christian University, Montgomery, AL 36117-3553
Southern College, Orlando, FL 32807
Southern College of Seventh-day Adventist, Collegedale, TN 37315
Southern College of Technology, Marietta, GA 30060-2896
Southern Connecticut State University, New Haven, CT 06515
Southern Illinois University
    Carbondale, Carbondale, IL 62901-4710
    Edwardsville, Edwardsville, IL 62026-1600
Southern Maine Technical College, South Portland, ME 04106
Southern Methodist University, Dallas, TX 75275-0296
Southern Nazarene University, Bethany, OK 73008-2694
Southern Ohio College, Cincinnati, OH 45237
Southern Oregon State College, Ashland, OR 97520-5032
Southern State Community College, Hillsboro, OH 45133
Southern Union State Community College, Wadley, AL 36276
Southern University
    New Orleans, New Orleans, LA 70126
    Shreveport, Shreveport, LA 71107
Southern University and Agricultural and Mechanical College, Baton Rouge,
    LA 70813
Southern Utah University, Cedar City, UT 84720
Southern Vermont College, Bennington, VT 05201
Southern Virginia College, Buena Vista, VA 24416-3097
Southern Wesleyan University, Central, SC 29630-1020
Southern West Virginia Community College, Mount Gay, WV 25637
Southside Virginia Community College, Alberta, VA 23821
Southwest Baptist University, Bolivar, MO 65613-2496
Southwest Mississippi Community College, Summit, MS 39666
Southwest Missouri State University, Springfield, MO 65804-0094
Southwest State University, Marshall, MN 56258-1598
Southwest Texas Junior College, Uvalde, TX 78801
Southwest Texas State University, San Marcos, TX 78666-5709
Southwest Virginia Community College, Richlands, VA 24641-1510
Southwest Wisconsin Technical College, Fennimore, WI 53809
Southwestern Adventist College, Keene, TX 76059

Southwestern Assemblies of God College, Waxahachie, TX 75165
Southwestern Christian College, Terrell, TX 75160
Southwestern College, Chula Vista, CA 91910
Southwestern College, Phoenix, AZ 85032-7042
Southwestern College, Winfield, KS 67156-9988
Southwestern College of Christian Ministries, Bethany, OK 73008
Southwestern Community College, Sylva, NC 28779
Southwestern Community College, Creston, IA 50801
Southwestern Indian Polytechnic Institute, Albuquerque, NM 87184
Southwestern Michigan College, Dowagiac, MI 49047-9793
Southwestern Oklahoma State University, Weatherford, OK 73096
Southwestern Oregon Community College, Coos Bay, OR 97420-2956
Southwestern University, Georgetown, TX 78626
Spalding University, Louisville, KY 40203
Sparks State Technical College, Eufaula, AL 36072-0580
Spartanburg Methodist College, Spartanburg, SC 29301
Spartanburg Technical College, Spartanburg, SC 29305
Spelman College, Atlanta, GA 30314-4399
Spokane Community College, Spokane, WA 99207-5399
Spokane Falls Community College, Spokane, WA 99204-5288
Spoon River College, Canton, IL 61520
Spring Arbor College, Spring Arbor, MI 49283
Spring Hill College, Mobile, AL 36608
Springfield College, Springfield, MA 01109
Springfield College in Illinois, Springfield, IL 62702-2694
Springfield Technical Community College, Springfield, MA 01105-1296
Standing Rock College, Fort Yates, ND 58538
Stanford University, Stanford, CA 94305
Stanly Community College, Albemarle, NC 28001
Stark Technical College, Canton, OH 44720
State Community College, East St. Louis, IL 62201
State Fair Community College, Sedalia, MO 65301-2199
State Technical Institute at Memphis, Memphis, TN 38134
State University of New York
    Albany, Albany, NY 12222
    Binghamton, Binghamton, NY 13902-6001
    Buffalo, Buffalo, NY 14260
    Oswego, Oswego, NY 13126-3599
    Purchase, Purchase, NY 10577-1400
    Stony Brook, Stony Brook, NY 11794-1901
    College of Agriculture and Technology at Cobleskill, Cobleskill, NY
        12043
    College of Agriculture and Technology at Morrisville, Morrisville, NY
        13408
    College at Brockport, Brockport, NY 14420-2915
    College at Buffalo, Buffalo, NY 14222-1095
    College at Cortland, Cortland, NY 13045
    College of Environmental Science and Forestry, Syracuse, NY 13210-
        2779
    College at Fredonia, Fredonia, NY 14063
    College at Geneseo, Geneseo, NY 14454-1471
    College at New Paltz, New Paltz, NY 12561-2499
    College at Old Westbury, Old Westbury, NY 11568-0307
    College at Oneonta, Oneonta, NY 13820-4016
    College at Plattsburgh, Plattsburgh, NY 12901
    College at Potsdam, Potsdam, NY 13676-2294
    College of Technology at Alfred, Alfred, NY 14802-1196
    College of Technology at Canton, Canton, NY 13617-1098
    College of Technology at Delhi, Delhi, NY 13753-1190
    College of Technology at Farmingdale, Farmingdale, NY 11735-1021
    Empire State College, Saratoga Springs, NY 12866-6390
    Health Science Center at Brooklyn, Brooklyn, NY 11203-2098
    Health Science Center at Syracuse, Syracuse, NY 13210
    Health Sciences Center at Stony Brook, Stony Brook, NY 11794-8276
    Institute of Technology at Utica/Rome, Utica, NY 13504-3050
    Maritime College, Throggs Neck, NY 10465-4198
Stenotype Academy, New York, NY 10038
Stephen F. Austin State University, Nacogdoches, TX 75962-3051
Stephens College, Columbia, MO 65215-9986
Sterling College, Craftsbury Common, VT 05827-0072
Sterling College, Sterling, KS 67579-9989
Stetson University, DeLand, FL 32720
Stevens Institute of Technology, Hoboken, NJ 07030-5991
Stevens-Henager College of Business, Provo, UT 84606-6157
Stillman College, Tuscaloosa, AL 35403
Stone Child College, Box Elder, MT 59521-9796
Stonehill College, North Easton, MA 02357-5610
Stratton College, Milwaukee, WI 53202-2608
Strayer College, Washington, DC 20005
Sue Bennett College, London, KY 40741

Suffolk County Community College
Eastern Campus, Riverhead, NY 11901
Selden, Selden, NY 11784
Western Campus, Brentwood, NY 11717
Suffolk University, Boston, MA 02108-2772
Sul Ross State University, Alpine, TX 79832
Sullivan County Community College, Loch Sheldrake, NY 12759-4002
Suomi College, Hancock, MI 49930
Surry Community College, Dobson, NC 27017
Susquehanna University, Selinsgrove, PA 17870-1001
Sussex County Community College, Newton, NJ 07860
Swarthmore College, Swarthmore, PA 19081-1397
Sweet Briar College, Sweet Briar, VA 24595
Syracuse University, Syracuse, NY 13244-1120
Tabor College, Hillsboro, KS 67063
Tacoma Community College, Tacoma, WA 98465-9971
Taft College, Taft, CA 93268
Talladega College, Talladega, AL 35160
Tallahassee Community College, Tallahassee, FL 32304-2895
Talmudic College of Florida, Miami Beach, FL 33139
Talmudical Academy of New Jersey, Adelphia, NJ 07710
Talmudical Institute of Upstate New York, Rochester, NY 14607
Talmudical Seminary Oholei Torah, Brooklyn, NY 11213-3397
Talmudical Yeshiva of Philadelphia, Philadelphia, PA 19131
Tampa College, Tampa, FL 33614
Tarleton State University, Stephenville, TX 76402
Tarrant County Junior College, Fort Worth, TX 76102-6599
Taylor Business Institute, New York, NY 10119-0118
Taylor University, Upland, IN 46989-1001
Technical Career Institutes, New York, NY 10001
Technical College of the Lowcountry, Beaufort, SC 29902-1288
Technical Trades Institute, Colorado Springs, CO 80909
Technological College of the Municipality of San Juan, Hato Rey, PR 00936
Teikyo Marycrest University, Davenport, IA 52804-4096
Teikyo Westmar University, Le Mars, IA 51031
Teikyo-Post University, Waterbury, CT 06723-2540
Telshe Yeshiva-Chicago, Chicago, IL 60625
Temple Junior College, Temple, TX 76504-7435
Temple University, Philadelphia, PA 19122-1803
Tennessee Institute of Electronics, Knoxville, TN 37918
Tennessee State University, Nashville, TN 37203
Tennessee Technological University, Cookeville, TN 38505
Tennessee Temple University, Chattanooga, TN 37404
Tennessee Wesleyan College, Athens, TN 37371-0040
Terra Community College, Fremont, OH 43420-9670
Texarkana College, Texarkana, TX 75599
Texas A&M International University, Laredo, TX 78040-9960
Texas A&M University
College Station, College Station, TX 77843-0100
Galveston, Galveston, TX 77553-1675
Texas A&M University-Corpus Christi, Corpus Christi, TX 78412
Texas A&M University-Kingsville, Kingsville, TX 78363-8201
Texas Christian University, Fort Worth, TX 76129
Texas College, Tyler, TX 75712-2404
Texas Lutheran College, Seguin, TX 78155
Texas Southern University, Houston, TX 77004
Texas Southmost College, Brownsville, TX 78520
Texas State Technical College
Amarillo, Amarillo, TX 79111
Harlingen, Harlingen, TX 78550-3697
Sweetwater, Sweetwater, TX 79556
Waco, Waco, TX 76705
Texas Tech University, Lubbock, TX 79409-5005
Texas Wesleyan University, Fort Worth, TX 76105-1536
Texas Woman's University, Denton, TX 76204-0599
Thaddeus Stevens State School of Technology, Lancaster, PA 17602
Thiel College, Greenville, PA 16125
Thomas Aquinas College, Santa Paula, CA 93060
Thomas College, Waterville, ME 04901-9986
Thomas College, Thomasville, GA 31792-7499
Thomas Jefferson University: College of Allied Health Sciences, Philadelphia, PA 19107
Thomas More College, Crestview Hills, KY 41017
Thomas More College of Liberal Arts, Merrimack, NH 03054
Thomas Nelson Community College, Hampton, VA 23670-0407
Three Rivers Community College, Poplar Bluff, MO 63901-1308
Three Rivers Community-Technical College, Norwich, CT 06360-2479
Tidewater Community College, Portsmouth, VA 23703
Tiffin University, Tiffin, OH 44883
Toccoa Falls College, Toccoa Falls, GA 30598-0368
Tompkins-Cortland Community College, Dryden, NY 13053-0139
Tougaloo College, Tougaloo, MS 39174

Touro College, New York, NY 10010
Towson State University, Towson, MD 21204-7097
Transylvania University, Lexington, KY 40508-1797
Treasure Valley Community College, Ontario, OR 97914
Trenholm State Technical College, Montgomery, AL 36108
Trenton State College, Trenton, NJ 08650-4700
Trevecca Nazarene College, Nashville, TN 37210
Triangle Tech: Pittsburgh Campus, Pittsburgh, PA 15214-3897
Tri-County Community College, Murphy, NC 28906
Tri-County Technical College, Pendleton, SC 29670
Trident Technical College, Charleston, SC 29423-8067
Trinidad State Junior College, Trinidad, CO 81082
Trinity Bible College, Ellendale, ND 58436-7150
Trinity Christian College, Palos Heights, IL 60463
Trinity College, Deerfield, IL 60015
Trinity College, Hartford, CT 06106
Trinity College, Washington, DC 20017-1094
Trinity College of Vermont, Burlington, VT 05401
Trinity International University, Miami, FL 33101-9674
Trinity University, San Antonio, TX 78212-7200
Trinity Valley Community College, Athens, TX 75751
Tri-State University, Angola, IN 46703-0307
Triton College, River Grove, IL 60171
Trocaire College, Buffalo, NY 14220
Troy State University
Dothan, Dothan, AL 36304-0368
Montgomery, Montgomery, AL 36103-4419
Troy, Troy, AL 36082
Truckee Meadows Community College, Reno, NV 89512
Truett-McConnell College, Cleveland, GA 30528
Tufts University, Medford, MA 02155-5555
Tulane University, New Orleans, LA 70118-5680
Tulsa Junior College, Tulsa, OK 74135-6198
Tunxis Community-Technical College, Farmington, CT 06032-3187
Turabo University, Gurabo, PR 00778
Turtle Mountain Community College, Belcourt, ND 58316-0340
Tusculum College, Greeneville, TN 37743
Tuskegee University, Tuskegee, AL 36088
Tyler Junior College, Tyler, TX 75711-9020
UAB: Walker College, Jasper, AL 35501
Ulster County Community College, Stone Ridge, NY 12484
Umpqua Community College, Roseburg, OR 97470
Union College, Barbourville, KY 40906
Union College, Schenectady, NY 12308-2311
Union College, Lincoln, NE 68506-4300
Union County College, Cranford, NJ 07016-1599
Union Institute, Cincinnati, OH 45206-1947
Union University, Jackson, TN 38305-3697
United States International University, San Diego, CA 92131-1799
United States Merchant Marine Academy, Kings Point, NY 11024-1699
United Tribes Technical College, Bismarck, ND 58504
Unity College, Unity, ME 04988-0532
Universidad Adventista de las Antillas, Mayaguez, PR 00681
Universidad Metropolitana, Rio Piedras, PR 00928
Universidad Politecnica de Puerto Rico, Hato Rey, PR 00918
University of Akron
Akron, Akron, OH 44325-2001
Wayne College, Orrville, OH 44667
University of Alabama
Birmingham, Birmingham, AL 35294-1150
Huntsville, Huntsville, AL 35899
Tuscaloosa, Tuscaloosa, AL 35487-0132
University of Alaska
Anchorage, Anchorage, AK 99508-4675
Fairbanks, Fairbanks, AK 99775-0060
Southeast, Juneau, AK 99801
University of Arizona, Tucson, AZ 85721
University of Arkansas
Fayetteville, Fayetteville, AR 72701
Little Rock, Little Rock, AR 72204
Medical Sciences, Little Rock, AR 72205-7199
Monticello, Monticello, AR 71655
Pine Bluff, Pine Bluff, AR 71601-2799
University of the Arts, Philadelphia, PA 19102
University of Baltimore, Baltimore, MD 21201-5779
University of Bridgeport, Bridgeport, CT 06601
University of British Columbia, Vancouver, BC, Canada 00000

University of California
  Berkeley, Berkeley, CA 94720-5800
  Davis, Davis, CA 95616
  Irvine, Irvine, CA 92717
  Los Angeles, Los Angeles, CA 90024
  Riverside, Riverside, CA 92521
  San Diego, La Jolla, CA 92093-0337
  San Francisco, San Francisco, CA 94143-0404
  Santa Barbara, Santa Barbara, CA 93106
  Santa Cruz, Santa Cruz, CA 95064
University of Central Arkansas, Conway, AR 72035-0001
University of Central Florida, Orlando, FL 32816
University of Central Oklahoma, Edmond, OK 73034-0151
University of Central Texas, Killeen, TX 76540-1416
University of Charleston, Charleston, WV 25304-1099
University of Chicago, Chicago, IL 60637
University of Cincinnati
  Access Colleges, Cincinnati, OH 45221-0091
  Cincinnati, Cincinnati, OH 45221-0091
  Clermont College, Batavia, OH 45103-0162
  Raymond Walters College, Cincinnati, OH 45236
University of Colorado
  Boulder, Boulder, CO 80309-0030
  Colorado Springs, Colorado Springs, CO 80933-7150
  Denver, Denver, CO 80217-3364
  Health Sciences Center, Denver, CO 80262
University of Connecticut, Storrs, CT 06269-3088
University of Dallas, Irving, TX 75062-4799
University of Dayton, Dayton, OH 45469-1611
University of Delaware, Newark, DE 19716-6210
University of Denver, Denver, CO 80208-0132
University of Detroit Mercy, Detroit, MI 48219-0900
University of the District of Columbia, Washington, DC 20008
University of Dubuque, Dubuque, IA 52001-5050
University of Evansville, Evansville, IN 47722
University of Findlay, Findlay, OH 45840-3695
University of Florida, Gainesville, FL 32611
University of Georgia, Athens, GA 30602
University of Guam, Mangilao Guam, GU 00000
University of Hartford, West Hartford, CT 06117-0395
University of Hawaii
  Hawaii Community College, Hilo, HI 96720-4091
  Hilo, Hilo, HI 96720-4091
  Honolulu Community College, Honolulu, HI 96817
  Kapiolani Community College, Honolulu, HI 96816-4421
  Kauai Community College, Lihue, HI 96766
  Leeward Community College, Pearl City, HI 96782
  Manoa, Honolulu, HI 96822
  Maui Community College, Kahului, HI 96732
  West Oahu, Pearl City, HI 96782
  Windward Community College, Kaneohe, HI 96817
University of Houston
  Clear Lake, Houston, TX 77058-1080
  Downtown, Houston, TX 77002
  Houston, Houston, TX 77204-2161
  Victoria, Victoria, TX 77901-4450
University of Idaho, Moscow, ID 83844-3133
University of Illinois
  Chicago, Chicago, IL 60680
  Urbana-Champaign, Urbana, IL 61801
University of Indianapolis, Indianapolis, IN 46227-3697
University of Iowa, Iowa City, IA 52242-1396
University of Judaism, Los Angeles, CA 90077
University of Kansas
  Lawrence, Lawrence, KS 66045
  Medical Center, Kansas City, KS 66160
University of Kentucky, Lexington, KY 40506-0054
University of La Verne, La Verne, CA 91750-4443
University of Louisville, Louisville, KY 40292
University of Maine
  Augusta, Augusta, ME 04330-9410
  Farmington, Farmington, ME 04938-1994
  Fort Kent, Fort Kent, ME 04743-1292
  Machias, Machias, ME 04654
  Orono, Orono, ME 04469-5713
  Presque Isle, Presque Isle, ME 04769-2888
University of Mary, Bismarck, ND 58504-9652
University of Mary Hardin-Baylor, Belton, TX 76513

University of Maryland
  Baltimore, Baltimore, MD 21201
  Baltimore County, Baltimore, MD 21228-5398
  College Park, College Park, MD 20742-5235
  Eastern Shore, Princess Anne, MD 21853-1299
  University College, College Park, MD 20742-1672
University of Massachusetts
  Amherst, Amherst, MA 01003
  Boston, Boston, MA 02125-3393
  Dartmouth, North Dartmouth, MA 02747-2300
  Lowell, Lowell, MA 01854
University of Medicine and Dentistry of New Jersey: School of Nursing,
  Newark, NJ 07107-3006
University of Memphis, Memphis, TN 38152
University of Miami, Coral Gables, FL 33124
University of Michigan
  Ann Arbor, Ann Arbor, MI 48109-1316
  Dearborn, Dearborn, MI 48128-1491
  Flint, Flint, MI 48502-2186
University of Minnesota
  Crookston, Crookston, MN 56716
  Duluth, Duluth, MN 55812-2496
  Morris, Morris, MN 56267-2199
  Twin Cities, Minneapolis-St. Paul, MN 55455-0213
University of Mississippi
  Medical Center, Jackson, MS 39216
  University, University, MS 38677
University of Missouri
  Columbia, Columbia, MO 65211
  Kansas City, Kansas City, MO 64110-2944
  Rolla, Rolla, MO 65401
  St. Louis, St. Louis, MO 63121
University of Mobile, Mobile, AL 36663-0220
University of Montana-Missoula, Missoula, MT 59812
University of Montana College of Technology, Missoula, MT 59801
University of Montevallo, Montevallo, AL 35115-6030
University of Nebraska
  Medical Center, Omaha, NE 68198-4230
  Kearney, Kearney, NE 68849
  Lincoln, Lincoln, NE 68588-0417
  Omaha, Omaha, NE 68182-0005
University of Nevada
  Las Vegas, Las Vegas, NV 89154-1021
  Reno, Reno, NV 89557-0002
University of New England, Biddeford, ME 04005
University of New Hampshire
  Durham, Durham, NH 03824
  Manchester, Manchester, NH 03102
University of New Haven, West Haven, CT 06516
University of New Mexico, Albuquerque, NM 87131-2039
University of New Orleans, New Orleans, LA 70148
University of North Alabama, Florence, AL 35632-0001
University of North Carolina
  Asheville, Asheville, NC 28804-3299
  Chapel Hill, Chapel Hill, NC 27599-2200
  Charlotte, Charlotte, NC 28223
  Greensboro, Greensboro, NC 27412-5001
  Wilmington, Wilmington, NC 28403-3297
University of North Dakota
  Grand Forks, Grand Forks, ND 58202-8357
  Lake Region, Devils Lake, ND 58301-1598
  Williston, Williston, ND 58802-1326
University of North Florida, Jacksonville, FL 32224-2645
University of North Texas, Denton, TX 76203-6797
University of Northern Colorado, Greeley, CO 80639
University of Northern Iowa, Cedar Falls, IA 50614-0018
University of Notre Dame, Notre Dame, IN 46556-5602
University of Oklahoma
  Health Sciences Center, Oklahoma City, OK 73190
  . Norman, Norman, OK 73069-0520
University of Oregon
  Eugene, Eugene, OR 97403-1217
  Robert Donald Clark Honors College, Eugene, OR 97403-1293
University of Osteopathic Medicine and Health Sciences, Des Moines, IA
  50312
University of the Ozarks, Clarksville, AR 72830
University of the Pacific, Stockton, CA 95211-0197
University of Pennsylvania, Philadelphia, PA 19104-6376
University of Phoenix, Phoenix, AZ 85072-2069

University of Pittsburgh
    Bradford, Bradford, PA 16701-2898
    Greensburg, Greensburg, PA 15601-5898
    Johnstown, Johnstown, PA 15904
    Pittsburgh, Pittsburgh, PA 15260
    Titusville, Titusville, PA 16354-9990
University of Portland, Portland, OR 97203-5798
University of Puerto Rico
    Aguadilla, Aguadilla, PR 00604
    Arecibo Campus, Arecibo, PR 00613
    Bayamon Technological University College, Bayamon, PR 00959-1919
    Carolina Regional College, Carolina, PR 00984-4800
    Cayey University College, Cayey, PR 00633
    Humacao University College, Humacao, PR 00791
    La Montana Regional College, Utuado, PR 00641-2500
    Mayaguez Campus, Mayaguez, PR 00681-5000
    Medical Sciences Campus, Rio Piedras, PR 00936-5067
    Ponce Technological University College, Ponce, PR 00732
    Rio Piedras Campus, Rio Piedras, PR 00931-1907
University of Puget Sound, Tacoma, WA 98416-0003
University of Redlands, Redlands, CA 92373-0999
University of Rhode Island, Kingston, RI 02881-0806
University of Richmond, Richmond, VA 23173
University of Rio Grande, Rio Grande, OH 45674
University of Rochester, Rochester, NY 14627-0251
University of the Sacred Heart, Santurce, PR 00914
University of St. Thomas, St. Paul, MN 55105-1096
University of St. Thomas, Houston, TX 77006-4696
University of San Diego, San Diego, CA 92110
University of San Francisco, San Francisco, CA 94117-1080
University of Science and Arts of Oklahoma, Chickasha, OK 73018
University of Scranton, Scranton, PA 18510-4699
University of Sioux Falls, Sioux Falls, SD 57105-1699
University of the South, Sewanee, TN 37383-1000
University of South Alabama, Mobile, AL 36688
University of South Carolina
    Aiken, Aiken, SC 29801
    Beaufort, Beaufort, SC 29902
    Columbia, Columbia, SC 29208
    Lancaster, Lancaster, SC 29721
    Salkehatchie Regional Campus, Allendale, SC 29810
    Spartanburg, Spartanburg, SC 29303
    Sumter, Sumter, SC 29150-2498
    Union, Union, SC 29379
University of South Dakota, Vermillion, SD 57069-2390
University of South Florida, Tampa, FL 33620-6900
University of Southern California, Los Angeles, CA 90089-0911
University of Southern Colorado, Pueblo, CO 81001-4901
University of Southern Indiana, Evansville, IN 47712
University of Southern Maine, Gorham, ME 04038
University of Southern Mississippi, Hattiesburg, MS 39406-5166
University of Southwestern Louisiana, Lafayette, LA 70504
University of the State of New York: Regents College, Albany, NY 12203-5159
University of Tampa, Tampa, FL 33606-1490
University of Tennessee
    Chattanooga, Chattanooga, TN 37403
    Knoxville, Knoxville, TN 37996-0230
    Martin, Martin, TN 38238
    Memphis, Memphis, TN 38163
University of Texas
    Arlington, Arlington, TX 76019-0088
    Austin, Austin, TX 78712-1157
    Brownsville, Brownsville, TX 78520
    Dallas, Richardson, TX 75083-0688
    El Paso, El Paso, TX 79968
    Health Science Center at San Antonio, San Antonio, TX 78284-7702
    Medical Branch at Galveston, Galveston, TX 77555-1305
    Pan American, Edinburg, TX 78539
    Permian Basin, Odessa, TX 79762
    San Antonio, San Antonio, TX 78249-0617
    Southwestern Medical Center at Dallas, Dallas, TX 75235-9096
    Tyler, Tyler, TX 75701-6699
    Houston Health Science Center, Houston, TX 77225
University of Toledo, Toledo, OH 43606-3398
University of Tulsa, Tulsa, OK 74104-3189
University of Utah, Salt Lake City, UT 84112
University of Vermont, Burlington, VT 05401-3596
University of the Virgin Islands, Charlotte Amalie, VI 00000
University of Virginia, Charlottesville, VA 22906
University of Washington, Seattle, WA 98195-5840
University of West Alabama, Livingston, AL 35470

University of West Florida, Pensacola, FL 32514-5750
University of West Los Angeles, Inglewood, CA 90301
University of Wisconsin
    Eau Claire, Eau Claire, WI 54701
    Green Bay, Green Bay, WI 54311-7001
    La Crosse, La Crosse, WI 54601
    Madison, Madison, WI 53706-1490
    Milwaukee, Milwaukee, WI 53201
    Oshkosh, Oshkosh, WI 54901-8602
    Parkside, Kenosha, WI 53141-2000
    Platteville, Platteville, WI 53818
    River Falls, River Falls, WI 54022
    Stevens Point, Stevens Point, WI 54481
    Stout, Menomonie, WI 54751
    Superior, Superior, WI 54880
    Whitewater, Whitewater, WI 53190-1791
University of Wisconsin Center
    Baraboo/Sauk County, Baraboo, WI 53913-1098
    Barron County, Rice Lake, WI 54868
    Fond du Lac, Fond du Lac, WI 54935-2998
    Fox Valley, Menasha, WI 54952-8002
    Manitowoc County, Manitowoc, WI 54220-6699
    Marathon County, Wausau, WI 54401-5396
    Marinette County, Marinette, WI 54143
    Marshfield/Wood County, Marshfield, WI 54449
    Richland, Richland Center, WI 53581
    Rock County, Janesville, WI 53546-5699
    Sheboygan County, Sheboygan, WI 53081-4789
    Washington County, West Bend, WI 53095
    Waukesha, Waukesha, WI 53188-2799
University of Wyoming, Laramie, WY 82071-3435
Upper Iowa University, Fayette, IA 52142-1859
Urbana University, Urbana, OH 43078-2091
Ursinus College, Collegeville, PA 19426
Ursuline College, Pepper Pike, OH 44124-4398
Utah State University, Logan, UT 84322
Utah Valley State College, Orem, UT 84058
Utica College of Syracuse University, Utica, NY 13502-4892
Utica School of Commerce, Utica, NY 13501
Valdosta State University, Valdosta, GA 31698
Valencia Community College, Orlando, FL 32802-3028
Valley City State University, Valley City, ND 58072-4098
Valley Forge Christian College, Phoenixville, PA 19460-2399
Valley Forge Military College, Wayne, PA 19087-3695
Valparaiso University, Valparaiso, IN 46383-6493
Vance-Granville Community College, Henderson, NC 27536
Vanderbilt University, Nashville, TN 37203-1700
VanderCook College of Music, Chicago, IL 60616-3886
Vassar College, Poughkeepsie, NY 12601
Vennard College, University Park, IA 52595
Ventura College, Ventura, CA 93003
Vermilion Community College, Ely, MN 55731-9989
Vermont Technical College, Randolph Center, VT 05061
Vernon Regional Junior College, Vernon, TX 76384-4092
Victor Valley College, Victorville, CA 92392-9699
Victoria College, Victoria, TX 77901
Villa Julie College, Stevenson, MD 21153
Villa Maria College of Buffalo, Buffalo, NY 14225-3999
Villanova University, Villanova, PA 19085-1672
Vincennes University, Vincennes, IN 47591
Virginia College, Birmingham, AL 35234
Virginia Commonwealth University, Richmond, VA 23284-2526
Virginia Highlands Community College, Abingdon, VA 24210-0828
Virginia Intermont College, Bristol, VA 24201-4298
Virginia Marti College of Fashion and Art, Lakewood, OH 44107
Virginia Military Institute, Lexington, VA 24450-9967
Virginia Polytechnic Institute and State University, Blacksburg, VA 24061-0202
Virginia State University, Petersburg, VA 23806-9018
Virginia Union University, Richmond, VA 23220
Virginia Wesleyan College, Norfolk, VA 23502-5599
Virginia Western Community College, Roanoke, VA 24038
Vista Community College, Berkeley, CA 94704
Viterbo College, La Crosse, WI 54601
Volunteer State Community College, Gallatin, TN 37066
Voorhees College, Denmark, SC 29042
Wabash College, Crawfordsville, IN 47933-0352
Wadhams Hall Seminary-College, Ogdensburg, NY 13669-9308
Wagner College, Staten Island, NY 10301-4495
Wake Forest University, Winston-Salem, NC 27109
Wake Technical Community College, Raleigh, NC 27603
Waldorf College, Forest City, IA 50436

Walla Walla College, College Place, WA 99324-1198
Walla Walla Community College, Walla Walla, WA 99362-9267
Wallace State College at Hanceville, Hanceville, AL 35077-2000
Walsh College of Accountancy and Business Administration, Troy, MI 48007-7006
Walsh University, North Canton, OH 44720-3396
Walters State Community College, Morristown, TN 37813-6899
Warner Pacific College, Portland, OR 97215-4026
Warner Southern College, Lake Wales, FL 33853-8725
Warren County Community College, Washington, NJ 07882-9605
Warren Wilson College, Ashville, NC 28815-9000
Wartburg College, Waverly, IA 50677
Washburn University of Topeka, Topeka, KS 66621
Washington Bible College, Lanham, MD 20706
Washington College, Chestertown, MD 21620-1197
Washington and Jefferson College, Washington, PA 15301
Washington and Lee University, Lexington, VA 24450
Washington State Community College, Marietta, OH 45750
Washington State University, Pullman, WA 99164-1036
Washington University, St. Louis, MO 63130-4899
Washtenaw Community College, Ann Arbor, MI 48106-0978
Waubonsee Community College, Sugar Grove, IL 60554-9799
Waukesha County Technical College, Pewaukee, WI 53072
Waycross College, Waycross, GA 31503
Wayland Baptist University, Plainview, TX 79072-6998
Wayne Community College, Goldsboro, NC 27533-8002
Wayne County Community College, Detroit, MI 48226
Wayne State College, Wayne, NE 68787
Wayne State University, Detroit, MI 48202
Waynesburg College, Waynesburg, PA 15370
Weatherford College, Weatherford, TX 76086
Webber College, Babson Park, FL 33827-0096
Weber State University, Ogden, UT 84408-1015
Webster University, Webster Groves, MO 63119-3194
Wellesley College, Wellesley, MA 02181-8292
Wells College, Aurora, NY 13026
Wenatchee Valley College, Wenatchee, WA 98801
Wentworth Institute of Technology, Boston, MA 02115
Wentworth Military Academy, Lexington, MO 64067-1799
Wesley College, Florence, MS 39073-0070
Wesley College, Dover, DE 19901-3875
Wesleyan College, Macon, GA 31297-4299
Wesleyan University, Middletown, CT 06459
West Chester University of Pennsylvania, West Chester, PA 19383
West Coast University, Los Angeles, CA 90020-1765
West Georgia College, Carrollton, GA 30118-0001
West Hills Community College, Coalinga, CA 93210
West Liberty State College, West Liberty, WV 26074
West Los Angeles College, Culver City, CA 90230
West Shore Community College, Scottville, MI 49454-0277
West Side Institute of Technology, Cleveland, OH 44102
West Suburban College of Nursing, Oak Park, IL 60302
West Texas A&M University, Canyon, TX 79016
West Valley College, Saratoga, CA 95070-5698
West Virginia Institute of Technology, Montgomery, WV 25136-2436
West Virginia Northern Community College, Wheeling, WV 26003
West Virginia State College, Institute, WV 25112-1000
West Virginia University
    Morgantown, Morgantown, WV 26506-6009
    Parkersburg, Parkersburg, WV 26101-9577
West Virginia Wesleyan College, Buckhannon, WV 26201-2998
Westark Community College, Fort Smith, AR 72913-3649
Westbrook College, Portland, ME 04103
Westchester Business Institute, White Plains, NY 10602
Westchester Community College, Valhalla, NY 10595-1698
Western Baptist College, Salem, OR 97301-9392
Western Carolina University, Cullowhee, NC 28723
Western Connecticut State University, Danbury, CT 06810
Western Dakota Technical Institute, Rapid City, SD 57701
Western Illinois University, Macomb, IL 61455-1390
Western International University, Phoenix, AZ 85021
Western Iowa Tech Community College, Sioux City, IA 51102
Western Kentucky University, Bowling Green, KY 42101
Western Maryland College, Westminster, MD 21157-4390
Western Michigan University, Kalamazoo, MI 49008
Western Montana College of the University of Montana, Dillon, MT 59725
Western Nebraska Community College: Scottsbluff Campus, Scottsbluff, NE 69361
Western Nevada Community College, Carson City, NV 89703
Western New England College, Springfield, MA 01119-2688
Western New Mexico University, Silver City, NM 88062
Western Oklahoma State College, Altus, OK 73521

Western Oregon State College, Monmouth, OR 97361-1394
Western Piedmont Community College, Morganton, NC 28655-9978
Western State College of Colorado, Gunnison, CO 81231
Western Texas College, Snyder, TX 79549
Western Washington University, Bellingham, WA 98225-9009
Western Wisconsin Technical College, La Crosse, WI 54602-0908
Western Wyoming Community College, Rock Springs, WY 82901
Westfield State College, Westfield, MA 01086
Westminster Choir College of Rider University, Princeton, NJ 08540-3899
Westminster College, New Wilmington, PA 16172-0001
Westminster College, Fulton, MO 65251-1299
Westminster College of Salt Lake City, Salt Lake City, UT 84105
Westmont College, Santa Barbara, CA 93108-1099
Westmoreland County Community College, Youngwood, PA 15697
Wharton County Junior College, Wharton, TX 77488-0080
Whatcom Community College, Bellingham, WA 98226
Wheaton College, Wheaton, IL 60187-5593
Wheaton College, Norton, MA 02766
Wheeling Jesuit College, Wheeling, WV 26003-6295
Wheelock College, Boston, MA 02215-4176
White Pines College, Chester, NH 03036
Whitman College, Walla Walla, WA 99362-2085
Whittier College, Whittier, CA 90608-0634
Whitworth College, Spokane, WA 99251-0002
Wichita State University, Wichita, KS 67260-0124
Widener University, Chester, PA 19013
Wilberforce University, Wilberforce, OH 45384-1091
Wiley College, Marshall, TX 75670
Wilkes Community College, Wilkesboro, NC 28697-0120
Wilkes University, Wilkes-Barre, PA 18766-0001
Willamette University, Salem, OR 97301-3922
William Carey College, Hattiesburg, MS 39401-5499
William Jewell College, Liberty, MO 64068
William Paterson College of New Jersey, Wayne, NJ 07470
William Penn College, Oskaloosa, IA 52577
William Rainey Harper College, Palatine, IL 60067-7398
William Tyndale College, Farmington Hills, MI 48331-9985
William Woods University, Fulton, MO 65251-1098
Williams Baptist College, Walnut Ridge, AR 72476
Williams College, Williamstown, MA 01267
Williamsburg Technical College, Kingstree, SC 29556-4197
Williamson Free School of Mechanical Trades, Media, PA 19063-5299
Willmar Community College, Willmar, MN 56201
Willmar Technical College, Willmar, MN 56201-1097
Wilmington College, Wilmington, OH 45177
Wilmington College, New Castle, DE 19720
Wilson College, Chambersburg, PA 17201-1285
Wilson Technical Community College, Wilson, NC 27893
Wingate College, Wingate, NC 28174-0157
Winona State University, Winona, MN 55987
Winston-Salem State University, Winston-Salem, NC 27110
Winthrop University, Rock Hill, SC 29733
Wisconsin Indianhead Technical College, Shell Lake, WI 54871
Wisconsin Lutheran College, Milwaukee, WI 53226-4699
Wisconsin School of Electronics, Madison, WI 53704
Wittenberg University, Springfield, OH 45501-0720
Wofford College, Spartanburg, SC 29303-3663
Wood College, Mathiston, MS 39752
Wood Tobe-Coburn School, New York, NY 10016-0190
Woodbury University, Burbank, CA 91510-7846
Worcester Polytechnic Institute, Worcester, MA 01609-2280
Worcester State College, Worcester, MA 01602-2597
Worthington Community College, Worthington, MN 56187
Wor-Wic Community College, Salisbury, MD 21801
Wright State University
    Dayton, Dayton, OH 45435
    Lake Campus, Celina, OH 45822
Wytheville Community College, Wytheville, VA 24382
Xavier University, Cincinnati, OH 45207-5311
Xavier University of Louisiana, New Orleans, LA 70125-1098
Yakima Valley Community College, Yakima, WA 98907
Yale University, New Haven, CT 06520-8234
Yavapai College, Prescott, AZ 86301
Yeshiva Beth Yehuda-Yeshiva Gedolah of Greater Detroit, Oak Park, MI 48237
Yeshiva Derech Chaim, Brooklyn, NY 11218
Yeshiva Gedolah Zichron Moshe, South Fallsburg, NY 12779
Yeshiva Ohr Elchonon Chabad/West Coast Talmudical Seminary, Los Angeles, CA 90046
Yeshiva Shaar Hatorah, Kew Gardens, NY 11418
Yeshiva Toras Chaim Talmudical Seminary, Denver, CO 80204
Yeshiva University, New York, NY 10033-3299

Yeshivath Beth Moshe, Scranton, PA 18505
York College, York, NE 68467-2699
York College of Pennsylvania, York, PA 17403-3426
York Technical College, Rock Hill, SC 29730
Young Harris College, Young Harris, GA 30582-0116
Youngstown State University, Youngstown, OH 44555-0001
Yuba College, Marysville, CA 95901

CSS/FINANCIAL AID PROFILE - 1996-97

Registration

Read carefully the General Information and CSS Code List and the instructions on the back of this page.

(1) Student's name — Last — First — M.I.

(4) Title (optional) — 1 ☐ Mr. — 2 ☐ Miss, Ms., or Mrs.

(2) Student's permanent mailing address (Mail will be sent to this address.) — Number, street, and apartment number — City — State — Zip Code

(5) Student's date of birth — Month — Day — Year

(3) Student's home telephone number — Area Code

(6) Student's social security number

---

(7) What will be the student's year in school during 1996-97? (Mark only one box.)

- 1 ☐ 1st year (never previously attended college)
- 2 ☐ 1st year (previously attended college)
- 3 ☐ 2nd year
- 4 ☐ 3rd year
- 5 ☐ 4th year
- 6 ☐ 5th year or more undergraduate
- 7 ☐ first-year graduate/professional (beyond a bachelor's degree)
- 8 ☐ second-year graduate/professional
- 9 ☐ third-year graduate/professional
- 0 ☐ fourth-year or more graduate/professional

(8) What is the student's current marital status? (Mark only one box.)

- 1 ☐ unmarried (single, divorced, widowed)
- 2 ☐ married
- 3 ☐ separated

(9) Is the student a veteran of the U.S. Armed Forces?
Yes ☐ 1 No ☐ 2

(10) Is the student an orphan, or a ward of the court, or was the student a ward of the court until age 18?
Yes ☐ 1 No ☐ 2

(11) Does the student have legal dependents (other than a spouse) that fit the definition in the instructions?
Yes ☐ 1 No ☐ 2

(12) Are the student's natural or adoptive parents separated or divorced?
Yes ☐ 1 No ☐ 2

(13) Do the student's parents own all or a part of a business or farm? (See instructions.)
Yes ☐ 1 No ☐ 2

(14) What will be the student's 1996-97 financial aid status?

- 1 ☐ First-time applicant, entering student
- 2 ☐ Renewal applicant, continuing student
- 3 ☐ First-time applicant, continuing student

---

(15) Colleges, universities, and programs to receive PROFILE information. Write in the Code Number and Housing Code for up to 10 schools to which the student wants CSS to send information. Use only the CSS Code List. At least one code must be entered.

	CSS Code No.	Housing Code*		CSS Code No.	Housing Code*
1.			6.		
2.			7.		
3.			8.		
4.			9.		
5.			10.		

* Housing codes for 1996-97 (Enter only one code per school.)

1 = Campus housing 3 = With parents
2 = Off-campus housing 4 = With relatives

(16) Fee and type of payment

A. Registration Fee (Non-refundable) — $ 5.00

B. Schools' and Programs' Processing Fee (Multiply number from Question 15 above by $14.50. Enter result. Must be at least $14.50.) — $

C. Express Delivery Service (Mark box and enter $10.00 to receive service.) ☐ — $

D. Data Confirmation Report (Mark box and enter $5.50 to receive report.) ☐ — $

Total (Add amounts on lines A-D.) — $

CSS Use Only

Mark below the box showing the type of payment.

☐ Enclosed is a check or money order for the correct fee. (Make payable to College Scholarship Service.)

☐ Charge the following credit card:
1 ☐ MasterCard 2 ☐ VISA 3 ☐ American Express

Credit Card Number — M M Y Y Expiration Date

A check, money order, or a credit card number must be provided with this Registration when it is mailed to CSS. If you fail to do so, this Registration will be returned unprocessed.

Mail the completed Registration to CSS in the addressed envelope. Alternatively, your Registration may be faxed to CSS at 609-771-7733 if payment is being made by credit card.

(17) Certification: All the above information is true and complete to the best of my knowledge. I give permission to send information from this Registration and from my PROFILE Application to the schools and programs given in **15**, and I agree to pay all appropriate fees.

Student's signature — Date

Instructions for the PROFILE Registration

Do not fill out more than one PROFILE Registration. If you are applying to more than 10 schools, or want to add a school later, the <u>General Information and CSS Code List</u> will tell you what to do.

This form collects information about the student who is applying for aid. On this form, the word "school" means a college, university, graduate or professional school, or any other school beyond high school.

Not all questions require instructions. Where additional information is necessary, you will find it below.

2. If you are requesting the optional express delivery service (See Question 16), a street address must be given. Do not enter a P.O. box number.

7. Mark the student's year in school from July 1, 1996, through June 30, 1997. If the student is currently a senior in high school or will be a first-time, entering freshman, check "1st (never previously attended college)."

9. Mark "Yes" if the student was released from **active military service** under a condition other than dishonorable, or if the student is not a veteran now, but will be one by June 30, 1997.

10. Mark "Yes" if both of the student's parents are dead and the student doesn't have an adoptive parent or legal guardian. Also check "Yes" if the student is currently a ward of the court or was a ward of the court until age 18.

11. Mark "Yes" if the student has any children who get more than half of their support from the student. Also mark "Yes" if other people (not the student's spouse) live with the student and get more than half of their support from the student and will continue to get that support during the 1996-97 school year.

12. Mark "Yes" if the student's natural or adoptive parents have separated or divorced, even if one or both have since remarried.

13. Mark "Yes" if the student's parents own all or part of a business, corporation, partnership, or are a farm or ranch owner, operator, or farm tenant.

14. If the student is a high school senior or has never attended college before, mark box one (1).

15. Give the CSS Code Number and Housing Code for up to 10 schools and programs to which the student wants CSS to send information. CSS will send the student a customized PROFILE Application packet based on the requirements of the schools and programs listed in this question. At least one code number must be given, or the Registration will be returned unprocessed.

    Don't list a code for a school or program unless it is included on the CSS Code List or unless the school or program has told the student to do so. **CSS will not refund any fee the student pays for reporting to a school or program that does not use the PROFILE Service.**

    Write in the Housing Code that best describes where the student plans to live while attending school during 1996-97. If the student is considering more than one school, provide a housing code for each school the student lists. Answer "Campus housing" if the student will live in housing controlled by the school the student will attend. Answer "Off-campus housing" if the student will not be living with parents, in campus housing, or with relatives (other than a spouse or children). Answer "With parents" if the student will live with one or both parents while attending school. Answer "With relatives" if the student will live with relatives other than parents, spouse, or children.

16. The PROFILE Registration Fee covers the cost of preparing and mailing the PROFILE Application packet. The fee for schools and programs covers processing and reporting the student's PROFILE information to the schools and programs that have been requested. CSS's responsibility to the student in this regard does not extend beyond the amount of the student's fee.

    See the <u>General Information and CSS Code List</u> for a description of the optional fee based services.

    Mark the box showing the type of payment. If paying by check or money order, send it with the PROFILE Registration. Don't staple the check or money order to the form. If a check is sent that the bank won't accept, the student will be charged an additional $5.00 fee. Checks must not be written on foreign banks. Students outside the U.S. (except for Canada and U.S. possessions) should use an international money order.

    A Registration received without payment will be returned unprocessed to the student.

Mail to CSS the completed PROFILE Registration with payment or credit card number in the envelope provided. If no envelope is available, mail to: College Scholarship Service, P.O. Box 6920, Princeton, NJ 08541-6920. Alternatively, you may fax the Registration to CSS at 609-771-7733, if payment is being made by credit card.

CSS can not accept the PROFILE Registration before September 22, 1995, or after February 1, 1997.

CSS/FINANCIAL AID PROFILE™

Application 0

(Computer print special instructions regarding specific sections of the form to be completed by the student.)

Section A — Student's Information

1. How many family members will the student (and spouse) support in 1996-97? <u>Always include the student (and spouse).</u> List their names and give information about them in Section M. See instructions. ☐☐

2. Of the number in 1, how many will be in college at least half-time for at least one term in 1996-97? Include yourself. ☐

3. What is the student's state of legal residence? ☐☐

4. What is the student's citizenship status?

a. 1 ☐ U.S. citizen (Skip to Question 5.)

    2 ☐ Permanent resident (Skip to Question 5.)

    3 ☐ Neither of the above (Answer "b" and "c" below.)

b. Country of citizenship?

☐☐☐☐☐☐☐☐☐☐☐☐☐☐☐

c. Visa classification?

1 ☐ F1 2 ☐ F2 3 ☐ J1 4 ☐ J2 5 ☐ G 6 ☐ Other

Section B — Student's 1995 Income & Benefits

If married, include spouse's information in Sections B, C, D, and E.

5. The following 1995 U.S. income tax return figures are (Mark only one box.)

  1 ☐ estimated. Will file IRS Form 1040EZ or 1040A. Go to 6.

  2 ☐ estimated. Will file IRS Form 1040. Go to 6.

  3 ☐ from a completed IRS Form 1040EZ or 1040A. Go to 6.

  4 ☐ from a completed IRS Form 1040. Go to 6.

  5 ☐ a tax return will not be filed. Skip to 10.

Tax Filers Only

6. 1995 total number of exemptions (IRS Form 1040, line 6e or 1040A, line 6e or 1040EZ — see instructions) ☐☐

7. 1995 Adjusted Gross Income from IRS Form 1040, line 31 or 1040A, line 16 or 1040EZ, line 3 (Use the worksheet in the instructions.) $ _____ .00

8. 1995 U.S. income tax paid (IRS Form 1040, line 46 or 1040A, line 25 or 1040EZ, line 9) $ _____ .00

9. 1995 itemized deductions (IRS Form 1040, Schedule A, line 29. Write in "0" if deductions were not itemized.) $ _____ .00

10. 1995 income earned from work by student (See instructions.) $ _____ .00

11. 1995 income earned from work by student's spouse $ _____ .00

12. 1995 dividend and interest income $ _____ .00

13. 1995 untaxed income and benefits (Give total amount for year.)

  a. Social security benefits (See instructions.) $ _____ .00

  b. Aid to Families with Dependent Children $ _____ .00

  c. Child support received for all children $ _____ .00

  d. Earned Income Credit (IRS Form 1040, line 56 or 1040A, line 28c or 1040EZ, line 7) $ _____ .00

  e. Other – write total from worksheet, page X. $ _____ .00

14. 1995 earnings from Federal Work-Study or other need-based work programs plus any grant and scholarship aid required to be reported on your U.S. income tax return $ _____ .00

Section C — Student's Assets

15. Cash, savings, and checking accounts $ _____ .00

16. Total value of IRA, Keogh, 401k, 403b, etc. accounts as of December 31, 1995. $ _____ .00

	What is it worth today?	**What is owed on it?**
17. Investments (Including Uniform Gifts to Minors. See instructions.)	$ _____ .00	$ _____ .00
18. Home (Renters write in "0.")	$ _____ .00	$ _____ .00
19. Other real estate	$ _____ .00	$ _____ .00
20. Business and farm	$ _____ .00	$ _____ .00

21. If a farm is included in 20, is the student living on the farm? Yes ☐ 1 No ☐ 2

22. If student owns home, give

  a. year purchased ☐1☐9☐☐ b. purchase price $ _____ .00

Section D — Student's Trust Information

23. a. Total value of all trust(s) $ _____ .00

  b. Is any income or part of the principal currently available?

    Yes ☐ 1 No ☐ 2

  c. Who established the trust(s)?

    1 ☐ Student's parents 2 ☐ Other

Section E — Student's 1995 Expenses

24. 1995 child support paid by student $ _____ .00

25. 1995 medical and dental expenses not covered by insurance (See instructions.) $ _____ .00

Section F — Student's Expected Summer/School-Year Resources for 1996-97

	Amount per month	Number of months
26. Student's veterans benefits (July 1, 1996 – June 30, 1997)	$ _____ .00	⌴

27. Student's (and spouse's) resources
(Don't enter monthly amounts.)

	Summer 1996 (3 months)	School Year 1996-97 (9 months)
a. Student's wages, salaries, tips, etc.	$ _____ .00	$ _____ .00
b. Spouse's wages, salaries, tips, etc.	$ _____ .00	$ _____ .00
c. Other taxable income	$ _____ .00	$ _____ .00
d. Untaxed income and benefits	$ _____ .00	$ _____ .00
e. Grants, scholarships, fellowships, etc. from other than the colleges or universities to which the student is applying (List sources in Section P.)		$ _____ .00
f. Tuition benefits from the parents' and/or the student's or spouse's employer		$ _____ .00
g. Contributions from the student's parent(s)		$ _____ .00
h. Contributions from other relatives, spouse's parents, and all other sources		$ _____ .00

Section G — Parents' Household Information — See page X of the instruction booklet.

28. How many family members will your parents support in 1996-97? ⌴
<u>Always include the student and parents.</u>
List their names and give information about them in Section M.

29. Of the number in 28, how many will be in college at least half-time for at least one term in 1996-97? Include the student. ⌴

30. How many parents will be in college at least half-time in 1996-97? (Mark only one box.)

₁ ☐ Neither parent   ₂ ☐ One parent   ₃ ☐ Both parents

31. What is the current marital status of your parents? (Mark only one box.)

₁ ☐ single   ₃ ☐ separated   ₅ ☐ widowed
₂ ☐ married   ₄ ☐ divorced

32. What is your parents' state of legal residence? ⌴

Section H — Parents' Expenses

		1995	Expected 1996
33. Child support paid by the parent(s) completing this form	33.	$ _____ .00	$ _____ .00
34. Repayment of parents' educational loans (See instructions.)	34.	$ _____ .00	$ _____ .00
35. Medical and dental expenses not covered by insurance (See instructions.)	35.	$ _____ .00	$ _____ .00
36. Total elementary, junior high school, and high school tuition paid for dependent children			
a. Amount paid (Don't include tuition paid for the student.)	36.	$ _____ .00	$ _____ .00
b. For how many dependent children? (Don't include the student.)		⌴	⌴

Section I — Parents' Assets — If parents own all or part of a business or farm, write in its name and the percent of ownership in Section P.

37. Cash, savings, and checking accounts $ _____ .00

38. Monthly home mortgage or rental payment (If none, explain in Section P.) $ _____ .00

	What is it worth today?	What is owed on it?
39. Investments	$ _____ .00	$ _____ .00
40. a. Home (Renters write in "0.")	$ _____ .00	$ _____ .00

b. year purchased |1|9|_|_| c. purchase price $ _____ .00

	What is it worth today?	What is owed on it?
41. Business	$ _____ .00	$ _____ .00
42. a. Farm	$ _____ .00	$ _____ .00

b. Does family live on the farm?
Yes ☐ ₁   No ☐ ₂

43. a. Other real estate $ _____ .00 $ _____ .00

b. year purchased |1|9|_|_| c. purchase price $ _____ .00

Section J — Parents' 1994 Income & Benefits

44. 1994 Adjusted Gross Income (IRS Form 1040, line 31 or 1040A, line 16 or 1040EZ, line 3) $ _____ .00

45. 1994 U.S. income tax paid (IRS Form 1040, line 46, 1040A, line 25 or 1040EZ, line 9) $ _____ .00

46. 1994 itemized deductions (IRS Form 1040, Schedule A, line 29. Write "0" if deductions were not itemized.) $ _____ .00

47. 1994 untaxed income and benefits (Include the same types of income & benefits that are listed in 55 a – k.) $ _____ .00

Section K — Parents' 1995 Income & Benefits

48. The following 1995 U.S. income tax return figures are (Mark only one box.)

1 ☐ estimated. Will file IRS Form 1040EZ or 1040A. Go to 49. 2 ☐ estimated. Will file IRS Form 1040. Go to 49. 3 ☐ from a completed IRS Form 1040EZ or 1040A. Go to 49. 4 ☐ from a completed IRS Form 1040. Go to 49. 5 ☐ a tax return will not be filed. Skip to 53.

Tax Filers Only

49. 1995 total number of exemptions (IRS Form 1040, line 6e or 1040A, line 6e or 1040EZ)   **49.** ☐☐

50. 1995 Adjusted Gross Income (IRS Form 1040, line 31 or 1040A, line 16 or 1040EZ, line 3)   **50.** $ _____ .00

Breakdown of income in 50

   a. Wages, salaries, tips (IRS Form 1040, line 7 or 1040A, line 7 or 1040EZ, line 1)   **50. a.** $ _____ .00

   b. Interest income (IRS Form 1040, line 8a or 1040A, line 8a or 1040EZ, line 2)   **b.** $ _____ .00

   c. Dividend income (IRS Form 1040, line 9 or 1040A, line 9)   **c.** $ _____ .00

   d. Net income (or loss) from business, farm, rents, royalties, partnerships, estates, trusts, etc. (IRS Form 1040, lines 12, 18, and 19) If a loss, enter the amount in (parentheses).   **d.** $ _____ .00

   e. Other taxable income such as alimony received, capital gains (or losses), pensions, annuities, etc. (IRS Form 1040, lines 10, 11, 13, 14, 15b, 16b, 17, 20b, and 21 or 1040A, line 10b)   **e.** $ _____ .00

   f. Adjustments to income (IRS Form 1040, line 30 or 1040A, line 15c)   **f.** $ _____ .00

51. 1995 U.S. income tax paid (IRS Form 1040, line 46, 1040A, line 25 or 1040EZ, line 9)   **51.** $ _____ .00

52. 1995 itemized deductions (IRS Form 1040, Schedule A, line 29. Write in "0" if deductions were not itemized.)   **52.** $ _____ .00

53. 1995 Income earned from work by father   **53.** $ _____ .00

54. 1995 Income earned from work by mother   **54.** $ _____ .00

55. 1995 untaxed income and benefits (Give total amount for the year. Do not give monthly amounts.)

   a. Social security benefits   **55. a.** $ _____ .00

   b. Aid to Families with Dependent Children   **b.** $ _____ .00

   c. Child support received for all children   **c.** $ _____ .00

   d. Deductible IRA and/or Keogh payments (See instructions.)   **d.** $ _____ .00

   e. Payments to tax-deferred pension and savings plans (See instructions.)   **e.** $ _____ .00

   f. Amounts withheld from wages for dependent care and medical spending accounts   **f.** $ _____ .00

   g. Earned Income Credit (IRS Form 1040, line 56 or 1040A, line 28c or 1040 EZ, line 7)   **g.** $ _____ .00

   h. Housing, food and other living allowances (See instructions.)   **h.** $ _____ .00

   i. Tax-exempt interest income (IRS Form 1040, line 8b or 1040A, line 8b)   **i.** $ _____ .00

   j. Foreign income exclusion (IRS Form 2555, line 43)   **j.** $ _____ .00

   k. Other – write in the total from the worksheet in the instructions, page X.   **k.** $ _____ .00

WRITE ONLY IN THE ANSWER SPACES. DO NOT WRITE ANYWHERE ELSE.

Section L — Parents' 1996 Expected Income & Benefits
(If the expected total income and benefits will differ from the 1995 total income and benefits by $3,000 or more, explain in Section P.)

56. 1996 income earned from work by father $ _____ .00

57. 1996 income earned from work by mother $ _____ .00

58. 1996 other taxable income $ _____ .00

59. 1996 untaxed income and benefits (See 55a – k.) $ _____ .00

Section M — Family Member Listing — Give information for all family members but don't give information about yourself. List up to seven other family members here. If there are more than seven, list first those who will be in school or college at least half-time. List the others in Section P.

60.

	Full name of family member **You — the student applicant**	Use codes from below.	Age	Claimed by parents as tax exemption in 1995? Yes? / No?	1995-96 school year Name of school or college	Year in school	Scholarships and grants	Parents' contri-bution	1996-97 school year Attend college at least one term full-time / half-time	Name of school or college
1										
2		☐		☐ ☐					1☐ 2☐	
3		☐		☐ ☐					1☐ 2☐	
4		☐		☐ ☐					1☐ 2☐	
5		☐		☐ ☐					1☐ 2☐	
6		☐		☐ ☐					1☐ 2☐	
7		☐		☐ ☐					1☐ 2☐	
8		☐		☐ ☐					1☐ 2☐	

Write in the correct code from the right. ↑ 1 = Student's parent, 2 = Student's stepparent, 3 = Student's brother or sister, 4 = Student's husband or wife, 5 = Student's son or daughter, 6 = Student's grandparent, 7 = Other

Section N — Parents' Information

61. Mark one: ☐ Father ☐ Stepfather ☐ Legal guardian ☐ Other (Explain in P.)

a. Name _____ Age ☐☐

b. Mark if: ☐ Self-employed ☐ Unemployed – Date last employed: _____

c. Occupation _____

d. Employer _____ No. years _____

e. Work telephone ☐☐☐ – ☐☐☐ – ☐☐☐☐

f. Retirement plans: ☐ Social security ☐ Union/employer ☐ Civil service/state ☐ IRA/Keogh/tax-deferred ☐ Military ☐ Other

62. Mark one: ☐ Mother ☐ Stepmother ☐ Legal guardian ☐ Other (Explain in P.)

a. Name _____ Age ☐☐

b. Mark if: ☐ Self-employed ☐ Unemployed – Date last employed: _____

c. Occupation _____

d. Employer _____ No. years _____

e. Work telephone ☐☐☐ – ☐☐☐ – ☐☐☐☐

f. Retirement plans: ☐ Social security only ☐ Union/employer ☐ Civil service/state ☐ IRA/Keogh/tax-deferred ☐ Military ☐ Other

Section O — Divorced, Separated, or Remarried Parents

(to be answered by the parent who completes this form if the student's natural or adoptive parents are divorced, separated, or remarried)

63. a. Year of separation ☐☐ Year of divorce ☐☐

b. Other parent's name _____

Home address _____

_____

Occupation/Employer _____

c. According to court order, when will support for the student end? ☐☐ ☐☐ Month Year

d. Who last claimed the student as a tax exemption? _____

_____ Year? ☐☐

e. How much does the other parent plan to contribute to the student's education for the 1996-97 school year? $ _____ .00

f. Is there an agreement specifying this contribution for the student's education? Yes ☐ No ☐

Section P — Explanations/Special Circumstances
Use this space to explain any unusual expenses such as high medical or dental expenses, educational and other debts, child care, elder care, or special circumstances. Also, give information for any outside scholarships you have been awarded.

Certification:

All the information on this form is true and complete to the best of my knowledge. If asked, I agree to give proof of the information that I have given on this form. I realize that this proof may include a copy of my U.S., state, or local income tax returns. I certify that all information is correct at this time, and that I will send timely notice to my schools/programs of any signifi-cant change in family income or assets, financial situation, college plans of other children, or the receipt of other scholarships or grants.

1 _____
Student's signature

2 _____
Student's spouse's signature

3 _____
Father's (stepfather's) signature

4 _____
Mother's (stepmother's) signature

Date this form was completed:

☐☐ ☐☐ Month Day

1 ☐ 1995
2 ☐ 1996
3 ☐ 1997
Year

– 4 –

1996–97 College Scholarship Service PROFILE Code List

The institutions on the following list all require or accept PROFILE information. An asterisk(*) next to an entry means that the college uses the PROFILE service only for Early Decision/Early Action applicants. If a college is not listed below, do not use its CSS code number on the Registration unless the college specifically tells you to do so. **Do not use code numbers from any other list.** Read the instructions on the back of the Registration before using this code list.

Alabama

1813 Tuskegee University

Arkansas

6273 Hendrix College

California

4017 Biola University
4034 California Institute of Technology
4054 Claremont McKenna College
4063 College of Notre Dame
4069 Concordia University
4341 Harvey Mudd College
4403 Loyola Marymount University
4493 Mount Saint Mary's College
4581 Occidental College
4612 Pacific Oaks College
4620 Patten College
4619 Pitzer College
4607 Pomona College
4750 Samuel Merritt College
4036 San Francisco Art Institute
4851 Santa Clara University
4693 Scripps College
4850 University of San Francisco
University of Southern California:
4852 —Undergraduate students
4950 Westmont College
4952 Whittier College

Colorado

4072 Colorado College
4073 Colorado School of Mines

Connecticut

3390 Fairfield University
3780 Sacred Heart University
3899 Trinity College
3663 University of New Haven
3959 Wesleyan University
Yale University:
3987 —New freshmen and transfers only
3213 —Continuing undergraduates only

District of Columbia

5104 Catholic University of America

George Washington University:
5246 —All undergraduates
Georgetown University:
5244 —Undergraduates only
5422 Mount Vernon College

Florida

5080 Florida Institute of Technology
5327 International Fine Arts College
5437 Lynn University
5679 Southern College
*5815 University of Miami

Georgia

5002 Agnes Scott College
5014 Atlanta College of Art
5187 Emory University
5417 Morris Brown College
5186 Oxford College of Emory University
5616 Shorter College
5990 Young Harris College

Hawaii

*4105 Chaminade University of Honolulu

Illinois

1070 Bradley University
1140 Concordia University
1206 Eureka College
1707 Illinois Benedictine College
1318 Illinois Institute of Technology
1320 Illinois Wesleyan University
1392 Lake Forest College
1404 Lewis University
1412 Loyola University of Chicago
1456 McKendree College
1470 Millikin University
1484 Monmouth College
Northwestern University:
1565 —Incoming freshmen and transfer applicants
3593 —Continuing and returning undergraduates
1630 Principia College
1667 Rosary College
1717 Shimer College

1810 Trinity College
1832 University of Chicago, The College

Indiana

1079 Bethel College
1073 Butler University
1166 DePauw University
1251 Goshen College
1290 Hanover College
1702 Saint Mary's College
1208 University of Evansville
1841 University of Notre Dame (undergraduates only)
1895 Wabash College

Iowa

6101 Coe College
6252 Grinnell College
6306 Iowa State University
6926 Wartburg College

Kentucky

1808 Transylvania University

Louisiana

6832 Tulane University
6975 Xavier University of Louisiana

Maine

3076 Bates College
3089 Bowdoin College
3755 Saint Joseph's College

Maryland

5114 College of Notre Dame of Maryland
5257 Goucher College
5296 Hood College
5370 Loyola College
5421 Mount Saint Mary's College
5598 Saint John's College
5888 Washington College

Massachusetts

3003 Amherst College

3005 Anna Maria College
3009 Assumption College
3075 Babson College
3078 Bay Path College
3096 Bentley College
3083 Boston College
Boston University:
3087 —All undergraduates
3091 Bradford College
3279 Clark University
3282 College of the Holy Cross
3352 Dean College
3283 Elms College
3367 Emerson College
3368 Emmanuel College
3369 Endicott College
3417 Gordon College
3447 Hampshire College
Harvard University:
3434 —Harvard and Radcliffe
        Colleges
3481 Lasell College
3512 Massachusetts College of
        Pharmacy and Allied Health
        Sciences
3514 Massachusetts Institute of
        Technology
3525 Merrimack College
9101 Montserrat College of Art
3529 Mount Holyoke College
3667 Northeastern University
3689 Pine Manor College
3723 Regis College
3795 Simon's Rock College of Bard
3762 Smith College
3763 Springfield College
3770 Stonehill College
3771 Suffolk University
Tufts University:
3901 —Tufts/Jackson,
        undergraduates
3957 Wellesley College
3964 Wheelock College
3965 Williams College
3969 Worcester Polytechnic
        Institute

Michigan
1007 Albion College
1095 Calvin College
1094 Concordia College
1253 Corner Stone College and Grand
        Rapids Seminary
1295 Hillsdale College
1301 Hope College
1365 Kalamazoo College
1595 Olivet College
1672 Reformed Bible College
1753 Saint Mary's College

Minnesota
6081 Carleton College
6104 College of Saint Benedict
6253 Gustavus Adolphus College
6390 Macalester College
6624 Saint John's University
6638 Saint Olaf College

Missouri
6611 Rockhurst College

New Hampshire
3351 Dartmouth College
3649 New Hampshire College
3670 Notre Dame College
3748 Saint Anselm College
3977 White Pines College

New Jersey
2193 Drew University: Undergraduates
Fairleigh Dickinson University:
2232 —Edward Williams College
2262 —Madison
2263 —Teaneck
2672 Princeton University
2819 Stevens Institute of Technology

New Mexico
4737 Saint John's College

New York
2005 *Alfred University:*
2060 —SUNY College of Ceramics
2489 Allied Health Education, NYU
        Medical Center
2037 Bard College
2038 Barnard College-Columbia
        University
*0707 Clarkson University
2086 Colgate University
Columbia University:
2116 —Columbia College
2097 Cooper Union
2098 Cornell University
2011 Dowling College
2226 Elmira College
Fordham University:
2259 —Rose Hill Campus
2286 Hamilton College
2288 Hartwick College
2294 Hobart College
*Jewish Theological Seminary of
        America:*
2339 —Albert A. List College
2366 Le Moyne College
Long Island University:
*2369 —Brooklyn
2070 —C.W. Post Campus, Brookville

2604 —C.W. Post Campus, Brentwood
2853 —Southampton
2395 Manhattan College
2396 Manhattan School of Music
2397 Manhattanville College
2398 Mannes College of Music
2511 Nazareth College of Rochester
New School for Social Research:
9384 —The Eugene Lang College/
        New School (undergraduates)
2638 —Parsons School of Design
2561 New York Institute of Technology
        (all campuses)
Pace University:
*2635 —Undergraduate, New York City
*2685 —Undergraduate, Pleasantville
Polytechnic University:
2668 —Brooklyn
2695 —Farmingdale
2669 Pratt Institute
2796 Saint Francis College
2894 Saint John's Riverside Hospital,
        Cochran School of Nursing
2805 Saint Lawrence University
2810 Sarah Lawrence College
2815 Skidmore College
2920 Union College
2928 University of Rochester
2956 Vassar College
2971 Wells College
2978 William Smith College

North Carolina
5067 Brevard College
5103 Catawba College
5150 Davidson College
5156 Duke University
5183 Elon College
5260 Greensboro College
5261 Guilford College
*5410 Meredith College
5435 Mount Olive College
5214 Saint Andrews Presbyterian
        College
5600 Saint Mary's College
5607 Salem College
5816 University of North Carolina,
        Chapel Hill
Wake Forest University:
5885 —Undergraduates only

Ohio
1021 Ashland University
1067 Bluffton College
Case Western Reserve University:
1105 —All undergraduates
1112 —Applied social sciences
1152 Cleveland Institute of Art
1124 Cleveland Institute of Music

1134 College of Wooster
1162 Defiance College
1297 Hiram College
1370 Kenyon College
1391 Lake Erie College
1439 Malone College
1444 Marietta College
1492 Mount Union College
1496 Muskingum College
1587 Oberlin College
1591 Ohio Northern University
1594 Ohio Wesleyan University
1597 Otterbein College
1817 Tiffin University
1834 University of Dayton
1223 University of Findlay
1845 University of Toledo
1926 Walsh University
1922 Wittenberg University

Oregon

4387 Linfield College
4601 Pacific University
4654 Reed College
4595 Warner Pacific College
*4954 Willamette University

Pennsylvania

2004 Albright College
2021 Allentown College of Saint
     Francis de Sales
2039 Beaver College
2049 Bryn Mawr College
2050 Bucknell University
2071 Cabrini College
2100 Curtis Institute of Music
2186 Dickinson College
2225 Elizabethtown College
2261 Franklin and Marshall College
2275 Gettysburg College
2289 Haverford College
2297 Holy Family College
2341 Juniata College
2361 Lafayette College
2365 Lehigh University
2372 Lycoming College
2410 Mercyhurst College
2418 Moravian College
2424 Muhlenberg College
2763 Rosemont College
2801 Saint Joseph's University
2812 Seton Hill College
2820 Susquehanna University
2821 Swarthmore College
2910 Thiel College
University of Pennsylvania:
Undergraduates
2926 —Incoming freshmen and
     transfer applicants

2933 —Returning undergraduates
2931 Ursinus College
2967 Washington and Jefferson
     College
2975 Westminster College
2991 York College of Pennsylvania

Rhode Island

Brown University:
3094 —Continuing undergraduates only
3189 —New freshmen and transfers
     only
3095 Bryant College
3693 Providence College
3724 Rhode Island College
3726 Rhode Island School of Design
3759 Salve Regina University

South Carolina

5117 Columbia College
5121 Converse College
5222 Furman University
5846 University of South Carolina,
     Union
5912 Wofford College

Tennessee

1102 Carson-Newman College
1818 Tennessee Temple University
1809 Trevecca Nazarene College
1842 University of the South
Vanderbilt University:
1871 —All undergraduates

Texas

6831 Trinity University

Vermont

3509 Marlboro College
3526 Middlebury College
3669 Norwich University
3796 Southern Vermont College

Virginia

*5115 College of William and Mary
5291 Hampden-Sydney College
5566 Randolph-Macon College
5625 Southern Virginia College
5887 Washington and Lee University

Washington

4801 Cornish College of the Arts
4067 University of Puget Sound
4951 Whitman College

West Virginia

5060 Bethany College

5151 Davis and Elkins College
5905 West Virginia Wesleyan College
5906 Wheeling Jesuit College

Wisconsin

1012 Alverno College
1059 Beloit College
1100 Cardinal Stritch College
1103 Carthage College
1202 Edgewood College
7590 Milwaukee Institute of Art &
     Design
1490 Mount Mary College
1706 Saint Norbert College
1300 Silver Lake College
University of Wisconsin:
1918 —River Falls
1921 —Whitewater

CANADA

0935 McGill University
0982 University of Toronto

FRANCE

0866 American University of Paris

HONG KONG

3984 International Asian Studies
     Program at the University of
     Hong Kong

SWITZERLAND

0922 Franklin College

VIRGIN ISLANDS

0879 University of the Virgin Islands,
     Saint Thomas

Plan Ahead For Success In College
WITH BOOKS FROM THE COLLEGE BOARD

Summer on Campus
College Experiences for High School Students
Introduction by Shirley Levin

Want to get a firsthand glimpse of college life? Improve your study skills? Try out new fields of study? You can—by enrolling in academic summer programs at colleges throughout the country.

Summer on Campus gives you complete information about more than 450 programs offered at over 350 colleges, with facts supplied by the institutions. Entries include:

- types of courses
- cost and financial aid availability
- length of summer session
- housing and supervision
- student composition
- application procedures

Handy indexes will help you quickly locate:

- course offerings
- host colleges
- available financial aid
- programs for minority students, in-state and commuter students, as well as junior high school students
- program length

A special introduction describes the benefits of summer study, provides tips on financing the experience, and includes comments from students who have attended programs described in the book.

005260, 1995, 288 pages, $15

The College Board Guide to 150 Popular College Majors

This unique guide will help you make informed choices about college majors. Detailed descriptions of the most widely offered undergraduate majors are written by a leading professor in the field.

Majors are grouped into 17 fields, ranging from the arts, business, and engineering to health services and the physical sciences. Each entry:

- describes the major's content
- explains what you will study
- lists related majors to consider

In addition to an overview of the major, each description lists:

- interests and skills associated with success in the major
- recommended high school preparation
- typical courses in the major
- careers the major may lead to
- where to get more information

Readers will also find expert advice on what a major is, how to choose one, and the connection of majors to careers and further education. In an introductory chapter, college students tell how they chose their major.

004000, 1992, 328 pages, glossary, indexes, $16

Order Form

Mail order form to: College Board Publications, Department T89, Box 886, New York, New York 10101-0886

Qty.	Item No.	Title	Price	Amount
____	005260	**Summer on Campus**	$ 15.00	$_____
____	004000	**The College Board Guide to 150 Popular College Majors**	$ 16.00	$_____
____	005066	**The College Handbook, 1996**	$ 20.00	$_____
____	005074	**Index of Majors and Graduate Degrees, 1996**	$ 17.00	$_____
____	005082	**College Costs and Financial Aid Handbook, 1996**	$ 16.00	$_____
____	239387	**3-Book Set: College Handbook, Index of Majors/Graduate Degrees, College Costs and Financial Aid Handbook, 1996**	$ 39.00	$_____
____	005104	**The College Handbook for Transfer Students, 1996**	$ 17.00	$_____
____	005090	**The College Handbook Foreign Student Supplement, 1996**	$ 16.00	$_____
____	004671	**The College Board Guide to Jobs and Career Planning, Second Edition**	$ 14.00	$_____
____	004736	**ABC's of Eligibility for College-Bound Student Athletes video, Revised & Updated**	$ 49.95	$_____
____	004744	**The College Guide for Parents, Third Edition**	$ 14.00	$_____
____	005112	**Real SATs**	$ 14.00	$_____
____	005295	**Look Inside the SAT I video**	$ 10.00	$_____
____	004418	**Breaking the Science Barrier: How to Explore and Understand the Sciences**	$ 14.00	$_____
____	003330	**Choosing a College: The Student's Step-by-Step Decision-Making Workbook**	$ 9.95	$_____
____	004280	**Your College Application**	$ 9.95	$_____
____	003276	**Your College Application video**	$ 29.95	$_____
____	004299	**Writing Your College Application Essay**	$ 9.95	$_____
____	002601	**Campus Visits and College Interviews**	$ 9.95	$_____
____	002261	**The College Admissions Organizer**	$ 16.95	$_____
____	003047	**College Bound: Getting Ready, Moving In, and Succeeding on Campus**	$ 9.95	$_____
____	003357	**Countdown to College: Getting the Most Out of High School**	$ 9.95	$_____
____	003179	**Campus Health Guide**	$ 14.95	$_____
____	003837	**Inside College: New Freedom, New Responsibility**	$ 10.95	$_____
____	003535	**The Student's Guide to Good Writing**	$ 9.95	$_____
____	002598	**Succeed with Math: Every Student's Guide to Conquering Math Anxiety**	$ 12.95	$_____
____	005139	**One-on-One with the SAT (MS-DOS)**	$ 49.95	$_____
____	005155	**College Explorer, 1996 (MS-DOS)**	$ 125.00	$_____
____	005171	**College Cost Explorer FUND FINDER*, 1996 (MS-DOS)**	$ 495.00	$_____
____	005163	**College Explorer PLUS**, 1996 (MS-DOS)**	$ 295.00	$_____

*Available September   **Available October

Payment must accompany all orders not submitted on an institutional purchase order or charged to a credit card. The College Board pays UPS regular ground postage on credit card and prepaid orders. Credit card and purchase orders must be for a minimum of $25. Postage is charged on all orders received on purchase orders or requesting faster than UPS ground shipment. Allow two weeks from receipt of order for delivery.

CA residents, add 7.25% sales tax; PA residents, add 6%; Canada residents, 7% Goods & Services tax $_____
Subtotal $_____
Handling Charge $ 3.95
Total $_____

___ Enclosed is my check or money order made payable to the College Board
___ Enclosed is an institutional purchase order (orders for $25 or more), or
___ Please charge my ___ MasterCard ___ Visa. My credit card number is ___ ___ ___ ___/___ ___ ___ ___/___ ___ ___ ___/___ ___ ___ ___

Card expiration date: ___/___ _____
month/year   Card holder's signature

Credit card holders only can place orders by calling toll-free 1-800-323-7155 Monday through Friday, 8am to 11pm EST. Please have your credit card number ready when you call and give operator the department number **T89**. This special 800 number is for credit card calls only. For other information or assistance, call (212) 713-8165, Monday through Friday, 9am to 5pm EST, FAX (212) 713-8143.

SHIP TO:
Name _____   City _____

Street Address (NO P.O. BOX NUMBERS) _____   State _____ Zip _____

_____   Telephone _____

Order Form

Mail order form to: College Board Publications, Department T89, Box 886, New York, New York 10101-0886

Qty.	Item No.	Title	Price	Amount
____	005260	**Summer on Campus**	$ 15.00	$_____
____	004000	**The College Board Guide to 150 Popular College Majors**	$ 16.00	$_____
____	005066	**The College Handbook, 1996**	$ 20.00	$_____
____	005074	**Index of Majors and Graduate Degrees, 1996**	$ 17.00	$_____
____	005082	**College Costs and Financial Aid Handbook, 1996**	$ 16.00	$_____
____	239387	**3-Book Set: College Handbook, Index of Majors/Graduate Degrees, College Costs and Financial Aid Handbook, 1996**	$ 39.00	$_____
____	005104	**The College Handbook for Transfer Students, 1996**	$ 17.00	$_____
____	005090	**The College Handbook Foreign Student Supplement, 1996**	$ 16.00	$_____
____	004671	**The College Board Guide to Jobs and Career Planning, Second Edition**	$ 14.00	$_____
____	004736	**ABC's of Eligibility for College-Bound Student Athletes video, Revised & Updated**	$ 49.95	$_____
____	004744	**The College Guide for Parents, Third Edition**	$ 14.00	$_____
____	005112	**Real SATs**	$ 14.00	$_____
____	005295	**Look Inside the SAT I video**	$ 10.00	$_____
____	004418	**Breaking the Science Barrier: How to Explore and Understand the Sciences**	$ 14.00	$_____
____	003330	**Choosing a College: The Student's Step-by-Step Decision-Making Workbook**	$ 9.95	$_____
____	004280	**Your College Application**	$ 9.95	$_____
____	003276	**Your College Application video**	$ 29.95	$_____
____	004299	**Writing Your College Application Essay**	$ 9.95	$_____
____	002601	**Campus Visits and College Interviews**	$ 9.95	$_____
____	002261	**The College Admissions Organizer**	$ 16.95	$_____
____	003047	**College Bound: Getting Ready, Moving In, and Succeeding on Campus**	$ 9.95	$_____
____	003357	**Countdown to College: Getting the Most Out of High School**	$ 9.95	$_____
____	003179	**Campus Health Guide**	$ 14.95	$_____
____	003837	**Inside College: New Freedom, New Responsibility**	$ 10.95	$_____
____	003535	**The Student's Guide to Good Writing**	$ 9.95	$_____
____	002598	**Succeed with Math: Every Student's Guide to Conquering Math Anxiety**	$ 12.95	$_____
____	005139	**One-on-One with the SAT (MS-DOS)**	$ 49.95	$_____
____	005155	**College Explorer, 1996 (MS-DOS)**	$ 125.00	$_____
____	005171	**College Cost Explorer FUND FINDER*, 1996 (MS-DOS)**	$ 495.00	$_____
____	005163	**College Explorer PLUS**, 1996 (MS-DOS)**	$ 295.00	$_____

*Available September   **Available October

Payment must accompany all orders not submitted on an institutional purchase order or charged to a credit card. The College Board pays UPS regular ground postage on credit card and prepaid orders. Credit card and purchase orders must be for a minimum of $25. Postage is charged on all orders received on purchase orders or requesting faster than UPS ground shipment. Allow two weeks from receipt of order for delivery.

CA residents, add 7.25% sales tax;
PA residents, add 6%; Canada
residents, 7% Goods & Services tax $_____
Subtotal $_____
Handling Charge $ 3.95
Total $_____

___ Enclosed is my check or money order made payable to the College Board
___ Enclosed is an institutional purchase order (orders for $25 or more), or
___ Please charge my ___ MasterCard ___ Visa. My credit card number is ___ ___ ___ ___/___ ___ ___ ___/___ ___ ___ ___/___ ___ ___ ___

Card expiration date: ___/___   _____
        month/year   Card holder's signature

Credit card holders only can place orders by calling toll-free 1-800-323-7155 Monday through Friday, 8am to 11pm EST. Please have your credit card number ready when you call and give operator the department number **T89**. This special 800 number is for credit card calls only. For other information or assistance, call (212) 713-8165, Monday through Friday, 9am to 5pm EST, FAX (212) 713-8143.

SHIP TO:
Name _____   City _____

Street Address (NO P.O. BOX NUMBERS) _____   State _____ Zip _____

_____   Telephone _____